# Meet the *Southern Living* Foods Staff

On these pages we present the *Southern Living* Foods Staff (left to right in each photograph).

*Kaye Adams, Test Kitchens Director; Patty Vann, Assistant Test Kitchens Director*

*Jean Wickstrom Liles, Senior Foods Editor*

*Karen Brechin, Editorial Assistant; Rebecca Hood Eiland, Editorial Assistant*

*Beverly Nesbit, Assistant Foods Editor; Dana Adkins Campbell, Assistant Foods Editor*

*Susan J. Reynolds, Foods Editor; Susan Dosier,*
*Associate Foods Editor*

*Diane Hogan, Test Kitchens Home Economist; Peggy*
*Smith, Marketing Manager*

*Jane Cairns, Test Kitchens Home Economist; Judy*
*Feagin, Test Kitchens Home Economist*

*Charles Walton IV, Senior Foods Photographer; Leslie*
*Byars, Photo Stylist*

# Southern Living

## 1992 ANNUAL RECIPES

Oxmoor House

©1992 by Oxmoor House, Inc.
Book Division of Southern Progress Corporation
P.O. Box 2463, Birmingham, Alabama 35201

*Southern Living®, Summer Suppers®,* and *Holiday Dinners®*
are federally registered trademarks of Southern Living, Inc.

Library of Congress Catalog Number: 79-88364
ISBN: 0-8487-1102-5
ISSN: 0272-2003

Manufactured in the United States of America
First printing 1992

*Southern Living®*

Senior Foods Editor: Jean Wickstrom Liles
Foods Editor: Susan J. Reynolds
Associate Foods Editor: Susan Dosier
Assistant Foods Editors: Dana Adkins Campbell,
    Beverly Nesbit, R.D.
Editorial Assistants: Karen Brechin, Rebecca Hood Eiland
Test Kitchens Director: Kaye Adams
Assistant Test Kitchens Director: Patty Vann
Test Kitchens Staff: Jane Cairns, Judy Feagin,
    Diane Hogan, Peggy Smith
Photo Stylist: Leslie Byars
Senior Foods Photographer: Charles E. Walton IV
Additional photography by Ralph Anderson, pages 298 and
    299; Jim Bathie, page 258; Sylvia Martin, pages 224,
    257, 259; Jan Wyatt Traynor, pages 74 and 75
Production Manager: Kay Fuston
Assistant Production Manager: Amy Roth
Production Traffic Manager: Vicki Weathers

Oxmoor House, Inc.

Editor-in-Chief: Nancy J. Fitzpatrick
Senior Foods Editor: Susan Carlisle Payne
Director of Manufacturing: Jerry R. Higdon
Art Director: James Boone

*Southern Living® 1992 Annual Recipes*

Senior Editor: Olivia Kindig Wells
Copy Editor: Donna Baldone
Editorial Assistants: Carole Cain, Meredith Walker

Production Manager: Rick Litton
Associate Production Manager: Theresa L. Beste
Production Assistant: Pam Beasley Bullock

Indexer: Mary Ann Laurens
Designer and Illustrator: Carol Middleton

---

Cover: *Cherry-Berry Pie (page 316), topped with a simple lattice
design, pastry leaves, and fresh raspberries dusted
with powdered sugar, makes an impressive addition to any
dessert table.*

Back cover: *Poached Pears With Honey-Yogurt Sauce (page
306) is a dessert as enchanting as the evening.*

Page 1: *Garnished with fresh strawberries and chocolate curls,
Chocolate-Sour Cream Pound Cake (page 153) is a chocolate
lover's dream.*

Page 4: *Make Shrimp-and-Rice Salad (page 307) ahead, and let
it chill so that the tangy dressing blends with the delicate fresh
shrimp, crisp green vegetables, and creamy white rice.*

# Table of Contents

# Our Year At Southern Living®

Welcome to *1992 Southern Living® Annual Recipes*, the fourteenth volume of our cookbook collection. While this cookbook is a rich assortment of all the food stories we published in 1992, the series continues to spotlight more and more outstanding recipes, beautiful photographs, and creative entertaining ideas.

Most of the recipes come as favorites from our readers, while many are handpicked by the foods staff as we travel the region gleaning story ideas or judging cooking contests. Join us now on a culinary tour of our favorite taste memories spanning January through December.

In **January**, we usher in the New Year with an uptown menu using down-home black-eyed peas and greens, keeping alive the tradition that these foods promise good luck and good fortune for the year.

**February** offers a month to eat chocolate and not feel guilty. Satisfy your Valentine's sweet tooth with our array of chocolate treats.

We wake up tastebuds in **March** with 24 cloves of garlic in Garlic-Spinach Chicken. Not only do we share some of the mystique of this bulb, but we remind you that garlic doesn't have to be pungent and is sweetened by heat, slow cooking, or roasting.

Enjoy springtime and **April** with five New Orleans brunches. Kick off your celebration with Turtle Soup or Louisiana Oyster-and-Artichoke Soup, and cap the affair with Cafe Pontalba or Bread Pudding With Whiskey Sauce.

What could be more fun in **May** than a visit to Southern food festivals? We showcase several: shrimp in Florida, strawberries in West Virginia, crab in Maryland, and watermelon in Arkansas. If you can't travel to these events, we invite you to sample our recipes from the celebrations.

Our **June** special section, *On the Light Side,* is packed with nutritional information, calorie-trimmed recipes, and exercise tips geared to an active life-style. Enjoy a variety of recipes all low in fat and high in fiber.

Join us in **July** at a block party. Our *Summer Suppers®* special section features block parties in Virginia, Georgia, and Tennessee; it also offers ideas on food and fun from other neighborhood festivities across the South.

Beat the heat in **August** with our too-hot-to-cook entrées or giant sandwich creations. We also suggest chilled pies for a cool, refreshing treat.

In **September**, our search for the best chocolate chip cookie led us to six favorites. Teamed with a glass of milk, cookies are perfect for an after-school snack. And to start the school day off right, we offer some simple and healthful breakfast ideas.

**October** brings a spectrum of wonderful flavors and aromas as you sample the region's fall harvest—pumpkin, pear, apple, sweet potato, and butternut squash.

Ring in the holidays with the **November** *Holiday Dinners®* special section offering recipes and decorating ideas to set the mood for this glorious season.

In **December**, give your home a warm holiday glow with a tree-trimming party featuring our easy-to-assemble buffet menu. And to wrap up the year with sweet gifts from your kitchen, choose from our smorgasbord of holiday confections.

For me, this *1992 Annual Recipes* winds up a special relationship with **you**, our readers, that spans over 20 years of warm and wonderful memories. Among these memories are more than half a million recipes you've submitted and thousands of cordial notes you've written thanking us for the pleasures *Southern Living* has provided. Starting in 1993, I look forward to leisure time in my own kitchen stirring up many of your favorite recipes I've taste-tested over the years. I'll miss your phone calls and letters. I'll miss the excitement of taste-testing recipes for each upcoming issue. And I'll miss the fellowship and camaraderie of the *Southern Living* staff. Many thanks for your enthusiastic support and loyalty all these years.

*Jean Wickstrom Liles*

# JANUARY

*As you ring in the new year, perk up traditional holiday fare*

*with some flavor variations. Our Spicy Black-Eyed Peas and*

*Uptown Collards promise good luck, as well as great taste.*

*Or if the bustle of the season has left you frazzled, try our*

*make-ahead Sunday dinner. It's a warming winter meal that's*

*delicious and easy on the cook. Then continue the celebration*

*throughout the year with our collection of festive cupcakes.*

# Yes, There Is A Sunday Dinner

Years ago, when you mentioned Sunday dinner in the South, a definite picture came to mind: family members filling their plates from heaping platters of steaming fried chicken, fresh farm vegetables, and of course, home-baked breads, cakes, and pies.

For some, this image still rings true today, but others find themselves victims of a mobile society and hectic schedules. Fewer people have time to cook a weekly feast, and these days relatives are rarely just down the road. But you probably don't have to look farther than your own neighborhood to find someone homesick for the traditional Sunday dinner.

Invite a few couples over, including the children. Don't forget the woman down the street who lives alone; the time with the little ones will be like a visit with her own grandchildren. In no time, it will be a family Sunday dinner.

This make-ahead menu for a Sunday feast is perfect for today's cooks with their busy lifestyles. Just like the old days, everyone brings a dish, so no one gets saddled with all the work.

We've included helpful preparation tips for each easy recipe. You won't find homemade bread in this menu, but a novice cook would love the easy task of bringing dinner rolls from the deli or bakery.

## SUNDAY DINNER FOR A DOZEN

**Mulled Cranberry Drink**
**Apricot Chicken**
**Garden Rice**
**Green Beans With Bacon and Mushrooms**
**Spinach-Apple Salad**
**Commercial rolls**
**Peach Crisp and/or Chocolate Chess Pie**

■ Prepare this hot beverage before guests arrive and serve it as a "sipper" while the group puts finishing touches on the potluck meal.

### MULLED CRANBERRY DRINK

6 cups cranberry juice
3 cups apple juice
3 cups orange juice
¾ cup maple syrup
1½ teaspoons ground cinnamon
¾ teaspoon ground cloves
¾ teaspoon ground nutmeg
12 (6-inch) sticks cinnamon
  (optional)

Combine all ingredients except cinnamon sticks in a Dutch oven; bring mixture to a boil. Serve mixture hot with 6-inch cinnamon sticks, if desired. Yield: 3 quarts. *Charlotte Hunt*
*Medon, Tennessee*

■ The hostess can prepare Apricot Chicken ahead and put it in the oven to bake 30 minutes before guests arrive. During remaining 25 minutes baking time, serve Mulled Cranberry Drink and set out the rest of the meal. Serve chicken over hot Garden Rice.

### APRICOT CHICKEN

12 chicken breast halves, skinned
  and boned
1 (12-ounce) can apricot nectar
1 teaspoon ground allspice
½ teaspoon salt
¼ teaspoon ground ginger
¼ teaspoon pepper
¾ cup apricot preserves
½ cup chopped pecans, toasted
Garnish: celery leaves

Place chicken breasts in a 13- x 9- x 2-inch baking dish. Combine apricot nectar and next 4 ingredients; stir well, and pour over chicken. Cover and chill 8 hours.

Remove chicken from refrigerator; let stand at room temperature 30 minutes. Cover and bake at 350° for 30 minutes. Uncover and drain liquid from baking dish, discarding liquid.

Heat preserves in a small saucepan over low heat until warm. Brush over chicken. Bake, uncovered, 25 minutes, basting occasionally with preserves. Sprinkle with pecans; garnish, if desired. Yield: 12 servings.
*Steve Turner*
*St. Louis, Missouri*

■ Put prepared Garden Rice in a large zip-top plastic bag. To serve, unzip bag, and reheat upright in a microwave oven. Spoon onto platter, and top with Apricot Chicken.

### GARDEN RICE

1 cup finely chopped onion
1 cup finely chopped celery
2 large cloves garlic, minced
¼ cup butter or margarine, melted
4⅔ cups chicken broth
2 cups brown rice, uncooked
¾ teaspoon salt
¼ teaspoon white pepper
1 cup finely chopped carrot

Sauté onion, celery, and garlic in butter in a Dutch oven; add broth, brown rice, salt, and pepper. Cover and cook over low heat 40 minutes. Stir in chopped carrot, and cook an additional 10 minutes. Yield: 12 servings.
*JaLayne Eddy*
*Jacksonville, Texas*

■ Transport cooked beans and crumbled bacon in separate zip-top plastic bags. To serve, unzip bag with beans and reheat upright in a microwave oven. Put beans in a serving bowl, and toss with bacon.

## GREEN BEANS WITH BACON AND MUSHROOMS

12 slices bacon
1 cup chopped onion
2 (4½-ounce) cans sliced
   mushrooms, drained
3 (9-ounce) packages frozen whole
   green beans, thawed
1 tablespoon sugar

Cook bacon in a large skillet until crisp; remove bacon, reserving 1 tablespoon drippings in skillet. Crumble bacon, and set aside.

Sauté onion in drippings in skillet over medium heat until tender. Add mushrooms; cook 2 minutes. Stir in green beans and sugar. Cover and cook 10 minutes or until desired degree of doneness, stirring occasionally. Transfer beans to serving dish. Add bacon, tossing gently, and serve immediately. Yield: 12 servings.

*Vikki Jacobsen*
*Wilton Manors, Florida*

■ Take the dressing in a jar and torn spinach, apples, and almonds in separate zip-top plastic bags. (To prevent browning, pour enough dressing over sliced apples in bag to thoroughly coat.) To serve, toss spinach with dressing and top with apples and, if desired, almonds.

## SPINACH-APPLE SALAD

⅔ cup vegetable oil
⅔ cup raspberry vinegar
1½ tablespoons honey
¼ teaspoon salt
⅛ teaspoon pepper
1½ pounds fresh spinach
4 medium apples, unpeeled
½ cup sliced almonds, toasted
   (optional)

Combine first 5 ingredients in a jar; cover tightly, and shake vigorously. Chill thoroughly.

Remove stems from spinach; wash leaves thoroughly, and pat dry. Tear into bite-size pieces. Toss spinach in enough dressing to coat, reserving remaining dressing; place spinach on a serving platter.

Core and slice apples. Toss in reserved dressing, and arrange on spinach. Sprinkle with almonds, if desired. Yield: 12 servings.

■ Assemble Peach Crisp at home, and bake in the hostess's oven after dinner. The 20 minutes of baking time will give everyone a chance to make room for this Southern favorite.

## PEACH CRISP

2 cups all-purpose flour
1 cup firmly packed dark brown
   sugar
1 cup quick-cooking oats,
   uncooked
½ teaspoon ground cinnamon
1 cup butter or margarine
1 cup chopped pecans
4 (16-ounce) cans sliced peaches,
   drained
Vanilla ice cream

Combine flour, sugar, oats, and cinnamon in a medium bowl; cut butter into oat mixture with a pastry blender until mixture resembles coarse meal. Stir in pecans.

Spoon peaches into a lightly greased 13- x 9- x 2-inch baking dish. Spoon crumb mixture on top. Bake at 400° for 18 to 20 minutes. Serve with ice cream. Yield: 12 servings.

*Freda L. Bell*
*Chattanooga, Tennessee*

■ Make pie a day ahead and store in a piekeeper. If you choose to garnish the pie, take the whipped cream in a separate container, and chill until serving time.

## CHOCOLATE CHESS PIE

1 unbaked 9-inch pastry shell
3 eggs, beaten
1½ cups sugar
2 tablespoons all-purpose flour
3½ tablespoons cocoa
¼ cup butter or margarine, melted
½ cup evaporated milk
1 teaspoon vanilla extract
Garnish: whipped cream

Bake pastry shell at 350° for 5 minutes. Set aside.

Combine eggs and next 6 ingredients in a medium bowl, and stir well. Spoon egg mixture evenly into prepared pastry shell. Bake at 350° for 45 minutes. Garnish, if desired. Yield: one 9-inch pie. *Ruth Porter*
*Elizabethtown, North Carolina*

## Baking Tips

■ Sifting flour, with the exception of cake flour, is no longer necessary. Simply stir the flour, gently spoon it into a dry measure, and level the top. Powdered sugar, however, should be sifted to remove the lumps.

■ Regular and quick-cooking oats are essentially interchangeable, but regular oats add chewy texture and are best for granola, cookies, desserts, and pie crust.

■ Unless otherwise specified, always preheat the oven at least 10 minutes before baking.

■ Every time the door of the oven is opened, the oven temperature drops 25 to 30 degrees. Use the oven window so as not to waste energy.

# A Calendar Of Cupcakes

Holidays and birthdays call for fun—in your child's classroom, around the coffeepot at work, and at church suppers. If a list goes around for volunteers to cook, sign up for dessert. You'll be in business all year with these cupcakes.

We started with one basic cupcake recipe, plus a couple of frostings. From there we went to the candy counter to find colorful decorations. Then our Test Kitchens group went to work to create whimsical designs.

If you're not much of a baker, you can still make these cupcakes. Just buy a box of your favorite cake mix, and get started. A 16-ounce container of ready-made vanilla frosting will substitute nicely for our homemade version. One container will yield 1½ cups frosting that you can color as each recipe directs. You also can purchase cans and tubes of precolored frostings; most include several basic decorating tips. Tubes cost a little more but will save you time.

### VANILLA CUPCAKES

¾ cup shortening
1½ cups sugar
3 eggs
2 cups all-purpose flour
1½ teaspoons baking powder
¼ teaspoon salt
1 cup milk
1½ teaspoons vanilla extract

Beat shortening in a large bowl at medium speed with an electric mixer; gradually add 1½ cups sugar, beating well. Add eggs, one at a time, beating well after each addition.

Combine flour, baking powder, and salt; add to creamed mixture alternately with milk, beginning and ending with flour mixture. Mix after each addition. Add vanilla, and mix just until blended. Spoon batter into paper or foil-lined muffin pans, filling each two-thirds full. Bake at 350° for 18 to 20 minutes or until a wooden pick inserted in center comes out clean. Remove from pans, and let cool on wire racks. Yield: 26 to 36 cupcakes.

**Chocolate Cupcakes:** Reduce all-purpose flour to 1⅓ cups; add ½ cup cocoa and ½ teaspoon baking soda to dry ingredients.

**Note:** To make **heart-shaped cupcakes** for Valentine's Day, make enough ½-inch balls of aluminum foil for each cupcake. Place paper baking cups in muffin pans. Put a foil ball in each cup between liner and one side of pan. Spoon in cake batter, and bake as usual.

### BOILED FROSTING

¾ cup sugar
¼ teaspoon cream of tartar
⅛ teaspoon salt
¼ cup hot water
2 egg whites
¼ teaspoon vanilla or almond
   extract

Combine first 4 ingredients in a heavy saucepan. Cook mixture over medium heat, stirring constantly, until clear. Cook, without stirring, to soft ball stage (240°).

Beat egg whites until soft peaks form; continue to beat, slowly adding hot syrup mixture. Add vanilla, and beat mixture until stiff peaks form and frosting is thick enough to spread. Yield: 2½ cups.

### VANILLA FROSTING

¾ cup butter or margarine,
   softened
¾ cup shortening
1 (16-ounce) package powdered
   sugar, sifted
2 tablespoons milk
1 teaspoon vanilla extract

Beat butter and shortening at medium speed with an electric mixer; gradually add sugar, beating mixture until light and fluffy. Stir in milk and vanilla. Yield: 3 cups.

### TANNENBAUM TEMPTATIONS

1 recipe Vanilla or Chocolate
   Cupcakes
2 recipes Vanilla Frosting, divided
Green and red paste food coloring
1 (6-ounce) package bugle-shaped
   snacks
Nonpareils
Tiny, multicolored, candy-coated
   gum pieces

Prepare cupcakes and Vanilla Frosting. Tint 3 cups frosting green and ¾ cup red, leaving remainder white. Set aside ½ cup white frosting; frost cupcakes smoothly with remaining white frosting.

Insert a bugle in center of each cupcake. Pipe branches around bugles with green frosting using tip No. 65. Decorate trees with nonpareils. Arrange 6 to 8 gum pieces around base of each tree as packages. Pipe bows on gum with red and white frostings using tip No. 2.

## NEW YEAR'S CONFETTI CUPCAKES

1 recipe Vanilla Cupcakes
2 to 3 tablespoons decorating candy nonpareils
1 recipe Vanilla Frosting
Blue paste food coloring
Decorating candy confetti
Large red gumdrops

Prepare Vanilla Cupcakes as directed, stirring in nonpareils at the end. Bake as directed. Prepare Vanilla Frosting. Tint 1 cup frosting blue, and spoon into a large decorating bag fitted with tip No. 14.

Spread white frosting on top of cupcakes, and sprinkle with confetti. Using kitchen shears, trim gumdrops to make party hats. Place on cupcakes; pipe a blue ruffle at base of hat and a blue pom-pom on top.

## SWEETHEART CUPCAKES

1 recipe Chocolate Cupcakes
1 recipe Vanilla Frosting
Red paste food coloring
Silver décors

Prepare heart-shaped cupcakes and Vanilla Frosting. Tint half of frosting red; leave remainder white. Smoothly frost cupcakes with white frosting. Pipe a lattice design over white frosting using red frosting and tip No. 2. Pipe a red border around edge of cupcakes using tip No. 14. Place silver décors around edge. Yield: 26 to 36 cupcakes.

## BIRTHDAY BALLOON CAKES

1 recipe Vanilla or Chocolate Cupcakes
1 recipe Boiled Frosting
Yellow paste food coloring
About 12 dozen gumballs
26 to 30 feet thin red licorice

Prepare cupcakes and Boiled Frosting. Tint frosting yellow, and frost cupcakes. Arrange 5 gumballs off center of each cupcake. Cut licorice into 12-inch strips; tie each into a bow. Microwave 5 bows at a time for 13 to 15 seconds or until warm to touch; secure bow knots with clothespins until cool. Attach a bow to each bundle of balloons. Use candles as desired.

## A TISKET, A TASKET

1 recipe Vanilla Cupcakes
1 recipe Vanilla Frosting
Green paste food coloring
1 (12-ounce) package small jellybeans
About 10 feet thin red licorice
1 (7-ounce) roll marzipan

Prepare Vanilla Cupcakes and Vanilla Frosting. Tint frosting green; spoon into decorating bag fitted with tip No. 233. Pipe frosting on cupcakes to look like grass.

Pile jellybean "eggs" on grass. Cut licorice into 4-inch strips for basket handles; insert handles in cakes. Roll marzipan to ¼-inch thickness. Cut rabbits using a cookie cutter. Prop a bunny in each basket near the handle.

## FOURTH-OF-JULY ICE-CREAM CONE CAKES

1 recipe Vanilla or Chocolate Cupcakes
34 flat-bottom ice-cream cones
1 recipe Boiled Frosting
34 maraschino cherries
34 miniature flags

Prepare cupcake batter as directed. Bake cupcake batter in ice-cream cones as follows: Place cones in muffin pans; spoon 2 tablespoons batter into each cone. Bake at 350° for 20 to 25 minutes or until a wooden pick inserted in center comes out clean. Remove cones from pans, and cool on wire racks.

Prepare Boiled Frosting. Frost cupcakes to look like ice-cream cones, letting a little frosting drip down sides. Top each with a cherry and a flag.

## GRAVEYARD GRUMBLINGS

1 recipe Chocolate Cupcakes
1 recipe Vanilla Frosting, divided
Orange and green paste food coloring
About 5 dozen cookies of assorted shapes

Prepare Chocolate Cupcakes and Vanilla Frosting. Tint ½ cup frosting orange; spoon into decorating bag fitted with tip No. 10. Tint remaining frosting green; spoon 1 cup green frosting into decorating bag fitted with tip No. 2. Spread remaining green frosting on cupcakes. Pipe green letters on cookies to look like tombstones; insert cookies into cupcakes. Pipe pumpkins with stems at base of tombstones.

## TURKEY TALK

1 recipe Chocolate Cupcakes
2 recipes Vanilla Frosting, divided
Red, brown, orange, and yellow paste food coloring
Thin black licorice

Prepare Chocolate Cupcakes and Vanilla Frosting. Tint 1 cup frosting red, 1 cup brown, ¾ cup orange, and ¾ cup yellow. Smoothly frost cupcakes with remaining white frosting. Pipe a smooth brown body and head for turkey using tip No. 10, letting body build up at base using heavy pressure, and releasing pressure at top for head. Pipe red for comb and wattle using tip No. 2. Trim tiny pieces of licorice for turkey feet. Pipe red, yellow, and orange tail feathers at back of turkey using tip No. 65.

# Nuts Over Pound Cake

In 1824, in *The Virginia Housewife*, Mary Randolph talks of adding "the common black walnut" to ice cream. Use this jewel in pound cake to add flavor and a texture variation.

Black walnuts grow on trees in the backyards of many Southern homes. They offer a pungent, earthy flavor. Black walnuts also are available at grocery stores for those not fortunate enough to own a tree. They make a grand addition to this pound cake.

### BLACK WALNUT POUND CAKE

1 cup butter, softened
½ cup shortening
3 cups sugar
5 eggs
3 cups all-purpose flour
½ teaspoon baking powder
1 cup milk
½ teaspoon vanilla extract
½ cup black walnuts, chopped

Beat butter and shortening at medium speed with an electric mixer about 2 minutes or until soft and creamy. Gradually add sugar, beating at medium speed 5 to 7 minutes. Add eggs, one at a time, beating just until yellow disappears.

Combine flour and baking powder; add to creamed mixture alternately with milk, beginning and ending with flour mixture. Mix just until blended after each addition. Stir in vanilla and walnuts.

Pour batter into a greased and floured 10-inch tube pan. Bake at 325° for 1 hour and 30 minutes or until a wooden pick inserted in center comes out clean. Cool in pan 10 to 15 minutes; remove from pan, and let cool completely on a wire rack. Yield: one 10-inch cake.

**Note:** Baked cake may be frozen 3 to 5 months. Thaw, and, if desired, reheat to serve.

# Dill Bread And All The Trimmings

When Mary Belle Purvis's Olive-Dill Casserole Bread was tested in our kitchens, we decided it was worthy of building an entire meal around. Baked in a casserole dish rather than a loafpan, the bread can be used as a sandwich base and as an accompaniment to a steaming bowl of soup.

Easy Potato Soup relies on canned soups and frozen hash brown potatoes to save time, yet the recipe doesn't scrimp on wholesome flavor. It's easy to keep the ingredients for this recipe in your pantry for last-minute meal planning.

To make Curried Turkey Spread, use leftover turkey—or pick up a prepackaged, cooked breast in the meat section at the grocery store.

Cashew Crunch Cookies provide a sweet ending to the meal. If time is a premium, bake the bread and the cookies on a weekend, and freeze them up to 3 months.

### DILL BREAD AND THE FIXINGS

**Olive-Dill Casserole Bread**
**Curried Turkey Spread**
**Easy Potato Soup**
**Cashew Crunch Cookies**

### OLIVE-DILL CASSEROLE BREAD

2 packages dry yeast
2 cups warm water (105° to 115°)
¼ cup minced fresh dillweed or
    1½ tablespoons dried dillweed
2 tablespoons sugar
3 tablespoons chopped pimiento-stuffed olives
2 tablespoons butter or margarine, melted
2 teaspoons salt
4½ cups all-purpose flour, divided
1 teaspoon dillseeds

Dissolve yeast in warm water in a large bowl, and let stand 5 minutes. Stir in dillweed, sugar, olives, butter, salt, and 2 cups flour. Beat at medium speed with an electric mixer until mixture is smooth. Gradually stir in enough remaining flour to make a soft dough.

Place dough in a well-greased bowl, turning to grease top. Cover and let rise in a warm place (85°), free from drafts, 45 minutes or until doubled in bulk. (Dough may be light and bubbly.) Punch dough down and vigorously stir with a wooden spoon 30 seconds. Turn out into a lightly greased 2-quart round casserole. Sprinkle top of dough with 1 teaspoon dillseeds.

Bake at 375° for 55 to 60 minutes, covering top of bread with aluminum foil to prevent overbrowning, if necessary. Remove bread from casserole and let cool on a wire rack. Yield: 1 round loaf.

**Note:** Baked bread may be frozen up to 3 months.
*Mary Belle Purvis*
*Greeneville, Tennessee*

### CURRIED TURKEY SPREAD

2 cups diced cooked turkey or chicken
⅔ to ¾ cup mayonnaise or salad dressing
1 teaspoon curry powder
½ teaspoon grated lemon rind
1 teaspoon lemon juice
2 tablespoons capers

Combine cooked turkey, mayonnaise, curry powder, grated lemon rind, and lemon juice; add capers, and stir mixture gently. Yield: 2 cups.
*Elizabeth R. Drawdy*
*Spindale, North Carolina*

**Tip:** *Freeze small portions of leftover meat or fowl until you have enough for a pot pie, curry, or casserole.*

## EASY POTATO SOUP

16 ounces frozen hash brown
   potatoes
1 cup chopped onion
1 (14½-ounce) can ready-to-serve
   chicken broth
2 cups water
1 (10¾-ounce) can cream of celery
   soup, undiluted
1 (10¾-ounce) can cream of
   chicken soup, undiluted
2 cups milk
Garnishes: shredded Cheddar cheese,
   diced cooked ham or bacon

Combine potatoes, chopped onion,
chicken broth, and water in a Dutch
oven; bring to a boil. Cover, reduce
heat, and simmer 30 minutes. Stir in
soups and milk; heat thoroughly. Garnish, if desired. Yield: 2½ quarts.
*Harriett Blanford*
*Owensboro, Kentucky*

## CASHEW CRUNCH COOKIES

1 cup butter or margarine, softened
¾ cup firmly packed light brown
   sugar
½ cup sugar
1 egg
1 teaspoon vanilla extract
2¼ cups all-purpose flour
½ teaspoon baking soda
½ teaspoon cream of tartar
1½ cups finely chopped cashews

Beat butter at medium speed with an
electric mixer; gradually add sugars,
mixing well. Add egg and vanilla; beat
well. Combine flour, soda, and cream
of tartar; gradually add to creamed
mixture, mixing after each addition.
Stir in cashews.
   Drop cookie dough by rounded teaspoonfuls onto lightly greased cookie
sheets, and bake at 350° for 10 to 12
minutes or until lightly browned.
Yield: 7 dozen.      *Fay Redding*
*Gastonia, North Carolina*

## ON THE LIGHT SIDE

# Vegetarian Entrées For Everyone

As more Americans turn to healthful
living, vegetarian and semi-vegetarian
dishes are gaining popularity. Some
studies show that vegetarians have
lower cholesterol and blood pressure
levels, less diabetes and cancer, and
lower rates of obesity and heart disease than the general population.
   The vegetables, grains, legumes,
and fruits that are the mainstay of vegetarian eating are low in fat, high in
fiber, and rich in vitamins and minerals, which are all characteristics of
healthful food.
   Today's vegetarian has come a long
way from the tofu and sprouts days of
the sixties and seventies. Meatless
dishes such as Chiles Rellenos Casserole, Cannelloni, and Eggplant Parmesan not only taste delicious but glean
high marks from nutritionists.
   If converting to vegetarianism
seems a bit drastic, try eating a vegetarian meal two or three times a
week. Keep in mind that the milk and
cheese substituted for meat should be
the low-fat varieties.

### CANNELLONI

1 (10-ounce) package frozen
   chopped spinach, thawed
Vegetable cooking spray
¾ cup diced fresh mushrooms
¼ cup diced onion
3 cloves minced garlic
¼ cup egg substitute
2 tablespoons freshly grated
   Parmesan cheese
½ teaspoon dried oregano
¼ teaspoon dried basil
8 cooked manicotti shells (cooked
   without salt or fat)
2 cups commercial low-fat spaghetti
   sauce, divided
Parmesan Sauce
2 tablespoons chopped fresh parsley

Place thawed spinach between paper
towels and squeeze until barely moist;
set aside.
   Coat a large nonstick skillet with
cooking spray; place over medium
heat until hot. Add mushrooms, onion,
and garlic; sauté 2 minutes. Add spinach; sauté until mushrooms are tender
and liquid evaporates. Remove mixture from heat, and cool slightly. Stir
in egg substitute, Parmesan cheese,
oregano, and basil. Stuff each manicotti shell with an equal amount of the
spinach mixture.
   Spread 1 cup spaghetti sauce in a
12- x 8- x 2-inch baking dish. Place
stuffed shells on spaghetti sauce.
Spread remaining spaghetti sauce
over shells. Spoon Parmesan Sauce
down center of casserole. Cover and
bake at 375° for 30 minutes or until
thoroughly heated. Sprinkle with parsley. Yield: 8 servings (155 calories per
1 cannelloni with sauce).

□ *9.1 grams protein, 6.5 grams fat,
16.6 grams carbohydrate, 11 milligrams cholesterol, 552 milligrams sodium, and 252 milligrams calcium.*

### Parmesan Sauce

2 tablespoons nonfat dry milk
   powder
1 cup skim milk
1½ tablespoons reduced-calorie
   margarine
2 tablespoons all-purpose flour
⅓ cup freshly grated Parmesan
   cheese
¼ teaspoon ground nutmeg
¼ teaspoon white pepper

Combine first 2 ingredients; set aside.
Melt margarine in a saucepan over
medium heat; add flour and cook 1
minute, stirring constantly. Gradually
add milk and cook until thickened, stirring constantly with a wire whisk. Add
Parmesan cheese, nutmeg, and pepper; cook until cheese melts, stirring
constantly. Yield: 1 cup plus 1 tablespoon (24 calories per tablespoon).

□ *1.6 grams protein, 1.2 grams fat,
1.9 grams carbohydrate, 2 milligrams
cholesterol, 51 milligrams sodium, and
51 milligrams calcium.*

## EGGPLANT PARMESAN

2 tablespoons all-purpose flour
1 (1-pound) eggplant
⅓ cup egg substitute
2 tablespoons skim milk
⅔ cup dry breadcrumbs
½ teaspoon Italian seasoning
Vegetable cooking spray
Marinara Sauce
1 cup (4 ounces) shredded part-skim
  mozzarella cheese
2 tablespoons Parmesan cheese

Place flour in a large zip-top plastic bag; set aside. Peel and cut eggplant into 12 (½-inch-thick) slices. Place slices in plastic bag; shake to coat.

Combine egg substitute and milk; set aside. Combine breadcrumbs and Italian seasoning. Dip each eggplant slice into egg mixture and dredge lightly in breadcrumbs. Place slices on a baking sheet coated with cooking spray. Bake at 400° for 12 to 14 minutes or until lightly browned.

Coat a 13- x 9- x 2-inch baking dish with cooking spray. Layer half of eggplant slices in dish, overlapping slightly; spoon half of hot Marinara Sauce over eggplant. Repeat with remaining eggplant and sauce. Sprinkle with cheeses and bake 5 minutes or until cheeses melt. Yield: 6 servings (182 calories per serving).

□ *9.9 grams protein, 5.8 grams fat, 24 grams carbohydrate, 17 milligrams cholesterol, 429 milligrams sodium, and 222 milligrams calcium.*

### Marinara Sauce

Vegetable cooking spray
¾ cup chopped onion
½ cup coarsely grated carrot
3 cloves garlic, minced
1 (28-ounce) can tomatoes with
  basil, undrained and chopped
1 teaspoon Italian seasoning
1 bay leaf
1½ teaspoons red wine vinegar

Coat a Dutch oven with cooking spray; place over medium-high heat until hot. Add onion, carrot, and garlic; sauté until tender. Add tomatoes, Italian seasoning, and bay leaf; bring to a boil. Reduce heat and cook 30 minutes, stirring occasionally.

Remove bay leaf; place sauce in an electric blender or food processor. Blend about 5 seconds (mixture will not be smooth). Return sauce to Dutch oven; add vinegar and cook 5 minutes. Yield: 3 cups (43 calories per ½-cup serving).

□ *1.7 grams protein, 0.46 gram fat, 9.1 grams carbohydrate, 0 milligrams cholesterol, 220 milligrams sodium, and 51 milligrams calcium.*

## CHILES RELLENOS CASSEROLE

8 large fresh Anaheim green chiles
1 cup (4 ounces) shredded reduced-
  fat Monterey Jack cheese
½ cup light ricotta cheese
½ cup egg substitute
3 tablespoons water
3 tablespoons all-purpose flour
8 egg whites
¼ teaspoon salt
¼ teaspoon white pepper
Vegetable cooking spray
⅓ cup (1½ ounces) shredded
  reduced-fat sharp Cheddar cheese
⅛ teaspoon chili powder

Place chiles on a baking sheet, and broil 5 to 6 inches from heat, turning often with tongs until chiles are blistered on all sides. Immediately place chiles in a heavy-duty plastic bag; fasten securely, and let steam 10 to 15 minutes.

Remove peel of each chile (chiles will be limp). Split chiles, and carefully remove stem and seeds. Drain on paper towels.

Combine Monterey Jack cheese and ricotta cheese in a small bowl; place an equal amount of cheese mixture down center of each chile, and fold over to close. Set aside.

Combine egg substitute, water, and flour in a large bowl; stir with a wire whisk until smooth. Set aside.

Beat egg whites, salt, and white pepper in a large mixing bowl until stiff peaks form; fold into egg substitute mixture. Coat a 12- x 8- x 2-inch baking dish with cooking spray; spread half of egg white mixture in dish. Place stuffed chiles over mixture; sprinkle with Cheddar cheese. Spread remaining egg white mixture over chiles; sprinkle with chili powder. Bake at 325° for 25 to 30 minutes or until golden brown. Serve immediately. Yield: 4 servings (240 calories per 2 stuffed chiles).

□ *26.1 grams protein, 9.3 grams fat, 14.7 grams carbohydrate, 30 milligrams cholesterol, 582 milligrams sodium, and 380 milligrams calcium.*

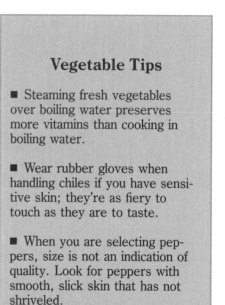

## Vegetable Tips

■ Steaming fresh vegetables over boiling water preserves more vitamins than cooking in boiling water.

■ Wear rubber gloves when handling chiles if you have sensitive skin; they're as fiery to touch as they are to taste.

■ When you are selecting peppers, size is not an indication of quality. Look for peppers with smooth, slick skin that has not shriveled.

■ Eggplant flesh darkens rapidly when cut, so don't peel until just before cooking. Rub cut surfaces with lemon or lime juice to prevent darkening.

■ Remember that leftover vegetables go nicely in a salad. Or make a chef's salad with leftover meats, cheeses, and cold cuts cut in strips and tossed with leftover vegetables, greens, and salad dressing.

# Carrots Make The Cake

Carrot Cake with cream cheese frosting has been a Southern favorite for years, but making a traditional carrot cake healthier involves some trade-offs. Coconut and nuts were eliminated in order to retain the cream cheese frosting (the best part). And low-fat cottage cheese was added to the frosting to decrease the fat.

By using egg substitute for whole eggs and reducing sugar and oil, the calories, fat, and cholesterol are kept to a minimum. Grated carrots, crushed pineapple, and raisins keep the cake tender and moist while adding natural sweetness. Grated orange rind adds a flavor variation to the frosting.

### FROSTED CARROT CAKE

1½ cups all-purpose flour
⅔ cup whole wheat flour
2 teaspoons baking soda
2 teaspoons ground cinnamon
¼ teaspoon salt
1 cup firmly packed brown sugar
¾ cup egg substitute
¾ cup nonfat buttermilk
1 (8-ounce) can crushed pineapple in juice, drained
2 cups grated carrots
⅓ cup raisins
3 tablespoons vegetable oil
2 teaspoons vanilla extract
Vegetable cooking spray
Orange-Cream Cheese Frosting

Combine flours, soda, cinnamon, and salt, and set aside. Combine brown sugar and next 7 ingredients in a large mixing bowl; stir in dry ingredients, and beat at medium speed with an electric mixer until well blended. Pour batter into a 13- x 9- x 2-inch pan coated with cooking spray. Bake at 350° for 30 to 35 minutes or until a wooden pick inserted in center comes out clean. Cool cake completely in pan on wire rack. Spread Orange-Cream Cheese Frosting over top of cake. Cover and chill. Yield: 18 servings (205 calories per serving).

□ *5.3 grams protein, 4.8 grams fat, 35.9 grams carbohydrate, 8 milligrams cholesterol, 255 milligrams sodium, and 78 milligrams calcium.*

### Orange-Cream Cheese Frosting

½ cup 1% fat cottage cheese
2 teaspoons vanilla extract
1 (8-ounce) package light cream cheese, softened
1 teaspoon grated orange rind
1 cup sifted powdered sugar

Position knife blade in food processor bowl, and add cottage cheese. Process about 1 minute or until smooth. Add vanilla, cream cheese, and orange rind, and process until mixture is smooth. Add powdered sugar, and pulse 3 to 5 times until mixture is smooth. Yield: 1½ cups (44 calories per tablespoon).

□ *1.6 grams protein, 1.6 grams fat, 5.9 grams carbohydrate, 6 milligrams cholesterol, 73 milligrams sodium, and 16 milligrams calcium.*

| COMPARE THE NUTRIENTS (per serving) | | |
|---|---|---|
| | Traditional | Light |
| Calories | 455 | 205 |
| Fat | 25.6g | 4.8g |
| Cholesterol | 65 mg | 8 mg |

# No-Knead Yeast Bread

*Now* we're talking easy. Here's a yeast bread with made-from-scratch flavor without the usual kneading and shaping. When you take out those two steps, waiting is the hardest part. Just mix the batter, then let the yeast go to work. The interesting thing about Parmesan Bread? It's baked in a casserole dish, so you get a different look *and* great taste.

### PARMESAN BREAD

1 package dry yeast
1 cup warm water (105° to 115°)
3 cups all-purpose flour, divided
¼ cup butter or margarine, melted
1 egg, beaten
2 tablespoons sugar
2 teaspoons dried onion flakes
1 teaspoon salt
1 teaspoon Italian seasoning
½ teaspoon garlic salt
⅔ cup grated Parmesan cheese, divided
1 tablespoon butter or margarine, melted

Dissolve yeast in warm water in a large mixing bowl; let stand 5 minutes. Stir in 2 cups flour and next 7 ingredients. Beat at medium speed with an electric mixer 2 minutes. Gradually stir in ⅓ cup Parmesan cheese and remaining 1 cup flour. Cover and let rise in a warm place (85°), free from drafts, 1 hour or until doubled in bulk.

Punch dough down, and place in a greased 2-quart casserole. Brush with 1 tablespoon melted butter; sprinkle with remaining ⅓ cup Parmesan cheese. Cover and let rise in a warm place, free from drafts, 45 minutes or until doubled in bulk. Bake at 350° for 30 minutes or until golden. Cool in casserole 10 minutes. Remove and cool on wire rack. Serve warm or cool. Yield: 1 loaf. *Velma McGregor Gretna, Virginia*

# QUICK!

## Winter Warm-Ups

At what other time of the year other than winter can you skip the fancy appetizers and simply dig out that old fondue pot? Or enjoy a good chat and a mug of warm cider with a friend? These recipes remind us to take the time in the cold-weather months to enjoy tempting foods that very often get overlooked during warmer weather.

So stir up a pot of chili, or make beef stroganoff. These recipes beat the chill—and in less than 30 minutes.

### APPLE-ORANGE CIDER

1 quart apple cider
¼ cup orange juice
2 (4-inch) sticks cinnamon
6 whole cloves
Cinnamon sticks (optional)

Combine first 4 ingredients in a 2-quart saucepan. Cook over medium heat until thoroughly heated. Serve hot. Serve with cinnamon sticks, if desired. Yield: 1 quart.
*Ann C. McConnell*
*Kensington, Maryland*

### QUICK BEEF STROGANOFF

1 pound top round steak
2 tablespoons vegetable oil
1 onion, sliced
1 (8-ounce) carton sour cream
1 (10¾-ounce) can cream of
 mushroom soup, undiluted
2 tablespoons catsup
2 teaspoons Worcestershire sauce
Hot cooked noodles
Poppy seeds

Trim excess fat from steak; slice across grain into 2- x ¼-inch strips. Brown steak in oil; add onion and cook 5 minutes, stirring constantly.

Combine sour cream, soup, catsup, and Worcestershire sauce; add to steak. Cook over low heat, stirring constantly, until mixture is thoroughly heated. Serve over noodles sprinkled with poppy seeds. Yield: 4 servings.
*Ann Carolyn Jones*
*Lawrenceburg, Tennessee*

### PARTY CHEESE FONDUE

1 (11-ounce) can Cheddar cheese
 soup, undiluted
1 (8-ounce) carton French onion dip
1 cup (4 ounces) shredded sharp
 Cheddar cheese
½ teaspoon dry mustard
⅛ teaspoon red pepper

Combine all ingredients in a small, heavy saucepan; cook over medium heat, stirring constantly, until thoroughly heated and cheese melts. Transfer to fondue pot; place over heating unit to keep hot. Serve with breadsticks, apple slices, or nacho chips. Yield: 2⅓ cups. *Jamie Tarence*
*Montgomery, Alabama*

### QUICK-AND-EASY CHILI

1 pound lean ground beef
1 (16-ounce) can tomatoes,
 undrained and chopped
2 (15-ounce) cans red kidney beans,
 undrained
1 (10-ounce) can tomatoes and
 green chiles, undrained
1½ cups water
1 (1¾-ounce) envelope chili
 seasoning mix
1 (0.27-ounce) envelope instant
 onion soup mix

Cook ground beef in a Dutch oven until meat is browned, stirring until it crumbles; drain. Add tomatoes and remaining ingredients. Bring to a boil; reduce heat, and simmer, uncovered, 10 minutes, stirring occasionally. Yield: 9 cups. *Carolyn Pearce*
*Shreveport, Louisiana*

## Chicken Soups From "Dr. Mom"

Whether it's "starve a fever, feed a cold" or "feed a fever, starve a cold," a bowl of the proverbial "Mom's chicken soup" will cure what ails you. The usual chicken-noodle version will do, but here are four exciting variations sure to lift your spirits *and* your fever. If the cook is the one in bed, don't worry. These recipes use leftover chicken and several canned ingredients, so they're easy enough for a pinch hitter to handle.

### CREAMY CHICKEN-VEGETABLE CHOWDER

2 cups chopped cooked chicken
1 (10¾-ounce) can cream of potato
 soup, undiluted
1 (10¾-ounce) can cream of
 chicken soup, undiluted
1 (11-ounce) can Mexican-style
 corn, undrained
1 (4½-ounce) jar sliced mushrooms,
 undrained
1 (4-ounce) can chopped green
 chiles, undrained
1½ cups milk
1 cup chicken broth
⅓ cup sliced green onions
1½ cups (6 ounces) shredded
 Cheddar cheese
Garnish: sliced green onions

Combine chopped chicken, potato soup, chicken soup, corn, mushrooms, green chiles, milk, chicken broth, and green onions in a Dutch oven, stirring well. Cook over medium heat 5 to 8 minutes or until thoroughly heated. Remove from heat; add cheese, stirring until cheese melts. Garnish, if desired, and serve immediately. Yield: 9 cups.
*Lilann Taylor*
*Savannah, Georgia*

## CHICKEN-ALMOND CREAM SOUP

1 cup chopped celery
½ cup chopped onion
3 tablespoons butter or margarine, melted
3 tablespoons all-purpose flour
¼ teaspoon pepper
1 quart milk
2 teaspoons chicken-flavored bouillon granules
½ teaspoon Worcestershire sauce
1 cup chopped cooked chicken
½ cup sliced almonds, toasted

Cook celery and onion in butter in a Dutch oven over low heat until tender. Stir in flour and pepper; cook 1 minute, stirring constantly. Gradually stir in milk. Add bouillon granules and Worcestershire sauce; cook over medium heat, stirring constantly, until thickened and bubbly.

Stir in chicken and almonds; cook until thoroughly heated, stirring often. Yield: 1½ quarts.       *Patsy Bell Hobson*
*Liberty, Missouri*

## CURRIED CHICKEN-AND-CORN CHOWDER

1 cup chopped onion
1 tablespoon butter or margarine, melted
2 to 3 teaspoons curry powder
2 (6¾-ounce) cans chunk white chicken, drained
1 (17-ounce) can cream-style yellow corn
1 (14½-ounce) can ready-to-serve chicken broth
1 cup chopped tomato
1 cup whipping cream

Cook onion in butter in a Dutch oven over low heat until tender. Add curry powder; cook 1 minute, stirring constantly. Stir in chicken and remaining ingredients; bring mixture to a boil. Reduce heat and simmer, uncovered, 5 to 7 minutes, stirring often. Yield: about 7 cups.       *Sandi Pichon*
*Slidell, Louisiana*

## CHEESY CHICKEN CHOWDER

4 cups chicken broth
1½ cups diced potatoes
1 cup diced celery
1 cup diced carrots
½ cup diced onion
¼ cup butter or margarine
⅓ cup all-purpose flour
3 cups milk
1 tablespoon soy sauce
1 (8-ounce) loaf process cheese spread, cubed
2 cups chopped cooked chicken

Combine first 5 ingredients in a large saucepan; cover and cook over medium heat 15 minutes or until vegetables are tender.

Melt butter in a Dutch oven over low heat; add flour, stirring until smooth. Cook 1 minute, stirring constantly. Gradually stir in milk; cook over medium heat, stirring constantly, until thickened and bubbly. Gradually stir in vegetable mixture, soy sauce, cheese, and chicken. Cook until cheese melts and mixture is thoroughly heated. Yield: 2½ quarts.

*Mrs. William Yoder, Jr.*
*Montezuma, Georgia*

# Packing New Ideas For Lunch

There are many good reasons for packing lunches to take to school or work—to appease finicky eaters, to monitor nutrition, to save money, and to provide lunch when no other source is available. But don't get caught in the rut of taking peanut butter-and-jelly sandwiches day after day. Here are several alternatives for your lunchbox.

Whether packing lunches for children or adults, don't forget the importance of proper storage of foods that might spoil. For foods that need to stay cold, a refrigerator is the best choice. If refrigeration is not possible, you can rely on frozen gel packs to keep foods cool for short periods of time. Check them regularly for signs of splitting and leakage, and discard any food that comes in contact with a damaged gel pack. Or you may prefer to freeze rectangular cardboard containers of juice (commonly known as juice boxes) to use in the same fashion as gel packs. They help keep foods cool for a short period of time and provide a thirst quencher, too, when thawed. Remember that items that are likely to spoil need to stay below 45° to be safe.

Store in the refrigerator foods that are to be served hot; then reheat them in a microwave. Many companies provide microwave ovens for employee use. A thermos also helps keep hot foods hot for short periods of time. Most stainless-steel models keep food hotter than those made of plastic. Fill the thermos with hot water, and let it stand five minutes; then pour out the water, and quickly fill the thermos with food that has just been brought to a boil. To ensure safety, hot foods need to stay above 140°.

## Lunch for the Little Ones

Prevent lunchtime doldrums by sending Nutty Snack Mix or a container of Peanut Butter Spread for little ones to slather over rice cakes or fresh fruit. A bag of Raisin-Granola Treats also makes a good option for dessert—they look like cookies but are full of healthful ingredients.

## PEANUT BUTTER SPREAD

½ cup peanut butter
½ cup butter or margarine, softened
½ cup dark corn syrup

Combine peanut butter and butter, stirring until smooth. Stir in corn syrup, mixing well. Serve as a spread for rice cakes, fruit, toast, or waffles. Yield: 1½ cups.       *Nora Henshaw*
*Castle, Oklahoma*

## NUTTY SNACK MIX

3 cups corn-and-rice cereal
1 cup honey-graham cereal or bear-shaped graham cereal
1 (12-ounce) jar unsalted, dry-roasted peanuts
¼ cup grated Parmesan cheese
¼ teaspoon garlic powder
¼ cup butter or margarine, melted

Combine first 5 ingredients in a 15- x 10- x 1-inch jellyroll pan. Pour butter evenly over mixture; stir gently to coat. Bake at 300° for 15 minutes, stirring every 5 minutes. Remove from oven; cool. Store in an airtight container. Yield: 6¼ cups.

## RAISIN-GRANOLA TREATS

1 cup raisins
½ cup butter or margarine
1 (6-ounce) can frozen apple juice concentrate, thawed
1 large egg, lightly beaten
1¼ cups all-purpose flour
1 teaspoon baking soda
½ teaspoon ground cinnamon
½ teaspoon finely shredded orange rind
2 cups granola

Combine first 3 ingredients in a medium saucepan; cook over medium heat until butter melts. Cool. Add egg, mixing well. Set aside.
Combine flour, soda, and cinnamon; stir into raisin mixture. Stir in orange rind and granola. Let dough stand 2 minutes. Drop by rounded tablespoonfuls 2 inches apart on ungreased cookie sheets. Bake at 350° for 10 minutes. Let cool on wire racks. Yield: 3½ dozen.          *Sandra Russell*
*Gainesville, Florida*

## Lunch for Light Appetites
Dried Fruit Mix and Tortellini-Pesto Salad make good choices for adults who watch their nutrients closely. A

Chutney-Chicken Croissant is also a tasty alternative; pack the croissant, sprouts, and chicken mixture separately, and chill until ready to serve.

## TORTELLINI-PESTO SALAD

1 (9-ounce) package fresh cheese-filled tortellini
1 small sweet red pepper, cut into julienne strips
¾ cup broccoli flowerets
⅓ cup carrot slices
⅓ cup sliced pimiento-stuffed olives
½ cup mayonnaise or salad dressing
¼ cup commercial pesto sauce
¼ cup milk
2 tablespoons grated Parmesan cheese
1 tablespoon olive oil
1 teaspoon white vinegar
1 clove garlic, minced
Fresh spinach leaves (optional)

Cook tortellini according to package directions; drain. Rinse tortellini in cold water; drain well. Combine tortellini and next 4 ingredients in a medium bowl; set aside.
Combine mayonnaise and next 6 ingredients; spoon over tortellini mixture, and toss gently. Cover and chill until ready to serve. Serve on fresh spinach leaves, if desired. Yield: 4 to 6 servings.          *Travis Baker*
*Meeker, Oklahoma*

## DRIED FRUIT MIX

⅔ cup pecan halves
½ cup flaked coconut
⅓ cup sunflower kernels
1 cup pitted prunes
1 cup dried apricots
½ cup banana chips

Combine first 3 ingredients in a shallow pan. Bake at 350° for 5 to 7 minutes or until lightly toasted, stirring twice. Cool. Stir in prunes, apricots, and banana chips. Store in an airtight container. Yield: 3½ cups.

## CHUTNEY-CHICKEN CROISSANTS

1 (8-ounce) container whipped cream cheese
3 tablespoons commercial chutney, chopped
1½ teaspoons curry powder
2 cups chopped cooked chicken
Commercial croissants, cut in half horizontally
Alfalfa sprouts

Combine first 3 ingredients, stirring until blended. Add chicken; stir well. Spread mixture on bottom halves of croissants. Top with alfalfa sprouts and tops of croissants. Yield: 6 to 8 servings.

## Lunch for Hearty Eaters
For the meat-and-potatoes crowd who prefers heavy entrées during the day, either corned beef piled on a kaiser roll or Mexican Casserole reheated in a microwave would fit the bill nicely. Pack the corned beef filling separately to keep the bread from getting soggy, and pack the corn chips to top the casserole in a separate container, as well.

## MEXICAN CASSEROLE

1 cup elbow macaroni, uncooked
1 pound ground beef
¼ cup chopped onion
1 (15½-ounce) can Mexican-style chili beans, undrained
1 (10-ounce) can enchilada sauce
2 to 3 teaspoons chili powder
½ teaspoon salt
¼ teaspoon pepper
1 cup (4 ounces) shredded Cheddar cheese
¾ cup corn chips, crushed

Cook macaroni according to package directions, omitting salt. Drain macaroni and set aside.
Crumble beef into a 2-quart casserole; add onion. Cover tightly with heavy-duty plastic wrap; fold back a small corner of wrap to allow steam to

escape. Microwave at HIGH 5 to 7 minutes or until done. Drain well. Stir in macaroni, beans, and next 4 ingredients. Microwave at MEDIUM-HIGH (70% power) 9 to 11 minutes, giving dish a quarter-turn after 5 minutes. Sprinkle with cheese, and microwave at HIGH 1 minute. Sprinkle corn chips on top. Yield: 6 servings.

**Conventional Directions:** Prepare macaroni according to package directions, omitting salt. Drain and set aside. Cook ground beef and onion in a large skillet until meat is browned, stirring to crumble meat; drain well. Stir in macaroni, chili beans, and next 4 ingredients; spoon into a greased 2-quart casserole. Bake at 350° for 25 minutes; sprinkle with cheese, and bake an additional 5 minutes. Sprinkle corn chips on top. *Peggy C. Harris Fayetteville, North Carolina*

## CORNED BEEF SANDWICHES

1 (7-ounce) can chopped cooked
   corned beef
⅓ cup minced celery
1 tablespoon minced onion
¼ cup mayonnaise or salad
   dressing
1½ teaspoons prepared mustard
5 kaiser rolls, split

Combine first 5 ingredients; mix well. Spread mixture on bottom half of each roll; cover with top of roll. Yield: 5 servings. *Charlotte Pierce Greensburg, Kentucky*

**Tip:** *When selecting onions, consider all of the flavor possibilities. The large Spanish or Bermuda onion and the small white onion are usually mild in flavor, while Globe types, such as red, brown, and small yellow onions, are stronger flavored.*

# Uptown Menu, Down-Home Food

If you're one who likes the New Year's tradition of eating greens and black-eyed peas, you'll like this menu.

For financial fortune, you'll enjoy Uptown Collards, simmered in Chablis and dotted with red pepper for color. Good luck comes from Spicy Black-eyed Peas. After all this flavor, try Lemon Cheesecake for dessert.

## HERBED PORK PINWHEELS

3 small sweet red or yellow
   peppers
¾ cup finely chopped onion
¾ cup finely chopped celery
1½ teaspoons dried thyme, crushed
¾ teaspoon garlic salt
¾ teaspoon red pepper
¾ teaspoon paprika
3 tablespoons vegetable oil
3 (¾-pound) pork tenderloins
1½ tablespoons fennel seeds,
   crushed
1½ tablespoons lemon-pepper
   seasoning

Sauté first 7 ingredients in hot oil until tender; set aside.

Slice each pork tenderloin lengthwise down center, cutting to but not through bottom. Place each between sheets of heavy-duty plastic wrap; pound to a 12- x 8-inch rectangle of even thickness using a meat mallet.

Spoon one-third of pepper mixture onto tenderloin, spreading to within ½-inch of sides; roll tenderloin, jelly-roll fashion, starting with short side. Tie with heavy string at 1½-inch intervals. Repeat procedure with remaining tenderloins and pepper mixture. Combine last 2 seasonings; rub onto top and sides of tenderloins.

Place seam side down, on a lightly greased rack in a shallow pan. Bake, uncovered at 325° for 45 minutes or until done. Let stand 10 minutes; remove strings, and slice. Yield: 8 to 10 servings. *M. K. Quesenberry Dugspur, Virginia*

## UPTOWN COLLARDS

7 pounds fresh collards
1 medium onion, quartered
1 cup water
1 cup Chablis or other dry white
   wine
1 tablespoon sugar
1 tablespoon bacon drippings
1 small sweet red pepper, diced

Remove stems from greens. Wash leaves thoroughly, and cut into 1-inch-wide strips; set aside.

Position knife blade in food processor bowl; add onion, and process until smooth. Combine onion and next 4 ingredients in a large Dutch oven; bring to a boil. Add greens and red pepper; cover and cook over medium heat 45 minutes to 1 hour or until greens are tender, adding additional water, if necessary. Yield: 8 to 10 servings. *John Alex Floyd, Jr. Trussville, Alabama*

## SPICY BLACK-EYED PEAS

1 (16-ounce) bag dried black-eyed
   peas
5 cups water
2 tablespoons minced green onions
1 tablespoon Creole seasoning
1 teaspoon dried parsley flakes
1 teaspoon garlic powder
1 teaspoon chili powder
1 teaspoon coarsely ground pepper
3 chicken-flavored bouillon cubes

Sort and wash peas; place in a large Dutch oven. Add water to cover peas 2 inches; let soak 8 hours. Drain peas, and return to Dutch oven. Add 5 cups water and remaining ingredients. Bring to a boil; cover, reduce heat, and simmer 45 minutes to 1 hour or until tender, stirring occasionally. Yield: 8 to 10 servings. *Lynne Teal Weeks Columbus, Georgia*

## LEMON CHEESECAKE

¾ **cup graham cracker crumbs**
2 **tablespoons sugar**
1 **tablespoon ground cinnamon**
1 **tablespoon butter or margarine,**
   **softened**
5 **(8-ounce) packages cream cheese,**
   **softened**
1⅔ **cups sugar**
5 **eggs**
⅛ **teaspoon salt**
1½ **teaspoons vanilla extract**
¼ **cup lemon juice**

Combine first 3 ingredients; stir well, and set aside. Grease bottom and sides of a 10-inch springform pan with butter. Add crumb mixture; tilt pan to coat sides and bottom. Chill.

Beat cream cheese at medium speed with an electric mixer until light and fluffy; gradually add 1⅔ cups sugar, beating well at high speed. Add eggs, one at a time, beating well after each addition. Stir in salt, vanilla, and lemon juice; pour mixture into prepared crust. Bake at 300° for 1 hour and 20 minutes. (Center may be soft but will set when chilled.) Cool on a wire rack; cover and chill 8 hours. Yield: 10 servings.       *Dale Safrit*
*Columbus, Ohio*

# Time Out For Super Bowl Snacks

When a crowd gathers to watch the Super Bowl, all eyes are typically glued to the TV. Most folks don't even look down as fingers dig into munchies. But serve these recipes, and we predict guests will take notice.

### GREEN ONION-CHEESE SPREAD

2 **(8-ounce) packages cream cheese,**
   **softened**
¼ **cup milk**
¾ **cup minced green onions**

Beat cream cheese at medium speed with an electric mixer until smooth; gradually add milk, beating until light and fluffy. Stir in green onions. Cover and chill up to 2 days. Serve with crackers. Yield: 2½ cups.
*Clara B. Givens*
*Lubbock, Texas*

### EASY ANTIPASTO

1 **(14-ounce) can artichoke hearts,**
   **drained and quartered**
1 **cup cherry tomatoes, halved**
½ **cup pitted ripe olives**
½ **cup pimiento-stuffed olives**
8 **to 12 pepperoncini salad peppers,**
   **drained**
1 **(2½-ounce) jar sliced mushrooms,**
   **drained**
1 **(8-ounce) bottle reduced-calorie**
   **Italian salad dressing**
1 **(8-ounce) package mozzarella**
   **cheese**
1 **(6-ounce) package thinly sliced**
   **boiled ham**
**Leaf lettuce**

Arrange first 6 ingredients in a 12- x 8- x 2-inch dish. Drizzle dressing over vegetables. Cover and refrigerate 8 hours, stirring occasionally.

Cut mozzarella into sticks. Cut ham slices in half; roll into logs, and secure with decorative wooden picks.

Drain vegetables, reserving marinade. Arrange vegetables, cheese, and ham on a lettuce-lined tray. Drizzle reserved marinade over cheese and ham. Yield: 6 to 8 appetizer servings.       *Laura B. Harris*
*Rock Hill, South Carolina*

# Horseradish Packs A Powerful Punch

Once you've tried horseradish, you never forget it. If you stir just a little prepared horseradish into a recipe, the result is usually a mild flavor that pleasantly tingles your tongue. But a heavy hand with the ingredient will open both your eyes and sinuses.

For the easiest approach to these recipes, use prepared horseradish found in your grocer's refrigerated section. If you prefer to make your own, we also offer a recipe calling for horseradish root, found in many produce departments. But be warned: Horseradish is better than onions for a good cry.

### BAKED HORSERADISH SQUARES

1 **small onion, quartered**
½ **pound cooked ham, coarsely**
   **chopped**
8 **ounces extra-sharp Cheddar**
   **cheese, coarsely chopped**
1½ **tablespoons prepared**
   **horseradish**
½ **teaspoon salt**
¼ **teaspoon pepper**
½ **teaspoon hot pepper sauce**
1 **(16-ounce) loaf very thinly sliced**
   **sandwich bread**
**Paprika**

Position knife blade in food processor bowl; add onion and ham. Process until finely chopped. Remove from bowl; set aside. Add cheese to processor bowl; process until finely chopped. Return onion and ham to processor bowl. Add horseradish, salt, pepper, and hot pepper sauce; process just until mixture begins to form a ball.

Spread about 1 tablespoon mixture on each bread slice. Place slices on ungreased baking sheets; cover and freeze about 20 minutes or until spread is firm. Remove crusts, and cut each slice into 4 small squares or triangles. Sprinkle with paprika; bake at 400° for 12 to 14 minutes. Remove from oven; serve immediately. Yield: 9 dozen appetizers.

**Note:** Appetizers may be frozen up to 1 week. To serve, remove from freezer. Let stand 10 minutes, quarter slices, and bake as above.
*Betty Rabe*
*Plano, Texas*

## STUFFED CHERRY TOMATOES

2 dozen cherry tomatoes
1 (8-ounce) package cream cheese, softened
1½ to 2 tablespoons prepared horseradish
¼ cup bacon bits

Cut top off each tomato; scoop out pulp, reserving pulp for other uses. Invert tomato shells on paper towels to drain.

Combine cream cheese, horseradish, and bacon bits in small bowl; beat at medium speed with an electric mixer until light and fluffy. Spoon or pipe cream cheese mixture into tomato shells. Yield: 2 dozen appetizers.          *Mary Loftin Bruff*
*Westminster, Maryland*

## HOMEMADE HORSERADISH

6 ounces horseradish root
½ cup half-and-half
⅓ cup white vinegar
1 tablespoon brown sugar
2 tablespoons vegetable oil
1 teaspoon salt
½ teaspoon dry mustard

Scrub horseradish root; peel with a knife or vegetable peeler, and coarsely chop. Position knife blade in food processor bowl; add horseradish and remaining ingredients. Cover with lid and process until finely chopped. Spoon into a small saucepan, and cook over medium heat until thoroughly heated (do not boil). Store in covered container in refrigerator up to 1 month. Yield: 1⅓ cups.

## ZESTY CLAM DIP

1 (15-ounce) can New England clam chowder
1½ (8-ounce) packages cream cheese, softened
2 tablespoons minced onion
2 tablespoons prepared horseradish
2 tablespoons Worcestershire sauce

Combine all ingredients in container of an electric blender or food processor; process until smooth. Serve with raw vegetables or chips. Yield: 4 cups.
*Betty Huffcut*
*Pensacola, Florida*

# Quick-Rise Yeast Bread

Sure you're busy, but you still have time to bake yeast bread. This recipe for Quick Whole Wheat Bread uses rapid-rise yeast, which shaves a significant amount of time from traditional bread-baking techniques. You stir the yeast directly into the dry ingredients without dissolving it, and the dough has to rise just one time. Four or five twists of the wrist are all the kneading required.

The time it takes the bread to rise is shorter using this yeast. Even though the texture is slightly coarser than bread made with regular yeast, the end product has virtually the same yeast flavor.

## QUICK WHOLE WHEAT BREAD

2¼ cups water
½ cup butter or margarine
4 cups bread flour, divided
2 cups whole wheat flour
2½ teaspoons salt
2 teaspoons sugar
1 package rapid-rise yeast

Combine water and butter in a saucepan; heat until butter melts, stirring occasionally. Remove from heat and cool to 125° to 130°.

Combine 3 cups bread flour and remaining ingredients in a large mixing bowl; stir well. Gradually add liquid mixture to flour mixture, beating well at high speed with an electric mixer. Beat an additional 2 minutes at medium speed. Gradually stir in enough remaining flour to make a soft dough. Cover bowl, and let dough rest 10 minutes.

Punch dough down; turn out onto a lightly floured surface, and knead lightly 4 or 5 times. Divide dough in half, shaping each into a loaf. Place each loaf in a greased 8½- x 4½- x 3-inch loafpan.

Cover and let rise in a warm place (85°), free from drafts, 45 minutes or until doubled in bulk. Uncover and bake at 350° for 45 minutes or until loaves sound hollow when tapped. Remove from pans immediately; cool on wire racks. Yield: 2 loaves.

# Potatoes: Plain To Fancy

A little name-calling may be in order for one of our favorite vegetables. Some say just plain "potatoes," while others opt for the spunkier "spuds."

## POTATOES WITH EGGS AND MEAT

¼ pound bulk pork sausage
1 tablespoon vegetable oil
2 medium potatoes, peeled and diced
4 eggs, slightly beaten
8 (6-inch) flour tortillas
Picante sauce

Brown sausage in a large nonstick skillet, stirring until it crumbles. Drain and set aside.

Heat oil in skillet; add potatoes, and cook until tender, stirring often. Return sausage to skillet; pour eggs over potatoes and sausage. Draw a spatula across bottom of skillet until egg forms large curds; then remove skillet from heat.

Heat tortillas according to package directions. Spoon potato mixture evenly down center of each tortilla; top with picante sauce. Roll up tortillas, and serve immediately. Yield: 4 servings.
*Sharon Franklin*
*Lewisville, Texas*

## BAKED POTATO SOUP

4 large baking potatoes
⅔ cup butter or margarine
⅔ cup all-purpose flour
6 cups milk
¾ teaspoon salt
½ teaspoon pepper
4 green onions, chopped and divided
12 slices bacon, cooked, crumbled, and divided
1¼ cups (5 ounces) shredded Cheddar cheese, divided
1 (8-ounce) carton sour cream

Wash potatoes and prick several times with a fork; bake at 400° for 1 hour or until done. Let cool. Cut potatoes in half lengthwise; scoop out pulp, and set aside. Discard skins.

Melt butter in a heavy saucepan over low heat; add flour, stirring until smooth. Cook 1 minute, stirring constantly. Gradually add milk; cook over medium heat, stirring constantly, until mixture is thickened and bubbly.

Add potato pulp, salt, pepper, 2 tablespoons green onions, ½ cup bacon, and 1 cup cheese. Cook until thoroughly heated, and stir in sour cream. Add extra milk, if necessary, for desired consistency. Serve with remaining green onions, bacon, and cheese. Yield: 10 cups.                *La Juan Coward*
*Jasper, Texas*

## CRAB-STUFFED POTATOES

6 large baking potatoes
Vegetable oil
½ cup butter or margarine
½ cup sour cream
1 cup (4 ounces) shredded Cheddar cheese
½ teaspoon salt
½ teaspoon Old Bay seasoning
¼ teaspoon pepper
½ pound fresh lump crabmeat *
¼ cup finely sliced green onions
2 tablespoons fine, dry breadcrumbs
¼ teaspoon paprika
¼ teaspoon Old Bay seasoning

Wash potatoes, and rub skins with vegetable oil. Prick each potato several times with a fork. Bake at 400° for 1 hour or until potatoes are done. Let cool. Cut a 1-inch lengthwise strip from top of each potato. Carefully scoop out pulp, leaving a ¼-inch shell intact; mash pulp.

Combine potato pulp, butter, and next 5 ingredients; gently stir in lump crabmeat and green onions. Stuff shells with potato mixture. Sprinkle with breadcrumbs, paprika, and ¼ teaspoon Old Bay seasoning. Bake stuffed potatoes at 425° for 15 minutes. Yield: 6 servings.

* One 6-ounce can lump crabmeat, drained, may be substituted for ½ pound fresh lump crabmeat.
                *Sandra Rhodes Potter*
*Cambridge, Maryland*

## BARBECUED POTATOES

1 tablespoon butter or margarine, melted
1 tablespoon honey
2 teaspoons chili powder
⅛ to ¼ teaspoon garlic powder
⅛ teaspoon pepper
3 medium-size baking potatoes, cut into ½-inch slices

Combine first 5 ingredients; add potatoes, tossing to coat. Spread potatoes evenly on a lightly greased 15- x 10- x 1-inch jellyroll pan. Bake at 425° for 20 minutes or until tender. Yield: 4 servings.                *Dee Gilbert*
*Knightdale, North Carolina*

# Standby Vegetable Casseroles

When you run out of creativity, when you just can't make another involved recipe, when one more dinner party is more than you can take, turn to an old standby—casseroles.

All these recipes—except Greek-Style Squash—can be made ahead. (The phyllo pastry gets soggy if you let it sit.) Simply prepare the casseroles, and refrigerate 8 hours. Let them stand 30 minutes to come to room temperature before cooking for the amount of time directed.

## GREEK-STYLE SQUASH

2½ pounds yellow squash, sliced or 3 (10-ounce) packages frozen sliced yellow squash, thawed
1 large onion, chopped
1 teaspoon salt
1 cup water
1 (16-ounce) container ricotta cheese
1 cup cottage cheese
½ cup grated Parmesan cheese
¼ teaspoon salt
¼ teaspoon white pepper
1 (16-ounce) package frozen phyllo pastry, thawed
Butter-flavored vegetable cooking spray

Combine first 4 ingredients in a Dutch oven. Bring to a boil over medium heat. Reduce heat, and simmer 5 to 7 minutes or until squash is tender; drain. Set aside.

Combine ricotta cheese and next 4 ingredients. Set aside.

Keep phyllo covered with a slightly damp towel until ready for use. Place 1 phyllo sheet horizontally on a flat surface. Coat phyllo with cooking spray. Layer 5 more phyllo sheets on first sheet, spraying each sheet with cooking spray; place phyllo in a lightly greased 13- x 9- x 2-inch baking dish, letting excess phyllo pastry fall over sides of dish.

Spoon half each of squash mixture and cheese mixture over phyllo in dish. Repeat procedure with 6 more sheets of phyllo and remaining squash mixture and cheese mixture. Coat remaining phyllo with cooking spray, and place on top of casserole. Using scissors, trim overhanging edges of phyllo

around dish. Bake at 350° for 40 minutes or until golden. Yield: 10 to 12 servings.
*Carol Yarbro*
*Birmingham, Alabama*

## VEGETABLE-CURRY CASSEROLE

1 (16-ounce) package frozen broccoli, green beans, celery, red pepper, and mushrooms
1 (10¾-ounce) can cream of chicken soup, undiluted
1 cup (4 ounces) shredded sharp Cheddar cheese
¼ to ⅓ cup mayonnaise or salad dressing
½ teaspoon curry powder
¼ cup fine dry breadcrumbs
2 tablespoons butter or margarine, melted

Cook vegetables according to package directions; drain. Combine vegetables and next 4 ingredients; spoon into a lightly greased 1-quart casserole. Combine breadcrumbs and butter; sprinkle over casserole. Bake at 350° for 30 minutes or until bubbly and lightly browned. Yield: 4 servings.
*Lois M. Peele*
*Greensboro, North Carolina*

## LAYERED VEGETABLE CASSEROLE

1 (10¾-ounce) can cream of mushroom soup, undiluted
1 (6-ounce) roll garlic cheese, sliced
1 (5-ounce) can evaporated milk
1 (16-ounce) can whole green beans, drained
2 (14-ounce) cans artichoke hearts, drained and quartered
1 (8-ounce) can sliced water chestnuts, drained
2 (4-ounce) cans sliced mushrooms, drained
1 (16-ounce) package frozen broccoli cuts
¾ cup sliced green onions
½ cup soft breadcrumbs
¼ cup butter or margarine, melted

Combine first 3 ingredients in a medium saucepan. Cook over medium heat until mixture is smooth, stirring often. Remove from heat.

Combine green beans and next 5 ingredients. Spoon half of vegetable mixture into a lightly greased 12- x 8- x 2-inch casserole; pour half of sauce over vegetables. Repeat procedure with remaining vegetables and sauce.

Combine breadcrumbs and butter; sprinkle over casserole. Bake at 350° for 40 minutes or until bubbly and lightly browned. Yield: 8 to 10 servings.
*Carol Barclay*
*Portland, Texas*

# Cook Up Some Fun This Weekend

After a hectic week of catch-as-catch-can meals, it's time to slow the pace and actually enjoy your kitchen this weekend. Recreational cooks pull out pots and pans the way shoppers hit the malls and sports enthusiasts head to the gym for fun.

These recipes are involved enough to be interesting, but not so complicated to be frustrating. They serve from 6 to 12 people, so weekend chefs can treat the whole family and even invite a few friends.

## ITALIAN PORK ROAST

1 (3- to 3½-pound) rolled boneless pork loin roast
4 cloves garlic, halved
1 tablespoon olive oil
1 to 2 tablespoons dried Italian seasoning
1 teaspoon coarsely ground pepper

Place roast in a shallow roasting pan. Cut 8 small slits into roast at 2-inch intervals; insert garlic halves deep into slits. Brush olive oil evenly over roast, and sprinkle with Italian seasoning and pepper. Insert meat thermometer, making sure it does not touch fat. Bake at 325° for 1½ hours (30 minutes per pound) or until meat thermometer reaches 155°. Remove from oven, and cover loosely with aluminum foil. Let stand 15 minutes or until thermometer reaches 160°. Yield: 10 to 12 servings.
*Sara Cairns*
*Montevallo, Alabama*

## DEVILED CRAB CASSEROLE

1 pound fresh crabmeat, drained and flaked *
2 cups soft breadcrumbs, divided
½ cup chopped celery
2 tablespoons finely chopped green pepper
2 tablespoons chopped fresh parsley
2 tablespoons chopped chives
2 hard-cooked eggs, chopped
½ cup mayonnaise or salad dressing
2½ tablespoons lemon juice
1 tablespoon prepared mustard
½ teaspoon salt
½ teaspoon Worcestershire sauce
½ teaspoon hot sauce
1 egg, beaten
2 tablespoons butter or margarine, melted

Combine crabmeat, 1 cup breadcrumbs, celery, green pepper, parsley, chives, and egg in a lightly greased 2-quart baking dish. Combine mayonnaise and next 6 ingredients, and stir into crabmeat mixture.

Combine butter and remaining breadcrumbs; sprinkle on top. Bake at 375° for 35 minutes or until thoroughly heated. Yield: 6 servings.

* You can substitute one (16-ounce) container pasteurized crabmeat, drained and flaked, for fresh crabmeat. To make casserole ahead, assemble and chill 8 hours before baking. Remove from refrigerator, and let sit at room temperature 30 minutes before baking as instructed.
*Marge Killmon*
*Annandale, Virginia*

## SAVORY YOGURT CHICKEN

1 cup fine, dry breadcrumbs
¼ cup grated Parmesan cheese
1 to 2 tablespoons instant minced
  onion
1 teaspoon garlic powder
1 teaspoon seasoned salt
¼ teaspoon dried whole oregano,
  crushed
¼ teaspoon dried thyme, crushed
Dash of pepper
1 (8-ounce) carton plain yogurt
8 chicken breast halves, skinned
¼ cup butter or margarine, melted
1 teaspoon sesame seeds
Creamy Yogurt Sauce

Combine first 8 ingredients in a shallow dish; set aside.

Brush yogurt on both sides of chicken breast halves; coat with breadcrumb mixture. Place in a lightly greased 15- x 10- x 1-inch pan. Drizzle with butter, and sprinkle with sesame seeds. Bake, uncovered, at 350° for 50 to 60 minutes or until done. Serve casserole with Creamy Yogurt Sauce. Yield: 8 servings.

### Creamy Yogurt Sauce

1 (8-ounce) carton plain yogurt
1 (10¾-ounce) can cream of
  chicken soup, undiluted
½ teaspoon chicken-flavored
  bouillon granules
½ teaspoon lemon juice
½ teaspoon Worcestershire
  sauce
Dash of garlic powder
Dash of seasoned salt

Combine yogurt (at room temperature) and remaining ingredients in a small saucepan; cook over low heat, stirring constantly, until thoroughly heated. Yield: 2 cups.

*Mrs. Earl L. Faulkenberry*
*Lancaster, South Carolina*

# From Our Kitchen To Yours

The three Rs—reduce, reuse, and recycle—are keys to solving the growing problem of shrinking landfill space.

Recycling is a fundamental change in the way we deal with trash. To do your part, set a plan in motion, beginning with environmentally sound shopping and practical kitchen routines to reduce, reuse, and recycle. Here are some simple things we do now—and your family can, too.

Before buying items, ask yourself a few questions. Is the packaging just cleverly designed garbage that will end up in a landfill? Is it more economical to buy in bulk? Can the container be reused or recycled?

Make choosing a convenient location for the home recycling center a family project. Place these materials in the center—not in the trash can:

■ Aluminum products (cans, foil, piepans, and TV dinner trays). Check locally to find out if you need to keep cans separate and remove labels.
■ Tin cans (soup, fruit, vegetable, and pet food). Keep them separate from aluminum cans.
■ Glass bottles and jars. Remove lids and caps. Plastic cap liners, neck rings, and paper or plastic labels can be left on bottles and jars. Find out if you have to separate glass containers by color.
■ Brown paper bags and corrugated cardboard.
■ Paperboard (cereal and cracker boxes, egg and berry cartons). Remove liners.
■ Plastic. Look on the bottom for the imprinted recycling symbol with a number in the middle; numbers 1 through 6 represent different plastics, and 7 means it's

not recyclable. Check with your recycling center to find out which plastics are accepted. PET (Polyethylene terephthalate) products are marked number 1 and account for most of the currently recycled plastic.

## Additional recycling tips:

■ Shop with a canvas tote or string bag.
■ Look for biodegradable products (capable of decomposing by natural biological processes) and photodegradable products (capable of decomposing in the sun's ultraviolet rays).
■ Avoid purchasing squeezable plastic containers; they are not recyclable or biodegradable.
■ Select products sold in concentrated forms, such as some beverages, liquid soaps, cleaning products, or in compact packages.
■ Purchase products made from recycled materials; always look for recycled, unbleached paper products.
■ Buy eggs in paper cartons instead of polystyrene-foam cartons, which are nonbiodegradable.
■ Avoid using disposable products when possible. If they are necessary, buy disposable tableware made from recycled paper; choose unlaminated paper, which is biodegradable.

When you begin recycling, if you have not already, check on collection services available in your community. Services differ in each area, and practices vary from state to state. To find the nearest recycling center, look in the Yellow Pages under "Recycling Centers" or "Environmental Groups." If you want more information, contact your state recycling agency.

# FEBRUARY

*While the weather outside is frosty, fill your home with the aroma of homemade breads and desserts. Select from our sampling of muffins, coffee cake, and cherry pie recipes. While they bake, prepare a romantic dinner for two, featuring an elegant shrimp and pasta entrée accompanied by a colorful vegetable salad and your fresh-baked treats.*

# A Slice Of Americana

Looking for the perfect recipe for cherry pie? By George, we've got it. And our timing is perfect, since February is also the season to wish George Washington "Happy Birthday." But no candle-laden cake will do. We want cherry pie in honor of his legendary tree-chopping confession.

We haven't chopped down any cherry trees, but we *have* cut down the time it takes to make these fruit desserts. Because fresh cherries aren't available until late spring and summer, we've substituted canned cherries and pie filling in these recipes as another time-saver.

for 5 minutes. Cook pie filling in a saucepan over medium heat just until hot. Pour into pastry shell; sprinkle coconut mixture over filling. Bake at 375° for 25 minutes or until top is lightly browned. Cool on a wire rack. Yield: one 9-inch pie.

*Mrs. Earl L. Faulkenberry*
*Lancaster, South Carolina*

## LEMONY CHERRY PIE
*(pictured on page 40)*

2 (16-ounce) cans tart, red pitted
  cherries
1 cup sugar
3 tablespoons cornstarch
2 tablespoons butter or margarine
1 tablespoon lemon juice
⅛ teaspoon red food coloring
  (optional)
Pastry for double-crust 9-inch pie

Drain cherries, reserving ½ cup juice. Set both aside.

Combine sugar and cornstarch in a large saucepan; stir in reserved cherry juice. Cook over medium heat, stirring constantly, until mixture comes to a boil; boil 1 minute, stirring constantly. Remove from heat, and stir in cherries, butter, lemon juice, and if desired, food coloring; cool.

Roll half of pastry to ⅛-inch thickness on a lightly floured surface. Place in a 9-inch pieplate; trim off excess pastry along edges. Pour cherry mixture into pastry shell.

Roll remaining pastry to ⅛-inch thickness; cut into ½-inch strips. Arrange in lattice design over cherries; trim strips even with edges. Make shaped cutouts with remaining pastry. Moisten edge of piecrust with water, and gently press cutouts around edges. Bake at 375° for 30 to 35 minutes. Yield: one 9-inch pie.

## CHERRY-PECAN PIE

1 (14-ounce) can sweetened
  condensed milk
1 (8-ounce) container frozen
  whipped topping, thawed
¼ cup lemon juice
1 cup chopped pecans
1 (21-ounce) can cherry pie filling
2 (8-inch) graham cracker crusts

Combine sweetened condensed milk and whipped topping; gradually stir in lemon juice. Fold pecans and pie filling into mixture. Spoon into graham cracker crusts; chill 2 hours. Yield: two 8-inch pies.
*Carolyn Few*
*St. Petersburg, Florida*

## COCONUT CRUMB
## CHERRY PIE

½ cup all-purpose flour
¼ cup sugar
¼ cup butter or margarine, melted
1 cup flaked coconut
1 unbaked 9-inch pastry shell
1 (21-ounce) can cherry pie filling

Combine first 3 ingredients; add coconut, and stir until mixture is crumbly. Set aside. Bake pastry shell at 450°

## CHERRY CREAM PIE
## WITH ALMOND PASTRY

1 (14-ounce) can sweetened
  condensed milk
⅓ cup lemon juice
1 teaspoon vanilla extract
½ teaspoon almond extract
½ cup whipping cream, whipped
Almond Pastry
1 (16-ounce) can tart, red pitted
  cherries
¼ cup sugar
1 tablespoon cornstarch
3 or 4 drops of red food coloring

Combine sweetened condensed milk, lemon juice, vanilla extract, and almond extract. Gently fold whipped cream into mixture. Spoon into Almond Pastry; chill.

Drain cherries; reserve ⅔ cup juice (add water, if necessary, to equal ⅔ cup). Set cherries and juice aside.

Combine sugar and cornstarch in a heavy saucepan; stir in reserved cherry juice. Cook over low heat, stirring constantly, until mixture comes to a boil; boil 1 minute, stirring constantly. Stir in cherries and food coloring; cool slightly. Spoon mixture over cream filling; chill 3 to 4 hours. Yield: one 9-inch pie.

### Almond Pastry

½ (11-ounce) piecrust mix (1 cup)
⅓ cup slivered almonds, finely
  chopped
2 to 3 tablespoons cold water

Combine piecrust mix and almonds. Sprinkle cold water (1 tablespoon at a time) evenly over surface; stir with a fork until dry ingredients are moistened. Shape into a ball; chill.

Roll pastry to ⅛-inch thickness on a lightly floured surface. Place in a 9-inch pieplate; trim off excess pastry along edges. Fold edges under and flute. Prick bottom of pastry generously with a fork. Bake at 425° for 9 minutes or until lightly browned. Cool before filling. Yield: pastry for one 9-inch pie.                    *Mrs. Scriven Taylor*
*Natchitoches, Louisiana*

# Rise To The Occasion

Hot bread from the oven piques the senses with smells as rich as steaming coffee, sizzling bacon, and cinnamon wafting from an apple cobbler. There is something about stirring a batter, watching dough rise, and then smearing the hot bread with butter that awakens our palates.

Our readers have shared some favorite recipes that tap that love of fresh-baked breads—and remembered aromas. Try them, knowing that many hands have stirred the same kind of batter before you.

■ In Woodland, Mississippi, the bakers are getting younger all the time. Just ask 11-year-old Heidi Huffman. Heidi and her mom came up with this recipe, but Heidi is "the head roll baker now."

### WHOLESOME WHOLE WHEAT ROLLS

2½ cups milk
2 packages dry yeast
½ cup honey
½ cup shortening
2 teaspoons salt
3 cups whole wheat flour
2 eggs
3½ to 4 cups all-purpose flour
Melted butter or margarine

Heat milk to 110° to 115°; remove from heat. Dissolve yeast in ½ cup warm milk in a small bowl; let stand 5 minutes. Combine remaining milk, honey, shortening, salt, and whole wheat flour; beat at medium speed with an electric mixer until smooth. Add yeast and eggs; mix well. Gradually stir in enough all-purpose flour to make a stiff dough. Place in a well-greased bowl, turning to grease top. Cover and let rise in a warm place (85°), free from drafts, 1 hour or until doubled in bulk.

Punch dough down; turn out onto a well-floured surface, and knead 4 or 5 times. Roll to ½-inch thickness; cut with a 2½-inch biscuit cutter. Place on a lightly greased baking sheet.

Cover and let rise in a warm place (85°), free from drafts, about 30 minutes or until doubled in bulk. Bake at 400° for 12 to 15 minutes or until browned. Brush rolls with melted butter. Yield: 2 dozen.      *Heidi Huffman*
*Woodland, Mississippi*

■ Kregg Owens thinks everyone ought to be able to make a good biscuit. He says the secret of making a foolproof product is to avoid overworking the dough and to layer two baking sheets under biscuits when baking.

### BISCUITS
*(pictured on pages 38 and 39)*

2 cups self-rising soft wheat flour
⅛ teaspoon baking powder
1 tablespoon sugar
¾ cup shortening
1 cup buttermilk
1 tablespoon butter or margarine, melted

Combine first 3 ingredients in a large bowl; cut in shortening with a pastry blender until shortening is the size of peas. Add buttermilk, stirring with a fork until dry ingredients are moistened. (Dough will resemble cottage cheese and be sticky.) Turn dough out onto a heavily floured surface, and knead lightly 4 or 5 times.

Roll dough to ¾-inch thickness; cut with a 2½-inch round cutter. Stack two baking sheets, one on top of the other. Place biscuits on top of one, lightly greased, and bake at 450° for 10 to 12 minutes. Brush with butter. Yield: 10 biscuits.     *Kregg Owens*
*Albany, Georgia*

■ After sampling sweet potato muffins at a restaurant, Ethelwyn Langston developed her own version.

### SWEET POTATO MUFFINS
*(pictured on pages 38 and 39)*

1¾ cups all-purpose flour
1 teaspoon baking soda
½ teaspoon ground cinnamon
¼ teaspoon salt
2 eggs
1 cup sugar
½ cup firmly packed brown sugar
½ cup vegetable oil
1 (17-ounce) can sweet potatoes, drained and mashed
½ cup chopped pecans
1 cup dates, chopped
¼ cup all-purpose flour

Combine first 4 ingredients in a large bowl; make a well in center of mixture. Combine eggs and next 4 ingredients in a bowl; beat at medium speed with an electric mixer until blended. Add sweet potato mixture to dry ingredients, and stir just until moistened.

Dredge pecans and dates in ¼ cup flour; fold into muffin mixture. Spoon into greased muffin pans, filling three-fourths full. Bake at 350° for 27 to 30 minutes. Remove from pans immediately. Yield: 1½ dozen.
**Note:** Bake batter in miniature muffin pans at 350° for 12 to 14 minutes. Yield: 4 dozen.     *Ethelwyn Langston*
*Birmingham, Alabama*

■ Christine Kenyon inherited this breakfast bread recipe from her great-grandmother, who immigrated from Sweden. Cardamom adds the distinctive aroma you'll notice as the bread bakes. Christine prefers to grind about 35 cardamom seeds for even more flavor.

### MANDELKRANTZ
*(pictured on pages 38 and 39)*

2 packages dry yeast
1 teaspoon sugar
¼ cup warm water (105° to 115°)
2 cups milk, divided
¾ cup shortening
1 cup sugar
1 teaspoon salt
35 cardamom seeds, ground, or ¼
    teaspoon ground cardamom
3 eggs, slightly beaten
6 to 7 cups soft wheat flour,
    divided
⅓ cup butter or margarine,
    softened
1 teaspoon almond extract
¾ cup sugar, divided
¾ cup chopped walnuts, divided

Dissolve yeast and 1 teaspoon sugar in warm water in a small bowl; let stand 5 minutes.

Combine 1 cup milk, shortening, and next 3 ingredients in a Dutch oven; cook over low heat until shortening dissolves. Remove from heat. Add remaining 1 cup milk, eggs, 4 cups flour, and yeast mixture, stirring well with a wooden spoon. Stir in enough remaining flour to make a soft dough. Cover and let rise in a warm place (85°), free from drafts, 1 hour or until doubled in bulk.

Punch dough down; turn out onto a lightly floured surface and knead 4 to 5 minutes; divide dough into thirds. Roll one portion of dough into a 12- x 8-inch rectangle. Combine butter and almond extract; spread one-third of mixture over dough to within ½ inch of sides. Sprinkle with ¼ cup each of sugar and walnuts. Roll up dough, jellyroll fashion, starting at long side. Press firmly to eliminate air pockets; fold ends under. Place dough, seam side down, in a well-greased 9- x 5- x 3-inch loafpan. Repeat procedure with remaining two portions of dough and filling.

Cover and let dough rise in a warm place, free from drafts, 45 minutes or until doubled in bulk. Bake at 350° for 30 to 35 minutes. Cover with aluminum foil to prevent overbrowning, if needed. Remove bread from pans immediately; cool slightly on a wire rack before slicing. Yield: 3 loaves.
*Christine Kenyon*
*Lawrenceville, Georgia*

■ You're in luck if you live near Lucille Terry. A good cook who has dabbled in catering, she often shares her coffee cake with neighbors and relatives. She says Granny Smith or Jonathan apples add just the right tartness.

### FRESH APPLE COFFEE CAKE

½ cup butter or margarine,
    softened
2 cups sugar
4 eggs
2 cups all-purpose flour
2 teaspoons baking powder
½ teaspoon salt
5 cups peeled and chopped apple
    (about 4 large apples)
1 teaspoon vanilla extract
1½ tablespoons sugar
½ teaspoon ground cinnamon

Beat butter at medium speed with an electric mixer. Gradually add 2 cups sugar; beat well. Add eggs, one at a time; beat after each addition.

Combine flour, baking powder, and salt; add to creamed mixture. Stir in apple and vanilla. Spoon batter into a greased and floured 13- x 9- x 2-inch pan. Combine 1½ tablespoons sugar and cinnamon; sprinkle over cake batter. Bake at 350° for 45 minutes or until a wooden pick inserted in center comes out clean. Serve warm or cool. Yield: 15 servings. *Lucille Terry*
*Frankfort, Kentucky*

### Bake Like the Pros

**Here's the scoop on flour:** Several recipes specifically call for soft wheat flour. This flour yields light, tender biscuits and breads. You'll find it under labels such as White Lily, Martha White, or other regional brands.

**About yeast:** Make sure the freshness date on the package hasn't expired. When dissolving yeast, use a thermometer to ensure that the water or other liquid is between 105° and 115°. A higher temperature can kill the yeast and cause the bread not to rise. A lower temperature causes slow or minimal rising.

**Kneading:** Place the dough on a flat, floured surface. Coat your hands with flour. Form the dough into a round ball, and then fold it toward you. Using the heels of your hands, push the dough away with a rolling motion. Turn dough a quarter-turn, and repeat the motion as the recipe specifies. If the dough gets sticky, lightly flour your hands and the surface again beneath the dough as needed.

**Baking and freezing:** Preheat the oven before baking, and use the correct pan size. To keep some breads from getting too brown, you may need to cover or shield them with aluminum foil during the last 10 to 15 minutes of baking. After the breads are completely cool, they may be frozen. We froze each bread recipe on this page and the preceding one to see if it would maintain its quality, and all of them did well. Use a freezer bag or wrap them in heavy-duty foil. They will keep up to 3 months. Thaw the loaves and reheat to serve.

# New Twist On Meat Loaf

Meat loaf no longer has to be bland and lifeless. With a little creativity, you can turn a meat loaf dinner into a memorable event.

Meat Loaf Supreme features Italian flavors. A spiral of red pepper, onion, mushrooms, and cheese appears in each slice of meat loaf. A Parmesan-seasoned beef mixture is patted into a rectangle on wax paper, and topped with the colorful ingredients. Using the wax paper as a guide, lift and roll the meat into a loaf. As the loaf bakes, the filling flavors the meat. Let it stand about 10 minutes before slicing. For a flavor variation, try salmon loaf.

As a side dish, zucchini and carrot strips can be sautéed in olive oil and garlic. Add a loaf of crusty Italian bread, and dinner is complete.

## MEAT LOAF SUPREME

1½ pounds ground round
¾ cup Italian-seasoned
  breadcrumbs
¼ cup catsup
1 egg, beaten
2 tablespoons grated Parmesan
  cheese
1 teaspoon Worcestershire sauce
1 teaspoon dried minced garlic
¼ teaspoon dried basil
¼ teaspoon dried thyme
¼ teaspoon dried parsley flakes
¼ teaspoon salt
¼ teaspoon pepper
1 small sweet red pepper, cut into
  thin 2-inch strips
1 small onion, sliced and separated
  into rings
3 fresh mushrooms, sliced
2 (6- x 3½-inch) slices Swiss
  cheese

Combine first 12 ingredients; mix well. Shape mixture into an 18- x 12-inch rectangle on a sheet of wax paper. Layer red pepper, onion, mushrooms, and cheese on rectangle, leaving a 1-inch margin around edges. Roll meat mixture up jellyroll fashion, starting at short side and using wax paper to lift and roll. Pinch edges and ends to seal.

Place loaf, seam side down, on rack of a lightly greased broiler pan. Bake at 350° for 40 to 45 minutes. Yield: 6 servings. *Jan Griffin*
*Jacksonville, Florida*

## TURKEY LOAF

1 teaspoon chicken-flavored
  bouillon granules
¼ cup boiling water
1 egg, slightly beaten, or ¼ cup
  egg substitute
3 slices whole wheat bread, cubed
¼ cup chopped onion
½ teaspoon dried sage
¼ teaspoon salt
1 pound ground turkey
3 tablespoons chili sauce

Dissolve bouillon granules in boiling water. Combine bouillon, egg, and remaining ingredients, mixing well. Shape mixture into a 6-inch loaf, and place on rack of a lightly greased broiler pan. Bake at 350° for 55 minutes. Yield: 4 to 6 servings.
*Juanita Lowery*
*McRae, Georgia*

## SAVORY SALMON LOAF

1 (15½-ounce) can salmon
2 cups saltine cracker crumbs,
  divided
¼ cup butter or margarine, melted
2 eggs, beaten
¼ cup chopped green pepper
2 tablespoons grated onion
1 tablespoon butter or margarine,
  melted
¼ teaspoon salt
¼ teaspoon pepper
¼ teaspoon baking powder
1 tablespoon dried parsley flakes
1 tablespoon Worcestershire sauce
2 tablespoons catsup
¼ teaspoon hot sauce
3 slices bacon
Cucumber Cream Sauce

Drain salmon, reserving ⅓ cup liquid; set aside. Remove skin and bones, if desired; flake salmon with a fork.

Brown 1½ cups cracker crumbs in ¼ cup butter in a large skillet, and set mixture aside.

Combine salmon, reserved liquid, remaining ½ cup unbrowned cracker crumbs, eggs, and next 10 ingredients. Sprinkle ¼ cup browned cracker crumbs in center of a greased 13- x 9- x 2-inch pan. Shape salmon mixture into a 9-inch loaf, and place on top of crumbs. Press remaining browned cracker crumbs on top and sides of loaf. Arrange bacon slices diagonally across loaf. Bake at 350° for 55 to 60 minutes, covering loosely with foil the last 15 minutes if crumbs brown too quickly. Serve with Cucumber Cream Sauce. Yield: 6 servings.

## Cucumber Cream Sauce

½ cucumber
½ cup sour cream
1 tablespoon lemon juice
1 teaspoon grated onion
¼ teaspoon pepper

Peel and seed cucumber. Grate enough cucumber to measure ½ cup. Combine grated cucumber and remaining ingredients, stirring well. Cover and chill. Yield: about 1 cup.
*Jane Feagin*
*Birmingham, Alabama*

# Shrimp "Pastabilities"

Pair shrimp and pasta for an easy but elegant meal? Now that's using your noodle. Not only does it make a fun combination, the pasta also stretches the seafood so it's affordable, even for a weeknight. The hardest part of these recipes is peeling the shrimp. All that's left then is to sauté or simmer the shrimp and other ingredients while the pasta is boiling.

Here are a few tips to make perfect pasta every time:
■ Use a large pot with plenty of water so pasta has room to move around while cooking. Keep at a full boil so pasta won't stick together.
■ Add a drop of vegetable oil or a small pat of margarine to the water to prevent it from boiling over.
■ Follow package directions for cooking each type of pasta. It's ready when it's "al dente"—firm but tender "to the tooth."

## SHRIMP AND TORTELLINI

1 pound unpeeled medium-size
  fresh shrimp
1 (9-ounce) package fresh tortellini
  with cheese filling, uncooked
⅓ cup butter or margarine
1 shallot, minced
2 tablespoons chopped fresh basil
  or 2 teaspoons dried basil
½ cup grated Parmesan cheese
Garnish: fresh basil

Peel and devein shrimp, and set aside. Cook fresh pasta according to package directions; drain and set aside. Melt butter in a large skillet over medium-high heat, and add shrimp, minced shallot, and basil. Cook about 5 minutes, stirring constantly. Add pasta and Parmesan cheese. Toss gently, and garnish, if desired. Yield: 4 servings.          *Nancy Clark*
          *Columbia, South Carolina*

## SHRIMP AND MUSHROOMS WITH ANGEL HAIR PASTA

1 pound unpeeled medium-size
  fresh shrimp
4 ounces angel hair pasta,
  uncooked
¼ cup butter or margarine
2 small cloves garlic, minced
2 tablespoons minced fresh basil or
  2 teaspoons dried whole basil
1 cup fresh shiitake mushroom
  caps *
⅛ teaspoon pepper

Peel and devein shrimp; set aside. Cook pasta according to package directions; drain and set aside. Melt butter in a large skillet over medium-high heat. Add garlic and basil; cook 1 minute, stirring often. Add shrimp, mushrooms, and pepper; cook about 5 minutes, stirring occasionally. Serve over angel hair pasta. Yield: 2 or 3 servings.

* 1 cup sliced fresh mushrooms may be substituted for 1 cup shiitake mushrooms.          *Marie A. Davis*
          *Charlotte, North Carolina*

## SPICY SHRIMP AND LINGUINE

1 pound unpeeled medium-size
  fresh shrimp
6 ounces linguine, uncooked
1 stalk celery, sliced
1 medium onion, sliced and cut into
  quarters
1 tablespoon olive oil
1 (14½-ounce) can Italian-style
  tomatoes, undrained and chopped
1 (8-ounce) can tomato sauce
1½ teaspoons dried parsley flakes
¼ to ½ teaspoon crushed red
  pepper
¼ teaspoon pepper

Peel and devein shrimp; set aside. Cook pasta according to package directions; drain and set aside. Sauté shrimp, celery, and onion in oil in a large skillet about 3 minutes or until shrimp are pink. Add tomatoes and next 4 ingredients, stirring well. Bring to a boil; reduce heat, and simmer 10 minutes. Toss with linguine. Yield: 3 servings.          *Linda Pierce*
          *Germantown, Tennessee*

# The Stew Wars Go On

Those Virginians and Georgians are *still* at it. Although the age-old question of whose Brunswick Stew is best remains unsettled—as it has for centuries—stewmasters from both states vie endlessly for the title nonetheless. But don't look to us for a decision. We simply invite you to sample a warm bowl of both recipes; then jump into the friendly debate yourself.

## VIRGINIAN BRUNSWICK STEW

1 (4-pound) broiler-fryer
1½ teaspoons salt
4 quarts water
⅓ pound ground beef
¼ pound salt pork
8 small potatoes (2½ pounds),
  peeled and sliced
2 large onions, sliced
1 quart canned crushed tomatoes
2 (10-ounce) packages frozen baby
  lima beans
1 cup sliced carrot
⅓ cup sugar
¼ cup butter or margarine
1½ tablespoons paprika
1 tablespoon lemon juice
2 teaspoons salt
1 teaspoon black pepper
¾ teaspoon red pepper
2 (11-ounce) cans shoepeg corn,
  drained

Combine chicken, salt, and water in a large Dutch oven or stockpot; bring to a boil. Cover, reduce heat, and simmer 1 hour. Remove chicken from broth, reserving broth in Dutch oven. Cool chicken; skin, bone, and coarsely chop meat. Set aside.

Cook ground beef in a skillet over medium heat until browned, stirring until it crumbles. Drain well, and add to broth. Position knife blade in food processor bowl; add salt pork. Pulse 2 or 3 times until fat is finely ground; add to broth. Add potatoes and onion; cover and cook over medium heat 20 to 25 minutes.

Add chicken, tomatoes, and next 9 ingredients to broth; cover, reduce heat, and simmer 2 to 2½ hours, stirring occasionally. Add corn; cook, uncovered, 10 to 15 minutes. Yield: about 6 quarts.

*Alvin Lucy*
*Lawrenceville, Virginia*

## GEORGIAN BRUNSWICK STEW

1 pound round steak
1 pound boneless pork loin chops
3 medium onions, chopped
½ teaspoon salt
½ teaspoon pepper
7 cups water
1 (3-pound) broiler-fryer, skinned and halved
2 (28-ounce) cans whole tomatoes, undrained and chopped
1¾ cups catsup
⅓ cup Worcestershire sauce
½ cup chili sauce
1 tablespoon hot sauce
1 teaspoon dry mustard
2 bay leaves
2 (17-ounce) cans cream-style corn
2 (17-ounce) cans lima beans, drained
1 (17-ounce) can English peas, drained
3 small potatoes, peeled and diced
3 tablespoons white vinegar
1 (10-ounce) package frozen sliced okra, thawed

Combine first 6 ingredients in a large Dutch oven or stockpot; bring to a boil. Cover, reduce heat, and simmer 1½ hours. Add chicken, and simmer 1½ hours. Remove meat from broth, reserving broth in Dutch oven. Cool meat; bone and coarsely chop. Set meat aside.

Add tomatoes and next 6 ingredients to broth; bring to a boil. Simmer, uncovered, 1 hour, stirring occasionally. Stir in meat, corn, beans, peas, potatoes, and vinegar; simmer, uncovered, 45 minutes, stirring often. Add okra; cook 15 minutes. Remove bay leaves. Yield: 6½ quarts.

*Harriet Gilbert*
*St. Simons Island, Georgia*

# Broccoli And Cauliflower, Better Than Ever

What are two vegetables you can count on—even in winter months? Broccoli and cauliflower, of course. If you run out of new ideas, let salads provide inspiration. Whether you choose a flash-cooked, hot dish or a marinated, chilled version, these salads pack refreshing taste into meals.

Broccoli and cauliflower can be used interchangeably in many recipes. Both are delicious raw or cooked until barely tender. And to boost the vitamin payload, remember that uncooked or crisp-tender vegetables retain more nutrients. To make sure you'll be eating the freshest available, purchase compact, firm, and creamy-colored cauliflower, and select broccoli with dark-green, tightly packed buds. Refrigerate the vegetables, unwashed, in a plastic bag up to four days for best flavor and optimum nutrition.

## BROCCOLI-PEANUT SALAD

1½ pounds fresh broccoli
2 green onions, chopped
1 (4-ounce) jar diced pimiento, drained
½ cup raisins
½ cup dry roasted peanuts
½ cup mayonnaise or salad dressing
2 tablespoons honey

Trim off large leaves of broccoli, and remove tough ends of lower stalks; wash broccoli thoroughly. Cut stalks into ¼-inch slices. Cut remaining broccoli into flowerets; place in a large bowl. Add green onions, pimiento, raisins, and peanuts. Combine mayonnaise and honey in a small bowl; spoon dressing mixture over top of broccoli mixture. Toss gently to coat. Cover and chill 2 hours. Yield: 6 servings.

*Maxine D. Compton*
*Fredericksburg, Texas*

## WARM BROCCOLI SALAD

1½ pounds fresh broccoli
4 slices bacon
½ cup sliced green onions
¼ cup balsamic vinegar or red wine vinegar
1 teaspoon sugar
½ teaspoon salt
¼ teaspoon freshly ground pepper
1 (8-ounce) can sliced water chestnuts, drained
1 (2-ounce) jar sliced pimiento, drained
1 hard-cooked egg, grated

Trim off large leaves of broccoli and remove lower stalks. Wash thoroughly, and break into flowerets.

Cook broccoli in boiling water to cover 1 minute; drain immediately, and plunge broccoli into a bowl of ice water to stop cooking process. Drain; pat dry with paper towel.

Cook bacon in a large skillet until crisp; remove bacon, reserving 2 tablespoons drippings in skillet. Crumble bacon, and set aside. Add green onions and next 5 ingredients to drippings; cook until mixture boils, stirring constantly. Add broccoli and pimiento to skillet; cook just until broccoli is hot, stirring constantly. Spoon mixture into serving bowl; sprinkle with bacon and egg. Serve immediately. Yield: 6 to 8 servings.

## ITALIAN-STYLE CAULIFLOWER

1 medium cauliflower
3 tablespoons olive oil
2 tablespoons balsamic vinegar or
   red wine vinegar
¼ teaspoon salt
1 clove garlic, minced

Remove large outer leaves of cauliflower; break cauliflower into flowerets. Arrange cauliflower in a steaming rack. Place over boiling water; cover and steam 5 to 8 minutes or to desired degree of doneness. Transfer to a serving bowl; keep warm.

Combine olive oil and remaining ingredients in a saucepan; cook over medium heat until mixture is thoroughly heated. Pour the hot mixture over cauliflower; toss gently, and serve warm. Yield: 4 servings.

*Cindy Ward*
*Winston-Salem, North Carolina*

# Waldorf Salads To Please All

Crisp apples and celery plus creamy mayonnaise were the lone ingredients in the original Waldorf Salad. Its success is credited to Oscar Tschirky of the famous Waldorf-Astoria Hotel around the end of the 19th century. Although the recipe traveled the country, it has become standard fare in the South where the simple ingredients are abundant and of top quality.

Our recipes include an old and a new version. Should you want one reminiscent of the hotel creation, try Southern Classic Waldorf Salad. If a contemporary rendition suits you, prepare New Wave Waldorf Salad. In that recipe, red and green apples, along with a pear, celery, and golden raisins, show up in a honey-yogurt dressing.

## CAULIFLOWER SALAD

1 medium cauliflower
½ cup French salad dressing
½ cup pimiento-stuffed green
   olives, sliced
1 small avocado, diced
Leaf lettuce
3 medium tomatoes, cut into
   eighths
½ cup crumbled blue cheese

Remove large outer leaves of cauliflower; break cauliflower into flowerets. Add salad dressing, and toss gently. Add green olives and avocado; toss gently.

Arrange lettuce on individual plates; spoon cauliflower mixture onto lettuce. Place tomatoes around cauliflower, and sprinkle with blue cheese. Yield: 8 servings.

*Valerie Gail Stutsman*
*Norfolk, Virginia*

## NEW WAVE WALDORF SALAD

1 Red Delicious apple, unpeeled
   and chopped
1 Granny Smith apple, unpeeled
   and chopped
1 pear, unpeeled and chopped
1 tablespoon lemon juice
¼ cup golden raisins
1 stalk celery, diagonally sliced
1 (8-ounce) carton plain yogurt
1 tablespoon honey
1 teaspoon grated orange rind
¼ cup slivered almonds, toasted
Garnish: celery leaves

Combine first 3 ingredients in a medium-size bowl. Sprinkle lemon juice over fruit mixture, and toss gently. Stir in golden raisins and celery; set aside.

Combine yogurt, honey, and orange rind, stirring well. Stir ¼ cup yogurt mixture into fruit mixture. Spoon salad into a serving bowl, and sprinkle with almonds. Garnish, if desired. Serve with remaining dressing. Yield: 6 servings.

*Mildred Bickley*
*Bristol, Virginia*

## SOUTHERN CLASSIC WALDORF SALAD

2 tablespoons orange juice
3 large tart red apples, unpeeled
   and diced
½ cup diced celery
½ cup sour cream
½ cup raisins
¼ cup chopped pecans or walnuts
1½ teaspoons sugar
Lettuce leaves (optional)

Sprinkle orange juice over apples; toss gently and drain. Combine apples, celery, and next 4 ingredients; stir well. Cover and chill. Serve on lettuce leaves, if desired. Yield: 6 servings.

*Chris Bryant*
*Johnson City, Tennessee*

**Tip:** *Keep celery fresh and crisp by wrapping in paper towels; place in a plastic bag in the refrigerator. The towels absorb any excess moisture.*

*Teriyaki Beef Broil (page 56) borrows much of its flavor from minced cloves of garlic.*

*Biscuits, Sweet Potato Muffins, and Mandelkrantz bring the aroma of fresh-baked bread to your home. (Recipes, pages 31 and 32.)*

You can make Lemony Cherry Pie (page 30) the old-fashioned way with pastry from scratch, or take a shortcut with refrigerated piecrust.

# Wake To An Easy Brunch

Looking for some new, flavorful brunch ideas? Here are five brunch main dishes you can count on for minimum fuss. And, best of all, they're accompanied by menu suggestions.

■ Serve tomato juice or Bloody Marys and vegetable crudités before serving this main course. Miniature corn muffins and an assortment of jams and jellies complement the flavors in this soufflé.

### HAM SOUFFLÉ WITH CUCUMBER SAUCE

¼ cup butter or margarine
⅓ cup all-purpose flour
¼ teaspoon onion powder
1½ cups milk
1 teaspoon grated lemon rind
1 teaspoon lemon juice
4 large eggs, separated
2 cups ground cooked ham
Cucumber Sauce

Lightly oil a 2½-quart soufflé dish. Cut a piece of aluminum foil long enough to fit around rim of dish, allowing a 1-inch overlap. Fold foil lengthwise into thirds, and lightly oil one side. Wrap foil, oiled side against the outside of the dish, so it extends 3 inches above the rim. Securely attach foil with string. Set aside.

Melt butter in a heavy saucepan over low heat; add flour and onion powder, stirring until smooth. Cook mixture 1 minute, stirring constantly. Gradually add milk; cook over medium heat, stirring constantly, until thickened and bubbly. Stir in lemon rind and lemon juice.

Beat egg yolks until thick and pale. Gradually stir about one-fourth of hot mixture into yolks; add to remaining hot mixture.

Beat egg whites until stiff but not dry; fold ham and egg whites into cream sauce mixture. Pour into prepared soufflé dish. Bake at 350° for 45 to 50 minutes or until puffed and golden brown. Remove foil collar; serve immediately with Cucumber Sauce. Yield: 6 servings.

### Cucumber Sauce

1 (8-ounce) carton sour cream
2 tablespoons mayonnaise or salad dressing
½ cup finely chopped cucumber
½ teaspoon onion salt

Combine all ingredients, stirring mixture well. Refrigerate mixture. Yield: 1⅓ cups.          *Mrs. Clark Adams*
*Clearwater, Florida*

■ Welcome guests with orange juice or mimosas (champagne and orange juice cocktails). Serve the crêpes with a salad of watercress, tangelo sections, pear slices, and raspberry vinaigrette. Fruit sorbet and gingersnaps make a perfect light finish.

### TURKEY CRÊPES

½ cup sliced, fresh mushrooms
⅓ cup chopped onion
⅓ cup chopped celery
Vegetable cooking spray
2½ cups chopped cooked turkey breast
1 (4-ounce) jar sliced pimiento, drained
White Wine Sauce
Crêpes
⅓ cup grated Parmesan cheese
¾ cup (3 ounces) shredded Cheddar cheese
⅓ cup slivered almonds, toasted
Garnishes: fresh parsley, cherry tomatoes

Sauté first 3 ingredients in a large skillet coated with cooking spray until vegetables are tender. Add turkey, pimiento, and 1 cup White Wine Sauce, stirring gently. Spoon mixture down center of spotty side of each crêpe, dividing mixture equally among crêpes. Fold sides over, and place seam side up in a lightly greased 13- x 9- x 2-inch baking dish. Spoon remaining White Wine Sauce over crêpes. Cover and bake at 350° for 20 minutes. Sprinkle cheese over crêpes; bake, uncovered, an additional 5 minutes. Remove from oven; sprinkle with almonds. Garnish, if desired. Yield: 6 to 8 servings.

### White Wine Sauce

⅓ cup butter or margarine
⅓ cup all-purpose flour
1½ cups half-and-half
1¼ cups milk
¼ cup dry white wine
1½ tablespoons white wine Worcestershire sauce
½ teaspoon salt
¼ teaspoon white pepper

Melt butter in a heavy saucepan over low heat; add flour, stirring until smooth. Cook 1 minute, stirring constantly. Gradually add half-and-half, milk, and wine. Cook over medium heat, stirring constantly, until thickened and bubbly. Stir in Worcestershire sauce, salt, and pepper. Remove from heat. Yield: 3 cups.

### Crêpes

2 large eggs
1⅓ cups milk
1½ cups all-purpose flour
¼ teaspoon salt
1½ tablespoons vegetable oil
Vegetable cooking spray

Combine first 5 ingredients in container of an electric blender; process 30 seconds. Scrape down sides of blender container with rubber spatula; process an additional 30 seconds. Refrigerate batter 1 hour.

Coat bottom of a 6-inch crêpe pan or nonstick skillet with cooking spray; place over medium heat until just hot, not smoking. Pour 3 tablespoons batter into pan. Quickly tilt pan in all directions so batter covers pan in a thin film; cook batter about 1 minute or until crêpe can be shaken loose from pan. Flip crêpe, and cook about 30 seconds.

Place crêpes on a towel to cool. Stack between layers of wax paper to prevent sticking. Repeat until all batter is used. Yield: 12 (6-inch) crêpes.
*Dee Buchfink*
*Oologah, Oklahoma*

■ Fill cherry tomatoes and mushroom caps with a cream cheese-and-herb spread for a quick appetizer. Accompany the saucy chicken rolls with hot French bread and tomato aspic or marinated broccoli. Chocolate mousse would add an indulgent, yet light accent to the meal.

## CHICKEN-AND-HAM ROLLS Á LA SWISS

1 large egg, beaten
2 tablespoons water
2 tablespoons Dijon mustard, divided
½ cup fine, dry breadcrumbs
¼ cup grated Parmesan cheese
1 teaspoon salt, divided
½ teaspoon white pepper, divided
6 chicken breast halves, skinned and boned
6 (4-inch-square) slices cooked ham
¼ cup butter or margarine, melted
2 tablespoons butter or margarine
2 tablespoons all-purpose flour
1½ cups milk
½ cup dry white wine
1 cup (4 ounces) shredded Swiss cheese

Combine egg, water, and 1 tablespoon mustard, mixing well; set aside. Combine breadcrumbs, Parmesan cheese, ½ teaspoon salt, and ¼ teaspoon white pepper; set aside.

Place each piece of chicken between two sheets of wax paper; flatten to ¼-inch thickness using a meat mallet or rolling pin. Place a ham slice on each chicken breast. Roll up from short side, and secure rolls with wooden picks. Dip chicken rolls in egg mixture, and dredge in crumb mixture. Place chicken rolls in a lightly greased 12- x 8- x 2-inch baking dish. Drizzle chicken rolls with ¼ cup melted butter. Bake at 350° for 45 minutes or until tender.

Melt 2 tablespoons butter in a heavy saucepan over low heat; add flour, remaining 1 tablespoon mustard, remaining ½ teaspoon salt, and remaining ¼ teaspoon white pepper, stirring until smooth. Gradually add milk; cook over medium heat, stirring constantly, until mixture is thickened and bubbly. Stir in wine and Swiss cheese; continue to cook 1 minute or until cheese melts, stirring constantly. Serve over chicken. Yield: 6 servings.

*Jeanne S. Hotaling*
*Augusta, Georgia*

■ Set the mood for this festive brunch with baskets of tortilla chips and goblets of margaritas or limeade. Toss a tropical fruit salad to accompany this showy alternative to quiche. End the meal with an assortment of chocolates and Mexican coffee.

## CHICKEN-CHILE CHEESECAKE

1⅓ cups finely crushed tortilla chips
¼ cup butter or margarine, melted
3 (8-ounce) packages cream cheese, softened
4 large eggs
1 teaspoon chili powder
1 teaspoon Worcestershire sauce
¼ teaspoon salt
3 tablespoons minced green onions
1½ cups finely shredded cooked chicken
2 (4-ounce) cans chopped green chiles, drained
1½ cups (6 ounces) shredded Monterey Jack cheese
1 (16-ounce) carton sour cream
1 teaspoon seasoned salt
Garnish: minced green onions
Picante sauce

Combine tortilla chips and butter; press on bottom and 1 inch up sides of a 9-inch springform pan. Set aside.

Beat cream cheese at high speed with an electric mixer until light and fluffy; add eggs, 1 at a time, beating well after each addition. Stir in chili powder and next 3 ingredients.

Pour half of cream cheese mixture into prepared pan. Sprinkle with chicken, chiles, and cheese; carefully pour remaining cream cheese mixture on top. Bake at 350° for 10 minutes; reduce heat to 300°, and bake an additional hour or until set. Cool completely on a wire rack.

Combine sour cream and seasoned salt, stirring well; spread evenly on top of cheesecake. Cover and chill at least 8 hours. Garnish, if desired, and serve with picante sauce. Yield: 8 to 10 servings.

■ Offer sparkling cider or red wine coolers before or during this meal. For starters, dip skewered strawberries, papaya, and melon chunks in sour cream and then brown sugar. Serve spinach-and-mushroom salad topped with toasted almonds during the meal, and end with an assortment of cookies and a cup of cappuccino.

## CREAMED CHIPPED BEEF

1 (5-ounce) jar dried beef, chopped
2 tablespoons butter or margarine, melted
4½ cups milk, divided
½ cup all-purpose flour
1 teaspoon beef-flavored bouillon granules
½ teaspoon salt
¼ teaspoon white pepper
8 commercial frozen puff pastry shells, baked

Sauté beef in butter in a large skillet 1 to 2 minutes. Stir in 3½ cups milk; simmer 2 minutes, stirring often. Combine flour and bouillon granules in a small bowl; gradually stir in remaining 1 cup milk. Gradually stir flour mixture into beef mixture. Cook over medium heat, stirring constantly, until thickened and bubbly. Stir in salt and white pepper. Spoon mixture into baked puff pastry shells. Yield: 8 servings.

*Barbara Carson*
*Hollywood, Florida*

# Winning Grits Recipes

If you visit the Annual Greater Grits Cookoff in Columbia, South Carolina, you'll be greeted by the aroma of sausage frying, biscuits baking, and grits cooking.

### GRITS FIESTA PIE

1½ cups water
¼ teaspoon garlic powder
½ cup quick-cooking grits
¼ cup all-purpose flour
½ cup (2 ounces) shredded Cheddar cheese
1 large egg, lightly beaten
¾ pound lean ground beef
1 (1¼-ounce) package taco seasoning mix
1 cup (4 ounces) shredded Monterey Jack cheese, divided
⅓ cup chopped tomato
¼ cup sliced ripe olives
3 tablespoons finely chopped green pepper
2 large eggs, lightly beaten
2 tablespoons milk

Bring water and garlic powder to a boil in a large saucepan; stir in grits. Return to a boil; reduce heat and cook 4 minutes, stirring occasionally. Remove from heat. Combine flour and Cheddar cheese; stir into grits. Stir 1 egg into mixture until well blended.

Spoon mixture into a lightly greased 9-inch pieplate; press with back of a spoon to form a shell; set aside.

Cook ground beef and taco seasoning mix in a large skillet until meat browns, stirring to crumble meat; drain. Spread meat mixture into pie shell. Top with ¾ cup Monterey Jack cheese, tomato, ripe olives, and green pepper; set aside.

Combine 2 eggs and milk; pour over pie. Bake at 375° for 25 minutes. Remove from oven; sprinkle with remaining ¼ cup Monterey Jack cheese, and let stand 5 minutes before slicing. Yield: 6 servings. *Joy Gillespie*
*Neeses, South Carolina*

### GRITS ITALIANO

1 pound hot bulk pork sausage
1½ pounds lean ground beef
¾ cup regular grits
1 (14-ounce) jar pizza sauce
⅛ teaspoon salt
⅛ teaspoon pepper
¼ teaspoon garlic powder
1 large green pepper, chopped
1 medium onion, chopped
2½ cups (10 ounces) shredded Cheddar cheese

Brown sausage and ground beef in a large skillet, stirring until it crumbles; drain well.

Cook grits according to package directions; spoon into a lightly greased 13- x 9- x 2-inch baking dish. Combine pizza sauce and next 3 ingredients. Layer half each of pizza sauce, meat, green pepper, onion, and cheese over grits. Repeat layers, omitting remaining cheese. Cover and bake at 325° for 25 minutes. Add remaining cheese and bake, uncovered, an additional 5 minutes. Yield: 8 servings.
*Andriena Samuel*
*Columbia, South Carolina*

### SURPRISE COCONUT CREAM PIE

2½ cups water
½ cup regular grits
1 cup sugar
2 tablespoons butter or margarine
2 large eggs, beaten
1½ cups flaked coconut
½ cup sour cream
1 (6-ounce) chocolate-graham cracker crust
Garnishes: sweetened whipped cream, maraschino cherries

Bring water to a boil in a medium saucepan; stir in grits. Cover, reduce heat, and simmer 15 minutes, stirring occasionally.

Remove from heat, and stir in sugar and butter. Gradually stir about one-fourth of hot mixture into eggs; add to remaining hot mixture, stirring constantly. Cook over low heat until mixture thickens and reaches 160° (about 8 minutes). Remove from heat, and stir in coconut and sour cream. Spoon mixture into prepared crust; cover and chill. Garnish, if desired. Yield: one 9-inch pie. *Rachel Major*
*Prosperity, South Carolina*

# Yesteryear's Sodas And Shakes

Think of an old-fashioned soda fountain, and you probably envision teenagers in poodle skirts and letter sweaters perched on chrome bar stools sipping colorful ice cream drinks. But that decade was hardly the beginning of the sweet tradition.

Roll back the years to 1825, when a French pharmacist first thought to use soda water for fun instead of "medicinal purposes." When combined with ice cream, the bubbly beverage may not cure what ails you, but it certainly brings a smile to your face as it has for years in American drugstores and ice-cream parlors.

### PATIO BLUSH

1 (6-ounce) can frozen orange juice concentrate, thawed and undiluted
¼ cup lemon juice
¼ cup honey
¼ cup maraschino cherry juice
2 (33.8-ounce) bottles ginger ale, chilled
1 pint pineapple sherbet

Combine first 4 ingredients; divide among six 16-ounce glasses. Fill glasses with ginger ale; top each with a scoop of sherbet. Serve immediately. Yield: 6 servings.
*Berta F. Hester*
*Austin, Texas*

## MOCHA FROSTY

3 tablespoons sugar
3 tablespoons cocoa
⅔ cup water
1 tablespoon instant coffee granules
2 cups milk
1 pint vanilla ice cream
Frozen whipped topping, thawed

Combine first 3 ingredients in a small saucepan; bring to a boil, stirring constantly. Add coffee granules, stirring to dissolve; chill.

Combine chocolate mixture, milk, and ice cream in container of an electric blender; process until smooth. Top each serving with a dollop of whipped topping. Serve immediately. Yield: 5 cups.          *Mrs. Roy Nieman*
*Dunnellon, Florida*

## SUNSHINE FIZZ

1 cup orange juice, chilled
1 cup pineapple juice, chilled
1 cup orange sherbet
½ cup club soda, chilled
Orange sherbet
Garnishes: pineapple wedges, maraschino cherries

Combine first 3 ingredients in container of an electric blender; process until smooth. Stir in club soda, and pour into soda glasses. Add a scoop of orange sherbet to each glass, and garnish, if desired. Serve immediately. Yield: 3 servings.  *Mark J. Grigoraci*
*Charleston, West Virginia*

## STRAWBERRY-CHEESECAKE SHAKE

1 (10-ounce) package frozen sliced strawberries, thawed
1 (3-ounce) package cream cheese, softened
1 pint vanilla ice cream
½ cup milk

Combine all ingredients in container of an electric blender; process mixture until smooth. Serve immediately. Yield: 3½ cups.    *Nancy Monroe*
*Salisbury, North Carolina*

## DATE SHAKE

1 teaspoon instant coffee granules
1 tablespoon hot water
⅓ cup whole pitted dates, chopped
½ cup orange juice
½ cup plain yogurt
1 pint vanilla ice cream

Dissolve coffee granules in hot water; cool. Combine coffee mixture, dates, and remaining ingredients in container of an electric blender; process mixture until smooth. Serve immediately. Yield: 3½ cups.  *Sara A. McCullough*
*Broaddus, Texas*

## LEMON FRAPPÉ

1 (6-ounce) can frozen lemonade concentrate, undiluted
1½ cups water
1 pint lemon ice cream or sherbet
1 (12-ounce) can ginger ale

Combine first 3 ingredients in container of an electric blender; process until smooth. Spoon into pitcher; stir in ginger ale. Serve immediately. Yield: 5 cups.        *Kathleen Stone*
*Houston, Texas*

# Survival Of The Sweetest

In the 1850s, Gail Borden invented sweetened condensed milk, a canned version of milk that safely keeps for a long time at room temperature. It's produced by cooking fresh milk and sugar until some of the water evaporates. Don't confuse sweetened condensed milk with evaporated milk, which has no sugar added. Both come in cans but are quite different and shouldn't be substituted for each other in recipes.

## COCONUT-CARAMEL DESSERT

1½ cups self-rising flour
¾ cup butter or margarine, softened
¾ cup chopped pecans
¼ cup butter or margarine
1 (7-ounce) package flaked coconut
½ cup chopped pecans
1 (8-ounce) package cream cheese, softened
1 (14-ounce) can sweetened condensed milk
1 (12-ounce) container frozen whipped topping, thawed
1 (12.25-ounce) jar caramel sauce

Combine first 3 ingredients; press into a lightly greased 13- x 9- x 2-inch baking dish. Bake at 350° for 18 to 20 minutes or until lightly browned; cool completely.

Melt ¼ cup butter; add coconut and ½ cup chopped pecans. Cook over low heat, stirring often until coconut is golden; cool completely.

Combine cream cheese and sweetened condensed milk; beat at medium speed with an electric mixer until smooth. Fold in whipped topping. Layer one-third each of cheese mixture, caramel sauce, and coconut mixture over crust. Repeat procedure twice with remaining ingredients. Cover and freeze until firm. Yield: 15 servings.          *Linda Walton*
*Fort Valley, Georgia*

## FROZEN ORANGE DESSERT

60 round buttery crackers, crushed (about 3 cups)
½ cup butter or margarine, melted
¼ cup sugar
1 (14-ounce) can sweetened condensed milk
1 (6-ounce) can frozen orange juice concentrate, thawed and undiluted
1 (8-ounce) container frozen whipped topping, thawed
2 (11-ounce) cans mandarin oranges, drained

Combine first 3 ingredients; set aside ¾ cup. Press remaining crumb mixture into an ungreased 13- x 9- x 2-inch baking dish; set aside.

Combine sweetened condensed milk and orange juice concentrate; fold in whipped topping and oranges. Spoon mixture over crust, and sprinkle with reserved crumb mixture. Cover and freeze until firm. Yield: 12 servings.
*Carol Barclay*
*Portland, Texas*

### AUSTRALIAN OUTBACK SALAD

6 cups mixed salad greens
1 small carrot, grated
2 oranges, peeled, seeded, and sectioned
1 avocado, peeled and sliced
1½ cups diced fresh pineapple
Creamy Dressing

Place salad greens on individual plates; sprinkle with carrot. Arrange oranges, avocado, and pineapple on top. Serve with Creamy Dressing. Yield: 6 servings.

#### Creamy Dressing

1 (14-ounce) can sweetened condensed milk
⅔ cup cider vinegar
⅛ teaspoon dry mustard
⅛ teaspoon salt
Dash of pepper

Combine all ingredients, stirring well; cover and chill. Serve with Australian Outback Salad or fresh fruit salad. Yield: about 2 cups.     *Judi Grigoraci*
*Charleston, West Virginia*

# Don't Forget Dessert

Do you find yourself making desserts only when company's coming? If you do, here's an easy plan to remedy your family's dessertless dinners. Surprise your crew tonight with one of our down-home choices designed especially with families in mind. Your family will love their flavor; you'll love their ease and simplicity.

### MEMORY BOOK COOKIES

1 cup butter or margarine, softened
2 cups firmly packed brown sugar
2 large eggs
1 teaspoon vanilla extract
3½ cups all-purpose flour
1 teaspoon baking soda
½ teaspoon salt
1 cup chopped pecans

Beat butter at medium speed with an electric mixer; gradually add sugar, beating well. Add eggs and vanilla; mix well.

Combine flour, soda, and salt; gradually add to creamed mixture, mixing well. Stir in pecans. Shape dough into two 16-inch rolls; wrap in wax paper, and chill at least 4 hours.

Unwrap and cut into ⅓-inch slices; place on ungreased cookie sheets. Bake at 375° for 6 to 8 minutes. Cool on wire racks. Yield: 8 dozen.

**Note:** Dough may be frozen up to 3 months. Slice dough while frozen, and bake as directed.     *Kitty Cromer*
*Anderson, South Carolina*

### CHOCOLATE CHESS SQUARES

1 cup all-purpose flour
⅓ cup sifted powdered sugar
½ cup butter or margarine
1½ cups sugar
3 tablespoons cocoa
⅛ teaspoon salt
2 tablespoons butter or margarine, melted
2 large eggs, beaten
1 (5-ounce) can evaporated milk
1 teaspoon vanilla extract
½ cup chopped pecans

Combine flour and powdered sugar; cut in ½ cup butter with pastry blender until mixture resembles coarse crumbs. Press mixture evenly into bottom of a 9-inch square pan lined with heavy-duty aluminum foil. Bake at 350° for 15 minutes or until lightly browned.

Combine sugar, cocoa, and salt. Add 2 tablespoons butter and eggs; beat 2½ minutes at medium speed with an electric mixer. Add milk and vanilla, mixing well. Stir in pecans. Pour mixture over crust; bake at 350° for 45 minutes or until set. Cut into squares while warm. Let cool completely on a wire rack before removing from pan. Yield: 3 dozen.
*Celeste Pittman*
*Rocky Mount, North Carolina*

### EASY AMBROSIA

1 (20-ounce) can pineapple chunks, drained
1 (11-ounce) can mandarin oranges, drained
1½ cups seedless green grapes
1 cup flaked coconut
1 cup miniature marshmallows
½ cup chopped pecans
1 tablespoon sugar
¾ cup vanilla yogurt

Combine all ingredients in a large bowl; serve immediately or chill several hours. Yield: 8 servings.
*Patricia Ann Hill*
*Roan Mountain, Tennessee*

### STIRRED CUSTARD

3 large eggs, well beaten
¾ cup sugar
1 quart milk
1 tablespoon vanilla extract
Dash of ground nutmeg

Combine eggs and sugar in a large saucepan; gradually stir in milk. Cook over medium heat, stirring constantly, until mixture thickens and coats a metal spoon (about 20 minutes). Cool custard slightly. Stir in vanilla and nutmeg; cover and chill. (This mixture is pouring consistency.) Yield: 5 cups.
*Jane Figg Seale*
*Lafayette, Louisiana*

# Hurried, But Not Hungry

Not that you'd admit it, but how many mornings have you run out the door without breakfast only to pull into a fast-food drive-through or stop at the office vending machine? And when you've gobbled down "the most important meal of the day," as they say, you realize you've had too little taste and too little nutrition for too much cost. If only you'd had time for breakfast from home. Well, believe it or not, you do.

For the busiest of days, simply spoon Honey-Yogurt Apples into a nonbreakable container, and you're ready to go. To save even more time, chop the apples the night before, and toss them in lemon juice to prevent browning.

Another suggestion is to take a half-hour one evening to make Raisin-Nut Muffins. Store in an airtight container, and for the next few days, you can grab a muffin and head out for the day's tasks.

### HAM-AND-CHEESE FLIPS

1½ teaspoons butter or margarine, softened
1 teaspoon dried onion flakes
¾ cup diced cooked ham (about 4 ounces)
½ cup (2 ounces) shredded Cheddar cheese
1 (6-ounce) can refrigerated biscuits
1 tablespoon milk

Combine first 4 ingredients in a small bowl; set aside.

Separate biscuits, and place on an ungreased baking sheet. Press or roll each biscuit into a 5-inch circle. Spoon about ½ cup ham mixture onto half of each biscuit. Brush edges of biscuits with water; fold dough over filling, pressing edges with a fork to seal.

Make a 1-inch crescent-shaped slit on top of each turnover. Brush with milk, and bake turnovers at 375° for 15 minutes or until golden. Yield: 5 servings. *Paulette Surratt*
*Toast, North Carolina*

### CARIBBEAN FRENCH TOAST

½ cup orange juice
¼ cup whipping cream
2 tablespoons sugar
1 large egg
½ teaspoon ground cinnamon
Dash of ground nutmeg
6 (1-inch-thick) slices French bread
2 tablespoons butter or margarine, divided
Powdered sugar

Combine first 6 ingredients in a 13- x 9- x 2-inch baking dish. Place bread slices in mixture; turn slices to coat evenly. Let stand 5 minutes or until all liquid is absorbed.

Melt 1 tablespoon butter in a large skillet. Add 3 slices bread; cook over medium heat 3 minutes on each side or until golden brown. Remove from pan; keep warm. Repeat procedure with remaining bread slices.

Sift powdered sugar over toast; serve with maple syrup. Yield: 3 to 4 servings. *Betty Beske*
*Arlington, Virginia*

### HONEY-YOGURT APPLES

½ cup plain yogurt
2 tablespoons honey
2 apples, unpeeled and chopped
2 tablespoons shreds of wheat bran cereal

Combine yogurt and honey; spoon over apples. Sprinkle with cereal. Yield: 2 to 3 servings.

*Beverly Bardakjy*
*Miami, Florida*

### RAISIN-NUT MUFFINS

1 cup biscuit mix
¼ cup raisins
¼ cup chopped pecans
2 tablespoons brown sugar
1 large egg, beaten
¼ cup milk
2 tablespoons honey
Vegetable cooking spray

Combine first 4 ingredients in a large bowl; make a well in center of mixture. Combine egg, milk, and honey; add to dry ingredients, stirring just until moistened. Coat paper muffin pan liners with cooking spray; spoon batter into liners, filling two-thirds full. Bake at 400° for 12 to 15 minutes. Remove from pan immediately. Yield: 6 muffins. *Mrs. L. D. Fulton*
*Sturgis, Mississippi*

---

## ON THE LIGHT SIDE

# Dishes To Cluck About

When was the last time you sat down to a plate of eggs without feeling guilty? Once thought to be nature's perfect food, the egg has been relegated to the back of the refrigerator because of its high cholesterol content. Nowadays egg whites are most often used, particularly in healthful recipes. And if the whole egg is used, it's usually no more than one egg.

All the cholesterol found in an egg is in the yolk. The newest estimate on the amount of cholesterol in a single egg yolk is about 213 milligrams—less than the 274 milligrams it was originally thought to contain. For this reason the American Heart Association recently increased its guidelines for egg consumption from three to four eggs per week.

Egg whites are often substituted for whole eggs because they contain no cholesterol. Using two egg whites in place of a whole egg works well in many recipes. However, using only egg whites in dishes such as Fiesta Quiche, Italian Omelet, Vegetable Frittata, or plain scrambled eggs results in a pale, unappetizing product. Egg substitutes, either homemade (see recipe) or commercial, are best for recipes such as these.

Several varieties of commercial egg substitutes are available (see chart). In addition to egg whites, most contain oil, coloring, sodium, and preservatives to help them taste and perform like whole eggs. Egg substitutes can take the place of whole eggs in many egg dishes, but unfortunately they can be expensive.

We tested these recipes with both commercial egg substitute and our homemade egg substitute and got equally good results. We think you'll agree these low-cholesterol egg dishes are nutritious and tasty, too.

## HOMEMADE EGG SUBSTITUTE

6 egg whites
¼ cup instant nonfat dry milk powder
2 tablespoons water
1½ teaspoons vegetable oil
¼ teaspoon ground turmeric

Combine all ingredients in container of an electric blender or food processor. Process 30 seconds. Refrigerate up to 1 week or freeze in an airtight container up to 1 month. Yield: ¾ cup (90 calories per ¼ cup).

□ *10.6 grams protein, 2.4 grams fat, 6 grams carbohydrate, 2 milligrams cholesterol, 162 milligrams sodium, and 130 milligrams calcium.*

## FIESTA QUICHE

Vegetable cooking spray
4 (8½-inch) flour tortillas
½ cup (2 ounces) shredded reduced-fat Cheddar cheese
1 (4-ounce) can chopped green chiles, drained
¼ cup sliced green onions
½ cup picante sauce
1 cup egg substitute
⅓ cup skim milk
½ teaspoon chili powder
¼ teaspoon cracked black pepper
6 tomato slices
2 tablespoons plain nonfat yogurt
Fresh cilantro

Coat a 12-inch quiche dish with cooking spray; layer tortillas in dish. Sprinkle cheese, chiles, and green onions over tortillas; dollop with picante sauce. Combine egg substitute and next 3 ingredients; pour into quiche dish. Bake at 350° for 30 to 35 minutes. Remove from oven, and arrange tomato slices around edge of quiche; top each tomato slice with 1 teaspoon yogurt and a sprig of cilantro. Cut into wedges. Yield: 6 servings (225 calories per wedge).

□ *11.3 grams protein, 5.2 grams fat, 35.8 grams carbohydrate, 7 milligrams cholesterol, 388 milligrams sodium, and 169 milligrams calcium.*
*LuAnn Roberts*
*Rayville, Louisiana*

## ITALIAN OMELET

1 cup egg substitute
¼ teaspoon salt
⅛ teaspoon pepper
¼ teaspoon Italian seasoning
½ teaspoon olive oil
½ cup chopped onion
2 tablespoons chopped green pepper
2 cloves garlic, minced
¾ pound red potatoes, diced (about 4 small potatoes)
1 tablespoon grated Parmesan cheese
¼ cup commercial marinara sauce

Combine first 4 ingredients in a small bowl, and set aside.

Heat oil in a large nonstick skillet. Add onion, green pepper, and garlic; sauté until crisp-tender. Add potatoes; cook 5 to 8 minutes, stirring often, until potatoes begin to brown. Reduce heat; pour egg substitute mixture over vegetables in skillet, and sprinkle with Parmesan cheese. Cover and cook 7 to 8 minutes or until set. Invert onto serving plate; serve immediately with marinara sauce. Yield: 4 servings (127 calories per one-fourth omelet and 1 tablespoon marinara sauce).

□ *9.1 grams protein, 1.7 grams fat, 19.6 grams carbohydrate, 1 milligram cholesterol, 374 milligrams sodium, and 62 milligrams calcium.*
*Fredabeth Avant*
*Cordova, Tennessee*

| Nutritional Content and Cost of Eggs and Egg Substitutes | | | | |
|---|---|---|---|---|
| | Calories | Fat (grams) | Cholesterol (milligrams) | Estimated Cost* |
| Whole egg (1 large) | 79 | 5.6 | 213 | $.06 |
| Two egg whites | 32 | 0 | 0 | $.12 |
| Egg Beaters (¼ cup) | 25 | 0 | 0 | $.30 |
| Scramblers (¼ cup) | 60 | 3 | 0 | $.27 |
| Healthy Choice (¼ cup) | 30 | less than 1 | 0 | $.30 |
| Second Nature (¼ cup) | 60 | 2 | 0 | $.22 |
| Homemade Egg Substitute (¼ cup) | 90 | 2.4 | 2 | $.14 |

* Based on 1992 prices.

## VEGETABLE FRITTATA

1 cup egg substitute
1 tablespoon skim milk
⅛ teaspoon garlic powder
¼ teaspoon dried whole oregano
⅛ teaspoon salt
⅛ teaspoon pepper
Olive oil-flavored vegetable cooking
  spray
¼ cup chopped sweet red pepper
¼ cup chopped broccoli flowerets
¼ cup alfalfa sprouts
2 tablespoons sliced fresh
  mushrooms
2 ounces (½ cup) shredded reduced-
  fat Swiss cheese

Combine first 6 ingredients in a medium bowl; beat well. Coat a small nonstick skillet with cooking spray; add red pepper and broccoli, and sauté until tender. Remove vegetables from skillet, and add egg mixture. Reduce heat to low; cover and cook 8 to 10 minutes or until set. Top with alfalfa sprouts, sautéed vegetables, and mushrooms. Sprinkle evenly with cheese. Remove from heat; cover and let stand 3 to 5 minutes or until cheese melts. Serve immediately. Yield: 2 servings (about 186 calories per serving).

□ 21.4 grams protein, 8.7 grams fat, 5.4 grams carbohydrate, 26 milligrams cholesterol, 345 milligrams sodium, and 332 milligrams calcium.

# LIGHT FAVORITE

# Lean Yet Creamy Potatoes

For years potatoes have gotten a bad rap—they've been rumored to be fattening. In reality, a large potato has less than one gram of fat and about 220 calories. It's also a good source of complex carbohydrates, vitamins, and minerals.

What makes a potato a fattening food are the favorite accompaniments we use on it—sour cream, butter, cheese, and bacon. Two tablespoons each of butter, sour cream, and cheese added to a plain baked potato turn it into a 600-calorie side dish with about 40 grams of fat.

Traditional scalloped potatoes can be lightened by using skim milk, reduced-calorie margarine, and reduced-fat Cheddar cheese to cut back on fat content. In this lighter version, the original amount of cheese was decreased without sacrificing flavor by using reduced-fat sharp Cheddar cheese; it takes less of a strong cheese to produce the flavor of mild cheese.

## SCALLOPED POTATOES

¼ cup instant nonfat dry milk
  powder
2 cups skim milk
2 tablespoons reduced-calorie
  margarine
¼ cup all-purpose flour
½ teaspoon salt
½ teaspoon white pepper
1 (2-ounce) jar diced pimiento,
  drained
Vegetable cooking spray
1¾ pounds medium-size potatoes,
  cut into ¼-inch slices (about 4
  potatoes)
1½ cups thinly sliced onion,
  separated into rings
¾ cup (3 ounces) shredded reduced-
  fat sharp Cheddar cheese
¼ cup soft breadcrumbs

Dissolve milk powder in skim milk; set aside. Melt margarine in a heavy saucepan over low heat; add flour, stirring well. Cook 1 minute, stirring constantly (mixture will appear lumpy). Gradually add reserved milk, beating constantly with a wire whisk. Cook over medium heat, stirring constantly, until thickened and bubbly. Stir in salt, pepper, and pimiento; remove from heat.

Coat a 12- x 8- x 2-inch baking dish with cooking spray. Spread ¼ cup white sauce in baking dish. Top with half each of potatoes, onion, sauce, and cheese. Repeat layers of potatoes, onion, and remaining sauce. Cover and bake at 375° for 1 hour or until potatoes are tender. Uncover and sprinkle with remaining cheese and breadcrumbs. Coat with cooking spray. Bake an additional 5 minutes or until cheese melts. Yield: 12 servings (122 calories per ½-cup serving).

□ 6.4 grams protein, 2.9 grams fat, 18.3 grams carbohydrate, 6 milligrams cholesterol, 212 milligrams sodium, and 158 milligrams calcium.

### COMPARE THE NUTRIENTS
(per serving)

|  | Traditional | Light |
|---|---|---|
| Calories | 211 | 122 |
| Fat | 11.5g | 2.9g |
| Cholesterol | 35.6mg | 6mg |

# LIGHT MENU

# Warming Winter Supper

After a cold day outdoors, nothing warms like a hot bowl of soup. And, served as a main dish, soup provides an easy, healthy start to a meal.

French Market Soup is chock-full of nutritious dried beans—the kind that contain soluble fiber for lowering cholesterol. Wait to add the tomatoes until the last 30 minutes of cooking so the acid in the tomatoes won't keep the beans from softening. Double the recipe, and freeze the second batch.

With its crisp texture, shredded cabbage with oil-free salad dressing complements French Market Soup.

Cabbage is a member of the cruciferous vegetable family that is thought to have cancer-preventing potential. Add cabbage and its relatives—broccoli, kale, brussels sprouts, and cauliflower—to your menus often.

The recipe for Cornmeal Yeast Muffins yields three dozen muffins that freeze well. For a quick warmup, wrap frozen muffins in a paper towel and heat them in the microwave.

## FAMILY SOUP SUPPER

**French Market Soup**
**Shredded cabbage**
**Cornmeal Yeast Muffins**
**Jicama-Fruit Compote**

## FRENCH MARKET SOUP

1 (12-ounce) package dried bean
   soup mix
9 cups water
1 cup cubed lean cooked ham
½ teaspoon salt
¼ teaspoon white pepper
1 (16-ounce) can no-salt-added
   whole tomatoes, undrained
1½ cups chopped onion
¾ cup chopped celery
2 large cloves garlic, minced
3 tablespoons lemon juice
1 teaspoon hot sauce

Sort and wash bean soup mix; place in a Dutch oven. Cover with water 2 inches above beans; let soak 8 hours.

Drain beans and return to Dutch oven. Add 9 cups water, ham, salt, and white pepper. Bring to a boil; reduce heat, and simmer, uncovered, 2 hours or until beans are tender. Chop tomatoes and add with remaining ingredients; simmer 30 minutes, stirring occasionally. Yield: 5 servings (312 calories per 1½-cup serving).

□ *21.1 grams protein, 2.9 grams fat, 53.4 grams carbohydrate, 14 milligrams cholesterol, 498 milligrams sodium, and 138 milligrams calcium.*
*Linda Dorrough*
*Montgomery, Alabama*

## CORNMEAL YEAST MUFFINS

1 package dry yeast
¼ cup warm water (105° to 115°)
1¾ cups skim milk
⅓ cup sugar
¼ cup vegetable oil
¼ cup reduced-calorie margarine
1 teaspoon salt
½ cup egg substitute
1½ cups plain cornmeal
5 to 5½ cups all-purpose flour,
   divided
Butter-flavored vegetable cooking
   spray

Dissolve yeast in warm water in a large bowl; let stand 5 minutes. Combine milk and next 4 ingredients in a saucepan; cook over low heat until margarine melts. Cool to 105° to 115°. Add milk mixture to yeast mixture. Stir in egg substitute, cornmeal, and 2 cups flour. Beat mixture at medium speed with an electric mixer until smooth. Stir in enough remaining flour to make a soft dough.

Turn dough out onto a lightly floured surface and knead until smooth and elastic (about 8 minutes). Place in a bowl coated with cooking spray, turning to grease top. Cover and let rise in a warm place (85°), free from drafts, 1 hour or until doubled in bulk.

Punch dough down; shape into 72 balls. Place 2 balls in each muffin cup coated with cooking spray. Let rise in a warm place (85°), free from drafts, 45 minutes or until doubled in bulk. Bake at 375° for 12 to 15 minutes or until muffins are golden. Coat muffins with cooking spray, and remove from pans immediately. (These muffins freeze well.) Yield: 3 dozen (116 calories per muffin).

□ *3 grams protein, 2.8 grams fat, 19.4 grams carbohydrate, 0 milligrams cholesterol, 89 milligrams sodium, and 19 milligrams calcium.*

## JICAMA-FRUIT COMPOTE

1½ cups diced jicama
1½ tablespoons sugar
1½ teaspoons lemon juice
3 (2-inch) sticks cinnamon
⅓ cup orange juice
3 cups unpeeled sliced apple
¾ cup frozen pitted dark sweet
   cherries, thawed
⅛ teaspoon dried orange peel

Combine first 5 ingredients in a medium saucepan; cover and cook over medium heat about 10 minutes. Add remaining ingredients; cook 2 to 3 minutes. Serve warm. Yield: 6 servings (76 calories per ½-cup serving).

□ *0.8 gram protein, 0.4 gram fat, 18.7 grams carbohydrate, 0 milligrams cholesterol, 2 milligrams sodium, and 12 milligrams calcium.*

# Spreads For Breads

Everyone *loves* a biscuit or bread slathered with a sweet spread. Start with butter or cream cheese, and add a few ingredients for some easy options in bread toppers. They're simple and good.

Dried fruit and zest from citrus fruit, such as lemons, limes or oranges, add an extra-special flavor to a plain spread. And best of all, they're nutritious.

## PRUNE-ORANGE BUTTER

½ cup butter or margarine,
   softened
⅓ cup honey
1 teaspoon grated orange rind
½ cup chopped pitted prunes

Beat butter at medium speed with an electric mixer. Gradually add honey, beating until smooth. Stir in orange rind and prunes. Yield: 1 cup.
*Cheryl Richardson*
*Fairfax Station, Virginia*

## AMBROSIA SPREAD

1 (11-ounce) can mandarin orange
   sections, drained
1 (8-ounce) container soft cream
   cheese with pineapple
¼ cup flaked coconut, toasted
¼ cup slivered almonds, chopped
   and toasted

Set aside 3 orange sections for garnish. Chop remaining orange sections;
set aside. Stir together cream cheese,
coconut, and almonds until smooth.
Fold in reserved chopped oranges.
Arrange reserved orange sections on
top. Chill. Serve spread with date nut
bread, banana bread, or gingersnaps.
Yield: 1⅔ cups.      *Jennifer Mungo*
*Columbia, South Carolina*

# QUICK!

## Sweets To The Sweet

Valentine's Day is the perfect excuse
to unabashedly eat chocolate. And
these recipes will make quick work of
your cravings. All of them cook in just
20 minutes or less, but they'll need
some time to cool or chill.

A few of these recipes call for a
double boiler to melt the chocolate. If
you don't have one, use a heavy
saucepan, and keep the heat *low*. If
you get impatient and turn the heat
too high, it will ruin the chocolate.

## CHOCOLATE CRUNCHIES

10 (2-ounce) squares
   chocolate-flavored candy coating
1 cup light corn syrup
¼ cup butter or margarine
2 teaspoons vanilla extract
1 (7.2-ounce) package crispy rice
   cereal

Combine chocolate-flavored candy
coating, corn syrup, and butter in top
of a double boiler; bring water to a
boil. Reduce heat to low; cook until
coating melts. Remove from heat; stir
in vanilla.

Place cereal in a large mixing bowl;
pour chocolate mixture on top, and
stir until well coated. Quickly spoon
mixture into a buttered 13- x 9- x
2-inch dish; press firmly, using the
back of a spoon. Cool completely; cut
into bars. Yield: 4 dozen.
*Albert C. Noble*
*Bristol, Tennessee*

## CHOCOLATE DIP

2 tablespoons cocoa
2 teaspoons cornstarch
¼ cup water
⅓ cup light corn syrup
2 tablespoons butter or
   margarine
1 teaspoon vanilla extract

Combine cocoa and cornstarch in a
small saucepan. Add water, stirring
until smooth. Stir in the corn syrup.
Cook over medium heat, stirring constantly, until mixture boils; boil 30
seconds, stirring constantly. Remove
from heat; add butter, and stir until
melted. Stir in vanilla. Cool mixture to
room temperature. Serve with whole
strawberries. Yield: ½ cup.

## CHOCOLATE-MARSHMALLOW SQUARES

1 (12-ounce) package semisweet
   chocolate morsels
1 cup butterscotch morsels
½ cup peanut butter
1 (10½-ounce) package miniature
   marshmallows
1 cup salted peanuts

Combine first 3 ingredients in a
3-quart glass bowl. Microwave at ME-
DIUM (50% power) 3½ to 4½ minutes or until morsels soften, stirring

after 2 minutes. Stir until mixture is
smooth. Stir in marshmallows and
peanuts. Spread mixture in a lightly
greased 12- x 8- x 2-inch dish. Refrigerate until firm. Cut into 2-inch
squares. Store squares in refrigerator. Yield: 2 dozen.      *Lilann Taylor*
*Savannah, Georgia*

## WHITE CHOCOLATE SALTIES

8 (2-ounce) squares vanilla-flavored
   candy coating
2 (3-ounce) packages salted Spanish
   peanuts
3 cups thin pretzel sticks

Place candy coating in top of a double
boiler; bring water to a boil. Reduce
heat to low; cook until coating melts.
Remove from heat. Cool 2 minutes;
add peanuts and pretzel sticks, and
stir until coated. Drop by teaspoonfuls
onto wax paper. Chill 20 minutes or
until firm. Yield: 1½ pounds.

**Note:** Vanilla-flavored candy coating
usually can be found in the baking section at the supermarket.
*Carol Barclay*
*Portland, Texas*

## MICROWAVE CHOCOLATE FUDGE

3 cups semisweet chocolate
   morsels
1 (14-ounce) can sweetened
   condensed milk
¼ cup butter or margarine, cut into
   pieces
1 cup chopped walnuts

Combine first 3 ingredients in a
2-quart glass bowl. Microwave at ME-
DIUM (50% power) 4 to 5 minutes,
stirring at 1½-minute intervals. Stir in
chopped walnuts, and pour mixture
into a buttered 8-inch square dish.
Chill at least 2 hours. Cut into
squares. Yield: 2 pounds.
*Suzan L. Wiener*
*Spring Hill, Florida*

# Cheesecake With A New Taste

Next time you find yourself searching for a special luncheon entrée, try Layered Vegetable Cheesecake. Not only is it tasty, but it can also be made a day ahead.

### LAYERED VEGETABLE CHEESECAKE

1⅓ cups dry breadcrumbs
⅓ cup butter or margarine, melted
2 (8-ounce) packages Neufchâtel cheese, softened
2 large eggs
⅓ cup all-purpose flour
1 (8-ounce) carton sour cream
¼ cup minced onion
¼ teaspoon salt
¼ teaspoon white pepper
¾ cup shredded carrot
¾ cup diced green pepper
¾ cup diced sweet red pepper
Cucumber-Dill Sauce
Garnishes: cucumber slices, fresh dillweed

Combine breadcrumbs and butter; press on bottom and 1 inch up sides of a 9-inch springform pan. Set aside.

Beat cheese at high speed with an electric mixer until fluffy. Add eggs, one at a time, beating well after each addition. Add flour and next 4 ingredients; beat until blended.

Pour about one-fourth of cream cheese mixture into prepared pan; sprinkle with carrot. Top with one-third remaining cream cheese mixture; sprinkle with green pepper. Top with half of remaining cream cheese mixture; top with red pepper. Top with remaining cream cheese mixture. Bake at 300° for 1 hour or until set. Turn oven off, and partially open oven door; leave cheesecake in oven 1 hour. Remove from oven, and let cool completely. Cover and chill. Serve with Cucumber-Dill Sauce. Garnish, if desired. Yield: 6 to 8 servings.

### Cucumber-Dill Sauce

1 (8-ounce) carton plain yogurt
⅓ cup mayonnaise or salad dressing
½ cup chopped, unpeeled cucumber
¼ teaspoon salt
¼ teaspoon dried whole dillweed

Combine all ingredients, stirring well. Cover and chill. Yield: 1½ cups.

# Onions: In Season All Year

Most vegetables, such as sweet winter squash or succulent ripe tomatoes, have a peak season. However, the humble onion is at its best the entire year. During warm-weather months, a Southern-grown crop fulfills the demand. As it turns cold, fresh onions shipped from South Florida or Western states maintain the supply. Thanks to speedy transportation and a lengthy shelf life, onions are always plentiful in the produce section of the supermarket.

Take advantage of their bounty and try a recipe in this crop. From Honey-Paprika Sweet Onions to Beer-Battered Onion Rings, top quality onions play leading roles.

### ONION SHORTCAKE

1 large sweet onion, sliced
¼ cup butter or margarine, melted
1 large egg, lightly beaten
⅓ cup milk
1 (8¾-ounce) can cream-style corn
2 drops of hot sauce
2 (6-ounce) packages corn muffin mix
1 (8-ounce) carton sour cream
¼ teaspoon salt
¼ teaspoon dried dillweed
1 cup (4 ounces) shredded sharp Cheddar cheese, divided

Sauté onion in butter in a large skillet over medium heat until tender, and set aside.

Combine egg and next 3 ingredients; add corn muffin mix and stir just until moistened. Pour mixture into a lightly greased 8-inch square baking dish; set aside.

Combine reserved onion mixture, sour cream, salt, dillweed, and half of Cheddar cheese; spread evenly over batter. Bake at 350° for 25 minutes; sprinkle with remaining cheese, and bake an additional 5 minutes. Yield: 8 to 10 servings.

*Ruth Ann Cunningham*
*Scottsmoor, Florida*

### CREAMY ONION-AND-POTATO SOUP

2 tablespoons butter or margarine
2 tablespoons all-purpose flour
1 cup chopped onion
1 large clove garlic, minced
2 (14½-ounce) cans ready-to-serve chicken broth
4 cups peeled, cubed potatoes (about 3 large)
½ cup sliced green onions
⅛ teaspoon salt
¼ teaspoon white pepper
1 cup liquid non-dairy creamer or milk
Garnish: green onion strips

Melt butter in a Dutch oven over low heat; add flour, stirring until smooth. Cook 1 minute, stirring contantly. Add onion and garlic; cook 1 minute or until onion is tender. Gradually add broth, stirring constantly. Add potatoes and next 3 ingredients. Bring to a boil; cover, reduce heat, and simmer 15 minutes, stirring occasionally, or until potatoes are tender. Stir in non-dairy creamer, and heat thoroughly. Garnish, if desired. Yield: 7 cups.

*Cathy Darling*
*Grafton, West Virginia*

## BEER-BATTERED ONION RINGS

2 large sweet onions
1 large egg, lightly beaten
1 (12-ounce) can beer
1 tablespoon baking powder
1 tablespoon seasoned salt
1½ cups all-purpose flour
Vegetable oil

Cut onions into ½-inch slices, and separate into rings. Set aside. Combine egg and next 3 ingredients in a large bowl; add flour and stir with a wire whisk until smooth. Dip onion rings in batter. Pour oil to depth of 2 to 3 inches into a Dutch oven; heat to 375°. Fry, turning once, until golden brown. Drain well on paper towels. Serve onion rings immediately. Yield: 4 to 6 servings. *Sharon McClatchey Muskogee, Oklahoma*

## HONEY-PAPRIKA SWEET ONIONS

4 (1-pound) sweet onions, cut in half crosswise
¼ cup butter or margarine, melted
¼ cup honey
2 tablespoons water
1 teaspoon paprika
½ teaspoon salt

Place onions, cut side up, in a lightly greased 13- x 9- x 2-inch baking dish. Combine butter and remaining ingredients; pour over onions. Cover with aluminum foil, and bake at 350° for 45 minutes or until tender. Yield: 8 servings. *Mabel A. Scarborough Bel Air, Maryland*

# Try Tasty Blue Corn Muffins

You may be surprised to learn that blue cornmeal has long been a common food staple in the Southwest. The gray-blue meal is just beginning to find its way east. Stephan Pyles's Blue Corn Muffins are a specialty at his Dallas, Texas, restaurant, Routh Street Café.

Blue cornmeal has kernels of blackish purple, blue, and yellow. It's nuttier tasting than white or yellow meal; the corn is smoked and treated with lime before grinding.

## BLUE CORN MUFFINS

½ cup diced sweet red pepper
½ cup diced sweet yellow pepper
¼ cup diced onion
1 tablespoon vegetable oil
¼ cup plus 2 tablespoons butter or margarine
½ cup shortening
1½ cups blue cornmeal *
1 cup all-purpose flour
⅓ cup sugar
1 tablespoon baking powder
1 teaspoon salt
2 large eggs, lightly beaten
1 cup milk
½ cup half-and-half
1 cup diced cooked ham

Sauté peppers and onion in oil until tender; set aside.

Combine butter and shortening in a small saucepan; melt over low heat. Set aside to cool.

Combine cornmeal and next 4 ingredients; mix well, and set aside.

Combine eggs, milk, half-and-half, and ham. Stir in sautéed vegetables and melted butter mixture. Add to dry ingredients, stirring mixture just until moistened.

Spoon into greased and floured muffin pans, filling three-fourths full. Bake at 350° for 20 to 25 minutes. Yield: 2 dozen.

* White or yellow cornmeal can be substituted for blue cornmeal.

# From Our Kitchen To Yours

The Test Kitchens staff is always on the lookout for techniques to simplify food preparation. If your schedule is as busy as ours, you'll find these labor-saving suggestions helpful. When you use these methods, your time in the kitchen will be hassle free.

■ Grilling fragile foods and small items such as vegetables, shrimp, and fish can be difficult because they sometimes fall through the grates of the grill. A hinged wire grilling basket locks these foods in and makes flipping them a snap.

■ When making biscuits or pastry, cut the shortening into the dry ingredients by using a chopping motion with a pastry blender. Continue this action until the flour absorbs the shortening and the mixture becomes dry and crumbly; the texture will resemble coarse meal.

■ Sticky, wet dough (handled as little as possible) makes the best biscuits. To keep biscuit or yeast bread dough from sticking to your hands, begin kneading with a metal dough scraper or a spatula. (The metal scraper is available at kitchen shops.) With the stainless steel blade secured in a hardwood handle, you can lift the dough and fold it over on a floured surface. When the dough becomes less sticky, complete the kneading by hand.

■ Use kitchen shears to peel and devein shrimp. Quickly snip down the back of the shrimp and expose the vein. Lift the dark vein from the slit and discard it; then remove the shell, leaving the tail intact, if desired.

■ To cut vegetables such as carrots into julienne strips, lay the vegetables flat on a cutting board. Using a sharp paring knife, first cut the vegetables into ¼-inch-thick, finger-length pieces; then you can slice them lengthwise into ¼-inch-wide matchstick strips.

# MARCH

*Welcome spring with a casual gathering of friends. Fire up the grill and try a simple menu of poultry or seafood with fresh vegetables and fruits. For a spectacular finale to any occasion, prepare Satin Ribbon Cake, a magnificent centerpiece that is guaranteed to steal the show.*

# A Salute To Spring

Welcome spring with a menu that, like the season, is simply glorious—and gloriously simple. Gone are lengthy ingredient lists and vigils over hot pots. It's time for fresh foods that need little else. This menu is abundant in fruits and vegetables, and most of the recipes have five or fewer ingredients. Quickly make the side dishes; then enjoy spring sunshine while you grill catfish outdoors. Finally, let your guests help themselves to dessert.

### SPRING MENU FOR 6

**Grilled Catfish With Relish**
**Garlic New Potatoes**
**Buttered Green Beans**
**Bacon-Cheese French Bread**
**Minted Tea**
**Sweet-and-Sour**
**Strawberry Dessert**

## GRILLED CATFISH WITH RELISH

3 ears fresh corn
1 large tomato, chopped
2 to 3 green onions, chopped
½ cup commercial Italian salad dressing
6 (6-ounce) catfish fillets
Vegetable cooking spray
⅓ cup lemon juice
3 tablespoons butter or margarine, melted
1 tablespoon lemon-pepper seasoning

Remove husks and silks from corn, and cut corn from cob. Cook in a small amount of boiling water 8 to 10 minutes; drain and cool. Combine corn, tomato, green onions, and salad dressing; cover and chill 2 hours.

Place fish in a fish basket coated with cooking spray. Combine lemon juice, butter, and seasoning; brush fillets with lemon mixture. Place fish basket on grill, and close cover of grill. (Because of the shape of the fish basket, the grill will not close completely.) Grill fish over medium coals (300° to 400°) for 7 to 9 minutes on each side or until fish flakes easily with a fork, basting often with remaining lemon mixture. Serve with chilled corn relish. Yield: 6 servings.

## GARLIC NEW POTATOES

18 new potatoes, quartered
2 cloves garlic, minced
¼ cup butter or margarine, melted
1 tablespoon chopped parsley
¼ teaspoon freshly ground pepper

Cook potatoes, covered, in boiling salted water to cover 15 minutes or until tender; drain. Sauté garlic in butter in a small skillet until tender. Add parsley and pepper to skillet; pour mixture over potatoes, tossing gently to coat. Yield: 6 servings.

## BUTTERED GREEN BEANS

1½ pounds fresh green beans
¾ cup water
¼ cup butter or margarine, melted

Wash green beans; trim ends, and remove strings. Bring water to a boil in a Dutch oven. Add beans. Cover, reduce heat to medium, and cook 10 minutes, stirring occasionally. Drain, and toss beans with butter. Yield: 6 servings.

## BACON-CHEESE FRENCH BREAD

1 (16-ounce) loaf unsliced French bread
5 slices bacon, cooked and crumbled
2 cups (8 ounces) shredded mozzarella cheese
¼ cup butter or margarine, melted

Cut bread into 1-inch slices. Place sliced loaf on a large piece of aluminum foil. Combine bacon and cheese; place between bread slices. Drizzle butter over loaf, and wrap in foil. Bake at 350° for 20 minutes or until thoroughly heated. Yield: 1 loaf.

## MINTED TEA

5 cups boiling water
5 regular-size mint tea bags
1 cup sugar
5 cups water
1 cup pineapple juice
¾ cup lemon juice
2 (10-ounce) bottles ginger ale, chilled
Garnish: fresh mint sprigs

Pour boiling water over tea bags; cover and set aside 5 minutes. Remove tea bags, squeezing gently. Stir in sugar and next 3 ingredients. Chill. To serve, stir in ginger ale, and garnish, if desired. Yield: 3½ quarts.
*Ouida Hamilton*
*Birmingham, Alabama*

## SWEET-AND-SOUR STRAWBERRY DESSERT

1 quart fresh strawberries
1 (8-ounce) carton sour cream
1 cup firmly packed dark brown sugar
Garnish: fresh mint sprigs

Wash and hull strawberries; pat dry and slice. Top individual servings with sour cream and brown sugar. Garnish, if desired. Yield: 6 servings.

# Garlic: Peel A World Of Flavor

For about 5,000 years—as long as the portly bulb from the lily family has been alternately praised and defamed—garlic has sparked pungent debate between those who can't eat enough and those who are offended by it. This is for garlic lovers.

In our country, French settlers first grew garlic in New Orleans for their cooking needs. Wise to the way garlic blends the flavors of meat, seafood, and tomatoes into one aromatic bouquet, the French knew what cooks and physicians had touted for centuries—garlic's magic is like no other.

In ancient Rome, soldiers, athletes, and sailors ate garlic regularly in attempts to increase their strength and endurance. The Egyptian slaves who labored to build the pyramids were fed garlic to provide and prolong their strength. In the biblical book of Numbers, Israelites reminisce about the leeks, garlic, and onions they ate during their captivity in Egypt.

Several cultures claim garlic's healing powers. As early as 2000 B.C., Chinese scholars praised garlic for its medicinal value. Hippocrates wrote, "Let food be your medicine." He thought garlic an apt prescription for many medical problems, but worried that it was bad for the eyes. Whatever the case, Hippocrates saw the future.

The National Institute of Cancer has launched a research project that will focus on ways to extract natural compounds from foods to prevent cancer. Known as the "designer food" program, the project will examine citrus, licorice root, certain vegetables, and garlic.

The garlic faithful appreciate its changing flavor most. Its taste evolves at the hand of an appreciative cook. Garlic is sweetened by heat, slow cooking, or roasting. Tasted raw, it boasts an intense, almost arrogant flavor that overpowers any other.

The edible bulb or "head" grows beneath the ground. The bulb or "head" is made up of sections called cloves, and each is encased in its own parchment-like skin. Garlic is a member of the lily family.

The major suppliers of garlic are the United States (California, Texas, and Louisiana), France, Spain, Italy, and Mexico.

The following recipes represent garlic at the best of its extremes. Try these recipes as a sort of culinary journey over time and history, and when you taste them, toast the memory of that Frenchman who first sautéed garlic in New Orleans.

## A Louisiana Chef Shares His Tips

"Being from Louisiana, I use a lot of garlic," says Chef Efrem Cutler. Formerly the Executive Chef for Lafittes Landing/White Oak Plantation in his home state, Cutler consults his heritage when weaving garlic into the fabric of his restaurant's menu.

"I use heavy garlic," he admits. "I sauté it to secrete the oil. Sometimes I caramelize it. There's an explosion in your mouth when you bite into it."

Cutler says to look for fresh, firm heads with the papery skins intact. A sharp knife is his best tool. He prefers mincing over using a garlic press, arguing that the press damages the skin and allows the garlic to secrete too much oil. To mince, he makes several cuts across the clove one way, turns it and cuts the other way. When cooking garlic, he keeps the heat low to medium because burned garlic imparts a bitter flavor.

Here is his recipe for Roast Garlic Puree. If you prefer not to puree the roasted cloves, simply squeeze the garlic from the skins and spread it on buttered, toasted bread. Otherwise, use the puree to season soups, mayonnaise, roasts, and stews; or offer it as a condiment.

### ROASTED GARLIC PUREE

4 large heads garlic
¼ cup olive oil
⅛ to ¼ teaspoon salt
⅛ to ¼ teaspoon pepper
1 tablespoon fresh lemon juice

Chop off bottom of garlic head, and separate whole cloves, leaving tight outer covering intact. Place cloves in a shallow 8-inch square baking dish, and drizzle with olive oil. Bake at 350° for 20 minutes. Cool and drain; remove skins. Roast garlic may be eaten as is or pureed for smoother texture.

To puree, position knife blade in food processor bowl; add garlic, salt, pepper, and lemon juice. Process 30 seconds or until almost smooth, scraping sides of processor bowl occasionally. Use as a spread for buttered, toasted French bread or as a condiment for lamb, pork, or beef. Serve puree hot or cold. Yield: about ¾ cup.

Note: Elephant garlic may be substituted in Roasted Garlic Puree. This is a cross between a shallot and garlic, and it has less moisture than garlic. Elephant garlic will not substitute for regular garlic in some uses, such as sautéing. The white-skinned elephant garlic is a mild-flavored one. It has bulbs the size of a small grapefruit with huge cloves averaging 1 ounce each. Elephant garlic is the mildest-flavored variety among the three major types of garlic—American, Mexican, and Italian.

■ Garlic usually comes in whole heads of 8 to 12 cloves enclosed in a parchment-like covering. Individual cloves (also called toes or buds) are minced to give this recipe its flavor.

## TERIYAKI BEEF BROIL
*(pictured on page 37)*

1¾ pounds top round steak (1-inch thick)
¼ cup soy sauce
¼ cup vegetable oil
2 tablespoons molasses
2 teaspoons ground ginger
2 teaspoons dry mustard
6 cloves garlic, minced
Strips of chives (optional)

Partially freeze steak; slice diagonally across grain into ¼-inch strips. Place steak in a shallow container. Combine soy sauce and next 5 ingredients; pour over steak. Cover and chill 1 hour.

Remove steak from marinade, and thread onto 9-inch bamboo skewers. Place skewers on a lightly greased rack of a broiler pan. Broil 4 inches from heat 6 to 7 minutes, turning once. Serve over strips of chives, if desired. Yield: 6 servings or 24 appetizer servings.
*Doris Garton*
*Shenandoah, Virginia*

■ To press or not to press? Some say that using a press damages garlic's texture. Others like its pungency. Our Test Kitchens home economists voted to press the garlic for this salad dressing. To enliven a commercial dressing, press a clove and add it to dressing.

## GARLIC SAUCE

5 cloves garlic
¼ cup water
½ teaspoon salt
2 slices white bread, trimmed
⅓ cup slivered almonds
2 tablespoons white vinegar
½ cup olive oil

Position knife blade in food processor bowl; add garlic, and process until garlic is minced. Add water and next 4

ingredients; process until smooth. With processor running, pour olive oil through food chute in a slow steady stream until combined; chill. Serve sauce over vegetables, fish, or meat. Yield: 1¼ cups.
*Nancy B. Hall*
*Calvert City, Kentucky*

■ The French term for homemade garlic mayonnaise is aioli; this shortcut Garlic Mayonnaise relies on the commercial product seasoned with tomato paste and garlic. Serve it as a dip for artichokes or as a sandwich spread.

## RICH FISH SOUP
## WITH GARLIC MAYONNAISE

½ cup vegetable oil
¾ cup all-purpose flour
5 cups water
2 tablespoons fish-flavored bouillon granules
¼ cup dry red wine
1 (6-ounce) can tomato paste
¼ teaspoon red pepper
⅛ teaspoon ground saffron
Crostini
Garlic Mayonnaise

Heat oil in a Dutch oven over medium heat until hot. Add flour and cook, stirring constantly, until roux is chocolate colored (about 15 minutes). Remove from heat; gradually stir in water. Add bouillon granules and next 4 ingredients. Cook over medium heat. To serve, ladle into bowls, and top with Crostini and Garlic Mayonnaise. Yield: 6 cups.

### Crostini

1 baguette French bread
Butter-flavored vegetable cooking spray
¼ cup (2 ounces) shredded Cheddar cheese

Cut bread into ½-inch slices. Coat both sides with cooking spray, and

place on a baking sheet. Bake at 250° for 20 minutes; sprinkle with cheese. Broil 4 inches from heat 1 minute or until cheese melts. Yield: 2 dozen.

### Garlic Mayonnaise

½ cup mayonnaise
1 to 2 tablespoons tomato paste
3 cloves garlic, minced

Combine all ingredients. Yield: ½ cup.

■ This recipe is a spinach-packed variation on a popular recipe for garlic chicken that uses 40 cloves. Although this version calls for a total of 24 cloves of garlic, Bonita Phillips sometimes uses as many as 42.

## GARLIC-SPINACH CHICKEN

2 (10-ounce) packages frozen chopped spinach, thawed
6 chicken breast halves, skinned
12 to 18 cloves garlic, unpeeled
1 (10¾-ounce) can cream of chicken soup, undiluted
1½ cups dry white wine or champagne
6 cloves garlic, peeled
1 teaspoon ground ginger
6 (1-ounce) slices Swiss cheese
4 green onions, chopped

Drain spinach well, pressing between layers of paper towels; set aside.

Place chicken in a lightly greased 13- x 9- x 2-inch baking dish. Arrange unpeeled garlic around chicken; spread spinach evenly over top.

Combine soup and next 3 ingredients in container of an electric blender or food processor; process until smooth. Pour mixture over chicken. Cover and bake at 350° for 1 hour. Top with cheese, and bake, uncovered, an additional 5 minutes. Sprinkle with green onions. Yield: 6 servings.
*Bonita Phillips*
*Miami, Florida*

■ This surprising sauce is like a mayonnaise without eggs. Instead, bread and almonds are processed with garlic to lend a strong, pungent flavor. Serve it with vegetables or use it to give burgers a gourmet flavor.

## GARLIC-BLUE CHEESE VINAIGRETTE

1 cup vegetable oil
¾ cup white vinegar
½ cup olive oil
2 teaspoons celery salt
1 teaspoon sugar
1 teaspoon dry mustard
½ teaspoon freshly ground pepper
2 to 3 large cloves garlic, crushed
1 (4-ounce) package crumbled blue cheese

Combine first 8 ingredients in a jar. Cover tightly, and shake vigorously. Add blue cheese; stir mixture before serving. Serve with mixed greens. Yield: about 3 cups.

# Hooked On Gruyère

It's not so easy to say "cheese" when the variety has a name like Gruyère. Pronounced groo-YEHR, this cousin of Swiss cheese comes from Switzerland and France. It has smaller holes than regular Swiss cheese, and a sharper flavor.

Gruyère is sold in individually wrapped wedges at large supermarkets and specialty foods shops. If you can't find it in your store, substitute regular Swiss cheese. We tried these recipes with both cheeses and liked them equally well. Those who prefer a less pungent flavor might try the Swiss cheese first.

These recipes pair the breezy flavors of shrimp and scallops with the full-bodied taste of cheese. They're perfect when you want to serve something out of the ordinary.

## BAKED GRUYÈRE SCALLOPS

1 pound fresh bay scallops
¼ cup butter or margarine, melted and divided
1 medium onion, finely chopped
½ pound fresh mushrooms, sliced
1½ cups (6 ounces) shredded Gruyère or Swiss cheese
½ cup mayonnaise or salad dressing
¼ cup Chablis or other dry white wine

Sauté scallops in 2 tablespoons butter in a large skillet 2 to 3 minutes. Drain and set aside.

Sauté onion and mushrooms in remaining 2 tablespoons butter until tender; remove from heat. Add scallops, cheese, mayonnaise, and wine; stir well. Spoon mixture into 4 lightly greased individual casseroles. Broil 4 inches from heat 2 to 4 minutes or until lightly browned. Yield: 4 servings.

*Cynthia Zimmerman*
*Springfield, Virginia*

## SHRIMP-AND-GRUYÈRE CHEESECAKE

1¼ cups round buttery cracker crumbs
¼ cup butter or margarine, melted
1½ pounds unpeeled, medium-size fresh shrimp
⅓ cup minced green pepper
⅓ cup minced sweet red pepper
¼ cup minced onion
1 large clove garlic, minced
3 tablespoons butter or margarine, melted
2 (8-ounce) packages cream cheese, softened
½ cup mayonnaise
4 large eggs
⅓ cup milk
1¼ cups (5 ounces) shredded Gruyère or Swiss cheese
1 teaspoon white pepper
Garnishes: sweet red pepper strips, shrimp, fresh basil leaves
Italian Tomato Sauce

Combine cracker crumbs and ¼ cup butter; press into bottom of a 9-inch springform pan. Set aside.

Peel, devein, and chop shrimp. Sauté shrimp and next 4 ingredients in 3 tablespoons butter 4 to 5 minutes; drain well, and set aside.

Beat cream cheese and mayonnaise at high speed with an electric mixer until light and fluffy; add eggs, one at a time, beating after each addition. Gradually add milk, beating at low speed just until blended. Stir in shrimp mixture, Gruyère, and 1 teaspoon white pepper.

Pour mixture into prepared pan. Bake at 300° for 1 hour and 20 to 30 minutes or until set. Turn oven off, and partially open oven door; leave cheesecake in oven 1 hour.

Let cool completely on a wire rack; cover and chill. Garnish, if desired. Serve with Italian Tomato Sauce. Yield: 8 servings.

### Italian Tomato Sauce

¼ cup chopped onion
1 clove garlic, minced
1 tablespoon olive oil
2 (14-ounce) cans tomatoes, drained and chopped
1½ teaspoons dried Italian seasoning
1 bay leaf

Sauté onion and garlic in hot oil in a large skillet until onion is tender. Add tomatoes and remaining ingredients; simmer, uncovered, 20 minutes or until most of liquid evaporates, stirring occasionally. Remove bay leaf; serve warm. Yield: about 2 cups.

**Note:** To quickly chop tomatoes, use kitchen shears, and snip them into small pieces.

# Appealing Appetizers

A basket of chips and dip or a tray of cheese and crackers served to your guests before dinner is customary for casual entertaining. However, when the occasion demands fancy appetizers, try these palate-pleasing ones, which provide both distinctive flavor and stylish appearance.

Creamy Caviar Spread is an eye-catching example. Made with a sour cream and cottage cheese base and a wine-flavored gelatin mixture, the seafood spread can chill overnight. The beauty of this easy appetizer recipe is its appearance; the spread is crowned with the colorful toppings of hard-cooked egg, green onions, and black caviar.

For a definite showstopper, try Baked Cream Cheese Appetizer. Its elegant appearance masks simple preparation, which includes using refrigerated dinner rolls for the crust of the appetizer.

When serving appetizers, remember to garnish with a fresh sprig or two of an herb used in the recipe, or perhaps serve them on an interesting tray. And for additional appeal, try varying the size and shape of the crackers offered.

Be ready to receive rave reviews.

## CREAMY CAVIAR SPREAD

2 envelopes unflavored gelatin
⅓ cup white wine
1½ cups sour cream
1½ cups cottage cheese
3 tablespoons grated onion
1 tablespoon Worcestershire sauce
1 tablespoon lemon juice
⅛ teaspoon salt
⅛ teaspoon red pepper
Dash of garlic powder
1 hard-cooked egg, peeled and
   finely chopped
2 green onions, finely chopped
1 (2-ounce) jar black caviar,
   drained

Sprinkle gelatin over wine in a small saucepan; let stand 1 minute. Cook over low heat, stirring until gelatin dissolves.

Combine sour cream and next 7 ingredients in container of an electric blender; process until smooth. Gradually add gelatin mixture. Pour mixture into a lightly greased 9-inch quiche dish. Cover and chill 8 hours.

When ready to serve, invert spread onto serving platter. Sprinkle egg along outer edge of top to form a 2-inch border. Arrange a circle of green onions inside egg border; fill center with caviar. Serve with water crackers. Yield: about 4 cups.

*Pat Rush Benigno*
*Gulfport, Mississippi*

## SMOKED WHITEFISH SPREAD

6 small smoked whitefish (about
   1½ pounds)
⅓ cup mayonnaise or salad
   dressing
⅓ cup horseradish sauce
2 tablespoons cream cheese,
   softened
1 teaspoon lemon juice
⅛ teaspoon garlic powder
¼ cup chopped green onions

Carefully remove heads, tails, skin, and bones from fish. Flake fish with a fork; set aside.

Combine mayonnaise and next 4 ingredients; beat with a wire whisk until smooth. Add green onions and fish to mayonnaise mixture; stir well. Chill and spoon into serving bowl. Serve with assorted crackers. Yield: 2 cups.

*Kaki Mehlburger*
*Little Rock, Arkansas*

## ARTICHOKE APPETIZER FRITTATA

2 (6-ounce) jars marinated
   artichoke hearts, undrained
3 green onions, chopped
1 clove garlic, crushed
4 large eggs
⅛ teaspoon pepper
2 cups (8 ounces) shredded sharp
   Cheddar cheese
6 saltine crackers, crumbled
2 tablespoons chopped fresh parsley

Drain artichoke hearts, reserving liquid. Chop artichokes, and set aside. Pour artichoke liquid into a 9-inch skillet; add green onions and garlic, and cook until tender. Drain.

Combine eggs and pepper in a large bowl; beat mixture well. Stir in artichokes, onion mixture, cheese, crackers, and parsley. Pour mixture into a greased 8-inch square baking dish. Bake at 325° for 35 to 40 minutes or until set. Cut into 1½-inch squares. Yield: about 2 dozen.

*Sharon McClatchey*
*Muskogee, Oklahoma*

## BAKED CREAM CHEESE APPETIZER

1 (4-ounce) can refrigerated
   crescent dinner rolls
1½ teaspoons minced fresh
   dillweed or ½ teaspoon dried
   dillweed
1 (8-ounce) package cream cheese
1 egg yolk, beaten
Garnish: fresh dillweed sprig

Unroll dough on a lightly floured surface; press seams together to form a 12- x 4-inch rectangle. Sprinkle and gently press minced dillweed onto top of cream cheese. Place cream cheese, dillweed side down, in center of dough; bring up sides of dough snugly around cheese, pinching to seal.

Place seam side down on a lightly greased baking sheet. Brush with egg yolk. Bake at 350° for 20 to 22 minutes. Garnish, if desired. Serve warm with crackers. Yield: 16 appetizer servings.
*Erma Jackson*
*Huntsville, Alabama*

# Go Ahead; Grill It!

The best meals begin with great entrées, and these recipes start you in the right direction. Pair them with your favorite pasta or green salad, grilled vegetables, and garlic bread to complete the menu.

Seasonings are the key to flavor in Grilled Teriyaki Chicken. In Grilled London Broil, red wine vinegar tenderizes the meat in addition to providing a nice complement to soy sauce in the marinade.

## GRILLED CORNISH HENS

4 (1¼-pound) Cornish hens
½ cup olive oil
¼ cup lime juice
1 tablespoon ground cumin
2 teaspoons dried thyme
½ teaspoon salt
1 teaspoon pepper
1 teaspoon hot sauce
1 tablespoon Worcestershire sauce

Remove giblets from hens; reserve for other uses. Rinse hens with cold water, and pat dry. Place hens in a shallow dish; set aside. Combine remaining ingredients, stirring well; pour mixture over hens, coating thoroughly. Cover and chill 8 hours, turning occasionally.

Remove hens from marinade, reserving marinade. Place hens, breast side down, on a microwave-safe rack placed inside a 12- x 8- x 2-inch baking dish. Cover hens with a tent of wax paper. Microwave at HIGH 10 minutes. Turn hens over, and rotate dish; brush with marinade. Cover and microwave at HIGH 7 minutes.

Grill hens, breast side down, over medium coals (300° to 350°) for 10 minutes on covered grill, basting occasionally. Turn hens, and grill an additional 10 minutes or until internal temperature reaches 185°. Yield: 4 servings.

## GRILLED TERIYAKI CHICKEN

4 cups dry white wine
½ cup lemon juice
¼ cup teriyaki sauce
1 tablespoon minced onion
1 clove garlic, minced
2 bay leaves
1 tablespoon bouquet garni
½ teaspoon seasoned salt
½ teaspoon seasoned pepper
½ teaspoon lemon-pepper
   seasoning
2 black peppercorns
2 (2½- to 3-pound) broiler-fryers,
   halved
Garnishes: lemon slices, curly
   endive

Combine first 11 ingredients in a large shallow container; mix well. Add chicken; cover and chill 8 hours, turning chicken several times.

Remove chicken from marinade, reserving marinade. Remove and discard bay leaves. Grill chicken, covered, over hot coals (400° to 500°) for 50 to 60 minutes or until done, turning and basting often with marinade. Garnish, if desired. Yield: 4 to 8 servings.
*Chuck Behnke*
*Peachtree City, Georgia*

## GRILLED LONDON BROIL

½ cup red wine vinegar
½ cup soy sauce
½ cup vegetable oil
4 cloves garlic, sliced
½ teaspoon freshly ground pepper
1 (3½-pound) top round steak
½ teaspoon salt (optional)

Combine first 5 ingredients in a large shallow container, mixing well. Add steak; turn to coat each side. Cover and refrigerate 12 hours.

Remove steak from marinade, reserving marinade. Grill, covered, over medium-hot coals (350° to 400°) for 8 to 10 minutes on each side or until desired degree of doneness, basting occasionally with marinade. Remove from grill, and let stand 5 minutes; sprinkle with salt, if desired. Cut into thin slices. Yield: 10 servings.

**Note:** London Broil is made using top round or flank steak. Flank steak will cook slightly faster. *Alice Pahl*
*Raleigh, North Carolina*

# Just For The Two Of Us

Celebrate your anniversary with this casual menu perfect for the two of you on your special day. Toast the occasion with your favorite beverage.

It doesn't have to be your anniversary to enjoy this dinner. Once a week or once a month, plan to stay up late and have dinner—just the two of you.

### DINNER FOR TWO

Fish For Two
Dressed-Up Wild Rice
Sautéed Zucchini
Garden Salad
Your favorite dessert

### FISH FOR TWO

2 (8-ounce) grouper or halibut
  fillets
2 tablespoons butter or margarine,
  melted
2 tablespoons lemon juice
⅛ teaspoon lemon-pepper
  seasoning
¼ teaspoon garlic salt
Paprika
1 green onion, sliced
1 tablespoon chopped fresh parsley
Garnish: lemon wedges

Place fish fillets in a lightly greased 13- x 9- x 2-inch baking pan. Pour melted butter and lemon juice over fish; sprinkle lemon-pepper seasoning and next 4 ingredients evenly over fish. Bake at 350° for 20 to 25 minutes. Broil 3 to 5 minutes or until fish is lightly browned and flakes easily when tested with a fork. Garnish, if desired. Yield: 2 servings.

**Note:** To grill, wrap fillets in heavy-duty aluminum foil. Grill fillets over medium coals (300° to 350°) for 15 to 20 minutes.

### DRESSED-UP WILD RICE

3 green onions, sliced
1 cup sliced fresh mushrooms
2 tablespoons butter, melted
1 (6-ounce) package long-grain and
  wild rice mix
2 cups water
⅓ cup sherry or white wine

Sauté green onions and sliced mushrooms in butter in a medium saucepan until onions are tender. Add rice mix, and prepare according to package directions using 2 cups water and ⅓ cup sherry, omitting salt. Yield: 4 to 6 servings.

### SAUTÉED ZUCCHINI

2 tablespoons olive oil
2 small zucchini, sliced
¼ teaspoon dried whole basil
¼ teaspoon garlic powder
¼ teaspoon salt
⅛ teaspoon pepper

Heat olive oil in a skillet; add zucchini and sauté over high heat 3 minutes. Stir in basil, garlic powder, salt, and pepper; cook 1 minute, stirring constantly. Yield: 2 servings.

### GARDEN SALAD

2 cups torn iceberg lettuce
2 cups torn Bibb lettuce
1 stalk celery, sliced
1 carrot, shredded
½ cup mandarin oranges, drained
1 tablespoon sliced almonds,
  toasted
Zesty Salad Dressing

Place salad greens on two salad plates, and arrange sliced celery, shredded carrot, mandarin oranges, and sliced almonds over salad greens. Drizzle with Zesty Salad Dressing. Yield: 2 servings.

### Zesty Salad Dressing

¾ cup vegetable oil
¼ cup wine vinegar
¼ cup catsup
2 tablespoons water
1 tablespoon soy sauce
1 tablespoon Worcestershire sauce
⅓ cup sugar
1 clove garlic, minced
1 teaspoon dried whole basil

Combine all ingredients in a jar; cover tightly, and shake vigorously. Chill thoroughly. Yield: 1½ cups.

# New Potatoes, A New Way

If you're looking for new ways to serve potatoes, consider pairing them with fresh vegetables. Enjoy zucchini, carrots, and new potatoes in Potato Medley. Or mix new potatoes with broccoli and mushrooms in Creamy Potatoes and Broccoli. In these recipes, the potatoes and other vegetables are cooked together, keeping cleanup to a minimum.

Green peas, baby carrots, and pearl onions complement new potatoes in Potato-Vegetable Skillet. The lettuce in this dish enhances the sweetness of the peas during cooking. Lettuce becomes limp when cooked, so remove the leaves before serving.

### FRESH VEGETABLE PLATTER

1 pound new potatoes, peeled
2 cups water
½ teaspoon salt
½ pound baby carrots, scraped
1 small head cabbage, cut into
  wedges
¼ cup butter or margarine, melted
¼ cup chopped fresh parsley
Freshly ground pepper

Combine first 3 ingredients in a Dutch oven; bring to a boil. Cover, reduce heat, and simmer 5 minutes. Add carrots; cover and simmer 5 minutes. Add cabbage wedges; cover and simmer 5 to 7 minutes. Drain. Arrange vegetables on a serving plate.

Combine butter and parsley. Pour mixture over vegetables; sprinkle with pepper. Serve immediately. Yield: 6 servings. *Clota Engleman Spur, Texas*

## CREAMY POTATOES AND BROCCOLI

1 pound new potatoes, sliced
2 cups fresh broccoli flowerets
4 small mushrooms, sliced
2 tablespoons butter or margarine
2 tablespoons all-purpose flour
¾ cup milk
⅓ cup sour cream
¾ teaspoon salt
¼ teaspoon pepper
¼ teaspoon celery salt
3 slices bacon, cooked and crumbled

Arrange potatoes in a vegetable steamer over boiling water. Cover and steam 5 minutes. Add broccoli; cover and steam 6 minutes. Add mushrooms; cover and steam 3 minutes. Remove the steamer from heat and uncover.

Melt butter in a heavy saucepan over low heat; add flour, stirring until smooth. Cook 1 minute, stirring constantly. Gradually add milk; cook over medium heat, stirring constantly, until mixture is thickened and bubbly. Stir in sour cream, salt, pepper, and celery salt. Combine vegetables and sauce, stirring to coat. Sprinkle with crumbled bacon. Serve immediately. Yield: 4 to 6 servings.

## POTATO-VEGETABLE SKILLET

8 large iceberg lettuce leaves, divided
12 small new potatoes
12 pearl onions
1 pound baby carrots, scraped
2 parsley sprigs
½ cup boiling water
2 teaspoons sugar
½ teaspoon salt
Dash of pepper
¼ cup butter or margarine
1 (10-ounce) package frozen green peas, thawed

Line a 10-inch skillet with 4 lettuce leaves. Set aside. Peel a ½-inch-wide strip around center of each potato. Layer potatoes and next 3 ingredients over lettuce leaves. Add water and sprinkle with sugar, salt, and pepper. Dot with butter. Bring to a boil; cover, reduce heat, and simmer 15 minutes. Add peas and top with remaining lettuce leaves. Cover and simmer 10 minutes or until vegetables are tender. Remove top lettuce leaves and parsley sprigs. Serve immediately. Yield: 6 servings.
*Frances Myers Apache, Oklahoma*

## POTATO MEDLEY

¼ cup vegetable oil
3 tablespoons white wine vinegar
1 tablespoon grated orange rind
1½ teaspoons Dijon mustard
½ teaspoon mustard seed
½ teaspoon salt
⅛ teaspoon freshly ground pepper
4 new potatoes, sliced ¼-inch thick
3 carrots, scraped and thinly sliced
2 cups water
2 zucchini, sliced ½-inch thick
1 tablespoon chopped fresh dill
1 tablespoon chopped fresh parsley
1 tablespoon chopped fresh chives

Place oil, vinegar, orange rind, Dijon, mustard seed, salt, and pepper in food processor; process until well blended. Set aside.

Combine potatoes, carrots, and water in a saucepan; bring to a boil.

Cover, reduce heat, and simmer 3 minutes. Add zucchini; cover and cook 3 minutes. Drain.

Combine vegetables, dressing, and herbs, stirring to coat. Serve immediately. Yield: 6 servings.
*Caroline W. Kennedy Newborn, Georgia*

# QUICK!

## Snappy Vegetables

Capture fresh taste in no time with these easy side dishes. Inventive seasoning combinations and minimum ingredients guarantee satisfaction as well as a speedy cleanup.

The countdown for preparation begins 30 minutes before serving. However, if you can do the slicing and chopping in a spare moment earlier in the day, cooking time will be a snap. Be sure to store cut vegetables in airtight containers to preserve nutrients.

## GREEN BEANS WITH BUTTERED PECANS

½ pound green beans
2 cups water
¼ teaspoon salt
1 tablespoon butter or margarine
2 tablespoons chopped pecans
⅛ teaspoon pepper

Wash beans; trim ends, and remove strings. Bring water and salt to a boil in a medium saucepan. Add green beans; cook, uncovered, 10 minutes or just until crisp-tender. Drain and set aside.

Melt butter in a nonstick skillet; add pecans and cook until golden, stirring often. Add beans; toss gently, and cook until thoroughly heated. Sprinkle with pepper. Yield: 2 servings.
*Edith Askins Greenville, Texas*

## CREAMY CUCUMBERS

½ cup sour cream
1 tablespoon sugar
2 tablespoons chopped fresh parsley
1 tablespoon chopped fresh chives
2 tablespoons tarragon vinegar
3 small cucumbers, thinly sliced (about 3 cups)

Combine first 5 ingredients; add cucumber slices, tossing to coat. Cover and chill thoroughly. Serve with a slotted spoon. Yield: 6 to 8 servings.

*Mrs. John R. Allen*
*Dallas, Texas*

## CAJUN VEGETABLE SAUTÉ

2 tablespoons olive oil
1 large zucchini, sliced
1 large yellow squash, sliced
1 medium onion, chopped
1 clove garlic, crushed
¼ cup chopped fresh chives
1 teaspoon Creole seasoning
½ teaspoon pepper
¼ teaspoon hot sauce

Heat olive oil in a large skillet until hot; add remaining ingredients, and toss gently. Cover, reduce heat, and cook 10 minutes or until crisp-tender. Yield: 3 to 4 servings. *Marie Wiker*
*Gaithersburg, Maryland*

## SAUTÉED ZUCCHINI AND CARROTS

1 pound carrots, scraped and thinly sliced
2 tablespoons butter or margarine, melted
1 small onion, thinly sliced
2 small zucchini, thinly sliced
½ teaspoon salt
¼ teaspoon pepper
2 tablespoons minced fresh basil
Garnish: fresh basil sprig

Sauté carrot in butter over medium heat 4 minutes. Add onion; cook 1 minute. Add zucchini and next 3 ingredients; cover and cook 3 to 4 minutes or until crisp-tender. Garnish, if desired. Yield: 6 to 8 servings.

*Paula DeVivo*
*Savannah, Georgia*

## SKILLET SQUASH

4 slices bacon
2 pounds yellow squash, sliced
1 medium onion, chopped
½ cup sour cream
1½ teaspoons dried dillweed
1 teaspoon onion salt
¼ teaspoon pepper

Cook bacon in a large skillet until crisp; remove bacon, reserving 1 tablespoon drippings in skillet. Crumble bacon, and set aside.

Sauté squash and onion in reserved drippings 6 minutes or until tender; stir in sour cream and seasonings. Spoon into serving dish; sprinkle with crumbled bacon. Yield: 8 servings.

*Marie H. Webb*
*Roanoke, Virginia*

# Braid Your Own Challah

For those of the Jewish faith, baking bread does more than fill the kitchen with sweet aromas. Making Challah also fills the spirit.

Challah (sometimes spelled Hallah) is the sweet egg bread of the Sabbath. Since ancient times, practicing Jews have made a week's worth of bread on Friday, so that the bread would be fresh for the Sabbath observance. Today many cooks still follow this tradition. The sesame or poppy seeds sprinkled on top of the braided yeast bread represent manna, the bread God provided for the Jews during their 40-year exodus from Egypt.

## CHALLAH

1 package dry yeast
1 teaspoon sugar
½ cup warm water (105° to 115°)
½ cup vegetable oil
½ cup warm water (105° to 115°)
¼ cup sugar
2 large eggs
2 teaspoons salt
4 to 4½ cups all-purpose flour, divided
Vegetable cooking spray
1 egg white
1 teaspoon water
1 teaspoon sesame seeds or poppy seeds

Dissolve 1 package yeast and 1 teaspoon sugar in ½ cup warm water; let mixture stand 5 minutes.

Combine oil and next 4 ingredients in a large mixing bowl; beat at medium speed with an electric mixer until blended. Add yeast mixture and 2 cups flour; beat until smooth. Gradually stir in enough remaining flour to make a soft dough. (Dough should be sticky.) Cover dough, and let rest 10 minutes. Turn dough out onto a well-floured surface, and knead 5 minutes. Place in a well-greased bowl, turning to grease top. Cover and let rise in a warm place (85°), free from drafts, 1 to 1½ hours or until doubled in bulk.

Punch dough down; turn dough out onto a well-floured surface, and knead several times. Divide dough into thirds. Shape each third into a 14-inch rope. Place ropes on a greased baking sheet (do not stretch); pinch rope ends together at one end to seal. Braid ropes; pinch loose ends to seal. Lightly spray with vegetable cooking spray. Cover and let rise in a warm place, free from drafts, 30 to 40 minutes or until doubled in bulk.

Beat egg white and 1 teaspoon water; gently brush over bread. Sprinkle with sesame seeds. Bake at 375° for 30 to 35 minutes or until golden. Yield: 1 loaf. *Sally Wolfish*
*Dallas, Texas*

# Winning Combinations

When it comes to spring lunches, we've planned the strategy for you. This collection of soup, salad, and sandwich recipes offers a deck with plenty of wild cards to use.

## CRAB BENEDICT

1 pound fresh crabmeat, drained and flaked
½ cup chopped green pepper
½ cup chopped celery
2 tablespoons mayonnaise or salad dressing
1 tablespoon Worcestershire sauce
1 tablespoon butter or margarine, melted
1 (1⅛-ounce) package Hollandaise sauce mix
4 English muffins, split and toasted

Combine first 5 ingredients; sauté mixture in melted butter until thoroughly heated.

Prepare Hollandaise sauce according to package directions. Spoon crabmeat mixture over cut sides of English muffins; top with Hollandaise sauce. Yield: 4 servings. *Carole A. Brock*
*Mount Holly, Virginia*

## MEXICAN GRILLED CHEESE SANDWICH

1 (6-ounce) package Swiss cheese slices
1 (6-ounce) package thinly sliced ham
8 (10-inch) flour tortillas
2 tablespoons butter or margarine, softened

Arrange cheese and ham slices evenly over 4 tortillas; top with remaining tortillas. Spread butter on outside of top tortilla; invert sandwiches onto a hot skillet or griddle. Cook until tortilla is lightly browned. Spread butter on ungrilled side; carefully turn, and cook until lightly brown and cheese is slightly melted. Yield: 4 servings.
*Elaine Coltharp*
*Willis, Texas*

## E-Z HERO

1 (1-pound) loaf French bread
⅓ cup mayonnaise or salad dressing
2 tablespoons Dijon mustard
½ pound thinly sliced cooked ham
6 slices American cheese
1 large tomato, thinly sliced
1 slice purple onion, separated into rings
2 cups shredded iceberg lettuce
¼ to ⅓ cup commercial Italian salad dressing
Garnishes: alfalfa sprouts, olives

Slice bread horizontally to, but not through, other side. Combine mayonnaise and mustard; spread over bottom half of bread. Layer ham, cheese, tomato, onion, and lettuce on bread. Drizzle with salad dressing, and top with remaining bread half. Secure with long wooden pick. Garnish, if desired. To serve, cut into slices. Yield: 6 servings. *Jennifer Cairns*
*Jacksonville, Alabama*

## SWEET-AND-SOUR HOT SLAW

1 medium cabbage, shredded (about 2½ pounds)
¾ cup chopped onion
¾ cup chopped green pepper
1 cup sugar
1 cup white vinegar
1½ teaspoons salt
1 teaspoon celery seeds
1 teaspoon paprika
¾ teaspoon black pepper
½ teaspoon red pepper
Cabbage leaves

Combine first 3 ingredients in a large bowl; set aside. Combine sugar and remaining ingredients except cabbage leaves; stir until blended. Pour over cabbage mixture; cover and chill. Drain mixture, and spoon into cabbage-lined serving bowl. Yield: 8 to 10 servings. *Barbara McGrath*
*Memphis, Tennessee*

| MENU CARDS | | |
|---|---|---|
| Mexican Chef Salad<br>Gazpacho | Mexican Grilled Cheese Sandwich<br>Cold Zucchini Soup | Mexican Grilled Cheese Sandwich<br>Sweet-and-Sour Hot Slaw |
| E-Z Hero<br>Gazpacho | Garden Macaroni Salad<br>Gazpacho | Crab Benedict<br>Marinated Vegetable Salad |
| Crab Benedict<br>Gazpacho | E-Z Hero<br>Marinated Vegetable Salad | Mexican Grilled Cheese Sandwich<br>Gazpacho |
| Mexican Grilled Cheese Sandwich<br>Gazpacho<br>Marinated Vegetable Salad | Garden Macaroni Salad<br>Gazpacho<br>Marinated Vegetable Salad | Crab Benedict<br>Gazpacho<br>Marinated Vegetable Salad |

## MARINATED VEGETABLE SALAD

¾ cup lemon juice
¾ cup vegetable oil
3 tablespoons sugar
1 teaspoon dried oregano
1 teaspoon salt
½ teaspoon pepper
1 cup cauliflower flowerets
1 cup broccoli flowerets
1 cup thinly sliced carrot
1 cup sliced fresh mushrooms
1 small purple onion, sliced and
  separated into rings
1 cup thinly sliced zucchini
1 cup thinly sliced yellow squash

Combine first 6 ingredients in a jar; cover tightly, and shake vigorously. Set aside.

Combine cauliflower, broccoli, carrot, mushrooms, and onion; pour marinade over vegetables, and toss. Cover and chill 8 hours. Add zucchini and yellow squash; toss gently. Cover and chill 1 hour. Serve with a slotted spoon. Yield: 6 servings.

*Elizabeth M. Haney*
*Dublin, Virginia*

## MEXICAN CHEF SALAD

½ pound ground beef
⅓ cup water
2 tablespoons taco seasoning mix
8 cups torn iceberg lettuce
1 (16-ounce) can kidney beans,
  drained and rinsed
2 tomatoes, chopped
1 (2¼-ounce) can sliced olives,
  drained
½ cup (2 ounces) shredded Cheddar
  cheese
Guacamole Dressing
Tortilla chips

Cook ground beef in a skillet until meat is browned, stirring to crumble; drain. Return meat to skillet; add water and taco seasoning mix. Simmer 5 minutes or until liquid evaporates.

Layer lettuce, beans, beef mixture, tomato, olives, and cheese. Serve with Guacamole Dressing and tortilla chips. Yield: 4 servings.

## Guacamole Dressing

1 avocado, peeled and mashed
¼ teaspoon pepper
½ teaspoon salt
¾ teaspoon chili powder
1 teaspoon dried onion flakes
1 tablespoon lemon juice
2 tablespoons commercial Italian
  salad dressing
½ cup sour cream

Combine all ingredients, stirring until blended. Yield: 1¾ cups.

*Mrs. E. R. Lovell*
*Jackson, Mississippi*

## GARDEN MACARONI SALAD

1 cup elbow macaroni, uncooked
1 cup cubed ham
1 cup sliced carrot
1 cup chopped cucumber
2 tablespoons minced onion
½ cup mayonnaise or salad
  dressing

Cook macaroni according to package directions; drain. Rinse with cold water; drain. Add ham and remaining ingredients; toss well. Chill at least 4 hours. Yield: 6 servings.

*Peggy H. Amos*
*Martinsville, Virginia*

## GAZPACHO

4 tomatoes, unpeeled and diced
1 cucumber, unpeeled and diced
1 (2-ounce) jar chopped pimiento,
  undrained
½ cup diced purple onion
2 cloves garlic, minced
2 tablespoons olive oil
2 tablespoons red wine vinegar
¾ teaspoon salt
½ teaspoon pepper
Garnish: toast points

Combine first 5 ingredients in a bowl. Place half of mixture in container of an electric blender; process until smooth.

Return to bowl; add olive oil, vinegar, salt, and pepper. Chill 8 hours. Garnish, if desired. Yield: 5 cups.

*Doris Garton*
*Shenandoah, Virginia*

## COLD ZUCCHINI SOUP

3½ pounds zucchini, thinly sliced
1 cup chicken broth
¼ cup butter or margarine
1 tablespoon all-purpose flour
1 cup milk
1 teaspoon salt
¼ teaspoon white pepper
½ teaspoon dried marjoram
¼ teaspoon dried tarragon

Combine zucchini and chicken broth in a Dutch oven; bring to a boil. Cover, reduce heat, and simmer 15 minutes or until zucchini is tender. Spoon mixture into container of an electric blender; process until smooth.

Melt butter in a Dutch oven over low heat; add flour, stirring until smooth. Cook 1 minute, stirring constantly. Gradually add milk; cook 1 minute, stirring constantly. Gradually add zucchini mixture, salt, and remaining ingredients. Cook over medium heat, stirring constantly, until thoroughly heated. Remove from heat, and chill. Yield: 2 quarts.

*David H. Darst*
*Tallahassee, Florida*

# Showtime For Limes

If you usually think of oranges, grapefruit, and lemons when you think of citrus fruit, it's time to put limes in the spotlight. They'll earn compliments for you every time you use them. The tart, tangy flavor of lime juice can enhance many seafood, poultry, beef, and pork dishes, as well as salads and desserts. And a big squeeze of lime adds pizzazz to hot or iced tea.

## LIME-GINGER BEEF STIR-FRY

1 (1-pound) top loin steak
¼ teaspoon freshly ground pepper
½ teaspoon grated lime rind
¼ cup lime juice
1 tablespoon sugar
2 tablespoons dry sherry
2 teaspoons soy sauce
1 teaspoon grated fresh ginger
1 clove garlic, minced
1 tablespoon safflower or
  vegetable oil
2 green onions, cut into
  2-inch lengths
1 large carrot, cut into
  1½-inch strips
1 sweet red pepper, cut into
  1½-inch strips
1 tablespoon cornstarch
¼ cup water
Hot cooked rice (optional)
Garnish: lime slices

Slice steak diagonally across grain into thin strips; sprinkle with pepper, and set aside.

Combine lime rind and next 6 ingredients; set aside.

Pour oil into a wok or large skillet, coating bottom and sides; heat to medium-high (325°) for 1 minute. Add steak; stir-fry 2 to 3 minutes. Add vegetables; stir-fry 2 to 3 minutes. Add lime mixture, and stir-fry until mixture boils. Combine cornstarch and water; stir into vegetables and bring to a boil, stirring constantly. Boil 1 minute, stirring constantly. Serve with rice, if desired. Garnish, if desired. Yield: 4 servings.
*George M. Heilman*
*Owings Mills, Maryland*

### LIME-DILL DIP

½ cup sour cream
½ cup mayonnaise or salad
  dressing
1½ teaspoons chopped fresh
  dillweed or ½ teaspoon dried
  dillweed
2 tablespoons sliced green onions
2 teaspoons grated lime rind
1 tablespoon lime juice
1 tablespoon honey

Combine all ingredients, stirring well. Cover and chill 2 hours. Serve with tortilla chips or zucchini and jicama sticks. Yield: 1 cup.
*Marion Hall*
*Knoxville, Tennessee*

### LIME-CARROT SALAD

1 (8-ounce) can crushed pineapple,
  undrained
1 (3-ounce) package lime-flavored
  gelatin
2 tablespoons lime juice
1 cup shredded carrot
2 cups frozen whipped topping,
  thawed

Drain pineapple, reserving juice; add enough water to make 1¼ cups. Set pineapple aside. Bring liquid to a boil; add gelatin to liquid, stirring until gelatin dissolves. Add lime juice; chill mixture until the consistency of unbeaten egg white.

Fold in pineapple, carrot, and whipped topping. Spoon mixture into a lightly oiled 6-cup mold; cover and chill until firm. Yield: 8 servings.
*Bonnie Sellers*
*Clemmons, North Carolina*

### LIME PARTY PIES

1 (14-ounce) can sweetened
  condensed milk
1 (6-ounce) can frozen limeade
  concentrate, thawed and
  undiluted
½ cup lime juice
¼ teaspoon butter flavoring
2 or 3 drops of green food coloring
2 (8-ounce) containers frozen
  whipped topping, thawed and
  divided
2 (6-ounce) chocolate-flavored
  crumb crusts
Garnish: lime slices

Combine first 5 ingredients in a large mixing bowl; beat lime mixture at medium speed with an electric mixer until well blended. Set aside 1 cup whipped topping. Stir 2 cups whipped topping into lime mixture; gradually fold in remaining whipped topping, except for

reserved 1 cup. Spoon lime filling into prepared crusts. Dollop reserved 1 cup whipped topping around outer edges of pies. Cover pies and freeze. Garnish, if desired. Yield: two (9-inch) pies.
*Linda Magers*
*Clemmons, North Carolina*

## From Our Kitchen To Yours

With dietary guidelines recommending we reduce fat to 30% of the calories in our daily meals, the news of a tasty, low-fat ground beef is almost too good to be true. Can the new low-fat ground beef fool the taste buds?

As the Test Kitchens staff prepared familiar recipes to test this new product, we were skeptical. The bright cherry-red meat looks like regular ground beef, but how does it compare in other ways?

For our test, we made spaghetti sauce, pizza, meat loaf, and hamburgers using this revolutionary low-fat ground beef, containing less than 10% fat, and also lean ground beef. (According to the USDA, ground beef products are rated as extra lean, 15% fat; lean, 23% fat; and regular, not more than 30% fat. Ask the meat manager in your local supermarket for the specific fat content in the store's ground-beef products.)

The low-fat ground beef feels wetter because water is added to replace fat, and this additional moisture makes rolled meat loaves more difficult to handle. While cooking both products side by side, we noticed that the only difference was the absence of fat drippings in the skillet holding the low-fat ground beef. (To prevent sticking, we suggest coating the skillet or Dutch oven with vegetable cooking spray before browning.)

Although the low-fat ground beef hamburgers were a little less juicy, our trained palates couldn't detect a difference in taste between the low-fat and the lean ground beef dishes.

We skeptics are convinced that we now have a choice of preparing our favorite ground beef recipe, with low-fat ground beef, and trimming fat without losing flavor.

Quick favorites using heart-healthy, low-fat ground beef include Speedy Chili and Easy Spaghetti. Using these recipes, supper can be served in less than 35 minutes. For even speedier future meals, double the recipe, and freeze the extra portion.

## EASY SPAGHETTI

1 pound low-fat ground beef
1 small onion, chopped
1 (28-ounce) can tomatoes, undrained and chopped
2 (6-ounce) cans tomato paste
1 teaspoon dried whole oregano
1 teaspoon dried whole basil
½ teaspoon garlic powder
Hot cooked spaghetti
Grated Parmesan cheese

Combine ground beef and chopped onion in a large skillet; cook until beef is browned, stirring until it crumbles. Drain, if necessary. Stir in tomatoes and next 4 ingredients; cook mixture over medium heat, stirring occasionally, about 20 minutes. Serve over spaghetti and sprinkle with cheese. Yield: 4 servings.

■ This chili also can be served on hot dogs or baked potatoes. If desired, add one 16-ounce can kidney beans, drained, after simmering 25 minutes.

## SPEEDY CHILI

1 pound low-fat ground beef
1 large onion, chopped
1 clove garlic, crushed
1 (16-ounce) can tomato sauce
¼ teaspoon salt
⅛ teaspoon pepper
3 to 4 tablespoons chili powder
1 cup water

Combine first 3 ingredients in a Dutch oven; cook until beef is browned, stirring until it crumbles. Drain, if necessary. Add tomato sauce and remaining ingredients; cover, reduce heat, and simmer 30 minutes, stirring occasionally. Yield: about 4 cups.

## Shopping Know-how

Many supermarkets carry a version of low-fat ground beef made from the "AU Lean" recipe. You'll find packages with the required nutritional label marked "Ultra Lean 93% Lean Low-fat Ground Beef" or "Healthy Choice Extra Lean 96% Fat-free Ground Beef." These products combine lean beef with carrageenin (care-ah-GEE-nun), oat flour, or oat bran. Salt and hydrolyzed vegetable protein (derived from soybeans) may be used to enhance flavor. Carrageenin, a carbohydrate extract made from seaweed, holds the beef together and retains moisture in the absence of fat; oat bran acts as a sponge for the added water. This meat must be labeled low-fat ground beef product because it contains plant-derived products; it must be less than 10% fat and 30% other products.

## Cook's Notes

Here are some helpful tips. Many are familiar because low-fat ground beef is handled much like regular ground beef.

■ When purchasing low-fat ground beef, make sure it is tightly wrapped, cold to the touch, and free of excessive liquid in the tray.
■ Store in the coldest part of the refrigerator for up to 12 hours. This leaner beef will turn dark more quickly, but that doesn't mean it's harmful. For longer storage, freeze in the original packaging up to 2 weeks, or rewrap in freezer paper, aluminum foil, or plastic freezer bags, and freeze up to 4 months.
■ Thaw frozen beef in the refrigerator; a 1- to 1½-inch-thick package will thaw within 24 hours.
■ Don't overhandle; the meat has a firm, compact texture.
■ Use additional liquids, such as tomato sauce or milk, sparingly in meat loaf and meatball recipes so the texture won't get too soft.
■ Brown beef over medium heat to avoid hard, crusty pieces, but don't cook beef too slowly or the product may dry out.

# Spring Fling Coolers

Fruit coolers are fruit juice-based drinks that get a kick from sparkling water, club soda, ginger ale, or spirits. They're a refreshing switch from the chill-chasers of winter.

## SPICED PINEAPPLE PUNCH

1¼ cups water
1 cup sugar
4 (3-inch) sticks cinnamon
12 whole cloves
1 (46-ounce) can pineapple juice
1½ cups orange juice
½ cup lemon juice
1 (33.8-ounce) bottle ginger ale, chilled

Combine first 4 ingredients in a saucepan; bring to a boil. Reduce heat and simmer 30 minutes. Remove spices. Add pineapple juice, orange juice, and lemon juice; chill. Just before serving, stir in ginger ale; serve over ice. Yield: 3¼ quarts. *Vicki R. Helton San Antonio, Texas*

## FROZEN ORANGE-WHISKEY SOURS

1 (25.4-ounce) bottle whiskey sour mix
2 quarts orange juice
8 (12-ounce) cans lemon-lime carbonated beverage
2 cups whiskey

Combine all ingredients. Divide mixture evenly into 2 gallon-size, zip-top, heavy-duty plastic bags; freeze. Remove each bag from freezer 30 minutes before serving. Break into chunks. Gradually place chunks in container of an electric blender; process until smooth. Serve immediately. Yield: 7 quarts or 3½ quarts per bag.
*Paula Massanari Cockeysville, Maryland*

## BERRY PUNCH

1 (10-ounce) package frozen strawberries in syrup, thawed
1 (12-ounce) can frozen cranberry juice cocktail concentrate, thawed and undiluted
1 (12-ounce) can frozen lemonade concentrate, thawed and undiluted
2 (33.8-ounce) bottles club soda or seltzer, chilled
1 (33.8-ounce) bottle ginger ale, chilled

Place strawberries and syrup in container of an electric blender; process until smooth. Pour mixture into a punch bowl; add cranberry juice cocktail and remaining ingredients. Yield: about 5 quarts. *Velma Price Kestner Berwind, West Virginia*

## STRAWBERRY COOLERS

2½ cups sliced fresh strawberries
1½ cups water
¼ cup sugar
1 teaspoon grated lemon rind
2 tablespoons lemon juice
½ cup ginger ale
Garnish: fresh strawberries

Place sliced strawberries in container of an electric blender; process 30 seconds. Add water and next 3 ingredients; blend until smooth. Stir in ginger ale. Serve beverage over crushed ice. Garnish, if desired. Yield: 4 cups.
*Marie Davis Charlotte, North Carolina*

## GRAPEFRUIT TEA

1 quart boiling water
3 regular-size tea bags
2 regular-size mint tea bags
¾ cup sugar
½ cup lemon juice
¾ cup grapefruit juice
1 quart cold water

Pour boiling water over tea bags; cover and steep 5 minutes. Remove tea bags, squeezing gently. Add sugar and remaining ingredients. Serve over ice. Yield: 2 quarts.
*Jennifer M. Young Birmingham, Alabama*

## FRUIT JUICE COOLER

1 (12-ounce) can peach nectar
1 cup orange juice
¼ cup grapefruit juice
2 tablespoons lemon juice
1 (12-ounce) can ginger ale, chilled

Combine first 4 ingredients in a pitcher; refrigerate. Just before serving, add ginger ale. Serve over ice. Yield: 4½ cups. *Azine G. Rush Monroe, Louisiana*

# There's A Party In The Cards

We'll cut a deal with you. You name the game, we provide the menu, and you've got all the makings for a great card party. You and your guests will all be winners.

Citrus Spritzers
Apple-Date Spread
Double-Decker Club Sandwiches
Marinated Orange-Onion Salad
Peanut-Fudge Bites

## CITRUS SPRITZERS

2 (750-milliliter) bottles white wine, chilled
1 (2-liter) bottle lemon-lime carbonated beverage, chilled
½ cup lemon juice

Combine all ingredients, stirring well. Serve immediately. Yield: 4 quarts.

## APPLE-DATE SPREAD

1 (8-ounce) package cream cheese, softened
¼ cup milk
1½ cups finely chopped pecans
1 cup finely chopped, unpeeled apple
¾ cup finely chopped dates
Garnish: apple slices

Combine cream cheese and milk, mixing well. Stir in chopped pecans, apple, and dates. Garnish, if desired, and serve with assorted crackers. Yield: 2¾ cups. *Jennifer Mungo Columbia, South Carolina*

## DOUBLE-DECKER CLUB SANDWICHES

1 (8-ounce) carton sour cream
2 tablespoons prepared
   horseradish
2 teaspoons honey mustard
¼ teaspoon garlic salt
⅛ teaspoon white pepper
¾ pound thinly sliced ham
12 slices whole wheat bread
4 slices Swiss cheese
8 lettuce leaves
¾ pound thinly sliced turkey
8 slices tomato
4 slices bacon
16 pitted ripe olives
16 pimiento-stuffed olives

Combine first 5 ingredients; stir well. Place 3 ounces of ham on each of 4 slices of bread. Top each with 1 teaspoon spread, 1 slice cheese, a lettuce leaf, and another slice of bread. Place 3 ounces of turkey on each slice, and add 1 teaspoon spread, lettuce leaf, 2 slices tomato, and 1 slice bacon. Top with the remaining slices of bread.

Skewer a ripe olive and pimiento-stuffed olive on each of 16 wooden picks. Cut each sandwich into 4 triangles, and secure each quarter with a pick. Yield: 8 servings.

## MARINATED ORANGE-ONION SALAD

2 cups fresh orange sections
1 small purple onion, sliced and
   separated into rings
¼ cup red wine vinegar
¼ cup olive oil
2 tablespoons chopped fresh parsley
8 cups mixed salad greens

Combine orange sections and onion rings in a medium bowl; set aside.

Combine vinegar and oil; pour over orange mixture, and sprinkle with parsley. Cover and refrigerate up to 3 hours, tossing occasionally.

Place salad greens in a shallow dish; arrange orange and onion evenly over greens, and drizzle dressing over salad. Serve immediately. Yield: 8 servings.
*Marion Hall*
*Knoxville, Tennessee*

## PEANUT-FUDGE BITES

1 (12-ounce) package peanut
   butter morsels
1 (14-ounce) can sweetened
   condensed milk
3 tablespoons butter or margarine
1 cup semisweet chocolate
   morsels
1 tablespoon shortening

Combine peanut butter morsels, sweetened condensed milk, and butter in a 2-quart glass bowl. Microwave at HIGH 1½ minutes or until morsels melt; stir well.

Pour mixture on a cookie sheet lined with wax paper; spread into a 13- x 11-inch rectangle. Smooth surface with a rolling pin. Chill 45 minutes or until firm.

Turn mixture onto a cutting board; remove wax paper. Cut into desired shapes with 1-inch and 1½-inch cookie cutters.

Combine semisweet chocolate morsels and shortening in a 2-cup glass measure. Microwave at HIGH 1 minute; stir until smooth. Spoon chocolate mixture into a decorating bag, and pipe mixture onto peanut butter shapes.

Chill until candy piping is set. Store in refrigerator in an airtight container. Yield: about 11 dozen.
*Mildred Bickley*
*Bristol, Virginia*

# Celebrate With Satin Ribbon Cake

Fancy cakes smoothly coated with Rolled Fondant fit the bill for all types of special occasions—from a little girl's birthday to her grandparents' anniversary. This type of cake carries a steep price tag when crafted by professionals, but these directions tell you how to make it at home.

Orange-flavored pound cake forms the layers for the cake, while the smooth, rolled icing is made of fondant, a sweet, creamy sugar paste used to make icing or candy. The delicate flowers are made from additional rolled and shaped fondant. Satin ribbons ring the cake layers.

Set the cake out to be the center of attention prior to cutting it. Just before slicing, gently remove the ribbon by pulling it from a cut end.

This type of cake may look extremely difficult to make, yet it is surprisingly simple. The key element is the fondant coating. Fondant is made predominately of sugar, water, gelatin, and glycerin, a special syrupy liquid that is found in drugstores or specialty cake-decorating supply stores. The glycerin helps keep the fondant soft and is essential to the success of the recipe.

The fondant is kneaded until smooth and pliable, and is rolled thinly and eased over the cake to form an airtight shield that seals in freshness. (See page 75 for technique photos.) When working with fondant, make sure the surface and equipment are clean—even a fleck of lint can mar the smooth surface of the fondant.

## SATIN RIBBON CAKE
*(pictured on page 74)*

½ cup apricot preserves
Orange Pound Cake
Rolled Fondant
Vegetable cooking spray
Piping Icing
⅛ teaspoon cherry-pink powdered
   food coloring
1 tablespoon cornstarch

Heat apricot preserves in a small saucepan; strain, discarding pulp.

Place 9-inch Orange Pound Cake layer on serving plate, top side up; spread top and sides thinly with apricot preserves.

Roll about half of fondant on a smooth surface, sprayed with cooking spray, to at least a 12-inch round of ⅛-inch thickness. Carefully peel fondant from surface, and transfer to 9-inch cake layer, smoothing sides straight down. Using a pastry wheel, carefully trim excess fondant evenly at base of cake. Reserve crumb-free fondant scraps.

Set 6-inch cake layer on a smooth surface. Spread top and sides of layer thinly with preserves. Roll about half of remaining fondant to at least a 9-inch round of ⅛-inch thickness. Transfer to 6-inch cake layer, smoothing sides straight down. Using a pastry wheel, carefully trim fondant evenly at base of cake. Carefully set 6-inch layer in center of 9-inch layer.

Cut a piece of ⅜-inch-wide pink satin ribbon for the circumference of each of the two tiers of cake. Pin the ribbons about 1 inch from the base of the cake layers using pins that have colored heads for easy visibility. Pipe tiny dots of Piping Icing using round metal tip No. 2 along the top and bottom of ribbons, letting dots overlap onto fondant to keep the ribbon attached once icing has hardened and pins are removed.

Pipe decorative border of icing at base of both cake layers using metal tip No. 16.

Roll remaining fondant to ⅛-inch thickness. Cut flowers, using 3¼-inch, 2¼-inch, and 2-inch daisy cutters from a set of 6 graduated daisy canapé or cookie cutters. For each flower, gently roll edge of a wooden pick back and forth across petals of daisy to ruffle the edges.

Combine powdered food coloring and cornstarch; using a small art brush, lightly brush a small amount of mixture in center of flower. Hold flower in hand, and carefully fold in half, colored side in, being careful not to press edges together. Fold half-circle in half, and then fold in half again to gather edges of flower together. Pinch pointed end together to ruffle petals. Using a wooden pick, carefully separate petals to shape flower. Insert a wooden pick in bottom of each flower, and place flower on two stacked mesh wire racks to dry, inserting pick into mesh to hold flower upright. (Flowers will be soft and limp until dry.)

Remove pins from ribbon when icing is dry. Place flowers on cake in clusters on top and sides. Gently pull ribbon from the cake just before slicing. Yield: 30 to 40 servings.

## Orange Pound Cake

1 pound butter, softened
3 cups sugar
6 large eggs
4 cups all-purpose flour
½ cup milk
¼ cup orange juice
2 teaspoons grated orange rind
1 teaspoon almond extract
1 teaspoon vanilla extract

Beat butter at medium speed with an electric mixer; gradually add sugar, beating well. Add eggs, one at a time, beating after each addition. Add flour to creamed mixture alternately with milk and orange juice, beginning and ending with flour mixture. Mix after each addition. Stir in orange rind and flavorings.

Spoon 3 cups batter into a greased and floured 6-inch round cakepan with 2-inch sides. Pour remaining batter into a greased and floured 9-inch round cakepan with 2-inch sides. Bake at 300° for 1 hour and 25 minutes or until a wooden pick inserted in center comes out clean. Cool in pans 10 minutes; transfer to wire racks to cool completely. Yield: one 9-inch and one 6-inch cake layer.

## Rolled Fondant

1 package unflavored gelatin
3 tablespoons cold water
½ cup light corn syrup
2 tablespoons shortening
1 tablespoon glycerin
6 cups sifted powdered sugar

Sprinkle gelatin over water in a 2-cup glass bowl; let stand 5 minutes. Set bowl in a saucepan of simmering water, stirring until gelatin dissolves. Add corn syrup, shortening, and glycerin, stirring until shortening melts. Remove from heat.

Place sugar in a large mixing bowl; add gelatin mixture, and beat at low speed with an electric mixer until most of sugar is incorporated. Stir with a wooden spoon until completely blended. Turn out onto a smooth surface lightly dusted with powdered sugar. Knead until smooth and satiny. Wrap fondant tightly with plastic

wrap, and place in an airtight container; let rest at least 2 hours. (Fondant may be stored at room temperature up to 1 month prior to using.) Yield: 2½ pounds.

## Piping Icing

6½ cups sifted powdered sugar
2 tablespoons lemon juice
¼ teaspoon vanilla extract
¼ cup water

Combine first 3 ingredients; beat until blended. Gradually add water, beating until smooth. Yield: 2 cups.

## Work Schedule for Satin Ribbon Cake

You can make Satin Ribbon Cake all in one day, or you can spread out the preparation over a span of a month.

■ **Prepare Rolled Fondant**— This confection needs to rest at least 2 hours before rolling it, but you can store it covered up to a month at room temperature.

■ **Bake Orange Pound Cake**— Let the layers cool completely before assembling the cake. If desired, seal in an airtight plastic bag, and store at room temperature up to 24 hours before assembling. Or freeze the layers up to a month; let thaw completely in plastic bag before assembling.

■ **Assemble layers and fondant**—Prepare apricot preserves, and coat cake layers with preserves and fondant as directed. Carefully stack 6-inch layer on top of 9-inch layer.

■ **Prepare Piping Icing**—Icing dries quickly, so keep it covered with a damp cloth when not in use. Decorate the cake using Piping Icing and the remaining fondant as directed.

# Filled With Flavor Of The Tropics

In Spanish, piña colada means "strained pineapple." The flavor of piña colada (pineapple-coconut) is a popular favorite for desserts.

## PIÑA COLADA CHEESECAKE

1⅔ cups dry fine breadcrumbs
¼ cup sugar
½ cup butter or margarine, melted
4 (8-ounce) packages cream cheese, softened
¾ cup sugar
4 large eggs
1 (8-ounce) carton sour cream
1 (16-ounce) can cream of coconut
1 (15¼-ounce) can crushed pineapple, well drained
2 tablespoons cornstarch
1 teaspoon vanilla extract
1 teaspoon rum flavoring
1 teaspoon lemon juice
Topping

Combine first 3 ingredients; press into bottom and 1 inch up sides of a 10-inch springform pan. Bake at 350° for 10 to 12 minutes. Cool on a wire rack.

Beat cream cheese at medium speed with an electric mixer until smooth. Gradually add ¾ cup sugar, beating well. Add eggs, one at a time, beating after each addition. Stir in sour cream and next 6 ingredients; spoon into crust. Bake at 350° for 1 hour and 20 minutes; turn oven off. Sprinkle on topping; return to oven. Leave cheesecake in oven with door closed 1 hour; then cool to room temperature on a wire rack. Chill. Yield: 10 to 12 servings.

### Topping

¼ cup butter or margarine
½ cup flaked coconut
½ cup finely chopped almonds
¼ cup sugar

Melt butter; add remaining ingredients, and sauté until golden, stirring frequently. Yield: about 1 cup.

# ON THE LIGHT SIDE

## Healthy Cooking Under Pressure

New models of pressure cookers feature a locking system that allows pressure to build up only when the lid is properly sealed. The lock also prevents a pressure cooker from being opened until pressure is reduced.

There are advantages to cooking in a pressure cooker: It is fast and helps retain nutrients that are lost in conventional cooking. It also eliminates the need for added fat, and it tenderizes lean cuts of meat without compromising their texture.

**Note:** The following recipes were tested in a 6-quart stainless-steel pressure cooker.

## BLACK-EYED PEA JAMBALAYA

1½ cups dried black-eyed peas
4 (10½-ounce) cans ready-to-serve, no-salt-added chicken broth
2 cups chopped tomato
1 cup cubed lean cooked ham
1 cup chopped onion
¾ cup chopped green pepper
¼ cup chopped celery
2 cloves garlic, minced
1 bay leaf
½ teaspoon salt
¼ teaspoon dried thyme
⅛ teaspoon ground cloves
1½ cups long-grain rice, uncooked
1½ teaspoons hot sauce
½ cup sliced green onions

Sort and wash peas; place in a 5- or 6-quart pressure cooker. Add next 11 ingredients; stir well. Close lid securely; according to manufacturer's directions, bring to high pressure over high heat (about 10 to 12 minutes). Reduce heat to medium-low or level needed to maintain high pressure; cook 15 minutes. Remove from heat; run cold water over pressure cooker

to reduce pressure instantly. Remove lid so that steam escapes away from you. Drain mixture, reserving 3 cups cooking liquid. Remove black-eyed pea mixture from cooker, and keep warm. Remove and discard bay leaf.

Add rice and 3 cups reserved cooking liquid to cooker. Close lid securely; bring to high pressure over high heat (about 5 minutes). Reduce heat to medium-low or level needed to maintain high pressure; cook 5 minutes. Remove from heat; let stand 10 minutes or until pressure drops normally. Remove lid; add pea mixture, hot sauce, and green onions, and toss gently. Yield: 8 servings (223 calories per 1¼-cup serving).

□ *9.9 grams protein, 1.8 grams fat, 40.2 grams carbohydrate, 10 milligrams cholesterol, 333 milligrams sodium, and 32 milligrams calcium.*

## CHICKEN MARENGO

Vegetable cooking spray
1 (3¼-pound) broiler-fryer, cut up and skinned
1 (16-ounce) can whole tomatoes, undrained and chopped
½ cup pearl onions, peeled
1 clove garlic, minced
¼ cup dry sherry
1 bay leaf
½ teaspoon salt
½ teaspoon dried thyme
¼ teaspoon pepper
1 cup fresh mushrooms, sliced
2 tablespoons cornstarch
3 cups hot cooked rice (cooked without salt or fat)

Coat a 5- or 6-quart pressure cooker with cooking spray; add next 9 ingredients. Close lid securely; according to manufacturer's directions, bring to high pressure over high heat (about 8 to 10 minutes). Reduce heat to medium-low or level needed to maintain high pressure; cook 9 minutes. Remove from heat; run cold water over pressure cooker to reduce pressure instantly. Remove lid so that steam escapes away from you. Transfer chicken to serving platter; keep warm. Remove ¼ cup liquid; set aside to cool. Add mushrooms to cooker; cook over medium-high heat about 5 minutes or until tender.

Combine cornstarch and reserved liquid; stir into pressure cooker and return to a boil. Cook 1 minute, stirring constantly. Remove and discard bay leaf.

Pour sauce over chicken. Serve with rice. Yield: 6 servings (354 calories per 3 ounces chicken, ½ cup sauce, and ½ cup rice).

□ *38.1 grams protein, 5.5 grams fat, 35.2 grams carbohydrate, 112 milligrams cholesterol, 447 milligrams sodium, and 61 milligrams calcium.*

*Rita W. Cook*
*Corpus Christi, Texas*

## QUICK BEEF STEW
*(pictured on page 73)*

2 pounds lean boneless top round
  steak
¼ cup all-purpose flour
Vegetable cooking spray
1 tablespoon vegetable oil
1 pound carrots, cut into 1-inch
  slices
1¾ pounds red potatoes, unpeeled
  and cubed
2 cups onion slices
3 cloves garlic, minced
¼ cup chopped parsley
½ teaspoon dried thyme
¼ teaspoon salt
¼ teaspoon pepper
1½ cups ready-to-serve, no-salt-
  added beef broth
1 cup light beer
1 cup frozen English peas, thawed
1 tablespoon red wine vinegar

Trim fat from meat; cut into 1-inch cubes. Combine meat and flour in a zip-top plastic bag; close bag, and shake. Coat a 5- or 6-quart pressure cooker with cooking spray; add oil and place over high heat until hot. Add meat and cook until browned, stirring often. Add carrots and next 9 ingredients. Close lid securely; according to manufacturer's directions, bring to high pressure over high heat (about 10 to 12 minutes). Reduce heat to medium-low or level needed to maintain high pressure; cook 15 minutes. Remove from heat; run cold water over pressure cooker to reduce pressure instantly. Remove lid so that steam escapes away from you. Stir in peas and vinegar; cook 10 to 15 minutes. Yield: 6 servings (411 calories per 1½-cup serving).

□ *40.5 grams protein, 8.9 grams fat, 40.5 grams carbohydrate, 86 milligrams cholesterol, 237 milligrams sodium, and 63 milligrams calcium.*

LIGHT FAVORITE

# Caesar Salad

Many health-conscious meal planners have taken Caesar salad off their menus because of its high fat and cholesterol content and the threat of salmonella in the raw egg. However, with a few adjustments, it can easily fit healthy eating habits.

## CAESAR SALAD
*(pictured on page 73)*

⅓ cup hot water
1 teaspoon chicken-flavored
  bouillon granules
3 tablespoons fresh lemon juice
2 teaspoons reduced-sodium
  Worcestershire sauce
1 teaspoon Dijon mustard
2 cloves garlic, minced
1 anchovy fillet, rinsed and drained
⅛ teaspoon salt
⅛ teaspoon freshly ground pepper
3 tablespoons olive oil
8 cups torn romaine lettuce leaves
Garlic Croutons
3 tablespoons freshly grated
  Parmesan cheese

Combine water and bouillon granules in container of an electric blender; process 30 seconds. Add lemon juice and next 6 ingredients. With blender running, gradually add olive oil in a slow, steady stream. Cover and chill thoroughly. To serve, shake dressing vigorously and drizzle over romaine lettuce. Add Garlic Croutons and Parmesan cheese, and toss. Yield: 6 servings (101 calories per 1½-cup serving).

□ *2.9 grams protein, 8.2 grams fat, 4.8 grams carbohydrate, 2 milligrams cholesterol, 308 milligrams sodium, and 67 milligrams calcium.*

### Garlic Croutons

2 cloves garlic, halved
1 teaspoon olive oil
1 tablespoon water
5 (½-inch) slices day-old French
  bread, cubed

Sauté garlic in olive oil in a large non-stick skillet until tender. Add water, mixing well. Add bread cubes, tossing to coat; remove and discard garlic. Spread bread cubes evenly on a baking sheet, and bake at 325° for 20 minutes or until golden. Yield: 1½ cups (51 calories per ¼ cup).

□ *1.4 grams protein, 1.1 grams fat, 8.5 grams carbohydrate, 0 milligrams cholesterol, 86 milligrams sodium, and 8 milligrams calcium.*

| COMPARE THE NUTRIENTS | | |
|---|---|---|
| (per serving) | Traditional Version | Light Version |
| Calories | 389 | 101 |
| Fat | 35.8g | 8.2g |
| Cholesterol | 38mg | 2mg |

# Feast From The Mideast

Here's a menu with a Mideastern flair that offers distinctly different flavors your family is sure to enjoy.

Coriander, paprika, cumin, ginger, and turmeric season chunks of lean lamb in Stewed Lamb With Five Spices. It bakes in a covered casserole for 1 to 1½ hours. Lemon wedges and olives are added just before serving. Leg of lamb, the leanest cut of lamb, is the best choice for this dish, but shoulder or chops may be used if all the fat is drained.

Dilled Cucumber Salad offers a cool, refreshing accompaniment to this robust lamb dish. Pear Tart, an eye-catching end to this special meal, is sure to get raves from diners.

## STEWED LAMB WITH FIVE SPICES
*(pictured on page 73)*

1 (3½-pound) leg of lamb
Vegetable cooking spray
2 cups chopped onion
4 cloves garlic, minced
1 teaspoon ground coriander
½ teaspoon salt
½ teaspoon paprika
½ teaspoon ground cumin
½ teaspoon ground ginger
⅛ teaspoon ground turmeric
1 (16-ounce) can tomatoes, undrained and chopped
1 lemon, sliced into wedges
12 pimiento-stuffed olives, sliced
½ cup chopped fresh parsley
3 cups hot cooked rice (cooked without salt or fat)

Trim fat from lamb; bone and cut lamb into bite-size pieces. Set aside 1½ pounds of lamb; reserve remainder for other uses.

Coat a nonstick skillet with cooking spray; heat over medium-high heat until hot. Add lamb; cook until browned. Drain well. Return lamb to skillet; add onion and garlic, and cook until onion is transparent. Stir in coriander and next 6 ingredients. Transfer lamb mixture to a 3-quart casserole; cover and bake at 375° for 1 to 1½ hours or until lamb is tender. Squeeze juice of lemon wedges into casserole; stir in lemon wedges, olives, and parsley. Return to oven and cook 5 minutes or until thoroughly heated. Serve over rice. Yield: 6 servings (340 calories per ⅔ cup lamb with ½ cup rice).

□ *28.6 grams protein, 7.8 grams fat, 38.8 grams carbohydrate, 76 milligrams cholesterol, 437 milligrams sodium, and 80 milligrams calcium.*
*Marsha Goldstein*
*Bessemer, Alabama*

## DILLED CUCUMBER SALAD

¼ teaspoon salt
4½ cups thinly sliced cucumber (about 3 medium)
1 (8-ounce) carton plain nonfat yogurt
2 tablespoons tarragon vinegar or cider vinegar
1 tablespoon chopped fresh dill or 1 teaspoon dried dill
1 clove garlic, minced
6 lettuce leaves

Sprinkle salt over cucumber slices; toss gently to evenly coat all sides. Let stand 20 minutes. Drain cucumber slices between layers of paper towels; set aside.

Combine yogurt, vinegar, dill, and garlic. Pour dressing over cucumbers; toss gently, and chill up to 1 hour. Arrange on lettuce leaves. Yield: 6 servings (40 calories per ¾-cup serving with lettuce leaf).

□ *3.1 grams protein, 0.2 gram fat, 7.2 grams carbohydrate, 1 milligram cholesterol, 135 milligrams sodium, and 102 milligrams calcium.*
*Mrs. Hugh Bozeman*
*Charleston, South Carolina*

## PEAR TART

Butter-flavored vegetable cooking spray
3 sheets commercial frozen phyllo pastry, thawed
¼ cup finely chopped blanched almonds
¼ cup egg substitute
2 tablespoons sugar
1½ cups water
2 tablespoons lemon juice
3 medium-size fresh pears
2 tablespoons sugar
¼ teaspoon ground cinnamon
1 tablespoon sliced almonds
¼ cup low-sugar apple jelly, melted

Coat a 10-inch pieplate with cooking spray. Place 1 sheet of phyllo pastry over pieplate, leaving edges overhanging; coat sheet with cooking spray. Place second sheet of phyllo on top in opposite direction; coat with cooking spray. Top with third sheet; spray with cooking spray. Roll and fold edges loosely under themselves to form a ruffled edge; set aside.

Combine chopped almonds, egg substitute, and 2 tablespoons sugar; spread over bottom of shell.

Combine water and lemon juice in medium bowl. Peel and core pears; dip pears in lemon juice mixture and drain well. Cut pears in half vertically; cut each half into ⅛- to ¼-inch slices, keeping slices in order as they are cut. Arrange slices over almond mixture in shape of 6 pear halves, letting slices fan out slightly.

Combine 2 tablespoons sugar and cinnamon; sprinkle over pears. Coat lightly with cooking spray. Shield edges of phyllo with aluminum foil. Bake at 400° for 35 minutes. Remove shield from edges; sprinkle with sliced almonds. Bake 5 minutes or until edges are golden. Remove from oven; brush pears with apple jelly. Yield: 6 servings (177 calories per slice).

□ *3.4 grams protein, 3.6 grams fat, 35.3 grams carbohydrate, 0 milligrams cholesterol, 16 milligrams sodium, and 29 milligrams calcium.*

Top left: *Topped with Garlic Croutons and Parmesan cheese, this light Caesar Salad (page 71) rivals those in many restaurants.*

Top right: *In Quick Beef Stew (page 71), lean round steak becomes tender enough to cut with a fork in just 45 minutes.*

Right: *Stewed Lamb With Five Spices and commercial wheat rolls show that healthy eating and ethnic foods go hand in hand. (Recipes, page 72.)*

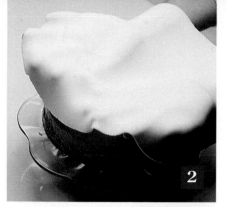

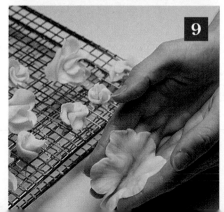

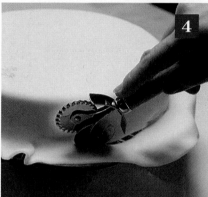

*A special celebration calls for a fancy cake to mark the occasion. Satin Ribbon Cake is the perfect creation for the event. (Follow step-by-step photos on this page and recipe on page 68.)*

**(Step 1)** *Roll about half of fondant to ⅛-inch thickness on smooth, crumb-free surface sprayed with vegetable cooking spray.*

**(Step 2)** *Carefully peel fondant from surface, and transfer fondant to 9-inch cake layer.*

**(Step 3)** *Smooth fondant to cover sides of cake, guiding fondant with your hands.*

**(Step 4)** *Carefully trim excess fondant at base of cake using a pastry wheel. Repeat process with 6-inch cake, and place on top of 9-inch cake.*

**(Step 5)** *Carefully pin pink satin ribbon around sides of cake layers 1 inch from base of cake layers.*

**(Step 6)** *Pipe dots of Piping Icing along top and bottom of ribbon, letting icing touch fondant to attach ribbons.*

**(Step 7)** *Pipe decorative borders of icing along base of each tier of cake. Remove pins from ribbon when icing is dry.*

**(Step 8)** *To make flowers, cut fondant with daisy cutter, and roll the edge of a wooden pick back and forth across petals of daisy to ruffle edges of flower.*

**(Step 9)** *Hold flower and carefully fold in half, colored side in, being careful not to press edges together; fold in half two more times to gather edges of flower together. Pinch pointed end to ruffle petals.*

**(Step 10)** *Carefully separate petals with a wooden pick to shape flowers. Let flowers dry on mesh wire racks, and place on cake according to photograph.*

The fat and cholesterol in Pound Cake, Buttermilk Pie, and Fresh Strawberry Ice Milk have been whittled down so that these desserts can be served often without guilt. (Recipes, pages 94 and 95.)

# APRIL

*Join us this month for a culinary tour of one of the
South's most colorful cities—New Orleans. In our
"Brunches & Lunches" special section, you'll find a bounty
of menu ideas for daytime entertaining—each accented with
the style and flavor of this grand city. And for a special treat,
we've taken some of the South's classic desserts and made
them lighter and healthier.*

# Get Fresh With Pasta

Today's refrigerated fresh pastas are moist and tender, and they come in a variety of shapes—half-moons, corkscrews, birds' nests, squares, and belly buttons. They boast formal names: rigatoni, rotini, ravioli, and tortellini.

With the introduction of refrigerated pastas a few years ago, cooking time decreased from 20 to about 10 minutes. Squeezed from commercial pasta machines, cut, cooled, and then packaged, refrigerated pasta doesn't go through drying machines as does dry pasta. Thus, refrigerated versions have higher moisture content and take less time to cook. Equally important, most pasta buffs say refrigerated ones taste more flavorful.

The differences between refrigerated, fresh pastas and dried varieties come down to cost, convenience, and personal preference. The refrigerated, fresh versions cost more than dry. Dry pastas last a long time—indefinitely when stored in a cool, dry place—compared to most refrigerated ones, which stay fresh from about 40 to 55 days.

These recipes pair refrigerated pastas with commercial products to make a quick and simple supper. The pairings will leave your palate tingling.

### TASTE-OF-TEXAS PASTA AND CHICKEN

¼ cup olive oil
1 tablespoon lime juice
⅛ teaspoon red pepper
4 chicken breast halves, skinned and boned
1 (9-ounce) package refrigerated linguine, uncooked
2 tablespoons butter, melted
1 to 1½ teaspoons grated lime rind
1 tablespoon olive oil
1 clove garlic, crushed
1 (16-ounce) jar mild, thick and chunky salsa
Garnish: lime slices

Combine first 3 ingredients in a zip-top, heavy-duty plastic bag; shake well. Add chicken; seal and refrigerate 15 minutes.

Cook pasta according to package directions; drain. Add butter and lime rind; toss well, and keep warm.

Remove chicken from marinade; discard marinade. Heat 1 tablespoon oil in a large skillet over medium heat. Add chicken, and cook 10 to 15 minutes or until done, turning once. Remove chicken, and set aside. Add garlic to skillet and cook, stirring until lightly browned. Add salsa, and bring to a boil. Arrange pasta and chicken on plates; top with salsa mixture. Garnish, if desired. Yield: 4 servings.

### ITALIAN PASTA VINAIGRETTE

1 (9-ounce) package refrigerated, cheese-filled ravioli, uncooked
3 tablespoons olive oil
3 tablespoons white wine vinegar
½ teaspoon dried Italian seasoning
¼ teaspoon freshly ground pepper
6 cherry tomatoes, halved
¼ cup sliced green onions
12 pepperoni slices, halved, or ½ cup cubed cooked ham

Cook pasta according to package directions; drain. Rinse with cold water, and drain.

Combine oil and next 3 ingredients; pour over pasta, tossing to coat. Stir in tomato and remaining ingredients. Cover and chill at least 2 hours. Yield: 3 servings.

### GARLIC PASTA WITH MARINARA SAUCE

1 (9-ounce) package refrigerated angel hair pasta, uncooked
½ teaspoon salt
4 cloves garlic, minced
2 tablespoons olive oil
½ teaspoon freshly ground pepper
1 (15-ounce) carton commercial marinara sauce
Grated Parmesan cheese

Cook pasta according to package directions using ½ teaspoon salt; drain.

Cook garlic in oil in a skillet over medium-high heat, stirring constantly; pour over pasta, and sprinkle with pepper, tossing gently. Serve with marinara sauce, and sprinkle with cheese. Yield: 3 servings.

## RAVIOLI WITH
## CREAMY PESTO SAUCE

1 cup whipping cream
1 (2.82-ounce) jar pesto sauce
1 (3-ounce) jar capers, drained
   (optional)
2 (9-ounce) packages refrigerated,
   cheese-filled ravioli, uncooked
2 tablespoons pine nuts, toasted

Combine whipping cream and pesto
sauce in a saucepan; add capers, if desired. Cook mixture over low heat until thoroughly heated, stirring
frequently.
   Cook pasta according to package directions, and drain. Toss pasta with
sauce, and sprinkle with toasted pine
nuts. Serve immediately. Yield: 4 to 6
servings.

**Note:** You can find commercial pesto
sauce on the grocery shelf or in the
refrigerated section of supermarkets.

# QUICK!
## Salads In Seconds

As the clock ticks down toward din-
nertime and you find yourself reaching
for the old reliable head of iceberg lettuce, stop. In the time it takes to
make the same old salad, you can
whip up one of these. Even though
the preparation time is short, there's
no sacrifice in flavor or appearance.
   With only five ingredients, Tomato-
Asparagus Salad is a cinch to prepare
and makes an attractive presentation.
Canned asparagus can be used, but
try fresh, if it is available. Spring is the
peak season for asparagus.
   Mandarin Orange-Lettuce Salad and
Garlic-Tarragon Green Salad are both
tossed. To speed up the preparation,
wash the salad greens ahead of time
and store in plastic bags in the crisper
drawer of your refrigerator.

## TOMATO-ASPARAGUS SALAD
### (pictured on page 116)

1 pound fresh asparagus *
8 romaine lettuce leaves
12 cherry tomatoes, sliced
⅓ cup commercial reduced-calorie
   Italian salad dressing
¼ cup freshly grated Parmesan
   cheese

Snap off tough ends of asparagus; remove scales from stalks with a knife
or vegetable peeler, if desired. Cook
asparagus, covered, in a small amount
of boiling water 6 to 8 minutes or until
crisp-tender; drain. Plunge asparagus
into ice water to stop the cooking process; drain and set aside.
   Arrange lettuce leaves on individual
plates. Arrange asparagus spears and
tomatoes on top; drizzle with salad
dressing, and sprinkle with Parmesan
cheese. Yield: 4 servings.

* 1 (16-ounce) can asparagus spears
may be substituted for fresh
asparagus.
   *Patricia B. Lewis*
   *Sarasota, Florida*

## QUICK
## SUMMER ITALIAN SALAD

15 small fresh mushrooms
1 large cucumber, unpeeled and
   sliced
1 large green pepper, cut into strips
2 medium tomatoes, cut into
   wedges
½ cup chopped green onions
1 cup commercial Italian salad
   dressing

Clean mushrooms with damp paper
towels. Remove stems, and reserve
for other uses. Combine mushroom
caps and remaining ingredients in a
large bowl; toss gently. Cover and
chill. Yield: 6 to 8 servings.
   *Ruth Harville*
   *Longview, Texas*

## MANDARIN ORANGE-LETTUCE
## SALAD

6 cups torn Belgian endive (about 1
   head)
1 (11-ounce) can mandarin oranges,
   drained
⅓ cup golden raisins
1 (2-ounce) package cashew nuts,
   toasted (⅓ cup)
½ cup commercial Italian salad
   dressing or sweet-and-sour salad
   dressing

Combine first 4 ingredients in a large
bowl. Just before serving, pour dressing over salad and toss. Yield: 4 to 6
servings.
   *Ginny Whitt*
   *Mount Washington, Kentucky*

## GARLIC-TARRAGON
## GREEN SALAD

1 clove garlic, minced
¼ teaspoon salt
⅛ teaspoon freshly ground pepper
Pinch of dry mustard
1 tablespoon tarragon vinegar
¼ cup vegetable oil
3 heads Bibb lettuce, torn *

Combine first 4 ingredients in a large
bowl; blend with a fork. Add vinegar
and oil, mixing well. Add lettuce; toss
gently. Yield: 4 to 6 servings.

* 8 cups mixed salad greens may be
substituted for Bibb lettuce.
   *Mrs. C. M. Conklin, II*
   *Dallas, Texas*

**Tip:** *To speed up salad making,
wash, trim, and dry all ingredients
for the salad as soon as you buy
them; tie the ingredients together in
a plastic bag, and store them in the
refrigerator. At mealtime, just pull
out the bag, gently toss the ingredients, and serve with a variety of
salad dressings.*

# After-Taxes Banquet For The Burdened

If tax-filing time has left you money hungry, here's a rich assortment of economical dishes for an after-taxes get-together.

Start with "Eye-Opener" Coffee Punch to wake up those filers who were trying to beat the midnight deadline to file their returns.

"Bean Counter" Soup (named for your favorite accountant) makes a great appetizer or light entrée for the hungry filer. After the exhaustion of making the April 15 deadline, you'll be relieved to know that none of these recipes is too taxing.

## "BEAN COUNTER" SOUP

½ cup finely chopped onion
2 cloves garlic, minced
1 tablespoon olive oil
1 medium tomato, finely chopped
2 (14½-ounce) cans ready-to-serve chicken broth
1¾ cups water
½ teaspoon dried whole basil
½ teaspoon dried oregano
½ teaspoon dried celery flakes
3 (16-ounce) cans Great Northern beans, rinsed and drained
1 cup elbow macaroni, uncooked
¼ teaspoon pepper
Grated Parmesan cheese

Cook onion and garlic in oil in a Dutch oven over medium-high heat until tender, stirring constantly. Add tomato; simmer 5 minutes, stirring occasionally. Add chicken broth, water, basil, oregano, and celery flakes. Bring to a boil; reduce heat and simmer, uncovered, 5 minutes. Add beans, macaroni, and pepper; return to a boil. Cover, reduce heat, and simmer 15 minutes or until macaroni is tender, stirring once. To serve, spoon into bowls, and sprinkle with cheese. Yield: 8 cups.

*Judi Grigoraci*
*Charleston, West Virginia*

## "BRING-HOME-THE-BACON" AVOCADO DIP

2 ripe avocados, peeled and mashed
½ cup mayonnaise
¼ cup finely chopped onion
2 tablespoons lime juice
½ teaspoon salt
⅛ teaspoon hot sauce
4 slices bacon, cooked and crumbled

Combine first 6 ingredients in a small bowl; cover and chill up to 2 hours. Stir in bacon. Serve with tortilla chips. Yield: 2 cups.

*Clairiece Gilbert Humphrey*
*Charlottesville, Virginia*

## "IN-THE-RED" CHILI OVER "ROLLING-IN-DOUGH" BISCUITS

3 pounds lean ground beef
3 cups chopped onion
1 tablespoon minced garlic
2 carrots, scraped and sliced
1 (15-ounce) can tomato sauce
1½ cups beef broth
¼ cup chili powder
2 tablespoons paprika
1 tablespoon ground cumin
1 tablespoon dried oregano
3 tablespoons cider vinegar
1 teaspoon dried crushed red pepper
1 (19-ounce) can kidney beans, drained
2 green peppers, chopped
½ teaspoon pepper
¼ teaspoon salt
"Rolling-in-Dough" Biscuits

Combine first 4 ingredients in a Dutch oven. Cook until meat browns, stirring to crumble; drain. Return mixture to Dutch oven; stir in tomato sauce and next 7 ingredients. Bring to a boil. Cover, reduce heat, and simmer 50 minutes; stir occasionally. Stir in beans and next 3 ingredients; simmer, uncovered, 15 minutes.

To serve, split "Rolling-in-Dough" Biscuits; spoon chili over bottom, and cover with top. Yield: 12 servings.

## "Rolling-in-Dough" Biscuits

3 cups all-purpose flour
1½ tablespoons baking powder
1 teaspoon baking soda
1 teaspoon salt
¼ cup butter or margarine
1 (16-ounce) carton sour cream
3 cups (12 ounces) shredded Cheddar cheese
2 jalapeño peppers, seeded and diced

Combine first 4 ingredients in a large bowl; cut in butter with a pastry blender until mixture is crumbly. Add sour cream, Cheddar cheese, and peppers, stirring until dry ingredients are moistened. Turn dough out onto a floured surface, and knead 3 or 4 times. Roll dough to ½-inch thickness; cut with a 4-inch round cutter. Place on lightly greased baking sheet. Bake at 425° for 15 minutes. Yield: 1 dozen.

*Rublelene Singleton*
*Scotts Hill, Tennessee*

## "EYE-OPENER" COFFEE PUNCH

1 cup water
3 cups sugar
¼ cup instant coffee granules
1 gallon milk
½ gallon vanilla ice cream, softened
½ gallon chocolate ice cream, softened

Bring water to a boil in a medium saucepan. Add sugar and coffee granules; reduce heat and simmer, stirring constantly until sugar and coffee dissolve. Remove from heat, and cool.

Combine milk and coffee mixture in a punch bowl. Just before serving, gently stir ice cream into bowl. Serve immediately. Yield: 7 quarts.

*Clota Engleman*
*Spur, Texas*

# Brunches & Lunches

## The Old-World Flavor Of New Orleans

Standing on the balcony of her historic French Quarter home, Mary Adele Baus watches over the courtyard wall for her friends, children, and grandchildren to arrive for a traditional after-church brunch.

### FRENCH BRUNCH FOR TWELVE

Louisiana Oyster-and-Artichoke Soup
Hickory-Grilled Ham
Omelette aux Fines Herbes   Eggplant Provençal
Bakery rolls and pastries
Oranges Grand Marnier   Oatmeal Cookies
Louisiana Pecan Pie   Cafe Pontalba

### LOUISIANA OYSTER-AND-ARTICHOKE SOUP

2 (12-ounce) containers fresh Standard oysters
½ cup finely chopped shallots
1 bay leaf
⅛ to ¼ teaspoon red pepper
Pinch of dried thyme
3 tablespoons butter or margarine, melted
2 tablespoons all-purpose flour
1 (14½-ounce) can ready-to-serve chicken broth
1 (14-ounce) can artichoke hearts, drained and cut into eighths
1 tablespoon chopped fresh parsley
½ teaspoon salt
⅛ to ¼ teaspoon hot sauce
½ cup whipping cream

Drain oysters, reserving 1 cup liquid. Cut oysters into fourths.

Sauté shallots and next 3 ingredients in butter in a Dutch oven until tender. Add flour, stirring until smooth. Cook, stirring constantly, 1 minute. Gradually add broth and oyster liquid; simmer, stirring occasionally, 15 minutes. Remove bay leaf. Add oysters, artichokes, parsley, salt, and hot sauce; simmer 10 minutes. Stir in whipping cream; cook until thoroughly heated. Yield: 6 cups.

**Microwave Directions:** Drain oysters, reserving 1 cup liquid. Cut oysters into fourths.

Place shallots and next 3 ingredients in a 3-quart casserole. Add butter, and microwave at HIGH 3 minutes, stirring after 2 minutes. Add flour, stirring until smooth. Gradually add broth and oyster liquid, stirring well. Microwave at HIGH 9 to 10 minutes, stirring after 5 minutes. Remove bay leaf. Add oysters, artichokes, parsley, salt, and hot sauce; microwave at HIGH 5 to 8 minutes, stirring mixture after 4 minutes. Stir in whipping cream.

### HICKORY-GRILLED HAM

Hickory wood chips
1 (7- to 8-pound) smoked, fully cooked ham half
½ cup dry mustard
½ cup firmly packed brown sugar
½ cup water
1 tablespoon whole cloves
4 slices fresh or canned pineapple
10 maraschino cherries
Grapefruit sections, peeled
Avocado slices, peeled

Soak hickory chips in water 1 to 24 hours before grilling. Cut ham bone loose from meat (or ask butcher to do this), but do not remove the bone; secure bone in ham before grilling using wooden picks or skewers. Combine dry mustard and brown sugar; add water, stirring mixture until smooth. Brush over ham.

Prepare charcoal fire; place hickory chips on coals around edges of grill. Grill ham, covered, over low coals (8 inches from heat) 1 hour, turning and brushing often with mustard mixture; remove ham from grill.

Stud ham with cloves; arrange pineapple and cherries on ham, securing with wooden picks. Return ham to grill, and grill an additional 30 minutes or until meat thermometer registers 140°. Remove bone before slicing ham. Serve with grapefruit sections and avocado slices. Yield: 16 servings.

# Brunches & Lunches

## OMELETTE AUX FINES HERBES

6 large eggs
¼ teaspoon salt
¼ teaspoon pepper
¼ cup butter or margarine
1 tablespoon finely chopped fresh basil *
1 tablespoon finely chopped fresh parsley *
1 tablespoon finely chopped fresh chives *
Garnish: parsley sprig

Whisk together eggs, salt, and pepper just until blended. Heat a 12-inch omelet pan or heavy skillet over medium heat. Add butter, and rotate pan to coat bottom. Pour egg mixture into skillet. As egg mixture starts to cook, gently lift edges of omelet with a spatula, and tilt pan so uncooked portion of mixture flows underneath the cooked portion.

Sprinkle omelet with herbs. Fold omelet in half, and transfer to plate. Garnish with parsley, if desired. Yield: 4 servings. (Prepare 3 omelets for 12 servings.)

* 1 teaspoon each of dried basil, parsley, and chives may be substituted for fresh versions of herbs.

**Tip:** *Use finely chopped fresh herbs whenever possible. Dried whole herbs are usually the next best choice since they maintain their strength longer than the commercially ground form.*

## EGGPLANT PROVENÇAL

1 tablespoon chopped fresh basil *
1 tablespoon chopped fresh thyme *
1 tablespoon chopped fresh oregano *
1 tablespoon chopped fresh rosemary *
1 small eggplant, peeled and cut into 12 slices
¼ cup olive oil
Salt and pepper
3 small onions, cut into 4 slices each
2 medium tomatoes, peeled and cut into 6 slices each
3 small green peppers, cut into 4 rings each
6 large cloves garlic, minced
¼ cup grated Parmesan cheese
¼ cup (1 ounce) shredded Gruyère cheese

Combine basil, thyme, oregano, and rosemary; set aside.

Place 6 eggplant slices in a lightly greased 12- x 8- x 2-inch baking dish; drizzle each slice with ¼ teaspoon olive oil. Sprinkle each slice lightly with salt and pepper and ¼ teaspoon herb mixture. Layer 6 onion slices, 6 tomato slices, and 6 green pepper slices on top, repeating olive oil and seasonings on onion, tomato, and green pepper slices as for eggplant. Sprinkle each stack of vegetables with ¼ teaspoon minced garlic.

Repeat seasoned layers with remaining ingredients to make 6 vegetable stacks in a second lightly greased 12- x 8- x 2-inch dish. Sprinkle each stack of layers with ¼ teaspoon garlic. Cover, and bake at 350° for 40 minutes. Uncover and sprinkle with 2 tablespoons each of Parmesan and Gruyère cheese; bake an additional 5 minutes. Yield: 12 servings.

* 1 teaspoon each of dried basil, thyme, and oregano may be substituted for fresh versions of herbs and 1 tablespoon dried rosemary for fresh.

To sprinkle herbs on vegetables, use only ⅛ teaspoon for each layer instead of ¼ teaspoon.

## ORANGES GRAND MARNIER

12 medium navel oranges
⅓ to ½ cup Grand Marnier or other orange-flavored liqueur
1½ quarts orange sherbet, softened

Cut a ½-inch slice from the stem end of each orange. Scoop out pulp, removing membrane and seeds; reserve orange shells. Chop pulp, and drain well. Combine pulp, Grand Marnier, and sherbet; stir until blended. Spoon mixture into orange shells, and place in muffin pans. Freeze 8 hours. Remove from freezer 20 to 30 minutes before serving. Yield: 12 servings.

## OATMEAL COOKIES

1¼ cups butter or margarine, softened
¾ cup firmly packed brown sugar
½ cup sugar
1 large egg
1 teaspoon vanilla extract
1½ cups all-purpose flour
1 teaspoon baking soda
¼ teaspoon salt
1 teaspoon ground cinnamon
¼ teaspoon ground nutmeg
3 cups regular oats, uncooked
½ cup currants or raisins

Beat butter at medium speed with an electric mixer. Gradually add sugars, beating mixture well. Add egg and vanilla; mix well.

Combine flour and next 4 ingredients; gradually add to butter mixture, mixing well. Stir in oats and currants.

Drop dough by tablespoonfuls onto ungreased cookie sheets. Bake at

375° for 10 minutes or until lightly browned. Cool slightly on cookie sheets; remove to wire racks to cool completely. Yield: about 4 dozen.

## LOUISIANA PECAN PIE

1½ tablespoons butter or margarine
¾ cup sugar
¾ cup light corn syrup
3 large eggs, lightly beaten
1 teaspoon vanilla extract
1 unbaked 9-inch, deep-dish pastry shell
1 cup chopped pecans

Combine first 3 ingredients in a medium saucepan; cook over low heat, stirring constantly, until sugar dissolves. Cool slightly. Add eggs and vanilla, stirring well.

Pour filling into unbaked pastry shell; top with pecans. Bake at 350° for 45 minutes. Yield: one 9-inch pie.

## CAFE PONTALBA

12 cups hot coffee with chicory
½ cup Kahlúa or crème de cacao
12 sugar cubes
Whipped cream
Grated chocolate
12 (4-inch) sticks cinnamon

Combine coffee and Kahlúa; ladle into cups. Add a sugar cube to each cup. Top each serving with a dollop of whipped cream; sprinkle with chocolate. Serve with cinnamon stick stirrers. Yield: 12 servings.

# The Art Of The Brunch

When Bill Fagaly was a little boy, his bedroom showcased the usual collections—seashells, marbles, and Indian artifacts.

Today Fagaly's whole house is filled with a collection of serious art. And every day he is surrounded by an even bigger and better collection at the New Orleans Museum of Art, where he is the assistant director. Away from the job, Fagaly enjoys still another art form—cooking. You can guess that from his stacks of cookbooks and from the beautiful meals he creates. His work is a sight to behold.

Fagaly's Easter brunch theme is the product of his love for food, art, and New Orleans. What's Easter—or brunch—without eggs? Fagaly thinks first of the inedible type, namely the famous Russian Fabergé eggs. They are his inspiration for "eggs as art" in his centerpiece and the party to go with it. Nothing is lost between the artist's palette and the diner's palate with this theme.

A Russian menu is a natural for the occasion, but he gives it a local twist. Traditional borscht (beet soup) is laced with crawfish, and his charlotte russe highlights Louisiana strawberries. You can serve the usual caviar with the Cheese Blintzes, but Fagaly likes Choupique caviar, which is the roe of a Louisiana fish, rather than from sturgeon.

### RUSSIAN EASTER BRUNCH FOR EIGHT

**Caviar Mousse
Piroshki
Crawfish Borscht
Cheese Blintzes
Vegetable Salad
With Horseradish Dressing
Charlotte Russe
With Strawberry Sauce**

## CAVIAR MOUSSE

1 (16-ounce) carton sour cream
1 (6-ounce) jar red caviar, undrained
¼ cup chopped parsley
1 teaspoon grated lemon rind
1 tablespoon grated onion
1 envelope unflavored gelatin
¼ cup cold water
1 cup whipping cream, whipped
⅛ teaspoon freshly ground pepper
Leaf lettuce
Garnish: fresh parsley leaves

Combine sour cream, caviar, parsley, lemon rind, and onion in a large bowl; set aside. Sprinkle gelatin over cold water in a small saucepan; let stand 1 minute. Cook over low heat, stirring until gelatin dissolves. Add to sour cream mixture. Fold in whipped cream and ⅛ teaspoon pepper.

Spoon mixture into 8 lightly greased ½-cup molds, and chill until set. Invert the molds, and unmold onto lettuce-lined plates. Garnish with parsley leaves, if desired, and serve with triangles of pumpernickel bread. Yield: 8 servings.

## PIROSHKI

½ pound fresh mushrooms, finely
  chopped
3 green onions, sliced
1 tablespoon butter, melted
2 teaspoons all-purpose flour
¼ teaspoon salt
⅛ teaspoon pepper
1 teaspoon fresh dillweed or
  ½ teaspoon dried dillweed
⅓ cup sour cream
Pastry
1 egg yolk, beaten
1 teaspoon water

Sauté mushrooms and green onions in
butter until tender. Remove from
heat; stir in flour and next 3 ingredients. Cool. Stir in sour cream.

Roll pastry to ⅛-inch thickness on a
lightly floured surface. Cut into
2½-inch circles with a biscuit cutter.
Place 1 teaspoon mushroom mixture
in center of each circle. Combine egg
yolk and water; brush edges of pastry
with mixture, and fold in half. Press
edges to seal. Place on lightly greased
baking sheets, and brush tops with
egg yolk mixture. Bake at 375° for 30
minutes. Yield: 3 dozen.

### Food Terms

Here's an easy way to come to
terms with this foreign menu:

**Blintz** (blints)—a thin rolled pancake filled with cream cheese or
cottage cheese mixture

**Piroshki** (pih-ROSH-kee)—a
small, filled pastry or turnover

**Charlotte russe** (roos)—a cold
dessert of creamy filling set in a
ladyfinger-lined mold

## Pastry

2 cups all-purpose flour
½ teaspoon baking powder
½ teaspoon salt
¼ cup butter, softened
1 large egg, lightly beaten
½ cup sour cream

Position knife blade in food processor
bowl; add all ingredients. Process 1 to
2 minutes or until dough forms a ball;
chill 1 hour. Yield: enough pastry for 3
dozen turnovers.

## CRAWFISH BORSCHT

1½ pounds fresh beets
2 cups chicken broth
1 cup water
½ pound fresh or frozen peeled
  crawfish tails, thawed *
1½ cups peeled and diced
  cucumber
½ cup sliced green onions
2 tablespoons red wine vinegar
1 tablespoon chopped
  fresh dill
1½ teaspoons sugar
2 cups buttermilk
Garnish: fresh dillweed

Peel beets, and cut into eighths. Combine beets, chicken broth, and water
in a Dutch oven; bring to a boil.
Cover, reduce heat, and simmer 20 to
25 minutes or until tender. Drain, reserving liquid.

Position knife blade in food processor bowl; add beets. Process until
smooth. Chop crawfish, and add
beets, reserved liquid, cucumber,
green onions, vinegar, dill, sugar, and
buttermilk. Cover and chill. Garnish, if
desired. Yield: 7½ cups.

* ½ pound peeled and deveined
shrimp may be substituted for peeled
crawfish tails.

## CHEESE BLINTZES

1 large egg, lightly beaten
1⅓ cups milk
1 cup all-purpose flour
¼ teaspoon salt
Vegetable oil or cooking
  spray
Blintz Filling

Combine egg and milk; gradually add
flour and salt, stirring with a wire
whisk until smooth. Brush bottom of a
6-inch crêpe pan or heavy skillet with
oil, or coat with cooking spray; place
over medium heat just until hot,
not smoking.

Pour 2 tablespoons batter into pan;
quickly tilt pan in all directions so batter covers pan with a thin film. Cook
about 1 minute or until crêpe can be
shaken loose from pan. Flip crêpe,
and cook about 30 seconds.

Place crêpes on a towel to cool.
Stack between layers of wax paper to
prevent sticking. Repeat until all batter is used.

Place about 1 tablespoon Blintz Filling in center of each crêpe. Fold top of
crêpe over filling, and then fold left
and right sides of crêpe over filling and
roll up crêpe.

Repeat procedure with remaining
crêpes and filling. Brush bottom of a
nonstick skillet with oil, or coat with
cooking spray; heat over medium heat
just until hot. Cook blintzes on all
sides until lightly browned. Serve
warm with apple sauce, sour cream,
and caviar. Yield: 16 crêpes.

### Blintz Filling

1 (12-ounce) container large-curd
  cottage cheese
2 tablespoons egg substitute
1½ tablespoons sugar
1 teaspoon vanilla extract

Combine cottage cheese, egg substitute, sugar, and vanilla, stirring well.
Yield: about 2 cups.

# Brunches & Lunches

## VEGETABLE SALAD WITH HORSERADISH DRESSING

2 quarts water
1 teaspoon salt
1 pound potatoes, peeled and cubed
3 medium carrots, scraped and cubed
1 (10-ounce) package frozen green peas
¼ cup egg substitute
1 tablespoon lemon juice
2 teaspoons Dijon mustard
1 to 2 teaspoons prepared horseradish
½ teaspoon salt
¼ teaspoon white pepper
3 tablespoons vegetable oil
2 tablespoons olive oil
¼ cup sour cream
1 (16-ounce) can sliced beets, well drained and cubed

Bring water and 1 teaspoon salt to a boil in a large saucepan. Add potatoes, and cook 5 minutes or just until tender. Remove with a slotted spoon, reserving boiling water; rinse in cold water, and drain. Set aside.

Add carrots to boiling water, and cook 4 minutes or just until tender. Remove with a slotted spoon, reserving boiling water; rinse in cold water, and drain. Set aside.

Add peas to boiling water, and cook 1 to 2 minutes or just until tender. Drain, rinse in cold water, and drain again. Set aside.

Combine potatoes, carrots, and peas in a large bowl; chill. Combine egg substitute, lemon juice, mustard, horseradish, salt, and pepper in container of an electric blender; process 1 minute. Remove plastic cap of blender lid. With blender running, pour oils in a slow, steady stream through opening in lid. Add sour cream, and process 10 seconds; chill.

To serve, stir beets into vegetable mixture, and serve with dressing mixture. Yield: 6 to 8 servings.

## CHARLOTTE RUSSE WITH STRAWBERRY SAUCE

2 envelopes unflavored gelatin
¼ cup cold water
⅔ cup sugar
4 egg yolks
1⅓ cups milk
1 teaspoon vanilla extract
½ cup sour cream
⅓ cup chopped almonds, toasted
1 cup whipping cream, whipped
16 ladyfingers, split
Strawberry Sauce
Garnish: fresh raspberries

Sprinkle gelatin over cold water; let stand 1 minute. Set aside.

Combine sugar and egg yolks in a heavy saucepan; beat at medium speed with an electric mixer until thick and pale. Add milk, and cook over medium heat, stirring constantly, until thermometer reaches 160° (about 5 minutes). Add reserved gelatin mixture, stirring until gelatin dissolves. Stir in vanilla, sour cream, and almonds; cool mixture slightly. Fold in whipped cream.

Line a 2-quart mold with 20- x 2-inch strips of wax paper, slightly overlapping. Line sides and bottom of mold with ladyfingers. Spoon cream mixture over ladyfingers. Arrange remaining ladyfingers over cream mixture. Chill at least 8 hours. Invert mold, and remove dessert. Carefully peel off wax paper. Serve with Strawberry Sauce, and garnish, if desired. Yield: 8 to 10 servings.

### Strawberry Sauce

1 pint fresh strawberries
1 tablespoon lemon juice
½ cup sugar
2 tablespoons framboise or other raspberry brandy *

Wash and hull strawberries. Put in container of an electric blender, and process until smooth. Add lemon juice

and remaining ingredients, and blend until smooth. Yield: 1⅓ cups.

* Black raspberry schnapps may be substituted for framboise.

# The Local Word On Brunch

If you ask a local where to have brunch in New Orleans, you better have time to chat, because that's one of the locals' favorite topics.

It all started at a breakfast restaurant called Madame Bégué's, where merchants and tradesmen who had been working since before dawn sought a big midmorning meal. The idea caught on for others, who had time for an early breakfast but preferred the leisurely hour instead, and brunch has evolved into a grand event. Today, there are plenty of places to choose from for weekend brunch and a few that serve brunch daily, so we asked the locals for their suggestions. Their favorites include Commander's Palace, Kabby's in the New Orleans Hilton Riverside and Towers, Petunia's, The Grill Room at the Windsor Court Hotel, Andrea's, Mr. B's, The Pelican Club, and the Blue Room in the Fairmont Hotel.

Nearly 20 years ago the famous Brennan clan turned brunch into a celebration at Commander's Palace, and most locals still name it as their number one choice.

If your appetite is whetted for brunch and you can't wait to get to New Orleans, we've given you the recipes for Commander's specialties—Eggs Creole and Creole Bread Pudding Soufflé. To satisfy your cravings, try them at home. If you order the soufflé at Commander's, it's topped with a thin, baked meringue not included in the recipe from the restaurant's cookbook. Both versions are spectacular.

The city's hotels are known for their lavish brunch buffets, and Kabby's in the New Orleans Hilton Riverside and Towers is a favorite of many. The restaurant is situated right on the Mississippi River, and affords diners a great view.

Looking for the out of the ordinary? Try Petunias for a casual, inexpensive brunch. Petunias is known for its dessert crêpes, and Hot Apples and Rum Flambé. You can make these giant treats in your own kitchen with the recipe the restaurant shared with us.

Locals enjoy The Pelican Club for its nontraditional, eclectic menu. The Banana Walnut French Toast, which includes champagne, a choice of appetizer, a basket of homemade goodies, and coffee or tea, is popular.

Another favorite is The Grill Room at the Windsor Court Hotel. You'll love the recipe for Black Bean Pancakes With Gazpacho Butter that Chef Kevin Graham shares. Graham often serves it alongside grilled pork loin.

Other brunch spots are popular for various reasons. Some try a different twist and go Italian at Andrea's in nearby Metairie. Mr. B's is a popular spot run by brother and sister Ralph and Cindy Brennan, and it is pegged as a favorite by New Orleanians. Several locals recommend Grillades and Grits, while others suggest Crabcakes and Eggs. For the best view of the city, head to Le Jardin on the 11th floor of The Westin Canal Place. Enjoy a panoramic view with a jazz brunch.

If it's atmosphere you want, Court of Two Sisters is the place to go. The Blue Room in the venerable Fairmont Hotel is a delicious trip down memory lane for many. Once a nationally noted club showcasing entertainers such as Bob Hope and the Dorsey Brothers, it's now a historical setting for a Sunday jazz brunch.

## BLACK BEAN PANCAKES WITH GAZPACHO BUTTER

1 cup dried black beans
3 cups chicken broth
1 large onion, chopped
1 sweet red pepper, chopped
3 jalapeño peppers, seeded and chopped
3 cloves garlic, minced
1 tablespoon chopped fresh cilantro
1 tablespoon ground cumin
3 tablespoons butter or margarine, melted
2 cups port or other sweet red wine
¼ teaspoon salt
⅛ teaspoon pepper
1½ cups all-purpose flour
1¾ teaspoons baking powder
1 teaspoon salt
3 tablespoons sugar
1 large egg, beaten
3 tablespoons butter or margarine, melted
Gazpacho Butter

Sort and wash beans; place in a Dutch oven. Add chicken broth; cover and soak 8 hours.

Cook onion and next 5 ingredients in 3 tablespoons butter over medium-high heat, stirring constantly, until tender. Add to bean mixture. Stir in port, ¼ teaspoon salt, and pepper; bring to a boil. Cover, reduce heat, and simmer 1 hour or until beans are tender. Drain, reserving 1¼ cups liquid; cool. Puree 1¾ cups bean mixture in an electric blender, reserving remainder for other uses. Set reserved liquid and bean puree aside.

Combine flour, baking powder, 1 teaspoon salt, and sugar in a bowl. Combine egg, 3 tablespoons butter, and 1¼ cups reserved bean liquid; add to dry ingredients, stirring just until moistened. Stir in bean puree.

For each pancake, pour ¼ cup batter onto a hot, lightly greased griddle. Turn when edges look cooked. Serve immediately with Gazpacho Butter. Yield: 8 (4-inch) pancakes.

## Gazpacho Butter

½ cup butter, softened
1 tablespoon tomato puree
½ cup finely chopped sweet red pepper
½ cup finely chopped sweet yellow pepper
2 tablespoons finely chopped cucumber

Combine all ingredients in a small bowl. Yield: 1½ cups.

## EGGS CREOLE

3¾ cups water
¾ cup regular grits, uncooked
1 cup diced hot smoked sausage
¼ cup (1 ounce) shredded Cheddar cheese
2 tablespoons butter or margarine
¼ teaspoon salt
¼ cup all-purpose flour
1 large egg, beaten
1 tablespoon milk
¾ cup Italian-seasoned breadcrumbs
Vegetable oil
Poached Eggs
Creole Sauce

Bring water to a boil in a large saucepan; gradually stir in grits, and return to a boil. Cover, reduce heat, and simmer, stirring occasionally, 10 minutes or until done. Remove from heat, and stir in sausage and next 3 ingredients. Spoon mixture into a lightly greased 13- x 9- x 2-inch pan, pressing firmly and smoothing surface. Cover and chill 24 hours.

Turn grits out onto wax paper. Cut out 12 (2½-inch) rounds with a biscuit cutter, reserving remaining grits for other uses. Sprinkle rounds with flour. Combine egg and milk; dip rounds into egg mixture, and dredge in breadcrumbs.

Pour oil to depth of 1 inch into a large, heavy skillet. Fry grits rounds in hot oil over medium-high heat 1 to 2 minutes on each side or until lightly browned. Drain rounds on paper towels. Place 2 rounds on each plate; top each with a poached egg and Creole Sauce. Serve immediately. Yield: 6 servings.

### Poached Eggs

12  large eggs

Lightly grease a large saucepan; add water to depth of 2 inches. Bring water to a boil; reduce heat and maintain at a light simmer. Break eggs, one at a time, into a saucer; slip eggs, one at a time, into water, holding saucer close to surface of water. Simmer 5 minutes or until cooked. Remove eggs with a slotted spoon; trim edges, if desired. Yield: 12 eggs.

### Creole Sauce

1  medium onion, cut into thin strips
1  medium-size green pepper, cut into thin strips
2  stalks celery, cut into thin strips
2  cloves garlic, sliced
1  bay leaf
2  tablespoons butter or margarine, melted
2  teaspoons paprika
2  medium tomatoes, diced
1  cup tomato juice
1½ tablespoons Worcestershire sauce
1 to 1½ tablespoons hot sauce
1½ tablespoons cornstarch
½  cup water

Cook onion, green pepper, celery, garlic, and bay leaf in butter in a large skillet over medium-high heat, stirring constantly, until crisp-tender. Stir in paprika, tomato, tomato juice, Worcestershire sauce, and hot sauce; simmer 5 minutes or until mixture is reduced by one-fourth.

Combine cornstarch and water. Stir into sauce, and return to a boil, stirring constantly. Boil, stirring constantly, 1 minute. Remove from heat. Remove and discard bay leaf. Serve warm. Yield: 3¾ cups.

### CREOLE BREAD PUDDING SOUFFLÉ

½  cup butter or margarine, softened
1  cup sugar
5  large eggs
2  cups whipping cream
1  tablespoon vanilla extract
⅛  teaspoon ground cinnamon
¼  cup raisins
12  (1-inch-thick) slices French bread
1  tablespoon butter or margarine
1½ tablespoons sugar
6  large eggs, separated
½  cup sugar
½  cup sifted powdered sugar
Whiskey Sauce

Beat ½ cup butter at medium speed with an electric mixer; gradually add 1 cup sugar, beating well. Add eggs, one at a time, beating after each addition. Gradually add cream, mixing well. Stir in vanilla, cinnamon, and raisins. Pour mixture into a lightly greased 13- x 9- x 2-inch pan.

Arrange bread slices in pan over cream mixture; let stand 10 minutes. Turn slices over; let stand 10 minutes. Cover pan with aluminum foil, and place in a larger shallow pan. Pour hot water to depth of 1 inch into larger pan. Bake at 350° for 40 minutes. Remove aluminum foil, and bake an additional 10 minutes.

Place 2½ cups baked bread mixture in a large bowl; set aside. Reserve remainder for other uses. (For a quick dessert, reheat remainder and serve with leftover Whiskey Sauce.)

Grease a 1½-quart soufflé dish with 1 tablespoon butter; coat bottom and sides of dish with 1½ tablespoons sugar, and set aside.

Combine egg yolks and ½ cup sugar in top of a double boiler; place over simmering water, and beat at high speed with an electric mixer about 4 minutes or until mixture thickens. Add yolk mixture to bread mixture in bowl, and beat at medium speed until smooth. Set aside.

Beat egg whites at high speed with an electric mixer until foamy. Gradually add powdered sugar, beating until stiff peaks form; fold into bread mixture. Pour into prepared soufflé dish. Bake at 375° for 40 minutes; serve with Whiskey Sauce. Yield: 6 to 8 servings.

### Whiskey Sauce

1  cup sugar
1  cup whipping cream
⅛  teaspoon ground cinnamon
1  tablespoon butter or margarine
1½ teaspoons cornstarch
¼  cup water
1  tablespoon bourbon

Combine first 4 ingredients in a heavy saucepan. Cook over medium heat until sugar dissolves, stirring often. Combine cornstarch and water; stir into cream mixture, and bring to a boil, stirring constantly. Boil, stirring constantly, 1 minute. Remove from heat, and stir in bourbon. Serve warm. Yield: 1⅔ cups.

## HOT APPLES AND RUM FLAMBÉ

½ cup butter or margarine
¼ cup sugar
¼ cup firmly packed brown sugar
1½ teaspoons vanilla extract
4 large Granny Smith apples, cored and sliced
¾ teaspoon ground ginger
¾ teaspoon ground cinnamon
¼ teaspoon ground nutmeg
¼ cup light rum
Crêpes
Whipped cream (optional)

Combine first 4 ingredients in a large saucepan; cook over medium heat until sugar dissolves, stirring occasionally. Add apple, ginger, cinnamon, nutmeg, and rum; cover, reduce heat, and simmer 30 minutes or until apple is tender.

Spoon warm mixture onto spotty side of each crêpe. Fold crêpes in half, and top with additional apple mixture. Serve with whipped cream, if desired. Yield: 6 servings.

### Crêpes

¾ cup all-purpose flour
¼ cup sugar
Pinch of salt
¾ cup milk
¼ cup water
2 tablespoons orange juice
2 large eggs
2 tablespoons vegetable oil
Melted butter

Combine first 6 ingredients, beating mixture until smooth. Add eggs, and beat well; stir in oil. Refrigerate batter at least 2 hours.

Brush bottom of a 12-inch crêpe pan or heavy skillet with melted butter; place over medium heat until just hot, not smoking. Pour ⅓ cup batter into pan, quickly tilting pan in all directions so batter covers pan in a thin film. Cook 1 minute or until crêpe can be shaken loose from pan. Flip crêpe, and cook about 30 seconds.

Place crêpes on a towel to cool. Stack between layers of wax paper to prevent sticking. Repeat until all batter is used. Yield: 6 (12-inch) crêpes.

**Note:** You may freeze crêpes, if desired. To serve, thaw at room temperature; fill as directed.

# Only In New Orleans

Anywhere you go in New Orleans, cooks are quick to serve you a plate loaded with tradition. Centuries-old recipes still thrive in the Crescent City and you'll want to try them all. If you've never eaten your way through New Orleans, then start with these old favorites on your first trip. Chances are you'll be back to enjoy them again. After all, there is a reason these time-tested dishes are still around—they're still great.

## Beignets *(ben-YAYS)*

The best way to describe *beignets* is "little puffed rectangular doughnuts without holes," and the best place to eat them, as it has been since the 1860s, is Café Du Monde.

Just remember three rules for eating the powdered sugar-laden treats: *don't* wear black, *don't* laugh while taking a bite, and *do* have fun. If you can't go to New Orleans for beignets, make your own from scratch with Emily Robinson's recipe. She and her mother created it years ago in their Baton Rouge, Louisiana, kitchen because they couldn't hop down to New Orleans every time they craved the doughnuts.

## FRENCH MARKET BEIGNETS

1 package dry yeast
2 tablespoons warm water (105° to 115°)
1 cup milk
¼ cup sugar
1 teaspoon salt
¼ teaspoon ground nutmeg
1 large egg, beaten
2 tablespoons vegetable oil
3 to 3½ cups all-purpose flour, divided
Vegetable oil
Sifted powdered sugar

Dissolve yeast in warm water in a large mixing bowl; let stand 5 minutes. Heat milk; add ¼ cup sugar, 1 teaspoon salt, and ¼ teaspoon ground nutmeg, and stir until sugar dissolves. Cool milk mixture to 105° to 115°, and add to yeast mixture. Add egg, 2 tablespoons oil, and 1 cup flour; beat at medium speed with an electric mixer until smooth. Stir in enough remaining flour to make a soft dough.

Place dough in a well-greased bowl, turning to grease top. Cover and let dough rise in a warm place (85°), free from drafts, about 1 hour or until doubled in bulk.

Punch dough down; turn out onto a lightly floured surface, and knead 4 or 5 times. Roll dough to an 18- x 12-inch rectangle; cut into 32 3- x 2-inch rectangles. Place on a floured surface; cover and let rise in a warm place (85°), free from drafts, 30 minutes or until doubled in bulk.

Pour oil to depth of 3 inches into a Dutch oven; heat to 375°. Fry 4 or 5 beignets at a time in hot oil about 1 minute on each side or until golden brown. Drain well on paper towels; sprinkle with powdered sugar. Serve warm. Yield: 32 beignets.

# Brunches & Lunches

## Calas (call-AYS or call-AHS)

A close cousin to beignets, *calas* are fried rice cakes, named from an African word for rice. Nineteenth-century black women headed through the city streets early in the morning carrying covered bowls of hot calas on their heads shouting, "Belles calas tout chaud!" (roughly translated as "beautiful calas, piping hot").

The traditional version uses yeast, but our recipe saves time with biscuit mix. When you're in New Orleans, drop by The Coffee Pot at 714 St. Peter Street, and sample their version.

### EASY CALAS

2 cups cooked rice
2 cups biscuit mix
2 tablespoons sugar
1 teaspoon ground cinnamon
½ teaspoon ground nutmeg
2 large eggs
½ cup evaporated milk
1 teaspoon vanilla extract
Vegetable oil
1 cup sifted powdered sugar
½ teaspoon vanilla extract
1 to 2 tablespoons water

Combine rice, biscuit mix, sugar, cinnamon, and nutmeg in a large bowl. Combine eggs, milk, and 1 teaspoon vanilla; add to dry ingredients, stirring well. Chill dough 1 hour.

Pour oil to depth of 2 inches into a Dutch oven; heat to 400°. Carefully drop batter by tablespoonfuls into hot oil. Fry a few at a time, turning once, 3 to 5 minutes or until golden brown. Drain well on paper towels.

Combine powdered sugar, ½ teaspoon vanilla, and water, stirring to desired consistency; drizzle glaze over hot calas. Serve warm. Yield: about 4 dozen.  *Joyce Markwood*
*China, Texas*

## À la Carte

To sample all the wonderful food New Orleans has to offer, or even just a portion of it, you'll have to stay awhile. Plenty of restaurants are within walking distance of the French Quarter, and the exercise is a must to make room for the next delectable, fattening meal.

After *beignets* at Café Du Monde, stroll through the French Market on Decatur Street, then head down the street to Central Grocery for lunch, and have a *muffuletta.*

Italians invented the 10-inch round sandwich at the turn of the century in this tiny grocery store, and it is still served there today. You can order the loaf filled with salami, ham, cheese, garlic, and olive salad (the key ingredient) to go, or grab a stool at the counter in the back. The Napoleon House at 500 Chartres is another historic place to enjoy a muffuletta.

If you'd like a hot lunch instead, check local menus for *red beans and rice.* You'll find it any day of the week, but especially on Mondays. Again, it goes back to tradition. Monday used to be wash day in New Orleans, leaving little time for cooking the evening meal. But if you simmered Sunday's leftover ham bone with some beans all day, dinner was ready when the laundry was done. Jazz great Louis Armstrong was so fond of the dish, he signed his autographs "Red beans and ricely yours."

For a light dessert, try a *praline* (PRAW-leen), a candy highlighting Louisiana pecans. Watching the preparation is as much fun as eating the confection at Aunt Sally's in the French Market, or at the New Orleans School of Cooking and The Louisiana General Store in nearby Jax Brewery.

If you'd rather drink your dessert than eat it, *café brûlot* (kaf-AY broo-LO) is for you. The typical New Orleans coffee is laced with brandy, rum, cinnamon, cloves, lemon and orange rind, and often dramatically flamed at the table for a spectacular presentation. Brûlot means "burnt brandy" in French.

New Orleans jazz musician Al Hirt calls it a "Creole tea ceremony with a kick." The beverage is so revered that it's often served from a brûlot set—a special bowl and ladle for serving and tall, narrow cups for sipping. A brûlot set is a popular wedding gift in the city. (A chafing dish and demitasse cups are good substitutes if you don't have access to a brûlot set.)

# Wild About Quail

Bee Fitzpatrick loves quail hunting in the fall with her husband, Michael, and knows that she'll reap the benefits even months later. With a good supply of game in the freezer, she looks forward to some easy but delicious meals, especially in the spring when she'd rather be outside with family and friends than in the kitchen.

Michael grills the birds, while Bee and the girls set a table in their Garden District courtyard. She calls a few close friends to join them for brunch but doesn't fight the clock to finish the food before they arrive.

### WILD GAME BRUNCH FOR EIGHT

**Grilled Quail**
**Wild Rice-Green Apple Salad**
**Carrot-Sweet Potato Puree**
**Steamed fresh asparagus**

### GRILLED QUAIL

16 quail, dressed
16 jalapeño peppers
16 slices bacon
1 (8-ounce) bottle Italian salad
  dressing
½ cup Chablis or other dry white
  wine
⅓ cup soy sauce
¼ cup lemon juice
¼ teaspoon pepper
Garnish: banana peppers

Rinse quail thoroughly with cold water; pat dry. Place a jalapeño pepper into body cavity of each quail. Wrap 1 bacon slice around each quail, and secure with a wooden pick. Place quail in a large shallow dish.

Combine Italian dressing and next 4 ingredients; pour over quail. Cover and marinate in refrigerator 8 hours. Remove quail from dish, reserving marinade.

Prepare charcoal fire in one end of grill; let burn 15 to 20 minutes or until flames disappear and coals are white. Grill quail, covered, on opposite end 1 hour, turning once, and basting often with marinade. Garnish, if desired. Yield: 8 servings.

**Note:** You may bake quail on rack of a roasting pan in the oven at 350° for 1 hour, turning once, and basting often with marinade.

### WILD RICE-GREEN APPLE SALAD

2 cups wild rice, uncooked
2 cups chicken broth
4 cups water
1 teaspoon salt
2 cups golden raisins
⅓ cup sherry
1 tablespoon grated orange rind
½ cup orange juice
½ cup commercial Caesar salad
  dressing
¼ teaspoon pepper
2 Granny Smith apples, chopped
1 bunch green onions, sliced
1 cup sunflower kernels

Wash wild rice in 3 changes of hot water; drain. Combine wild rice and next 3 ingredients in a saucepan; bring mixture to a boil. Cover, reduce heat, and simmer 50 to 60 minutes or until rice is tender; drain, if necessary, and set mixture aside.

Combine raisins and sherry; set aside. Combine orange rind and next 3 ingredients; set aside.

Combine rice, reserved raisin mixture, apple, green onions, and sunflower kernels. Add orange rind mixture; toss gently. Cover and chill at least 8 hours. Stir before serving. Yield: 8 to 10 servings.

### CARROT-SWEET POTATO PUREE

½ cup sour cream
½ cup whipping cream
4 pounds sweet potatoes
2 pounds carrots, scraped and
  sliced
½ teaspoon salt
⅓ cup sugar
2 tablespoons butter or margarine
¼ teaspoon salt
¼ teaspoon freshly grated nutmeg
⅛ teaspoon black pepper
⅛ teaspoon red pepper
½ cup butter or margarine

Combine sour cream and whipping cream. Cover and chill 8 hours.

Wash sweet potatoes; then bake at 375° for 1 hour or until done. Let potatoes cool to touch; peel and mash. Set aside.

Combine carrots, ½ teaspoon salt, sugar, 2 tablespoons butter, and water to cover in a heavy saucepan. Bring to a boil; cover, reduce heat, and simmer 15 minutes or until carrots are tender. Drain well, and set carrots aside.

Position knife blade in food processor bowl. Add half each of carrots and sweet potatoes; process until smooth. Remove to a large bowl. Process remaining carrots and potatoes, ¼ teaspoon salt, seasonings, and ½ cup butter until smooth. Add to carrot and potato mixture in bowl, and stir in sour cream mixture.

Spoon into a lightly greased 3-quart shallow baking dish, reserving 2 cups mixture for piping decoration on top, if desired. Bake at 350° for 25 to 30 minutes. Yield: 8 to 10 servings.

**Note:** You may freeze this recipe prior to baking. To serve, thaw overnight in the refrigerator, and then bake as directed.

## All Dazzle, No Frazzle

Caught up in the party spirit, but also caught in a rush putting a party together? Not Dee Lynott. Brunch is supposed to be a relaxing meal, and she sees that it is—for both her guests *and* herself.

Dee prepares the entire menu a day ahead and chills it until serving time. The only last-minute detail is heating her Easy Cheesy Brunch Casserole; the other dishes are all served cold.

### MAKE-AHEAD BRUNCH FOR FOUR

Shrimp Butter
Easy Cheesy
Brunch Casserole
Marinated Vegetable Salad
Commercial French bread
Raspberry Pudding
Commercial cookies

### SHRIMP BUTTER

2½ cups water
¾ pound unpeeled medium-size fresh shrimp
1 hard-cooked egg, coarsely chopped
1 (3-ounce) package cream cheese, softened
½ cup butter, softened
¼ cup coarsely chopped onion
¼ cup mayonnaise
1 clove garlic
⅛ teaspoon salt
⅛ teaspoon pepper
⅛ teaspoon Worcestershire sauce

Bring water to a boil; add shrimp, and cook 3 to 5 minutes. Drain well; rinse with cold water. Chill. Peel, devein, and coarsely chop shrimp.

Position knife blade in food processor bowl; add shrimp and remaining ingredients. Process until smooth.

Line a 2-cup mold or bowl with heavy-duty plastic wrap, allowing wrap to hang over rim at least 2 inches. Spoon butter mixture into mold; cover and chill at least 4 hours. Invert mold onto serving plate. Remove mold, and carefully peel plastic wrap off butter mixture. Let stand 20 to 30 minutes. Smooth surface with a knife, if necessary. Serve with assorted crackers. Yield: 1⅔ cups.

### EASY CHEESY BRUNCH CASSEROLE

4 slices white sandwich bread
1 medium onion, chopped
1 cup sliced fresh mushrooms
2 tablespoons butter or margarine, melted
1 cup chopped cooked ham
1 cup (4 ounces) shredded Cheddar cheese
1 cup (4 ounces) shredded Swiss cheese
1 tablespoon all-purpose flour
1¼ cups milk
4 large eggs, beaten
1 tablespoon prepared mustard
½ teaspoon garlic salt
Garnish: parsley sprigs

Place bread slices in bottom of a lightly greased 8-inch square baking dish; set aside.

Sauté onion and mushrooms in butter until tender; spoon evenly over bread. Top with ham. Combine cheeses and flour; sprinkle over ham.

Combine milk and next 3 ingredients; pour over cheese. Cover and chill 8 hours. Remove from refrigerator, and let stand at room temperature 30 minutes. Bake at 375° for 35 minutes or until set. Let stand 10 minutes before serving. Garnish, if desired. Yield: 4 to 6 servings.

### MARINATED VEGETABLE SALAD

2 stalks celery
2 large carrots, scraped
⅛ pound fresh green beans
1 green pepper
1 small head cauliflower, cut into flowerets
Wine Vinegar Dressing
5 green onions, cut into 1-inch pieces
1 (8¾-ounce) can garbanzo beans
½ cup pitted ripe olives
Romaine lettuce

Cut celery and carrots into 1-inch diagonal slices; place in a Dutch oven. Trim ends of green beans and remove strings; cut into 1-inch diagonal pieces and add to Dutch oven. Cut green pepper into 1-inch square pieces; add pepper and cauliflower flowerets to Dutch oven.

Add Wine Vinegar Dressing to Dutch oven, and bring to a boil. Cover, reduce heat, and simmer 5 to 6 minutes. Add green onions, drained garbanzo beans, and olives, and simmer 3 minutes. Remove from heat; transfer mixture to a bowl. Cover and chill at least 8 hours. Serve in a lettuce-lined bowl with a slotted spoon. Yield: 6 to 8 servings.

#### Wine Vinegar Dressing

¾ cup white wine vinegar
¾ cup water
¼ cup vegetable oil
¼ cup chopped fresh parsley
2 cloves garlic, minced
1 tablespoon sugar
1 teaspoon dried oregano
½ teaspoon dried basil
½ teaspoon salt
⅛ teaspoon pepper

Combine all ingredients in a jar. Cover tightly; shake vigorously before tossing with vegetables. Yield: 2 cups.

## RASPBERRY PUDDING

2 (10-ounce) packages frozen
  raspberries, thawed
¼ cup sugar
3 tablespoons cornstarch
Sugar (optional)
Whipping cream

Mash raspberries in a saucepan. Stir in ¼ cup sugar and cornstarch; cook over medium heat, stirring constantly, until mixture is thickened and bubbly. Remove mixture from heat; cool. Cover and chill at least 2 hours.

Spoon pudding into 4 individual stemmed glasses or dessert bowls; sprinkle lightly with additional sugar, if desired. Serve with whipping cream. Yield: 4 servings.

## Kitchen Helpers

■ When cooking for a crowd, make the most of your kitchen appliances. Plan your menu so that you can utilize several cooking appliances, rather than just your oven. Don't forget to use the cook top, microwave oven, electric skillet, and toaster oven, as well as smaller bread warmers.
■ The key to the best tasting coffee is buying fresh coffee beans and grinding them just before brewing. Use cold water and clean equipment for best results. To keep beans fresh, store tightly covered in the freezer.
■ It's easy to determine the amount of coffee needed. When making it for your next party, allow 1 pound of coffee and 2 gallons of water for 40 servings.

# Here's To Old Times

It seems like a typical Sunday morning in the French Quarter home of Julie and Cliff Collins. Today is one of those fun Sundays when the Collinses invite their friends over to relax and celebrate life in New Orleans.

When it comes to her menu, she likes tradition. She's fascinated by the city's history and its food, so tried-and-true recipes from old friends grace her table. Turtle Soup, Eggs Sardou, and bread pudding have long been favorites in New Orleans.

### TRADITIONAL NEW ORLEANS BRUNCH FOR EIGHT

Orange juice
Turtle Soup
Mint-Gin Fruit Salad
Eggs Sardou
Bread Pudding
With Whiskey Sauce

## TURTLE SOUP

¼ cup butter or margarine, melted
1 pound ground turtle meat
⅓ pound ground veal
1¼ cups diced onion
1 cup diced celery
3 cloves garlic, minced
1½ teaspoons ground cumin
1 teaspoon dried oregano
½ teaspoon dried thyme
½ teaspoon salt
½ teaspoon pepper
3 bay leaves
1 (16-ounce) can tomato puree
4 cups beef broth
1 cup butter or margarine
¾ cup all-purpose flour
Dry sherry
Hard-cooked eggs, chopped

Combine first 3 ingredients in a Dutch oven; cook over medium heat until meat is browned, stirring until it crumbles. Add onion and next 8 ingredients; cook until vegetables are tender, stirring often. Stir in tomato puree; cook 10 minutes.

Add beef broth, and bring to a boil; reduce heat and simmer, uncovered, 1 hour. Remove and discard bay leaves. Remove soup from heat, and set aside.

Melt 1 cup butter in a Dutch oven over medium heat. Add flour; cook, stirring constantly, until mixture is chocolate-colored (about 25 minutes). Add turtle mixture; cook until thickened, stirring often. Serve dry sherry and chopped hard-cooked egg as condiments. Yield: about 8 cups.

## MINT-GIN FRUIT SALAD

2 cups diced fresh pineapple
2 cups diced cantaloupe
2 cups diced honeydew melon
2 cups diced, seeded
  watermelon
1 pint fresh strawberries,
  sliced
1 cup seedless red grapes
1 cup seedless green grapes
3 kiwifruit, sliced
1 cup gin
Fresh mint leaves

Combine fruits and gin in a large bowl; toss gently. Chill mixture at least 2 hours. Add mint to salad mixture. Yield: 8 servings.

# Brunches & Lunches

## EGGS SARDOU

¼ cup chopped green onions
1½ tablespoons butter or
  margarine, melted
3 (10-ounce) packages frozen
  chopped spinach, thawed and
  well drained
1 (16-ounce) carton sour cream
½ cup whipping cream
½ cup grated Parmesan cheese
½ teaspoon ground nutmeg
¼ teaspoon salt
⅛ teaspoon pepper
3 (14-ounce) cans artichoke
  bottoms, drained
Poached Eggs
Hollandaise Sauce
Paprika

Sauté green onions in butter in a Dutch oven until tender; stir in spinach and next 6 ingredients. Cook over low heat until thoroughly heated (do not boil).

Place 16 artichoke bottoms on baking sheets, reserving any extra for other uses. Bake at 350° for 10 minutes or until artichoke bottoms are heated; keep warm.

For each serving, spoon 2 tablespoons spinach mixture onto a warm dinner plate; top with 2 artichoke bottoms. Arrange a poached egg on each artichoke bottom. Spoon 3 tablespoons Hollandaise Sauce over eggs. Sprinkle with paprika. Serve immediately. Yield: 8 servings.

### Poached Eggs

16 large eggs

Lightly grease a large saucepan; add water to a depth of 2 inches. Bring to a boil; reduce heat and maintain at a light simmer. Break eggs, one at a time, into a saucer; slip eggs, one at a time, into water, holding saucer close to water. Simmer 5 minutes or until cooked. Remove eggs with a slotted spoon; trim edges of eggs, if desired.

Repeat procedure with remaining eggs. Yield: 16 eggs.

### Hollandaise Sauce

6 egg yolks
¼ teaspoon salt
⅛ teaspoon red pepper
¼ cup lemon juice
1 cup butter or margarine, divided

Beat first 3 ingredients in top of a double boiler; gradually add lemon juice, stirring constantly. Add about one-third of butter to egg mixture; cook over hot (not boiling) water, stirring constantly until butter melts.

Add another third of butter, stirring constantly. As sauce thickens, stir in remaining butter. Cook until temperature reaches 160°. Remove from double boiler, and serve immediately. Yield: 1⅔ cups.

## BREAD PUDDING WITH WHISKEY SAUCE

1 (16-ounce) loaf French bread
3 cups milk
1 cup cream sherry
3 large eggs, beaten
2 cups sugar
2 tablespoons butter, melted
2 tablespoons vanilla extract
1 cup raisins
2 tablespoons butter or margarine, melted
½ cup honey
Whiskey Sauce

Break bread into small chunks, and place in a large bowl. Add milk and sherry; soak 10 minutes. Stir until thoroughly mixed. Combine eggs, sugar, 2 tablespoons butter, and vanilla; add to bread mixture, stirring well. Stir in raisins. Spoon mixture into a lightly greased 12- x 8- x 2-inch baking dish. Combine 2 tablespoons

butter and honey; pour over pudding. Bake at 350° for 45 minutes or until set. Serve with Whiskey Sauce. Yield: 10 to 12 servings.

### Whiskey Sauce

½ cup butter
1 cup milk
1 cup sugar
2 tablespoons cornstarch
¼ cup cold water
¾ cup bourbon

Combine butter, milk, and sugar in a heavy saucepan, and cook over low heat until butter melts and sugar dissolves. Combine cornstarch and water, stirring well; add to butter mixture. Add bourbon, and bring mixture to a boil over medium heat; cook 1 minute. Yield: 2¾ cups.

### Secret's in the Roux

A New Orleans cook's favorite culinary advice may be, "First, you make a roux."

That doesn't tell you much unless you're a native, but roux is just flour cooked in fat used to thicken gumbos and soups.

The color, texture, and flavor of a roux is determined by the length of time the mixture is cooked. As you stir the fat (often oil) and flour constantly over medium to medium-high heat, the fat browns the flour to a rich caramel or chocolate-brown color. There are three classic roux—white, blond, and brown.

# Down-Home Classic Desserts

In our Test Kitchens, we tested some treasured family desserts. In keeping with today's goals of healthful eating, we trimmed fat, cholesterol, and calories from these Southern recipes, and did so without sacrificing flavor.

To keep saturated fat to a minimum, the pastry shell for Buttermilk Pie is prepared with corn oil margarine instead of shortening. The dough is shaped into a ball and chilled before rolling out; chilling makes the dough easier to handle and keeps the crust from becoming soggy. Light process cream cheese product, nonfat buttermilk, and egg substitute are used in place of their fat- and cholesterol-laden counterparts to keep total fat to only 9 grams per serving.

Gelatin and egg substitute thicken Fresh Strawberry Ice Milk, and a combination of skim milk and evaporated skimmed milk gives it a creaminess similar to the ice cream of years gone by. Allow it to stand packed in ice and rock salt about an hour before serving.

Old-fashioned Banana Pudding uses fat-free sour cream to make a rich pudding. A golden meringue tops layers of vanilla wafers, bananas, and pudding.

## POUND CAKE
### (pictured on page 76)

Vegetable cooking spray
½ cup corn oil margarine, softened
⅔ cup sugar
⅓ cup egg substitute
2½ cups sifted cake flour
½ teaspoon baking powder
¼ teaspoon baking soda
¼ teaspoon salt
1 (8-ounce) carton low-fat vanilla yogurt
1 tablespoon vanilla extract
¾ teaspoon almond extract

Coat the bottom of a 9- x 5- x 3-inch loafpan with cooking spray; dust with flour, and set aside.

Beat margarine at medium speed with an electric mixer until fluffy. Gradually add sugar; beat well. Add egg substitute; beat until blended.

Combine flour, baking powder, baking soda, and salt; add to creamed mixture alternately with yogurt, beginning and ending with flour mixture. Mix just until blended after each addition. Stir in flavorings.

Spoon batter into prepared pan. Bake at 350° for 1 hour and 5 minutes or until a wooden pick inserted in center comes out clean. Cool in pan on a wire rack 10 minutes; remove from pan, and let cool on wire rack. Serve with ½ cup chopped or sliced fruit. Yield: 18 servings (136 calories per ½-inch slice).

□ *2.2 grams protein, 5.4 grams fat, 19.1 grams carbohydrate, 1 milligram cholesterol, 128 milligrams sodium, and 36 milligrams calcium.*

*Mrs. Abner Belcher*
*Americus, Georgia*

## FRESH STRAWBERRY ICE MILK
### (pictured on page 76)

4 cups fresh strawberries
1½ cups sugar, divided
3 cups skim milk
2 envelopes unflavored gelatin
½ cup egg substitute
2 (12-ounce) cans evaporated skimmed milk
1½ tablespoons vanilla extract
3 drops of red food coloring
Garnish: 16 whole fresh strawberries

Place strawberries in container of an electric blender or food processor, and process just until chopped. Sprinkle strawberries with ½ cup sugar, and set aside.

Combine remaining 1 cup sugar and skim milk in a saucepan; sprinkle gelatin over mixture, and let stand 1 minute. Cook mixture over medium heat, stirring constantly, until sugar and gelatin dissolve. Gradually stir in egg substitute; cook mixture 1 minute. Remove from heat; chill. Stir in strawberries, evaporated skimmed milk, vanilla, and food coloring. Pour into container of a 1-gallon hand-turned or electric freezer. Freeze according to manufacturer's instructions. Pack ice milk with additional ice and rock salt; let stand 1 hour before serving (ice milk will be soft). Garnish, if desired. Yield: 16 servings (148 calories per 1-cup serving).

□ *6.6 grams protein, 0.4 gram fat, 29.9 grams carbohydrate, 3 milligrams cholesterol, 86 milligrams sodium, and 190 milligrams calcium.*

## OLD-FASHIONED BANANA PUDDING

½ cup sugar
3 tablespoons cornstarch
⅓ cup water
1 (12-ounce) can evaporated skimmed milk
⅓ cup egg substitute
½ cup fat-free sour cream
1 teaspoon vanilla extract
22 vanilla wafers
3 medium bananas, sliced
3 egg whites
¼ teaspoon cream of tartar
1 tablespoon sugar

Combine ½ cup sugar and cornstarch in a heavy saucepan; gradually stir in water, evaporated skimmed milk, and egg substitute. Cook over medium heat, stirring constantly, until mixture comes to a boil. Boil, stirring constantly, 1 minute. Remove from heat; fold in sour cream and vanilla.

Place a layer of vanilla wafers in bottom of a 1½-quart dish. Spoon one-third of pudding over wafers; top with half of bananas. Repeat layers; spread remaining pudding on top, and arrange remaining vanilla wafers around edge; set aside. Beat egg whites and cream of tartar at medium speed with an electric mixer until foamy. Gradually add 1 tablespoon sugar, beating until stiff peaks form. Spread meringue over pudding, sealing to edge. Bake at 325° for 25 to 28 minutes. Yield: 10 servings (172 calories per ½-cup serving).

□ *6 grams protein, 2.2 grams fat, 32.2 grams carbohydrate, 1 milligram cholesterol, 117 milligrams sodium, and 108 milligrams calcium.*

### BUTTERMILK PIE
*(pictured on page 76)*

⅔ **cup sugar**
¼ **cup cornstarch**
2½ **cups nonfat buttermilk**
3 **tablespoons light process cream cheese product**
⅔ **cup egg substitute**
1 **teaspoon grated lemon rind**
2 **tablespoons lemon juice**
½ **teaspoon lemon extract**
**Light Pastry**
3 **egg whites**
½ **teaspoon cream of tartar**
1 **tablespoon sugar**
⅛ **teaspoon lemon extract**
**Garnishes: Lemon rind curls, fresh mint sprigs**

Combine ⅔ cup sugar and cornstarch in a heavy saucepan; gradually stir in buttermilk. Add cream cheese, and cook over medium heat, stirring constantly, until mixture thickens and comes to a boil. Boil, stirring constantly, 1 minute. Gradually stir about one-fourth of hot mixture into egg substitute; add to remaining hot mixture, stirring constantly. Cook over low heat, stirring constantly, 2 minutes. Remove from heat; stir in lemon rind, juice, and ½ teaspoon lemon extract. Spoon into baked shell.

Beat egg whites and cream of tartar at medium speed with an electric mixer until foamy. Gradually add 1 tablespoon sugar, beating until stiff peaks form. Stir in ⅛ teaspoon lemon extract. Spread meringue over filling, sealing to edge. Bake at 325° for 25 to 28 minutes. Garnish, if desired. Yield: 8 servings (279 calories per serving).

### Light Pastry

1¼ **cups all-purpose flour**
⅓ **cup corn oil margarine**
3 **tablespoons cold water**

Place flour in a small bowl; cut in margarine with pastry blender until mixture is resembles coarse meal. Sprinkle cold water (1 tablespoon at a time) evenly over surface; stir with a fork until dry ingredients are moistened. Shape into a ball; gently press between 2 sheets of heavy-duty plastic wrap into a 4-inch circle. Chill 15 minutes.

Roll dough into an 11-inch circle; freeze 5 minutes. Remove top sheet of plastic wrap, and invert into a 9-inch pieplate. Remove plastic wrap. Fold edges under, and crimp; prick bottom and sides with a fork. Bake at 425° for 15 minutes or until golden. Cool on a wire rack. Yield: one 9-inch pastry shell.

□ *8.6 grams protein, 9 grams fat, 40.5 grams carbohydrate, 5 milligrams cholesterol, 263 milligrams sodium, and 110 milligrams calcium.*

---

### LIGHT FAVORITE

# Dip Into A Healthy Spread

Fat-free mayonnaise is beneficial for low-fat recipes. Artichoke-Parmesan Spread could never be considered a low-fat spread with a cup of mayonnaise—even if the reduced-calorie version replaced regular mayonnaise. Because the recipe uses fat-free mayonnaise, Parmesan cheese is the only source of fat.

But even the amount of Parmesan cheese in this light version has been halved, and it calls for freshly grated cheese because it has a stronger flavor than the grated Parmesan available in canisters.

A conventional oven or microwave can be used to heat this dish. Serve it with an assortment of crisp, fresh vegetables or low-fat crackers.

### ARTICHOKE-PARMESAN SPREAD

1 **cup fat-free mayonnaise**
½ **cup freshly grated Parmesan cheese**
1 **cup soft breadcrumbs**
¼ **teaspoon reduced-sodium Worcestershire sauce**
¼ **teaspoon hot sauce**
⅛ **teaspoon garlic powder**
2 **(14-ounce) cans artichoke hearts, drained and chopped**
**Vegetable cooking spray**

Combine first 6 ingredients; gently fold in artichokes. Spoon into a 1-quart casserole coated with cooking spray. Cover and bake at 350° for 20 minutes or until thoroughly heated. Serve with assorted raw vegetables or low-fat crackers. Yield: 3¼ cups (64 calories per ¼-cup serving).

**Microwave Directions:** Combine first 6 ingredients; gently fold in artichokes. Spoon into a 1-quart casserole coated with cooking spray. Cover with wax paper, and microwave at MEDIUM (50% power) 12 to 14 minutes, stirring twice.

□ *3 grams protein, 1.4 grams fat, 10.5 grams carbohydrate, 3 milligrams cholesterol, 435 milligrams sodium, and 55 milligrams calcium.*

### COMPARE THE NUTRIENTS
(per serving)

|  | Traditional | Light |
|---|---|---|
| Calories | 180 | 64 |
| Fat | 16.6g | 1.4g |
| Cholesterol | 16mg | 3mg |

# LIGHT MENU

## Put Lasagna On The Menu

Take a break from your standard lasagna with meat sauce by serving Spinach-Bean Lasagna. Chopped kidney beans are substituted for meat in the sauce. Spinach, part-skim ricotta cheese, and egg substitute are combined for the filling, and shredded part-skim mozzarella cheese is layered in the middle.

Tomato-Cucumber Salad With Yogurt-Herb Dressing and commercial Italian rolls accompany this healthy lasagna for a menu that easily meets the American Heart Association's dietary recommendations.

### HEALTHY LASAGNA DINNER

**Spinach-Bean Lasagna
Tomato-Cucumber Salad
With Yogurt-Herb Dressing
Commercial Italian rolls
Lemon Cake Pudding**

### SPINACH-BEAN LASAGNA

2 (15-ounce) cans kidney beans
1¾ cups water
1 (27.5-ounce) jar reduced-fat, reduced-sodium pasta sauce
1 (10-ounce) package frozen chopped spinach, thawed and well drained
1 (15-ounce) container part-skim ricotta cheese
¼ cup egg substitute
Vegetable cooking spray
10 lasagna noodles, uncooked
1 cup (4 ounces) shredded part-skim mozzarella cheese
¼ cup grated Parmesan cheese

Rinse and drain beans. Position knife blade in food processor bowl; add beans. Pulse 2 or 3 times; gradually add water and pulse several times until beans are coarsely chopped. Combine bean mixture and pasta sauce in a saucepan; bring to a boil. Reduce heat and simmer, stirring occasionally, 10 minutes; set aside.

Combine spinach, ricotta cheese, and egg substitute; set aside.

Coat a 13- x 9- x 2-inch baking dish with cooking spray, and spread a thin layer of sauce on bottom of dish. Arrange 5 noodles over sauce. Spread half of spinach mixture over noodles; top with mozzarella. Spoon half of sauce over cheese. Repeat noodle, spinach, and sauce layers. Cover and refrigerate 24 hours. Remove from refrigerator, and let stand at room temperature 30 minutes. Cover and bake at 350° for 1 hour. Uncover, sprinkle with Parmesan cheese, and bake an additional 15 minutes. Yield: 8 servings (365 calories per serving).

□ 22.3 grams protein, 9.8 grams fat, 47.2 grams carbohydrate, 30 milligrams cholesterol, 643 milligrams sodium, and 328 milligrams calcium.

### TOMATO-CUCUMBER SALAD WITH YOGURT-HERB DRESSING

1 head Boston lettuce
4 small tomatoes, cut into wedges
1 medium cucumber, scored and sliced
½ small purple onion, sliced and separated into rings
Yogurt-Herb Dressing

Line individual plates with lettuce leaves; arrange tomato, cucumber, and onion in pinwheel fashion on plates. Top with 2 tablespoons Yogurt-Herb Dressing. Yield: 8 servings (47 calories per serving).

□ 2.5 grams protein, 0.4 gram fat, 9.4 grams carbohydrate, 0 milligrams cholesterol, 121 milligrams sodium, and 54 milligrams calcium.

### Yogurt-Herb Dressing

¾ cup plain nonfat yogurt
¼ cup fat-free mayonnaise
1 teaspoon chopped fresh dillweed
1 teaspoon chopped fresh chives
⅛ teaspoon white pepper

Combine ingredients; chill. Yield: 1 cup (9 calories per tablespoon).

□ 0.6 gram protein, 0 grams fat, 1.6 grams carbohydrate, 0 milligrams cholesterol, 56 milligrams sodium, and 22 milligrams calcium.

### LEMON CAKE PUDDING

1⅓ cups sugar
⅓ cup all-purpose flour
1½ tablespoons grated lemon rind
⅓ cup lemon juice
½ cup egg substitute
2 cups skim milk
6 egg whites
Vegetable cooking spray

Combine first 5 ingredients; gradually stir in milk. Beat egg whites at high speed with an electric mixer until stiff but not dry; fold into lemon mixture. Pour into 8 (10-ounce) custard cups coated with cooking spray. Place cups in a large shallow pan; add hot water to a depth of 1 inch into pan. Bake at 350° for 35 minutes or until edges are browned. Yield: 8 servings (191 calories per 1-cup serving).

□ 6.7 grams protein, 0.4 gram fat, 41.3 grams carbohydrate, 1 milligram cholesterol, 96 milligrams sodium, and 85 milligrams calcium.

# A Sampling Of Cool Salads

As the weather gets warmer, what's better than a cool salad? Our readers provide an assortment of salads to choose from—fruit or vegetable, crisp or creamy.

## TROPICAL ORANGE SALAD

6 oranges
1 cup pitted dates, cut in half lengthwise
½ cup flaked coconut
1 (8-ounce) carton sour cream
2 tablespoons brown sugar
1 to 2 tablespoons grated orange rind, divided

Peel, slice, and seed oranges; cut orange slices in half. Layer oranges, dates, and coconut in a 2-quart bowl. Cover and chill 2 to 4 hours.

Combine sour cream, brown sugar, and ½ to 1 teaspoon orange rind; spoon over fruit. Sprinkle with remaining orange rind. Yield: 6 to 8 servings.
*Charlotte Pierce*
*Greensburg, Kentucky*

## PINEAPPLE WALDORF SALAD

1 (20-ounce) can pineapple chunks, drained
1 orange, peeled and sectioned
1 tart red apple, unpeeled and coarsely chopped
1 banana, sliced
1 cup strawberries, hulled
1 cup diagonally sliced celery
¼ cup chopped walnuts
1 (8-ounce) carton strawberry yogurt

Combine first 7 ingredients in a large bowl; add yogurt, and toss gently to coat. Cover and chill. Yield: 8 servings.
*Patricia Hill*
*Roan Mountain, Tennessee*

## BROCCOLI-CAULIFLOWER SALAD

1½ pounds fresh broccoli
1 medium cauliflower, cut into flowerets
1 red onion, sliced
½ cup sliced celery
1 (2-ounce) jar diced pimiento, drained
1 cup mayonnaise or salad dressing
2 tablespoons sugar
1 teaspoon dry mustard
¼ teaspoon salt
⅛ teaspoon pepper
2 tablespoons vegetable oil
Lettuce leaves

Remove broccoli leaves, and cut off tough ends of stalks; discard. Wash thoroughly, and cut into 1-inch pieces. Combine broccoli, cauliflower, and next 3 ingredients in a large bowl.

Combine mayonnaise and next 5 ingredients; spoon over vegetables, tossing to coat. Cover and chill. Serve salad with a slotted spoon on lettuce-lined plates. Yield: 8 to 10 servings.
*Maggie Hatley*
*Sikeston, Missouri*

## CREAMY CUCUMBER SALAD

1 (3-ounce) package lime-flavored gelatin
¾ cup boiling water
2 (3-ounce) packages cream cheese, softened
1 cup mayonnaise or salad dressing
2 tablespoons lemon juice
1 teaspoon prepared horseradish
¼ teaspoon salt
¾ cup finely chopped cucumber (about 1 medium cucumber, peeled)
½ cup finely chopped onion
Lettuce leaves

Dissolve gelatin in boiling water; set aside. Combine cream cheese and next 4 ingredients in a large mixing bowl; beat at low speed with an electric mixer until blended. Gradually add gelatin mixture, beating well. Cover and chill 30 minutes. Stir in cucumber and onion.

Spoon mixture into 8 lightly oiled individual molds, 8 lightly oiled 6-ounce custard cups, or a lightly oiled 8-inch square dish. Cover and chill 8 hours. Unmold onto lettuce leaves. Yield: 8 servings.
*Azine G. Rush*
*Monroe, Louisiana*

# Bread With Italian Roots

Focaccia, an unadorned cousin to pizza, has been around since medieval times. Traditionally it's a hearth-baked bread with a sprinkling of salt, a few drops of olive oil, and perhaps a little chopped onion.

## MUSTARD-AND-ONION FOCACCIA

1 medium onion, sliced and cut into quarters
1 tablespoon butter or margarine
¼ cup Dijon mustard
⅛ teaspoon red pepper
1 (16-ounce) loaf frozen bread dough, thawed
1 tablespoon olive oil
⅛ teaspoon salt
Dash of black pepper

Cook onion in butter in a large skillet over medium-high heat, stirring constantly, until tender; set aside.

Combine mustard and red pepper; set aside. Place bread dough on a lightly floured baking sheet; roll to a 15- x 10-inch rectangle. Brush dough with olive oil; spread mustard mixture over dough. Arrange onion evenly over mustard. Sprinkle with salt and black pepper. Bake at 400° for 15 minutes or until golden. Cut into rectangles. Yield: 6 to 8 servings.
*Patricia Saylor*
*Crofton, Maryland*

# Basil At Its Best

Sure, you're familiar with basil. It's an herb in one of those many bottles on your spice rack, and you usually take it down when you're making spaghetti sauce or homemade pizza. But spring is here, and new experiences await you. Taste the flavor of *fresh* basil in these recipes.

If you're not already growing your own, you can buy small, individual packets of cut basil in the produce section of the grocery store. Once you discover how these aromatic green leaves magically make your favorite dishes even better, you'll want to grow your own. Here, we tell you how and give you some innovative uses for this herb. Remember, if you do use dried basil instead of fresh, use only one-third as much because the dried form is stronger and more concentrated than fresh.

## PESTO AND PASTA

½ cup packed chopped fresh basil
¼ cup minced fresh parsley
¼ cup grated Parmesan cheese
2 tablespoons pine nuts or walnuts
1 clove garlic, halved
2 tablespoons olive oil
2 tablespoons butter, softened
¼ teaspoon salt
¼ teaspoon pepper
6 ounces linguine, uncooked

Combine all ingredients except linguine in container of an electric blender. Process at high speed until mixture is smooth.

Cook linguine according to package directions; drain. Spoon pesto mixture over linguine; toss gently, and serve immediately. Yield: 3 to 4 servings.

*Georgianne McGee*
*Waycross, Georgia*

## BASIL-ORANGE ROUGHY WITH VEGETABLES

1 medium onion, sliced
¼ pound fresh mushrooms, sliced
2 small zucchini, sliced
3 tablespoons minced fresh basil
3 tablespoons vegetable oil, divided
1½ pounds orange roughy fillets
¼ teaspoon salt
¼ teaspoon pepper
2 tomatoes, peeled and sliced
½ cup grated Parmesan cheese

Cook onion, mushrooms, zucchini, and basil in 2 tablespoons oil in a large skillet over medium-high heat, stirring constantly, 4 minutes or until crisp-tender. Remove vegetables to serving platter; keep warm.

Sprinkle fish fillets with salt and pepper; add remaining 1 tablespoon oil and fish to skillet; place tomato slices on fish. Cover and simmer 8 to 9 minutes or until fish flakes easily with a fork. Place fish and tomato slices over vegetables on serving platter; sprinkle with cheese. Serve immediately. Yield: 4 to 6 servings. *Sarah Evans*
*Dallas, Texas*

## Growing Basil

Even one basil plant will flavor many meals, but you may want more for the attractive addition it can make to a garden. Plant seeds or transplants in a sunny spot anytime after danger of frost has passed, leaving about 18 inches between plants. Mix a little slow-release fertilizer in the soil at planting, or water monthly with liquid fertilizer, as directed on the label. Water basil at first sign of wilting. Pinch off flower spikes as soon as they appear to keep plants bushy. And don't be afraid to cut as much as one-third of the foliage several times during the season.

You can choose between different types of basil. Sweet Basil with smooth edges and Green Ruffles basil with curled edges are both large plants with good-size leaves. Green Bouquet and Spicy Globe are compact mounds with small leaves that are as ornamental as they are flavorful. These compact forms of basil are your best choices for a windowsill garden. Purple Ruffles is an improvement over the old Dark Opal. This new type offers colorful foliage that will turn herb vinegar pink.

*Sweet Basil*

*Spicy Globe*

*Purple Ruffles*

## SAUTÉED ZUCCHINI AND CARROTS

6 carrots, thinly sliced
2 tablespoons butter or margarine, melted
1 small onion, sliced
2 medium zucchini, sliced
3 tablespoons chopped fresh basil
½ teaspoon salt
¼ teaspoon pepper

Cook carrots in butter over medium-high heat, stirring constantly, 4 minutes or until crisp-tender. Add onion; cook, stirring constantly, 1 minute. Stir in zucchini and remaining ingredients; cook, stirring constantly, 1 minute. Serve immediately. Yield: 6 servings.
*Paula De Viro*
*Savannah, Georgia*


## EASY HERB PIZZA

1 (10-ounce) can refrigerated pizza crust *
1 (8-ounce) can tomato sauce
⅓ cup chopped fresh basil
1½ cups (6 ounces) shredded provolone cheese

Shape pizza crust into a lightly greased 12-inch pizza pan; bake at 425° for 7 minutes. Spread tomato sauce over pizza crust; sprinkle evenly with basil. Bake 8 minutes. Sprinkle with cheese; bake 5 minutes. Yield: 1 (12-inch) pizza.

* One (12-inch) commercial pizza crust may be substituted for refrigerated crust. It's available in cellophane packaging in your grocer's bread or deli/bakery section. *Shannon Gayle*
*Alexandria, Louisiana*

**Tip:** *Refrigerate cheese in its original wrap until opened. After opening, rewrap the cheese tightly in plastic wrap, plastic bags, or aluminum foil, or place in airtight containers and refrigerate.*


# Bring On The Shrimp

Remember when the only place to buy fresh shrimp was on the coast? Happily, shrimp is now available year-round in most supermarkets.

When buying shrimp, select those that are firm and light colored with no strong odors. Take them home, and refrigerate shrimp immediately, making sure they're not out of the refrigerator for more than two hours. If necessary have your grocer place ice in the package of shrimp. (You may want to carry an ice chest if you have several stops to make.)

Cook the shrimp within two days, or freeze them. To freeze, remove and discard the heads. Wash shrimp and place in freezer bags or cartons. Use within three months.


## CREOLE SHRIMP JAMBALAYA

1½ pounds unpeeled medium-size fresh shrimp
2 tablespoons vegetable oil
1 cup chopped onion
½ cup chopped green pepper
1 carrot, cut into thin strips
½ cup chopped celery
3 cloves garlic, minced
1 (8-ounce) can tomato sauce
1 (14½-ounce) can tomatoes, undrained and chopped
1 (14½-ounce) can ready-to-serve chicken broth
1¼ cups water
1 cup long-grain rice, uncooked
1 teaspoon salt
½ teaspoon dried thyme
½ teaspoon red pepper
¼ teaspoon chili powder
¼ teaspoon sugar
½ cup chopped fresh parsley
⅛ teaspoon hot sauce (optional)

Peel and devein shrimp. Cook shrimp in oil in a small Dutch oven over medium heat, stirring constantly, 5 minutes or until shrimp turn pink. Remove shrimp with a slotted spoon; refrigerate. Add onion, green pepper, carrot, celery, and garlic to Dutch oven; cook over medium heat 3 minutes. Stir in tomato sauce and next 9 ingredients. Bring to a boil; cover, reduce heat, and simmer, stirring frequently, 45 minutes or until rice is tender and most of liquid is absorbed. Stir in parsley and shrimp; cook about 10 minutes or until thoroughly heated. Add hot sauce, if desired. Yield: 4 servings.
*Irene B. Prejean*
*Abbeville, Louisiana*


## SHRIMP-STUFFED EGGPLANT

1 pound unpeeled medium-size fresh shrimp
2 medium eggplants
½ cup chopped onion
⅓ cup chopped celery
1 clove garlic, minced
1 tablespoon butter or margarine, melted
⅓ cup Italian-seasoned breadcrumbs
¼ teaspoon garlic powder
¼ teaspoon celery salt
⅛ teaspoon red pepper
2 tablespoons Italian-seasoned breadcrumbs
1½ tablespoons butter or margarine

Peel and devein shrimp; set aside. Cut eggplants in half lengthwise. Remove pulp, leaving a ¼- to ½-inch shell; set shells aside. Chop pulp.

Cook onion, celery, garlic, and eggplant pulp in 1 tablespoon butter in a large skillet over medium-high heat, stirring constantly, 10 to 12 minutes or until tender. Add shrimp; cook, stirring constantly, 3 to 5 minutes or until shrimp turn pink. Remove from heat; stir in ⅓ cup breadcrumbs and next 3 ingredients.

Place eggplant shells on a baking sheet; spoon hot mixture into shells. Sprinkle with breadcrumbs, and dot with butter. Bake at 350° for 20 to 25 minutes. Yield: 4 servings.
*Pat Rush Benigno*
*Gulfport, Mississippi*

## CREAMY SHRIMP AND NOODLES

1 pound unpeeled medium-size fresh shrimp
6 ounces fettuccine, uncooked
2 tablespoons butter or margarine
1 small sweet red pepper, cut into strips
1¼ cups milk
2 (0.6-ounce) envelopes cream of chicken-flavored instant soup mix
½ cup frozen English peas
3 tablespoons grated Parmesan cheese
¼ teaspoon garlic powder

Peel and devein shrimp; set aside. Cook fettuccine according to package directions; drain and set aside.

Melt butter in a large skillet over medium-high heat; add shrimp and red pepper. Cook, stirring constantly, 3 minutes. Combine milk and soup mix; add to shrimp mixture. Stir in peas, cheese, and garlic powder. Bring to a boil; reduce heat and simmer, stirring often, 5 minutes or until thickened. Toss with fettuccine. Serve immediately. Yield: 3 to 4 servings.

*Carolyne M. Carnevale*
*Ormond Beach, Florida*

## ANGEL HAIR PASTA WITH SHRIMP AND ASPARAGUS

8 unpeeled jumbo fresh shrimp
4 ounces angel hair pasta, uncooked
¼ cup olive oil
2 tablespoons minced garlic
1 teaspoon chopped shallots
6 stalks asparagus, cut into 2-inch pieces
¼ cup peeled, seeded, diced tomato
½ cup sliced shiitake mushroom caps *
¼ teaspoon salt
⅛ teaspoon dried crushed red pepper
½ cup dry white wine
1 tablespoon chopped fresh basil
1 tablespoon chopped fresh oregano
1 tablespoon chopped fresh thyme
1 tablespoon chopped fresh parsley
¼ cup freshly grated Parmesan cheese

Peel and devein shrimp; set aside. Cook pasta according to package directions; drain and set aside.

Heat a 9-inch skillet over high heat 1 minute; add oil, and heat 10 seconds. Add shrimp, garlic, and shallots; cook, stirring constantly, 2 to 3 minutes or until shrimp turn pink. Add asparagus and next 4 ingredients; stir in wine, scraping bottom of skillet to loosen any particles, if necessary. Add pasta, basil, and remaining ingredients; toss gently. Serve immediately. Yield: 2 servings.

* ½ cup sliced fresh mushrooms may be substituted for shiitake mushrooms. *Efrem Cutler* *Dunwoody, Georgia*

# Florida Starts The Season

In the spring, fresh green beans, corn, sweet peppers, and zucchini from Florida are abundant in grocery stores and farmers markets. Suppliers from other parts of the country make these vegetables available year-round, but springtime is Florida's peak season for these Southern favorites.

## CORN-AND-ZUCCHINI TIMBALES

2½ cups corn cut from cob (about 6 ears)
⅔ cup water
5 large eggs
1 tablespoon all-purpose flour
1 teaspoon sugar
½ teaspoon salt
1 large zucchini
½ teaspoon dried thyme

Place corn and water in container of an electric blender; process 1 minute.

Add eggs and next 3 ingredients; process until blended.

Using a vegetable peeler, cut 16 paper-thin, lengthwise zucchini strips; set aside. Grate remaining zucchini to measure 1 cup; squeeze between paper towels to remove excess moisture. Stir grated zucchini and thyme into corn mixture.

Arrange two zucchini slices around the inside of 8 lightly greased 6-ounce soufflé or custard cups. Pour corn mixture equally into cups. Place soufflé cups in a shallow pan; add hot water to pan to depth of 1 inch. Bake at 350° for 35 minutes or until a knife inserted in center comes out clean. Remove cups from water; loosen edges with a spatula, and invert onto serving plate. Yield: 8 servings.

*Rublelene Singleton*
*Scotts Hill, Tennessee*

## SIMPLE GREEN BEANS

1 pound fresh green beans
1 cup water
2 slices bacon, cut into 1-inch pieces
½ cup chopped onion
¼ cup chopped green pepper
½ cup whipping cream
½ teaspoon salt
Dash of pepper
Dash of ground nutmeg

Wash beans; trim ends, and remove strings. Cut into 1-inch pieces. Bring water to a boil in a large saucepan; add beans. Cover, reduce heat to medium, and cook 10 minutes or until tender. Drain and set aside.

Cook bacon in a large skillet until partially done (about 2 minutes); add onion and green pepper. Cook over medium-high heat, stirring constantly, until tender. Stir in beans, whipping cream, and remaining ingredients; cook 5 minutes or until thoroughly heated. Yield: 4 servings.

*Cathy Powell*
*Claxton, Georgia*

## FRESH VEGETABLE KABOBS

⅓ cup butter or margarine, melted
1½ tablespoons chopped fresh
    cilantro or parsley
¼ teaspoon ground cumin
¼ teaspoon dried crushed red
    pepper
⅛ teaspoon freshly ground pepper
Dash of salt
2 small ears of corn
1 small sweet red pepper
1 small sweet yellow pepper

Combine butter and next 5 ingredients, and set aside.

Cut corn into 1-inch-thick rounds, and peppers into 1½-inch squares; alternate on skewers. Brush with butter mixture. Grill over medium coals, basting occasionally, 10 to 15 minutes. Serve with remaining butter mixture. Yield: 2 servings.

*Linda Keith*
*Carrollton, Texas*

---

### Corn Tips

■ To select fresh corn, look for fresh green husks, dry silks, and even rows of plump kernels.

■ If you must store fresh corn, buy the ears in the husks and store in the refrigerator. This prevents sugar in the corn from turning to starch.

■ To remove the corn silk from corn on the cob, dampen a clean toothbrush and brush downward on the cob to remove all strands.

■ Keep in mind that the yield of kernels cut from corn-on-the-cob will depend upon the size of the ears. Generally, two average-size ears of corn will yield about 1 cup of kernels.

# Pavlova: A Classic Dessert

Anna Pavlova was a Russian ballerina whose delicate grace was admired the world over during the first quarter of this century. In honor of her visit to his country, an Australian chef created this special dessert—a cloudlike meringue topped with cream and fruit.

### PAVLOVA

1 teaspoon cornstarch
4 egg whites
1 cup sugar
1 teaspoon white vinegar
1 teaspoon vanilla extract
1½ cups whipping cream
2 tablespoons strawberry jam
1 tablespoon water
1 banana
Lemon juice
2 kiwifruit, peeled and sliced
1 pint strawberries, halved
Garnish: 2 strawberry fans

Mark an 11- x 7-inch rectangle on wax paper; place on baking sheet. Grease wax paper, and dust with cornstarch. Set aside.

Beat egg whites at high speed with an electric mixer until foamy. Gradually add sugar, ¼ cup at a time, beating until stiff peaks form and sugar dissolves (2 to 4 minutes). Beat in vinegar and vanilla. Spread meringue into an 11- x 7-inch rectangle on prepared wax paper. Bake at 275° for 45 minutes. Carefully remove meringue from baking sheet, and cool completely on wire rack. Carefully turn meringue over, and remove wax paper. Place meringue, right side up, on serving platter.

Beat whipping cream at medium speed with an electric mixer until soft peaks form. Set aside 1 cup whipped cream. Spread remaining whipped cream over meringue, leaving a 1-inch border. Pipe or dollop reserved whipped cream around edges.

Combine jam and water in a small saucepan; heat just until jam melts, stirring constantly. Strain mixture; set liquid aside to cool.

Slice banana, and sprinkle with lemon juice. Arrange banana, kiwifruit, and strawberry halves on whipped cream. Brush strawberries with strawberry liquid. Garnish, if desired. Yield: 10 to 12 servings.

*Carolyn Chester*
*Doraville, Georgia*

# A Cool Pie Beats The Heat

When you want a creamy frozen pie to cool a warm, spring evening, try Frozen Lemonade Pie. It can be made ahead and kept in the freezer. (Allow at least eight hours for any frozen pie to freeze.) The recipe makes two pies, so enjoy one with your family now and keep the extra one on hand for company.

### FROZEN LEMONADE PIE

1 (14-ounce) can sweetened
    condensed milk
1 (6-ounce) can frozen lemonade
    concentrate, thawed and
    undiluted
1 (8-ounce) container frozen
    whipped topping, thawed
2 (9-inch) prepared graham cracker
    crusts
Garnishes: lemon slices, fresh mint

Fold sweetened condensed milk and lemonade concentrate into whipped topping; spoon into crusts. Freeze until firm. Garnish, if desired. Yield: two 9-inch pies.

*Barbara Booth*
*Homer, Louisiana*

## You'll Brag About This "Bonus" Bread

Another good name for Wheat-and-Oat Bran Bread might be Bonus Bread. It tastes great, and it's good for you, too. Both oat bran and whole wheat flour give added fiber.

This recipe also offers flexibility. You can bake either two dozen dinner rolls or two 9-inch loaves. Better yet, divide the dough in half and bake both.

### WHEAT-AND-OAT BRAN BREAD

2 packages dry yeast
2 cups warm water (105° to 115°)
¼ cup firmly packed brown sugar
2 teaspoons salt
¼ cup olive oil
1 cup oat bran
1 cup whole wheat flour
3 to 3½ cups bread flour
Olive oil
Butter-flavored vegetable cooking
  spray (optional)

Dissolve yeast in warm water in a large mixing bowl; let stand 5 minutes. Add brown sugar, salt, and ¼ cup olive oil. Stir in oat bran and whole wheat flour. Gradually stir in enough bread flour to make a soft dough.

Turn dough out onto a floured surface, and knead until smooth and elastic (about 5 minutes). Place in a bowl coated with olive oil, turning to grease top. Cover and let rise in a warm place (85°), free from drafts, 45 minutes or until doubled in bulk.

Punch dough down, and divide into 24 balls; place in well-greased muffin pans. Cover and let rise in a warm place, free from drafts, 30 minutes or until doubled in bulk. Bake at 375° for 15 minutes or until golden brown. Spray tops with cooking spray, if desired. Remove from pans, and let cool on wire racks. Yield: 2 dozen.

*Evelyn Wilson*
*Burnsville, North Carolina*

**Note:** To shape loaves, divide dough in half, and shape each portion into a loaf. Place in 2 well-greased 9- x 5- x 3-inch loafpans. Cover and let rise as directed. Bake at 375° for 30 minutes or until loaves sound hollow when tapped, shielding with aluminum foil after 20 minutes. Yield: 2 loaves.

## From Our Kitchen To Yours

Cooking is a wonderful activity for parent and child to share. While having fun in the kitchen, there is also time to talk, teach, listen, and learn. Mixing Glazed Bunny Bread is simple because a convenience product is combined with ingredients usually kept on hand. As you read the directions together, you'll discover that it can be made several weeks ahead and frozen; if you have time, share one with grandparents or friends. Making this bread also is a project your family can enjoy together on Easter morning.

### GLAZED BUNNY BREAD

1 (16-ounce) package hot roll mix
¼ cup sugar
1 cup water
1½ teaspoons vanilla extract
1 large egg, lightly beaten
2 tablespoons butter, melted
2 tablespoons all-purpose flour
Raisins
1 cup sifted powdered sugar
1½ tablespoons lemon juice or milk
Jelly beans

Combine contents of hot roll mix package, yeast packet from mix, and sugar in a large bowl. Measure 1 cup hot water. (Temperature of water should be between 120° and 130°.) Add water, vanilla, egg, and butter to roll mix, and stir until dough pulls away from sides of bowl.

Sprinkle about 2 tablespoons all-purpose flour onto a pastry board. Turn dough out onto floured surface; turn over, coating the outside with flour. Knead until smooth by pushing the heels of your hands into dough; fold dough over, and repeat. If dough begins to stick to surface, sprinkle with more flour. Knead until dough is smooth and elastic (about 5 minutes).

Shape dough into a ball. Cover with a bowl or dishtowel, and let rest 5 minutes. Using kitchen shears, cut dough in half. Set one half aside. Shape other half into a ball for body, and place near end on a lightly greased 15- x 10- x 1-inch jellyroll pan; pat into a circle. Cut remaining half into three equal portions; set two portions aside. Shape one portion into a ball, and place on pan for head; pat into a circle. Divide second portion into two pieces; shape each piece into an ear, and attach to head. Cut remaining portion into four pieces, and shape into paws; attach to body. Gently push raisins into dough for eyes, nose, and mouth.

Cover dough with damp towel, and let rise in a warm place (85°), free from drafts, 20 minutes or until doubled in size. Bake at 350° for 25 to 30 minutes. (Check to make sure bread is browning evenly; if it begins to darken after 10 minutes, cover with aluminum foil.) Carefully remove bread to a cooling rack.

Combine powdered sugar and lemon juice in a bowl; brush over warm bread. Arrange jelly beans for collar. Yield: 1 loaf.

**To freeze:** Bake loaf as directed; let cool. Wrap in aluminum foil, and seal tightly in a plastic bag. To serve, let thaw at room temperature; reheat in foil at 350° for 15 minutes or until thoroughly heated.

# MAY

*With summer just around the corner, now is the perfect time
to keep cooking light and easy. In this chapter, we offer menu
ideas and recipes designed to keep your time in the kitchen to
a minimum, with such offerings as "Healthy Entreés To
Make Ahead." Seasonal variety, too, is reflected in "Festival
Favorites" and other regional specialties.*

# Mint: A Crush On Tradition

Breathe in mint—it's refreshing. Brush against a patch and the fresh fragrance floats up, inviting you to pluck it and gently pinch its leaves. This subtle, pleasant herb is rooted in lore and steeped in tradition.

Who in the South doesn't think first of the famous mint julep—equal parts sugar, water, and mint cooked into a syrup, strained, and served with bourbon? Connoisseurs argue over whether to make it with powdered or granulated sugar, and whether to crush or chop the mint. Whatever the preference, the beverage is the toast of Southern gentry and a must on Derby Day.

Spearmint is the choice most commonly used for cooking, although types such as lemon, orange, curly, apple, pineapple, ginger, gold, blue, balsam, Lebanese, variegated, and peppermint also intrigue gardeners and cooks.

## MINT SAUCE OVER VEGETABLES

2½ tablespoons Mint Vinegar (see recipe)
⅓ cup honey
2 tablespoons chopped fresh mint
1 tablespoon hot water
1 pound carrots, scraped and sliced *
Garnish: fresh mint sprig or chopped fresh mint

Combine first 3 ingredients in a saucepan; bring to a boil. Reduce heat and simmer 10 minutes or until slightly thickened; stir in water. Pour mixture through a wire-mesh strainer, discarding mint.

Arrange sliced carrot in a vegetable steamer over boiling water. Cover and steam 8 minutes or until crisp-tender; drain. Combine sliced carrot and mint sauce in a bowl; toss to coat. Garnish, if desired. Yield: 4 servings.

* 1 pound fresh or frozen English peas, cooked, may be substituted for steamed carrots.

## MINT VINEGAR

6 cups white wine vinegar
3 lemons
1½ cups loosely packed fresh mint leaves
½ cup honey
Fresh mint sprigs (optional)

Heat vinegar to 150° in a medium saucepan, and set aside. Using a citrus zester or a paring knife, cut strips of rind from lemon, reserving lemon for other uses.

Combine lemon rind, 1½ cups mint leaves, and honey; add hot vinegar. Stir with a wooden spoon, gently bruising leaves; pour into two 1-quart jars. Cover and store at room temperature 2 weeks. Pour mixture through a wire-mesh strainer into decorative bottles or jars, discarding mint. Place a mint sprig in each bottle, if desired. Store in a cool, dark place up to 6 months. Yield: 6 cups.

## MINTED CHICKEN SALAD

4 chicken breast halves
1 small sweet onion, quartered
5 sprigs fresh mint
1 teaspoon salt
4 cups water
1 cup seedless green grapes
⅓ cup chopped celery
⅔ cup lemon yogurt
2 tablespoons chopped fresh mint
⅛ teaspoon garlic powder
1 (11-ounce) can mandarin oranges, drained
Leaf lettuce
1 (2-ounce) package slivered almonds, toasted
1 small cantaloupe, peeled and sliced

Combine first 5 ingredients in a Dutch oven; bring to a boil. Cover, reduce heat, and simmer 45 minutes or until chicken is tender.

Drain chicken; discard onion and mint. Skin and bone chicken; cut into bite-size pieces. Combine chicken, grapes, and celery; set aside.

Combine yogurt, chopped mint, and garlic powder; add to chicken mixture, and toss gently. Fold in mandarin oranges; spoon onto lettuce-lined plates, and sprinkle with almonds. Arrange cantaloupe slices around salad. Yield: 6 servings.

## MINT-FRESH GREEN SALAD

¼ cup vegetable oil
2 tablespoons Mint Vinegar (see recipe)
1½ teaspoons sugar
¼ teaspoon salt
⅛ teaspoon hot sauce
8 cups mixed salad greens
2 tablespoons chopped fresh mint

Combine first 5 ingredients in a jar. Cover tightly, and shake vigorously; chill. Combine salad greens and mint in a large bowl. Drizzle dressing over salad greens; toss gently. Yield: 6 servings.


## MINTED ORANGE SALAD

4 navel oranges
⅓ cup thinly sliced radishes
2 tablespoons finely chopped fresh mint
3 tablespoons olive oil
Leaf lettuce

Peel oranges; cut into ¼-inch slices. Combine oranges, radishes, and mint; drizzle with olive oil, and toss gently. Cover and chill 2 to 3 hours, stirring occasionally. Serve salad on lettuce leaves. Yield: 6 servings.

*Valerie Stutsman*
*Norfolk, Virginia*


## MINTY MARINADE

⅓ cup Mint Vinegar (see recipe)
2 cloves garlic, crushed
2 to 4 tablespoons chopped fresh mint
⅛ teaspoon salt
⅛ teaspoon white pepper
⅓ cup olive oil

Combine first 5 ingredients in container of an electric blender; cover and process 10 seconds. With blender running, gradually add oil in a slow steady stream. Use as a marinade for fresh tuna or chicken. Yield: ⅔ cup.


## PINEAPPLE-ORANGE MINT JELLY

1 cup pineapple juice
1 cup orange juice
¼ cup water
1½ cups firmly packed fresh mint leaves and stems
3½ cups sugar
1 (3-ounce) package liquid pectin

Combine pineapple juice, orange juice, and water in a large saucepan; bring to a boil. Add mint; cover and remove from heat. Let stand 10 minutes. Pour mixture through a wire-mesh strainer, discarding mint. Combine 1¾ cups juice mixture and sugar in saucepan. Cook over medium-high heat, stirring frequently, until sugar dissolves and mixture comes to a boil. Add liquid pectin; bring to a full rolling boil, and boil, stirring constantly, 1 minute. Remove from heat. Skim off foam with a metal spoon.

Quickly pour jelly into hot sterilized jars, filling to ¼ inch from top; wipe jar rims. Cover at once with metal lids, and screw on bands. Process in boiling-water bath 5 minutes. Let stand 8 hours. Yield: 4 half pints.

**Note:** If jelly is not processed, store in refrigerator.


## CITRUS-MINT TEA COOLER

1 cup boiling water
3 regular-size tea bags
2 tablespoons chopped fresh mint
⅔ cup sugar
⅔ cup fresh grapefruit juice
½ cup fresh lemon juice
2 cups water

Pour boiling water over tea bags and mint; cover and steep 5 minutes. Pour mixture through a wire-mesh strainer, discarding tea bags and mint. Stir in sugar and next 3 ingredients. Serve over ice. Yield: 1 quart.

*Cathy Williams*
*Vale, North Carolina*


## The Legend Of Minthe

Mint is named after Minthe, a nymph in Greek mythology. Loved by Hades, god of the underworld, Minthe falls prey to Hades's jealous wife, Persephone, who banishes her to the plant world. There, Minthe must constantly seek underground water and shady places in search of her lost lover. In another tale, Persephone discovers the two lovers together. In a rage, she throws Minthe to the ground and tramples her. However, the soul of Minthe lives on in the tiny mint plant, its leaves always to be crushed.


## All About Mint

**To grow:** The herb may be grown indoors—just combine a rooted plant from a nursery and moist soil in a pot, and place on the kitchen windowsill.

**To harvest:** The tiny leaves of mint boast the most concentrated flavor right before the plants bloom. Cut the mint then, pruning the plant to just above the first or second pair of leaves. Crushing, chopping, or bruising the mint with the back of a spoon increases its pungency. Preserve the fresh flavor in our Mint Vinegar, or dry the herb on a screen placed in the sun. These recipes call for fresh mint, but if you use dried, substitute 1 teaspoon dried mint for 1 tablespoon chopped fresh mint.

**To buy and store:** You'll notice variety in the shapes and colors of mint available in your supermarket. Buy green, leafy bunches with no signs of yellow. If a bunch of mint seems slightly wilted, cut off the bottom of the stems, place mint in ice water, and chill. Or refrigerate it in a plastic bag lined with moistened paper towels.

# Keep The Salad Simple

Busy days often leave only enough time to prepare simple recipes. Rest assured that when salad is on the day's menu, these recipes will serve you well.

On a busy day, Tossed Fruit Salad and Sweet-and-Sour Potato Salad are quick enough to prepare just before serving. If you'd like to get a head start on preparation, however, choose Marinated Mixed Vegetables or Creamy Broccoli-Raisin Salad. Both recipes are best made ahead and chilled for the flavors to blend.

## TOSSED FRUIT SALAD

4 cups torn iceberg lettuce
1 cup sliced strawberries
1 cup sliced peaches
1 banana, sliced
1 small onion, thinly sliced
½ cup raisins
⅓ cup sunflower kernels, toasted
Commercial spicy-sweet French
    dressing

Combine first 7 ingredients in a large bowl; toss gently. Serve with dressing. Yield: 6 to 8 servings.

*Evelyn Snellings*
*Richmond, Virginia*

## CREAMY BROCCOLI-RAISIN SALAD

1 pound fresh broccoli
⅓ cup raisins
2 tablespoons chopped onion
2 slices bacon, cooked, crumbled,
    and divided
1 (3-ounce) package cream cheese,
    softened
2 tablespoons sugar
2 tablespoons white vinegar
2 tablespoons vegetable oil
1 tablespoon prepared mustard
1 clove garlic, minced

Remove broccoli leaves, and cut off tough ends of stalks; discard. Wash broccoli thoroughly, and cut into ½-inch pieces. Combine broccoli, raisins, onion, and half of bacon; toss gently. Set aside.

Combine cream cheese and remaining ingredients in a blender or food processor; process until smooth. Pour over broccoli mixture, stirring well. Chill 3 hours. Sprinkle with remaining bacon. Yield: 6 to 8 servings.

*Mrs. John B. Wright*
*Greenville, South Carolina*

## MARINATED MIXED VEGETABLES

1 large head cauliflower
1¼ pounds fresh broccoli
1 (14-ounce) can artichoke hearts,
    drained and chopped
5 stalks celery, chopped
5 green onions, chopped
1 (16-ounce) bottle Italian salad
    dressing
¾ cup mayonnaise or salad
    dressing
¼ cup chili sauce
2 tablespoons lemon juice
1½ to 2 teaspoons dried
    dillweed

Separate cauliflower and broccoli into flowerets; cut into bite-size pieces. Combine cauliflower, broccoli, and next 3 ingredients in a large shallow container. Spoon salad dressing over vegetables; cover and refrigerate 8 hours, stirring occasionally.

Drain vegetables, and set aside. Combine mayonnaise and remaining 3 ingredients; spoon over drained vegetables, tossing gently. Yield: 8 to 10 servings.

*Gail Thomas*
*White Hall, Maryland*

## SWEET-AND-SOUR POTATO SALAD

6 medium potatoes (about 2¼
    pounds)
10 slices bacon, cut into ½-inch
    pieces
1 small onion, chopped
2 large eggs, beaten
⅔ cup white vinegar
½ cup sugar

Cook potatoes in boiling water to cover 30 minutes or until tender. Drain and cool slightly. Peel and quarter potatoes; set aside. Cook bacon and onion in a large skillet until bacon is crisp; drain. Set aside.

Combine eggs, vinegar, and sugar in a heavy saucepan. Cook over medium heat, stirring constantly, until mixture thickens and reaches 160° (about 4 minutes).

Combine potatoes and bacon mixture. Pour vinegar mixture over potato mixture, tossing gently. Serve salad immediately. Yield: 6 to 8 servings.

*Mrs. David Williams*
*Baton Rouge, Louisiana*

# Artichoke: Getting To The Heart Of It

The artichoke has an intimidating reputation and appearance. Some people think it's reserved for stuffed-shirt occasions, but they shouldn't. Others look at it and wonder how to cook and eat it. There is an easy way to its delectable center.

We offer two simple cooking methods: boiling and microwaving. Our sauces can accompany artichokes for casual or formal occasions. To eat, pull off a leaf, dip the base in sauce, and pull the leaf through your front teeth to remove the soft pulp. Discard and start again. When all leaves have been removed, use a spoon to scrape out the "choke." Remaining is the "heart." Cut it into pieces, and dip it into the sauce.

## ARTICHOKES
*(pictured on page 109)*

4 artichokes
Lemon wedge
Lemon juice

Wash artichokes by plunging them up and down in cold water. Cut off stem end, and trim about ½ inch from top of each artichoke. Remove loose bottom leaves. With scissors, trim one-fourth off top of each outer leaf, if desired. Rub top and edges of leaves with lemon wedge to prevent discoloration.

Place artichokes in a large Dutch oven; cover with water, and add 3 tablespoons lemon juice. Bring to a boil; cover, reduce heat, and simmer 35 minutes or until lower leaves pull out easily. Drain and serve with desired sauce. Yield: 4 servings.

**Microwave Directions:** Wash and trim artichokes following instructions above. Place artichokes in an 11- x 7- x 1½-inch baking dish; add ¼ cup water and 1 tablespoon lemon juice. Cover with heavy-duty plastic wrap; fold back a small corner of wrap. Microwave at HIGH 14 to 16 minutes or until lower leaves pull out easily, giving dish a half-turn after 7 minutes.

## EASY DILLED
## HOLLANDAISE SAUCE

⅓ cup butter or margarine
1 (0.9-ounce) package hollandaise sauce mix
1 cup milk
1 tablespoon chopped fresh dill *
½ teaspoon grated lemon rind
1 tablespoon lemon juice

Melt butter in a small saucepan over low heat; stir in sauce mix. Remove from heat, and gradually stir in milk. Bring to a boil over medium-high heat, stirring constantly; reduce heat, and simmer 1 minute. Stir in dill, lemon rind, and lemon juice. Serve warm. Yield: 1¼ cups.

* 1 teaspoon dried dillweed may be substituted for fresh dill.

## WHITE BUTTER SAUCE
*(pictured on page 109)*

¼ cup Chablis or other dry white wine
¼ cup white wine vinegar
3 shallots, minced
⅓ cup half-and-half
1½ cups butter, softened

Combine first 3 ingredients in a medium saucepan; bring to a boil. Reduce heat, and simmer 8 minutes or until mixture is reduced to ⅓ cup. Stir in half-and-half, and simmer, stirring frequently, 8 minutes or until mixture is reduced to 3 tablespoons.

Remove from heat; add butter (1 tablespoon at a time), beating constantly with a wire whisk until butter melts and mixture is smooth. Serve immediately. Yield: about 1⅔ cups.

*Mrs. Robert Plummer*
*Franklin, Tennessee*

## CREAMY CITRUS MAYONNAISE

¾ cup mayonnaise
2 tablespoons frozen orange juice concentrate, thawed and undiluted
1 tablespoon lemon juice
¼ to ½ teaspoon lemon-pepper seasoning

Combine all ingredients; cover and chill at least 2 hours. Yield: ⅞ cup.

### Artichoke Facts

■ Choose artichokes that are deep green and heavy for their size, and have compact leaves.
■ To store fresh artichokes, sprinkle them with water, seal in a plastic bag, and refrigerate up to a week.
■ A 12-ounce fresh artichoke has only 25 calories, no fat, and 4 grams of dietary fiber.

# Seaside Salad Suppers

Ah, summer vacation—time to pack your bags and head to the beach for leisurely, sun-drenched days of building sandcastles, seeking seashell treasures, and finally getting to that book you've been meaning to read. As the sun lowers each afternoon, thoughts turn to food.

### GREEK STEAK SALAD

1 (1-pound) flank steak
1 cup olive oil
⅓ cup red wine vinegar
2 tablespoons chopped fresh mint
2 tablespoons chopped fresh parsley
1 tablespoon Dijon mustard
1 teaspoon dried oregano
¼ teaspoon salt
¼ teaspoon pepper
¼ teaspoon dried rosemary, crushed
1 (14-ounce) can artichoke hearts, drained and cut in half
¼ pound fresh green beans, cut into ½-inch pieces and blanched
1 small purple onion, sliced
⅓ cup pitted ripe olives, cut in half
½ sweet red pepper, cut into thin strips
4 cups torn mixed greens
2 medium tomatoes
½ cup crumbled feta cheese

Place steak on lightly greased rack of a broiler pan. Broil 4 to 5 inches from heat (with electric oven door partially opened) 10 to 12 minutes, turning once; cool. Thinly slice steak across grain; set aside.

Combine olive oil and next 8 ingredients in a shallow dish. Add steak, artichoke hearts, and next 4 ingredients; cover mixture and refrigerate 3 hours.

Arrange greens on platter; top with meat mixture. Cut tomato into wedges; arrange wedges around meat mixture, and sprinkle with feta cheese. Yield: 4 servings.

*Janice Elder*
*Charlotte, North Carolina*

## PASTA SALAD WITH HAM

8 ounces shell macaroni, uncooked
1 cup chopped cooked ham
½ cup green pepper, chopped
1 large tomato, chopped
½ cup mayonnaise or salad
  dressing
¼ cup grated Parmesan cheese

Cook macaroni according to directions; drain. Rinse with cold water; drain. Combine macaroni and remaining ingredients; toss well. Cover and chill. Yield: 6 servings.  *Pat Boschen*
*Ashland, Virginia*

## BROILED SALMON SALAD
*(pictured on pages 112 and 113)*

2 (6-ounce) salmon steaks
1 cup Lemon-and-Herb Dressing,
  divided
1 medium zucchini
1 medium-size yellow squash
1 carrot, scraped
½ sweet red pepper
1 tablespoon chopped fresh cilantro
  or parsley
2 cups torn fresh spinach
2 cups torn Bibb lettuce
1 tomato, cut into wedges
1 small avocado, peeled and sliced
Garnishes: lemon twists, fresh
  parsley sprigs

Place salmon steaks in a shallow 1-quart dish; pour ¼ cup dressing over steaks. Cover and refrigerate 1 hour, turning once.

Cut zucchini and next 3 ingredients into thin strips; combine with cilantro and ¼ cup dressing, tossing gently.

Remove steaks from marinade; place on lightly greased rack of a broiler pan. Broil 4 inches from heat (with electric oven door partially opened) 5 to 6 minutes; turn and brush with marinade. Broil an additional 5 to 6 minutes or until fish flakes easily. Cool slightly.

Arrange salad greens and marinated vegetables on serving plates. Top with salmon steaks, tomato wedges, and avocado slices. Garnish, if desired, and serve with remaining dressing. Yield: 2 servings.

### Lemon-and-Herb Dressing

¾ cup lemon juice
½ cup vegetable oil
1 teaspoon chopped fresh parsley
¼ teaspoon minced garlic
1½ tablespoons sugar
¾ teaspoon paprika
¾ teaspoon dried basil
½ teaspoon dried tarragon
½ teaspoon seasoned salt
⅛ teaspoon pepper

Combine all ingredients in a jar; cover tightly, and shake mixture vigorously. Yield: 1⅓ cups.  *Joyce M. Maurer*
*Christmas, Florida*

## FRUITED PASTA SALAD

1⅓ cups rotini, uncooked
2 cups chopped cooked chicken
1½ cups sliced celery
1 cup seedless green grapes,
  halved
¼ cup chopped green pepper
¼ cup chopped purple onion
1 (11-ounce) can mandarin oranges,
  drained
1 (8-ounce) can sliced water
  chestnuts, drained
¼ cup commercial buttermilk
  dressing
¼ cup mayonnaise
1 teaspoon Beau Monde
  seasoning
¼ teaspoon salt
⅛ teaspoon pepper

Cook pasta according to package directions; drain. Rinse pasta with cold water; drain. Combine pasta, cooked chicken, celery, grapes, green pepper, onion, oranges, and chestnuts, tossing gently.

Combine buttermilk dressing, mayonnaise, seasoning, salt, and pepper. Pour over pasta mixture, tossing gently. Cover and chill. Yield: 4 to 6 servings.  *Daphne K. Harbinson*
*Fletcher, North Carolina*

## TUNA PASTA SALAD

5 ounces bow tie pasta, uncooked
1 (7.3-ounce) jar marinated hearts
  of palm, drained
1 (6-ounce) jar marinated artichoke
  hearts, drained
1 (6⅛-ounce) can solid white tuna,
  drained and flaked
½ cup frozen English peas, thawed
¼ cup sliced pimiento-stuffed olives
¼ cup sliced pitted ripe olives
¼ cup seeded and coarsely chopped
  Greek salad peppers
¼ cup (1 ounce) shredded
  mozzarella cheese
¼ cup (1 ounce) shredded Cheddar
  cheese
2 tablespoons chopped green
  onions
2 tablespoons grated Parmesan
  cheese
½ cup commercial Italian salad
  dressing
⅛ teaspoon pepper

Cook pasta according to package directions; drain. Rinse with cold water, and drain. Combine pasta and next 11 ingredients in a bowl; add salad dressing and pepper, tossing to coat. Cover and chill 2 hours. Yield: 4 servings.
*L. Kristen Jahn*
*Myakka City, Florida*

### Salad Tips

■ Remember that salad greens should never be cut with a knife because it may discolor and bruise the leaves. Gently tearing the leaves is better and makes a prettier salad.
■ Add marinated vegetable salads to your next dinner party. They can be prepared in advance and chilled until serving time—an important bonus for the busy cook.
■ Add garlic flavor to a green salad by rubbing halved garlic cloves around the inside of the salad bowl.

*Artichokes and White Butter Sauce have long been a perfect pair. Serve the sauce in individual bowls for dipping. (Recipes, page 107.)*

*Serve Rice-Shrimp Salad, bread-sticks, and a beverage for a filling meal. A salad serving contains 13.5 grams of protein. (Recipe, page 142.)*

*Boasting crabmeat and shrimp, Seafood Chowder (page 122) is an impressive make-ahead dish you'll want to keep on hand.*

*For a romantic evening, enjoy
Broiled Salmon Salad (page 108) by
the fading light of a beach sunset.*

Right: *For an attractive presentation, serve Congealed Gazpacho Salad on lettuce leaves. Top with Avocado Cream, and garnish with green onion fans. (Recipes, page 158.)*

Far right: *Chicken with Orange, Lime, and Ginger Sauce (page 123) and Grilled Vegetables (page 124) cook quickly and offer delicious eating with very little fat.*

*Serve Italian-Style Grilled Vegetables (page 143) along with Peppercorn-Crusted Lamb Chops (page 142).*

Once you've tried Tomato-Asparagus
Salad (page 79), you'll serve it when
you need a quick recipe or even when
you have time to cook.

# Festival Favorites

Traveling to summer food festivals will have your mouth watering for the season's freshest strawberries, crab, watermelon, and shrimp. You've come to the right place to find out what's cooking where.

We sampled these seafood and desserts dishes from many festival booths, recipe contests, cookbooks, as well as some sent by readers from the featured states of West Virginia, Maryland, Arkansas, and Florida.

One bite of the many tasty varieties of food available and we're sure you'll pack up the car and head for the festivals to feast.

## SHRIMP SCAMPI

2 pounds unpeeled, medium-size fresh shrimp
1 (8-ounce) package linguine, uncooked
8 cloves garlic, minced
1 cup butter or margarine, melted
1 cup white wine
¼ teaspoon salt
⅛ teaspoon pepper
¼ cup chopped fresh parsley

Peel and devein shrimp; set aside. Cook linguine according to package directions; keep warm.

Cook garlic in butter and wine in a large skillet over medium-high heat, stirring constantly, until garlic is tender. Add reserved shrimp, and cook over medium heat 3 to 5 minutes or until shrimp turn pink. Add salt and pepper, and spoon mixture over reserved linguine. Sprinkle with chopped parsley, and serve immediately. Yield: 4 servings.

## BALTIMORE CRAB CAKES

1 pound fresh, lump crabmeat, drained
½ cup Italian-seasoned breadcrumbs
½ teaspoon baking powder
⅓ cup milk
1 large egg, beaten
¼ cup mayonnaise or salad dressing
2 tablespoons finely chopped green onions
¼ teaspoon garlic salt
⅛ teaspoon white pepper
2 teaspoons dried onion flakes
¾ teaspoon dried parsley flakes
¼ cup all-purpose flour
¼ cup butter or margarine, melted

Combine first 11 ingredients; shape into 6 patties. Coat with flour; chill at least 1 hour. Cook patties in butter in a skillet over medium-high heat 4 minutes on each side or until golden. Yield: 6 servings. *Roland S. Ormrod*
*Towson, Maryland*

## DEVILED CRAB

¾ cup chopped celery
¾ cup chopped onion
¼ cup chopped sweet red pepper
⅓ cup butter, melted
1 pound fresh, lump crabmeat, drained
1 cup saltine cracker crumbs, divided
½ cup chopped fresh parsley
¼ cup whipping cream
1 teaspoon dry mustard
½ teaspoon freshly ground pepper
¼ teaspoon salt
1 tablespoon Dijon mustard
½ teaspoon hot sauce
1 tablespoon butter, melted
Paprika

Cook first 3 ingredients in ⅓ cup butter in a large skillet over medium-high heat, stirring constantly, until tender. Remove from heat. Gently stir in crabmeat, ¾ cup cracker crumbs, and parsley.

Combine whipping cream and next 5 ingredients; gently stir into crabmeat mixture. Spoon into 6 baking shells or individual baking dishes.

Brown remaining ¼ cup cracker crumbs in 1 tablespoon butter in a small skillet, stirring often. Sprinkle each serving with cracker crumbs and paprika. Bake at 350° for 15 to 20 minutes. Yield: 6 servings.
*Mrs. Herbert W. Rutherford*
*Baltimore, Maryland*

## SHERRIED WATERMELON

4 cups watermelon balls
¼ cup sugar
½ cup dry sherry

Combine all ingredients; cover and chill several hours. To serve, spoon into individual compotes or drain and thread watermelon onto wooden skewers. Yield: 4 servings.
*Donna Presley*
*Perrytown, Arkansas*

## STRAWBERRY DREAM TART

1 (8-ounce) package cream cheese, softened
1 (14-ounce) can sweetened condensed milk
1 (5.1-ounce) package vanilla instant pudding mix
½ cup water
1 (8-ounce) container frozen whipped topping, thawed
Brown Sugar Crust
1 quart fresh strawberries, sliced

Beat cream cheese at medium speed with an electric mixer until smooth. Add next 3 ingredients; beat until smooth. Chill 5 minutes; fold in whipped topping.

Spread filling over Brown Sugar Crust; arrange strawberries over filling. Chill at least 30 minutes before slicing. Yield: one 12-inch tart.

### Brown Sugar Crust

4 cups corn flakes cereal
¾ cup butter or margarine, softened
¼ cup firmly packed brown sugar
2 egg yolks
¼ teaspoon salt
¼ teaspoon almond extract
1⅓ cups all-purpose flour

Crush corn flakes; set aside. Beat butter and brown sugar at medium speed with an electric mixer until fluffy; add egg yolks, salt, and almond extract, beating until smooth. Gradually add flour and cereal. Shape mixture into a ball; press into a well-buttered 12-inch pizza pan. Bake at 375° for 10 to 12 minutes or until golden. Cool completely. Yield: one 12-inch crust.

*Betty Osburn*
*Buckhannon, West Virginia*

## CHOCOLATE BASKETS WITH BERRY CREAM

Vegetable cooking spray
1 (6-ounce) package semisweet chocolate morsels
3 (2-ounce) squares chocolate-flavored candy coating
¼ cup strawberry preserves
1 tablespoon Cointreau or other orange-flavored liqueur
1 cup whipping cream, whipped
1 pint fresh strawberries, sliced
Garnishes: mint, strawberry fans

Invert six 6-ounce custard cups; cover each with a paper baking cup and then with heavy-duty plastic wrap. Make sure paper cup stays in place. Place inverted cups on baking sheet. Coat with cooking spray.

Combine chocolate morsels and candy coating in a heavy saucepan; stir over low heat until melted. Remove from heat; let stand 10 minutes. Spoon into a decorating bag fitted with a small writing tip. (Or use a heavy-duty, zip-top plastic bag, snipping a tiny hole in one corner.)

Slowly drizzle chocolate over each cup. (If it drizzles too fast, let cool a little longer. If it becomes too firm to pipe, reheat it.) Chill 10 minutes.

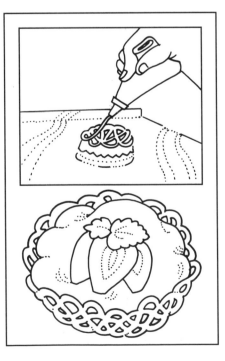

Pipe a second layer of chocolate; chill 1 hour. Carefully remove custard cups and paper cups from baskets, and gently peel away plastic wrap. Store in an airtight container in refrigerator until ready to serve.

Gently fold preserves and liqueur into whipped cream. Place chocolate baskets on plates; spoon cream mixture into cups. Arrange strawberries over cream mixture. Garnish, if desired; serve immediately. Yield: 6 servings.

*Belenda Sandy*
*Buckhannon, West Virginia*

# Add Fruit To The Batter

Plain muffins will hardly seem the same once you sample these fruit-filled varieties. Bursting with blueberries, raspberries, and other juicy prizes from the garden, these moist and tender breads fit menus that span from morning to evening, and even snacktime along the way.

Best of all, each of these recipes makes a dozen and a half muffins. Unless you're expecting company or have a very large family, you'll probably have enough leftover to stick in the freezer for another meal. Seal them in an airtight freezer bag, and freeze up to three months. You can let them thaw in the bag overnight, or remove them from the bag and pop them, still frozen, into the microwave as needed.

The perfect muffin boasts a pebbly brown top, a smooth, even texture, and a rounded shape. Those muffins that are peaked and have tunnels running throughout have not been mixed properly.

When making muffins, stir the dry ingredients together, and make a well in the center of the mixture. Pour the liquid ingredients into the well, and stir just until dry ingredients are moistened. Don't try to get all the lumps out of the batter, or you'll probably see those peaks and tunnels in the muffins. Remove muffins from the pans immediately after baking to keep condensation from forming and making them soggy.

## ORANGE-DATE MUFFINS

2 cups all-purpose flour
1 teaspoon baking powder
1 teaspoon baking soda
½ teaspoon salt
1 teaspoon grated orange rind
¾ cup sugar
1 orange, peeled and sectioned
½ cup butter or margarine
½ cup pitted dates, chopped
½ cup orange juice
1 large egg

Combine first 6 ingredients in a large bowl; make a well in center of mixture. Set aside.

Position knife blade in food processor bowl; add orange sections and remaining ingredients. Process 30 seconds or until mixture is blended, but not smooth. Add to dry ingredients, stirring just until moistened. Place paper baking cups in muffin pans. Spoon batter into paper cups. Bake at 400° for 15 minutes or until golden brown. Remove from pans immediately. Yield: 1½ dozen.

*Sharon McClatchey*
*Muskogee, Oklahoma*

## LEMON-RASPBERRY MUFFINS

2 cups all-purpose flour
1 tablespoon baking powder
½ teaspoon salt
¾ cup sugar
1 cup fresh raspberries
2 large eggs, beaten
1 cup half-and-half
½ cup vegetable oil
1 teaspoon lemon extract
Vegetable cooking spray

Combine first 5 ingredients in a large bowl, and make a well in center of

mixture. Combine eggs and next 3 ingredients; add to dry ingredients, stirring just until moistened. Place paper baking cups in muffin pans, and coat with cooking spray; spoon batter into paper cups, filling three-fourths full. Bake at 425° for 20 to 22 minutes. Remove from pans immediately. Yield: 1½ dozen.

*Linda Magus*
*Clemmons, North Carolina*

## BLUEBERRY-OAT MUFFINS

2 cups all-purpose flour
1 tablespoon baking powder
½ teaspoon baking soda
¼ teaspoon salt
½ teaspoon ground cinnamon
1 cup quick-cooking oats, uncooked
¾ cup sugar
2 large eggs, lightly beaten
1 cup buttermilk
¼ cup vegetable oil
1 teaspoon vanilla extract
1 teaspoon butter flavoring
1 cup fresh blueberries

Combine first 7 ingredients in a large bowl; make a well in center of mixture. Combine eggs and next 4 ingredients; add to dry ingredients, stirring just until moistened. Fold blueberries into mixture. Spoon into greased muffin pans, filling three-fourths full. Bake at 400° for 18 to 20 minutes. Remove from pans immediately. Yield: 1½ dozen.

*Eileen Wehling*
*Austin, Texas*

# Cakes To Match The Event

Gardening, softball, bridal showers—there are so many spring activities, and cake can accompany them all.

For a quick snack after yard work or other outdoor activities, try

Brownie Carrot Cake or Applesauce-Oatmeal Cake. For those special occasions when you want a fancy, frosted dessert, make Coconut Cake or Banana-Nut Cake.

Remember this helpful tip: You can substitute all-purpose flour in place of cake flour by using two tablespoons less of all-purpose flour per cup. For example, our recipe for Banana-Nut Cake on page 120 lists two cups of cake flour as an ingredient. If you need to substitute all-purpose flour, be sure to use only 1¾ cups.

## APPLESAUCE-OATMEAL CAKE

1¼ cups applesauce
¾ cup quick-cooking oats, uncooked
¾ to 1 cup raisins
½ cup butter or margarine, softened
¾ cup firmly packed light brown sugar
1 large egg
1½ cups all-purpose flour
1 teaspoon baking soda
½ teaspoon salt
1 teaspoon ground cinnamon
¼ teaspoon ground cloves

Bring applesauce to a boil in a small saucepan; remove from heat. Stir in oats and raisins; cover and let stand 20 minutes. Beat butter at medium speed with an electric mixer until fluffy. Gradually add sugar, beating well. Add egg, and beat well.

Combine flour, baking soda, salt, cinnamon, and ground cloves. Gradually add to creamed mixture; mix just until blended after each addition. Stir in applesauce mixture.

Pour batter into a greased and floured 9-inch square pan; bake at 350° for 30 to 35 minutes or until a wooden pick inserted in center comes out clean. Cool in pan on a wire rack. Yield: 9 servings.

*Bertha Bench*
*Mineral Wells, Texas*

## BROWNIE CARROT CAKE

1 (19.8-ounce) package fudge
  brownie mix
4 large eggs
2 cups grated carrots
1½ cups mayonnaise
1 cup sugar
1 teaspoon ground cinnamon
1 teaspoon vanilla extract
1 cup chopped pecans
Powdered sugar (optional)

Combine first 7 ingredients in a large mixing bowl; beat at low speed with an electric mixer 2 minutes. Stir in chopped pecans.

Pour into a greased 13- x 9- x 2-inch pan; bake at 350° for 50 to 55 minutes or until a wooden pick inserted in center comes out clean. Cool in pan on a wire rack. Cut into squares. Dust with powdered sugar, if desired. Yield: 15 to 18 servings.
*Dessie Smedley*
*Pasadena, Texas*

## COCONUT CAKE

1 cup butter or margarine, softened
2 cups sugar
4 large eggs
3¼ cups all-purpose flour
1 tablespoon baking powder
1¼ cups milk
1 teaspoon vanilla extract
Sour Cream-Coconut Filling

Beat butter at medium speed with an electric mixer until fluffy, and gradually add sugar, beating well. Add eggs, one at a time, beating mixture after each addition.

Combine flour and baking powder; add to creamed mixture alternately with milk, beginning and ending with flour mixture. Mix just until blended after each addition. Stir in vanilla.

Pour batter into 3 greased and floured 9-inch round cakepans. Bake at 350° for 18 minutes or until a wooden pick inserted in center comes out clean. Cool in pans on wire racks 10 minutes; remove from pans, and let cool completely on wire racks.

Split each layer in half horizontally. Spread Sour Cream-Coconut Filling between layers and on top of cake. Cover and chill at least 3 hours before serving. Yield: one 3-layer cake.

### Sour Cream-Coconut Filling

2 cups sifted powdered sugar
1 (16-ounce) carton sour cream
1 (8-ounce) container frozen
  whipped topping, thawed
2 (6-ounce) packages frozen
  coconut, thawed

Combine first 3 ingredients; stir in coconut. Yield: about 5½ cups.
*Bea Chalupa*
*Sealy, Texas*

## BANANA-NUT CAKE

1⅓ cups sugar, divided
2 cups sifted cake flour
1 teaspoon baking powder
1 teaspoon baking soda
1 teaspoon salt
½ cup chopped pecans
2 large eggs, separated
1 cup mashed banana
⅔ cup buttermilk
⅓ cup vegetable oil
1 teaspoon vanilla extract
Cream Cheese Frosting
½ cup chopped pecans

Combine 1 cup sugar, cake flour, baking powder, baking soda, salt, and ½ cup chopped pecans in a large bowl; make a well in center of mixture. Combine egg yolks and next 4 ingredients; add to dry ingredients, stirring just until moistened.

Beat egg whites with an electric mixer until foamy. Gradually add remaining ⅓ cup sugar, and beat until stiff (but not dry) peaks form. Fold egg white mixture into batter. Pour batter into 2 greased and floured 9-inch round cakepans.

Bake at 325° for 25 minutes or until a wooden pick inserted in center comes out clean. Cool in pans on wire racks 10 minutes; remove from pans, and cool completely on wire racks.

Spread Cream Cheese Frosting between layers and on top and sides of cake. Press ½ cup chopped pecans into frosting on sides of cake. Yield: one 2-layer cake.

### Cream Cheese Frosting

1 (8-ounce) package cream cheese,
  softened
1 (16-ounce) package powdered
  sugar, sifted
2 teaspoons vanilla extract
1¼ teaspoons lemon juice

Beat cream cheese with an electric mixer until smooth; gradually add powdered sugar, beating until light and fluffy. Stir in vanilla and lemon juice. Cover and chill until spreading consistency. Yield: enough for one 2-layer cake.
*Janet Griffin*
*Ormond Beach, Florida*

# Inspired By Almonds

Pay attention, cheesecake lovers: Sour Cream-Almond Dessert is one of the creamiest and richest cheesecake-like desserts you'll find.

## SOUR CREAM-ALMOND DESSERT

¾ cup butter or margarine,
  softened
1½ cups all-purpose flour
½ cup chopped almonds
2 tablespoons sugar
¾ to 1 cup almond paste, broken
  into small pieces
4 large eggs
1 cup sugar
2 tablespoons cornstarch
1 (16-ounce) carton sour cream
1 pint whipping cream
3 tablespoons powdered sugar
¼ cup sliced almonds, toasted

Combine first 4 ingredients in a large mixing bowl; beat at medium speed with an electric mixer until blended. Spread mixture evenly on bottom and 1½ inches up sides of an ungreased 9-inch springform pan. Bake at 400° for 10 minutes or until lightly browned; set aside.

Combine almond paste, eggs, and 1 cup sugar; beat at medium speed with an electric mixer until blended (about 4 minutes). Combine cornstarch and sour cream; stir into almond paste mixture, and pour into prepared crust. Bake at 325° for 1 hour or until lightly browned (center will be a little soft). Let cool to room temperature on a wire rack. Cover and refrigerate at least 8 hours.

Remove ring from springform pan. Beat whipping cream until foamy; gradually add powdered sugar, beating until soft peaks form. Set aside 1 cup whipped cream, and spread remaining whipped cream on top of dessert. Pipe or dollop reserved whipped cream around outer edges, and sprinkle with toasted almonds. Yield: 8 to 10 servings.
*Bettie Sechrist*
*Montgomery, Alabama*

# From Our Kitchen To Yours

If the supermarket doesn't have a ground seasoning blend, such as Beau Monde, what can you substitute? Or if you are in the middle of a recipe calling for the seasoning blend fines herbes, which you don't have on hand, what can you use instead?

We're frequently asked these questions, so we developed some easy recipes for homemade seasoning blends using herbs and spices you probably have on hand. The Test Kitchens staff has prepared and compared recipes using each seasoning blend—one a commercial brand and the other a homemade version. In our opinion, the homemade blends consistently had the best flavor.

Store the blends in tightly sealed containers in a dark, cool, dry place up to six months. Because heat weakens spice flavors, avoid displaying seasonings on open racks above or near cooking tops or ovens. We store seldom-used seasonings in the freezer to maintain freshness.

## GROUND SEASONING BLEND

2 tablespoons ground celery seeds
1 tablespoon onion powder
1 tablespoon salt

Combine all ingredients, and store in an airtight container. Use in stews, chowders, or sandwich spreads. Yield: ¼ cup.

## FIVE-SPICE POWDER BLEND

2 teaspoons anise seeds, crushed
2 teaspoons freshly ground pepper
2 teaspoons fennel seeds, crushed
2 teaspoons ground cloves
2 teaspoons ground cinnamon
1½ teaspoons ground ginger
½ teaspoon ground allspice

Combine all ingredients; store in an airtight container. Use to flavor fish or pork. Yield: ¼ cup.

## CREOLE SEASONING BLEND

1 tablespoon salt
1½ teaspoons garlic powder
1½ teaspoons onion powder
1½ teaspoons paprika
1¼ teaspoons dried thyme
1 teaspoon red pepper
¾ teaspoon black pepper
¾ teaspoon dried oregano
½ teaspoon ground bay leaves
¼ teaspoon chili powder

Combine all ingredients, and store in an airtight container. Use with seafood, chicken, beef, or vegetables. Yield: ¼ cup.

## GREEK SEASONING BLEND

2 teaspoons salt
2 teaspoons dried oregano
1½ teaspoons onion powder
1½ teaspoons garlic powder
1 teaspoon cornstarch
1 teaspoon pepper
1 teaspoon beef-flavored bouillon granules
1 teaspoon dried parsley flakes
½ teaspoon ground cinnamon
½ teaspoon ground nutmeg

Combine all ingredients, and store in an airtight container. Serve with steaks, pork chops, chicken, or fish. Yield: ¼ cup.

## BAY SEAFOOD SEASONING BLEND

1 tablespoon ground bay leaves
2½ teaspoons celery salt
1½ teaspoons dry mustard
1½ teaspoons black pepper
¾ teaspoon ground nutmeg
½ teaspoon ground cloves
½ teaspoon ground ginger
½ teaspoon paprika
½ teaspoon red pepper
¼ teaspoon ground mace (optional)
¼ teaspoon ground cardamom (optional)

Combine all ingredients; store in an airtight container. Use with seafood or chicken. Yield: ¼ cup.

## HERBS SEASONING BLEND

1 tablespoon dried thyme
1 tablespoon dried oregano
2 teaspoons rubbed sage
1 teaspoon dried rosemary
1 teaspoon dried marjoram
1 teaspoon dried basil
1 teaspoon dried parsley flakes

Combine all ingredients; store in an airtight container. Use in omelets and to season fish, vegetables, or chicken. Yield: ¼ cup.

# Healthy Entrées To Make Ahead

To avoid last-minute meal preparation or the temptation to grab fast food, stock your freezer with these nutritious make-ahead entrées.

Seafood Chowder will become a favorite. Team it with French bread and a salad tossed with a low-fat dressing for an easy meal that looks impressive. Divide the chowder into several portions for freezing so you can thaw it one meal at a time.

Cornbread-Tamale Pie requires a little preparation after thawing, yet it's still a quick meal. Double the frozen portion of the recipe so that one can be served and the other frozen. To avoid leaving pans in freezer, line them with aluminum foil sprayed with cooking spray; add the food, seal tightly, and freeze. Once frozen, the wrapped entrée can be removed from pan, labeled, and stored.

It's best to freeze foods as quickly as possible after cooking to preserve flavor and texture. Store about an inch apart to allow air to circulate. Label packages with recipe name, date, instructions, and number of servings.

turkey and shrimp. Spoon into an 11- x 7- x 1½-inch baking dish coated with cooking spray; sprinkle with breadcrumbs. Bake at 350° for 35 to 45 minutes or until bubbly. Yield: 6 servings (273 calories per serving).

**Note:** Cover and freeze casserole before sprinkling with breadcrumbs. Thaw in refrigerator 24 hours, and let stand at room temperature 30 minutes. Sprinkle with breadcrumbs, and bake at 350° for 35 to 45 minutes or until bubbly.

□ *34.4 grams protein, 9.4 grams fat, 12.2 grams carbohydrate, 154 milligrams cholesterol, 682 milligrams sodium, and 218 milligrams calcium.*

## TURKEY-AND-SHRIMP FLORENTINE CASSEROLE

1 pound unpeeled, medium-size fresh shrimp
1 pound turkey breast fillets
¼ teaspoon garlic powder
¼ teaspoon pepper
¼ cup Chablis or other dry white wine
2 (10-ounce) packages frozen chopped spinach
1 (8-ounce) container light process cream cheese product
1 (10¾-ounce) can 99% fat-free cream of mushroom soup, undiluted
3 tablespoons Parmesan cheese
Vegetable cooking spray
2 tablespoons fine, dry breadcrumbs

Peel and devein shrimp; set aside. Sprinkle turkey with garlic powder and pepper; set aside. Place wine in a large, nonstick skillet; add turkey, and bring to a boil. Add shrimp; cover, reduce heat, and cook 3 to 5 minutes or until shrimp turn pink. Remove shrimp from heat; cool slightly. Drain pan juices, and set aside. Cut turkey into bite-size pieces, and set turkey and shrimp aside.

Cook spinach according to package directions, omitting salt; drain well between layers of paper towels.

Place cream cheese in a large saucepan; cook over low heat, stirring constantly, until cheese melts. Remove from heat; stir in pan juices, mushroom soup, Parmesan cheese, and spinach. Gently stir in reserved

## SEAFOOD CHOWDER
*(pictured on page 111)*

1½ pounds unpeeled, medium-size fresh shrimp
Vegetable cooking spray
1 teaspoon olive oil
1 cup chopped onion
1 cup chopped celery
1 cup diced sweet red pepper
3 cloves garlic, minced
½ cup all-purpose flour
2 (10½-ounce) cans ready-to-serve, no-salt-added chicken broth
1½ cups water
3 cups peeled, diced red potatoes
1 cup diced carrot
½ teaspoon white pepper
½ teaspoon dried thyme
2 bay leaves
2 (12-ounce) cans evaporated skimmed milk
2 (8¾-ounce) cans no-salt-added, cream-style corn
1 teaspoon hot sauce
1 pound fresh crabmeat, drained and flaked

Peel and devein shrimp; set aside. Coat a Dutch oven with cooking spray; add oil, and place over medium-high heat until hot. Add onion and next 3 ingredients; cook until tender. Add flour and cook, stirring constantly, 1 minute. Gradually stir in chicken broth, water, and next 5 ingredients.

Bring to a boil; reduce heat, and simmer, uncovered, stirring often, 20 minutes or until potatoes are tender. Stir in milk, corn, and hot sauce; return to a boil. Add reserved shrimp and crabmeat; cook 5 minutes or until shrimp turn pink, stirring constantly. Remove and discard bay leaves. Yield: 10 servings (279 calories per 1½-cup serving).

**Note:** Freeze chowder in airtight containers. Thaw in refrigerator 24 hours. Place in a saucepan, and cook over low heat until thoroughly heated (do not overcook).

□ *28 grams protein, 2.8 grams fat, 35.1 grams carbohydrate, 126 milligrams cholesterol, 314 milligrams sodium, and 302 milligrams calcium.*

### CORNBREAD-TAMALE PIE

Vegetable cooking spray
1 pound low-fat ground beef
1 cup chopped onion
1 cup chopped green pepper
1 clove garlic, minced
2 (8-ounce) cans no-salt-added tomato sauce
1 (12-ounce) can no-salt-added whole kernel corn, drained
15 ripe olives, sliced
1 tablespoon sugar
1 tablespoon chili powder
⅛ teaspoon salt
¼ teaspoon pepper
1 cup (4 ounces) shredded, reduced-fat sharp Cheddar cheese
¾ cup yellow cornmeal
½ teaspoon salt
2 cups water
1 tablespoon reduced-calorie margarine

Coat a large, nonstick skillet with cooking spray; place over medium heat. Add ground beef; cook until browned, stirring until it crumbles. Drain and pat dry with paper towels. Wipe pan drippings from skillet with a paper towel. Coat skillet with cooking spray. Add onion, green pepper, and garlic; cook until vegetables are tender. Stir in ground beef, tomato

sauce, and next 6 ingredients. Simmer, uncovered, 15 to 20 minutes. Add Cheddar cheese, stirring until cheese melts. Spoon into an 8-inch square baking dish coated with cooking spray.

Combine cornmeal, salt, and water in a saucepan; bring to a boil, stirring constantly. Reduce heat and cook, stirring constantly, until mixture thickens (about 3 minutes). Stir in margarine. Spoon over meat mixture to within 1 inch of edge. Bake at 375° for 40 minutes or until topping is golden. Yield: 6 servings (333 calories per serving).

**Note:** Freeze pie before topping with cornmeal mixture. Thaw in refrigerator 24 hours. Remove from refrigerator, and let stand at room temperature 30 minutes; proceed as directed, baking 45 to 50 minutes.

□ *23.3 grams protein, 11.9 grams fat, 34.7 grams carbohydrate, 61 milligrams cholesterol, 674 milligrams sodium, and 191 milligrams calcium.*
*Ruth M. Witt*
*Hutchinson, Kansas*

---

# LIGHT MENU

# Supper Hot Off The Grill

As often as possible, Southerners escape from the kitchen and cook outdoors. With the help of our readers, we've come up with a cookout menu that's easy to plan, easy to do, and easy on the heart.

Chicken With Orange, Lime, and Ginger Sauce is a simple recipe that's loaded with flavor. The tangy sauce gives it some zip. Brush it on at the beginning of cooking and again when the chicken is turned.

Vegetables are outstanding on the grill. In preparing them, steam vegetables before grilling them. That way, they're all cooked when it's time to eat, and they still absorb the smoky flavor from grilling.

### EASY COOKOUT MENU

**Chicken With Orange, Lime, and Ginger Sauce**
**Grilled Vegetables**
**Commercial rolls**
**Watermelon Sherbet**

### CHICKEN WITH ORANGE, LIME, AND GINGER SAUCE
*(pictured on page 115)*

2½ tablespoons reduced-calorie orange marmalade
⅛ teaspoon grated lime rind
1½ tablespoons fresh lime juice
½ tablespoon grated fresh gingerroot
4 (4-ounce) skinned, boned chicken breast halves

Combine first 4 ingredients. Place chicken on grill, and brush with half of marmalade mixture. Cook, covered, over medium-hot coals (350° to 400°) 6 minutes. Turn chicken, and brush with remaining marmalade mixture; cook 6 minutes or until done. Yield: 4 servings (147 calories per serving).

□ *25.5 grams protein, 3.7 grams fat, 1.1 grams carbohydrate, 70 milligrams cholesterol, 65 milligrams sodium, and 17 milligrams calcium.*   *Beth Evins*
*Atlanta, Georgia*

**Tip:** *When choosing meat for grilling, allow 4 ounces raw meat or 3 ounces cooked meat per serving.*

## GRILLED VEGETABLES
*(pictured on page 115)*

1 medium onion
4 ears fresh corn
2 medium-size red, yellow, or green peppers, seeded and halved
1 medium zucchini, quartered lengthwise
1 medium-size yellow squash, quartered lengthwise
4 large fresh mushrooms
1½ teaspoons salt-free lemon-and-herb blend

Peel onion, and place a vegetable steamer over boiling water; cover and steam 8 minutes. Remove onion from steamer; cool slightly, and cut into 4 (¾-inch) slices. Set aside.

Remove husks and silks from corn; place in steamer over boiling water. Cover and steam 8 minutes; remove from rack, and set aside.

Place peppers, zucchini, and yellow squash in steamer over boiling water. Cover and steam 3 minutes; add mushrooms, and steam 1 minute longer. Remove vegetables from rack; sprinkle with salt-free lemon-and-herb blend. Grill vegetables, covered, over medium-hot coals (350° to 400°) 8 minutes, turning once. Yield: 4 servings (122 calories per serving).

□ *4.3 grams protein, 1.4 grams fat, 27.5 grams carbohydrate, 0 milligrams cholesterol, 19 milligrams sodium, and 23 milligrams calcium.* Kim Cain
Greenville, North Carolina

## WATERMELON SHERBET

5 cups seeded, cubed watermelon
¾ cup sugar
1 tablespoon lemon juice
1 envelope unflavored gelatin
¼ cup water
1 (12-ounce) can evaporated skimmed milk

Combine first 3 ingredients; cover and chill 30 minutes. Place watermelon mixture in container of an electric blender or food processor. Cover and process until smooth; set aside.

Sprinkle gelatin over water in a small saucepan; let stand 1 minute. Cook over medium heat, stirring until gelatin dissolves; remove from heat.

Combine watermelon mixture, gelatin, and milk. Pour into freezer container of a 5-quart hand-turned or electric freezer. Freeze according to manufacturer's instructions. Yield: 9 servings (125 calories per ½-cup serving).

□ *4.1 grams protein, 0.5 gram fat, 27.4 grams carbohydrate, 2 milligrams cholesterol, 46 milligrams sodium, and 117 milligrams calcium.*

---

## LIGHT FAVORITE

# A Low-Fat Mexican Entrée

When shopping for flour tortillas to use for Oven-Fried Beef Chimichangas, choose those made with oil instead of lard, a saturated fat that contains cholesterol.

## OVEN-FRIED BEEF CHIMICHANGAS

1 (2-pound) lean top sirloin steak
Vegetable cooking spray
1 cup chopped onion
2 cloves garlic, minced
1 (4-ounce) can chopped green chiles, undrained
1 teaspoon ground cumin
½ teaspoon dried oregano
¼ teaspoon salt
¼ teaspoon dried crushed red pepper
8 (8-inch) flour tortillas
8 cups shredded lettuce
1 cup picante sauce
½ cup nonfat sour cream alternative
Garnish: chopped green onions

Trim excess fat from steak. Place steak in an ovenproof Dutch oven coated with cooking spray. Cover and bake at 325° for 1½ to 2 hours or until tender. Remove steak from Dutch oven, and let cool to touch.

Pour pan juices through a gravy skimmer; reserve pan juices, and discard fat. Shred meat, and combine with reserved pan juices; set aside.

Cook onion and garlic in a large, nonstick skillet coated with cooking spray over medium-high heat, stirring constantly, until tender. Add meat mixture, green chiles, and next 4 ingredients; cook over low heat, stirring often, 10 to 15 minutes.

Heat tortillas according to package directions. Place about ½ cup beef mixture just below center of tortilla. (Keep remaining tortillas warm.) Fold in left and right sides of tortillas to partially enclose filling. Fold remaining edges to form a rectangle. Repeat procedure with remaining tortillas and beef mixture.

Place filled tortillas on a baking sheet coated with cooking spray. Bake at 425° for 10 minutes or until crisp and lightly browned. Serve with shredded lettuce, picante sauce, and nonfat sour cream alternative. Garnish, if desired. Yield: 8 servings (308 calories per chimichanga with 1 cup shredded lettuce, 2 tablespoons picante sauce, and 1 tablespoon nonfat sour cream alternative).

□ *30.3 grams protein, 8.5 grams fat, 27.7 grams carbohydrate, 76 milligrams cholesterol, 575 milligrams sodium, and 61 milligrams calcium.*
Tracy Rogers
Hattiesburg, Mississippi

---

### COMPARE THE NUTRIENTS
(per serving)

|  | Traditional | Light |
|---|---|---|
| Calories | 547 | 308 |
| Fat | 37.7g | 8.5g |
| Cholesterol | 82mg | 76mg |

# Spectacular Made Simple

One look at impressive dishes made with phyllo and puff pastry brings a chorus of "oohs," "ahs," and unfortunately, some "aarghs."

Phyllo, a paper-thin pastry, has long been popular in many Greek recipes, such as baklava. You'll find it in your grocer's freezer section marked "fillo (phyllo) dough leaves." You can use it in many dishes, ranging from appetizers to desserts.

Puff pastry, also in the freezer section, is labeled "puff pastry sheets." Much thicker and more doughlike and pliable than phyllo, this fragile French pastry is actually many tissue-thin layers stacked and rolled together that "puff" to a delicate, flaky texture when heated.

## SPINACH-STUFFED CHICKEN IN PUFF PASTRY

4 skinned and boned chicken breast halves *
½ teaspoon salt
½ teaspoon pepper
1 (10-ounce) package frozen spinach, thawed and drained
¾ cup (3 ounces) shredded Gruyère or Swiss cheese
½ cup finely chopped prosciutto or cooked ham (3 ounces)
¼ teaspoon salt
⅛ teaspoon pepper
Dash of ground nutmeg
1 (17¼-ounce) package frozen puff pastry sheets, thawed
1 large egg, lightly beaten
1 teaspoon water
1 (0.9-ounce) package béarnaise sauce mix

Place chicken between two sheets of heavy-duty plastic wrap; flatten to ⅛-inch thickness using a meat mallet or rolling pin. Sprinkle chicken with ½ teaspoon each of salt and pepper, and set aside.

Combine spinach and next 5 ingredients; shape into 4 balls, placing 1 in center of each chicken breast. Fold chicken over spinach.

Roll each sheet of puff pastry into a 12-inch square. Cut a 1-inch strip from side of each sheet, setting aside for garnish. Cut each sheet in half, making 4 (5½- x 6-inch) rectangles.

Place stuffed chicken breasts in center of pastry rectangles; fold sides over chicken. Combine egg and water, and brush on pastry seams, pinching to seal. Place seam side down on a lightly greased 15- x 10- x 1-inch jellyroll pan.

Cut decorative stems and leaves or desired shapes from reserved pastry strips. Brush back of cutouts with egg mixture, and arrange on chicken bundles. Chill bundles and remaining egg mixture 1 hour. Brush bundles with egg mixture, and bake at 400° for 20 to 25 minutes or until golden.

Prepare béarnaise sauce according to package directions. Spoon 2 tablespoons sauce in each of four plates; top with chicken bundle. Serve immediately. Yield: 4 servings.

* Twelve (1-ounce) slices of veal scaloppine may be substituted for 4 chicken breasts. Overlap 3 slices of veal, and place on each puff pastry rectangle.
*Missy Wilson*
*Birmingham, Alabama*

## CHEESE TWISTS

½ cup grated Parmesan cheese
¾ teaspoon seasoned pepper
½ teaspoon dried parsley flakes
¼ teaspoon garlic powder
1 (17¼-ounce) package commercial frozen puff pastry sheets, thawed
1 egg white, lightly beaten

Combine first 4 ingredients in a small bowl. Unfold one puff pastry sheet onto cutting board. Brush pastry lightly with egg white; sprinkle with one-fourth cheese mixture. Lightly press cheese mixture into pastry; turn pastry over, and repeat procedure.

Cut pastry sheet in half; cut each half into 9 strips (about 1 inch wide); twist each strip into a spiral shape. Repeat procedure with remaining half pastry sheet.

Place twists on a lightly greased baking sheet. Bake at 350° for 15 minutes or until golden. Yield: 3 dozen.
*Sandra Russell*
*Gainesville, Florida*

## Phyllo Facts

■ Keep phyllo in the refrigerator if you'll use it within a month, or in the freezer for longer storage.
■ Thaw frozen phyllo completely in the refrigerator before using, not at room temperature. Quick thawing makes the pastry sticky and too difficult to handle.
■ Remove phyllo from the refrigerator two hours before using it for easiest handling.
■ While working, keep unused portion covered with a slightly damp towel to prevent pastry from getting dry and brittle.
■ Use vegetable cooking spray instead of brushing melted butter on the many layers for less messy and lower-calorie cooking.
■ Refreeze any unused phyllo pastry after thawing.

## Puff Pastry Pointers

■ For clean cuts, use only a sharp knife or pastry wheel. A dull knife can compact or seal the pastry edges, preventing them from "puffing" to the fullest height.
■ Thaw frozen puff pastry 20 minutes at room temperature before using in a recipe.
■ While preparing the recipe, leave thawed pastry in refrigerator until ready to use. Dough is easiest to work with when cool, not at room temperature.
■ Lightly flour surface before rolling puff pastry.
■ Don't reroll pastry; it won't rise as high when cooked.

## WRAPPED BRIE

8 sheets commercial frozen phyllo
   pastry, thawed
Butter-flavored cooking spray
1 (15-ounce) round herbed Brie
   cheese
Garnishes: fresh herbs, ribbon

Spray 1 sheet of phyllo with cooking spray, keeping remaining pastry covered with a slightly damp towel to prevent it from drying out. Place Brie in center of sheet; wrap phyllo around Brie. Repeat procedure 3 times, inverting Brie each time; set aside.

Layer remaining 4 sheets of phyllo pastry, spraying each with cooking spray; place wrapped Brie in center. Bring corners of phyllo to center of Brie to cover, gently gathering and pressing together in center to resemble a package. Carefully tie with kitchen string.

Coat wrapped Brie with cooking spray, and place on a lightly greased baking sheet. Bake at 375° for 25 minutes or until golden, shielding top of pastry with aluminum foil the last 15 minutes to prevent overbrowning. Remove from oven; let stand about 20 minutes before serving. Remove string, and garnish, if desired. Serve with crackers. Yield: 12 to 15 appetizer servings.
*Hazel Wilson*
*Nacogdoches, Texas*

# QUICK!

## Spice Up Your Stir-Fry

Stir-frying doesn't have to mean Oriental, so we have spiced up the usual formula to emphasize the culinary tastes of several cultures and countries. The result is a world tour for your taste buds.

When you stir-fry, be sure to have all meat and vegetables cut up before you begin to cook. Meat and poultry will be easier to slice if you freeze them for 10 minutes before cutting. And consider combining cornstarch mixtures ahead of time to eliminate frantic measuring during the middle of the cooking process.

## ITALIAN STIR-FRY

1 pound turkey cutlets
2 teaspoons cornstarch
¼ cup Marsala wine *
1 (14½-ounce) can Italian-style
   stewed tomatoes, undrained
1 cup Italian-style tomato sauce
3 tablespoons olive oil, divided
3 cloves garlic, minced
1 large zucchini, cut into thin strips
Hot cooked fettuccine

Cut turkey into thin strips; set aside. Combine cornstarch and wine; stir in tomatoes and sauce; set aside.

Pour 1 tablespoon olive oil around top of preheated wok or skillet, coating sides; heat at medium-high (325°) for 2 minutes. Add garlic and zucchini; stir-fry 2 to 3 minutes or until zucchini is crisp-tender. Remove from wok, and set aside. Pour remaining 2 tablespoons olive oil into wok; add turkey, and stir-fry 3 to 4 minutes. Drain.

Return reserved turkey to wok. Add reserved tomato mixture and zucchini; boil. Cook, stirring constantly, 1 minute. Serve over fettuccine. Yield: 4 servings.

* 3 tablespoons Chablis or other dry white wine plus 1 tablespoon brandy may be substituted for Marsala wine.

## INDIAN STIR-FRY

1 pound boneless lamb *
2 teaspoons cornstarch
2 tablespoons chopped chutney
½ cup beef broth
2 tablespoons olive oil, divided
2 cloves garlic, minced
1 large sweet red pepper, cut into
   strips
1 to 2 teaspoons curry powder
Hot cooked rice or pasta (optional)

Slice lamb diagonally across grain into thin strips, and set aside. Combine cornstarch, chutney, and beef broth; set aside.

Pour 1 tablespoon olive oil around top of preheated wok or skillet, coating sides; heat at medium-high (325°) for 2 minutes. Add garlic; stir-fry 30 seconds. Add red pepper strips; stir-fry 3 minutes. Remove from wok, and set aside.

Pour remaining 1 tablespoon olive oil into wok; add sliced lamb, and stir-fry 2 minutes. Stir in curry powder, coating well.

Return reserved minced garlic and red pepper strips to wok, and add broth mixture. Cook, stirring constantly, until mixture is thickened. Serve with hot cooked rice or pasta, if desired. Yield: 4 servings.

* 1 (1-pound) top sirloin steak (about 1 inch thick) may be substituted for boneless lamb.

## MEXICAN STIR-FRY
*(pictured on page 149)*

1 pound chicken breast halves,
   skinned and boned
2 tablespoons Mexican-seasoned
   chili powder
2 teaspoons cornstarch
½ cup chicken broth
2 tablespoons olive oil, divided
1 cup frozen whole kernel corn,
   thawed
2 medium tomatoes, seeded and
   diced
1 cup canned black beans, drained
¼ teaspoon salt

Cut chicken into thin strips; toss with chili powder, coating well. Let stand 10 minutes. Combine cornstarch and chicken broth; set aside.

Pour 1 tablespoon oil around top of preheated wok or skillet, coating sides; heat at medium-high (325°) for 2 minutes. Add chicken; stir-fry 3 to 4 minutes. Remove from wok, and set aside. Pour remaining 1 tablespoon olive oil into wok; add corn and tomato, and stir-fry 2 minutes. Return reserved chicken to wok. Add broth mixture, beans, and salt; cook, stirring constantly, until thickened. Yield: 4 servings.

## CAJUN SHRIMP STIR-FRY

4 slices bacon
2 teaspoons cornstarch
½ teaspoon fish-flavored bouillon
  granules
⅓ cup water
1½ pounds unpeeled medium-size
  fresh shrimp
2 teaspoons Creole seasoning
1 small green pepper, cut into 1-
  inch pieces
½ cup diced celery
1 (14-ounce) can Cajun-style
  stewed tomatoes, undrained
Hot cooked rice

Cook bacon in a large wok or skillet until crisp; remove bacon, reserving 3 tablespoons drippings. Crumble bacon, and set aside. Combine cornstarch, bouillon granules, and water; set aside.

Peel and devein shrimp. Pat shrimp dry; sprinkle with Creole seasoning. Pour 2 tablespoons reserved bacon drippings around top of preheated wok or skillet, coating sides; heat at medium-high (325°) for 1 minute. Add shrimp; stir-fry 2 minutes or until shrimp turn pink. Remove shrimp, and set aside.

Pour remaining 1 tablespoon reserved drippings into wok; add green pepper and celery, and stir-fry 2 minutes. Add tomatoes, and stir-fry 2 minutes. Return reserved shrimp to wok, and add cornstarch mixture; bring to a boil. Cook, stirring constantly, 1 minute. Sprinkle with reserved bacon. Serve over hot cooked rice. Yield: 4 servings.

# Warm-Weather Cooking Is Easy

Once the weather warms, cooking difficult meals probably isn't anywhere on your list of favorite activities. Who has the time or energy to cook for company? With these easy, elegant main dishes, *you* will. So pick one, team it with a microwaved potato or quickly sautéed vegetables and a tossed salad, and shout across the fence for your neighbors to join you.

## HERBED FLANK STEAK

1½ pounds flank steak
¼ cup finely chopped shallots
1 clove garlic, minced
3 tablespoons olive oil
2 tablespoons red wine vinegar
2 teaspoons chopped fresh basil or
  ¾ teaspoon dried basil
¾ teaspoon salt
½ teaspoon freshly ground
  pepper
½ teaspoon dried oregano

Trim excess fat from flank steak, and score steak on both sides. Place steak in a large shallow dish. Combine shallots and remaining ingredients, and pour mixture over steak; cover and marinate in refrigerator 4 hours, turning occasionally.

Place steak on lightly greased rack of a broiler pan; broil 6 inches from heat (with electric oven door partially opened) 10 to 14 minutes or until done, turning once. Serve immediately. Yield: 6 servings.

## LIME-BUTTERED TURKEY TENDERLOINS

¼ cup butter or margarine, melted
¼ cup lime juice
2 teaspoons dry mustard
2 teaspoons garlic salt
2 (¾-pound) turkey breast
  tenderloins
Garnishes: lime wedges, fresh
  parsley

Combine butter, lime juice, mustard, and garlic salt; divide mixture in half, and set aside.

Grill turkey, covered, over medium-hot coals (350° to 400°) 4 to 5 minutes on each side or until meat thermometer registers 170°, turning once and basting often with half of marinade.

Cook remaining marinade in a small saucepan until thoroughly heated; serve warm with sliced turkey. Garnish, if desired. Yield: 4 to 6 servings.
*Shirley McGehee*
*Spring Branch, Texas*

## SHRIMP PATTIES

3 cups water
1 pound unpeeled medium-size
  fresh shrimp
3 tablespoons butter or margarine
⅓ cup all-purpose flour
½ cup milk
2 green onions, chopped
1 tablespoon chopped fresh parsley
1 teaspoon lemon juice
½ teaspoon Beau Monde seasoning
¼ teaspoon salt
¼ teaspoon pepper
¼ teaspoon paprika
¼ teaspoon hot sauce
1 large egg, lightly beaten
1 cup Italian-seasoned
  breadcrumbs, divided
¼ cup vegetable oil

Bring water to a boil; add shrimp, and cook 3 to 5 minutes or until shrimp turn pink. Drain well; rinse with cold water. Peel and devein shrimp; chop and set aside.

Melt butter in a heavy saucepan over low heat; add flour, stirring until smooth. Cook 1 minute, stirring constantly. Gradually add milk to saucepan; cook over medium heat, stirring constantly, until mixture is thickened and bubbly. Stir in green onions and next 7 ingredients.

Combine shrimp, egg, and ½ cup breadcrumbs; stir in sauce mixture. Shape into 4 patties; dredge patties in remaining breadcrumbs. Pour oil to depth of ½-inch into a large, heavy skillet. Fry patties in hot oil over medium-high heat until golden brown, turning once. Drain on paper towels. Yield: 4 servings.

*Frances Berga-Rigsby*
*Daphne, Alabama*

**Tip:** *Did you know that scallions are the same as green onions? The only differences are that green onions are more mature, and each onion has a tiny bulb at its base.*

# Well-Seasoned Lamb

Lamb often is approached with uncertainty by some cooks. For years cookbooks have insisted that lamb be roasted until well-done. But anyone who has savored lamb roasted until juicy and pink will testify to its superior taste and texture.

A glance at these recipes shows that lamb is as versatile as beef, pork, or poultry. Try cooking Garlic-Rolled Lamb Roast just until the meat thermometer reads 140° to 150° to enjoy it at its juicy best.

For Lamb Kabobs, choose boneless lamb from the leg, rib, or loin. Like the kabobs, Destin Lamb Steak, cut from the leg, is broiled to seal in flavor. Both recipes are cooked under high heat, so be sure not to overcook.

Because of its age when marketed, lamb is naturally tender. Cuts from the leg, rib, or loin produce a subtle, delicate flavor when cooked the shortest amount of time that's suggested in your recipe. Insert a meat thermometer to eliminate any guesswork.

## BARBECUED LAMB SHANKS

6 lamb shanks
3 tablespoons all-purpose flour
2 tablespoons vegetable oil
1 cup catsup
½ cup water
¼ cup cider vinegar
¼ cup firmly packed brown sugar
2 tablespoons Worcestershire sauce
2 teaspoons salt
2 teaspoons dry mustard
1 medium onion, sliced
Hot cooked rice

Dredge lamb shanks in flour; set aside. Brown lamb shanks in oil in a large Dutch oven. Drain off drippings, and discard.

Combine catsup and next 6 ingredients; pour over lamb in Dutch oven. Add onion slices. Cover and simmer 2 hours, basting occasionally. Uncover and simmer an additional 15 minutes. Serve over rice. Yield: 6 servings.

*Nancy Swinney*
*Tallahassee, Florida*

## GARLIC-ROLLED LAMB ROAST

1 (4- to 6-pound) boned, rolled, and
  tied leg of lamb
6 to 8 cloves garlic, halved
1 (8-ounce) bottle Dijon vinaigrette
  salad dressing
2 tablespoons all-purpose flour
¼ cup water
¼ cup dry red wine
⅛ teaspoon pepper
Garnishes: fresh rosemary sprigs,
  sweet red pepper strips

Make several ½-inch slits on outside of lamb and insert garlic. Place lamb in a large shallow dish, and pour salad dressing over lamb. Cover and marinate 24 hours in refrigerator, turning lamb occasionally.

Remove lamb from marinade, reserving marinade. Place lamb, fat side up, on a rack in a shallow roasting pan, and insert meat thermometer, making sure it does not touch fat. Bake lamb at 350° for 1 hour and 45 minutes or until thermometer registers desired degree of doneness (rare 140°, medium 160°, and well-done 170°).

Transfer lamb to a serving platter, reserving drippings in pan; let stand 10 minutes before carving. Skim fat from pan drippings. Measure remaining liquid; add reserved marinade and enough water to measure 1¼ cups. Pour into small saucepan.

Combine flour and ¼ cup water, stirring well; add to pan drippings mixture. Add wine and pepper. Cook over medium heat, stirring constantly, until gravy is thickened and bubbly. Serve with lamb. Garnish, if desired. Yield: 8 to 10 servings. *Mrs. W. M. Alvine*
*Winter Springs, Florida*

## DESTIN LAMB STEAK

1½ tablespoons Dijon mustard
½ teaspoon dried whole rosemary
¼ teaspoon dried whole dillweed
¼ teaspoon ground ginger
⅛ teaspoon garlic powder
1 teaspoon Worcestershire sauce
¼ teaspoon prepared horseradish
1 (¾-inch-thick) center cut leg of lamb slice (about 12 ounces)
Olive oil

Combine first 7 ingredients; set aside. Brush lamb with olive oil, and place on lightly greased rack of a broiler pan. Broil 4 inches from heat 5 minutes. Turn and spread half of mustard sauce on lamb; broil 5 minutes. Turn and spread with remaining sauce; broil 1 to 2 minutes or until bubbly. Yield: 2 servings. *Frank Jacobson*
*Destin, Florida*

## LAMB KABOBS

1 pound boneless lamb, cut into 1-inch cubes
¾ teaspoon salt
⅛ teaspoon coarsely ground pepper
¼ teaspoon dried whole oregano
½ large onion
1 tomato
½ cup pineapple chunks
1 tablespoon vegetable oil

Place lamb in a shallow dish; sprinkle with seasonings, and stir gently. Cover, and chill 2 hours. Cut onion and tomato each into 8 wedges. Alternate lamb, onion, tomato wedges, and pineapple on 4 skewers. Brush with oil; broil 4 to 5 inches from heat 15 minutes or until desired degree of doneness, turning every 5 minutes. Yield: 4 servings. *Jean McIntosh*
*Spavinaw, Oklahoma*

# It's Rhubarb Time!

Wake up your taste buds with the invigorating flavor of rhubarb. It's no longer limited to recipes for pies and preserves. Our readers have found new ways to enjoy it, including a congealed salad.

## TART RHUBARB SALAD

4 cups sliced rhubarb (about 1 pound)
1 cup water
¾ cup sugar
¼ teaspoon salt
1 (6-ounce) package strawberry-flavored gelatin
1¾ cups cold water
¼ cup lemon juice
2 (11-ounce) cans mandarin oranges, drained
1 cup diced celery
Lettuce leaves
Sour cream

Combine first 4 ingredients in a large saucepan; bring to a boil. Reduce heat, and simmer 3 to 5 minutes or until rhubarb is tender. Remove from heat. Add gelatin, and stir until dissolved. Stir in cold water and lemon juice; chill until consistency of unbeaten egg white. Fold in oranges and celery; pour into a 12- x 8- x 2-inch dish; chill until firm. Cut into squares. Serve on lettuce leaves; dollop with sour cream. Yield: 12 servings.
*Barbara Sherrer*
*Bay City, Texas*

## RHUBARB SALAD

2 cups chopped rhubarb (about ½ pound)
¾ cup sugar
1 envelope unflavored gelatin
½ cup cold water
2 tablespoons lemon juice
2 drops red food coloring (optional)
1 cup chopped celery
½ cup chopped pecans
Lettuce leaves

Combine rhubarb and sugar in a saucepan; let stand 30 minutes, stirring several times. Sprinkle gelatin over cold water; let stand 5 minutes.

Cook rhubarb over low heat 5 to 10 minutes or until tender. Add gelatin mixture, lemon juice, and if desired, food coloring; stir well. Chill until consistency of unbeaten egg white. Fold in celery and pecans. Spoon into 5 (½-cup) oiled molds; chill until firm. Serve on lettuce leaves. Yield: 5 servings. *Mary P. Richmond*
*Paintsville, Kentucky*

## RHUBARB SQUARES

1 cup all-purpose flour
½ cup sifted powdered sugar
½ cup butter or margarine, softened
1 cup sugar
¼ cup all-purpose flour
¾ teaspoon baking powder
2 large eggs, beaten
3 cups diced rhubarb (about ¾ pound)

Combine 1 cup flour and powdered sugar; cut in butter with pastry blender until mixture resembles coarse meal. Press mixture evenly into a lightly greased 13- x 9- x 2-inch pan. Bake at 350° for 12 minutes.

Combine sugar, ¼ cup flour, and baking powder; add eggs, and mix well. Stir in rhubarb, and pour over prepared crust. Bake at 325° for 45 to 50 minutes. Cool and cut into squares. Yield: 12 servings.
*Mrs. Clayton J. Turner*
*DeFuniak Springs, Florida*

## RHUBARB CRISP

1 cup regular oats, uncooked
⅔ cup sugar
⅓ cup all-purpose flour
⅓ cup butter or margarine, melted
½ teaspoon ground cinnamon
6 cups chopped rhubarb (about 1½ pounds)
1 cup sugar

Combine uncooked oats, ⅔ cup sugar, flour, melted butter, and cinnamon, and set aside. Combine chopped rhubarb and 1 cup sugar; toss mixture gently, and place in a greased 8-inch square baking dish. Top rhubarb mixture with oats mixture. Bake at 350° for 45 minutes or until lightly brown. Yield: 8 servings. *Georgia S. Hagan*
*Bristol, Tennessee*

# A Little Mousse Magic

To some cooks, making a mousse is about as easy as pulling a rabbit out of a hat. But once you learn a few tricks of the trade, there's nothing to it. To solve the first mystery, mousse is simply a French term for "froth." Its consistency is light because of the air incorporated into it.

Traditionally, beaten egg whites gave mousses their volume, but to keep up with new safety standards of avoiding raw eggs in recipes, we've used another familiar option—whipped cream. It works just as well as beaten egg whites to lighten these sweets, but adds richer flavor and more calories than the egg whites.

Unflavored gelatin helps versions chilled in a mold hold their shape once removed from the containers. Whichever version you choose to prepare, these treats are sure to make dessert a magical finale.

## FROZEN WATERMELON MOUSSE

2½ cups seeded, diced watermelon
1 envelope unflavored gelatin
1 cup sugar
1 tablespoon lemon juice
1 cup whipping cream, whipped

Place watermelon in container of an electric blender, and process until smooth. Reserve 2¼ cups puree, discarding any remaining puree.

Combine gelatin and ¼ cup watermelon puree. Bring remaining 2 cups puree to a boil in a small saucepan. Remove from heat; add gelatin mixture, and stir until gelatin dissolves. Stir in sugar and lemon juice, and chill mixture until consistency of unbeaten egg white.

Fold whipped cream into chilled watermelon mixture. Spoon into a lightly oiled 6-cup mold. Cover and freeze 8 hours or until firm; unmold onto serving plate. Yield: 8 to 10 servings.
*Mrs. E.W. Hanley*
*Palm Harbor, Florida*

## LEMON MOUSSE WITH RASPBERRY SAUCE

1 envelope unflavored gelatin
2 tablespoons Chablis or other dry white wine
1½ tablespoons grated lemon rind
⅓ cup lemon juice
3 egg yolks
½ cup sugar, divided
1⅓ cups whipping cream
Raspberry Sauce

Sprinkle gelatin over wine in a heavy-duty, 1-quart saucepan; stir and let stand 1 minute. Stir in lemon rind and juice. Cook over low heat, stirring until gelatin dissolves.

Combine egg yolks and 3 tablespoons sugar; add to gelatin mixture, and cook, stirring constantly, until mixture reaches 160°. Cool 5 to 10 minutes, stirring often with a wire whisk. (Do not let mixture congeal.)

Beat whipping cream until foamy; gradually add remaining 5 tablespoons sugar, beating until soft peaks form.

Fold into lemon mixture. Spoon into individual serving dishes; chill until set. Serve with Raspberry Sauce. Yield: 6 servings.

### Raspberry Sauce

1 (10-ounce) package frozen raspberries, thawed and drained
2 tablespoons sugar
1 tablespoon lemon juice
1 tablespoon Grand Marnier or other orange-flavored liqueur

Combine raspberries, sugar, and lemon juice in container of an electric blender; process until smooth. Strain raspberry mixture, and discard seeds. Stir in Grand Marnier. Yield: ½ cup.
*Betty Watts*
*Panama City, Florida*

## PUMPKIN MOUSSE

1 envelope unflavored gelatin
¼ cup light rum
4 egg yolks
⅔ cup sugar
1 cup cooked, mashed pumpkin
½ teaspoon ground cinnamon
½ teaspoon ground ginger
¼ teaspoon ground mace
¼ teaspoon ground cloves
1½ cups whipping cream, whipped
Garnishes: whipped cream, walnut halves

Sprinkle gelatin over rum in a small saucepan; stir, and let stand 1 minute. Cook over low heat, stirring until gelatin dissolves; remove from heat.

Combine egg yolks and sugar in top of a double boiler; gradually stir in gelatin mixture. Bring water to a boil. Cook yolk mixture, stirring constantly, until mixture reaches 160° (about 20 minutes).

Gradually stir in pumpkin and spices. Fold whipped cream into pumpkin mixture. Spoon into a 1-quart soufflé dish, and chill until firm. Garnish, if desired. Yield: 6 to 8 servings.
*Margaret Cotton*
*Franklin, Virginia*

# JUNE

*If a more healthful lifestyle is important to you and your family, be sure to read this month's "On The Light Side" special section. The recipes are low in cholesterol and fat yet high in flavor, including some delectable fresh fruit desserts. Make Father's Day special by letting the children do the cooking. We've chosen an easy menu that even the younger ones can help prepare.*

# No Taste Like Home

It's time for homemade ice cream, so haul out the freezer, and take a turn at the crank. These recipes offer three distinctly new flavors.

Invite some friends over for an ice cream party and let them take part in making it. There's no better way to enjoy the fruits of your labor.

## STRAWBERRIES AND CREAM

1 quart milk
1 pint half-and-half
2 (14-ounce) cans sweetened condensed milk
2 teaspoons vanilla extract
⅛ to ¼ teaspoon almond extract
1 quart fresh strawberries, sliced

Combine first 5 ingredients in a large bowl. Pour mixture into freezer container of a 5-quart hand-turned or electric freezer. Freeze according to manufacturer's instructions. Pack freezer with additional ice and rock salt, and let stand 1 hour before serving. Serve with sliced strawberries. Yield: 3 quarts.

**Tip:** *Evaporated milk and sweetened condensed milk are different types of canned milk and cannot be used interchangeably. Evaporated milk is unsweetened milk thickened by removing some of its water content. Sweetened condensed milk is sweetened with sugar and thickened by evaporation of some of its water content.*

## PEANUT ICE CREAM

6 large eggs, lightly beaten
1 cup firmly packed brown sugar
3 cups milk
⅔ cup creamy peanut butter
3 cups whipping cream
2 cups unsalted peanuts, coarsely chopped
Commercial hot fudge sauce
Garnish: chopped peanuts

Combine eggs and brown sugar; set aside. Heat milk in a large saucepan over medium heat until hot. Gradually stir a small amount of hot milk into egg mixture; add to remaining hot milk, stirring constantly. Cook over medium heat, stirring often, until thermometer reaches 160° (about 3 to 5 minutes). Remove from heat; stir in peanut butter, and cool. Stir in whipping cream and peanuts.

Pour mixture into freezer container of a 1-gallon hand-turned or electric freezer. Freeze mixture according to manufacturer's instructions. Pack freezer with additional ice and rock salt, and let stand 1 hour. Serve with hot fudge sauce. Garnish, if desired. Yield: 2½ quarts. *Rublelene Singleton*
*Scotts Hill, Tennessee*

## BUTTER CRISP ICE CREAM

2 cups finely crushed corn flakes cereal
2 cups chopped pecans
1 cup firmly packed brown sugar
½ cup butter or margarine, melted
4 envelopes unflavored gelatin
2 cups sugar
¼ teaspoon salt
6 cups milk, divided
6 large eggs, lightly beaten
1 quart whipping cream
2 tablespoons vanilla extract

Combine first 3 ingredients; stir in butter. Spoon mixture into a 15- x 10- x 1-inch jellyroll pan. Bake at 350° for 25 minutes, stirring occasionally; cool. Set aside.

Combine gelatin, sugar, and salt in a large saucepan; stir in 2 cups milk. Let stand 1 minute. Cook over low heat, stirring until gelatin dissolves (about 5 minutes). Gradually stir a small amount of hot milk mixture into eggs; add to remaining hot milk mixture, stirring constantly. Cook over medium heat, stirring often, until thermometer reaches 160° (about 3 to 5 minutes). Add remaining 4 cups milk, whipping cream, and vanilla.

Pour mixture into freezer container of a 5-quart hand-turned or electric freezer. Freeze according to manufacturer's instructions.

Spoon ice cream into a large airtight container, and stir in reserved corn flakes mixture. Cover and freeze. Yield: 1 gallon. *Erma Jackson*
*Huntsville, Alabama*

# From Garden To Table

When the weather gets warmer, meals get lighter, and fresh vegetables are a natural. By planning a vegetable menu, you can skip the meat course and still have a nutritionally balanced meal.

Start preparation with Summer Salad With Citrus Marinade. Then assemble the individual corn dishes, and get the carrots and okra ready to cook. Put the corn dishes in to bake, cook Orange-Fennel Carrots, and fry Okra Fritters. Get ready to enjoy these vegetables at their best.

### VEGETABLE DINNER FOR FOUR

**Corn-and-Swiss Cheese Bake**
**Orange-Fennel Carrots**
**Okra Fritters**
**Summer Salad**
**With Citrus Marinade**

### CORN-AND-SWISS CHEESE BAKE

2 cups fresh corn, cut from cob
¾ cup (3 ounces) shredded
  Swiss cheese
½ cup whipping cream
1 large egg, beaten
⅛ teaspoon salt
⅛ teaspoon pepper
Garnish: red pepper strips

Combine first 6 ingredients; spoon into 4 lightly greased 6-ounce ramekins or custard cups. Bake at 350° for 20 to 25 minutes. Garnish, if desired. Yield: 4 servings.

**Note:** You can bake mixture in a lightly greased 1-quart casserole at 350° for 30 to 35 minutes.
*Sandi Pichon*
*Slidell, Louisiana*

### ORANGE-FENNEL CARROTS

1 pound carrots, scraped and cut
  into thin strips
2 tablespoons butter or
  margarine
3 tablespoons brown sugar
1½ teaspoons fennel seeds
1½ teaspoons orange juice

Cook carrots, covered, in a small amount of boiling water in a medium saucepan 6 to 8 minutes or until crisp-tender. Drain.

Melt butter in a small saucepan. Add next 3 ingredients, and bring to a boil. Reduce heat, and simmer 5 minutes. Pour mixture through a wire-mesh strainer over carrots; discard fennel seeds. Stir carrots; serve immediately. Yield: 4 servings.

**Microwave Directions:** Combine carrots and ¼ cup water in a 1-quart casserole. Cover and microwave at HIGH 7 to 8 minutes or until carrots are crisp-tender. Drain.

Place butter in a 1-cup glass measure; microwave at HIGH 30 seconds. Stir in next 3 ingredients, and microwave at HIGH 2 minutes, stirring after 1 minute. Pour mixture through a wire-mesh strainer over carrots; discard fennel seeds. Stir carrots; serve immediately.
*Barbara Allison*
*Ormond Beach, Florida*

### OKRA FRITTERS

¼ cup cornmeal
¼ cup all-purpose flour
½ cup finely chopped onion
½ cup evaporated milk
1 large egg, lightly beaten
3 tablespoons chopped fresh parsley
2 tablespoons grated Parmesan
  cheese
½ teaspoon salt
¼ teaspoon red pepper
2 cups sliced fresh okra (about ⅔
  pound) *
Vegetable oil
Salt (optional)

Combine first 9 ingredients; stir in okra. Pour oil to depth of 2 inches in a Dutch oven; heat to 350°. Drop mixture by tablespoonfuls into oil, and cook until golden brown, turning once. Drain on paper towels. Sprinkle with salt, if desired, and serve immediately. Yield: 4 to 6 servings.

* Two cups frozen sliced okra, thawed, may be substituted for sliced fresh okra.

### SUMMER SALAD WITH CITRUS MARINADE

2 to 3 medium tomatoes, sliced
1 small green pepper, sliced into
  rings
⅓ cup olive oil
½ teaspoon grated lemon rind
1½ tablespoons lemon juice
1 tablespoon chopped fresh chives
¼ teaspoon sugar
⅛ teaspoon white pepper
Lettuce leaves

Arrange tomato and green pepper in a shallow dish. Set aside.

Combine olive oil and next 5 ingredients; pour over vegetables. Cover and marinate in refrigerator 45 minutes. Serve with a slotted spoon, and arrange on lettuce. Yield: 4 servings.

### Vegetable Basics

■ Wash most vegetables; trim wilted parts or excess leaves before storing in refrigerator.

■ The darker the orange color of carrots, the greater the content of vitamin A.

■ Remove the tops of carrots before refrigerating. Tops drain the carrots of moisture, making them limp and dry.

■ Sand and dirt can be removed from fresh vegetables by soaking in warm salted water 5 minutes.

■ It's helpful to know when buying okra that 1 pound of the fresh okra pods yields about 2 cups slices.

■ Always be sure to cook okra quickly, as overcooking will result in a gummy texture.

# Kids Cook For Father's Day

"Look, Daddy, I cooked it myself!" What a special Father's Day when the children do the cooking. We've chosen an easy menu that some children can prepare alone. Others, especially young ones, will need help. Make the meal a family affair by letting older relatives assist the children.

Kids love using various candies, nuts, and morsels to design the face on our Father's Day Cake. Made from a cake mix, the cake can be frosted with either our buttercream frosting or a store-bought version.

If a child isn't old enough to use a grill, let him or her prepare the marinade for the ham; he or she can help an adult grill it. Hands too young to operate a microwave oven can measure the ingredients for Cheesy Vegetable Sauce.

### FATHER'S DAY MENU

**Easy Grilled Ham**
**Quick Baked Potatoes**
**with**
**Cheesy Vegetable Sauce**
**Sliced tomatoes with**
**Commercial Italian**
**salad dressing**
**Father's Day Cake**

### EASY GRILLED HAM

1 (2-inch-thick) boneless, fully
 cooked ham steak
½ cup ginger ale
½ cup orange juice
¼ cup firmly packed brown sugar
1 tablespoon vegetable oil
1½ teaspoons white vinegar
1 teaspoon dry mustard
¼ teaspoon ground ginger
⅛ teaspoon ground cloves

Place steak in a large shallow dish or heavy-duty, zip-top plastic bag. Combine ginger ale, orange juice, brown sugar, vegetable oil, white vinegar, dry mustard, ground ginger, and ground cloves, stirring until sugar dissolves; pour over steak. Cover or seal, and refrigerate 8 hours, turning meat occasionally.

Drain steak, discarding marinade. Grill, covered, over medium-hot coals (350° to 400°) 15 minutes on each side or until a meat thermometer registers 140°. Yield: 10 to 12 servings.

*Judy Grimes*
*Brandon, Mississippi*

### QUICK BAKED POTATOES

6 medium baking potatoes (about 3
 pounds)

Wash potatoes, and pat dry; prick each potato several times with a fork. Arrange potatoes on paper towels in a microwave. Microwave potatoes at HIGH 12 minutes (2 minutes per potato), turning and rearranging potatoes after 6 minutes. Carefully remove potatoes, and place on a baking sheet. Bake potatoes at 400° for 30 minutes or until done. Yield: 6 servings.

*Kelly Sullivan*
*Birmingham, Alabama*

### CHEESY VEGETABLE SAUCE

½ cup (2 ounces) shredded Cheddar
 cheese
½ cup sour cream
¼ cup butter or margarine
2 tablespoons chopped fresh
 parsley
½ teaspoon garlic powder

Combine shredded Cheddar cheese and remaining ingredients in a 1-quart glass bowl. Microwave at MEDIUM-HIGH (70% power) 2 minutes or until cheese melts, stirring at 1-minute intervals with a wire whisk. Serve sauce over baked potatoes or other vegetables. Yield: 1 cup.

*Catherine Bowen Drewry*
*Crawford, Georgia*

### FATHER'S DAY CAKE

1 (22.5-ounce) package chocolate
 cake mix with pudding
1½ cups butter or margarine,
 softened
2 tablespoons milk
1 teaspoon vanilla or almond
 extract
4 cups sifted powdered sugar
¾ cup chopped pecans
Garnishes: candy-coated chocolate
 pieces, gumdrops, red cinnamon
 candies, jelly beans, semisweet
 chocolate mini-morsels, gumballs,
 chocolate-covered peanuts

Prepare cake mix according to package directions; spoon batter into two greased and floured 9-inch round cakepans. Bake at 350° for 25 minutes or until a wooden pick inserted in center comes out clean. Cool in pans on wire racks 10 minutes. Remove from pans; cool completely on wire racks.

Beat butter, milk, and vanilla at medium speed with an electric mixer 30 seconds; gradually add powdered sugar, beating until blended. Beat an additional 2 minutes or until frosting is light and fluffy.

Place one cake layer on cake plate; spread cake layer with 1 cup frosting, and top cake with second layer. Frost top and sides of cake with remaining frosting. Pat chopped pecans on cake to resemble hair. Make face using assorted candies, if you wish. Yield: one 2-layer cake.

**Note:** Two (16-ounce) containers of ready-to-spread vanilla-flavored frosting may be substituted for our buttercream frosting.

# IIII On The Light Side

## Back To Basics: Eating For Better Health

Nutrition research has proven that many chronic diseases in the United States are linked to the foods we eat. Most nutrition experts agree that a high-fiber, low-fat diet is important in the prevention of heart disease and certain types of cancer. Many authorities also suggest that we keep a check on salt and sugar, and drink alcoholic beverages in moderation, if at all. In addition, it's important to stay active with regular exercise, and to maintain a proper weight.

In the 1990 "Dietary Guidelines for Americans," the U.S. Department of Health and Human Services still encourages us to eat a variety of foods.

What follows is a review of the different food groups and how each group fits into a healthful diet for the nineties. We've included the recommended number of servings from each food group as a guide. If you're active, follow the upper level of daily servings. Less-active individuals or those who are watching their weight should stay at the lower end of the range.

### Breads and Other Grain Products

In the seventies and eighties, many weight-conscious people considered a high-protein, low-carbohydrate diet a sure way to lose weight. When following such a diet, they avoided potatoes and bread but ate thick rib-eye steaks and other heavily marbled meats with great abandon.

Today's dietary guidelines recommend 6 to 11 servings of bread, cereal, rice, or pasta daily. Some examples of a serving include 1 slice of bread; ½ hamburger bun; ½ cup cooked cereal, rice, or pasta; and ¾ cup dry, ready-to-eat cereal.

Bread and pasta are loaded with complex carbohydrates, which should not be confused with the simple carbohydrates found in sugars. Many simple carbohydrate foods (candy, soft drinks) provide few nutrients other than calories and should be consumed only in moderation. The complex carbohydrates in breads and cereals are accompanied by B vitamins, iron, and protein. To make them even healthier, these foods are naturally low in fat. Whole grain products, such as whole wheat bread and brown rice, are also high in fiber.

### Fruits and Vegetables

We used to be told, "An apple a day keeps the doctor away." But today's guidelines suggest we eat two to four servings of fruit instead of just one. In addition, we need to eat three to five servings of vegetables daily. One piece of fruit, ½ cup diced fruit, or ¾ cup fruit juice is one serving of fruit. One-half cup of cooked vegetables or 1 cup of raw vegetables is considered one serving of vegetables.

Fruits and vegetables provide fiber, carbohydrates, vitamins, and minerals. They are also naturally low in fat.

### Meat, Poultry, Fish, Dried Beans, and Eggs

A healthful eating plan contains only two 3-ounce servings of cooked lean meat, poultry, or fish a day. If a food scale is not available, you can estimate the serving size by appearance. One serving (about 3 ounces without the skin or bone) is about the size of a deck of playing cards, which is less than most people eat.

Choose your protein foods wisely by purchasing lean cuts of meat, trimming the excess fat and skin when possible, and following low-fat cooking methods.

A word of caution about smoked or salt-cured meats, such as bacon, smoked ham, and processed luncheon meats: These foods contain substances some studies have linked to cancer of the stomach and esophagus, so limit the amounts of these you eat.

One-half cup cooked dried beans or peas substitutes well for one serving of meat. Dried beans and peas are low in fat and high in fiber and protein. Eggs also provide plenty of protein, but they are high in cholesterol. One egg or two egg whites are equivalent to one serving of meat.

### Milk and Milk Products

These dairy foods are rich in calcium, protein, B vitamins, and phosphorus. Fortified skim, low-fat, and whole milk also provide vitamins A and D. Many low-fat and nonfat choices—skim milk, nonfat and low-fat yogurt, and low-fat cheese—are available today. Two to three servings from low-fat and nonfat choices are recommended daily with 1 cup of milk or yogurt or 1½ ounces of cheese equivalent to a serving.

## Other Foods

Salt and sugars are popular ingredients in some of our favorite foods, but the latest dietary guidelines recommend that these ingredients be eaten only in moderation.

Salt is the main source of sodium in our diets, and while some sodium is necessary for normal body functions, most Americans eat far more than needed. In countries where people eat small amounts of salt, high blood pressure is less common than in those places with diets similar to our own. (Other factors that contribute to the development of high blood pressure include heredity, obesity, and excess consumption of alcohol.)

When individuals with high blood pressure cut back on the amount of sodium they eat, their blood pressure usually decreases. Even those who don't have high blood pressure benefit by eating less sodium and may decrease their risk of developing it. Because there is currently no way to predict who will and who won't develop high blood pressure, nutritionists generally recommend that we consume less sodium, unless advised otherwise by a physician.

Sugars, such as table sugar, syrup, fructose, and dextrose (found in many processed foods), are simple carbohydrates that provide calories with almost no nutrients. They should be eaten in moderation.

Alcohol, like sugars, supplies calories with little or no nutrients. Alcohol is linked to many health problems, is the cause of many accidents, and can lead to addiction. If you do drink alcohol, a healthy guide is to limit it to two drinks a day for men and one drink for women. (One drink is equal to 1½ ounces of pure alcohol [80 proof], 5 ounces of wine, or 12 ounces of regular beer.)

## Putting the Basics to Work

Good nutrition is important for growth and maintenance throughout life. What we eat contributes to the development or prevention of certain chronic diseases, particularly heart disease and cancer. We've given you a guide for eating a variety of healthy foods that are low in fat and high in fiber, vitamins, and minerals. Now we'll tell you how to turn those foods into dishes your family will enjoy.

# Low-Fat Cooking Techniques

Low fat doesn't have to mean less flavor. But preparing flavorful, low-fat meals requires different cooking techniques. Here's a description of some you'll want to try, along with some tips to help give foods more flavor.

## Poaching

Poaching is cooking food gently in a small amount of liquid at a temperature below the boiling point. No added fat is needed for poaching, and the food retains its flavor, shape, and texture. Poultry, firm fish, pears, apples, and peaches are some foods that poach well. Equipment: skillet, pan, or poacher with a lid; slotted spoon.
■ Suggested poaching liquids include wine, low-sodium chicken broth, unsweetened fruit juice, and water.
■ Herbs, spices, shallots, and onions can be added to the poaching liquid for extra flavor.
■ The poaching liquid should barely move during cooking time; if the liquid simmers or boils, the temperature is too high.
■ While cooking, keep the pan covered to prevent steam from escaping.
■ Do not overcook or the food will be dry and tough.
■ Use leftover poaching liquid as a base for soups.

## Steaming

This technique involves cooking food on a rack using the steam from boiling liquid in a covered pan. Food can also be steamed in the oven without any liquid in a parchment paper package (*en papillote*) or in a package made from heavy-duty aluminum foil. No added fat is needed for steaming, and the food retains its flavor, shape, and texture. Steaming limits the loss of water-soluble vitamins. Equipment needed: large saucepan with lid and steamer rack or basket, or parchment paper package, or heavy-duty aluminum foil package; potholder; and spoon or tongs.
■ Place food on steamer rack about 1 inch above the boiling liquid.
■ Do not let the steaming liquid boil away during cooking.
■ Herbs and spices can be added to the steaming liquid for extra flavor.
■ Bring the steaming liquid to a boil before adding the food.
■ Place the food in a single layer on steamer rack or in steamer basket.
■ To prevent steam burns, be sure to open the lid away from you.

**Note:** To steam food in a microwave oven, use a small amount of liquid in a microwavable container covered with heavy-duty plastic wrap and vented.

## Broiling/grilling

Broiling or grilling means cooking food by using direct heat on one side of the food at a time. Beef, pork, poultry, fish, vegetables, and some fruits broil or grill well. Equipment needed: broiler pan and rack or grill, rack, and charcoal; potholder; instant-read thermometer; timer; basting brush; and spatula or tongs.
■ Line the broiler pan with aluminum foil for easy cleanup, and coat the broiler rack with vegetable cooking spray to prevent sticking. Coat the grill rack with vegetable cooking spray away from the fire and preheat rack 4 to 5 minutes before adding food.

■ Trim excess fat from meats to minimize fire flare-ups and reduce the potential for carcinogens to form.
■ Cook food at the recommended distance from the heating element or charcoal.
■ Use tongs to turn the food instead of a fork to avoid piercing the food and releasing the juices.
■ Keep in mind that broiled or grilled fish is done when it is opaque and it flakes easily when tested with a fork.

## Braising

This method calls for browning food on the cook top for color and flavor, and then cooking it at a low temperature for a long period of time in a small amount of liquid in a pot covered with a tight-fitting lid. Braising is ideal for less-tender cuts of meat, such as boned, rolled, and tied meats; chuck roasts; rump roasts; round roasts; veal or lamb shanks; and whole chickens or Cornish hens. Vegetables that braise well include carrots, leeks, Belgian endive, and celery hearts. Equipment needed: an ovenproof Dutch oven or a cook top-safe or ovenproof casserole with a tight-fitting lid; meat fork or spoon.
■ Use a small amount of fat or vegetable cooking spray in which to brown the food. Add ¼ to ½ inch liquid to the pan after the food has browned, cover tightly, and finish cooking either on low heat on the cook top or at a low temperature in the oven.
■ Water, no-salt-added chicken or beef broth, unsweetened fruit juice, wine, and no-salt-added tomato juice make good braising liquids.
■ A nutrient-rich sauce can be made from the cooking liquid once the fat is removed.

## Baking/roasting

Baking or roasting means cooking food in an oven using dry heat. Equipment needed: an assortment of baking pans (baking sheets, cakepans, loafpans, or muffin pans) or roasting pans

(a broiler pan with a rack or shallow, ovenproof baking dishes).
■ Coat baking and roasting pans and racks with vegetable cooking spray to prevent food from sticking.
■ Preheat oven to desired temperature; use an oven thermometer to check oven temperature for accuracy.
■ Prepare baking pans before preparing the food; bake batters and doughs immediately because the leavening agents in the recipes are activated as soon as the dry and liquid ingredients are stirred together.
■ Set a timer for the recommended cooking time, and do not open the oven door until the end of the cooking time in order to avoid changes in oven temperature.
■ Place meats on a rack so that the fat can drip away during cooking, and place the rack in a shallow pan for adequate air circulation and even heat penetration.
■ Bake fish about 10 minutes per inch of thickness.
■ Because of the water whipped into reduced-calorie margarine, it does not work well in some baked products.
■ Keep in mind that baked goods may not brown as well when the amount of fat or sugar is reduced.

## Sautéing/stir-frying

Sautéing and stir-frying are terms for cooking food quickly over high heat in a small amount of hot fat in a wok or skillet. Small chops, pounded pieces of chicken or meat, fish fillets, sweet peppers, mushrooms, and summer squash are ideal for sautéing and stir-frying. Equipment needed: sauté pan, wok, or large, heavy skillet; spatula or wooden spoon.
■ The cookware can be coated with vegetable cooking spray instead of adding a small amount of fat. (**Note:** Hold cookware over the sink or counter top—not over the cook top or heating element—when coating it with cooking spray.) Food can sometimes be dry-sautéed in a well-seasoned,

cast-iron skillet or a heavy, nonstick skillet.
■ Watch carefully whenever you sauté using only vegetable cooking spray because food can burn quickly.
■ Cut food into uniform-size pieces for even cooking.
■ Cook food in small batches; if food is crowded, it will steam instead of sauté. Stir the food constantly during cooking time to prevent overbrowning and sticking.
■ Do not use a lid or the food will steam or sweat.

# Facts On Fat And Fiber

Eat more fiber—but be sure not to eat too much fat. Sounds like a difficult balancing act, doesn't it? It's really not as tough as it seems. Foods that are naturally high in fiber are also naturally low in fat; this is an important fact to consider about daily diets.

## Focus on Fiber

For years nutritionists have promoted fiber-rich fruits and vegetables because they are usually low in calories and promote regularity. Today, strong evidence links foods high in fiber to a decreased risk of certain types of cancer, as well as lower levels of blood cholesterol.

Fiber can be categorized into two major types: soluble and insoluble. Soluble fiber tends to swell when eaten and slows the digestion of foods in the stomach. It also helps control the blood sugar level of diabetics and lowers blood cholesterol levels. Examples include oat bran, dried beans and peas, barley, and some fruits and vegetables. Insoluble fiber promotes regularity and helps decrease the risk of colon cancer. An example is the wheat bran in whole wheat bread.

While soluble and insoluble fiber perform different jobs in the body, it's best to increase your intake of all fiber-rich foods rather than emphasize one type over the other. The recommended amount of fiber for most people is 20 to 35 grams a day. To meet this guideline, you need to eat six or more servings of whole grain products and five or more servings of fruits, vegetables, and/or legumes daily. Be sure to increase your fiber intake gradually to prevent abdominal pain, gas, and diarrhea. In addition, drink plenty of fluids because fiber needs water to work properly.

You may be tempted to get your recommended amount of fiber through supplements instead of food. But supplements do not contain all of the vitamins and minerals found in high-fiber foods and are generally not recommended. Furthermore, scientists are uncertain if fiber works alone or in combination with other substances to promote good health.

## Focus on Fat

The amount of fat suggested for most people is based on the number of calories eaten: Fat should contribute no more than 30% of total calories of your daily intake. As a rough guide, most people can eat 60 to 70 grams of fat a day.

Some foods, such as meat and cheese, are naturally high in fat, while others, such as vegetables and fruits, are almost fat-free. About 10 grams of fat are present in each of the following foods: 3 slices broiled bacon, 3 ounces roast beef, 1½ ounces Cheddar cheese, 1¼ cups whole milk, and 1 tablespoon margarine. On the lighter side it takes 18 ounces cooked red snapper, 25 cups skim milk, 20 medium apples, or 100 cups of lettuce to provide the same amount of fat.

## VEGETABLE BURRITOS
*(pictured on page 152)*

4½ cups sliced fresh mushrooms (1 pound)
1 cup chopped onion
1 cup chopped green pepper
2 cloves garlic, crushed
2 teaspoons olive oil
1 (15-ounce) can kidney beans
2 tablespoons finely chopped ripe olives
¼ teaspoon pepper
8 (8-inch) flour tortillas
½ cup nonfat sour cream alternative
1 cup commercial chunky salsa, divided
½ cup (2 ounces) shredded, reduced-fat sharp Cheddar cheese
Vegetable cooking spray

Cook mushrooms, onion, green pepper, and garlic in olive oil in a large, nonstick skillet over medium-high heat, stirring constantly, until tender. Remove from heat; drain. Combine cooked vegetables, drained kidney beans, olives, and pepper.

Spoon about ½ cup bean mixture evenly down center of each tortilla. Top with 1 tablespoon sour cream alternative, 1 tablespoon salsa, and 1 tablespoon cheese; fold opposite sides over filling.

Coat a large nonstick skillet or griddle with cooking spray. Heat over medium-high heat until hot. Cook tortillas, seam-side down, 1 minute on each side or until thoroughly heated. Top each tortilla with 1 tablespoon salsa. Yield: 8 servings (225 calories [22% from fat] per 1 burrito and 1 tablespoon salsa).

□ *9.7g protein, 5.4g fat (1.5g saturated, 2.4g monounsaturated, 0.9g polyunsaturated), 37.3g carbohydrate, 6g fiber, 5mg cholesterol, 480mg sodium, and 120mg calcium.*
*Linda Weathers*
*Birmingham, Alabama*

## MINTED MARINATED FRUIT

1 (20-ounce) can unsweetened pineapple chunks, undrained
1½ cups unpeeled, chopped red apple
1½ cups unpeeled, chopped green apple
1 cup unpeeled, chopped pear
1 cup sliced banana
½ cup orange juice
2 tablespoons chopped fresh mint
1 tablespoon honey

Drain pineapple chunks, reserving juice. Combine fruit in an 11- x 7- x 1½-inch dish. Combine reserved pineapple juice, orange juice, and remaining ingredients; pour over fruit. Cover and chill 3 hours, stirring occasionally. Yield: 7 servings (118 calories [3% from fat] per 1-cup serving).

□ *0.8g protein, 0.4g fat (0.1g saturated, 0g monounsaturated, 0.3g polyunsaturated), 30.4g carbohydrate, 2.9g fiber, 0mg cholesterol, 1mg sodium, and 19mg calcium.* *Daisy Reed*
*Southaven, Mississippi*

## TOSSED VEGETABLE SAUTÉ

1 pound fresh asparagus
3 medium carrots, scraped and cut into thin strips
1 clove garlic, minced
2 teaspoons margarine, melted
1 cup frozen snow pea pods, thawed
½ cup diagonally sliced green onions
¼ teaspoon salt
¼ teaspoon freshly ground pepper

Snap off tough ends of asparagus. Remove scales from stalks with a vegetable peeler or knife, if desired. Cut diagonally into ¾-inch pieces.

Cook asparagus, carrots, and garlic in melted margarine in a large, non-stick skillet over medium-high heat, stirring mixture constantly, 5 minutes or until crisp-tender. Stir in snow peas, green onions, salt, and pepper; cook, stirring constantly, 1 minute or until thoroughly heated. Yield: 4 servings (73 calories [27% from fat] per 1-cup serving).

□ 3.9g protein, 2.2g fat (0.5g saturated, 0.8g monounsaturated, 0.7g polyunsaturated), 11.2g carbohydrate, 4.3g fiber, 0mg cholesterol, 191mg sodium, and 56mg calcium.

*Hilda Marshall*
*Front Royal, Virginia*

### CAROLINA BLACK BEAN SOUP

1 pound dried black beans
8 cups water
1 cup chopped onion
1 cup chopped celery
1 cup chopped green pepper
1 clove garlic, minced
1 tablespoon olive oil
1 teaspoon salt
½ to 1 teaspoon pepper
3 (8-ounce) cans no-salt-added tomato sauce

Sort and wash beans; place in a large Dutch oven. Add water, and bring to a boil; cook 3 minutes. Remove from heat; cover and let stand 1 hour. Do not drain.

Cook onion and next 3 ingredients in olive oil in a nonstick skillet over medium-high heat, stirring constantly, until tender. Add onion mixture, salt, and pepper to beans; bring to a boil. Cover, reduce heat, and simmer 1½ hours or until beans are tender. Stir in tomato sauce, and simmer, stirring mixture occasionally, 30 minutes.

Yield: 11 servings (185 calories [9% from fat] per 1-cup serving).

□ 9.9g protein, 1.9g fat (0.3g saturated, 1g monounsaturated, 0.4g polyunsaturated), 33.7g carbohydrate, 6.2g fiber, 0mg cholesterol, 239mg sodium, and 62mg calcium.

*Tami Summerour*
*Little Mountain, South Carolina*

# Wake Up To A Healthy Breakfast

Whether you're rushing to the office, or getting the children ready for school—you probably have little time for breakfast. That's why Oat Bran Waffles have so much appeal. You can make a batch one day and freeze the leftovers; then pop them in the toaster or microwave for a quick, nutritious breakfast. For a cool, refreshing breakfast drink on busy mornings, try Strawberry-Pear Shake, which provides plenty of fiber and is easy to prepare.

### STRAWBERRY-PEAR SHAKE

1 cup fresh strawberries, sliced and frozen
1 medium-size ripe pear, peeled, and coarsely chopped
½ cup vanilla low-fat yogurt
½ cup skim milk
1 teaspoon sugar

Combine all ingredients in container of an electric blender; process until smooth. Serve beverage immediately.

Yield: 2 cups (148 calories [8% from fat] per 1-cup serving).

□ 5.6g protein, 1.4g fat (0.6g saturated, 0.3g monounsaturated, 0.2g polyunsaturated), 30.3g carbohydrate, 4g fiber, 4mg cholesterol, 70mg sodium, and 192mg calcium.

*Libby Winstead*
*Nashville, Tennessee*

### OAT BRAN WAFFLES

¾ cup oat bran
½ cup whole wheat flour
½ cup all-purpose flour
2 teaspoons baking powder
½ teaspoon salt
1½ cups skim milk
3 tablespoons safflower or vegetable oil
1 egg yolk, beaten
2 egg whites
Vegetable cooking spray

Combine oat bran and next 4 ingredients in a medium bowl. Combine milk, oil, and egg yolk; add to dry ingredients, stirring just until moistened. Beat egg whites at high speed with an electric mixer until stiff peaks form; gently fold into batter.

Coat a waffle iron with cooking spray, and allow waffle iron to preheat. Spoon 1⅓ cups batter onto hot waffle iron, spreading batter to edges. Bake until lightly browned. Repeat procedure with remaining batter. Yield: 12 (4-inch) waffles (106 calories [41% from fat] per waffle).

□ 3.9g protein, 4.8g fat (0.5g saturated, 0.6g monounsaturated, 2.7g polyunsaturated), 12.7g carbohydrate, 1.4g fiber, 19mg cholesterol, 174mg sodium, and 79mg calcium.

*Mary Beth Asma*
*Winter Garden, Florida*

## OPEN-FACED BREAKFAST SANDWICHES

½ cup light process cream cheese
  product
4 whole wheat English muffins,
  split and toasted
½ cup low-sugar orange marmalade
8 (1-ounce) slices lean Canadian
  bacon
1 cup alfalfa sprouts
32 mandarin orange segments

Spread 1 tablespoon cream cheese on cut side of each muffin half; spread 1 tablespoon orange marmalade over cream cheese. Top with Canadian bacon; place on a baking sheet. Broil 5 inches from heat (with electric oven door partially open) 3 minutes or until hot. Remove from oven; top each with 2 tablespoons alfalfa sprouts and 4 orange segments. Serve immediately. Yield: 8 servings (191 calories [24% from fat] per serving).

□ *10.2g protein, 5.1g fat (2.1g saturated, 0.9g monounsaturated, 0.3g polyunsaturated), 25.7g carbohydrate, 0.2g fiber, 22mg cholesterol, 647mg sodium, and 77mg calcium.*

---

### Calorie Checklist

■ Choose dairy products that are made from skim or low-fat milk as a way to keep fat and calories lower.
■ Save calories at mealtime by eating your meal from a small luncheon plate rather than a large dinner plate. Smaller portions of food will look larger.
■ Reduce the calories in meat dishes by trimming away and discarding any visible fat from the meat before cooking.

---

# Salads Make The Meal

Salads can help make your meals appetizing and nutritious. To keep main-dish salads low in fat, carefully select the source of protein. Lean meats, poultry, and seafood, as well as low-fat cheeses and cooked egg whites, are all good choices.

Also choose the dressing carefully. Many salad dressings, as well as mayonnaise, are almost all fat. One tablespoon of blue cheese dressing contains about 9 grams of fat. The fat content in mayonnaise is even higher, with 11 grams of fat per tablespoon. If you make a homemade dressing, use reduced-calorie mayonnaise or plain nonfat yogurt as a base instead of regular mayonnaise.

## ORIENTAL PORK SALAD

12 ounces lean, boneless pork loin,
  cut into 3- x ¼-inch strips
1 (6-ounce) can unsweetened
  pineapple juice
3 tablespoons dry sherry
2 tablespoons brown sugar
½ teaspoon dried crushed red
  pepper
6 cloves garlic, halved
½ teaspoon dark sesame oil
2 teaspoons reduced-sodium soy
  sauce
Vegetable cooking spray
3 green onions, cut into 1-inch
  pieces
¼ cup sliced water chestnuts, cut
  into thin strips
1 (6-ounce) package frozen snow
  pea pods, thawed
3 cups finely shredded cabbage
1 teaspoon sesame seeds,
  toasted
Garnish: dried crushed red pepper

Place pork in a shallow dish. Combine pineapple juice, sherry, brown sugar, crushed red pepper, and garlic; pour over pork. Cover and chill 2 hours, stirring occasionally.

Drain pork, reserving ½ cup marinade. Combine reserved marinade, sesame oil, and soy sauce; set aside.

Coat a large skillet with cooking spray; place over medium-high heat until hot. Add pork, and cook, stirring constantly, 3 minutes or just until done. Stir in green onions, water chestnuts, snow peas, and reserved marinade mixture. Cook pork mixture until thoroughly heated, stirring frequently.

Arrange ½ cup cabbage on individual serving plates. Top each with ⅔ cup pork mixture, and sprinkle with sesame seeds. Garnish by sprinkling with crushed red pepper, if desired. Yield: 6 servings (151 calories [31% from fat] per serving).

□ *13.5g protein, 5.2g fat (1.6g saturated, 2.2g monounsaturated, 0.8g polyunsaturated), 12.5g carbohydrate, 1.9g fiber, 34mg cholesterol, 115mg sodium, and 47mg calcium.*

## CRAB-AND-ASPARAGUS SALAD

18 fresh asparagus spears
   (¾ pound)
¼ cup nonfat mayonnaise
1 tablespoon lemon juice
1 teaspoon chopped capers
½ teaspoon prepared mustard
½ teaspoon white wine
   Worcestershire sauce
12 large lettuce leaves
¾ pound fresh crabmeat, drained
   and flaked
⅛ teaspoon paprika

Snap off tough ends of asparagus. Remove scales from stalks with a vegetable peeler or knife, if desired. Arrange asparagus in a vegetable steamer over boiling water. Cover and steam 8 minutes or until crisp-tender. Plunge asparagus into ice water to stop the cooking process; drain and chill.

Combine mayonnaise and next 4 ingredients. Arrange lettuce leaves on individual serving plates; top with equal amounts of asparagus and crab. Serve each salad with 1 tablespoon mayonnaise mixture, and sprinkle with paprika. Yield: 6 servings (83 calories [13% from fat] per serving).

□ *13g protein, 1.2g fat (0.2g saturated, 0.2g monounsaturated, 0.5g polyunsaturated), 5.1g carbohydrate, 0.8g fiber, 57mg cholesterol, 337mg sodium, and 78mg calcium.*

*Ginny Munsterman*
*Garland, Texas*

## TUNA-PASTA SALAD

2½ cups cooked tricolored rotini
   (cooked without salt or fat)
2 cups fresh broccoli flowerets
2 unpeeled, medium tomatoes, cut
   into wedges (¾ pound)
10 ripe olives, sliced
2 slices purple onion, separated
   into rings
1 (6½-ounce) can tuna in water,
   drained and flaked
⅓ cup apple cider vinegar
¼ cup lemon juice
2 tablespoons water
1 tablespoon olive oil
1½ tablespoons Dijon
   mustard
½ teaspoon freshly ground
   pepper

Combine rotini, broccoli, tomato, olives, onion, and tuna; set aside. Combine vinegar, lemon juice, water, olive oil, mustard, and pepper in a jar; cover tightly, and shake vigorously. Pour over pasta mixture; toss gently. Cover and chill 2 hours. Toss gently before serving. Yield: 6 servings (147 calories [26% from fat] per 1-cup serving).

□ *9.2g protein, 4.3g fat (0.7g saturated, 2.4g monounsaturated, 0.8g polyunsaturated), 19g carbohydrate, 2.6g fiber, 9mg cholesterol, 266mg sodium, and 29mg calcium.*

---

## A Trip to the Salad Bar

A trip to the salad bar doesn't mean you'll be eating nutritiously. Many high-fat foods await you. While eating small amounts of these items won't ruin your goal of eating healthfully, the calories and fat from high-fat foods quickly add up. Here's a guide to help you make low-fat selections.

| Full Speed Ahead | Proceed With Caution |
|---|---|
| Salad greens and other raw vegetables | Prepared salads, such as potato, carrot, and pasta; coleslaw; olives |
| Garbanzo beans | Marinated bean salad |
| Turkey and ham; boiled shrimp; cooked egg white | Chopped egg, bacon, and chicken, tuna, and seafood salads |
| Cottage cheese, mozzarella cheese | Most cheeses such as Cheddar, blue, Colby, and Monterey Jack |
| Fresh fruit | Gelatin desserts |
| Breadsticks, melba toast, saltine crackers, oyster crackers | Buttery crackers, buttered bread, croutons |
| Reduced-calorie salad dressing, vinegar and lemon juice | Regular salad dressing, mayonnaise |

## RICE-SHRIMP SALAD
*(pictured on page 110)*

2 unpeeled, medium tomatoes
  (¾ pound)
3 cups water
1 pound unpeeled, medium-size
  fresh shrimp
2 cups cooked long-grain rice
  (cooked without salt or fat)
1 cup unpeeled, chopped apple
¾ cup chopped green pepper
½ cup sliced celery
¼ cup chopped green onions
1 tablespoon chopped fresh parsley
3 tablespoons white wine vinegar
1 tablespoon olive oil
½ teaspoon salt
¼ teaspoon pepper
2 cloves garlic, minced
6 red cabbage leaves
6 lemon wedges (optional)

Cut tomatoes in half. Carefully squeeze each half over a small bowl to remove seeds; pour juice through a wire-mesh strainer into a small bowl, discarding seeds. Reserve 2 tablespoons juice. Chop tomatoes.

Bring water to a boil; add shrimp, and cook 3 to 5 minutes. Drain well, and rinse with cold water. Peel and devein shrimp.

Combine chopped tomatoes, shrimp, rice, and next 5 ingredients in a large bowl; set aside. Combine reserved tomato juice, vinegar, and next 4 ingredients; stir with a wire whisk until blended. Pour over shrimp mixture, and toss gently; chill. Spoon salad over cabbage leaves, and serve with a lemon wedge, if desired. Yield: 6 servings (190 calories [16% from fat] per 1¼-cup serving).

□ *13.5g protein, 3.4g fat (0.6g saturated, 1.9g monounsaturated, 0.6g polyunsaturated), 26.1g carbohydrate, 2.4g fiber, 101mg cholesterol, 329mg sodium, and 47mg calcium.*
                    *Thorunn Rafnar*
              *Chapel Hill, North Carolina*

## DILLED MACARONI-CHICKEN SALAD

1 (8-ounce) package elbow
  macaroni, uncooked
1 cup cooked, chopped chicken
  breast
½ cup evaporated skimmed milk
3 tablespoons white wine vinegar
2 tablespoons chopped green onions
1 tablespoon vegetable oil
1 tablespoon chopped pimiento
2 teaspoons sugar
1 teaspoon dried dillweed
½ teaspoon salt
½ teaspoon dry mustard
¼ teaspoon pepper

Cook macaroni according to package directions, omitting salt and fat. Drain; rinse in cold water, and drain again. Combine macaroni and chicken in a large bowl; set aside.

Combine milk and remaining ingredients in a small jar; cover tightly, and shake vigorously. Pour over macaroni mixture; toss gently. Cover; chill 2 hours. Yield: 5 servings (283 calories [16% from fat] per 1-cup serving).

□ *18.4g protein, 5.1g fat, (1.1g saturated, 1.4g monounsaturated, 2g polyunsaturated), 39.1g carbohydrate, 1.2g fiber, 30mg cholesterol, 296mg sodium, and 96mg calcium.*

# All Fired Up

Today's grilling isn't always throwing a burger on the fire—shrimp, pork chops, chicken, and even vegetables now share a spot over the coals. The lean meats and low-fat marinades in these grilling recipes make healthful eating tasty.

## PEPPERCORN-CRUSTED LAMB CHOPS
*(pictured on page 114)*

8 (4-ounce) lean lamb chops
2 tablespoons coarse-grained
  mustard
1 tablespoon cracked pepper
1 tablespoon reduced-sodium soy
  sauce
1 green onion, finely chopped
1 clove garlic, minced
Vegetable cooking spray
Garnish: green onion fans

Trim excess fat from lamb chops. Combine mustard and next 4 ingredients; coat one side of each chop.

Coat grill rack with cooking spray; place on grill over medium-hot coals (350° to 400°). Place chops on rack, coated side up; grill, uncovered, 5 minutes on each side or until desired degree of doneness. Garnish, if desired. Yield: 4 servings (258 calories [40% from fat] per serving).

□ *33.7g protein, 11.5g fat (3.9g saturated, 4.7g monounsaturated, 0.7g polyunsaturated), 2.4g carbohydrate, 0.5g fiber, 105mg cholesterol, 467mg sodium, and 33mg calcium.*

## RED SNAPPER VERACRUZ

Vegetable cooking spray
½ cup chopped green pepper
¼ cup chopped onion
2 cloves garlic, minced
1½ cups chopped, peeled tomato
  (about 2 medium)
2 tablespoons chopped green chiles,
  drained
1 tablespoon chopped fresh cilantro
  or parsley
¼ teaspoon salt
¼ teaspoon hot sauce
Dash of white pepper
4 (4-ounce) red snapper fillets
2 teaspoons margarine, melted

Coat a nonstick skillet with cooking spray; place over medium-high heat until hot. Add green pepper, onion, and garlic; cook, stirring constantly, until tender. Stir in tomato and next 5 ingredients; cook, stirring frequently, until thoroughly heated.

Brush fish with margarine; place in a fish basket coated with cooking spray. Grill, covered, over medium-hot coals (350° to 400°) 5 minutes on each side or until fish flakes easily when tested with a fork. Serve with tomato mixture. Yield: 4 servings (161 calories [23% from fat] per fish fillet and ½ cup tomato mixture).

□ *24.3g protein, 4.1g fat (0.8g saturated, 1.1g monounsaturated, 1.3g polyunsaturated), 6.1g carbohydrate, 1.5g fiber, 42mg cholesterol, 259mg sodium, and 49mg calcium.*

*Shirley Draper*
*Winter Park, Florida*

### ITALIAN-STYLE GRILLED VEGETABLES
*(pictured on page 114)*

⅓ cup white wine vinegar
¼ cup chopped fresh parsley
¼ cup lemon juice
1 tablespoon vegetable oil
2 teaspoons dried Italian seasoning
1 tablespoon chopped fresh oregano or 1 teaspoon dried oregano
4 cloves garlic, minced
1 medium eggplant, unpeeled and cut into ½-inch slices
2 medium-size sweet yellow peppers, quartered
2 medium-size sweet red peppers, quartered
Vegetable cooking spray
Garnish: fresh oregano sprigs

Combine first 7 ingredients in a shallow dish or a large heavy-duty, zip-top plastic bag. Add vegetables, tossing gently; cover or seal. Chill 30 minutes.

Coat grill rack with cooking spray; place on grill over medium-hot coals (350° to 400°). Drain vegetables, reserving marinade. Place vegetables on grill rack. Grill, uncovered, 10 minutes, turning once, and basting occasionally with reserved marinade. Garnish, if desired. Yield: 8 servings (52 calories [36% from fat] per 2 eggplant slices and 2 pepper quarters).

□ *1.3g protein, 2.1g fat (0.4g saturated, 0.5g monounsaturated, 1g polyunsaturated), 8.3g carbohydrate, 1.9g fiber, 0mg cholesterol, 6mg sodium, and 45mg calcium.*

# Treat Yourself To Dessert

What's the first thing you do when you cut calories? Forgo dessert, right? Well, don't. Most traditional desserts deserve their reputation of being high in fat and calories, but fresh fruit desserts, such as these, can be altogether different.

### FRESH ORANGE SORBET

2½ cups water
1 cup sugar
Orange rind strips from 2 oranges
2⅔ cups fresh orange juice
⅓ cup fresh lemon juice

Combine water and sugar in a saucepan; bring to a boil. Add orange rind strips; reduce heat, and simmer 5 minutes. Pour mixture through a wire-mesh strainer, discarding orange rind strips; cool completely.

Stir in orange juice and lemon juice, and pour mixture into freezer container of a 1-gallon hand-turned or electric freezer. Freeze according to manufacturer's instructions. Pack freezer with additional ice and rock salt, and let stand 1 hour before serving. Yield: 6 servings (82 calories [0% from fat] per 1-cup serving).

□ *0.8g protein, 0.1g fat (0g saturated, 0g monounsaturated, 0g polyunsaturated), 46.8g carbohydrate, 0.2g fiber, 0mg cholesterol, 2mg sodium, and 14mg calcium.*

### SUMMER STRAWBERRY DESSERT

1 (1.3-ounce) envelope whipped topping mix
½ cup skim milk
1 teaspoon vanilla extract
2 (6-ounce) cartons strawberry low-fat yogurt
½ (10½-ounce) commercial angel food cake, torn into bite-size pieces
2 cups fresh strawberries, sliced
3 kiwifruit, sliced
2 tablespoons sliced almonds, toasted

Prepare whipped topping mix according to package directions, using ½ cup skim milk and 1 teaspoon vanilla. Fold in yogurt, and set aside.

Layer half each of cake, yogurt mixture, strawberries, and kiwifruit in an 8-inch square dish. Repeat layers; sprinkle almonds on top. Cover and chill at least 2 hours. Yield: 8 servings (162 calories [17% from fat] per ¾-cup serving).

□ *4.3g protein, 3.1g fat (1.7g saturated, 0.8g monounsaturated, 0.3g polyunsaturated), 29.2g carbohydrate, 2.2g fiber, 2mg cholesterol, 65mg sodium, and 114mg calcium.*

*Nelda Shumake*
*Smyrna, Georgia*

## BLUEBERRY STREUSEL CAKE

¾ cup sugar, divided
¼ cup margarine, softened
1 large egg
1 teaspoon grated lemon rind
1½ cups all-purpose flour
½ teaspoon baking soda
½ cup plain nonfat yogurt
Vegetable cooking spray
1 tablespoon all-purpose flour
2 cups fresh blueberries
1 teaspoon ground cinnamon
⅛ teaspoon ground allspice
1 teaspoon powdered sugar

Combine ½ cup sugar and next 3 ingredients; beat at medium speed with an electric mixer 5 minutes. Combine 1½ cups flour and baking soda; add to egg mixture alternately with yogurt, beginning and ending with flour mixture. Pour batter into a 9½-inch round tart pan coated with cooking spray, spreading evenly over bottom and up sides of pan.

Combine remaining ¼ cup sugar, 1 tablespoon flour, and next 3 ingredients, tossing gently. Spoon over batter, leaving a ½-inch border.

Bake at 350° for 45 minutes or until lightly browned; cool 20 minutes on a wire rack. Sprinkle with powdered sugar. Yield: 10 servings (196 calories [25% from fat] per serving).

☐ *3.4g protein, 5.4g fat (1.2g saturated, 2g monounsaturated, 1.6g polyunsaturated), 34.2g carbohydrate, 1.9g fiber, 21mg cholesterol, 112mg sodium, and 43mg calcium.*

# Pack A Gourmet Picnic

What better way to take advantage of gorgeous weather, green grass, and blooming wildflowers than to go on a picnic—a gourmet one, at that. The gourmet recipes featured in our suggested menus are also light.

### BLUE SKIES PICNIC SUPPER FOR SIX

**Mesquite-Smoked Cornish Hens**
**Herbed Pasta-and-Tomato Salad**
**Commercial French breadsticks**
**Fresh pears and seedless red grapes**
**Chilled sparkling water**

### MESQUITE-SMOKED CORNISH HENS

3 (1½-pound) Cornish hens
3 small, unpeeled cooking apples, cored and quartered (¾ pound)
1 cup loosely packed fresh thyme
1 cup unsweetened apple juice
¼ cup low-sodium soy sauce
2 tablespoons chopped fresh parsley
½ teaspoon pepper
¼ teaspoon salt
Mesquite chips
Vegetable cooking spray

Remove giblets from hens, and discard. Rinse hens with cold water; remove skin, and trim excess fat. Stuff hens with apple quarters, and close the cavities. Secure with wooden picks, and truss (tie the legs together with string).

Combine thyme and next 5 ingredients in a large heavy-duty, zip-top plastic bag or shallow dish. Add hens,

turning to coat; seal or cover. Chill 2 to 4 hours, turning hens occasionally. Drain, reserving marinade.

Soak mesquite chips in water 30 minutes. Prepare charcoal fire in smoker; let burn 20 minutes. Place mesquite on coals. Place water pan in smoker; add reserved marinade and enough hot water to fill pan.

Coat grill rack with cooking spray; place rack in smoker. Place hens, breast side up, on rack. Cover with smoker lid; cook 2 hours or until meat thermometer registers 185° when inserted in breast. Remove hens from smoker, and cool; split in half lengthwise, discarding apple quarters. Serve at room temperature or chilled. Yield: 6 servings (223 calories [34% from fat] per serving).

☐ *33g protein, 8.5g fat (2.3g saturated, 3g monounsaturated, 1.9g polyunsaturated), 1.5g carbohydrate, 0g fiber, 101mg cholesterol, 222mg sodium, and 18mg calcium.*

### HERBED PASTA-AND-TOMATO SALAD

4 ounces rotini, uncooked
2 cups small cherry tomatoes, halved
1 cup peeled, chopped cucumber
½ cup chopped celery
1½ ounces provolone cheese, cut into thin strips
⅓ cup white wine vinegar
¼ cup chopped fresh basil
¼ cup chopped fresh parsley
1 tablespoon water
1 tablespoon olive oil
2 teaspoons chopped fresh oregano
¼ teaspoon salt
¼ teaspoon coarsely ground pepper

Cook rotini according to package directions, omitting salt. Drain; rinse in cold water, and drain again.

Combine rotini, tomatoes, and next 3 ingredients in a large bowl; set aside. Combine white wine vinegar and remaining ingredients, stirring with a wire whisk. Pour over pasta mixture; toss gently. Cover and chill at least 8 hours; toss before serving. Yield: 6 cups (135 calories [31% from fat] per 1-cup serving).

□ *5g protein, 4.7g fat (1.6g saturated, 2.3g monounsaturated, 0.5g polyunsaturated), 18.4g carbohydrate, 1.6g fiber, 5mg cholesterol, 179mg sodium, and 75mg calcium.*

## A MEADOW PICNIC LUNCH FOR EIGHT

**Cold Chicken-Leek Terrine**
**Dilled Baby Carrots**
**Commercial French rolls**
**Fresh pears and seedless red grapes**
**Chilled sparkling water**

## COLD CHICKEN-LEEK TERRINE

1½ cups chopped leeks
½ cup water
1 teaspoon sugar
½ teaspoon chicken-flavored bouillon granules
⅓ cup chopped fresh parsley
2 pounds lean ground chicken
2 (1-ounce) slices whole wheat bread, crumbled
2 egg whites
½ teaspoon paprika
¼ teaspoon salt
¼ teaspoon garlic powder
¼ teaspoon pepper
Vegetable cooking spray
5 tablespoons plus 1 teaspoon commercial honey mustard

Combine chopped leeks, water, sugar, and bouillon granules in a large skillet; bring to a boil. Cover, reduce heat, and simmer 10 minutes. Uncover and cook, stirring constantly, just until liquid evaporates. Remove mixture from heat; stir in parsley, and set aside.

Combine chicken, crumbled bread, egg whites, and seasonings in a large bowl; mix well. Shape mixture into a 15- x 10-inch rectangle on a sheet of wax paper. Spoon leek mixture evenly over rectangle, leaving a 1-inch margin around edge. Roll meat mixture up jellyroll fashion, starting at short side and using wax paper to lift. Pinch ends of terrine to seal.

Place terrine, seam side down, on a roasting rack coated with cooking spray; place rack in a shallow roasting pan. Bake at 350° for 1 hour and 15 minutes or until done. Cool slightly; cover and chill at least 8 hours. Cut into 16 slices, and serve with honey mustard. Yield: 8 servings (210 calories [31% from fat] per 2 slices and 2 teaspoons honey mustard).

□ *27.4g protein, 7.2g fat (1.7g saturated, 2.2g monounsaturated, 1.5g polyunsaturated), 7.8g carbohydrate, 0.6g fiber, 76mg cholesterol, 350mg sodium, and 37mg calcium.*

## DILLED BABY CARROTS

1½ pounds baby carrots, scraped
1 cup water
1½ teaspoons dried dillweed
2 dried red chile peppers
1 clove garlic, halved

Cook carrots in boiling water to cover 10 minutes or until crisp-tender; drain, and set aside.

Combine 1 cup water and remaining ingredients in a small saucepan; bring to a boil. Pour over carrots, and cool.

Cover and chill 8 hours. Remove dried red chile peppers and garlic; discard. Serve with a slotted spoon. Yield: 8 servings (37 calories [5% from fat] per ½-cup serving).

□ *0.9g protein, 0.2g fat (0g saturated, 0g monounsaturated, 0.1g polyunsaturated), 8.7g carbohydrate, 2.7g fiber, 0mg cholesterol, 30mg sodium, and 26mg calcium.*

## Savvy Picnic Safety

Whether you pack a gourmet meal or simply a sandwich and fruit, a picnic requires some advance planning. Here are a few suggestions on how you can make your next warm-weather outing a success.

■ Plan your menu by selecting foods that travel easily and safely in a picnic basket or cooler.

■ Pack food in airtight plastic containers or bags that seal tightly and will not break.

■ Remember that an iced-down cooler keeps perishable food cold for a few hours—but not all day—in the hot weather.

■ Keep in mind that meats, poultry, seafood, and dairy products spoil easily. When packing these foods in a cooler, allow plenty of room for the ice.

■ Make cleanup quick by using paper or plastic plates and plastic flatware. Take along a large trash bag for these and other disposables.

# Stressed Out? Get Some Exercise

Feeling tense and wired? Can't sleep? The best prescription for alleviating symptoms of stress is a dose of exercise. We've always heard that exercise benefits the *body;* we now know that exercise is just as effective for the *mind.* One study found that walking is actually more effective for relieving stress than a tranquilizer.

Recent studies show that regular physical activity can produce dramatic improvements in the moods of people who are anxious or depressed. They are more likely to feel in control of their destiny and have a better self-image. Increasing feelings of authority over the body often leads to a sense of competence in other areas of life.

When we experience stress, our heart rate and blood pressure rise dramatically, and muscles tense. In effect, the body is ready to do battle or make a quick escape—the "fight or flight" reaction. To the rescue comes exercise, which can provide an outlet for muscle tension and help remove excess levels of chemicals generated by stress.

Exercise can also relieve the physical and mental fatigue caused by stress. Vigorous activity raises body temperature, increasing the production of brain-calming chemicals.

Physically fit people have a lower heart rate and blood pressure than sedentary people. With a strengthened heart, circulatory system, and respiratory system, people can perform more tasks with less effort. In other words, you tolerate more work and stress when you're fit than when you're not. And because it provides an outlet for muscle tension and nervousness, which often accompany stress, exercise promotes sound sleep—another strong ally for coping with stress.

You don't have to be a top-notch athlete, nor do you need to exercise at the gym every day to enjoy the advantages of physical activity. Any type of rhythmic exercise—brisk walking, jogging, cycling, or rowing—can alleviate tension. Studies show that even a 10-minute walk can significantly reduce tension.

Here are some other fast refreshers when stress mounts:

■ **Deep breathing exercises**— Sitting relaxed or lying down, draw in a deep breath, using your stomach muscles, to a count of 8. When you feel a filling sensation in your abdomen, exhale slowly

to a count of 8. Repeat 5 to 10 times for full effect. Repeat a calming word or phrase to yourself to help you concentrate.

■ **Tensing and relaxing muscles**—Start with your toes; tense them hard for 5 seconds, and then release them. Gradually work your way up the legs, torso, and upper body, tensing and relaxing major muscles.

■ **Neck and shoulder exercises**—People with desk jobs most often feel stress in their neck and shoulders. Ease tightness with shoulder shrugs and shoulder rolls. Unlock tension in the neck by *gently* nodding the head back and forth, and *gently* rolling the head from side to side.

■ **Think yourself away to a calmer environment**—Give yourself a brief mental vacation from a stressful environment by envisioning calmer, refreshing surroundings. Try picturing your last vacation spot or a relaxing evening with friends or family. Constructive daydreaming can help boost your spirits.

■ **Giving yourself a laugh**— Exchange jokes and funny cartoons with friends. Build a library of some favorite comic strips or comedy albums, and keep them handy for 10-minute comedy breaks. Many researchers believe that humor is a great way to manage stress, prevent burnout, and heighten creative problem-solving abilities.

# Strength Training

Until recently, it seemed that aerobic exercise was the only kind that really mattered. Physical fitness meant a well-conditioned cardiovascular system. Strength training was for appearance, not health.

But in 1990 the American College of Sports Medicine (ACSM) revised its exercise recommendations for the first time in 12 years. The new guidelines advise adults to include strength training along with aerobic activities.

As the ACSM statement points out, you will lose both muscle and muscle tone in areas that are not exercised. To maintain your muscle mass requires "a well-rounded program that exercises all the major muscle groups," ACSM reported.

## Strength vs. Aging

The physical and psychological benefits you'll get from strength training will mean an improved quality of life. Instead of losing strength and stamina, you'll continue to participate in daily activities with more vigor. And stronger muscles and bones will help you perform better and longer in recreational activities while also reducing the chances of injury.

Strength training benefits bones, helping to preserve their density and strength. This type of fitness training results in a lower risk of developing osteoporosis in later years.

## Strength vs. Back Pain

Lower back injury has been called the common cold of the musculoskeletal system. It is caused not so much by abuse as by disuse. Strengthening the back and abdominal muscles that support the spine can help prevent or rehabilitate back injuries.

## Do It Now

You don't have to join a health club or even purchase a set of barbells to reap the benefits of strength training. Hand-held dumbbells of varying weights are inexpensive and work well. Several recommended exercises, such as push-ups, don't require any equipment—your body provides the resistance.

To start a strength training program, buy a step-by-step book on strength training with detailed descriptions and illustrations of each exercise. Be sure the author has good credentials in exercise science. Several such books are available.

Follow these tips for a safe and effective workout:

■ Warm up your muscles with calisthenics and stretches before starting. After the session, stretch muscles gently to maintain flexibility.

■ Perform a minimum of 8 to 10 different exercises that utilize the major muscle groups at least twice a week, and allow at least 48 hours for recovery before repeating the same exercise. Perform all movements slowly. Be sure to exhale during exertion, and inhale as you return to the starting point. Do not hold your breath during the exercise.

■ To develop both strength and muscular endurance, find a weight that nearly exhausts the muscle after 8 to 12 repetitions of the exercise.

# Game's Over; Let's Eat

Reward your Little Leaguers for their hard work with food that's a winner. Most children love pizza, and it wouldn't be summer without hamburgers. So we've combined them into All-American Pizza Burgers. Add a dip and ice cream with chocolate sauce, and this meal for 12 is ready.

To take the party to the ballpark, transport perishables in an ice chest. The chocolate sauce will stay warm in a widemouthed thermos.

Make the ice-cream mixture a day ahead and refrigerate. At the beginning of the party, churn the ice cream, and let it stand for an hour to ripen.

## RANCH-STYLE DIP

¾ cup low-fat cottage cheese
1 (8-ounce) carton sour cream
1 cup mayonnaise or salad dressing
1 (1-ounce) envelope Ranch-style dressing mix

Place cottage cheese in container of a blender or food processor; process until smooth. Add sour cream and remaining ingredients; process until blended, stopping once to scrape down sides. Serve dip with fresh vegetables. Yield: 2½ cups.

*Brenda Pogue*
*Fredericktown, Missouri*

## ALL-AMERICAN PIZZA BURGERS

1½ pounds lean ground beef
1½ pounds ground turkey sausage
Vegetable cooking spray
1 (14-ounce) jar pizza sauce, divided
¾ cup grated Parmesan cheese
1 medium onion, chopped (optional)
12 slices mozzarella cheese
12 hamburger buns

Combine ground beef and sausage; shape into 12 patties. Coat grill rack with cooking spray. Place on grill over medium-hot coals (350° to 400°). Place patties on rack, and cook, uncovered, 5 minutes on each side or until done, brushing patties occasionally with ¾ cup pizza sauce. (Discard any remaining pizza sauce used for brushing patties.)

Sprinkle with Parmesan cheese and, if desired, onion. Serve on buns with mozzarella cheese and remaining pizza sauce. Yield: 12 servings.

*Cindy Quebe*
*Greenville, Texas*

## VANILLA CUSTARD ICE CREAM

1½ cups sugar
¼ cup all-purpose flour
¼ teaspoon salt
1 quart milk
4 large eggs, lightly beaten
1 quart half-and-half
1 tablespoon vanilla extract

Combine sugar, flour, and salt in a large, heavy saucepan. Gradually add milk, stirring until smooth. Cook mixture over medium heat, stirring constantly, until thickened (about 10 minutes). Gradually stir one-fourth of hot mixture into beaten eggs; add to remaining hot mixture, stirring constantly. Cook over medium heat, stirring constantly, until mixture reaches 160° (about 1 minute). Remove from heat; stir in half-and-half and vanilla. Chill.

Pour mixture into freezer container of a 1-gallon hand-turned or electric freezer. Freeze according to manufacturer's instructions. Pack freezer with additional ice and salt; let stand 1 hour before serving. Yield: 2½ quarts.

*Jane Maloy*
*Wilmington, North Carolina*

## EASY CHOCOLATE SAUCE

2 (14-ounce) cans sweetened condensed milk
4 (1-ounce) squares unsweetened chocolate
¼ cup butter or margarine
Dash of salt
1 teaspoon vanilla extract

Combine sweetened condensed milk, chocolate, butter, salt, and vanilla in a heavy saucepan; cook mixture over low heat, stirring constantly with a wire whisk, until chocolate melts and mixture is smooth. Serve warm over ice cream. Yield: 3⅓ cups.

*Pat Boschen*
*Ashland, Virginia*

Serve Mexican Stir-Fry (page 126) with
tortilla chips and a salad for a festive
south-of-the-border meal.

For a classic dessert, serve Sour Cream Pound Cake with a variety of fabulous sauces. From left: Lemon-Blueberry Cream, Raspberry-Orange Sauce, and Amaretto-Chocolate Sauce. (Recipes, pages 153 and 154.)

Mushrooms, onion, and kidney beans are a few of the ingredients that make up the fiber-rich filling in Vegetable Burritos (page 138).

# Jazz Up Your Pound Cake

Time-honored foods are important to our heritage, but a fresh approach can add real inspiration to an old standard like pound cake. Both children and adults will love Butterscotch-Pecan Pound Cake. Chock-full of butterscotch morsels and nuts, one piece should satisfy the sweetest cravings. Sour Cream Pound Cake and Chocolate-Sour Cream Pound Cake show how a plain, perfectly textured cake can be turned into a fabulous dessert. A sampling of fruit purees, a rich chocolate sauce, and lemon-flavored whipped cream are silken toppings that add elegance and easy flavor to any pound cake recipe. (For step-by-step instructions on making a pound cake, turn to "From Our Kitchen to Yours," page 154.)

## SOUR CREAM POUND CAKE
*(pictured on pages 150 and 151)*

1 cup butter or margarine, softened
3 cups sugar
6 large eggs
3 cups all-purpose flour
¼ teaspoon baking soda
1 (8-ounce) carton sour cream
1 teaspoon vanilla extract
1 teaspoon almond extract

Beat butter at medium speed with an electric mixer about 2 minutes or until soft and creamy. Gradually add sugar, beating at medium speed 5 to 7 minutes. Add eggs, one at a time, beating just until yellow disappears.

Combine flour and baking soda; add to creamed mixture alternately with sour cream, beginning and ending with flour mixture. Mix at lowest speed just until blended after each addition. Stir in flavorings.

Spoon batter into a greased and floured 10-inch tube pan. Bake at 325° for 1 hour and 20 minutes or until a wooden pick inserted in center comes out clean. Cool in pan on a wire rack 10 to 15 minutes; remove from pan, and let cool completely on a wire rack. Yield: one 10-inch cake.

*Ernestine James*
*Gore Springs, Mississippi*

## BUTTERSCOTCH-PECAN POUND CAKE

1 cup butter or margarine, softened
1 (8-ounce) package cream cheese, softened
2¼ cups sugar
6 large eggs
2⅔ cups all-purpose flour
1 teaspoon vanilla extract
1 teaspoon vanilla, butter, and nut flavoring
1 cup chopped pecans, toasted
½ cup butterscotch morsels

Beat butter and cream cheese at medium speed with an electric mixer about 2 minutes or until soft and creamy. Gradually add sugar, beating at medium speed 5 to 7 minutes. Add eggs, one at a time, beating just until yellow disappears. Gradually add flour, mixing at lowest speed just until blended after each addition. Stir in flavorings, pecans, and morsels.

Spoon batter into a greased and floured 12-cup Bundt pan. Bake at 325° for 1 hour and 20 minutes or until a wooden pick inserted in center comes out clean. Cool in pan on a wire rack 10 minutes; remove from pan, and let cool completely on a wire rack. Yield: one 10-inch cake.

## CHOCOLATE-SOUR CREAM POUND CAKE
*(pictured on page 1)*

1 cup butter or margarine, softened
2 cups sugar
1 cup firmly packed brown sugar
6 large eggs
2½ cups all-purpose flour
¼ teaspoon baking soda
½ cup cocoa
1 (8-ounce) carton sour cream
2 teaspoons vanilla extract
Powdered sugar (optional)

Beat butter at medium speed with an electric mixer about 2 minutes or until soft and creamy. Gradually add sugars, beating at medium speed 5 to 7 minutes. Add eggs, one at a time, beating just until yellow disappears.

Combine flour, baking soda, and cocoa; add to creamed mixture alternately with sour cream, beginning and ending with flour mixture. Mix at lowest speed just until blended after each addition. Stir in vanilla.

Spoon batter into a greased and floured 10-inch tube pan. Bake at 325° for 1 hour and 20 minutes or until a wooden pick inserted in center comes out clean. Cool in pan on a wire rack 10 to 15 minutes; remove from pan, and cool completely on a wire rack. Sprinkle with powdered sugar, if desired. Yield: one 10-inch cake.

## LEMON-BLUEBERRY CREAM
*(pictured on pages 150 and 151)*

¾ cup whipping cream
⅓ cup sifted powdered sugar
1 cup fresh blueberries
½ cup sour cream
2 teaspoons freshly grated lemon rind
Garnishes: lemon zest, fresh blueberries

Beat whipping cream and powdered sugar at medium speed with an electric mixer until soft peaks form. Fold in 1 cup blueberries, sour cream, and lemon rind. Serve with pound cake. Garnish, if desired. Yield: 2½ cups.

## RASPBERRY-ORANGE SAUCE
*(pictured on pages 150 and 151)*

2 cups fresh or frozen raspberries,
    thawed
¾ cup sifted powdered sugar
¼ cup Cointreau or other orange-
    flavored liqueur
1 tablespoon frozen orange juice
    concentrate, thawed

Place raspberries in container of an electric blender or food processor; process until smooth. Add powdered sugar and remaining ingredients; process until blended. Pour through a wire-mesh strainer; press mixture with back of a spoon against the sides of the strainer to squeeze out liquid. Discard seeds. Serve with pound cake and additional fruit. Yield: 1 cup.

## AMARETTO-CHOCOLATE SAUCE
*(pictured on pages 150 and 151)*

1 cup whipping cream
⅓ cup sugar
2 (4-ounce) bittersweet chocolate
    bars, chopped
2 tablespoons butter or margarine
3 to 4 tablespoons amaretto
Garnish: fresh strawberries

Combine first 4 ingredients in a small saucepan. Cook mixture over low heat, stirring constantly, until thickened and smooth. Remove mixture from heat, and stir in liqueur. Serve warm or at room temperature with ice cream and pound cake. Garnish, if desired. Yield: 2¼ cups.

## STRAWBERRY-PEACH SAUCE

1 (10-ounce) package frozen
    strawberries in syrup, thawed
½ cup peach nectar
2 tablespoons peach brandy
1 tablespoon cornstarch
2 peaches, peeled and sliced

Place strawberries in container of an electric blender or food processor; process until smooth. Pour through a wire-mesh strainer; press strawberries with back of a spoon against the sides of the strainer to squeeze out juice. Discard seeds. Combine strawberry juice, peach nectar, peach brandy, and cornstarch in a saucepan. Add peaches; cook mixture over medium-low heat, stirring constantly, until thickened. Serve warm or at room temperature with pound cake. Yield: 1½ cups.

# From Our Kitchen To Yours

Have you ever tasted 12 different pound cakes in six days, and sampled several of them as many as three times? The Foods staff did, and selected three outstanding recipes, which begin on page 153.

The classic pound cake was originally made with one pound each of butter, sugar, flour, and eggs, thus earning its name. These contemporary adaptations create rich, moist variations on the traditional recipe, but don't call for the same amounts of ingredients. Instead, cream cheese or vegetable shortening replaces some of the butter, and milk or sour cream replaces some of the eggs. Small amounts of baking powder or baking soda add extra volume and lightness.

Although the ingredients vary, the procedure hasn't changed. Air bubbles caused by creaming or beating the butter and shortening or cream cheese with sugar help to produce a satiny appearance and cause the pound cake to rise.

## Tips from Experience

■ Use the correct pan size. Recipes suitable for a 10-inch tube pan, which holds 16 cups, won't always fit in a 12- or 13-cup Bundt pan. If the pan is too small, the batter will run over the sides, and the cake will fall; if the pan is too big, the sides shield the batter and slow the baking.

---

### Steps to a Good Pound Cake

**STEP 1:** Beat softened butter, cream cheese, or vegetable shortening at medium speed with an electric mixer about 2 minutes or until soft and creamy. This most important step whips air into the cake batter, so it will rise during baking. (In some recipes, cream cheese or vegetable shortening replaces some of the butter.)

**STEP 2:** Gradually add sugar to beaten butter, beating at medium speed 5 to 7 minutes or until mixture reaches a fluffy consistency similar to whipped cream. Add large eggs, one at a time, beating **just until yellow** disappears. Overmixing cake batter adds air, causing a tough crust and heavy texture.

**STEP 3:** Gradually add one-fourth flour mixture; beating mixture at lowest speed with an electric mixer and beginning and ending with flour mixture. Mix **just until blended** after each addition (about 10 seconds). Stir in flavorings. Scrape bottom and sides of bowl several times with a rubber spatula to uniformly mix cake batter.

**STEP 4:** Spoon batter evenly into a 10-inch tube pan greased with solid shortening and coated with flour. Smooth top. Place pan in center of oven, and bake as directed. (A temperature that is too low causes the cake to fall.) When placed on a rack too low in the oven, the crust browns too much on bottom.

- Grease pan with solid shortening, using a pastry brush for ease. Don't substitute butter, margarine, or vegetable cooking spray. Always flour a greased pan, because a slippery surface keeps the cake from adhering to the sides of the pan and rising to its full volume.
- Beat butter and sugar at medium speed 5 minutes with a heavy-duty mixer (such as KitchenAid), 6 minutes with a standard mixer (such as a Sunbeam), and 7 minutes with a portable, hand-held mixer.
- Keep the oven door closed until minimum baking time has elapsed. Bake cake as directed in recipe; a temperature that is too low causes the cake to fall.
- Test cake for doneness with a cake tester or wooden pick. Insert it in the center of the cake; it should come out with no batter or crumbs clinging to it. Underbaking results in a damp cake and sinking in center.
- Cool the cake in pan on a wire rack 10 to 15 minutes. Removing the cake too soon causes dampness and sinking in center.
- Remove from pan by first running a metal spatula around sides, pressing the spatula against sides of the pan. Invert onto a wire rack; invert cake onto another wire rack so the rounded top is up. Let cool completely, away from drafts.
- Don't substitute self-rising flour for all-purpose flour. To substitute cake flour for all-purpose flour, use 1 cup plus 2 tablespoons sifted cake flour in place of 1 cup all-purpose flour.
- Store in an airtight container up to three days; wrap with plastic wrap and aluminum foil, and refrigerate up to one week or freeze up to two months. Thaw without unwrapping.

# New Chips In Town

Not long ago, potato chips were the choice for an easy appetizer. Not anymore. An intriguing parade of chips has hit the market: pita chips, bagel chips, corn chips, pretzel chips, and tortilla chips.

These chips have inspired innovative combinations. Pair Zesty Bacon Dip with pretzel chips or Hummas with pita chips. Eggplant-Mushroom Spread, served in an eggplant shell, is a natural with bagel chips.

### CHILI-AND-BLACK-EYED PEA DIP

1 (16-ounce) can black-eyed peas, drained
1 (16-ounce) loaf process cheese spread, cubed
1 (10½-ounce) can chili without beans
1 (4-ounce) can chopped green chiles, undrained
1 large onion, chopped
1 teaspoon ground cumin
1 teaspoon dried oregano
¼ teaspoon garlic powder
½ teaspoon hot sauce

Position knife blade in food processor bowl; add peas; process until smooth. Combine peas, cheese, and remaining ingredients; spoon into a lightly greased 8-inch square baking dish. Bake, uncovered, at 350° for 40 to 45 minutes. Serve hot with tortilla chips. Yield: about 5½ cups.
*Mrs. George S. Crane*
*Fort Worth, Texas*

### HUMMAS

3 green onions, sliced
3 to 4 cloves garlic
1 (19-ounce) can garbanzo beans, drained
¼ cup chopped fresh parsley
2 tablespoons lemon juice
½ teaspoon salt
½ teaspoon pepper
Dash of hot sauce
¼ cup olive oil
Garnish: fresh parsley sprigs

Position knife blade in food processor bowl; add green onions and garlic. Cover and process until onions are minced. Add garbanzo beans and next 5 ingredients; process until smooth, scraping sides of processor bowl occasionally. Slowly pour olive oil through food chute with processor running; process until smooth. Spoon into a serving bowl; cover and chill. Garnish, if desired, and serve with pita chips. Yield: 1¾ cups.
*Mrs. Fred Mayse*
*Farmington, Missouri*

## EGGPLANT-MUSHROOM SPREAD

1 large eggplant (about 1½ pounds)
¼ cup olive oil
1 medium-size green pepper, chopped
1 medium onion, chopped
4 cloves garlic, minced
1 cup fresh mushrooms, chopped
1 (6-ounce) can tomato paste
½ cup water
2 tablespoons wine vinegar
2 teaspoons sugar
½ teaspoon salt
½ teaspoon dried oregano
¼ teaspoon pepper
Lettuce leaves

Cut a 2-inch lengthwise strip from top of eggplant. Carefully scoop out pulp, leaving a ¼-inch shell, and chop pulp to measure 3 cups, reserving remaining pulp for other uses. Set eggplant shell aside.

Heat oil in a heavy saucepan over medium-low heat; add 3 cups chopped eggplant, green pepper, onion, and garlic. Cover and cook, stirring occasionally, 15 minutes. Add mushrooms and next 7 ingredients; bring to a boil. Cover, reduce heat, and simmer, stirring occasionally, 15 minutes or until eggplant is tender. Cool slightly; cover and chill at least 2 hours. Spoon into lettuce-lined eggplant shell; serve with bagel chips. Yield: 3 cups.

*Mrs. J. A. Allard*
*San Antonio, Texas*

## ZESTY BACON DIP

6 slices bacon, cooked and crumbled
1 (8-ounce) carton sour cream
2 teaspoons prepared horseradish
1 teaspoon Worcestershire sauce

Combine all ingredients; cover and chill at least 2 hours. Serve dip with pretzel chips. Yield: 1 cup.

*Debbie Forrest*
*Hartford, Kentucky*

## HOT CHILE SAUCE

4 cups chopped, peeled tomatoes (about 2½ pounds)
½ cup chopped green pepper
½ cup chopped onion
½ cup chopped jalapeño peppers
2 cloves garlic, minced
⅔ cup white vinegar
2 tablespoons sugar
2 teaspoons salt
½ teaspoon mustard seeds
⅛ teaspoon ground allspice

Combine all ingredients in a large saucepan; bring to a boil over medium heat. Reduce heat, and simmer, stirring occasionally, 10 minutes or until vegetables are tender; cool. Spoon into a serving dish; cover and chill. Serve with tortilla chips. Yield: about 3½ cups.

*Geneva Emswiler*
*Porter, Texas*

# This Cook Shares His Secrets

Caribbean cuisine is the rage on the East and West coasts, and it soon will be in Richmond, Virginia, too, if William Moreno has his way.

Born in New York to Puerto Rican parents, Moreno was raised on his mother's spicy and colorful cuisine from the tropics. Since then, he has perfected her favorite Caribbean recipes and techniques, taking them with him when he moved to Richmond.

Empanadas, turnover-like pastries with a variety of fillings, are his favorite food to make because they are his favorite to eat. Moreno makes 6-inch empanadas for a main dish and 3-inch ones for appetizers. Fillings include beef, chicken, pork, seafood, and cheese. He says it's the special seasonings that color and flavor foods in the Caribbean style.

Following are Moreno's recipes for empanadas and other foods that make up what he calls a typical Caribbean menu. We've included his recipes for homemade seasonings that he makes in bulk and then freezes, but you might prefer to purchase commercial seasonings.

## EMPANADAS

¼ cup vegetable oil
4 cloves garlic, minced
1½ teaspoons commercial or 1 tablespoon homemade adobo
2 teaspoons commercial or 3 tablespoons homemade sazon
1½ pounds ground beef *
1 cup finely chopped onion
1 cup finely chopped green pepper
2 green onions, finely chopped
1 (8-ounce) can tomato sauce
1½ teaspoons commercial or 1 tablespoon homemade adobo
2 teaspoons commercial or 3 tablespoons homemade sazon
Pastry
Vegetable oil

Heat ¼ cup oil in a Dutch oven until hot. Stir in garlic, 1½ teaspoons adobo, and 2 teaspoons sazon; cook about 1 minute. Add ground beef, and cook until browned, stirring until it crumbles; drain well. Return mixture to Dutch oven; add onion and next 2 ingredients, and cook, stirring occasionally, 5 minutes. Add tomato sauce and remaining seasonings; simmer 5 minutes. Remove from heat.

Roll each portion of pastry to ⅛-inch thickness on a heavily floured surface; cut into 6-inch circles. Place about 2 tablespoons meat mixture in center of each circle, and fold pastry in half. Moisten edges with water, and press with a fork to seal.

Pour oil to depth of 3 inches in a Dutch oven; heat to 350°. Fry empanadas, a few at a time, in hot oil until golden, turning once; drain on paper towels. Yield: 2½ dozen.

* 4 cups shredded, cooked chicken may be substituted for ground beef.

### Pastry

6 cups all-purpose flour
1 tablespoon baking soda
1 tablespoon commercial sazon *
1 cup vegetable oil
2 cups water

Combine first 3 ingredients; set aside. Place oil in a small saucepan; heat over medium heat until hot. Stir hot oil into flour mixture (mixture will not be smooth). Gradually stir in water. Divide dough into 4 portions. (Dough will be soft.) Wrap each portion securely in plastic wrap and chill 8 hours. Yield: Enough pastry for 2½ dozen (6-inch) empanadas.

* 1½ teaspoons salt plus ½ teaspoon paprika may be substituted for commercial sazon.

**Note:** To make 3-inch empanadas, cut pastry into 3-inch circles. Place about 2½ teaspoons meat mixture in center of each circle; seal and fry empanadas as directed above. Makes about 75 appetizer empanadas.

### PERNIL (PORK ROAST)

1 (6-pound) Boston butt pork roast
2 cloves garlic, crushed
2 teaspoons dried oregano
1 teaspoon freshly ground pepper
1 tablespoon all-purpose flour
1 tablespoon olive oil
2 to 4 tablespoons commercial or ¼ to ½ cup homemade adobo

Cut tiny slits in Boston butt. Combine garlic and next 4 ingredients; rub on all sides of meat. Rub adobo on all sides of meat; cover and chill 8 hours.
   Place roast, fat side up, on a rack in a shallow roasting pan. Insert meat thermometer, making sure it does not touch fat or bone. Bake, uncovered, at 325° for 35 to 40 minutes per pound or until meat thermometer reaches 170° (about 3½ hours). Yield: 8 to 10 servings.

### RICE WITH PIGEON PEAS

¼ cup vegetable oil
2 teaspoons commercial or 3 tablespoons homemade sazon
1 teaspoon commercial or 2 teaspoons homemade adobo
¼ cup commercial or ½ cup homemade sofrito
½ cup finely chopped, cooked ham
1 (16-ounce) can pigeon peas, drained
4 cups water
2 cups long-grain rice, uncooked

Combine first 6 ingredients in a saucepan; cook, stirring occasionally, over medium heat 5 minutes. Stir in water and rice; cover and cook over medium heat 20 minutes or until water is absorbed. Yield: 8 servings.

### SAZON

¼ cup chopped onion
3 tablespoons chopped green pepper
3 tablespoons chopped sweet red pepper
3 tablespoons chopped green onions
3 tablespoons tomato paste
1 tablespoon plus 1 teaspoon chopped fresh parsley
1 tablespoon plus 1 teaspoon chopped fresh coriander
1 tablespoon plus 1 teaspoon olive or vegetable oil
1 tablespoon plus 1 teaspoon white vinegar
½ teaspoon dried oregano
½ teaspoon sweet paprika
⅛ teaspoon salt
⅛ teaspoon hot sauce
1 (2-ounce) jar diced pimiento, drained
1 clove garlic, minced

Combine all ingredients in container of a blender; process until smooth. Pour into a saucepan; bring to a boil. Reduce heat, and simmer, stirring constantly, 5 minutes or until thoroughly heated. Remove from heat; cool. Cover and chill. Yield: about 1 cup.

### Cooking Caribbean With William Moreno

**Adobo** (ah-DOH-boh)—a Caribbean seasoning most often used for meat. Commercial adobo, composed of salt, garlic, and other spices, is available in an 8-ounce container; his homemade version of adobo is a pureed mix of fresh onion, garlic, salt, and other seasonings.
**Annatto seeds** (uh-NAH-toh)—also called achiote, this term refers to dried seeds used mainly for their characteristic red color. You can substitute commercial sazon (which contains enough annatto seeds to give the desired color) if you can't find plain annatto seeds.
**Pernil** (per-NIL)—Caribbean term for a pork roast.
**Pigeon peas**—not actually peas at all, these small round seeds are about the size of peas and can be bought canned or frozen. Chick peas make a good substitute for pigeon peas.
**Plantains** (PLAN-tins)—a member of the banana family, plantains look like large bananas. They are hard and starchy when green, and are used much like a potato. They turn yellow, and then black, as they ripen.
**Sazon** (sa-ZON)—a common seasoning available in 1.41-ounce boxes containing several packets of the mixture. The commercial product is a dry mixture of MSG, salt, annatto seeds, and other spices. His homemade sazon is a puree of spices and vegetables.
**Sofrito** (soh-FREE-toh)—a basic Spanish sauce of onion, tomato, garlic, and other seasonings. The commercial product, which can be purchased in 6-ounce jars, is similar to Moreno's homemade sauce.

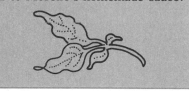

## TOSTONES DE PLÁTANO (PLANTAIN CHIPS)

1 large, firm green plantain
2 quarts water, divided
2 tablespoons salt, divided
Vegetable oil
Plantain Dip

Peel plantain, and diagonally cut into ⅛-inch-thick slices. Combine 1 quart water and 1 tablespoon salt in a large bowl, stirring until salt dissolves; add plantain slices. Cover and let stand 30 minutes. Drain plantain slices well, and pat dry.

Heat 2 tablespoons oil in a large skillet; add plantain slices, and cook over medium-high heat, stirring constantly, until tender, but not brown. Drain well on paper towels.

Combine remaining 1 quart water and 1 tablespoon salt, stirring until salt dissolves. Dip plantain slices into salted water; drain well, and pat dry.

Pour oil to depth of 2 inches in a Dutch oven, and heat to 375°. Fry plantain slices, a few at a time, until golden brown; drain on paper towels. Serve plantain chips with Plantain Dip. Yield: 3 dozen.

### Plantain Dip

¼ cup olive oil
¼ cup white vinegar
4 cloves garlic, minced
1 teaspoon commercial sazon

Combine all ingredients in a jar; cover tightly, and shake vigorously. Chill at least 2 hours. Shake just before serving. Yield: ½ cup.

**Tip:** *If you're faced with peeling a large quantity of tomatoes, try this method: Dip the tomatoes into boiling water for 1 minute; then plunge them into cold water. The skins will then slip off easily.*

## ADOBO

½ medium onion, quartered
5 cloves garlic
1 tablespoon dried oregano
1½ teaspoons salt
1½ teaspoons pepper
2 tablespoons orange juice
2 tablespoons lime juice
3 tablespoons peanut or vegetable oil

Combine first 5 ingredients in container of an electric blender; process until onion and garlic are chopped. Add juices. With blender on high, gradually add oil in a slow steady stream; process until blended. Cover and chill (or freeze up to one month). Yield: ⅔ cup.

## SOFRITO

⅓ cup chopped onion
3 tablespoons chopped tomato
2 tablespoons chopped green pepper
2 tablespoons tomato sauce
1 tablespoon olive oil
½ teaspoon annatto (achiote) seeds
¼ teaspoon ground coriander
Dash of dried oregano
Dash of freshly ground pepper
2 cloves garlic, minced

Combine all ingredients in container of an electric blender; process until smooth. Cover and chill (or freeze up to 1 month). Yield: ⅔ cup.

# Cool Salad For Hot Days

Gazpacho, a cold soup from Spain, typically includes such ingredients as garlic, tomatoes, and garden-fresh vegetables. Congealed Gazpacho Salad borrows those same ingredients to flavor this cool salad.

Green pepper, cucumber, and green onions are combined with vinegar and tomato juice to make a tangy congealed salad. To serve, dollop with Avocado Cream.

## CONGEALED GAZPACHO SALAD WITH AVOCADO CREAM
*(pictured on page 114)*

2 envelopes unflavored gelatin
1 quart tomato juice, divided
¼ cup white wine vinegar
1 clove garlic, crushed
¾ teaspoon salt
¼ teaspoon black pepper
Dash of red pepper
1 cup peeled, chopped tomato, drained
¾ cup finely chopped green pepper
¾ cup peeled, chopped cucumber
½ cup chopped green onions
1 (2-ounce) jar diced pimiento, drained
Lettuce leaves
Avocado Cream
Garnish: green onion fans

Sprinkle gelatin over 1 cup tomato juice in a medium saucepan; let stand 1 minute. Cook over low heat, stirring until gelatin dissolves. Remove from heat; stir in remaining tomato juice, white wine vinegar, and next 4 ingredients. Chill until the consistency of unbeaten egg white.

Fold in tomato and next 4 ingredients. Spoon into 10 lightly oiled ½-cup molds; chill until firm. Unmold onto lettuce-lined salad plates; top with Avocado Cream. Garnish, if desired. Yield: 10 servings.

### Avocado Cream

½ cup sour cream
⅓ cup mashed ripe avocado
Dash of red pepper

Combine all ingredients; stir until smooth. Yield: ⅔ cup. *Carol Barclay Portland, Texas*

# QUICK!

## Cheese To The Rescue

Need a sandwich, appetizer, or bread in a hurry? Each of these recipes takes less than 20 minutes to prepare. For a quick sandwich, try Feta-Tomato Crostini or Welsh Rarebit With Tomatoes and Bacon. Creamy Pimiento Cheese Spread takes only minutes to make in a food processor. Use it as a sandwich filling or cracker spread. And for a special dinner bread, spread refrigerator crescent rolls with flavored cream cheese before baking to make Cream Cheese Croissants.

### CREAM CHEESE CROISSANTS

1 (8-ounce) package refrigerator crescent rolls
¼ cup cream cheese with chives, softened

Unroll crescent rolls, separating into 8 triangles. Gently spread 1½ teaspoons cream cheese on top of each triangle. Roll up each triangle, beginning at wide end. Place rolls, point side down, on baking sheets. Bake at 375° for 11 minutes or until golden. Serve immediately. Yield: 8 rolls.

*Judi Grigoraci*
*Charleston, West Virginia*

### FETA-TOMATO CROSTINI

3 (6-inch) French bread rolls, split
Olive oil
1 (7-ounce) package feta cheese, crumbled
Coarse ground garlic powder with parsley
3 small tomatoes, chopped
1½ tablespoons balsamic vinegar
2 tablespoons chopped fresh mint
Lettuce leaves
Garnish: fresh mint sprigs

Brush cut side of each roll with olive oil; place on baking sheet. Broil 6 inches from heat (with electric oven door partially opened) 2 minutes or until lightly browned. Place cheese evenly on each roll; sprinkle lightly with garlic powder. Place tomatoes over cheese; drizzle with balsamic vinegar, and sprinkle with mint. Serve on lettuce leaves, and garnish, if desired. Serve immediately. Yield: 6 servings. *Fran Oppenheimer*
*Panama City, Florida*

### WELSH RAREBIT WITH TOMATOES AND BACON

6 slices bacon
1½ teaspoons butter or margarine
1 (8-ounce) loaf process cheese spread
¼ teaspoon Worcestershire sauce
¼ teaspoon dry mustard
Dash of ground red pepper
⅓ cup milk
6 bread slices, halved and toasted
2 tomatoes, sliced

Place bacon on a microwavable rack in an 11- x 7- x 1½-inch baking dish; cover with paper towels. Microwave at HIGH 5 to 6 minutes. Drain on paper towels; crumble and set aside.

Place butter in a 1½-quart glass bowl; microwave at HIGH 15 seconds. Add cheese; microwave at HIGH 1 minute. Using a wire whisk, stir in Worcestershire sauce, dry mustard, and red pepper. Gradually add milk, whisking constantly. Microwave at HIGH 3 minutes, whisking at 1-minute intervals.

Arrange toast in single layer. Spoon half of cheese sauce over toast; top with tomato slices and remaining cheese sauce. Sprinkle with bacon. Yield: 4 to 6 servings. *Lauri Pittman*
*Gladstone, Missouri*

### CREAMY PIMIENTO CHEESE SPREAD

2½ cups (10 ounces) shredded sharp Cheddar cheese
1 (12-ounce) container cottage cheese
¼ cup mayonnaise or salad dressing
⅛ teaspoon white pepper
4 drops of hot sauce
1 (4-ounce) jar diced pimiento, undrained

Position knife blade in food processor bowl; add first 5 ingredients. Process until smooth. Add pimiento; pulse 4 or 5 times. Yield: 3⅓ cups. *Kay Johnson*
*Montevallo, Alabama*

## MEATY CHEESE DIP

1 pound ground beef
½ pound hot bulk pork sausage
1 (8-ounce) jar medium salsa
1 (2-pound) loaf process cheese spread, cut into cubes

Brown ground beef and sausage in a large skillet, stirring until it crumbles; drain and return to skillet. Add remaining ingredients, and cook over low heat, stirring constantly, until cheese melts. Serve warm with corn chips. Yield: 4½ cups.   *April Black*
*Athens, Georgia*

# Toss Spinach Into A Salad

When you think about adding a spinach salad to the menu, use your imagination, just as our readers did when they created these recipes.

## WILTED SPINACH SALAD

1 pound fresh spinach
4 slices bacon
3 tablespoons finely chopped onion
⅓ cup white wine vinegar
⅓ cup water
1 (2-ounce) jar diced pimiento, drained
2 tablespoons sugar

Remove stems from spinach; wash leaves thoroughly, and pat dry. Tear into bite-size pieces, and place in a large bowl.
Cook bacon in a large skillet until crisp; drain, reserving drippings. Crumble bacon; set aside. Sauté onion in bacon drippings. Add vinegar and last 3 ingredients; bring to a boil. Pour over spinach, tossing gently. Sprinkle with bacon, and serve. Yield: 4 servings.   *Nancy Whorton*
*New Boston, Texas*

## ARRANGED SPINACH SALAD

1 pound fresh spinach
1 cup large curd cottage cheese
2 hard-cooked eggs, cut into wedges
1 cup (4 ounces) shredded mozzarella cheese
½ cup walnut pieces, toasted
2 slices bacon, cooked and crumbled
½ cup sour cream
2 to 4 tablespoons sugar
2 tablespoons white vinegar
2 teaspoons prepared horseradish
½ teaspoon dry mustard
¼ teaspoon salt
¼ teaspoon pepper

Remove stems from spinach; wash leaves thoroughly, and pat dry. Tear into bite-size pieces; arrange on individual salad plates. Arrange next 4 ingredients on top. Sprinkle with bacon.
Combine sour cream and remaining ingredients; stir until sugar dissolves. Drizzle over spinach salad. Yield: 4 to 6 servings.   *Della Taylor*
*Jonesboro, Tennessee*

## SPINACH-SESAME SALAD

1 pound fresh spinach
½ head iceberg lettuce, torn
1 green onion, sliced
⅓ cup olive oil
3 tablespoons lemon juice
1 tablespoon honey
1 tablespoon sesame seeds, toasted

Remove stems from spinach; wash leaves thoroughly, and pat dry. Tear into bite-size pieces. Combine spinach, lettuce, and green onion in a large bowl; set aside.
Combine olive oil, lemon juice, and honey in a jar; cover tightly, and shake. Pour dressing over salad just before serving, and toss gently. Sprinkle with sesame seeds. Yield: 6 to 8 servings.   *Barbara Beacom*
*Kernersville, North Carolina*

## SPINACH SALAD WITH POPPY SEED DRESSING

1 pound fresh spinach
1 cup sliced fresh mushrooms
1 small purple onion, sliced and separated into rings
¼ cup slivered almonds, toasted
2 hard-cooked eggs, sliced
⅓ cup vegetable oil
2 tablespoons white vinegar
1 tablespoon honey
1 tablespoon prepared mustard
2 teaspoons poppy seeds

Remove stems from spinach; wash leaves thoroughly, and pat dry. Tear into bite-size pieces. Combine spinach, mushrooms, onion, almonds, and eggs in a large bowl.
Combine oil and remaining ingredients in a jar. Cover tightly, and shake vigorously. Pour dressing over spinach mixture just before serving, and toss. Yield: 6 to 8 servings.
*Cathy Williams*
*Vale, North Carolina*

## Timesaving Tip

If you've ever purchased fresh spinach, you're no doubt familiar with the need to rinse each leaf very well. Particles of dirt cling tightly to the curly leaves, and spinach will be gritty if you don't wash the leaves carefully. After washing, pinch off the spiny stems from each leaf.
To help the harried consumer save time, many marketers now wash, trim, and bag fresh produce—including spinach. Most stores bag ready-to-use washed and trimmed spinach in 10-ounce packages, which are roughly equivalent to one pound of fresh, untrimmed spinach. So now you have a faster option on busy days.

# JULY

*Summertime's the perfect time to call your neighbors and plan a block party — all-American style. Our "Summer Suppers" special section in this chapter spotlights block parties, giving just-right recipes and menus along with plans and activities. But to entertain a smaller group, use our menu for "The Perfect Picnic," complete with step-by-step suggestions for an elegant lakeside dinner.*

# The Perfect Picnic

Don't let the lavish setting throw you—it's really simple to prepare this picnic. Find a nearby lake or pond for your backdrop; then add splashes of color with a cool, refreshing meal you can whip up tonight and casual dishes and tablecloths you already have on hand. Here's the plan, from preparation to cleanup.

## At Home

**1.** Keep the invitation list small. You'll need less food *and* equipment and have a more intimate setting.
**2.** Prepare Basil-Chicken-Vegetable Salad a day ahead. Chill the chicken, tomatoes, beans, and basil garnish in separate zip-top plastic bags.
**3.** Chill macaroni salad and melon balls in separate zip-top plastic bags.
**4.** Prepare and chill Ginger Cheese in a small bowl; cover with plastic wrap.
**5.** Pack muffins and gingersnaps in separate zip-top plastic bags.
**6.** Pack dishes, glasses, and flatware in a sturdy basket with a tablecloth and napkins, securing breakables in folds of the fabric. Put delicate, easy-to-eat fruit such as apples, oranges, or grapes on top.
**7.** Pack a napkin-lined basket for muffins and a bowl or basket for fruit.
**8.** Pack chilled foods in an ice chest.
**9.** Pack plastic garbage bags and paper towels for easy cleanup.
**10.** If you want a centerpiece, wrap stems of fresh-cut flowers in wet paper towels, and stand them in a vase. Bring a jar of water to fill the vase if the picnic site has no running water.

## At the Lake

**1.** Remove paper towels from fresh flowers, and arrange in vase.
**2.** Arrange apples, oranges, or grapes in bowl or basket.
**3.** Set the table and place floral centerpiece on table.
**4.** Arrange food on plates, disposing of zip-top plastic bags.
**5.** Put muffins in napkin-lined basket.
**6.** After enjoying a long, relaxing meal, scrape leftover food from plates into one garbage bag.
**7.** Stack plates, flatware, and glasses, and wrap securely in another garbage bag. Put back in the basket, and surround garbage bag with tablecloth and napkins.
**8.** Use paper towels for any last minute cleanup.

---

### PICNIC BY THE LAKE

**Basil-Chicken-Vegetable Salad**
**Shell Macaroni Salad**
**Sweet-and-Hot Melon**
**Oatmeal Muffins**
**Ginger Cheese with commercial gingersnaps**

---

### BASIL-CHICKEN-VEGETABLE SALAD

4 skinned and boned chicken breast
  halves
1 tablespoon olive oil
⅓ cup white wine vinegar
⅓ cup olive oil
2 tablespoons chopped fresh basil
1 tablespoon capers
½ teaspoon sugar
½ teaspoon salt
1 pound fresh green beans
½ teaspoon salt
2 medium tomatoes, cut into
  wedges
Garnish: fresh basil leaves

Cut chicken into ½-inch strips. Heat 1 tablespoon olive oil in a large skillet; add chicken, and cook 5 minutes or until chicken is tender, stirring often. Set aside.

Combine vinegar and next 5 ingredients in a jar; cover tightly, and shake vigorously. Pour dressing over chicken strips; toss gently. Cover and chill 1 to 2 hours.

Wash green beans; trim ends, and remove strings. Pour water to depth of 1 inch into a skillet. Add ½ teaspoon salt, and bring to a boil. Add green beans; cover, reduce heat, and cook 8 to 10 minutes or until crisp-tender. Drain beans immediately; plunge beans into ice water to stop cooking process.

Arrange beans and tomato wedges on plates; top with chicken strips. Drizzle with dressing, and garnish, if desired. Yield: 4 servings.

*Barbara Davis*
*Lilburn, Georgia*

## SHELL MACARONI SALAD

4 ounces small shell macaroni, uncooked
2 hard-cooked eggs, chopped
½ cup shredded cabbage
⅓ cup chopped green pepper
¼ cup chopped celery
¼ cup mayonnaise or salad dressing
1 tablespoon cubed sweet pickle
1 tablespoon commercial Thousand Island or Ranch-style dressing
¼ teaspoon salt
⅛ teaspoon pepper

Cook macaroni according to package directions; drain. Rinse with cold water; drain and cool.

Combine macaroni and remaining ingredients; toss mixture gently to coat. Cover and refrigerate 1 to 2 hours. Yield: 4 servings.

*Betty Jo Smith*
*La Grange, Georgia*


## SWEET-AND-HOT MELON

1 small cantaloupe, scooped into balls
¼ cup Marsala wine *
½ teaspoon dried crushed red pepper
Pinch of salt

Combine all ingredients; cover and refrigerate at least 2 hours, stirring occasionally. Remove melon balls from liquid; serve on wooden skewers, if desired. Yield: 4 to 6 servings.

* ¼ cup ginger ale may be substituted for Marsala wine. *Carol Noble*
*Burgaw, North Carolina*


**Tip:** *It's easy for food to reach warm temperatures in the hot sun, so keep picnic containers away from direct sunlight. Pack the food to be used first on the top to avoid excessive opening of the container.*

## OATMEAL MUFFINS

1 cup regular oats, uncooked
1 cup buttermilk
1 large egg
¼ cup vegetable oil
¼ cup honey
1 cup whole wheat flour
1½ teaspoons baking powder
½ teaspoon baking soda
½ teaspoon salt
¼ cup sesame seeds

Combine oats and buttermilk in a bowl. Let stand for 30 minutes. Stir in egg, oil, and honey. Combine flour and next 4 ingredients in a large bowl; make a well in center of mixture. Add oatmeal mixture, stirring just until moistened.

Spoon mixture into greased muffin pans, filling three-fourths full. Bake at 350° for 20 to 25 minutes. Remove from pans immediately. Yield: 15 muffins. *Alice Hobbs Little*
*Marion, North Carolina*


## GINGER CHEESE

1 (8-ounce) package cream cheese, softened
2 tablespoons half-and-half
3 tablespoons chopped crystallized ginger
2 tablespoons almond slices, toasted
Commercial gingersnaps

Combine cream cheese and half-and-half. Beat at medium speed with an electric mixer until smooth.

Stir in ginger; chill 8 hours. Sprinkle with almonds, and serve with gingersnaps. Yield: 1 cup. *Pat Boschen*
*Ashland, Virginia*


# Cool It With Dessert

Has spending all day on a recipe soured your taste for dessert? We've got sweet news. These delights rely on convenience products—canned fruit, instant pudding, or cake mix—to make preparation a snap. Additional ingredients mask any artificial taste. Some patience is needed; all the recipes require a stint in the refrigerator or freezer.


## COOKIES-AND-CREAM CAKE

½ gallon cookies-and-cream ice cream, softened
1 (18.25-ounce) package chocolate cake mix without pudding
3 large eggs
1⅓ cups water
½ cup vegetable oil
1 (8-ounce) container frozen whipped topping, thawed

Spread ice cream evenly into two 9-inch round cakepans lined with plastic wrap. Place in freezer for at least 1 hour. Remove from pans, and return to freezer.

Combine cake mix and next 3 ingredients in a large mixing bowl; beat at low speed with an electric mixer until moistened. Beat at medium speed 2 minutes. Pour batter into three greased and floured 9-inch round cakepans. Bake at 350° for 20 to 23 minutes or until a wooden pick inserted in center comes out clean. Cool cake layers on wire racks in pans 10 minutes; remove from pans, and let cool completely.

To assemble cake, remove ice cream from freezer, and remove plastic wrap. Place one cake layer on cake platter; top with ice-cream layer. Repeat with second cake layer, ice cream, and third cake layer.

Frost cake with whipped topping. Store cake in freezer. Yield: one 9-inch cake. *Janet Mussler*
*Louisville, Kentucky*

## ALMOND CREAM DIP WITH STRAWBERRIES

2 pints fresh strawberries
1 (3.4-ounce) package vanilla
  instant pudding mix
2 cups whipping cream
1 cup milk
½ teaspoon almond extract

Wash strawberries; do not hull. Pat dry, and chill.

Combine pudding mix and remaining ingredients in a large mixing bowl; beat at low speed with an electric mixer until blended. Beat at high speed until soft peaks form (about 8 minutes). Serve with strawberries. Yield: 6 to 8 servings or 25 appetizer servings.          *Sharron Kay Johnston*
                       *Fort Worth, Texas*


## APRICOT SHERBET

2 (16-ounce) cans apricot halves in
  light syrup, drained
2 cups sugar
1 quart milk
¼ cup lemon juice

Place apricots in container of an electric blender; process until smooth, stopping once to scrape down sides. Combine apricot puree, sugar, and remaining ingredients. Pour into freezer container of a 1-gallon hand-turned or electric freezer. Freeze according to manufacturer's instructions, and serve. Yield: 2 quarts.
                       *Mrs. Thomas Byrd*
                       *Nashville, Tennessee*


## PEANUT BUTTER DESSERT

35 cream-filled chocolate sandwich
  cookies, crushed
⅓ cup butter or margarine, melted
1 (5.1-ounce) package vanilla
  instant pudding mix
2 cups milk
1¼ cups creamy peanut butter
1 (8-ounce) container frozen
  whipped topping, thawed

Combine cookie crumbs and butter, and reserve ¼ cup crumb mixture. Press crumb mixture into bottom of a 13- x 9- x 2-inch pan. Bake at 375° for 5 minutes. Let cool on a wire rack 15 minutes.

Combine pudding mix and milk; beat with a wire whisk until smooth. Add peanut butter, beating with whisk until smooth and thickened. Fold in whipped topping. Spoon over crumb crust, and sprinkle with reserved crumb mixture. Cover and chill at least 3 hours. Yield: 15 servings.
                       *Betty Lang*
                       *Cocoa Beach, Florida*


# Serve Berries With A Sauce

Most of us love all kinds of fresh berries. For a special occasion, adding a sauce can take berries from simplicity to sophistication.

Chocolate fans will savor White Chocolate Sauce. With its flavor enhanced by a splash of crème de cacao and vanilla, it is sure to be a favorite.

Pear Sauce has the same texture as applesauce. It's good served over berries, gingerbread, spice cake, or pancakes. Or enjoy it plain—just like applesauce.


## WHITE CHOCOLATE SAUCE

1 (6-ounce) white chocolate-flavored
  baking bar, chopped
¼ cup plus 2 tablespoons whipping
  cream
2 tablespoons light corn syrup
1½ teaspoons crème de cacao or
  other chocolate-flavored liqueur
½ teaspoon vanilla extract

Place chocolate in a small, heavy saucepan; cook over low heat, stirring constantly, until chocolate melts. Remove from heat, and set aside.

Place whipping cream in a saucepan, and bring to a boil; add corn syrup, stirring until blended. Remove from heat, and gradually add to melted chocolate, stirring constantly, until smooth. Stir in crème de cacao and vanilla. Serve at room temperature with fresh berries. Yield: 1 cup.


## PEAR SAUCE

2 medium pears, peeled, cored, and
  sliced
1 teaspoon grated lemon rind
2½ tablespoons lemon juice
⅓ cup sugar
1 tablespoon cornstarch
1 cup water

Combine first 3 ingredients in container of an electric blender; process until smooth.

Combine pear mixture, sugar, cornstarch, and water in a medium saucepan. Bring mixture to a boil; reduce heat, and cook, stirring constantly, 1 minute. Remove from heat; cool. Yield: 2⅔ cups.


## CRÈME ANGLAISE

4 egg yolks, beaten
¼ cup sugar
¼ teaspoon salt
Dash of ground nutmeg
1½ cups warm milk
1 teaspoon vanilla extract

Combine first 4 ingredients in top of a double boiler; bring water to a boil. Gradually add milk, stirring constantly; cook over low heat, stirring occasionally, until sauce thickens and reaches 160° (about 15 minutes). Remove from heat, and stir in vanilla; cool. Cover with plastic wrap, gently pressing directly on sauce; chill. Serve with fresh berries and other fruit. Yield: about 2 cups.
                       *Mrs. James L. Twilley*
                       *Macon, Georgia*

# summer Suppers.

## Invite The Neighborhood

Gas streetlights and towering oaks line the 3300 block of West Franklin Street in Richmond, Virginia. It's an old-fashioned neighborhood of rowhouses-turned-dream homes. Folks sit on their porches and quietly visit in the evenings—every evening except July 3 and 4, that is.

When the sun drops on the eve of Independence Day, neighbors barricade their street for a rip-roaring celebration. Everyone gets into the act, from the tiniest toddler donning only patriotic diapers to 89-year-old Ruth Lane, who leads her team's cheer at the volleyball game.

But the residents of the 32 houses don't add up to the nearly 400 attendees at the 1991 event. Folks who have moved away since the block parties began 19 years ago keep in touch with old neighbors, hoping for invitations to this impressive reunion. And then there are the residents' parents, siblings, and cousins who come—casseroles in hand—to join the festivities. How this party has grown over the years.

### Let the Festivities Begin

Come along and experience a Richmond block party.

#### Fourth of July Eve

**3:00**—Barricade the street. It's a block party!

**6:30**—Each neighbor stages his own sidewalk cookout for family and friends. This simple event—looking more like a neighborly table-setting and menu-planning contest—sends aromas of grilled foods drifting down the street.

**9:00**—On Fred Rose's front porch, the Franklin (as in West Franklin Street) Art Repertory Theater premieres its annual entertainment, complete with lights, cameras, curtain calls, and lots of laughter.

#### The Glorious "Fourth"

**8:30**—A breakfast buffet on Ann Holiday's front porch, with beverages served by Dick Wilson from two doors down, gets this block party crew rolling. (Wilson's Bloody Marys earn him the title "The Painless Dentist" from fun-loving adults at this meal.)

**11:30**—Melissa Bannister and helpers turn children into Ninja Turtles and other characters at her face-painting booth, just in time for . . .

**12:15**— . . . the children's parade. A boom box sets the pace.

**12:30**—The crowd gathers in the middle of the street for hot dogs and ice cream.

**1:30**—Oh, the games people play! There's fun for all ages. A new watermelon-eating contest rivals the egg toss for popularity.

**3:30**—Grab a curbside seat for the annual "North vs. South" (sides of the street) volleyball game. Sudden rain showers dampen participants, but not spirits, as the South rises again.

**4:30**—Music sets the mood for a limbo contest and dancing.

**5:30**—The line forms for Carlisle Bannister's legendary barbecue chicken and pork and a spectacular covered dish spread of 84 side dishes and 28 desserts. What delicious decisions to make!

**7:15**—Neighborhood children volunteer for a magic show in front of Francyne Goldstein's home.

**9:00**—Barricades come down, but the party isn't quite over. The crowd disperses for spontaneous festivities that continue well into the morning.

The cleanup crew takes over as the festivites end, and the next day the only visible reminders of the block party are a few bits of eggshell and some watermelon seeds from the contests. But folks on West Franklin Street are already talking about how they can make next year's event even bigger and better.

■ Fred Rose grills this flank steak the evening before the Fourth for the sidewalk cookout, doubling or tripling the recipe as necessary to accommodate the number of guests he invites.

## GRILLED FLANK STEAK

2 (1-pound) flank steaks
⅔ cup vegetable oil
⅔ cup soy sauce
⅓ cup red wine vinegar
¼ cup commercial chutney
2 tablespoons finely chopped onion
¼ teaspoon garlic powder

Trim excess fat from steaks. Score steaks on both sides in 1½-inch squares, and place in a large shallow dish or a heavy-duty, zip-top plastic bag. Combine oil and remaining ingredients; pour over steaks, turning to coat. Cover or seal; marinate steaks in refrigerator 8 to 12 hours, turning occasionally.

Remove steaks from marinade, discarding marinade. Grill, uncovered, over hot coals (400° to 500°) 10 to 12 minutes on each side or to desired degree of doneness. To serve, cut steaks diagonally across grain into thin slices. Yield: 8 servings.

■ Carlisle Bannister has perfected this barbecue recipe. He always grills pork roasts, as well as chicken, for the big "Fourth" feast.

## BANNISTER'S BARBECUE

4 (6- to 6½-pound) Boston butt pork roasts
Bannister's Barbecue Sauce

Prepare charcoal fire in grill; let burn 15 to 20 minutes or until flames disappear and coals are white. Place pork on grill, fat side down. Grill, covered, over low coals (275° to 300°) 3 to 4

hours or until meat thermometer registers 160° when inserted in center of meat, turning pork every hour. Add charcoal to maintain temperature.

Remove from grill, and cool. Trim away bone and excess fat; coarsely chop meat. Add about 6 cups Bannister's Barbecue Sauce to pork, mixing well. Yield: 25 to 30 servings.

### Bannister's Barbecue Sauce

1½ quarts catsup
½ cup cider vinegar
½ cup light corn syrup
½ cup prepared mustard
⅓ cup Worcestershire sauce
1 tablespoon salt
1½ teaspoons garlic powder
1 to 1½ teaspoons ground cinnamon
1 to 1½ teaspoons celery seeds
1½ teaspoons black pepper
1 teaspoon ground red pepper

Combine all ingredients in a Dutch oven, and cook over low heat until thoroughly heated, stirring frequently. Chill 8 hours. Yield: 2 quarts.

■ Ann Holiday first tried this dish at a Tri Club (a Richmond women's organization) meeting and now shares it annually with West Franklin Street.

### TRI CLUB POTATO SALAD

8 medium-size red potatoes (about 3½ pounds)
1 teaspoon salt
1 (8-ounce) carton sour cream
1 cup mayonnaise or salad dressing
1 teaspoon celery seeds
½ teaspoon salt
¼ teaspoon ground white pepper
1 teaspoon prepared horseradish
1 purple onion, thinly sliced and separated into rings
1 cup chopped fresh parsley

Peel and slice potatoes; place in a Dutch oven. Add 1 teaspoon salt and water to cover. Bring to a boil; reduce heat, and cook 8 to 10 minutes or until tender. Drain and cool.

Combine sour cream and next 5 ingredients; set aside. Place one-third of potato slices in a large bowl; spread with one-third sour cream dressing mixture. Arrange one-third onion over dressing; sprinkle with one-third parsley. Repeat layers twice with remaining ingredients. Yield: 8 to 10 servings.

■ Daphne Howell prepares a huge batch of this old family favorite so out-of-town relatives can enjoy it at the annual sidewalk cookout and take some home with them.

## ZIPPY BARBECUE SAUCE

1 gallon catsup
1 quart water
2 large onions, finely chopped
1 small green pepper, finely chopped
1 serrano chile pepper, seeded and diced
¾ cup commercial hot salsa
1 (4-ounce) can diced green chiles, undrained
2 tablespoons Worcestershire sauce
1½ tablespoons minced garlic
2 teaspoons dried celery flakes
2 teaspoons dried basil
1 teaspoon ground cumin
1 teaspoon hot sauce

Combine all ingredients in a large Dutch oven. Bring to a boil over medium heat, stirring occasionally. Reduce heat and simmer, uncovered, stirring occasionally, 2 hours or to desired consistency. Refrigerate sauce and use within two weeks, or freeze. Yield: 1 gallon.

## VEGETABLE-PASTA SALAD

1 (16-ounce) package linguine, uncooked
1 small red cabbage, coarsely shredded (6 cups)
4 medium carrots, scraped and coarsely shredded
3 medium tomatoes, coarsely chopped
3 stalks celery, coarsely chopped
2 medium cucumbers, sliced
1 large purple onion, chopped
1 large green pepper, chopped
1 (8-ounce) bottle Italian salad dressing
1½ tablespoons Nature's Seasons seasoning blend

Break linguine into thirds, and cook according to package directions, omitting salt; drain. Rinse with cold water; drain. Combine linguine and remaining ingredients, tossing well. Serve immediately, or cover and refrigerate 8 hours. Yield: 16 servings.

*Jére S. Kitchen*

## CAULIFLOWER SLAW

1 medium cauliflower
1 cup thinly sliced radishes
1 small onion, grated
½ cup green pepper strips
1 (8-ounce) carton sour cream
1 tablespoon garlic-cheese salad dressing mix *
1½ tablespoons lemon juice
¼ teaspoon salt
¼ teaspoon seasoned salt
¼ teaspoon pepper
2 tablespoons vegetable oil

Remove cauliflower leaves; discard. Break cauliflower into flowerets, and thinly slice. Combine cauliflower and next 3 ingredients in a large bowl. Combine sour cream and remaining ingredients; add to vegetables, tossing

gently. Cover and chill at least 2 hours. Yield: 6 to 8 servings. *K Hall*

* Italian salad dressing mix may be substituted for garlic-cheese mix.

## APPLE-PECAN CAKE

3 large eggs
2 cups sugar
1 cup vegetable oil
2 teaspoons vanilla extract
2¾ cups all-purpose flour
1 teaspoon baking soda
1 teaspoon salt
2 teaspoons ground cinnamon
4 cups peeled, chopped apple
1 cup chopped pecans

Beat eggs at medium speed with an electric mixer until thick and pale. Gradually add sugar, beating until blended. Add oil and vanilla; beat at low speed until blended.

Combine flour and next 3 ingredients; add to beaten mixture, stirring until blended. Stir in apple and pecans. Pour batter into a greased and floured 10-inch tube pan. Bake at 350° for 1 hour and 25 minutes or until a wooden pick inserted in center comes out clean. Cool cake in pan on a wire rack 5 minutes; remove from pan, and cool completely on wire rack. Yield: one 10-inch cake. *Charles A. Morgan*

**Tip:** *Have your oven thermostat professionally checked at least once a year. Another way to occasionally check oven temperature is to prepare a cake mix according to package directions; the cake should bake the entire recommended time and test done. (A wooden pick inserted in the center should come out clean.)*

# International Potluck

Welcome to Fort Benning, Georgia, home of a major Army installation and 12 friendly families on Dial Street hosting their seventh block party of the year. It's no wonder these neighborhood events offer an international flair; residents here are liaison officers from European countries and students of the School of the Americas, a program that shares U.S. military tactics with Latin American cadets.

For the children, the highlight of each block party is the father-child soccer game.

Most of the adults say they relish the international foods and the chance to meet new friends. The party-goers enjoy sharing recipes from their childhood and a taste of home with their new friends, as well as sampling dishes from other countries. Come with us on a culinary tour of the small world waiting to be discovered at Fort Benning.

■ For the adults in the group, Tricia Collins likes to serve gin-based Pimms Punch like she remembers from merry old England. She describes it as a festive drink that makes for a lively party.

### PIMMS PUNCH

1 (750-milliliter) bottle Pimms, chilled
1 (2-liter) bottle lemon-lime carbonated beverage, chilled
Apple chunks
Fresh mint sprigs

Combine all ingredients just prior to serving. Serve punch over ice. Yield: 11 cups.

■ Kathy Henderson teaches friends about her Southern heritage by making enough fried fish and hush puppies for the whole crowd.

### SOUTHERN FRIED FISH

8 catfish or bream fillets (about 2 pounds)
1 quart water
½ teaspoon hot sauce
2 cups yellow cornmeal
1 cup all-purpose flour
2 teaspoons salt
1 teaspoon white pepper
1 teaspoon garlic powder
1 teaspoon paprika
Vegetable oil

Combine first 3 ingredients. Cover and refrigerate 1 hour; drain.

Combine cornmeal and next 5 ingredients in a plastic bag. Add fillets, one at a time, shaking well to coat completely.

Pour oil to depth of 2 to 3 inches into a Dutch oven; heat to 375°. Fry fillets, a few at a time, about 4 minutes on each side or until golden brown. Drain well on paper towels. Serve immediately. Yield: 8 servings.

### HUSH PUPPIES

2 cups yellow cornmeal
1 cup all-purpose flour
1 tablespoon baking powder
1 teaspoon salt
1½ teaspoons onion powder
½ teaspoon white pepper
1 small onion, grated
2 large eggs, beaten
1 to 1¼ cups milk
Vegetable oil

Combine first 7 ingredients; add eggs and 1 cup milk, stirring well. Add additional milk, if necessary, for desired consistency.

Pour oil to depth of 2 to 3 inches in a Dutch oven or heavy saucepan; heat to 375°. Carefully drop batter by rounded tablespoonfuls into oil. Fry a few at a time 1 to 2 minutes on each side or until golden brown. Drain on paper towels, and serve immediately. Yield: about 3 dozen.

■ Janet Rice, who calls Glennville, Georgia, home, knows about barbecued ribs. She shared her hickory-smoked version at this block party.

### SMOKED RIBS WITH HONEY-MUSTARD SAUCE

Hickory chips
5 pounds pork spareribs
½ cup honey
¼ cup firmly packed brown sugar
¼ cup prepared mustard
½ teaspoon maple flavoring

Soak hickory chips in water at least 15 minutes. Prepare charcoal fire in smoker; let burn 15 to 20 minutes or until coals are white. Place hickory chips on coals.

Place water pan in smoker; fill with water. Place ribs on food rack. Cover with smoker lid; cook ribs 3 hours.

Combine honey and remaining ingredients in a saucepan; cook over medium heat, stirring constantly, until sugar dissolves. Baste ribs with sauce; cover and cook 30 minutes. Turn ribs over, and baste again with sauce. Cover and cook an additional 30 minutes. Yield: 5 to 6 servings.

■ Tricia Collins's Shepherd's Pie hails from her country of origin, England. It adds an international flavor to the block party festivities. This updated version uses top sirloin. Traditionally, lamb or mutton was used.

### SHEPHERD'S PIE

2 pounds top sirloin steak, finely chopped
3 cups water
3 large carrots, chopped
1 medium onion, chopped
1 beef-flavored bouillon cube
2 (¾-ounce) packages beef-flavored gravy mix
1½ pounds red potatoes, peeled and sliced (about 4 large)
3 tablespoons butter or margarine
3 to 5 tablespoons milk
1 cup (4 ounces) shredded Cheddar cheese
Paprika

Combine steak and water in a large saucepan; cover and bring to a boil. Reduce heat, and simmer 15 minutes. Drain steak, and reserve broth.

Combine broth, carrots, and onion in saucepan; cover mixture and cook 12 minutes or until tender.

Drain carrots and onion, reserving 2 cups broth. (Add enough water to broth to measure 2 cups, if necessary.) Set vegetables aside.

Combine broth, bouillon cube, and gravy mix in saucepan; bring to a boil, stirring constantly. Reduce heat, and simmer mixture 1 minute. Stir in beef and cooked vegetables; spoon into a lightly greased 13- x 9- x 2-inch baking dish.

Cook potatoes in boiling water to cover 12 minutes or until potatoes are tender. Drain and mash potatoes. Stir in butter and milk. Spread potato mixture evenly over meat mixture; top with cheese, and sprinkle mixture with paprika. Bake at 350° for 20 to 25 minutes or until bubbly. Yield: 8 servings.

■ A native of Puerto Rico, Sandra Nevárez enjoys serving Southern barbecue with Puerto Rican side dishes. The recipe below is one of her favorite accompaniments.

## GREEN BANANAS ESCABECHE (PICKLED GREEN BANANAS)

¾ cup olive oil
⅓ cup white vinegar
¾ teaspoon salt
½ teaspoon black peppercorns
3 large cloves garlic
2 small bay leaves
3 small onions, sliced and
   separated into rings
8 cups water
2 tablespoons salt
12 medium-size green (unripe)
   bananas, peeled

Combine first 6 ingredients in a medium saucepan; bring to a boil. Reduce heat, and simmer, uncovered, 20 minutes. Add onions; cook, stirring occasionally, 10 minutes. Remove from heat, and cool. Remove and discard bay leaves.

Combine water and 2 tablespoons salt in a Dutch oven; add bananas, and let stand 10 minutes. Place over high heat, and bring to a boil; reduce heat, and simmer 10 minutes. Drain and cool. Cut bananas into ¾-inch slices. Combine bananas and onion mixture, tossing gently; cover and chill. Yield: 16 to 18 servings.

**Tip:** *Onions offer outstanding nutritive value. They are a good source of calcium and vitamins A and C. They contain iron, riboflavin, thiamine, and niacin; have a high percentage of water; and supply essential bulk. They are low in calories and have only a trace of fat.*

■ Steffi Braun makes German Potato Salad just the way she remembers it from her childhood in Germany.

## GERMAN POTATO SALAD

7 medium-size red potatoes (about
   2 pounds)
½ cup chopped onion
2 tablespoons chicken-flavored
   bouillon granules
¼ cup boiling water
3 tablespoons salad vinegar
1 tablespoon vegetable oil
¼ teaspoon salt
¼ teaspoon pepper
3 slices bacon, cooked and
   crumbled

Cook potatoes in boiling water to cover 25 minutes or until tender. Drain, and cool slightly. Peel potatoes, and cut into ¼-inch slices. Combine potatoes and onion in a large bowl; set aside.

Dissolve bouillon granules in boiling water; stir in vinegar and next 3 ingredients. Pour over potato mixture, and toss gently. Sprinkle with bacon. Yield: 8 servings.

■ Originally from Argentina, Ana Desmarás brought her flan recipe handwritten in Spanish to the party. Her 11-year-old daughter, Pia, is studying English in school and translated it for us.

## FLAN DE LECHE (FLAN WITH MILK)

1 cup sugar, divided
5 large eggs
3 cups milk
1 teaspoon vanilla extract

Sprinkle ½ cup sugar in a heavy skillet. Cook over medium heat, stirring constantly, until sugar melts and turns a light golden brown. Immediately

pour into a 6-cup Bundt pan; let melted sugar cool.

Combine remaining ½ cup sugar, eggs, milk, and vanilla in container of an electric blender; process until sugar dissolves. Pour into Bundt pan, and place pan in a large Dutch oven. Add water to Dutch oven to depth of 2 inches. Bake at 350° for 45 to 50 minutes or until a knife inserted in center comes out clean.

Carefully remove Bundt pan from Dutch oven; cool pan on a wire rack. Cover and chill 8 hours. Invert pan onto a serving dish, letting melted sugar drizzle over the top. Yield: 8 servings.

■ Roswitha Valdez loves to sample the block party dishes from other countries, and the Fort Benning crowd enjoys trying her German Green Bean Salad.

## GERMAN GREEN BEAN SALAD

2 (16-ounce) cans whole green
   beans
¼ cup finely chopped onion
2 tablespoons salad vinegar
1 tablespoon vegetable oil
¼ teaspoon salt
½ teaspoon pepper

Drain green beans, reserving 1 cup liquid. Place beans in a small bowl. Combine bean liquid, onion, and remaining ingredients; pour over beans, tossing gently. Cover and chill at least 2 hours. Yield: 6 servings

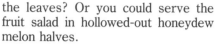

# Cooking Up Your Own Block Party

Our readers' family gatherings and neighborhood celebrations have inspired this collection of recipes perfect for your upcoming block party, and we've given you some ideas for serving in a colorful and attractive way. Start with ordinary containers, and add your personal touches for a special look.

For example, instead of the usual salad bowl, why not line the inside of a basket or clay pot with heavy-duty plastic wrap and large lettuce or cabbage leaves, and spoon Summer Fruit Salad or Pineapple-Almond Slaw onto the leaves? Or you could serve the fruit salad in hollowed-out honeydew melon halves.

Favorite Pound Cake doesn't have to be presented on the expected cake stand. For fun, serve it sliced or whole on a cutting board with fresh summer berries. Arrange Yummy Bars on a tray lined with festive fabric or a napkin, and for a decorative touch, tuck a few colorful flowers in the corners of the tray. Try nestling Four Cheese Casserole in a colorful cloth-lined flat basket to help insulate the dish.

## GRILLED CHICKEN

3½ to 4 pounds chicken pieces, skinned
1 cup white or red wine vinegar
½ cup vegetable oil
2 tablespoons salt
¼ cup pepper
2 tablespoons poultry seasoning

Place chicken in a 13- x 9- x 2-inch dish or heavy-duty, zip-top plastic bag. Combine vinegar and remaining ingredients; pour marinade over chicken. Cover and refrigerate 8 hours, turning occasionally.

Remove from marinade, discarding marinade. Grill, covered, over hot coals (400° to 500°) 30 to 40 minutes or until done, turning frequently. Yield: 5 to 6 servings.

*G. Stephen Crain*
*Williamston, South Carolina*

## BAKED MUSHROOM RICE

2 cups long-grain rice, uncooked
1 cup sliced green onions
2 tablespoons butter or margarine, melted
3 cups chicken broth
½ cup dry sherry
1 (4½-ounce) jar sliced mushrooms, undrained
1 (4-ounce) jar chopped pimiento, drained
1 teaspoon salt
1 teaspoon seasoned pepper

Place rice in a lightly greased 11- x 7- x 1½-inch baking dish; set aside.

Cook green onions in butter in a large skillet over medium-high heat, stirring constantly, until tender. Add broth and remaining ingredients, and bring to a boil; remove from heat, and pour over rice. Cover and bake at 375° for 25 minutes or until liquid is absorbed and rice is tender. Stir before serving. Yield: 8 servings.

*Nell H. Amador*
*Guntersville, Alabama*

## FOUR CHEESE CASSEROLE

1 (16-ounce) package wide egg noodles, uncooked
1 (15-ounce) container ricotta cheese
1 cup grated Parmesan cheese
1 cup whipping cream
¾ cup (3 ounces) shredded Swiss cheese
¾ cup (3 ounces) shredded mozzarella cheese
1 large egg, lightly beaten
3 (¾-ounce) slices mozzarella cheese, cut in half diagonally

Cook noodles according to package directions; drain.

Combine noodles and next 6 ingredients; spoon into a lightly greased 11- x 7- x 1½-inch baking dish. Bake at

400° for 20 minutes. Remove from oven; top with mozzarella cheese slices. Bake 5 minutes or until lightly browned. Yield: 10 servings.

*Eleanor K. Brandt*
*Arlington, Texas*

## PINEAPPLE-ALMOND SLAW

⅔ cup sour cream
⅔ cup mayonnaise or salad dressing
1 tablespoon lemon juice
1 teaspoon sugar
1 teaspoon finely chopped onion
⅛ teaspoon salt
5 cups shredded cabbage
2 cups shredded carrot (about 4 carrots)
1 (15¼-ounce) can pineapple tidbits, drained
1 (2-ounce) package slivered almonds, toasted

Combine first 6 ingredients in a small bowl; set aside. Combine cabbage and remaining ingredients in a large bowl; add sour cream mixture, tossing well. Cover and chill thoroughly. Yield: 8 to 10 servings.

*Jodie McCoy*
*Tulsa, Oklahoma*

## SUMMER FRUIT SALAD

1 pint fresh strawberries, sliced
1½ cups seedless green grapes
1 cup honeydew melon balls
2 oranges, peeled, seeded, and sectioned
2 kiwifruit, peeled and sliced
1 apple, unpeeled, cored, and sliced
¼ cup orange juice
2 tablespoons honey
1 tablespoon lime juice
2 bananas, sliced

Combine first 6 ingredients in a large bowl. Combine orange juice, honey, and lime juice; pour over fruit, tossing gently. Cover and chill 2 hours. Add bananas just before serving. Yield: 10 to 12 servings.

*Sandi Pichon*
*Slidell, Louisiana*

## FAVORITE POUND CAKE

1 cup butter or margarine, softened
1 (8-ounce) package cream cheese, softened
3 cups sugar
6 large eggs
3 cups all-purpose flour
¼ teaspoon baking soda
1½ teaspoons vanilla extract
¾ teaspoon lemon extract

Beat butter and cream cheese at medium speed with an electric mixer about 2 minutes or until soft and creamy. Gradually add sugar, beating at medium speed 5 to 7 minutes. Add eggs, one at a time, beating just until yellow disappears.

Combine flour and soda; gradually add to creamed mixture. Mix at lowest speed just until blended after each addition. Stir in flavorings.

Spoon batter into a greased and floured 13-cup Bundt pan. Bake at 325° for 1 hour and 20 minutes or until a wooden pick inserted in center comes out clean. Cool in pan on a wire rack 10 minutes; remove from pan, and let cool completely on a wire rack. Yield: one 10-inch cake.

*Aileen Halcomb*
*Huntsville, Alabama*

## YUMMY BARS

1 (14-ounce) package caramels
1 (5-ounce) can evaporated milk, divided
1 (18.25-ounce) package German chocolate cake mix with pudding
¾ cup butter or margarine, melted
1 large egg
1 (6-ounce) package semisweet chocolate morsels
1 cup coarsely chopped pecans

Combine caramels and ¼ cup evaporated milk in a small saucepan. Cook over low heat, stirring occasionally, until smooth; set aside.

Combine cake mix, butter, egg, and remaining evaporated milk. Spoon half of mixture into a greased 13- x 9- x 2-inch pan, spreading mixture evenly; bake at 350° for 6 minutes. Remove from oven; sprinkle with morsels and pecans. Spoon caramel mixture on top; carefully spoon remaining cake mixture over caramel layer. Bake at 350° for 20 to 25 minutes. Cool cake on a wire rack, and cut into bars. Yield: about 3 dozen.

*Ann Wheeler*
*Lexington, Kentucky*

## GINGER ALE-NECTAR PUNCH

2 (12-ounce) cans apricot nectar
1 (6-ounce) can frozen orange juice concentrate, thawed and undiluted
1 cup water
2 tablespoons lemon juice
Dash of salt
1 (2-liter) bottle ginger ale, chilled

Combine first 5 ingredients; chill. Stir in ginger ale just before serving. Serve over ice. Yield: 3½ quarts.

*Mary Andrew*
*Winston-Salem, North Carolina*

# Respect For Blockheads

Although residents of a Tennessee neighborhood called Roundtree put a couple of "blockheads" in charge of their big block party every year, their plans somehow seem to fall in place anyway. Elected annually to spearhead community and neighborhood efforts, the blockheads are actually among the most respected and appreciated homeowners in the area.

A beautifully landscaped subdivision tucked in the rolling countryside that overlooks Johnson City, Tennessee, the Roundtree neighborhood is home to about 100 families.

The party is held the weekend after Labor Day. It's no small task to plan an event for a neighborhood of this size, but this group really knows how to get the job done. You won't find any bumbling blockheads here—just organized, fun-loving residents with lots of great ideas.

### Rolling Out the Red Carpet

After the games are over, everyone gathers to formally welcome newcomers to the neighborhood. Roundtree rolls out the red carpet (actually a piece of red plastic) for new families to walk across in the spotlight (the glow of a flashlight). Newcomers introduce their families and tell something witty about themselves.

### Food and More Food

A feast marks the formal closing of the day's activities. Barbecue and fried chicken are catered, and every family brings two covered dishes to the dinner. (If your last name begins with A through K, you bring a dessert and side dish; L through Z supply a salad and side dish.)

The serving tables are decorated with beautiful baskets of wildflowers from Sandy Cox's garden.

### NO-FRY EGGPLANT PARMESAN

2 large eggplants (about 3 pounds)
3 large eggs, lightly beaten
1½ cups matzoh meal
1 (16-ounce) package sliced
   mozzarella cheese
1 (16-ounce) jar spaghetti sauce
½ cup grated Parmesan cheese

Peel eggplants; cut into ½-inch slices. Dip in egg, and dredge in matzoh meal. Place in a single layer on lightly greased baking sheets. Bake at 400° for 20 minutes. Turn eggplant slices, and bake an additional 15 minutes.

Layer one-third of eggplant slices in a lightly greased 13- x 9- x 2-inch baking dish. Top with one-third each of mozzarella cheese slices and spaghetti sauce; repeat layers twice. Sprinkle eggplant with grated Parmesan cheese, and bake, uncovered, at 325° for 30 minutes or until thoroughly heated. Yield: 8 servings.

*Sandra D. Fish*

## Food Safety

■ Always be careful not to cross-contaminate foods as you cook. Use separate cutting boards and knives for raw meats and vegetables, washing hands and equipment thoroughly between tasks.

■ Warm food should be put directly in the refrigerator, not left on the counter to cool. Just be sure not to add so much warm food that it raises the refrigerator temperature. If foods are too hot to be refrigerated immediately, place the pan in a sink of ice water and stir the food often (if recipe allows) until it cools.

■ Marinate meat, fish, or poultry in the refrigerator. If you want to serve some of the marinade or basting liquid with the food, set some aside in the refrigerator before adding or brushing it on the raw food.

■ When you take cooked foods off the grill, always use a clean platter and utensil. If not, bacteria from the raw product on the used platter could contaminate the cooked food.

■ Don't leave hot or cold foods at room temperature for more than two hours. Bacteria becomes a problem after that point. And remember, if you're serving food out in the summer heat, you only have one hour to let food sit safely. So don't serve the meal until everyone has arrived and is ready, and return foods to the refrigerator as soon as guests are finished eating.

## BAKED BEANS AND MORE BEANS

1 pound bacon, chopped
2 large onions, chopped
½ cup white vinegar
1 cup firmly packed brown sugar
1 teaspoon garlic powder
½ teaspoon dry mustard
3 (18-ounce) jars baked beans, undrained
2 (17-ounce) cans lima beans, rinsed and drained
1 (16-ounce) can kidney beans, rinsed and drained
1 (15-ounce) can butter beans, rinsed and drained

Cook bacon in a large skillet until crisp. Remove bacon, reserving 2 tablespoons drippings in skillet. Drain bacon on paper towels; set aside.

Cook onion in reserved drippings over medium-high heat, stirring constantly, until tender; drain. Combine onion, bacon, vinegar, and remaining ingredients, and spoon into 2 lightly greased 2-quart shallow baking dishes. Bake, uncovered, at 350° for 1 hour, stirring every 15 minutes. Yield: 18 servings.        *Karen Green*

## CONFETTI ORZO SALAD

1½ cups orzo, uncooked
1 carrot, scraped and chopped
1¼ cups chopped sweet red, green, or yellow pepper
½ cup peeled, seeded, and chopped cucumber
¼ cup thinly sliced green onions
¼ cup chopped purple onion
¼ cup chopped fresh parsley
½ teaspoon grated lemon rind
3 tablespoons lemon juice
2 tablespoons white wine vinegar
¾ teaspoon salt
⅛ teaspoon coarsely ground pepper
2 cloves garlic, minced
⅓ cup olive oil

Cook orzo according to package directions; drain. Rinse with cold water; drain. Combine orzo, carrot, and next 5 ingredients; set aside.

Combine lemon rind, lemon juice, vinegar, salt, coarsely ground pepper, and minced garlic. Gradually add oil, beating with a wire whisk until blended. Pour over orzo mixture, tossing gently. Cover and chill. Yield: 8 to 10 servings.        *Sandy Cox*

**Note:** Orzo is a rice-shaped pasta.

## MARINATED SLICED TOMATOES

6 medium tomatoes, sliced
⅓ cup vegetable oil
2 tablespoons lemon juice
1 teaspoon salt
1 teaspoon dried oregano
2 cloves garlic, crushed

Place tomatoes in an 11- x 7- x 1½-inch dish. Combine oil, lemon juice, salt, oregano, and crushed garlic. Pour over tomatoes. Cover and chill. Yield: 10 to 12 servings.        *Barby Wilson*

## CHILLED SQUASH SOUP

2 pounds yellow squash, thinly sliced
1 medium onion, chopped
2 (14½-ounce) cans ready-to-serve chicken broth
1 (8-ounce) package cream cheese, softened
⅛ to ¼ teaspoon freshly ground pepper

Combine first 3 ingredients in a saucepan; bring to a boil. Cover, reduce heat, and simmer 8 minutes or until

tender; cool. Spoon half each of squash mixture and cream cheese into container of an electric blender; process until smooth, stopping once to scrape down sides. Repeat procedure with remaining squash mixture and cream cheese. Stir in pepper, and chill well. Yield: 2 quarts.    *Denis Brock*

## CHOCOLATE-RASPBERRY CAKE

1 (18.25-ounce) package butter recipe chocolate cake mix with pudding
1 (12-ounce) package semisweet chocolate morsels, divided
¼ cup Chambord or other raspberry-flavored liqueur (optional)
½ cup seedless raspberry jam
1 (8-ounce) carton sour cream
2 tablespoons chopped pecans, toasted

Prepare cake mix according to package directions; stir in 1 cup chocolate morsels. Spoon batter into 2 greased and floured 9-inch round cakepans.

Bake at 350° for 25 to 30 minutes or until a wooden pick inserted in center comes out clean. Cool in pans on wire racks 10 minutes. Remove from pans, and cool completely on wire racks.

Brush tops of cake layers with Chambord or other raspberry-flavored liqueur, if desired. Place one cake layer on a plate; spread cake layer with raspberry jam, and top with second cake layer.

Melt remaining chocolate morsels in a heavy saucepan over low heat, stirring often. Remove melted chocolate from heat, and gradually stir in sour cream. Spread frosting on top and sides of cake; sprinkle top of cake with chopped pecans. Chill at least 2 hours. Yield: one 2-layer cake.
        *Jane Hales*

### POPPY SEED CAKE

3 large eggs
1½ cups milk
1 cup vegetable oil
1½ teaspoons vanilla extract
½ teaspoon butter flavoring
½ teaspoon almond extract
3 cups all-purpose flour
1½ teaspoons baking powder
1½ teaspoons salt
2¼ cups sugar
2 tablespoons poppy seeds
Glaze

Combine first 6 ingredients in a large mixing bowl. Combine flour and next 4 ingredients; add to egg mixture. Beat mixture at medium speed with an electric mixer 1 to 2 minutes. Spoon batter into a well-greased and floured 10-inch tube pan. Bake at 350° for 1 hour or until a wooden pick inserted in center comes out clean. Cool in pan on a wire rack 10 minutes; remove cake from pan, and place on wire rack. Immediately brush warm cake with Glaze; let cool completely. Yield: one 10-inch cake.

### Glaze

¾ cup sugar
¼ cup orange juice
½ teaspoon vanilla extract
¼ teaspoon butter flavoring
¼ teaspoon almond extract

Combine all ingredients in a small saucepan, stirring well. Bring to a boil; reduce heat, and simmer 1 to 2 minutes. Yield: ⅔ cup. *Karen Green*

### BLACK FOREST CAKE

1 (18.25-ounce) package devil's food cake mix without pudding
¼ cup sugar
½ cup water
2 tablespoons kirsch or other cherry-flavored liqueur (optional)
2½ cups whipping cream
¼ cup sifted powdered sugar
¼ cup kirsch or other cherry-flavored liqueur (optional)
1 cup chopped maraschino cherries, divided
¾ cup semisweet chocolate mini-morsels, divided

Prepare cake mix according to package directions. Spoon batter into 3 greased and floured 8-inch round cakepans. Bake at 375° for 20 to 25 minutes or until a wooden pick inserted in center comes out clean. Cool in pans on wire racks 10 minutes. Remove from pans, and cool completely on wire racks.

Combine sugar and water in a small saucepan. Bring to a boil; reduce heat, and simmer 5 minutes. Stir in 2 tablespoons kirsch, if desired; cool. Brush syrup on tops of cake layers; let stand 5 minutes.

Beat whipping cream at medium speed with an electric mixer until foamy; gradually add powdered sugar, beating until soft peaks form. Gently fold in ¼ cup kirsch, if desired.

Place one cake layer on cake plate; spread with about 1 cup whipped cream mixture. Sprinkle with ⅓ cup chopped cherries and ¼ cup chocolate morsels. Add second cake layer, and repeat whipped cream mixture, cherries, and chocolate morsels. Top with third cake layer, and spread top and sides of cake with remaining whipped cream mixture. Sprinkle with remaining cherries and chocolate morsels. Store in refrigerator. Yield: one 3-layer cake. *Pat Burleson*

### STIR-AND-DROP SUGAR COOKIES

2 large eggs
⅔ cup vegetable oil
2 cups all-purpose flour
2 teaspoons baking powder
¾ cup sugar
2 teaspoons grated lemon rind
2 teaspoons vanilla extract
2½ cups sifted powdered sugar
1 tablespoon butter or margarine, melted
2 tablespoons lemon juice
1 tablespoon water
½ teaspoon vanilla extract
1 to 2 drops desired food coloring

Combine eggs and oil in a large mixing bowl; beat at medium speed with an electric mixer until blended. Combine flour, baking powder, and sugar; add to egg mixture, beating well. Stir in lemon rind and 2 teaspoons vanilla. Drop dough by rounded teaspoonfuls onto ungreased baking sheets. Bake at 350° for 10 to 12 minutes. Transfer to wire racks and cool completely.

Combine powdered sugar and next 4 ingredients; stir until smooth. Stir in food coloring. (Add 1 additional tablespoon water, if needed, to make desired consistency.) Spread on cookies. Yield: 3½ dozen. *Pam Sherwood*

**Tip:** *You can bake and freeze many cakes, pies, cookies, breads, casseroles, and sauces a few weeks or even months before an event, depending on the recipe. Consult your particular recipe, or pick one you've successfully frozen before.*

# Celebrate Spain With Tapas

When we tried tapas in our Test Kitchens, the taste of sherry, garlic-soaked marinated olives, and crisp bread drizzled with olive oil tantalized us. We began sampling and wanted to know more.

*Tapas* (pronounced TAH-pahs) resemble what Southerners might call appetizers. They feature the best-tasting, authentic ingredients of Spain—garlic, sherry, olives, almonds, tomatoes, cheeses, and more.

*Tapa* means "lid." As the story goes, bartenders in the Andalusia region would place a tiny plate of olives or a slice of bread with ham on it on top of a glass of sherry to ward off flies. Bars then began to develop their own recipes to place on the lids, hoping to coax customers into their establishments and increase sales.

After doing a little homework, we came up with recipes that represent the Spanish delicacies you might sample if you visit. Here's what we learned:

■ Some ingredients are difficult to find in the United States except in specialty markets. We didn't hesitate to substitute French bread in place of crusty homemade breads, or a French goat cheese rather than a Spanish one. We did find Spanish manchego cheese after some searching; it's a cheese with a light, milky color that belies its tangy flavor.

■ Dry sherry is the perfect complement to *tapas.* It's bold enough to accompany the strong garlic, cheeses, and marinades. Try it on the rocks with a squirt of fresh lime for a cool, refreshing change. Even if you aren't serving a Spanish menu, sherry stimulates the appetite, and the crisp, dry flavor makes a perfect beverage to offer guests before dinner.

■ Sherry vinegar, a by-product of sherry, is a jewel of Spanish cooking. Use it in marinades and salad dressings. Food experts predict it will be a sought-after item in coming years as Americans come to appreciate its full, sweet-tart flavor. Other full-flavored vinegars such as balsamic or red wine vinegar (or white vinegar mixed with sherry) will substitute in these recipes if you can't find sherry.

■ Many *tapas* require no cooking at all. Just put the following on your grocery list: olives, almonds, crusty bread, goat and other cheeses, and extra virgin olive oil for dipping bread. The extra virgin oil is lighter than regular olive oil.

■ You can make a meal of *tapas,* too. Serve several of them, and let folks sample until they're full. You may want to serve them in courses. Finish with Almond Cookies and orange slices soaked in sherry vinegar for dessert.

■ Tortillas are perhaps the most famous *tapas,* but don't mistake them for Mexican tortillas. Tortilla Española is like a potato frittata and may be served at breakfast for fans of hash brown potatoes.

## GARLIC-HAM TAPAS

1 baguette French bread
¼ cup olive oil
2 cloves garlic, cut in half
4 to 6 roma or cherry tomatoes, sliced
24 (6-inch) slices prosciutto
24 fresh parsley leaves

Cut bread into 24 (1-inch) slices. Brush both sides with olive oil, and rub with cut side of garlic. Bake at 400° for 5 minutes; turn and bake 5 to 7 minutes or until lightly browned. Top each slice with a tomato slice, prosciutto, and a parsley leaf. Yield: 24 appetizer servings.

## SHERRIED GARLIC SHRIMP

8 unpeeled, large fresh shrimp
¼ cup extra virgin olive oil
2 cloves garlic, crushed
⅓ cup dry sherry
1 tablespoon chopped fresh parsley

Peel and devein shrimp. Cook in olive oil in a large skillet over medium heat, stirring constantly, 3 to 4 minutes or until shrimp turn pink. Transfer shrimp to a serving dish with a slotted spoon; keep warm.

Add garlic to oil remaining in skillet. Cook 1 minute over medium-high heat, stirring constantly. Remove from heat; let stand 1 minute to cool slightly. Slowly stir in sherry. Return to heat; cook just until mixture begins to boil. Pour over shrimp; sprinkle with parsley. Serve with French bread. Yield: 4 appetizer servings.

## TORTILLA ESPAÑOLA

2 tablespoons olive oil
6 medium potatoes, peeled and thinly sliced (about 2 pounds)
1 large onion, finely chopped
½ teaspoon salt
½ teaspoon pepper
6 large eggs
½ teaspoon salt
2 tablespoons olive oil

Heat 2 tablespoons olive oil in a 10½-inch, cast-iron skillet; add next 4 ingredients. Cook, stirring constantly, over medium heat 4 to 5 minutes; cover and cook 5 minutes or until potatoes are soft, but not browned.

Combine eggs and ½ teaspoon salt in a large bowl; beat until frothy. Stir in potato mixture.

Heat a clean 10½-inch, cast-iron skillet over medium heat until hot enough to sizzle a drop of water. Add 2 tablespoons olive oil; rotate pan to coat bottom and sides. Pour egg mixture into skillet. Cook 5 minutes over medium-low heat. Bake at 375° for 10 minutes or until set. Loosen with a spatula; invert onto serving plate. To serve, cut into wedges or bite-size squares. Yield: 16 appetizer servings.

## MARINATED ROASTED PEPPERS

2 large sweet red peppers
2 large green peppers
¼ cup olive oil
2 tablespoons chopped fresh
   parsley
1½ tablespoons white wine
   vinegar
1 clove garlic, minced
¼ teaspoon salt
¼ teaspoon pepper

Wash and dry peppers; place on a foil-lined baking sheet. Bake at 500° for 25 minutes. Place in a heavy-duty, zip-top plastic bag; seal and let stand 10 minutes to loosen skins. Peel peppers; open peppers, if needed. Remove and discard membranes and seeds. Cut peppers into ⅓-inch strips, and place in a shallow dish.

Combine olive oil and remaining ingredients; pour mixture over peppers. Cover and chill 8 hours. Yield: 8 appetizer servings.      *Carol S. Noble*
*Burgaw, North Carolina*

**Note:** For tips on preparing roasted peppers, see "From Our Kitchen to Yours" on this page.

## HERB-MARINATED OLIVES

½ cup olive oil
½ cup sherry vinegar *
½ teaspoon dried marjoram
½ teaspoon dried rosemary
½ teaspoon dried thyme
2 cloves garlic, cut in slivers
2 (5.75-ounce drained weight) cans
   colossal ripe, pitted olives,
   drained

Combine olive oil and next 5 ingredients in a heavy-duty, zip-top plastic bag or shallow dish. Add olives to mixture, tossing or stirring gently. Seal or cover; chill 8 hours. Yield: 16 appetizer servings.

* 6 tablespoons white vinegar and 2 tablespoons sherry may be substituted for sherry vinegar.

## ALMOND COOKIES

1 (8-ounce) package blanched whole
   almonds, finely ground
1 cup superfine sugar
3 egg yolks
1 egg white
Sliced almonds

Combine ground almonds, sugar, and egg yolks in a bowl, stirring well. Shape 1 tablespoon mixture into a ball; place on a lightly greased cookie sheet, and flatten. Brush with egg white, and top with an almond slice. Repeat procedure with remaining dough. Bake at 325° for 10 minutes or until cookies are lightly browned. Let stand on cookie sheet 5 minutes; remove cookies to wire racks to cool completely. Yield: 2 dozen.

**Note:** To grind almonds, position knife blade in a food processor bowl; add almonds. Process until mixture resembles coarse meal.

# From Our Kitchen To Yours

As we prepared Marinated Roasted Peppers (on this page), the Test Kitchens staff was surprised to learn how easy it is to roast them in the oven or microwave. The unexpected flavor of roasted sweet pepper strips adds a surprise when added to pasta or salads, layered on sandwiches, or pureed into pesto or soups. In addition, these vegetables are high in vitamin C and a good source of vitamin A.

Although peppers are produced year-round, prices vary according to local availability. When selecting peppers, look for well-shaped, firm ones with a bright color and shiny skin. Choose peppers heavy for their size. Avoid those with shriveled or limp skins. Store sweet peppers in a vegetable crisper or plastic bags; refrigerate up to two weeks.

Consider the varying flavors of sweet peppers when deciding which ones to add to a meal. Red peppers are sweeter than the bolder green ones. Yellow ones also have a milder, more delicate flavor. Both red and yellow peppers start out green, but as they mature, the peppers take on brilliant colors.

If you're choosing peppers for color, you may prefer to roast sweet red and yellow ones because they retain their rich hues. When cooked, green peppers turn a dull shade.

Baking sweet peppers at a high temperature intensifies their mild, sweet flavor and allows the charred skin to peel away from the soft flesh easily. Follow the step-by-step directions for roasting peppers, and add zip to your favorite recipes.

**Note:** Sweet red peppers already roasted are available at supermarkets. (A 6½-ounce jar yields ¾ cup; a 12-ounce jar yields 1½ cups.)

## Roasting Sweet Peppers in the Microwave
Because we have busy schedules and look for shortcuts in the kitchen, we experimented with roasting sweet peppers in the microwave.

It's a time-saver for sweet red and yellow peppers; however, we do not recommend this procedure for green peppers because it is difficult to remove the skin.

**Microwave Directions:** Rub two medium sweet red or yellow peppers (about 1 pound) with vegetable oil. Pierce each pepper several times with a fork, and arrange, stems facing out, in a 9-inch pieplate in the microwave. Cover with a paper towel. Microwave at HIGH 4 minutes. Turn peppers over; cover and rotate pieplate. Microwave at HIGH 6 to 8 minutes or until skin on peppers looks blistered. Immediately place peppers in a heavy-duty, zip-top plastic bag, and seal. Let stand 10 minutes to loosen skin. Peel away skin; open peppers, if needed. Remove membranes and seeds from peppers; discard skin and seeds. Cut peppers in strips, if desired. Yield: 1 cup.

# Put The Freeze On Vegetables

Freezing is probably the easiest method of food preservation, and vegetables are one of the most popular foods to preserve. So if you crave the taste of fresh cream-style corn or green beans during the winter, stock up on family-size freezer containers and learn how to freeze summer's bountiful crop.

The secrets to ensuring good quality are to start with fresh vegetables, freeze them as quickly as possible, and use the proper equipment and techniques. Here's how to get the best results for your efforts.

## Take Stock of Equipment

To maintain the flavor of the vegetables, you'll need to blanch them before freezing, so make sure you have a saucepan or Dutch oven and a steaming basket large enough to accommodate a big batch. Have another large container or sink available for cooling vegetables after blanching.

You'll also need the following items to help prepare the produce: sharp knife, cutting board, and blanching basket, as well as plastic or glass freezer containers.

Plastic freezer bags make good flexible packaging for tray-packed vegetables. You can use wax freezer cartons with the bags to provide extra protection during storage, but do not use the cartons without freezer bags.

## Freezing the Produce

Start with just-harvested vegetables at the peak of flavor, and prepare amounts to fill only a few containers at a time. Discard damaged produce. Wash and drain vegetables before peeling or shelling, and prepare according to directions on our Vegetable Freezing Chart on page 178.

For the best quality, most vegetables require **blanching** (exposure to boiling water or steam for a few minutes) to inactivate natural enzymes that cause loss of flavor, color, and texture. Blanching also gives vegetables a brighter color and helps retain nutrients.

Follow the recommended blanching time for each vegetable because overblanching causes a loss of color, flavor, and nutrients. Underblanching stimulates rather than inactivates enzymes in the vegetables.

To blanch the vegetables, bring 1 gallon of water to a boil for each pound of prepared vegetables. (Use 2 gallons per pound for leafy green vegetables.) Place vegetables in a blanching basket, and submerge in boiling water. Cover vegetables and begin timing immediately.

To stop the cooking process, plunge the basket in ice water, using 1 pound of ice for each pound of vegetables, or hold the vegetables under cold running water. Let vegetables cool the same number of minutes that they were blanched; then drain.

Blanching can also be done by steaming or in the microwave. Steam blanching is recommended for only a few vegetables. To steam blanch vegetables, suspend them in a basket above boiling water. (The vegetables in this article should not be steam blanched.) Microwave blanching may not inactivate enzymes. However, if you plan to use the microwave method, work with small quantities, and use the directions that were designed for your microwave oven.

After blanching, freeze vegetables in a dry pack or tray pack. For a **dry pack,** place cooled vegetables in freezer containers, filling to ½ inch from top, and freeze.

In a **tray pack,** vegetables are frozen individually so that they remain loose in the package. Simply spread the vegetables in a single layer on a shallow tray, and freeze until firm, checking every 10 minutes after 1 hour. Package in a tray pack, leaving no headspace, and freeze.

For preparation directions and blanching times, see chart below.

| VEGETABLE FREEZING CHART | | |
|---|---|---|
| **Vegetable** | **Preparation** | **Blanching Time** |
| Beans (butter, lima, and pinto) | Choose tender beans with well-filled pods. Wash and shell; then sort according to size. | Small beans, 2 minutes; medium beans, 3 minutes; large beans, 4 minutes |
| Beans (green, snap, and waxed) | Select tender young pods. Wash beans, and cut off tips. Cut lengthwise or in 1- or 2-inch lengths. | 3 minutes |
| Corn (on the cob) | Husk corn, and remove silks; trim and wash. | Small ears, 7 minutes; medium ears, 9 minutes; large ears, 11 minutes |
| Corn (whole kernel) | Blanch ears first. Then cut kernels from cob about ⅔ depth of kernels. | 4 minutes |
| Corn (cream-style) | Blanch ears first. Cut off tips of kernels. Scrape cobs with back of a knife to remove juice and hearts of kernels. | 4 minutes |
| Greens (beet, chard, collards, mustard, spinach, turnip) | Select tender green leaves. Wash thoroughly; remove woody stems. | Collards, 3 minutes; other greens, 2 minutes |
| Okra | Select tender, green pods. Wash and sort according to size. Remove stems being careful not to expose seed cells. After blanching, leave pods whole or slice crosswise. | Small pods, 3 minutes; large pods, 4 minutes |
| Peas | Select pods with tender, barely mature peas. Shell and wash peas; discard those that are immature, hard, or overly mature. | 2 minutes for black-eyed and field peas; 1½ minutes for green peas |
| Squash (summer) | Select young squash with small seeds and tender rind. Wash and cut into ½-inch slices. | 3 minutes |
| Tomatoes | Raw: Wash; dip tomatoes in boiling water 30 seconds to loosen skins. Core and peel. Chop or quarter tomatoes, or leave whole. Pack pints or quarts to 1 inch from top. | Stewed: Remove stem and core; peel and quarter. Cover; cook until tender (10 to 20 minutes). Place pan in cold water to cool. Pack pints to ½ inch from top, quarts to 1 inch from top. |

# Bite Into A Watermelon Cookie!

When Sandra Russell's family in Gainesville, Florida, thinks of watermelon, their recollections turn to Watermelon Cookies.

## WATERMELON COOKIES

⅓ cup butter or margarine, softened
⅓ cup shortening
¾ cup sugar
1 large egg
1 tablespoon milk
1 teaspoon vanilla extract
2 cups all-purpose flour
1½ teaspoons baking powder
½ teaspoon salt
Red paste food coloring
⅓ cup semisweet chocolate mini-morsels
1½ cups sifted powdered sugar
2 tablespoons water
Green paste food coloring

Beat butter and shortening in a large mixing bowl at medium speed with an electric mixer. Gradually add sugar, beating well. Stir in egg, milk, and vanilla. Combine flour, baking powder, and salt; gradually add to creamed mixture, mixing well. Add a small amount of red food coloring to color dough as desired, beating until blended. Shape dough into a ball; cover and chill at least 3 hours.

Divide dough in half; store one portion in refrigerator. Roll remaining portion to ¼-inch thickness on a lightly floured surface.

Cut dough with a 3-inch round cookie cutter; cut circle in half. Place on an ungreased cookie sheet. Press several chocolate mini-morsels in each cookie. Repeat with remaining dough.

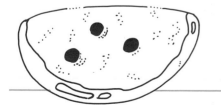

Bake at 375° for 8 to 10 minutes (do not brown). Cool on wire racks.

Combine powdered sugar and water, mixing until smooth. Add a small amount of green food coloring, mixing until blended. Dip round edge of each cookie in green frosting, and place cookie on wax paper until frosting is firm. Yield: 3 dozen.

**Note:** You can purchase paste food coloring at specialty shops, bakery supply stores, or craft stores.

# Peaches At Their Peak

Plump, juicy peaches are one of summer's most delightful treats. Baskets filled with the reddish-gold fruit adorn roadside fruit stands and beckon folks to stop and buy them.

## GEORGIA SUMMER SALAD

1 large honeydew melon, peeled and sliced
1 large cantaloupe, peeled and sliced
3 fresh peaches, peeled and sliced
12 fresh strawberries
Lettuce leaves
Peachy Dip

Arrange fruit on individual lettuce-lined salad plates. Serve with Peachy Dip. Yield: 12 servings.

### Peachy Dip

2 fresh peaches, peeled and cored
½ cup sour cream
2 tablespoons brown sugar
1½ teaspoons lemon juice

Combine all ingredients in container of an electric blender; process on low speed 30 seconds or until smooth. Cover and chill; stir before serving. Yield: 1½ cups. *Mrs. C. D. Hancock La Grange, Georgia*

## BAKED PEACHES

5 to 6 fresh peaches, peeled and sliced (about 2¼ pounds)
½ cup all-purpose flour
½ cup firmly packed brown sugar
⅛ teaspoon ground cinnamon
Dash of ground nutmeg
⅓ cup butter or margarine

Place peaches in a lightly greased 8-inch square baking dish; set aside. Combine flour and next 3 ingredients; cut in butter with a pastry blender until mixture is crumbly. Sprinkle flour mixture over peaches. Bake at 375° for 20 to 25 minutes. Serve with ice cream or whipped cream. Yield: 6 servings.
*Bettye Lewis Morrison, Tennessee*

## PEACH TRIFLE

1 (3-ounce) package vanilla pudding mix
1 ¾ cups milk
1 (12-ounce) container frozen whipped topping, thawed and divided
2 tablespoons sugar
5 fresh peaches, peeled and sliced (about 2 pounds)
1 (16-ounce) frozen pound cake loaf, thawed and cut into 1-inch cubes
½ cup orange juice

Combine pudding mix and milk in a saucepan; bring to a boil over medium heat, stirring constantly. Remove from heat, and let cool. Fold in half of whipped topping.

Sprinkle sugar over peaches; toss gently, and set aside. Place half of cake in bottom of 16-cup trifle bowl, and drizzle cake with half of orange juice. Arrange half of peaches over cake, and top with half of pudding mixture. Repeat layers. Spread remaining whipped topping on top. Cover and chill trifle at least 2 hours. Yield: 14 to 16 servings. *Mrs. J. C. Crawford Monroe, Louisiana*

## PEACH COBBLER WITH PRALINE BISCUITS

1½ cups sugar
2 tablespoons cornstarch
1 teaspoon ground cinnamon
1 cup water
8 cups sliced fresh peaches (about 5½ pounds)
3 tablespoons butter or margarine, melted
¼ cup firmly packed dark brown sugar
1 cup chopped pecans
2 cups self-rising flour
2 teaspoons sugar
½ cup shortening
¾ cup buttermilk

Combine first 3 ingredients in a Dutch oven. Gradually stir in water; add peaches. Bring to a boil, and cook 1 minute, stirring often. Remove from heat. Pour into a lightly greased 13- x 9- x 2-inch baking dish; set aside.

Combine butter, brown sugar, and pecans; set aside.

Combine flour and 2 teaspoons sugar; cut in shortening with a pastry blender until mixture is crumbly. Add buttermilk, stirring just until dry ingredients are moistened. Turn dough out onto a floured surface, and knead 3 or 4 times.

Roll dough to a 12- x 8-inch rectangle; spread with reserved pecan mixture, leaving a ½-inch border. Starting with long side, roll up jellyroll fashion. Cut into ½-inch slices; arrange slices over peach mixture. Bake at 400° for 25 to 30 minutes or until lightly browned. Yield: 12 servings.

*Lynne S. DeWitt*
*Greeneville, Tennessee*

# Save The Best Of Summer For Busy Days Ahead

Grab a jar of Tomato-Basil Sauce from your shelf and supper is ready in minutes. Each of these recipes starts with the seasoned tomato mixture. Even if you've never canned before, the simplicity and ease of using the Tomato-Basil Sauce will encourage you to preserve its flavor with a boiling-water bath.

## TOMATO-BASIL SAUCE

10 pounds tomatoes
1 tablespoon dried basil
6 tablespoons lemon juice, divided
3 teaspoons salt, divided

Wash tomatoes. Dip each tomato in boiling water 30 to 60 seconds or until skins split. Plunge immediately into ice water; core, peel, and quarter tomatoes. Place 4 cups of tomatoes in a large stockpot; crush tomatoes. Quickly bring to a boil over high heat, stirring vigorously; gradually add remaining quartered tomatoes, stirring constantly. Reduce heat, and simmer, uncovered, 2 hours.

Remove stockpot from heat; stir in basil. Add 1 tablespoon lemon juice and ½ teaspoon salt to each pint jar. Immediately pack hot tomatoes into hot jars, filling to ½ inch from top. Carefully run a nonmetallic spatula around inside of jars to remove air bubbles; wipe jar rims. Cover at once with metal lids, and screw on bands. Process in boiling-water bath 35 minutes. Yield: 6 pints.

## QUICK PASTA AND TOMATOES

¼ teaspoon minced garlic
2 tablespoons chopped onion
1 hot pepper, seeded and chopped
1 tablespoon olive oil
1 pint Tomato-Basil Sauce, drained
1 (8-ounce) package refrigerated tricolor cheese-filled tortellini, uncooked
¼ cup grated Parmesan cheese
2 tablespoons sliced ripe olives

## Boiling-Water Bath

A boiling-water bath is a simple process designed to preserve some foods for long-term storage. It's simpler than pressure canning and a good way to preserve high-acid foods, such as tomatoes. Pickles, jellies, jams, and preserves are also processed in a boiling-water bath. Call your local Extension agent if you have additional questions.

**1.** A boiling-water bath canner is any pot deep enough to permit water to cover jars by at least 1 inch with extra space allowed for boiling. The canner needs a lid, and a rack to hold jars at least ½ inch above the bottom of the pot. Prepare canner by filling it halfway with water and heating the water until hot but not boiling.

**2.** Pack clean jars with food filling to ½ inch from top, and carefully remove air bubbles by running a nonmetallic spatula around the inside of the jar. Wipe jar rims and threads clean with a damp cloth. Add canning lids and screw on metal bands. Place jars in hot water in canner.

**3.** Add or remove water so that it covers jars by 1 to 2 inches. Cover the canner, and begin timing when water around jars returns to a boil. Boil for time stated in the recipe.

**4.** Remove with a canning jar lifter (pair of tongs) and let stand, undisturbed, for 12 to 24 hours at room temperature. You may hear the lids pop as they "seal." If after standing, a lid moves when you press it, the product needs to be refrigerated and used within 3 days or re-canned within 24 hours. Otherwise, remove bands, and store jars in a cool, dark, dry place.

Cook first three ingredients in olive oil in a large skillet over medium-high heat, stirring constantly, until tender. Add Tomato-Basil Sauce, and cook 5 minutes or until thoroughly heated. Cook tortellini according to package directions; drain. Spoon sauce over tortellini. Top with cheese and olives. Yield: 2 servings.

## EASY PIZZA

1 pint Tomato-Basil Sauce
1 small onion, chopped
1 (10-ounce) can refrigerated pizza crust
1 (3½-ounce) package sliced pepperoni
1 green pepper, cut into rings
1 (2¼-ounce) can ripe sliced olives, drained
1 (8-ounce) package shredded mozzarella cheese

Combine Tomato-Basil Sauce and onion. Bring to a boil; reduce heat, and simmer, uncovered, 25 minutes or until liquid evaporates.

Prepare pizza crust according to package directions. Spread tomato mixture evenly over crust. Layer pepperoni, green pepper, and olives over tomato mixture. Bake at 450° for 15 minutes. Sprinkle with cheese, and bake an additional 3 to 5 minutes. Yield: one 12-inch pizza.

# QUICK!

## Thin Cuts Save Time

The thinner the cut of meat, the shorter the cooking time. Thin cuts better fit busy lifestyles and smaller families. Choose veal and turkey cutlets, boneless pork chops, chicken breasts, and cubed sirloin.

They are all speedy to prepare and lean, but they cost a little more and become tough if overcooked. For once, it pays to be in a hurry, so keep it quick and enjoy.

## CHICKEN IN MUSTARD CREAM SAUCE

4 skinned, boned chicken breast halves
⅛ teaspoon pepper
1 tablespoon Dijon mustard
2 tablespoons olive oil
¼ cup whipping cream
¼ cup Chablis or other dry white wine
2 teaspoons Dijon mustard
1 teaspoon green peppercorns in vinegar

Place chicken between two sheets of heavy-duty plastic wrap; flatten to ¼-inch thickness using a meat mallet or rolling pin. Sprinkle with pepper, and spread one side of chicken breasts evenly with 1 tablespoon mustard. Cook chicken in oil in a large skillet over medium heat, 10 minutes, turning frequently. Remove from skillet, and keep warm.

Combine whipping cream and remaining ingredients in skillet. Bring to a boil, and cook until mixture thickens. Spoon sauce over the chicken. Yield: 4 servings.
*Carol Durr*
*Pasadena, Maryland*

## APPLE-GLAZED PORK CUTLETS

½ cup catsup
¼ cup tomato juice
¼ cup finely chopped onion
2 tablespoons honey
2 tablespoons white vinegar
1 teaspoon dry mustard
1½ teaspoons Worcestershire sauce
½ cup applesauce
1 pound thinly sliced pork loin chops

Combine first 7 ingredients in a saucepan; bring to a boil over medium heat. Reduce heat, and simmer 5 minutes. Stir in applesauce. Set aside ½ cup sauce, and cook remainder over low heat 15 minutes.

Place pork on lightly greased rack of a broiler pan, and brush with half of reserved sauce. Broil 6 inches from heat (with electric oven door partially opened) 4 to 5 minutes. Turn and brush with remaining ¼ cup reserved sauce. Broil 4 to 5 minutes or until done. Transfer to a serving platter; spoon remaining sauce over pork. Yield: 4 servings.
*Frank H. Fogg*
*Tulsa, Oklahoma*

## VEAL PICCATA

4 veal cutlets (about ¾ pound)
¼ cup all-purpose flour
½ teaspoon salt
¼ teaspoon pepper
1½ tablespoons peanut or vegetable oil
3 tablespoons vermouth or dry white wine
2 tablespoons butter or margarine
2 tablespoons lemon juice
2 teaspoons grated lemon rind
Garnishes: lemon slices, parsley

Place cutlets between two sheets of heavy-duty plastic wrap; flatten to ⅛-inch thickness using a meat mallet or rolling pin. Combine flour, salt, and pepper; dredge cutlets in flour mixture. Cook in oil in a skillet over medium heat 1 minute on each side. Remove from skillet; keep warm.

Add vermouth to skillet; cook until thoroughly heated. Add butter and lemon juice; heat just until butter melts. Pour over cutlets, and sprinkle with lemon rind. Garnish, if desired. Yield: 2 servings.
*Jane Maloy*
*Wilmington, North Carolina*

## TURKEY WITH PEPPERS

1 pound turkey cutlets
¼ teaspoon salt
⅛ teaspoon pepper
2 tablespoons vegetable oil
½ pound fresh mushrooms, sliced
1 medium-size green pepper, cut
   into thin strips
¼ cup water
1 cup buttermilk
2 tablespoons chopped fresh parsley
1 tablespoon cornstarch
½ teaspoon dried marjoram
¼ teaspoon dried tarragon

Sprinkle cutlets with salt and pepper. Cook in oil in a large skillet over medium-high heat 2 minutes on each side or until no longer pink. Remove cutlets from skillet, and keep warm.

Combine mushrooms, green pepper and water in skillet; cook 2 minutes, stirring constantly. Combine buttermilk and remaining ingredients; stir into mushroom mixture. Bring to a boil; cook 1 minute, stirring constantly. Spoon over cutlets, and serve immediately. Yield: 4 servings.

*Kathleen Stone*
*Houston, Texas*

# ON THE LIGHT SIDE

# Give Me Five!

Five is the winning number of daily fruit and vegetable servings for reducing your risk of cancer, heart disease, and other chronic illnesses.

It's not difficult to meet the five-a-day challenge although only about 9% of Americans do so. Count 1 medium piece of fruit, ½ cup fruit or cooked vegetables, 1 cup raw vegetables, ¾ cup fruit or vegetable juice, or ¼ cup dried fruit as one serving. If the serving size on some of these recipes is 1 cup, count it as two servings.

In reaching your quota of five a day, be sure to include at least one serving of a high-fiber choice, such as pears, prunes, or dried beans and peas, and at least one daily serving of a food rich in vitamins A and C. Dark-green leafy vegetables are high in both vitamins; yellow-orange fruits and vegetables contain vitamin A; and citrus fruits and strawberries are rich in vitamin C. And several times a week include servings from the cabbage family, including broccoli, brussels sprouts, or cauliflower.

## PARMESAN-STUFFED TOMATOES

4 medium tomatoes (2½ pounds)
3 tablespoons chopped green onions
2 tablespoons chopped green pepper
1 teaspoon reduced-calorie
   margarine, melted
¼ cup Italian-seasoned
   breadcrumbs
2 tablespoons chopped fresh parsley
⅛ teaspoon dried oregano
⅛ teaspoon ground red pepper
⅛ teaspoon black pepper
Vegetable cooking spray
2 tablespoons grated Parmesan
   cheese

Slice off top of each tomato, and carefully scoop out pulp. Set tomato shells and pulp aside.

Cook green onions and green pepper in margarine in a large skillet over medium-high heat, stirring constantly, until tender. Remove from heat, and stir in tomato pulp, breadcrumbs, and next 4 ingredients. Spoon into shells, and place in an 8-inch square baking dish coated with cooking spray.

Cover and bake at 350° for 25 minutes. Sprinkle with cheese, and broil 5 inches from heat (with electric oven door partially opened) 3 minutes or until golden. Yield: 4 servings (96 calories [23% from fat] per tomato).

□ *4.2g protein, 2.5g fat (0.7g saturated, 0.5g monounsaturated, 0.5g polyunsaturated), 16.6g carbohydrate, 2mg cholesterol, 277mg sodium, and 60mg calcium.*   *Patricia Wenzel*
*Hurst, Texas*

## ZUCCHINI AND TOMATO WITH HERBS

¼ cup chopped onion
1 clove garlic, minced
2 teaspoons olive oil
5 cups sliced zucchini (1¾ pounds)
1 bay leaf
1 teaspoon dried basil
½ teaspoon dried oregano
¼ teaspoon pepper
⅓ cup water
2 cups unpeeled, chopped tomato
1 teaspoon sugar

Cook onion and garlic in oil in a Dutch oven over medium-high heat, stirring constantly, until tender. Stir in zucchini, bay leaf, basil, oregano, pepper, and water. Cover and cook over medium heat 10 minutes. Stir in chopped tomato and sugar; cover and cook 5 minutes. Remove and discard bay leaf. Serve immediately. Yield: 5 servings (58 calories [36% from fat] per 1-cup serving).

□ *2.3g protein, 2.3g fat (0.3g saturated, 1.4g monounsaturated, 0.3g polyunsaturated), 9.2g carbohydrate, 1.8g fiber, 0mg cholesterol, 11mg sodium, and 33mg calcium.*

*Joan McDonald*
*Weirton, West Virginia*

## CABBAGE-PINEAPPLE SLAW

1 (8-ounce) can unsweetened
   pineapple tidbits, undrained
3 cups finely shredded cabbage
1½ cups unpeeled, chopped Red
   Delicious apple
½ cup chopped celery
¼ cup golden raisins
¼ cup reduced-calorie mayonnaise
Lettuce leaves
Garnishes: apple wedges, celery
   leaves

Drain pineapple, reserving 3 tablespoons juice. Combine pineapple and next 4 ingredients in a large bowl. Combine reserved juice and mayonnaise; add to cabbage mixture, tossing gently. Cover and chill. Spoon into a lettuce-lined bowl, and garnish, if desired. Yield: 5 servings (112 calories [28% from fat] per 1-cup serving).

□ *1.1g protein, 3.5g fat (0.6g saturated, 0g monounsaturated, 2.2g polyunsaturated), 21.1g carbohydrate, 2.7g fiber, 4mg cholesterol, 111mg sodium, and 33mg calcium.*     Diann Laney
Rainsville, Alabama

## ITALIAN GREEN BEANS

1 pound fresh green beans
1 medium onion, sliced and
  separated into rings
3 cloves garlic
1 teaspoon vegetable oil
2 tablespoons water
1 teaspoon sugar
1 teaspoon dried basil
¼ teaspoon salt
2 tablespoons grated Parmesan
  cheese

Wash green beans; trim ends, and remove strings.

Add water to depth of 1 inch in a large skillet; bring to a boil, and add beans. Cover, reduce heat, and cook 6 to 8 minutes. Drain and immediately place in ice water. Let stand 5 minutes; drain well.

Cook onion and garlic in oil in a large skillet over medium-high heat, stirring constantly, until tender. Add green beans; cook 1 minute, stirring constantly.

Add 2 tablespoons water, sugar, basil, and salt; cook 1 to 2 minutes, stirring constantly. Remove and discard garlic; sprinkle with Parmesan cheese. Yield: 3 servings (97 calories [25% from fat] per 1-cup serving).

□ *4.6g protein, 2.7g fat (1g saturated, 0.8g monounsaturated, 0.9g polyunsaturated), 15.9g carbohydrate, 3.9g fiber, 3mg cholesterol, 267mg sodium, and 117mg calcium.*
Susan Buckmaster
Charlotte, North Carolina

---

# LIGHT MENU

# The Fresher, The Better

Velvety peaches, silk-tufted corn, scurrying crabs—Southern summers are brimming with wholesome foods. Although fresh offerings are plentiful, they don't last forever. So here's a healthy luncheon menu that accentuates the season's bounty.

## LIGHT LUNCHEON MENU

**Fresh Corn-and-Crab Soup
Healthy Slaw
Commercial breadsticks
Peach-Blueberry Dessert**

## FRESH CORN-AND-CRAB SOUP

2 cups fresh corn cut from cob
  (about 6 ears)
3¾ cups ready-to-serve, no-salt-
  added chicken broth
Vegetable cooking spray
1 tablespoon vegetable oil
1 cup chopped onion
3 cloves garlic, minced
3¾ cups 2% low-fat milk, divided
½ teaspoon freshly ground pepper
¼ teaspoon salt
½ teaspoon hot sauce
½ cup all-purpose flour
1 pound fresh lump crabmeat,
  drained
Garnish: paprika

Combine corn and chicken broth in a large saucepan. Bring to a boil over medium-high heat, stirring occasionally; reduce heat, and simmer mixture 20 minutes.

Coat a small skillet with cooking spray; add oil, and place over medium-high heat until hot. Add onion and garlic; cook, stirring constantly, until

tender. Add onion mixture, 3¼ cups milk, and next 3 ingredients to corn mixture; bring to a boil. Combine flour and remaining ½ cup milk, stirring with a wire whisk until smooth. Add to corn mixture, and cook, stirring often, over medium heat until thickened and bubbly. Stir in crabmeat. Garnish, if desired. Yield: 9 cups (280 calories [24% from fat] per 1½-cup serving).

□ *23.7g protein, 7.4g fat (2.5g saturated, 1.9g monounsaturated, 2.1g polyunsaturated), 28.7g carbohydrate, 2.5g fiber, 88mg cholesterol, 400mg sodium, and 277mg calcium.*

## HEALTHY SLAW

4 cups finely shredded cabbage
2 cups finely shredded red cabbage
¾ cup shredded carrot
3 tablespoons sliced green onions
¼ cup reduced-calorie mayonnaise
¼ cup plain low-fat yogurt
2 tablespoons white vinegar
1 teaspoon sugar
½ teaspoon pepper

Combine first 4 ingredients in a bowl; set aside. Combine mayonnaise and remaining ingredients; add to cabbage mixture, tossing well. Cover and chill. Yield: 6 servings (61 calories [44% from fat] per 1-cup serving).

□ *1.7g protein, 3g fat (0.8g saturated, 0.1g monounsaturated, 1.8g polyunsaturated), 7.6g carbohydrate, 2.1g fiber, 4mg cholesterol, 97mg sodium, and 58mg calcium.*

## PEACH-BLUEBERRY DESSERT

3½ cups peeled, sliced fresh
   peaches, divided *
1½ cups fresh blueberries, divided
¼ cup unsweetened apple juice
⅛ to ¼ teaspoon ground nutmeg
3 cups vanilla ice milk

Combine 1 cup peaches, 1 cup blueberries, apple juice, and nutmeg in a saucepan. Bring to a boil, and cook 2 minutes, stirring occasionally. Remove from heat. Stir in remaining 2½ cups peaches and ½ cup blueberries. Cover and chill.

Spoon into individual dishes; top with ice milk. Yield: 6 servings (160 calories [17% from fat] per ½ cup fruit with ½ cup ice milk).

□ 3.5g protein, 3.1g fat (1.8g saturated, 0.9g monounsaturated, 0.2g polyunsaturated), 31.8g carbohydrate, 3.3g fiber, 9mg cholesterol, 55mg sodium, and 96mg calcium.

* Frozen peaches and blueberries, thawed, may be substituted for fresh peaches and blueberries.

---

## LIGHT FAVORITE

# Strawberry Shortcake

Ruby-red strawberries and mounds of whipped topping heaped on oh-so-sweet layers of cake—Strawberry Shortcake is too delicious to pass up. And now you don't have to. Our healthy version of this classic is just as dreamy as the original favorite.

To lighten this dessert we began by revamping the rich, buttery cake. By using a smaller amount of margarine and substituting skim milk for whole milk, calories and fat are lowered.

Beaten egg whites folded into the batter help give it a tender texture.

Reduced-calorie frozen whipped topping replaces another high-fat culprit—whipping cream. Although the commercial topping contains some saturated fat, whipping cream has five times more total fat. This switch also cuts calories: A tablespoon of whipped cream has 28 calories while a tablespoon of topping has only 9.

Just a sprinkle of sugar brings out the natural sweetness of juicy fresh strawberries. Select the brightest-colored berries you can find, and you'll savor every bite of this favorite.

## STRAWBERRY SHORTCAKE
*(pictured on facing page)*

4 cups sliced fresh strawberries
¼ cup sugar
Vegetable cooking spray
¼ cup margarine, softened
⅓ cup sugar
1 large egg, separated
1¾ cups all-purpose flour
1½ teaspoons baking powder
¼ teaspoon salt
¾ cup skim milk
½ teaspoon vanilla extract
1 egg white
2 tablespoons sugar
1½ cups thawed, reduced-calorie
   frozen whipped topping
Garnish: strawberry fan

Combine strawberries and ¼ cup sugar; cover and refrigerate 2 to 3 hours, stirring occasionally.

Coat a 9-inch round cakepan with vegetable cooking spray; dust with flour, and set prepared pan aside.

Beat margarine at medium speed with an electric mixer until soft; gradually add ⅓ cup sugar, beating well. Add egg yolk, beating just until blended. Combine flour, baking powder, and salt in a small bowl; add dry ingredients to creamed mixture alternately with milk, beginning and ending with flour mixture. Mix after each addition. Stir in vanilla.

Beat egg whites until foamy. Gradually add 2 tablespoons sugar, one at a

time, beating until stiff peaks form. Stir about ½ cup beaten egg whites into batter; fold in remaining egg whites. Spoon batter into prepared pan. Bake at 350° for 30 minutes or until a wooden pick inserted in center comes out clean. Let cool in pan on a wire rack 10 minutes. Remove cake from pan; let cool completely on a wire rack.

Slice shortcake in half horizontally. Place bottom half, cut side up, on a serving plate. Drain strawberries, reserving juice, and drizzle half of juice over bottom layer. Set aside 1 tablespoon whipped topping; spread ¾ cup whipped topping over cake layer, and arrange half of strawberries over topping. Top with remaining cake layer, cut side down, and repeat procedure. Dollop with reserved 1 tablespoon whipped topping; garnish, if desired. Yield: 9 servings (250 calories [27% from fat] per slice).

□ 4.9g protein, 7.6g fat (2.5g saturated, 2.6g monounsaturated, 1.9g polyunsaturated), 41.3g carbohydrate, 2.3g fiber, 24mg cholesterol, 207mg sodium, and 82mg calcium.

| COMPARE THE NUTRIENTS | | |
|---|---|---|
| (per serving) | | |
| | Traditional | Light |
| Calories | 430 | 250 |
| Fat | 22.2g | 7.6g |
| Cholesterol | 115mg | 24mg |

**Tip:** *It is best to store most fruit in the refrigerator. Allow melons, avocados, and pears to ripen at room temperature; then refrigerate. Berries should be sorted to remove imperfect fruit before refrigerating. Wash and hull just before serving.*

*With a creamy topping and sweet red berries, this Strawberry Shortcake is luscious and light. (Recipe is on facing page.)*

*Carved watermelons can be both practical and beautiful. A melon half forms the perfect bowl for Watermelon Punch (recipe, page 190), and the carved swan makes an elegant container for fresh fruit. (See instructions below.)*

**Swan:** *Using a washable marker, draw pointed feathers around middle of melon. On brown paper, draw neck and head; cut out. Position pattern on melon, attaching with pushpins or tape. Make sure head connects to feathers. Trace around pattern. Using a sharp paring knife, cut along markings, carefully removing rind in small pieces. Hollow out melon, reserving pulp for melon balls. See finished swan in illustration.*

**Basket:** *Using a washable marker, draw a horizontal line around melon. From top of melon, draw two vertical lines starting 2 inches apart, gradually increasing width as lines connect with horizontal line. Wipe off horizontal line between vertical handle markings. Using a knife, cut on remaining lines; carefully lift out sections. Trim edges to make uniform; scoop out pulp, reserving for fruit mixture. See finished basket.*

**Flowers:** *Cut 1 (4- x 2½-inch) and 2 (3- x 2-inch) pieces of florist foam; soak in water. Arrange cuttings, such as fern, dusty miller, geranium, ageratum, dianthus, bachelor's button, wildflowers, and ivy, in foam. For swan or basket, cut a 2-inch square of florist foam; soak in water. Attach with wooden picks; arrange cuttings. Using 1½ yards of ribbon, make 5 loops, wrap wire around center of loops, and attach to swan or basket.*

*Simple carving techniques (see instructions on facing page) turn a plump watermelon into a flowering basket for chilled fresh fruit mixture.*

*Honey-Grilled Tenderloins,
Tomato-Cucumber Salad, yellow
squash, and fresh breadsticks make
a simple yet delightful meal.
(Recipes, page 199.)*

# AUGUST

*We have some secrets to share — secret recipes, that is, from*

*some well-known chefs at Southern inns. Other special recipes*

*include winners of a community cookbook contest. You'll be a*

*winner, too, when you serve chilled fresh fruit, sorbet, or*

*punch in beautiful containers carved from watermelons.*

# Whittle A Watermelon

Summer treasures—fresh-cut flowers and watermelons—bloom into masterpieces using some creative carving techniques. Covered with plastic wrap, carved watermelons will keep in the refrigerator up to three days. If you're going to serve punch or fresh fruit in a watermelon, add it just before serving. Follow our photos—or use your imagination—to make a festive, summertime centerpiece for your next party or afternoon tea.

## WATERMELON PUNCH
*(pictured on page 186)*

1 large watermelon
1 (6-ounce) can frozen orange juice concentrate, thawed and undiluted
½ cup lemon juice
3 cups ginger ale, chilled

Cut off top of melon; scoop out unseeded flesh, and place about 3 cups in container of an electric blender or food processor. Process until smooth (seeds will float). Pour watermelon puree through a wire-mesh strainer into a bowl, discarding pulp and seeds. Repeat procedure with remaining unseeded flesh.

Measure 15 cups watermelon juice, discarding any remaining juice; stir in orange juice concentrate and lemon juice. Refrigerate at least 2 hours. Stir in chilled ginger ale just before serving. Yield: 19 cups. *Tonya Vann*
*Birmingham, Alabama*

## WATERMELON SORBET

½ medium watermelon, sliced lengthwise
1 (6-ounce) can frozen pink lemonade concentrate, thawed and undiluted
1 (15¼-ounce) can crushed pineapple, undrained
½ cup sugar
Fresh fruit
Garnish: fresh mint sprigs

Scoop out unseeded watermelon flesh; place in container of an electric blender or food processor. Process until smooth (seeds will float). Pour watermelon puree through a wire-mesh strainer into a bowl, discarding pulp and seeds. Measure 8 cups watermelon juice, discarding any remaining juice; add lemonade concentrate, pineapple, and sugar, stirring until sugar dissolves.

Pour mixture into a 13- x 9- x 2-inch pan; cover and freeze until firm. Break frozen mixture into chunks. Place one-half of mixture in container of an electric blender or food processor; process until smooth. Repeat procedure. Serve immediately with fresh fruit, and garnish if desired. Yield: about 9 cups.
*Mrs. Thomas Lee Adams*
*Kingsport, Tennessee*

# Too Hot To Cook?

During the long, hot days of summer, why heat up the kitchen? These main dishes need little or no cooking.

Melon-and-Prosciutto Salad is a classic dish made from prosciutto (proh-SHOO-toh), an Italian-style ham that's salt-cured, air-dried, and unsmoked. For best flavor and texture, use within 24 hours of slicing. If prosciutto isn't available, substitute fully cooked, paper-thin ham slices.

Use leftover cooked chicken and rice to prepare Curried Chicken-Rice Salad. If you don't have leftovers on hand, choose quick-cooking rice and cooked chicken or turkey from the deli or meat department.

## CURRIED CHICKEN-RICE SALAD

4 chicken breast halves, skinned
½ teaspoon salt
1½ cups cooked rice
1 cup chopped celery
1 cup seedless green grapes, halved
½ cup chopped pecans, toasted
⅓ cup sweet pickle relish
¾ cup mayonnaise
1 teaspoon curry powder
½ teaspoon salt
¼ teaspoon pepper
Lettuce leaves
1 pint fresh strawberries
1 fresh pineapple, peeled and cut into spears

Combine chicken and ½ teaspoon salt in a Dutch oven; add water to cover. Bring to a boil; cover, reduce heat, and simmer 40 minutes or until tender. Drain, reserving broth for other uses. Bone chicken, and cut into bite-size pieces. Combine chicken, rice, and next 4 ingredients. Combine mayonnaise and next 3 ingredients; add to chicken mixture, stirring well. Serve on lettuce leaves with strawberries and pineapple. Yield: 4 to 6 servings.
*Mrs. Garwood Briggs*
*Moultrie, Georgia*

## MELON-AND-PROSCIUTTO SALAD

3 cups cantaloupe balls (1 small cantaloupe)
3 cups honeydew melon balls (1 small honeydew)
4 ounces prosciutto, cut into strips *
1 cup (4 ounces) shredded provolone cheese
Lettuce leaves
Poppy Seed Dressing

Combine first 4 ingredients; toss gently. Cover and chill. Serve salad in a lettuce-lined bowl with Poppy Seed Dressing. Yield: 6 servings.

### Poppy Seed Dressing

⅓ cup sugar
½ cup white vinegar
1 teaspoon salt
1 teaspoon dry mustard
1 teaspoon grated onion
1 cup vegetable oil
1 tablespoon poppy seeds

Combine sugar and next 4 ingredients in container of an electric blender; process 20 seconds. With blender on high, gradually add oil in a slow steady stream. Stir in poppy seeds. Yield: 1¾ cups.

* Four ounces fully cooked, paper-thin slices of ham can be substituted for 4 ounces prosciutto.

## HAM-DIJON PASTA SALAD

1 (7-ounce) package refrigerated rigatoni, uncooked
2 cups cubed cooked ham
1 cup (4 ounces) shredded Swiss cheese
1 carrot, scraped and thinly sliced
½ teaspoon freshly ground pepper
1 (8-ounce) carton plain low-fat yogurt or nonfat sour cream alternative
1 tablespoon Dijon mustard
Lettuce leaves

Cook pasta according to package directions; drain. Rinse with cold water; drain. Combine pasta and next 4 ingredients; set aside.

Combine yogurt and mustard; spoon over salad, and toss gently. Cover and chill. Serve on lettuce leaves. Yield: 6 servings.

## HEARTS OF PALM SANDWICH

1 (12-ounce) baguette French bread
8 Bibb lettuce leaves, torn in half
1 (14-ounce) can hearts of palm, drained and quartered
2 small carrots, scraped and shredded
1 small cucumber, thinly sliced
1 (6-ounce) package sliced provolone cheese, cut in half
¼ cup commercial vinaigrette salad dressing
Additional commercial vinaigrette salad dressing (optional)

Slice bread horizontally to within ¼ inch of edge. Arrange half of lettuce on bottom half of bread. Layer hearts of palm, carrots, cucumber, and provolone cheese on lettuce; drizzle with ¼ cup salad dressing, and top with remaining lettuce. Cut sandwich into fourths, and serve with additional salad dressing, if desired. Yield: 4 servings.

# Beat The Heat

Lower the heat and raise spirits with refreshing, cool pies. Kids will love Candy-Crust Mint Pie with its cereal shell and ice-cream filling. But you better leave Daring Daiquiri Pie to the adults; they'll get a kick (literally) out of its rum-laced flavor. You can make these desserts ahead, and leave them in the refrigerator or freezer until you need them.

## CANDY-CRUST MINT PIE

⅔ cup semisweet chocolate morsels
3 tablespoons butter
2 cups crisp rice cereal
1 quart mint-chocolate chip ice cream, softened
Garnish: chocolate curls

Combine chocolate morsels and butter in a small, heavy saucepan; cook over low heat until melted. Remove mixture from heat, and gradually add to cereal; stir well.

Line a 9-inch pieplate with aluminum foil; place a circle of wax paper over foil in bottom of pieplate. Press cereal mixture evenly into pieplate. Cool. Invert crust on the back of another 9-inch pieplate; remove foil and wax paper. Return crust to original 9-inch pieplate.

Spread ice cream into crust, and freeze until firm. Garnish, if desired. Yield: one 9-inch pie.

*Cheryl H. Richardson*
*Fairfax Station, Virginia*

## DARING DAIQUIRI PIE

1 (8-ounce) package cream cheese
1 (14-ounce) can sweetened condensed milk
1 (6-ounce) can frozen limeade concentrate, thawed and undiluted
¼ cup light rum
Green food coloring
1¾ cups frozen whipped topping, thawed and divided
1 baked 9-inch pastry shell

Beat softened cream cheese in a large mixing bowl at high speed with an electric mixer until light and fluffy. Add sweetened condensed milk and limeade concentrate; beat at medium speed until smooth.

Stir in rum and desired amount of food coloring. Fold in 1 cup whipped topping. Spoon filling into pastry shell, and chill. Spread remaining ¾ cup whipped topping over pie, and serve. Yield: one 9-inch pie. *Kate Morris*
*South Charleston, West Virginia*

# And The Winners Are...

It was a big moment for volunteer organizations across our region when the 1991 TABASCO Community Cookbook Awards were announced. Not surprisingly, seven of the winners came from the South, and we've given you an example of what each cookbook winner has to offer.

We haven't changed any ingredients or procedures, but we have tested the recipes and written them all in our style to make them consistent and a little easier to follow. We think you'll give them a blue ribbon, too.

■ The first-place winner, *Come On In!*, is by the Junior League of Jackson, Mississippi.

## MEAT LOAF WITH SUN-DRIED TOMATOES AND HERBS

1¼ cups (2½ ounces) dried tomato
    halves
1 medium onion, finely chopped
1 medium-size green pepper, finely
    chopped
1 tablespoon olive oil
1 slice white bread
2 tablespoons milk
2 large eggs, lightly beaten
1 pound lean ground beef
1½ cups (6 ounces) shredded
    provolone cheese
2 cloves garlic, minced
2 teaspoons dried basil
1 teaspoon dried oregano
1 teaspoon dried thyme
1 teaspoon salt
1 teaspoon freshly ground pepper
1 tablespoon all-purpose flour
1 cup half-and-half
1 tablespoon finely chopped green
    onions
1 teaspoon dried basil
¼ teaspoon salt
¼ teaspoon freshly ground pepper
Garnish: dried tomato halves

Place tomato halves in a heavy saucepan; add water to cover. Bring to a boil over medium heat; reduce heat, and simmer 5 minutes. Drain tomato halves and set aside.

Cook onion and green pepper in oil in a skillet over medium heat, stirring constantly, until tender. Set aside.

Tear bread into small pieces, and place in a large bowl; drizzle with milk. Add onion mixture, 1 cup reserved tomato halves, eggs, and next 8 ingredients; mix well. Press into a lightly greased 9- x 5- x 3-inch loafpan. Bake at 350° for 1 hour. Remove from oven, and invert onto a serving platter, reserving ¼ cup drippings for gravy mixture. Keep meat loaf warm.

Heat drippings in a nonstick skillet over medium heat. Add flour and cook, stirring constantly, 1 minute. Gradually stir in half-and-half; cook, stirring often, until thickened and bubbly. Add remaining ¼ cup tomato halves, green onions, 1 teaspoon basil, ¼ teaspoon salt, and ¼ teaspoon pepper; heat thoroughly. Serve over meat loaf. Garnish, if desired. Yield: 6 servings.

■ The second-place winner, *Preserving Our Italian Heritage,* was submitted by the Sons of Italy Florida Foundation of Tampa.

## ORZO PRIMAVERA

3 quarts water
1 teaspoon salt
2 cups orzo, uncooked
1 pound fresh asparagus, cut into
    1-inch pieces
3 cloves garlic, minced
½ cup chopped sweet red pepper
1 teaspoon butter or margarine,
    melted
1 tablespoon olive oil
1 cup frozen English peas, thawed
½ cup chicken broth
1 teaspoon grated lemon rind
¼ teaspoon ground white pepper
½ cup freshly grated Parmesan
    cheese

Combine water and salt in a large Dutch oven; bring to a boil. Add orzo, and cook 5 minutes. Add asparagus, and cook 4 minutes. Drain and set mixture aside in a large serving bowl.

Cook garlic and red pepper in butter and oil in Dutch oven over medium heat, stirring constantly, 1 minute or until crisp-tender. Add peas; cook, stirring constantly, 1 minute. Add broth, lemon rind, and white pepper; bring to a boil, and cook 1 minute. Add vegetable mixture to orzo mixture, tossing well. Sprinkle with Parmesan cheese. Serve immediately. Yield: 6 to 8 servings.

**Note:** Orzo is a rice-shaped pasta.

■ The Walter S. McIlhenny Hall of Fame selection, *Recipes and Reminiscences of New Orleans,* is produced by the Ursuline Academy Parents Club of Metairie, Louisiana.

### YAMS COINTREAU

4 large yams or sweet potatoes,
    unpeeled (about 3½ pounds)
¼ cup Cointreau or other orange-
    flavored liqueur
¼ cup butter or margarine, melted
1 teaspoon salt
⅛ teaspoon pepper
Garnish: chopped fresh parsley

Cook yams in boiling water to cover 30 minutes or until tender. Drain and let cool to touch; peel. Mash yams; stir in Cointreau and next 3 ingredients. Garnish, if desired. Yield: 6 to 8 servings.

---

## Yam Tips

■ When buying yams or sweet potatoes, select firm potatoes with smooth, bright-colored skins. Avoid any with blemishes.
■ Never store uncooked fresh sweet potatoes in the refrigerator as the coolness will cause them to lose their flavor and turn black.

■ The Walter S. McIlhenny Hall of Fame selection, *Virginia Hospitality,* is compiled by the Junior League of Hampton Roads of Hampton, Virginia.

## CREAM OF PEANUT SOUP

2 stalks celery, chopped
1 small onion, chopped
¼ cup butter or margarine, melted
2 tablespoons all-purpose flour
2 cups chicken broth
1 cup milk
1 cup half-and-half
1 cup creamy peanut butter
¼ teaspoon salt
⅛ teaspoon pepper
Garnish: paprika

Cook celery and onion in butter in a Dutch oven over medium heat, stirring constantly, 3 minutes. Add flour and chicken broth, stirring until smooth. Cook 1 minute, stirring constantly. Bring to a boil. Gradually stir in milk and half-and-half.

Pour mixture through a wire-mesh strainer into a bowl, discarding vegetables left in strainer and reserving liquid. Place peanut butter in Dutch oven, and gradually return reserved liquid to Dutch oven, stirring with a wire whisk. Simmer 5 minutes, stirring occasionally. Add salt and pepper. Garnish, if desired. Yield: 5 cups.

■ The Southwestern regional winner, *Potluck on the Pedernales,* is from the Community Garden Club of Johnson City, Texas.

## CHEESE VELVET SOUP

6 ounces Brie cheese
½ cup finely chopped celery
½ cup finely chopped carrot
¼ cup finely chopped onion
½ cup butter or margarine, melted
½ cup all-purpose flour
2 cups chicken broth
1 teaspoon dried thyme
1 bay leaf
½ cup whipping cream
Garnish: shredded carrot

Carefully cut rind from Brie and discard; set cheese aside.

Cook celery, carrot, and onion in butter in a saucepan over medium heat, stirring constantly, until tender. Add flour, and cook over low heat, stirring constantly, 1 minute. Gradually stir in broth, thyme, and bay leaf. Cook, stirring constantly, until mixture is thickened and bubbly. Add cheese, stirring until smooth. Add whipping cream, and heat thoroughly. Discard bay leaf; serve immediately. Garnish, if desired. Yield: 3 cups.

■ The Walter S. McIlhenny Hall of Fame selection, *Atlanta Cooknotes,* is by the Junior League of Atlanta. (The award honors the best community cookbooks selling more than 100,000 copies since first published.)

## ORANGE CURD TARTS

½ cup butter or margarine
½ cup sugar
1 egg yolk
3 large eggs
1 (6-ounce) can frozen orange juice concentrate, thawed and undiluted
12 baked (3-inch) pastry shells
1 (12-ounce) jar raspberry jam *
Garnish: orange rind strips

Combine butter and sugar in top of a double boiler; bring water to a boil. Reduce heat to low; cook until butter melts. Add egg yolk and next 2 ingredients; cook, stirring occasionally, about 10 minutes or until thickened. Spoon into shells.

Melt jam in a small saucepan over low heat; spread on orange filling. Chill at least 2 hours. Garnish, if desired. Yield: 12 (3-inch) tarts.

* 4 ounces semisweet chocolate morsels may be substituted for jam. Place morsels in a heavy-duty, zip-top plastic bag. Microwave at HIGH 1 to 2 minutes or until chocolate melts. Snip a tiny corner from bag, and gently squeeze bag, drizzling chocolate over orange filling. Chill 2 hours.

■ The Southern regional winner, *A Centennial Sampler,* is by The American Association of University Women of Elkins, West Virginia.

## DIAMOND FUDGE

1 6-ounce package semisweet chocolate morsels
1 cup creamy peanut butter
½ cup butter or margarine
1 cup sifted powdered sugar

Cook first 3 ingredients in a saucepan over low heat, stirring constantly, just until mixture melts and is smooth. Remove from heat. Add powdered sugar, stirring until smooth. Spoon into a buttered 8-inch square pan; chill until firm. Let stand about 10 minutes at room temperature before cutting into squares. Store in refrigerator. Yield: 1½ pounds.

## Cooking Checklist

■ Before starting a recipe, make sure you have the equipment needed to prepare it. Be sure to use the correct pan size, especially when preparing cakes, pies or breads.
■ Measure ingredients accurately. For liquids, use a glass measuring cup; this allows you to see that you are measuring correctly. Use a metal or plastic measuring cup for solids or dry ingredients.
■ When preparing a recipe, always try to follow directions carefully. Avoid substituting items; for example, don't use soft margarine for butter or margarine, or whipped cream cheese for cream cheese.
■ Before trying a new recipe, read through it at least once before beginning, and check carefully to be sure all ingredients called for are on hand.

# Chefs Share Their Secrets

If you can't dash off to Southern inns to sample the culinary creations of their restaurants, do the next best thing—cook them at home.

Our Test Kitchens staff adapted the recipes from several famous inns to suit your kitchen. We cut down on some of the complicated steps and simplified the ingredients.

## EGGPLANT CAVIAR WITH TAPENADE

1 large eggplant
3 tablespoons finely chopped onion
⅓ cup chopped tomato
2 tablespoons chopped fresh parsley
1 tablespoon chopped fresh basil (optional)
¼ teaspoon minced garlic
2 tablespoons olive oil
2 tablespoons lemon juice
¼ teaspoon salt
¼ teaspoon pepper
Tapenade
Toasted French bread slices

Prick eggplant several times with a fork, and place on a baking sheet. Bake at 450° for 20 minutes or until skin starts to darken and pulp feels soft. Let cool.

Peel eggplant, and coarsely chop pulp. Combine eggplant and next 9 ingredients. Serve with Tapenade and French bread. Yield: 3 cups.

### Tapenade

¾ cup Greek olives, pitted and finely chopped
2 anchovy fillets, chopped
1 tablespoon capers
1 tablespoon olive oil
2 teaspoons Dijon mustard

Combine all ingredients. Yield: ⅔ cup.
*Hotel Maison de Ville*
*New Orleans, Louisiana*

## CORN-AND-BOURBON SOUP

2 slices bacon
1 onion, chopped
2 shallots, chopped
⅓ cup chopped celery
⅓ cup chopped leeks
4 cups corn cut from cob (about 8 ears)
2 quarts chicken broth
1 medium potato, peeled and chopped
¼ teaspoon salt
¼ teaspoon ground white pepper
1 cup whipping cream
2 to 3 tablespoons bourbon
Garnishes: crème fraîche, chives

Cook bacon in a Dutch oven until lightly browned. Add onion and next 3 ingredients; cook over medium heat 2 minutes. Add corn, and cook 5 minutes, stirring occasionally. Add broth and next 3 ingredients; bring to a boil. Cover, reduce heat, and simmer 20 minutes or until potato is tender. Add cream, and cook 2 minutes.

Remove and discard bacon. Place half of mixture in container of an electric blender; process until smooth. Repeat with remaining mixture. Pour mixture through a wire-mesh strainer into Dutch oven, pressing pulp with the back of a spoon; discard pulp. Stir in bourbon; serve soup hot or cold. Garnish each serving, if desired. Yield: 9½ cups. *Little Palm Island*
*Little Torch Key, Florida*

## BAKED BREAST OF CHICKEN WITH MARINATED BERMUDA ONIONS

1 large head garlic
Olive oil
½ pound goat cheese, softened
1 tablespoon chopped fresh basil
1 tablespoon chopped fresh parsley
¼ teaspoon salt
⅛ teaspoon pepper
8 boned whole chicken breasts with skin
Marinated Bermuda Onions

Chop off bottom of garlic head, and separate whole cloves, leaving tight outer covering intact. Place in an 8-inch square pan, and drizzle with olive oil. Bake at 350° for 20 minutes. Cool and drain; remove skins from cloves. Set aside.

Position knife blade in food processor bowl; add garlic, goat cheese, and next 4 ingredients. Process 30 seconds or until almost smooth, stopping occasionally to scrape down sides.

Loosen skin from breasts, forming a pocket without detaching skin. Spread 2 tablespoons cheese mixture under skin of each piece of chicken. Place in a 15- x 10- x 1-inch jellyroll pan. Bake, uncovered, at 400° for 30 minutes or until done. Serve on a bed of Marinated Bermuda Onions. Yield: 8 servings.

### Marinated Bermuda Onions

1 cup balsamic vinegar
¼ cup olive oil
3 cloves garlic, minced
3 tablespoons chopped fresh basil
¼ teaspoon salt
⅛ teaspoon pepper
3 large Bermuda onions, thinly sliced and separated into rings
2 tablespoons olive oil

Combine first 6 ingredients; pour over onions. Cover and chill 1 hour; drain. Cook onions in 2 tablespoons olive oil in a large nonstick skillet over medium-high heat, stirring constantly 3 to 5 minutes or until crisp-tender. Yield: 4 cups. *Morrison House*
*Alexandria, Virginia*

**Tip:** *When buying garlic, select firm, plump bulbs that have dry, unbroken skins. Store in a cool, dry place that is well ventilated. The flavor will remain sharp up to four months.*

## VICTORIA CRAB CAKES

2 large eggs, beaten
½ cup chopped onion
½ cup chopped green pepper
½ cup chopped sweet red pepper
3 tablespoons white wine
    Worcestershire sauce
1 tablespoon lemon juice
1 teaspoon dry mustard
½ to 1 teaspoon ground red pepper
1 pound fresh lump crabmeat
2 cups Italian-seasoned
    breadcrumbs, divided
2 to 4 tablespoons butter or
    margarine, divided
Garnishes: lemon slices, butter
    curls, fresh parsley sprigs

Combine first 8 ingredients; stir in crabmeat and 1 cup breadcrumbs. Shape into 8 patties; dredge patties in remaining breadcrumbs. Fry in 2 tablespoons butter over medium heat until golden brown, adding additional butter as needed. Drain patties on paper towels. Garnish, if desired. Yield: 8 servings.
*The Victoria*
*Anniston, Alabama*

## SPINACH SALAD WITH GARLIC-GINGER VINAIGRETTE DRESSING

1 pound fresh spinach
1 head radicchio, torn
1 cup seedless red grapes, halved
8 cherry tomatoes, halved
4 ounces oyster mushrooms, sliced
1 tablespoon olive oil
1 (8-ounce) package Muenster
    cheese
Vegetable cooking spray
⅓ cup Italian-seasoned
    breadcrumbs
Garlic-Ginger Vinaigrette Dressing

Remove stems from spinach; wash leaves thoroughly, and pat dry. Tear into bite-size pieces. Combine spinach and next 3 ingredients in a large bowl.
Cook mushrooms in olive oil over medium-high heat, stirring constantly 2 to 3 minutes or until crisp-tender. Add to salad mixture.

Cut cheese into 16 (3½- x ½- x ¼-inch) strips. Spray cheese with cooking spray, and roll in breadcrumbs; place on a lightly greased baking sheet. Bake at 400° for 3 minutes or until cheese begins to soften. Pour dressing over salad; toss gently. Top with baked cheese. Serve immediately. Yield: 8 servings.

### Garlic-Ginger Vinaigrette Dressing

3 cloves garlic, minced
2 tablespoons chopped shallots
2 tablespoons chopped gingerroot
1 tablespoon olive oil
½ cup olive oil
¼ cup sesame oil
2 tablespoons chopped cilantro
2 tablespoons chopped fresh mint
1 tablespoon chopped fresh thyme
2 tablespoons rice vinegar
2 tablespoons balsamic vinegar
1½ tablespoons soy sauce
⅛ teaspoon salt
⅛ teaspoon pepper

Cook first 3 ingredients in 1 tablespoon olive oil over medium heat, stirring constantly, 2 to 3 minutes. Combine garlic mixture, ½ cup olive oil, and remaining ingredients in a jar. Cover tightly, and shake vigorously. Yield: 1⅓ cups.
*Fairmount Hotel*
*San Antonio, Texas*

## PEAR TART WITH WHITE CARAMEL SAUCE

2 small firm pears
4 cups water
½ cup sugar
1 egg yolk
2 tablespoons sugar
2 tablespoons whipping cream
1 (17¼-ounce) package commercial
    frozen puff pastry sheets
¼ cup marzipan
¼ cup unsalted butter, melted
White Caramel Sauce
Garnishes: raspberries, fresh mint
    sprigs

Peel pears, and set aside. Combine water and ½ cup sugar in a Dutch oven; bring mixture to a boil. Add pears; cover, reduce heat, and simmer 12 to 15 minutes or until pears are tender. Remove from heat; uncover and let cool. Drain pears, and cut in half lengthwise; core. Cut each pear half lengthwise into thin slices, cutting to but not through small end. Set aside.
Combine egg yolk, 2 tablespoons sugar, and whipping cream; set aside.
Thaw pastry at room temperature about 20 minutes before gently unfolding. Place on a lightly floured surface; cut with a 4½-inch round cutter into 8 rounds. Place 4 rounds on a parchment paper-lined baking sheet.
Roll 1 tablespoon marzipan into a 3-inch circle. Place in center of a pastry round; repeat with remaining 3 pastry rounds and marzipan.
Cut out centers of remaining 4 pastry rounds using a 3-inch round cutter; remove centers, and discard. Place pastry rings on top of pastry rounds with marzipan, and brush pastry with egg yolk mixture; seal with a fork. Place a pear half in center of each pastry, fanning out slices; brush pear with melted butter. Bake at 400° for 12 to 15 minutes or until golden brown. Serve with White Caramel Sauce. Garnish, if desired. Yield: 4 servings.

### White Caramel Sauce

¼ cup sugar
2 tablespoons water
½ cup whipping cream
2 teaspoons vanilla extract
¼ cup butter

Combine sugar and water in a small, heavy saucepan; cook over medium heat, stirring constantly, about 3 minutes or until mixture is reduced to 3 tablespoons. Add whipping cream and vanilla. (Mixture will become lumpy.) Cook over medium heat, stirring constantly, about 5 minutes or until mixture is reduced to 6 tablespoons. Remove sauce from heat. Add butter; stir until blended. Yield: about ⅔ cup.
*The Inn at Perry Cabin*
*St. Michael's, Maryland*

# Slice a Giant Sandwich

If your family is a typical one, sandwiches are everyday fare in the summer. For a change, try a "giant" sandwich. Ours are made from unsliced loaves of bread or layered tortillas. They're prepared whole and then divided into individual portions just before serving.

The Big Veggie Sandwich is a little tricky to assemble. To overcome its tendency to tear apart, cut the bread into slices, leaving the bottom ½ inch attached so the loaf resembles an accordion. Fill every other cut of bread with sandwich ingredients. Remember, the thinner you slice the vegetables, the easier it is to keep the sandwich together.

## TORTILLA STACK-UPS

2 cups (8 ounces) shredded
   Monterey Jack cheese
2 cups (8 ounces) shredded
   Cheddar cheese
½ to ¾ cup thinly sliced green
   onions
1 (4-ounce) can chopped green
   chiles
8 (8-inch) flour tortillas
2 tablespoons butter or margarine,
   melted
Sour cream
Picante sauce

Combine cheeses; set aside. Combine green onions and chiles; set aside. Layer 4 tortillas into each of two 8-inch round cakepans, sprinkling ⅔-cup cheese mixture and 2 heaping tablespoons chiles mixture between each tortilla. Brush top tortillas with melted butter. Bake at 400° for 20 minutes or until cheese melts and tops are lightly browned. Cool 5 minutes; invert onto serving platters, and cut into wedges. Serve immediately with sour cream and picante sauce. Yield: 6 to 8 servings. *Eileen Wehling*
*Austin, Texas*

## GIANT MEATBALL SANDWICH

1 pound ground beef
½ pound ground pork sausage
2 cups commercial spaghetti sauce
   with peppers and mushrooms
1 clove garlic, minced
1 (16-ounce) loaf unsliced Italian
   bread
1 (6-ounce) package sliced
   provolone cheese

Combine ground beef and sausage; shape into 1-inch balls. Cook in a large skillet over medium-high heat 8 to 10 minutes or until browned. Remove from heat; drain meatballs on paper towels. Discard drippings.

Combine spaghetti sauce and garlic in skillet; add meatballs. Cook over medium heat, stirring occasionally, 12 to 15 minutes or until done.

Cut bread in half lengthwise. Place on a baking sheet, cut sides up; broil 5 inches from heat 2 minutes or until lightly toasted.

Spoon meatball mixture onto bottom half of bread. Cut cheese slices in half; arrange on top of meatballs, overlapping as needed. Place top half of bread over cheese. Serve immediately. Yield: 6 to 8 servings.

## TURKEY HERO SANDWICHES

1 (12-ounce) package fresh
   mushrooms, thinly sliced
1 (8-ounce) bottle Italian salad
   dressing
1 (16-ounce) loaf unsliced French
   bread
4 lettuce leaves, coarsely
   shredded
1½ pounds thinly sliced smoked
   turkey
2 large tomatoes, thinly sliced
2 cups (8 ounces) shredded
   mozzarella cheese

Combine mushrooms and salad dressing; cover, and chill 1 hour. Drain.

Cut bread in half lengthwise. Scoop out center of each half, leaving at least ½-inch shells. Spoon mushrooms into shells, and layer lettuce and next 2 ingredients on top. Sprinkle with cheese. Broil 5 inches from heat 2 minutes or until cheese melts. Yield: 12 servings.

## BIG VEGGIE SANDWICH

1 (16-ounce) loaf unsliced whole
   wheat bread
1 (8-ounce) container
   chives-and-onion-flavored
   cream cheese
6 lettuce leaves
1 small green pepper,
   thinly sliced
1 large tomato, thinly sliced
2 avocados, peeled and sliced
1 small cucumber, thinly sliced
¾ cup alfalfa sprouts
¼ to ⅓ cup commercial Italian
   salad dressing

Cut bread vertically into 12 slices, cutting to within ½ inch of bottom crust. Starting at first cut, carefully spread a thin layer of cream cheese on facing sides of both pieces of bread. Repeat procedure with every other cut. Carefully pull cheese-spread bread slices apart; fill equally with vegetables. Drizzle dressing into each sandwich. Serve immediately, separating at unfilled cuts. Yield: 6 servings.

**Tip:** *Use a stiff vegetable brush to scrub vegetables rather than peel them. Peeling causes a loss of vitamins found in and just under the skin. For many vegetables, such as squash, peeling is not necessary.*

# Layer On The Flavor

If lasagna sounds good, but you're tired of the same old recipe, try one of these. We used vegetables for the meatless version, and chicken for a variation of the traditional meat variety. They're sure to become instant family favorites.

We assembled these recipes ahead of time and froze them. Lasagna is a good choice for freezing because the ingredients don't dry out or get mushy after being frozen. And it's perfect to bring to a covered-dish supper.

## EASY LASAGNA

½ pound lean ground beef or turkey
1 (30-ounce) jar spaghetti sauce
½ cup water
8 lasagna noodles, uncooked and divided
1 (15-ounce) container ricotta cheese
1 large egg, beaten
½ teaspoon ground white pepper
8 (1-ounce) slices mozzarella cheese, divided
½ cup grated Parmesan cheese

Crumble beef into a microwave-safe colander; place in a 9-inch pieplate, and cover with wax paper. Microwave at HIGH 3 to 5 minutes or until meat is no longer pink, stirring after 1½ minutes; drain well.

Combine spaghetti sauce and water. Spread ½ cup of sauce in a lightly greased 11- x 7- x 1½-inch baking dish. Arrange 4 uncooked lasagna noodles on sauce. Combine ricotta cheese, egg, and pepper; spread one-half over noodles. Layer with half each of mozzarella cheese, remaining sauce, and beef. Repeat layers. Cover tightly with heavy-duty plastic wrap. Fold back a small corner of wrap to allow steam to escape.

Microwave at MEDIUM (50% power) 30 to 40 minutes, giving a half-turn at 15-minute intervals. Sprinkle with Parmesan cheese; cover and let stand 10 minutes before serving. Yield: 8 servings.

**Note:** To bake in a conventional oven, prepare as directed. Cover and bake at 350° for 50 minutes. Sprinkle with Parmesan cheese, and bake, uncovered, 10 minutes. Let lasagna stand 10 minutes before serving.

*Brenda Rogers*
*Durham, North Carolina*

## CHICKEN LASAGNA

1 (2½- to 3-pound) broiler-fryer
6 cups water
1 teaspoon salt
1 clove garlic, minced
2 tablespoons butter, melted
1 (10¾-ounce) can cream of celery soup, undiluted
½ teaspoon dried oregano
¼ teaspoon pepper
8 lasagna noodles, uncooked
1 (8-ounce) loaf process American cheese, cut in ¼-inch slices, divided
2 cups (8 ounces) shredded mozzarella cheese, divided
2 tablespoons grated Parmesan cheese

Place chicken in a Dutch oven; add water and salt. Bring to a boil; cover, reduce heat, and simmer 45 minutes or until tender. Drain, reserving broth, and let cool slightly. Bone chicken, cutting meat into bite-size pieces; set aside.

Cook garlic in butter in a skillet over medium-high heat 2 minutes, stirring constantly. Add cream of celery soup, ¾ cup reserved chicken broth, oregano, and pepper.

Cook lasagna noodles according to package directions in remaining reserved chicken broth, adding more water, if necessary; drain. Spoon a small amount of sauce into a lightly greased 11- x 7- x 1½-inch baking dish. Layer with half each of lasagna noodles, sauce, chicken, American and mozzarella cheeses. Repeat procedure with noodles, sauce, and chicken, reserving remaining cheeses to add later. Bake at 350° for 25 minutes; top with remaining cheeses, and bake an additional 5 minutes. Let stand 10 minutes. Yield: 6 servings.

**Note:** To save time, cook chicken in a pressure cooker; follow manufacturer's instructions.
*Grace Scott*
*Houston, Texas*

## VEGETABLE LASAGNA CASSEROLE

3 quarts water
2 teaspoons salt
1 teaspoon olive oil
9 lasagna noodles, uncooked
4 medium carrots, scraped and
  thinly sliced
4 medium zucchini, thinly
  sliced
¼ cup reduced-calorie margarine
¼ cup all-purpose flour
2 cups skim milk
1 tablespoon dried basil or ¼ cup
  chopped fresh basil
¾ teaspoon salt
¾ teaspoon freshly ground
  pepper
Vegetable cooking spray
½ cup (2 ounces) shredded
  mozzarella cheese
Basil-Tomato Sauce

Bring water, salt, and olive oil to a boil in a large Dutch oven; add lasagna noodles, and return to a boil. Cook 15 minutes or just until tender. Drain and set aside.

Arrange carrot and zucchini slices in a vegetable steamer over boiling water. Cover and steam 8 minutes or until crisp-tender; set aside.

Melt margarine in a heavy saucepan over low heat; add flour, stirring until smooth. Cook 1 minute, stirring constantly. Gradually add milk; cook over medium heat, stirring constantly, until mixture is thickened and bubbly. Stir in basil, salt, and pepper.

Spread ½ cup white sauce in an 11- x 7- x 1½-inch baking dish coated with cooking spray. Arrange one-third of noodles on sauce; top with one-third of the vegetables and ½ cup white sauce. Repeat noodle, vegetable, and sauce layers twice. Cover and bake at 350° for 45 minutes. Uncover and sprinkle with cheese; bake an additional 5 minutes. Serve Basil-Tomato Sauce over individual servings. Yield: 6 servings.

### Basil-Tomato Sauce

1 (28-ounce) can whole tomatoes,
  drained and coarsely chopped
1½ teaspoons dried basil or 4
  teaspoons chopped fresh basil
1 tablespoon lemon juice
⅛ teaspoon freshly ground pepper

Combine all ingredients in container of an electric blender; process until smooth. Pour into a medium saucepan; bring to a boil, stirring occasionally. Cover, reduce heat, and simmer 5 minutes. Yield: 1⅓ cups.

*Doris Garton*
*Shenandoah, Virginia*

## LASAGNA SUPREME

12 lasagna noodles, uncooked
1 pound ground beef
1 clove garlic, minced
1 small onion, chopped
2 (6-ounce) cans tomato paste
1 (16-ounce) can whole tomatoes,
  undrained and chopped
1½ cups water
1 tablespoon dried basil
1 teaspoon salt
½ teaspoon dried rosemary
2 bay leaves
2 large eggs, lightly beaten
2 cups ricotta cheese
1 (8-ounce) carton sour cream
2 tablespoons dried parsley or
  ¼ cup chopped fresh parsley
½ teaspoon salt
¼ teaspoon pepper
1 cup (4 ounces) shredded Cheddar
  cheese, divided
½ cup grated Parmesan cheese,
  divided
½ cup grated Romano cheese,
  divided
2 (8-ounce) packages mozzarella
  cheese slices

Cook lasagna noodles according to package directions. Drain; set aside.

Cook ground beef, garlic, and onion in a large skillet over medium heat until meat is browned, stirring to crumble. Drain well. Wipe pan drippings from skillet with a paper towel. Combine tomato paste and next 6 ingredients in skillet; stir in meat. Bring to a boil, stirring occasionally; reduce heat and simmer, uncovered, 1 hour and 15 minutes, stirring often.

Combine eggs and next 5 ingredients; set aside.

Arrange 4 lasagna noodles in bottom of a lightly greased 13- x 9- x 2-inch baking dish. Layer with one-third each of meat mixture, egg mixture, and Cheddar, Parmesan, and Romano cheeses. Repeat layers twice. Bake at 375° for 30 to 35 minutes or until bubbly. Arrange mozzarella cheese slices over top; bake an additional 5 minutes. Let stand 10 minutes. Yield: 8 to 10 servings.

**Note:** To make an extra one to freeze, prepare half of lasagna in an

---

## Substitution Savvy

■ Substitute cottage cheese for ricotta. Cottage cheese yields a more moist product, while ricotta cheese is cheesier in taste.

■ Sprinkle on a variety of cheeses. Experiment with Cheddar, American, and Romano among others. You might also try Gouda, Swiss, or—for a little spicy heat—Monterey Jack with hot peppers.

■ Substitute spicy sausage when the recipe calls for ground beef. For a lower-fat choice, use the same amount of ground turkey or chicken.

■ Sample the new precooked noodles available at the grocery store. Follow the directions on the package to eliminate boiling the noodles before placing them in the baking dish.

8-inch square baking dish, and bake as directed above. Prepare remaining lasagna in an 8-inch square aluminum pan; freeze unbaked up to 2 months. To bake, thaw in refrigerator 24 hours; let stand at room temperature 30 minutes. Bake at 375° for 35 to 40 minutes; add mozzarella cheese slices, and bake an additional 5 minutes.

*Betty Beske*
*Arlington, Virginia*

# ON THE LIGHT SIDE

## Garden Supper At Sunset

When daylight wanes, it's time to put away the garden tools and think about supper. And if you plan ahead, you can enjoy an easy no-fuss meal with this light menu.

### SUNSET SUPPER FOR SIX

**Honey-Grilled Tenderloins**
**Tomato-Cucumber Salad**
**Grilled yellow squash**
**Commercial breadsticks**
**Easy Pineapple Sherbet**

### HONEY-GRILLED TENDERLOINS
*(pictured on page 188)*

2 (¾-pound) pork tenderloins
⅓ cup low-sodium soy sauce
½ teaspoon ground ginger
5 cloves garlic, halved
2 tablespoons brown sugar
3 tablespoons honey
2 teaspoons dark sesame oil
Vegetable cooking spray

Trim fat from tenderloins. Butterfly tenderloins by making a lengthwise

cut in each, cutting to within ¼ inch of other side. Place in a shallow container or large, heavy-duty, zip-top plastic bag. Combine soy sauce, ginger, and garlic; pour over tenderloins. Cover or seal, and refrigerate at least 3 hours, turning occasionally.

Remove tenderloins from marinade, discarding marinade. Combine brown sugar, honey, and oil in a small saucepan; cook over low heat, stirring constantly, until sugar dissolves.

Coat grill rack with cooking spray; place on grill over medium-hot coals (350° to 400°). Place tenderloins on rack, and brush with honey mixture. Cook 20 minutes or until a meat thermometer inserted in thickest portion registers 160°, turning once and basting frequently with honey mixture. Yield: 6 servings (201 calories [26% from fat] per 3-ounce serving).

□ *24.7g protein, 5.7g fat (1.6g saturated, 2.4g monounsaturated, 1.1g polyunsaturated), 11.9g carbohydrate, 0g fiber, 79mg cholesterol, 166mg sodium, and 11mg calcium.*

**Note:** Basting mixture becomes very thick when cool. Keep warm while grilling tenderloins by placing the saucepan directly on the grill rack.

### TOMATO-CUCUMBER SALAD
*(pictured on page 188)*

¼ teaspoon salt
2 cups thinly sliced cucumber
¾ cup sliced green pepper
½ cup sliced fresh mushrooms
⅓ cup thinly sliced green onions
2 medium tomatoes, cut into wedges
3 tablespoons white wine vinegar
1 tablespoon olive oil
1 tablespoon water
1 clove garlic, minced
½ teaspoon dried basil
¼ teaspoon dried oregano
¼ teaspoon pepper
Leaf lettuce

Sprinkle salt over cucumber; toss gently, and let stand 30 minutes.

Drain cucumber slices, and press dry between paper towels. Combine cucumber, green pepper, and next 3 ingredients in a bowl; set aside.

Combine vinegar and next 6 ingredients in a small jar. Cover tightly, and shake vigorously. Drizzle over vegetables; toss gently. Cover and chill 3 to 4 hours. Toss gently before serving, and arrange on lettuce leaves. Yield: 6 servings (44 calories [53% from fat] per 1-cup serving).

□ *1g protein, 2.6g fat (0.4g saturated, 1.7g monounsaturated, 0.3g polyunsaturated), 5.1g carbohydrate, 1.3g fiber, 0mg cholesterol, 107mg sodium, and 19mg calcium.*

### EASY PINEAPPLE SHERBET

1 (15¼-ounce) can unsweetened crushed pineapple, undrained
1¼ cups unsweetened pineapple juice
¼ cup sugar
1 (12-ounce) can lemon-lime carbonated beverage, chilled
¾ cup evaporated skimmed milk

Drain crushed pineapple, reserving ¾ cup juice; set pineapple aside. Combine reserved mixture juice, 1¼ cups pineapple juice, and sugar in a saucepan; bring to a boil. Reduce heat, and simmer, stirring occasionally, 3 minutes or until sugar dissolves. Pour into a large bowl; cover and chill. Stir in carbonated beverage and milk. Pour into freezer container of a 5-quart hand-turned or electric freezer. Freeze according to manufacturer's instructions. Transfer to a large bowl; fold in crushed pineapple. Store in freezer. Yield: 6¼ cups (113 calories [1% from fat] per ¾-cup serving).

□ *2g protein, 0.1g fat (0g saturated, 0g monounsaturated, 0g polyunsaturated), 26.9g carbohydrate, 0.1g fiber, 1mg cholesterol, 34mg sodium, and 80mg calcium.*

# Gifts From The Sea

What can Southerners learn from the Eskimo diet? Although the Eskimo's diet is high in fat, overly high in protein, and low in fiber-rich fruits and vegetables, the incidence of heart disease among Arctic people is one-third that of most Americans.

Strong indications point to the Eskimo's main dietary staple—fish. Certain varieties of fish contain oils that have the potential to reduce the risk of heart disease as well as rheumatoid arthritis, high blood pressure, and cancer. These fish oils are high in a class of polyunsaturated fats called omega-3 fatty acids.

The best way to get these fatty acids is to eat at least two (3-ounce) servings of a fatty fish per week. As a rule, dark-fleshed fish, such as tuna, mackerel, and salmon, are the best sources of omega-3 fatty acids. Halibut, bluefish, trout, ocean perch, and pollock contain moderate amounts.

## POLLOCK WITH SUMMER SQUASH RELISH

Vegetable cooking spray
2 teaspoons reduced-calorie margarine, divided
½ cup coarsely chopped green pepper
1 small zucchini, cut into thin strips
¾ cup thinly sliced yellow squash
1 tablespoon chopped fresh parsley
1 tablespoon chopped fresh basil or 1 teaspoon dried basil
1 tablespoon chopped fresh oregano or 1 teaspoon dried oregano
2 cloves garlic, minced
½ cup chopped tomato
1 tablespoon white wine vinegar
2 teaspoons brown sugar
4 (4-ounce) pollock fillets

Coat a large nonstick skillet with cooking spray; add 1 teaspoon margarine, and place over medium-high heat until hot. Add green pepper; cook 1 minute, stirring constantly. Add zucchini and next 5 ingredients; cook 3 minutes or until crisp-tender, stirring constantly. Stir in tomato, vinegar, and brown sugar. Remove from skillet, and set aside.

Recoat skillet with cooking spray, and add remaining margarine; place over medium-high heat until hot. Add fish, and cook 5 minutes on each side or until fish flakes easily when tested with a fork. Return squash mixture to pan. Cover and cook 1 minute or until thoroughly heated. Yield: 4 servings (143 calories [16% from fat] per fish fillet with ½-cup squash mixture).

□ 23.2g protein, 2.5g fat (0.4g saturated, 0.6g monounsaturated, 1g polyunsaturated), 6.3g carbohydrate, 1.3g fiber, 81mg cholesterol, 126mg sodium, and 92mg calcium.

## ROSEMARY-GARLIC MACKEREL

2 tablespoons white wine vinegar
2 tablespoons reduced-sodium soy sauce
3 cloves garlic, minced
4 (4-ounce) mackerel fillets
Vegetable cooking spray
1½ teaspoons dried rosemary, crushed
¾ teaspoon cracked pepper

Combine first 3 ingredients in a large shallow dish or heavy-duty, zip-top plastic bag. Add fish; cover or seal, and refrigerate 1 hour.

Drain fish, discarding marinade. Place fish, skin side up, on a broiler pan coated with cooking spray. Broil fish 3 inches from heat (with electric oven door partially opened) 3 minutes. Carefully turn fish over, and sprinkle with rosemary and pepper. Broil fish fillets (with electric oven door partially opened) 6 minutes or until fish flakes easily when tested with a fork. Yield: 4 servings (141 calories [36% from fat] per serving).

□ 20.3g protein, 5.6g fat (1.5g saturated, 1.8g monounsaturated, 1.5g polyunsaturated), 1g carbohydrate, 0.2g fiber, 62mg cholesterol, 147mg sodium, and 20mg calcium.

## SALMON-PESTO VERMICELLI

1 cup firmly packed fresh basil leaves
¼ cup commercial oil-free Italian dressing
2 tablespoons water
3 cloves garlic, crushed
1 (1-pound) salmon fillet
¼ teaspoon cracked pepper
Vegetable cooking spray
4 cups cooked vermicelli (cooked without salt or fat)
6 lemon wedges (optional)

Combine first 4 ingredients in food processor bowl fitted with knife blade. Process 2 minutes, scraping sides of bowl occasionally. Set aside.

Sprinkle fish with pepper, and place, skin side down, on a broiler pan coated with cooking spray. Broil 6 inches from heat (with electric oven door partially opened) 5 minutes. Carefully turn over, and broil (with electric oven door partially opened) 4 minutes or until fish flakes easily when tested with a fork. Remove from pan; cool. Remove and discard skin; break fish into bite-size pieces.

Combine fish, basil mixture, and vermicelli in a large bowl; toss gently. Serve with lemon wedges, if desired. Yield: 6 servings (254 calories [24% from fat] per 1-cup serving).

□ *19.8g protein, 6.9g fat (1.2g saturated, 3.1g monounsaturated, 1.6g polyunsaturated), 26.4g carbohydrate, 1.4g fiber, 49mg cholesterol, 146mg sodium, and 16mg calcium.*

## TUNA WITH TANGY MUSTARD SAUCE

4 (8-ounce) tuna steaks
½ cup Chablis or other dry white wine
¼ cup lemon juice
2 tablespoons reduced-sodium soy sauce
¼ teaspoon garlic powder
Butter-flavored cooking spray
½ teaspoon cracked pepper
Tangy Mustard Sauce

Cut each tuna steak in half, and place in a large shallow dish or heavy-duty, zip-top plastic bag. Combine wine and next 3 ingredients; pour mixture over fish. Cover or seal, and refrigerate 30 minutes.

Drain tuna, discarding marinade. Place tuna on a broiler pan coated with cooking spray. Lightly coat surface of tuna with cooking spray. Broil 5 inches from heat (with electric oven door partially opened) 5 minutes. Carefully turn over, and coat again with cooking spray. Sprinkle with pepper, and broil (with electric oven door partially opened) 5 minutes or until done. Serve with Tangy Mustard Sauce. Yield: 8 servings (191 calories [33% from fat] per 3-ounce tuna steak with 1½ tablespoons sauce).

□ *26.8g protein, 6.9g fat (1.7g saturated, 2g monounsaturated, 2g polyunsaturated), 3.4g carbohydrate, 0.2g fiber, 45mg cholesterol, 307mg sodium, and 9mg calcium.*

### Tangy Mustard Sauce

½ cup unsweetened orange juice
2 tablespoons lemon juice
2 tablespoons finely chopped onion
¼ cup Dijon mustard
½ teaspoon curry powder
2 tablespoons low-fat sour cream
1 tablespoon minced fresh parsley

Combine first 3 ingredients in a small saucepan; bring to a boil. Add mustard and curry powder, stirring with a wire whisk until smooth. Cook 2 minutes over low heat. Remove mixture from heat; stir in sour cream and parsley. Yield: ¾ cup (16 calories [40% from fat] per tablespoon).

□ *0.2g protein, 0.7g fat (0.2g saturated, 0.3g monounsaturated, 0.1g polyunsaturated), 2g carbohydrate, 0.1g fiber, 1mg cholesterol, 150mg sodium, and 5mg calcium.*

## LIGHT FAVORITE

# Thick, Rich, Light

The trick to this creamed corn recipe is getting all the corn off the cob. First, slice off the tips of the kernels, and then scrape the cob to extract the milk and pulp. Flavor heightens and cholesterol plummets when butter is replaced with low-fat milk simmered with onion slices. Add salt and pepper, and Southern-Style Creamed Corn proves that down-home cooking can be healthful.

## SOUTHERN-STYLE CREAMED CORN

6 medium ears fresh corn
1 cup 1% low-fat milk, divided
2 teaspoons cornstarch
2 (½-inch-thick) onion slices
¼ teaspoon salt
¼ teaspoon ground white or black pepper

Cut off tips of kernels into a large bowl; scrape milk and remaining pulp from cob, using a small paring knife. Set aside.

Combine ¼ cup milk and cornstarch; set aside.

Combine remaining ¾ cup milk and onion in a heavy saucepan; bring to a boil over medium heat. Cover, reduce heat, and simmer 5 minutes; remove and discard onion. Add corn, and cook over medium heat, stirring frequently, 5 minutes. Stir in cornstarch mixture, salt, and pepper. Cook, stirring constantly, until thickened and bubbly (about 3 minutes). Yield: 3 servings (180 calories [12% from fat] per 1-cup serving).

□ *6.8g protein, 2.4g fat (0.8g saturated, 0.7g monounsaturated, 0.8g polyunsaturated), 37.8g carbohydrate, 4.9g fiber, 3mg cholesterol, 257mg sodium, and 110mg calcium.*

| COMPARE THE NUTRIENTS (per serving) | | |
|---|---|---|
| | Traditional | Light |
| Calories | 325 | 180 |
| Fat | 21.5g | 2.4g |
| Cholesterol | 56mg | 3mg |
| Sodium | 584mg | 257mg |

# From Our Kitchen To Yours

Roasting, broiling, or grilling chicken and tender cuts of pork and beef is easy. The trick is not to overcook today's leaner and healthier meats, but to cook them so they are safe to eat. Armed with a meat thermometer and a few tips, you can produce entrées cooked to perfection.

## Instant-Read or Standard?

Two types of meat thermometers are available, and we use both types in our Test Kitchens. An instant-read thermometer gives a more accurate reading, and it's easier to use in smaller cuts of meat. Periodically insert the instant-read thermometer near the end of the cooking time to check for doneness; this type of thermometer does not remain in the meat. The standard meat thermometer stays inserted in the center of the meat (not touching fat or bone) throughout the cooking process. For an accurate reading, at least half of the stem of either thermometer must be in the meat. If you need a thermometer, consider the more versatile instant-read type.

Treat these sensitive instruments with care. Never force the pointed probe into place, and don't wash in the dishwasher. Test it occasionally by putting the probe in boiling water to see if it registers 212° F. If you use an instant-read type, always warm the probe in warm water before inserting it into hot meat.

## Meat Safety Reminders

■ As recommended by the USDA, marinate meat and fish in the refrigerator. Reserve a portion of the marinade for basting before adding raw meat to serve with cooked meat.
■ Remove visible fat before grilling to avoid charring and flare-ups.
■ Don't place cooked meat in the same container used to hold the raw meat unless the container has been washed with soap and hot water. This will prevent any cross-contamination from bacteria in raw meat.

---

## A Thermometer Knows

Cooking timetables are simply guides; actual cooking time will vary with individual cuts. Use the internal temperature to determine doneness.

| Meat | Internal Temperature |
|------|----------------------|
| *Beef, lamb* | 140° F. (rare—bacterial risk) |
| | 160° F. (medium) |
| | 170° F. (well-done) |
| *Pork* | 160° F. |
|    Crown roast, Boston butt | 160°-170° F. |
| *Poultry* | 185° F. |
|    Poultry breasts | 170° F. |
| *Smoked pork* | |
|    Ham (cook before eating) | 160° F. |
|       (fully cooked) | 140° F. |
| *Veal* | 170° F. |
| *Ground meat and meat mixtures* | |
|    Chicken, turkey | 170° F. |
|    Beef, pork, veal, lamb | 160° F. |

---

# A Lunch For Young Chefs

The moment of truth arrives when your children open their lunchboxes and take a peek at what's inside. It may be the same old peanut butter-and-jelly sandwich and squashed potato chips. If this gets the day (and lunch) off to a bad start, why not let your children try their hand at packing their lunch. Here's a menu and guide.

**Ham-and-Cheese Hoagie**
**Baby carrots**
**Apple slices**
**Pretzel sticks**
**Pine-orange-banana juice**
**Fruit-flavored yogurt**

## The Night Before

Wash your hands. Wipe out lunchbox; dry with towel.

With a spoon, stir together 1 tablespoon mustard and 1½ teaspoons plain low-fat yogurt. Spread mixture on bun with a spreader or table knife. Place ham slices on bottom of bun; top with cheese slices and lettuce. Place the other half of bun on top. Put sandwich in plastic container or plastic sandwich bag, and place in refrigerator overnight.

Remove top from fruit-flavored yogurt; stir it with a spoon, and put top back on. Place yogurt and can of pine-orange-banana juice in the freezer.

With help from an adult, slice the apple. Place apple slices in plastic container; pour 2 tablespoons pineapple juice over apple slices to prevent browning. Cover and place container in the refrigerator. Also put the carrots in a container, and refrigerate.

Measure ¾ cup pretzels in a dry measuring cup, and pack pretzels in a container. Put the pretzels and napkin in your lunchbox.

When you have finished packing your lunchbox, make sure the countertop is clean. Place the utensils you used to prepare your lunch in the dishwasher, and return food items to their proper places.

## The Next Morning

Remove the fruit juice and yogurt from the freezer and place them in your lunchbox.

Drain pineapple juice off apple slices; reseal the container, and put it in your lunchbox.

Take the sandwich and carrot containers out of the refrigerator; place these in your lunchbox, too. Now your carefully prepared lunch is ready to go and enjoy later at school.

---

### What You'll Need

Creamy mustard
Plain low-fat yogurt
1 whole wheat hoagie bun
Turkey ham
American cheese
Lettuce
1 container of fruit-flavored yogurt
1 can of pine-orange-banana juice
1 apple
Pineapple juice
Scraped baby carrots
Pretzel sticks

### What to Use

Small bowl
1 tablespoon
1 teaspoon
½ teaspoon
Spoons
Spreader or table knife
Sandwich container or bag
Cutting board
Sharp knife (with an adult's help)
Apple container
Carrot container
Pretzel container
¾ cup dry measuring cup
Napkin
Lunchbox

---

# QUICK!

## Pancakes And Toppings

People love the pancake and topping choices at pancake restaurants. The next time you have guests for breakfast, treat them to the same variety at home with our pancake buffet.

Instead of using commercial syrups and toppings, try ours. Each of them takes less than 25 minutes to prepare, and you can make them ahead of time and reheat before serving.

No pancake mix? Make our Easy Pancakes from biscuit mix. Because there's less measuring, they're easier than preparing pancakes from scratch.

### EASY PANCAKES

1 (5.5-ounce) package or 1¼ cups biscuit mix *
1 large egg, beaten
⅔ cup milk
1 tablespoon vegetable oil

Place biscuit mix in a bowl; make a well in center. Combine egg, milk, and oil; add to biscuit mix, stirring just until dry ingredients are moistened.

For each pancake, pour about ¼ cup batter onto a moderately hot, lightly greased griddle. Turn pancakes when tops are covered with bubbles and edges of pancakes look cooked. Yield: 8 pancakes.

* One (7-ounce) package bran muffin mix may be substituted for biscuit mix to make pancakes.

### CRANBERRY-APPLE SAUCE

1 (16-ounce) can whole-berry cranberry sauce
2 small cooking apples, cored and chopped
⅓ cup apple juice

Combine all ingredients in a small saucepan; bring to a boil, stirring constantly. Reduce heat and simmer, stirring occasionally, 6 minutes or until apples are tender. Serve warm over pancakes. Store sauce in refrigerator. Yield: 2½ cups.
*Erma Jackson*
*Huntsville, Alabama*

### PINEAPPLE SAUCE

1 (20-ounce) can unsweetened crushed pineapple, undrained
⅓ cup sugar
1 tablespoon tapioca
½ teaspoon lemon juice
¼ teaspoon ground ginger

Combine all ingredients in a medium saucepan; let stand 5 minutes. Bring to a boil over medium heat; reduce heat and simmer, stirring occasionally, 2 minutes or until thickened. Serve warm over pancakes. Store sauce in refrigerator. Yield: 2 cups.
*Dee Buchfink*
*Oologah, Oklahoma*

### PEACH SAUCE

3 cups frozen sliced peaches, thawed
¼ cup orange juice
¾ cup sugar
2 tablespoons honey
½ teaspoon grated orange rind
⅛ teaspoon ground allspice

Combine peaches and orange juice in a saucepan. Bring to a boil over medium heat; cover, reduce heat, and simmer, stirring occasionally, 5 to 10 minutes or until peach slices are tender. Spoon mixture into container of an electric blender; process until smooth, stopping once to scrape down sides.

Return mixture to saucepan; add sugar and remaining ingredients, and bring to a boil. Reduce heat and simmer, uncovered, stirring occasionally, 5 to 10 minutes or until thickened. Serve warm over pancakes. Store sauce in refrigerator. Yield: 1½ cups.
*Charlotte Pierce*
*Greensburg, Kentucky*

# Candy Bar Creations

Even the sweetest sweet tooth will meet its match when tasting these candy bar dessert treats. What else would you expect from the addition of candy bars to an assortment of already-rich desserts?

These sensational sweets are simple to make when you keep a few tips in mind. Save elbow grease by using a sharp, sturdy knife to chop candy bars with nuts or caramel. Crunchy chocolate bars will crush easily if pulsed several times in a food processor. And be sure to refrigerate cold desserts for the specified period of time to ensure a neat cut.

## CRUNCHY PEANUT-BUTTERY DESSERT

4 (2.1-ounce) chocolate-coated, crispy peanut-buttery candy bars, crushed
1 cup graham cracker crumbs
½ cup saltine cracker crumbs
½ cup butter or margarine, melted
2 (3.4-ounce) packages vanilla instant pudding mix
2 cups milk
1 pint vanilla ice cream, softened
1 (8-ounce) container frozen whipped topping, thawed

Combine first 4 ingredients; reserve ⅓ cup candy-crumb mixture for garnish. Press remaining candy-crumb mixture into the bottom of a 13- x 9- x 2-inch dish; chill.

Combine pudding and milk in a bowl; beat at low speed with an electric mixer until blended. Beat at medium speed 2 minutes. Add ice cream; beat at low speed 2 minutes. Spoon over crust; refrigerate until set. Spread whipped topping over pudding, and sprinkle with reserved candy-crumb mixture, if desired. Chill at least 8 hours. (Do not freeze.) Yield: 15 servings. *Carolyn Griffin*
*Macon, Georgia*

## CANDY BAR BROWNIES

4 large eggs, lightly beaten
2 cups sugar
¾ cup butter or margarine, melted
2 teaspoons vanilla extract
1½ cups all-purpose flour
½ teaspoon baking powder
¼ teaspoon salt
⅓ cup cocoa
4 (2.07-ounce) chocolate-coated caramel-peanut nougat bars, coarsely chopped
3 (1.55-ounce) milk chocolate bars, finely chopped

Combine first 4 ingredients in a large bowl. Combine flour and next 3 ingredients; stir into sugar mixture. Fold in chopped nougat bars. Spoon into a greased and floured 13- x 9- x 2-inch pan; sprinkle with chopped milk chocolate bars. Bake at 350° for 30 to 35 minutes. Cool and cut into squares. Yield: 2½ dozen. *Mardee Johnson*
*Winston-Salem, North Carolina*

## CANDY BAR CAKE

3 (2.15-ounce) chocolate-coated, caramel and creamy nougat bars, chopped
1 cup butter, softened and divided
2 cups sugar
4 large eggs
1 teaspoon vanilla extract
3 cups all-purpose flour
½ teaspoon baking soda
1 cup buttermilk
1 cup chopped pecans

Combine candy bars and ½ cup butter in a heavy saucepan; place over medium heat and stir constantly until candy bars melt. Set aside.

Beat remaining ½ cup butter at medium speed with an electric mixer about 2 minutes or until soft and creamy. Gradually add sugar, beating at medium speed 5 to 7 minutes. Add eggs, one at a time, beating just until yellow disappears. Stir in vanilla.

Combine flour and soda; add to creamed mixture alternately with buttermilk, beginning and ending with flour mixture. Mix at low speed just until blended after each addition. Stir in pecans and candy bar mixture.

Pour batter into a greased and floured 10-inch tube pan. Bake at 325° for 1 hour and 25 minutes or until a wooden pick inserted in center comes out clean. Cool in pan 15 minutes on wire rack. Remove from pan, and let cool completely on wire rack. Yield: one 10-inch cake. *Marie Bilbo*
*Meadville, Mississippi*

**Tip:** *Use odd pieces of candy to make a topping for ice cream. Plain chocolate, mints, or cream candies may be placed in top of a double boiler with a little cream and heated until well blended. Serve hot over ice cream or cake, or store in refrigerator and use later cold.*

# SEPTEMBER

*Fall kicks off and signals the perfect time to entertain. Toast the winning season and your favorite team with an array of hot and cold beverages. For your next party, add flair and color with a south-of-the-border theme, featuring Risotto prepared in a new and different way. To score big with the dessert lovers in the group, serve Chocolate Chip Cookies, or new versions of Chess Pie, an old Southern favorite.*

# A Chip Off
# The Old Block

We'd love to take a Southern bow for chocolate chip cookies, but must reluctantly give credit to the famed Toll-house Inn near Boston, Massachusetts. So, chefs' hats off to then-owner Ruth Wakefield for giving us this favorite American sweet.

Thanks to her, we've come a long way from finding baking chocolate only in blocks. The surprising success spurred her on, and she took her idea for chocolate "chips" to a well-known food company. Now, more than 60 years later, consumers can select from nearly a baker's dozen of chips products.

So load your grocery cart with mint chocolate chips, peanut butter chips, vanilla-milk chips, and more, and work your way through our collection of recipes to discover more new chips off an old block.

We like to share our baking secrets. For cookie baking tips and storage ideas, see "From Our Kitchen To Yours" on the facing page.

## CHOCOLATE-MINT COOKIES

⅔ cup butter or margarine, softened
1 cup sugar
⅓ cup firmly packed dark brown sugar
1 large egg
1 teaspoon vanilla extract
1 (1-ounce) square unsweetened chocolate, melted
1½ cups all-purpose flour
1 (10-ounce) package mint chocolate morsels

Beat butter at medium speed with an electric mixer until fluffy; gradually add sugars, beating well. Add egg, vanilla, and melted chocolate, mixing well. Gradually add flour, mixing well. Stir in morsels; drop by level tablespoonfuls onto lightly greased cookie sheets. Bake at 325° for 12 to 15 minutes. Cool on cookie sheets 3 minutes; remove to wire racks to cool completely. Yield: 3½ dozen.

*Gwen Louer*
*Roswell, Georgia*

## DOUBLE-CHOCOLATE SUGAR COOKIES

1 (12-ounce) package semisweet chocolate morsels, divided
1 cup butter or margarine, softened
1 cup sugar
1 large egg
2 tablespoons milk
1 teaspoon vanilla extract
3 cups all-purpose flour
1 teaspoon baking powder
½ teaspoon baking soda
½ teaspoon salt
½ cup sugar

Melt 1 cup semisweet chocolate morsels in a heavy saucepan over low heat, reserving remaining morsels. Set melted morsels aside.

Beat butter at medium speed with an electric mixer until fluffy; gradually add 1 cup sugar, beating well. Add egg, milk, and vanilla, mixing well. Add melted morsels, mixing until blended.

Combine flour and next 3 ingredients; gradually add to butter mixture, mixing well. Stir in remaining chocolate morsels.

Roll dough into balls, 1 tablespoon at a time; roll balls in ½ cup sugar. Place on lightly greased cookie sheets. Bake at 400° for 8 to 10 minutes. (Cookies will be soft and will firm up as they cool.) Remove to wire racks to cool. Yield: 4½ dozen.

*Jill D. Abell*
*Snellville, Georgia*

## CHOCOLATE CHIPPERS

1 cup butter or margarine, softened
1 (8-ounce) package cream cheese, softened
1 cup sugar
1 cup firmly packed brown sugar
2 large eggs
1½ teaspoons vanilla extract
2 cups all-purpose flour
1½ cups quick-cooking oats, uncooked
1 teaspoon baking powder
1 teaspoon baking soda
½ teaspoon salt
1 cup (6 ounces) semisweet chocolate mini-morsels
1 cup (6 ounces) milk chocolate morsels or rainbow semisweet chocolate morsels
1½ cups chopped walnuts

Beat butter and cream cheese at medium speed with an electric mixer until fluffy; gradually add sugar and brown sugar, beating well. Add eggs and vanilla, mixing well.

Combine flour and next 4 ingredients; gradually add to butter mixture, mixing well. Stir in chocolate morsels and walnuts; drop by rounded teaspoonfuls onto lightly greased cookie sheets. Bake at 350° for 12 to 14 minutes. Remove to wire racks to cool. Yield: 8 dozen.

## RICH DATE-NUT CHOCOLATE CHIP COOKIES

½ cup butter or margarine, softened
¾ cup firmly packed brown sugar
1 large egg
1 tablespoon vanilla extract
¾ cup chopped dates
1 cup all-purpose flour
½ teaspoon baking soda
¼ teaspoon baking powder
¼ teaspoon salt
1 (12-ounce) package semisweet chocolate morsels
¾ cup coarsely chopped walnuts
½ cup flaked coconut

Beat butter at medium speed with an electric mixer until fluffy; gradually add brown sugar, beating well. Add egg and vanilla, mixing well. Stir in dates; let stand 5 minutes. Beat at high speed 3 minutes.

Combine flour, baking soda, baking powder, and salt; gradually add to butter mixture, mixing well. Stir in morsels, chopped walnuts, and coconut; drop dough by level tablespoonfuls onto lightly greased cookie sheets. Bake at 350° for 10 to 12 minutes or until lightly browned. Remove to wire racks to cool. Yield: 3 dozen.

*Beverly Garver*
*Anderson, South Carolina*

## OATMEAL-PEANUT BUTTER CHOCOLATE CHIP COOKIES

½ cup butter or margarine, softened
1 (18-ounce) jar chunky peanut butter
1½ cups sugar
1½ cups firmly packed brown sugar
4 large eggs
1 teaspoon vanilla extract
6 cups quick-cooking oats, uncooked
2½ teaspoons baking soda
1 cup (6 ounces) semisweet chocolate morsels

Beat butter and peanut butter at medium speed with an electric mixer until fluffy; gradually add sugar and brown sugar, beating well. Add eggs and vanilla, mixing well.

Combine oats and baking soda; add to butter mixture, mixing well. Stir in morsels; drop by tablespoonfuls onto ungreased cookie sheets. Bake at 350° for 9 to 10 minutes. Cool on cookie sheets 5 minutes; remove to wire racks to cool completely. Yield: 7 dozen.

*Thomas F. Sheffield*
*Charleston, South Carolina*

## CHUNKY MACADAMIA NUT WHITE CHOCOLATE COOKIES

½ cup butter or margarine, softened
¾ cup firmly packed brown sugar
2 tablespoons sugar
1 large egg
1½ teaspoons vanilla extract
2 cups all-purpose flour
¾ teaspoon baking soda
½ teaspoon baking powder
⅛ teaspoon salt
1 cup (6 ounces) vanilla-milk morsels or 1 (6-ounce) package white chocolate-flavored baking bars, cut into chunks
1 (7-ounce) jar macadamia nuts, coarsely chopped

Beat butter at medium speed with an electric mixer until fluffy; gradually

add sugars, beating well. Add egg and vanilla, mixing well.

Combine flour and next 3 ingredients; gradually add to butter mixture, mixing well. Stir in morsels and nuts; drop by rounded teaspoonfuls onto lightly greased cookie sheets. Bake at 350° for 8 to 10 minutes or until lightly browned. Remove to wire racks to cool. Yield: 5 dozen.

*Elizabeth S. Evins*
*Atlanta, Georgia*

# From Our Kitchen To Yours

Turn on the oven, follow these simple tips, and fill the cookie jar with chocolate chip cookies (see recipes here and on facing page). While young chefs mix ingredients, drop dough, and bake cookies, older "kids-at-heart" enjoy supervising—and sampling goodies fresh from the oven.

## Hints From Pros
■ Products labeled spread, reduced-calorie, liquid, or soft-style tub butter or margarine contain less fat than regular butter or margarine. These do not always produce satisfactory results when substituted for butter.
■ To prevent stiff cookie dough from straining hand-held portable mixers, stir in the last additions of flour mixture by hand.
■ Keep mixing to a minimum; over-mixing toughens dough.
■ To have future batches of freshly baked cookies ready in minutes, place dough in a tightly covered container, and refrigerate up to one week or freeze up to six months; let stand at room temperature until dough is soft enough to handle. Dough can also be dropped onto a cookie sheet and frozen until firm; place frozen mounds in a heavy-duty, zip-top plastic bag, and store in freezer. When ready to bake,

place frozen mounds on cookie sheet, and follow recipe directions.

- Use vegetable cooking spray or solid shortening (not butter or margarine) to grease cookie sheets.
- Preheat oven 10 minutes before baking cookies.
- Drop cookies 2 inches apart on shiny, heavy aluminum cookie sheets. Dark sheets may absorb heat, causing overbrowning on the cookie bottoms; however, nonstick cookie sheets work well if not too dark. Cookies will not brown on the bottom and will take slightly longer to bake on insulated cookie sheets (made with two sheets of aluminum separated by an insulating layer of air).
- Bake one cookie sheet at a time on the middle oven rack; if you need to bake more than one, rotate the sheets from the top to the bottom rack halfway through baking time.
- Keep an eye on the first batch of cookies placed in the oven; check for doneness of cookies at the minimum baking time.
- Transfer baked cookies to a wire rack immediately after baking unless otherwise directed. (Delicate cookies must cool slightly on the cookie sheet to become firm enough to transfer.) If cookies remain on the cookie sheet too long, they may harden and stick; to loosen cookies, return cookie sheet to oven for 1 minute.
- Allow cookie sheets to cool before reusing between baking; wipe surface with a paper towel or scrape off crumbs with a metal turner to prevent sticking.
- Not enough wire racks? Place a sheet of wax paper on the kitchen counter, and sprinkle with sugar. Transfer cookies from cookie sheet to sugared wax paper; cookies will cool without getting soggy.

## Preserve That Just-Baked Freshness

For best results, cool cookies completely, and store each kind separately at room temperature. If cookies are moist or sticky, separate layers with wax paper. Soft cookies keep well in a container with a tight-fitting lid. After three days, these cookies may harden, but can be softened again by placing

an apple wedge on a piece of wax paper in the container. (Remove the apple after one day.) Store crisp cookies in a container with a loose-fitting lid.

Unfrosted cookies freeze well for 8 to 12 months. Pack cooled cookies in heavy-duty, zip-top plastic bags, metal tins, or plastic freezer containers. To serve, thaw in container for about 15 minutes, and add frosting or glaze, if needed.

# Cheers For Beverages

The Southern football season usually starts in the sweltering heat and ends in the bitter cold. So if you entertain, you'll need cold drinks for the first games and hot beverages for later in the season.

## EASY FROZEN SANGRÍA

1 (6-ounce) can frozen lemonade
  concentrate, undiluted
¾ cup burgundy wine
Ice cubes

Combine frozen lemonade and wine in container of an electric blender. Process 30 seconds. Gradually add enough ice to bring the mixture to 4 cup level; blend mixture until smooth. Yield: 4 cups.
*Margie Shedd*
*Athens, Georgia*

## MULLED APPLE CIDER

2 quarts apple cider
10 whole cloves
10 whole allspice
4 (4-inch) sticks cinnamon
¼ cup firmly packed brown sugar

Combine all ingredients in a Dutch oven. Bring to a boil; reduce heat, and simmer 5 minutes. Remove and discard spices; serve hot. Yield: 2 quarts.
*Elizabeth R. Drawdy*
*Spindale, North Carolina*

## BOURBON PUNCH

1 (6-ounce) can frozen orange juice
  concentrate, thawed and
  undiluted
1 (6-ounce) can frozen lemonade
  concentrate, thawed and
  undiluted
½ cup lemon juice
2 cups bourbon
1 (2-liter) bottle lemon-lime
  carbonated beverage, chilled
1 (10-ounce) bottle club soda,
  chilled

Combine first 4 ingredients; chill. To serve, stir in lemon-lime beverage and club soda; pour mixture over crushed ice. Yield: about 3 quarts.
*Kristy LeFevre*
*Arlington, Virginia*

## CAFE MEXICANO

½ cup instant coffee granules
12 cups boiling water
⅓ cup chocolate syrup
¼ cup sugar
½ teaspoon ground cinnamon
¼ teaspoon ground nutmeg
1½ cups Kahlúa or other coffee-
  flavored liqueur
Whipped cream
Ground cinnamon

Combine first 6 ingredients in a Dutch oven; stir until coffee and sugar dissolve. Add liqueur; cook over medium heat until thoroughly heated. To serve, top each with a dollop of whipped cream, and sprinkle with cinnamon. Yield: 13 cups.
*Mike Singleton*
*Memphis, Tennessee*

## RED RUBY

2 beef-flavored bouillon cubes
¼ cup boiling water
1 (46-ounce) can tomato juice, chilled
¼ cup lemon juice
1 (10-ounce) bottle club soda, chilled
1 cup vodka (optional)

Dissolve bouillon cubes in boiling water; let cool. Stir in juices. Just before serving, stir in club soda and, if desired, vodka. Serve over ice. Yield: about 7 cups.          *Ray Jackson*
*Birmingham, Alabama*


## CRAN-GRAPE-TEA PUNCH

1½ cups boiling water
2 family-size tea bags
10 whole cloves
2 (3-inch) sticks cinnamon
2 cups cranberry juice cocktail
1½ cups unsweetened white grape juice
½ cup sugar

Pour boiling water over tea bags and spices; cover and let stand 5 minutes. Remove tea bags, squeezing gently; remove and discard spices. Add fruit juices and sugar; stir mixture until sugar dissolves. Serve hot or cold. Yield: 5 cups.


# Football, Friends, And Food

All across the South, from small towns to big cities, football fans collect in front of TV sets to cheer their teams. No matter where folks congregate, football games wouldn't be the same without food.

These appetizers are sure to satisfy hungry sports enthusiasts. With some advance cutting, grating, and measuring, the recipes won't take time away from guests or the game. However, Layered Catfish Appetizer should be made ahead. Once the ingredients are prepared and chilled, all that's required on game day is layering and serving.


## APPETIZER CHEESE BAKE

1 large egg, lightly beaten
1 cup mayonnaise
⅛ teaspoon pepper
3 cups (12 ounces) shredded sharp Cheddar cheese
1 cup chopped onion

Combine first 3 ingredients; stir in cheese and onion. Spoon into a 1-quart soufflé dish. Bake at 325° for 25 minutes or until puffed and golden. Serve immediately with crackers. Yield: 3 cups.     *Mrs. John C. Neiman*
*Birmingham, Alabama*


## SAVORY CHICKEN BITES

1 (8-ounce) package cream cheese, softened
½ teaspoon lemon juice
½ teaspoon dried basil
¼ teaspoon onion salt
⅛ teaspoon dried oregano
⅛ teaspoon dried thyme
1 cup finely chopped, cooked chicken
⅓ cup finely chopped celery
1 (2-ounce) jar diced pimiento, drained
2 (8-ounce) cans refrigerated crescent dinner rolls
1 large egg, lightly beaten
1½ teaspoons sesame seeds

Combine first 6 ingredients, mixing until well blended. Stir in chicken, celery, and pimiento; set aside.

Separate crescent dough into 8 rectangles; press perforations to seal. Spread about ¼ cup cream cheese mixture over each dough rectangle, leaving ½-inch margin on one long side and no margin on other sides. Roll dough, jellyroll fashion, starting at long side with filling spread to edge; pinch seams to seal. Brush with egg, and sprinkle with sesame seeds. Cut each roll into 5 pieces; place seam side down on lightly greased baking sheets. Bake at 375° for 12 to 15 minutes or until golden brown. Yield: 40 appetizers.

**Note:** To reheat, bake, uncovered, at 375° for 4 to 6 minutes.
*Yvonne M. Greer*
*Mauldin, South Carolina*


## LAYERED CATFISH APPETIZER

4 (3-ounce) packages cream cheese, softened
2 tablespoons mayonnaise
2 tablespoons Worcestershire sauce
1 tablespoon lemon juice
Dash of garlic salt
1 small onion, finely chopped
½ cup water
¼ teaspoon salt
1 pound catfish fillets
½ cup chili sauce
Paprika (optional)

Combine first 5 ingredients; beat at medium speed with an electric mixer until smooth. Stir in chopped onion. On a serving platter, spread cream cheese mixture into a 6-inch circle, and pinch up a small rim. Cover and chill at least 3 hours.

Combine water and salt in a large skillet; bring to a boil, and add fish. Cover, reduce heat, and simmer 10 to 15 minutes or until fish flakes easily with a fork. Drain and flake fish with a fork; chill. To serve, spoon chili sauce over cream cheese mixture; top with fish. Sprinkle with paprika, if desired. Serve with crackers. Yield: 14 to 16 appetizer servings.     *Betsy Neill*
*Leland, Mississippi*

# Ready, Set, Risotto!

When Jade and Charlie McCulloch of Houston, Texas, host a party, the margaritas are cold, the humor is hot, and tall tales fly with the speed of a Texas jackrabbit. If you can keep up with the wit, you can pull up to the table—or to the skillet, if she recruits you to stir the risotto.

Risotto (pronounced rih-SAW-toh) is an Italian dish made by adding broth to rice that has been sautéed in butter. This recipe boasts the pungent, distinct flavors of the Southwest—leafy cilantro, ripe tomatoes, hot jalapeños—plus white wine and Parmesan cheese.

with cold water. Chill; peel and devein shrimp. Cut shrimp into quarters, and set aside.

Combine avocados and lime juice in a small bowl; set aside. Combine shrimp, tomatoes, and next 7 ingredients in a large bowl; gently stir in avocado-lime mixture. Chill at least one hour. Serve in a lettuce-lined bowl with tortilla chips. Yield: 11½ cups.

## SOUTHWESTERN RISOTTO PARTY FOR TEN

Margaritas
Beer or soft drinks
Salsa Picante With Shrimp
Grilled Shrimp-and-Scallop Kabobs
Southwestern Risotto
Steamed Asparagus
Margarita Cheesecake

## MARGARITAS

Lime wedges
Margarita salt
2¼ cups tequila
2¼ cups triple sec
1 cup freshly squeezed lime or
    lemon juice
1 (7-ounce) bottle lime juice
Garnish: lime wedges

Rub rims of 10 wide-mouth glasses with lime wedges. Place salt in saucer; spin rim of each glass in salt. Set glasses aside.

Combine tequila and next 3 ingredients. Serve over ice. Garnish each glass, if desired. Yield: 10 servings.

**Note:** Margarita salt is sold with other mixed beverage supplies.

## SALSA PICANTE WITH SHRIMP

4 cups water
1½ pounds unpeeled, large fresh
    shrimp
2 avocados, peeled and cubed
¼ cup lime juice
6 cups cubed tomatoes (about 3
    pounds)
3 large onions, chopped (4 cups)
8 to 10 cloves garlic, minced
¼ cup chopped fresh cilantro
3 jalapeño peppers, seeded and
    chopped
1 tablespoon ground cumin
2 teaspoons paprika
1 teaspoon salt
Lettuce leaves
Tortilla chips

Bring water to a boil, add shrimp, and cook 3 to 5 minutes or until shrimp turn pink. Drain shrimp well; rinse

## GRILLED SHRIMP-AND-SCALLOP KABOBS

30 unpeeled, jumbo fresh shrimp
30 sea scallops
1 cup olive oil
½ cup fresh lime juice
2 cloves garlic, crushed
½ teaspoon salt
¼ teaspoon freshly ground pepper

Peel shrimp, leaving tails intact, and devein. Combine shrimp and scallops in a shallow dish. Combine olive oil and remaining ingredients; pour over shrimp and scallops. Cover and refrigerate 1 hour, stirring occasionally.

Remove shrimp and scallops from marinade, discarding marinade. Alternate shrimp and scallops on 10 (14-inch) wooden skewers; grill, uncovered, over medium coals (300° to 350°) 8 to 10 minutes on each side. Yield: 10 servings.

**Note:** Cooking time may vary according to size of shrimp and scallops. They may be cooked on separate skewers to control the degree of doneness, if desired. Sea scallops are large (about 2 inches in diameter); bay scallops are about the size of a nickel.

## SOUTHWESTERN RISOTTO

½ cup chopped onion
2 cloves garlic, crushed
2 tablespoons butter or margarine, melted
1 cup medium-grain rice, uncooked
½ cup dry white wine
6 cups chicken broth, divided
½ cup whipping cream
2 medium tomatoes, seeded and chopped
1 jalapeño pepper, seeded and minced
½ cup sliced green onions
½ cup grated Parmesan cheese
2 to 3 tablespoons minced cilantro
Garnish: fresh cilantro sprigs, cubed tomatoes

Cook onion and garlic in butter in a large skillet or saucepan over medium heat, stirring constantly, until tender. Add rice; cook 2 to 3 minutes, stirring frequently with a wooden spoon. Add wine and cook, uncovered, until liquid is absorbed. Add 1 cup broth; cook, stirring constantly, over medium-high heat 5 minutes or until broth is absorbed. Add remaining broth, 1 cup at a time, cooking and stirring constantly until each cup is absorbed, about 25 to 30 minutes. (Rice will be tender and have a creamy consistency.) Stir in whipping cream and next 5 ingredients; cook 2 minutes. Garnish, if desired, and serve immediately. Yield: 6 servings.

Note: For a party of 10 to 12, make two batches.

## STEAMED ASPARAGUS

3 pounds small fresh asparagus (½ inch in diameter)
¼ cup butter or margarine, melted

Snap off tough ends of asparagus. Remove scales with a vegetable peeler or knife, if desired. Arrange asparagus in a steamer over boiling water. Cover and steam 6 to 8 minutes or until asparagus is crisp-tender. Transfer to serving dish, and drizzle with butter. Yield: 10 servings.

Note: If asparagus of a larger diameter is used, increase cooking time 3 to 5 minutes.

## MARGARITA CHEESECAKE

1½ cups pretzel crumbs
½ cup butter or margarine, melted
1 cup fresh strawberries, hulled
3 (8-ounce) packages cream cheese, softened
1 cup sugar
4 large eggs
¼ cup fresh lime juice
¼ cup tequila
¼ cup Triple Sec or other orange-flavored liqueur
Garnishes: lime slices, fresh strawberries

Combine pretzel crumbs and butter; firmly press on bottom and 1½ inches up sides of a 9-inch springform pan. Bake at 325° for 8 to 10 minutes; set crust aside.
Place strawberries in container of an electric blender; process until smooth, stopping once to scrape down sides. Reserve ½ cup puree.
Beat cream cheese at medium speed with an electric mixer until fluffy. Gradually add sugar, beating well. Add eggs, one at a time, beating after each addition. Stir in lime juice, tequila, and liqueur. Pour into prepared pan; pour reserved strawberry puree on top in a circle, and gently swirl batter with a knife. Bake at 325° for 1 hour and 10 minutes (center will be soft). Remove from oven, and run knife around edge of pan to release sides. Return to oven; turn oven off, and leave cheesecake in oven 30 minutes. Remove from oven, and let cool completely on a wire rack. Remove from pan; cover with plastic wrap, and chill 8 hours. (Do not cover with aluminum foil.) Garnish, if desired. Yield: 12 to 14 servings.

# Great Grains

Grains? You're probably familiar with several of these "edible seeds of grasses"—rice, wheat, corn, and oats. But the next time you toss the usual bag of rice into the grocery cart, stop and look at other options. Barley, bulgur, and wild rice may seem foreign to you now, but not once you know what to do with them. Try some of our suggestions, and discover that grains really can add much variety to any menu.

■ Wild rice isn't a true rice, but a grass seed instead. It's similar to real rice in appearance, but it requires several washings before cooking, takes much longer to cook, and remains fairly firm when thoroughly cooked. Wild rice's nutty flavor is especially good in the fall.

## PECAN-LEMON WILD RICE

1 cup wild rice, uncooked
3 cups chicken broth
1½ tablespoons lemon rind, divided
1 tablespoon lemon juice
1 tablespoon butter or margarine
½ cup chopped pecans, toasted
3 tablespoons chopped green onions
¼ cup chopped fresh parsley

Wash wild rice in 3 changes of hot water; drain. Combine broth, 2¼ teaspoons lemon rind, lemon juice, and butter in a medium saucepan. Bring to a boil; stir in rice. Cover, reduce heat, and simmer 50 to 60 minutes or until liquid is absorbed, and rice is tender. Stir in pecans, remaining 2¼ teaspoons lemon rind, green onions, and parsley. Yield: 4 to 6 servings.

*Sandi Pichon*
*Slidell, Louisiana*

■ Barley looks like a round form of oats, but is a different grain altogether. Before it reaches the market, it has a tough husk that is "polished" away and the bran removed, so it's often labeled "pearled" barley. Like oats, barley is available in both regular and quick-cooking varieties.

### BARLEY SALAD

3 cups water
1 teaspoon salt
1 cup quick-cooking barley, uncooked
⅔ cup chopped green pepper
⅔ cup chopped sweet red pepper
1 (16-ounce) can whole kernel corn, drained
3 tablespoons chopped fresh parsley
¼ cup white wine vinegar
⅓ cup olive oil
¼ teaspoon salt
¼ teaspoon pepper
⅛ teaspoon paprika

Combine water and salt in a saucepan; bring to a boil. Stir in barley; return to a boil. Cover, reduce heat, and simmer 12 to 15 minutes or until mixture is tender, stirring occasionally; drain. Combine barley and next 4 ingredients; set aside. Combine vinegar and remaining ingredients; pour over barley mixture and toss. Chill 8 hours. Yield: 12 servings.

**Note:** Regular barley may be used in place of quick-cooking barley. To cook, combine 4 cups water and ⅛ teaspoon salt in a saucepan; bring to a boil. Stir in barley; return to a boil. Cover, reduce heat, and simmer 30 to 35 minutes or until tender, stirring occasionally; drain. *Harriet Brenner*
*Kiawah Island, South Carolina*

**Tip:** *Prices of fresh vegetables and fruit change with the seasons. It is best to buy seasonal fresh foods when they are most plentiful and at peak quality in your area.*

■ Bulgur is whole wheat that's been precooked, then cracked into pieces. Recipes usually call for letting the grains stand in hot or boiling water long enough to reconstitute as in Tabbouleh Salad.

### TABBOULEH SALAD

2 cups hot water
1 cup bulgur wheat, uncooked
1 teaspoon salt
1 cup chopped cucumber
½ cup chopped fresh parsley
⅓ cup lemon juice
¼ teaspoon pepper
1 pint cherry tomatoes, halved

Combine first 3 ingredients in a bowl; let stand 30 minutes. Drain well, and cool. Add next 4 ingredients. Cover and chill 8 hours. Just before serving, stir in tomatoes. Yield: 8 servings.
*Patsy Bell Hobson*
*Liberty, Missouri*

■ If you hated school-day breakfasts of gummy oatmeal, give oats another chance in this homemade yeast bread. Warm *or* cold, the flavor and texture are much better than you remember. This recipe uses regular oats, but you'll also find quick-cooking ones for other, faster dishes.

### OATMEAL BREAD

1 (12-ounce) can evaporated milk
½ cup water
2 tablespoons shortening
2 cups regular oats, uncooked
⅓ cup firmly packed brown sugar
1½ teaspoons salt
1 package dry yeast
½ cup warm water (105° to 115°)
3¾ to 4¼ cups all-purpose flour
2 teaspoons regular oats, uncooked

Combine first 3 ingredients in a saucepan; bring to a boil. Pour mixture over 2 cups oats; stir in sugar and salt. Cool to 105° to 115°.
Combine yeast and warm water in a 1-cup liquid measuring cup; let stand 5

minutes. Combine yeast mixture and oatmeal mixture in a large mixing bowl. Stir in enough flour to make a soft dough.
Turn dough out onto a floured surface, and knead 5 minutes or until smooth and elastic. Place in a well-greased bowl, turning to grease top. Cover and let rise in a warm place (85°), free from drafts, 1 hour or until doubled in bulk.
Punch dough down, and divide in half. Shape each portion into a loaf, and place into 2 well-greased 8½- x 4½- x 3-inch loafpans. Cover and let rise in a warm place (85°), free from drafts, 30 minutes or until doubled in bulk. Uncover; sprinkle with 2 teaspoons oats. Bake at 350° for 35 minutes or until loaves sound hollow when tapped. Remove from pans, and cool. Yield: 2 loaves. *Betty Czebotar*
*Baltimore, Maryland*

# Start School Days Right

With school starting, resolve to begin your children's days with a healthy breakfast. No time in the morning? Do the work the night before. Mix Overnight Coffee Cake and pour it into a prepared pan. Pop it into the oven when you first get up. About 45 minutes later, serve the warm coffee cake with a glass of milk and fresh fruit.

### SAUSAGE-CHEESE MUFFIN SANDWICHES

½ pound ground pork sausage
½ cup water
1 teaspoon white vinegar
4 large eggs
4 English muffins, split and toasted
4 (1-ounce) slices process American cheese
Picante sauce (optional)

Shape sausage into 4 patties; cook in a heavy skillet over medium heat 8 minutes or until done, turning once. Drain and set aside.

Place 2 tablespoons water and ¼ teaspoon vinegar in each of 4 (6-ounce) custard cups. Space cups evenly on a microwave-safe platter. Microwave at HIGH 2 to 3 minutes or until water is boiling. Gently break an egg into each cup, and pierce each egg yolk with a wooden pick. Cover cups with heavy-duty plastic wrap; fold back a small edge of wrap to allow steam to escape. Microwave at MEDIUM HIGH (70% power) 3 to 3½ minutes and let cups stand 2 to 3 minutes. Drain.

Place a sausage patty on bottom half of each muffin. Top each with a poached egg, a slice of cheese, and top of muffin. Serve with picante sauce, if desired. Yield: 4 servings.

*Dorothy F. Havens*
*Huntsville, Alabama*

## FABULOUS GRANOLA

3 cups regular oats, uncooked
1 (2⅛-ounce) bottle sesame seeds
1 (3.75-ounce) package salted
  sunflower kernels
1 (2¼-ounce) package sliced
  almonds
½ cup flaked coconut
¾ cup pure maple syrup
½ cup vegetable oil
1 teaspoon ground cinnamon
½ teaspoon ground nutmeg
⅛ teaspoon salt
1 teaspoon vanilla extract
1 cup raisins
½ cup chopped dates

Combine first 5 ingredients in a large bowl. Combine syrup and next 5 ingredients; pour over oats mixture, and stir well. Spread evenly in a 15- x 10- x 1-inch jellyroll pan. Bake at 325° for 30 minutes or until golden brown, stirring every 10 minutes; turn oven off, and leave in oven 5 minutes. Remove from oven, and stir in raisins and dates. Let cool. Store granola in an airtight container in a cool, dry place. Serve granola with yogurt, milk, or as a snack. Yield: 7 cups.

*Nora Henshaw*
*Okemah, Oklahoma*

## OVERNIGHT COFFEE CAKE

2 cups all-purpose flour
1 cup sugar
½ cup firmly packed brown
  sugar
1 teaspoon baking soda
1 teaspoon baking powder
½ teaspoon salt
1 teaspoon ground cinnamon
1 cup buttermilk
⅔ cup butter or margarine,
  melted
2 large eggs
½ cup firmly packed brown sugar
½ cup chopped pecans
1 teaspoon ground cinnamon

Combine first 7 ingredients in a large mixing bowl; add buttermilk, butter, and eggs. Beat at low speed with an electric mixer until moistened; beat at medium speed 3 minutes. Spoon batter into a greased and floured 13- x 9- x 2-inch pan. Combine ½ cup brown sugar, pecans, and 1 teaspoon cinnamon; sprinkle over batter. Cover and refrigerate 8 to 12 hours. Uncover and bake at 350° for 30 to 35 minutes or until a wooden pick inserted in center comes out clean. Serve warm. Yield: 12 to 15 servings.

**Note:** Overnight Coffee Cake may be baked immediately at 350° for 30 minutes. To reheat, cover with aluminum foil, and bake at 350° for 5 minutes or until heated thoroughly.

*Ruth A. Smith*
*White Hall, Maryland*

# A Showy Fruit Platter

Marie Davis of Charlotte, North Carolina, says her Fresh Fruit Salad Platter is a fine choice for buffets. To select the right pineapple, look for a large, plump fruit with green leaves and a fresh fragrance. Avoid pineapples with soft spots or an overripe aroma. Don't rely on color; it might mislead you. Ripe pineapples vary in color from gold to green.

## FRESH FRUIT SALAD PLATTER

1 pineapple
1 apple, unpeeled and cubed
1 pear, unpeeled and cubed
1 pint fresh strawberries, hulled
  and halved
Lettuce leaves
2 oranges, unpeeled and sliced
½ cantaloupe, unpeeled and cut
  into thin wedges
Lime-Honey Dressing
Garnishes: fresh mint sprigs,
  strawberries

Cut pineapple in half lengthwise. Using a knife, remove core and discard. Remove pineapple pulp, leaving ¼- to ½-inch-thick shells; cut pulp into chunks, reserving shells. Combine pineapple chunks and next 3 ingredients; chill.

Line platter or basket with lettuce leaves. Place pineapple mixture in reserved shells. Arrange shells, orange slices, and cantaloupe wedges on lettuce leaves. Serve with Lime-Honey Dressing. Garnish, if desired. Yield: 8 servings.

### Lime-Honey Dressing

¼ cup honey
2 tablespoons fresh lime juice
Dash of salt

Combine honey, lime juice, and salt. Yield: ⅓ cup.

# Simple, Sweet Chess Pies

Generations ago, when life seemed less complicated, chess pie was popular because Southern cooks found it economical. Many of them used fresh eggs from the henhouse, milk, butter, sugar, and a sprinkling of golden cornmeal. Baked in made-from-scratch pastry, the pie was often the highlight of Sunday dinner.

Although still economical, chess pie remains a favorite for another reason—it's so easy. Use a commercial refrigerated piecrust, unfolded and pressed into a pieplate. (Or a commercial frozen piecrust is convenient, too.) Mixing the filling takes only minutes; then the pie is baked in the oven. Check for doneness after the minimum baking time by gently shaking the pie. The center should be set with a slight jiggle.

### PINEAPPLE-COCONUT CHESS PIE

*(pictured on page 224)*

1½ cups sugar
3 tablespoons cornmeal
2 tablespoons all-purpose flour
¼ teaspoon salt
4 large eggs, lightly beaten
1 teaspoon vanilla extract
¼ cup butter or margarine, melted
1 (3½-ounce) can flaked coconut
1 (15¼-ounce) can crushed
   pineapple, well drained
1 unbaked 9-inch pastry shell

Combine first 4 ingredients in a large bowl; add eggs and vanilla, stirring until blended. Stir in butter, coconut, and pineapple; pour into unbaked pastry shell. Bake at 350° for 1 hour or until set, covering with aluminum foil after 40 minutes. Cool on a wire rack. Yield: one 9-inch pie.
*Joy Knight Allard*
*San Antonio, Texas*

## BUTTERMILK CHESS PIE

2 cups sugar
2 tablespoons all-purpose flour
5 large eggs, lightly beaten
⅔ cup buttermilk
½ cup butter or margarine, melted
1 teaspoon vanilla extract
1 unbaked 9-inch pastry shell

Combine sugar and flour in a large bowl; add eggs and buttermilk, stirring until blended. Stir in butter and vanilla, and pour into unbaked pastry shell. Bake at 350° for 45 minutes or until set. Cool on a wire rack. Yield: one 9-inch pie.
*Carolyn Baker*
*Kingsport, Tennessee*

## CHOCOLATE CHESS TARTS

1 (5-ounce) can evaporated milk
2 (1-ounce) squares unsweetened
   chocolate
¼ cup butter or margarine
2 large eggs
1¼ cups sugar
1 teaspoon vanilla extract
12 unbaked (3-inch) tart shells

Combine first 3 ingredients in a small saucepan; cook over low heat, stirring frequently, until chocolate and butter melt. Cool slightly. Combine eggs and sugar in a large bowl; add chocolate mixture and vanilla, stirring until blended. Pour into tart shells; place filled pies on a baking sheet. Bake at 350° for 30 minutes or until set. Cool on a wire rack. Yield: 1 dozen tarts.
*Mrs. C. B. Williams*
*Richmond, Virginia*

# The Best Of Blue Plate Specials

Remember real diners where Andy and Barney might treat their dates before a movie? You can still find diners in big cities and Mayberry-size towns throughout the South. And the one thing they all have in common is the blue plate specials noted on chalkboard easels out front or announced by a friendly waitress.

A diner usually goes the extra mile for "the special," using fresh, wholesome vegetables. Its macaroni and cheese brims with loads of shredded Cheddar cheese, just like that of Aunt Bea, who never would have made potatoes from dehydrated flakes in a box. Neither would diner cooks. They insist on peeling, cooking, and mashing potatoes by hand, then drizzling them with butter. You won't find food fads and exotic ingredients in old-fashioned eateries.

### CHICKEN-FRIED STEAK

¼ cup all-purpose flour
½ teaspoon salt
½ teaspoon pepper
1 (1-pound) package cubed beef
   steaks
1 large egg, lightly beaten
2 tablespoons milk
1 cup saltine cracker crumbs
Vegetable oil
3 tablespoons all-purpose flour
1¼ cups chicken broth
½ cup milk
Dash of Worcestershire sauce
Dash of hot sauce

Combine first 3 ingredients; sprinkle on both sides of steaks. Combine egg and 2 tablespoons milk in a shallow dish. Dip steaks in egg mixture; dredge in cracker crumbs. Pour oil to depth of ½ inch into a large, heavy skillet. Fry steaks in hot oil over medium heat until browned, turning once. Cover, reduce heat, and simmer, turning occasionally, 15 minutes or until tender. Remove steaks, and drain on paper towels. Keep warm.

Drain off drippings, reserving 3 tablespoons in skillet. Add 3 tablespoons flour, stirring until smooth. Cook 1 minute, stirring constantly. Gradually add broth and ½ cup milk; cook over medium heat, stirring constantly, until thickened and bubbly. Stir in Worcestershire sauce and hot sauce. Serve gravy with steaks and rice or potatoes. Yield: 4 servings.

*Marie Davis*
*Charlotte, North Carolina*

## SALMON PATTIES

1 (14¾-ounce) can pink salmon, undrained
½ cup saltine cracker crumbs
¼ cup cornmeal
1 large egg, lightly beaten
¼ teaspoon salt
¼ teaspoon pepper
Vegetable oil

Drain salmon, reserving liquid; set liquid aside. Remove skin and bones from salmon, if desired; flake with a fork, and set aside.

Combine cracker crumbs and reserved liquid; let stand 5 minutes or until liquid is absorbed. Stir in salmon, cornmeal, and next 3 ingredients. Shape salmon mixture into 6 patties. Pour oil to depth of ¼ inch into a large, heavy skillet. Fry patties in hot oil over medium heat until browned, turning once. Drain patties on paper towels. Yield: 6 servings.

*Helen Dosier*
*Sparta, North Carolina*

## OLD-FASHIONED MACARONI AND CHEESE

1 (8-ounce) package elbow macaroni
2½ cups (10 ounces) shredded Cheddar cheese, divided
1½ cups milk
2 large eggs, lightly beaten
1 teaspoon salt
⅛ teaspoon ground white pepper
Paprika

Cook macaroni according to package directions; drain. Layer one-third of macaroni in a lightly greased 2-quart casserole. Sprinkle with one-third cheese; repeat procedure, and top with remaining macaroni. (Reserve remaining cheese.)

Combine milk, eggs, salt, and pepper; pour over macaroni and cheese. Cover and bake at 350° for 45 minutes. Uncover and sprinkle with remaining cheese and paprika. Cover and let stand 10 minutes before serving. Yield: 6 to 8 servings.

*Rebecca Patton*
*Tuscumbia, Alabama*

## GOOD OLD MASHED POTATOES

8 medium potatoes, peeled and quartered (about 3½ pounds)
¼ cup butter or margarine, melted and divided
½ cup milk
1 teaspoon salt
¼ teaspoon pepper

Cook potatoes in boiling salted water to cover 15 to 20 minutes or until tender. Drain and mash. Add 3 tablespoons butter and remaining ingredients, stirring until smooth. Spoon into a serving bowl; drizzle with remaining 1 tablespoon butter. Serve immediately. Yield: 6 to 8 servings.

## OKRA AND TOMATOES

1 pound fresh okra
¾ cup chopped onion
¼ cup chopped green pepper
2 cloves garlic, minced
2 tablespoons vegetable oil
2 ripe tomatoes, peeled and coarsely chopped
½ teaspoon salt
½ teaspoon pepper
¼ cup water
Dash of hot sauce (optional)

Wash okra and drain. Remove tips and stem ends. Cook onion, green pepper, and garlic in oil in a large skillet over medium-high heat, stirring constantly; add okra and remaining ingredients. Bring to a boil. Cover, reduce heat, and simmer 25 minutes, stirring occasionally. Yield: 6 servings.

*Betty Willis*
*Laurel Hill, Florida*

## TURNIP-AND-COLLARD GREENS

1 pound ham hocks
7 cups water
1 bunch fresh turnip greens (about 5 pounds)
1 bunch fresh collard greens (about 5 pounds)
1 teaspoon salt
1 teaspoon sugar
1 small whole red pepper
Pepper sauce (optional)

Combine ham hocks and water in a large Dutch oven; bring to a boil. Cover, reduce heat, and simmer 1 hour or until meat is tender.

Cut turnips from greens; reserve for other uses. Remove stems from turnip greens. Wash turnip and collard greens thoroughly; drain and tear into bite-size pieces. Add greens, salt, sugar, and red pepper to ham hocks; bring to a boil. Cover greens, reduce heat, and simmer 1 to 1½ hours or until greens are tender. Remove and discard red pepper. Serve with pepper sauce, if desired. Yield: 10 to 12 servings.

**Tip:** *During the week, keep a shopping list handy to write down items as you need them. This will eliminate unnecessary trips to the store. Before your weekly shopping trip, make a complete shopping list. If you arrange the list according to the layout of the store, you will save yourself time and steps.*

## MARINATED TOMATO-AND-CUCUMBER SALAD

3 medium tomatoes, cut into wedges
2 medium cucumbers, unpeeled and thinly sliced
1 small onion, sliced and separated into rings
¼ cup cider vinegar
¼ cup vegetable oil
3 tablespoons mayonnaise or salad dressing
2 tablespoons sugar
½ teaspoon salt

Combine tomato wedges, cucumber slices, and onion rings in a large bowl; set aside. Combine vinegar and remaining ingredients; beat, using a wire whisk, until mixture is smooth. Pour dressing over tomato mixture, tossing gently. Cover and chill at least 2 hours, stirring occasionally. Serve with a slotted spoon. Yield: 6 servings.

## CRACKLIN' CORNBREAD

1½ cups cornmeal
¼ cup all-purpose flour
1 teaspoon baking soda
1 teaspoon salt
1 large egg, lightly beaten
2 cups buttermilk
1 cup cracklings

Combine first 4 ingredients in a large bowl; add egg and buttermilk, stirring mixture just until dry ingredients are moistened. Stir in cracklings.
Place a well-greased, 10-inch cast-iron skillet in a 450° oven for 4 minutes or until hot. Remove from oven; pour batter into skillet. Bake at 450° for 25 minutes or until golden brown. Yield: 8 to 10 servings.
*Mrs. James L. Twilley*
*Macon, Georgia*

## CHOCOLATE MERINGUE PIE

1¾ cups sugar, divided
⅓ cup all-purpose flour
¼ cup cocoa
2 cups milk
4 large eggs, separated
2 tablespoons butter or margarine, melted and cooled
1 baked 9-inch pastry shell
½ teaspoon cream of tartar

Combine 1¼ cups sugar, flour, and cocoa in a heavy saucepan. Combine milk, egg yolks, and melted butter; beat, using a wire whisk, until mixture is well blended. Gradually add milk mixture to sugar mixture, stirring until smooth.
Cook mixture over medium heat, stirring constantly, until thickened and bubbly (about 10 minutes). Spoon into pastry shell; set aside.
Beat egg whites and cream of tartar at high speed with an electric mixer until foamy. Gradually add remaining ½ cup sugar, 1 tablespoon at a time, beating until stiff peaks form and sugar dissolves (2 to 4 minutes). Spread meringue mixture over chocolate filling, sealing to edge of pastry. Bake at 325° for 25 minutes or until golden brown. Yield: one 9-inch pie.
*Cammie Middleton*
*Red Oak, Texas*

# A New Setting For Black Beans

Black beans are humble no longer. Innovative chefs nationwide have accepted them into the world of sophisticated dining. Chef Bryan Frick of the Port Orleans Resort in Orlando's Walt Disney World, serves Black Bean Cakes With Greens and Apple Dressing as an appetizer or main dish. The recipe combines a savory pancake with chilled greens and a bacon-and-pecan-laced dressing.

## BLACK BEAN CAKES WITH GREENS AND APPLE DRESSING

½ pound dried black beans
2 quarts water
1 large egg
½ cup chopped onion
4 ounces smoked Andouille sausage, cut into 1-inch pieces
1 slice bacon, cooked and crumbled
¾ teaspoon salt
½ teaspoon hot sauce
2 cloves garlic
1 large egg
¼ cup milk
2 tablespoons butter or margarine, melted
¾ cup all-purpose flour
Dash of white pepper
3 cups torn dandelion or mixed greens
Apple Dressing

Sort and wash beans; place in a Dutch oven. Cover with water 2 inches above beans; let soak 8 hours. Drain beans, and return to Dutch oven. Add 2 quarts water. Bring to a boil; cover, reduce heat, and simmer 1 hour or until very tender. Drain, reserving ¼ cup cooking liquid. Position knife blade in food processor bowl; add beans, reserved cooking liquid, 1 egg, and next 6 ingredients. Process until smooth.
Combine egg, milk, and butter in a large bowl; add flour and pepper, mixing until blended. (Mixture will be thick.) Stir in bean mixture.
For each cake, pour about ¼ cup batter onto a hot, lightly greased griddle, spreading to a 4-inch circle. Turn pancakes when edges look cooked. To serve, arrange greens on serving platter; top with black bean cakes, and drizzle with Apple Dressing. Yield: 4 main-dish or 6 appetizer servings.

### Apple Dressing

1 cup apple cider
½ cup finely chopped onion
⅓ to ½ cup firmly packed brown sugar
5 slices bacon, cooked and crumbled
¼ cup finely chopped pecans, toasted

Combine first 3 ingredients in a small saucepan; bring to a boil. Reduce heat and simmer, uncovered, 5 minutes. Stir in crumbled bacon and toasted pecans. Yield: 1⅓ cups.

## BLACK BEAN-AND-CHEESE SALAD

1 (15-ounce) can black beans, drained
4 ounces Cheddar cheese, cut into ¼-inch cubes
1 (2-ounce) jar diced pimiento, drained
2 tablespoons minced onion
2 tablespoons fresh lime juice
2 tablespoons sugar
1 tablespoon vegetable oil
¼ teaspoon pepper
Lettuce leaves

Combine first 4 ingredients in a medium bowl; add lime juice and next 3 ingredients, and toss gently until combined. Cover and chill at least 4 hours. Using a slotted spoon, serve on lettuce leaves. Yield: 4 servings.

## BLACK BEAN SPAGHETTI

1 large onion, sliced
1 small sweet red pepper, cut into strips
1 small sweet yellow pepper, cut into strips
1 (8-ounce) package fresh mushrooms, sliced
2 tablespoons olive oil
1 (16-ounce) can whole tomatoes, undrained and chopped
1 (15-ounce) can black beans, drained and rinsed
1 (15½-ounce) can kidney beans, undrained
1 (3½-ounce) jar capers, undrained
¼ cup sliced ripe olives
¼ teaspoon dried rosemary
¼ teaspoon dried basil
¼ teaspoon pepper
Hot cooked angel hair pasta
Freshly grated Parmesan cheese
Garnish: fresh basil leaves

Cook first 4 ingredients in olive oil in a large skillet over medium-high heat, stirring constantly, until tender. Add tomatoes and next 7 ingredients; bring to a boil. Reduce heat, and simmer 30 minutes, stirring occasionally.

Serve over pasta, and sprinkle with Parmesan cheese. Garnish, if desired. Yield: 6 servings.          *Chris Johnson*
*Wilmington, North Carolina*

# A Harvest Of Soups

Get out your vegetable scraper, soup pot, and electric blender, and refine these fall vegetables into their purest, smoothest forms. These cream soups can serve as an autumn main dish or as an elegant appetizer course suitable for company.

## TURNIP SOUP

6 medium turnips, peeled and sliced (about 2 pounds)
4 cups chicken broth
2 tablespoons butter or margarine
½ teaspoon salt
½ teaspoon sugar
⅛ teaspoon ground white pepper
¼ cup whipping cream
Commercial croutons

Combine first 6 ingredients in a Dutch oven. Bring to a boil; cover, reduce heat, and simmer 20 to 25 minutes or until turnips are tender. Carefully spoon half of mixture into container of an electric blender; process until smooth. Repeat procedure with remaining mixture, returning smooth mixture to Dutch oven.

Stir whipping cream into turnip mixture. Cook over medium heat until thoroughly heated. Serve immediately, topping with croutons. Yield: about 1½ quarts.          *Daisy Cook*
*Tyler, Texas*

## POTATO-YOGURT SOUP

1 small onion, sliced
3 green onions, sliced
1 clove garlic, crushed
2 tablespoons butter or margarine, melted
2 medium potatoes, sliced (about ¾ pound)
1½ cups water
¼ to ½ teaspoon dried rosemary
2 teaspoons chicken-flavored bouillon granules
½ cup hot water
1 (8-ounce) carton plain yogurt

Cook onions and garlic in butter in a Dutch oven over medium-high heat, stirring constantly, until tender. Add potatoes and 1½ cups water. Bring to a boil over medium heat; cover, reduce heat, and simmer 12 to 15 minutes or until potatoes are tender. Carefully spoon potato mixture and rosemary into container of an electric blender; process until smooth. Return to Dutch oven.

Dissolve bouillon granules in ½ cup hot water; add to potato mixture. Cook over low heat until thoroughly heated, stirring occasionally. With a wire whisk, stir in yogurt (at room temperature). Serve immediately. Yield: 3¼ cups.

**Microwave Directions:** Place onions, garlic, and butter in a 2½-quart casserole. Cover with heavy-duty plastic wrap; fold back a small edge to allow steam to escape. Microwave at HIGH 3 to 5 minutes or until tender. Add potatoes and 1½ cups water; cover and microwave at HIGH 10 to 14 minutes or until potatoes are tender, stirring once. Spoon potato mixture and rosemary into container of an electric blender; process until smooth. Return to casserole.

Dissolve bouillon granules in ½ cup hot water; add to potato mixture. Microwave at HIGH 5 minutes or until thoroughly heated. With a wire whisk, stir in yogurt (at room temperature). Serve immediately.

## CREAMY CARROT SOUP

1 medium onion, chopped
2 tablespoons butter or margarine, melted
2 pounds carrots, scraped and sliced
3 cups chicken broth, divided
1 cup half-and-half
¼ teaspoon coarsely ground pepper
Pinch of salt
1 (8-ounce) carton plain yogurt
1 tablespoon minced fresh dillweed or 1 teaspoon dried dillweed
Garnish: fresh dillweed

Cook onion in butter in a Dutch oven over medium-high heat, stirring constantly, until tender. Add carrots and 1 cup broth; bring to a boil over medium heat. Cover, reduce heat, and simmer 8 minutes or until carrots are tender. Carefully spoon carrot mixture into container of an electric blender; process until smooth. Return to Dutch oven; add remaining broth, half-and-half, pepper, and salt. Cook over low heat until thoroughly heated, stirring constantly. With a wire whisk, stir in yogurt (at room temperature) and dillweed. Serve hot or chilled. Garnish, if desired. Yield: 2 quarts.

**Microwave Directions:** Place onion and butter in a 3-quart casserole. Cover with heavy-duty plastic wrap; fold back a small edge to allow steam to escape. Microwave at HIGH 2 minutes. Stir in carrots; cover and microwave at HIGH 12 minutes or until carrots are tender, giving dish a half-turn after 6 minutes. Place carrot mixture and 1 cup broth in container of an electric blender; process until smooth. Return to casserole; add remaining broth, half-and-half, pepper, and salt. Microwave at HIGH 8 to 10 minutes. With a wire whisk, stir in yogurt (at room temperature) and dillweed. Serve hot or chilled. Garnish, if desired.
*Gwen Louer*
*Roswell, Georgia*

# Begin With A Pork Loin Roast

Think beyond, "What can I fix for supper tonight?" and plan ahead. Buy a large boneless rolled pork loin roast or a boneless pork loin roast, and divide it into smaller cuts—a smaller roast, pork chops, cubes for stir-frying or kabobs, and thin strips for fajitas. By being your own butcher, you'll enjoy a slight price advantage. And to determine even further savings, compare price per serving rather than price per pound.

The labeling and packaging of cuts can vary, so you'll have to know how to identify a boneless rolled pork loin roast. It is two pieces of the loin tied together with a string or encased in netting. A boneless pork loin roast is the same cut of meat but in a single piece. Cut the large roast into smaller portions, cook one part for supper, package the other cuts, and freeze them up to six months. You'll be ready for any occasion.

■ Near the end of cooking time, periodically insert an instant-read thermometer into center of roast, not touching fat, to be sure meat is done.

## ROAST PORK LOIN WITH APPLES AND MUSHROOMS

1 (3-pound) boneless rolled pork loin roast, well trimmed
1 teaspoon dried thyme
¼ teaspoon salt
¼ teaspoon pepper
⅓ cup apple cider
2 tablespoons dry, white vermouth
1 cup chicken broth
1 cup whipping cream
3 tablespoons butter or margarine, divided
3 small cooking apples, peeled, cored, and cut into eighths
¾ pound fresh mushrooms, sliced
Garnish: fresh thyme sprigs

Sprinkle pork roast with seasonings, and place in a lightly greased 13- x 9- x 2-inch baking pan. Bake at 450° for 20 minutes; reduce heat to 325°, and bake 1 hour and 15 minutes or until a meat thermometer reaches 160°. Remove roast to platter; let stand 10 minutes before slicing.

Place baking pan over medium heat; add apple cider, stirring to scrape up any drippings. Add vermouth, chicken broth, and whipping cream. Bring mixture to a boil; cook 15 minutes or until thickened, stirring often. Remove from heat.

Melt 1½ tablespoons butter in a large skillet; add apples and cook until golden, turning once. Remove from skillet, keeping warm. Melt remaining butter in skillet; add mushrooms, and cook until tender. Stir in cream mixture, and cook ingredients over low heat until thoroughly heated.

Place 3 slices of pork roast on individual plates; spoon about ¼ cup sauce mixture over meat, and serve with apple slices. Garnish, if desired. Yield: 8 servings. *Ouida Hamilton*
*Birmingham, Alabama*

■ Butterflying increases marinated flavor and shortens grilling time.

## HONEY-GRILLED PORK LOIN

1 (3-pound) boneless pork loin roast
⅔ cup soy sauce
1 teaspoon ground ginger
3 cloves garlic, crushed
¼ cup firmly packed brown sugar
⅓ cup honey
1½ tablespoons sesame oil
Vegetable cooking spray

Trim fat from roast. Butterfly roast by making a lengthwise cut, cutting to within ½ inch of other side, and open roast. Place in a shallow dish or large, heavy-duty, zip-top plastic bag. Combine soy sauce, ginger, and garlic; pour over roast. Cover or seal, and refrigerate at least 3 hours, turning occasionally.

Remove roast, discarding marinade; set aside. Combine brown sugar, honey, and sesame oil in a saucepan; cook over low heat, stirring constantly, until sugar dissolves.

Coat a grill rack with cooking spray; place over medium-hot coals (350° to 400°). Place roast on rack; brush with mixture. Cook 20 to 25 minutes or until a meat thermometer reaches 160°, turning twice and basting frequently. Yield: 10 to 12 servings.

■ Serve strips as appetizers with wooden picks.

## MARINATED PORK STRIPS

¼ cup soy sauce
2½ tablespoons honey
1½ tablespoons sherry
⅛ teaspoon garlic powder
⅛ teaspoon ground ginger
1 pound boneless pork loin, cut into thin strips
1½ tablespoons sesame seeds
1½ tablespoons coarse-grained mustard

Combine first 5 ingredients in a shallow dish; add pork strips, tossing to coat. Cover and refrigerate 2 hours.

Drain, reserving ¼ cup marinade. Combine reserved marinade, sesame seeds, and mustard. Pour over pork strips; toss to coat. Place in a single layer on a lightly greased baking sheet. Bake at 350° for 20 minutes, turning once. Yield: 4 main-dish servings or 8 appetizer servings.

**Note:** Pork strips may be grilled in a lightly greased grilling basket over medium coals (300° to 350°), covered, 6 to 8 minutes, turning once.

■ It's easier to cut pork cubes and thin strips from partially frozen meat.

## SWEET-AND-SOUR PORK

1 tablespoon sherry
1 tablespoon soy sauce
1 tablespoon cornstarch
1 pound boneless pork loin, cut into ¾-inch pieces
¼ cup vegetable oil, divided
1 clove garlic, minced
1 small onion, sliced
2 green peppers, cut into 1-inch pieces
⅓ cup sugar
¼ cup catsup
1 tablespoon sherry
2 tablespoons soy sauce
2 tablespoons white vinegar
1 tablespoon cornstarch
⅓ cup water
1 (8-ounce) can pineapple slices, drained and quartered
Hot cooked rice

Combine first 3 ingredients; add pork, and let stand 20 minutes. Heat 2 tablespoons oil in a large nonstick skillet; add garlic, onion, and green pepper. Stir-fry 2 minutes or until crisp-tender; remove from skillet, and set aside.

Drain pork. Heat remaining 2 tablespoons oil in skillet; add pork. Cook over medium-high heat, stirring constantly, 3 to 5 minutes or until lightly browned. Pour off excess oil. Stir in cooked vegetables.

Combine sugar and next 6 ingredients, stirring until cornstarch dissolves; add to pork mixture. Cook

over medium heat, stirring constantly, until mixture comes to a boil. Add pineapple, and boil 1 minute, stirring constantly. Serve over hot cooked rice. Yield: 4 servings.

*Anna Robinson*
*Oak Ridge, Tennessee*

■ Butterflying pork chops is easier if the meat is well chilled.

## APRICOT-STUFFED PORK CHOPS

4 (1½-inch-thick) boneless pork chops (about 1¾ pounds)
1 (16-ounce) can apricot halves, drained and chopped
1 cup unseasoned croutons
⅓ cup coarsely chopped walnuts
1 (1-ounce) envelope onion soup mix
2 tablespoons butter or margarine, melted
½ cup apricot preserves
1 tablespoon hot water

Butterfly each chop by making a lengthwise cut on rounded side, cutting to within ½ inch of other side, and folding back to original shape. Turn chop over to uncut side, and cut a deep pocket on left side of center. Cut a second deep pocket on right side of center; set aside.

Combine apricots and next 4 ingredients. Fill each pocket with about 3 tablespoons stuffing mixture, and open chop up, butterfly style. (Pocket openings will be enclosed in center.) Grill, covered, over medium-hot coals (350° to 400°) for 18 minutes, turning once. Combine apricot preserves and water; brush over chops, and grill 5 minutes. Turn chops, brush with apricot mixture, and grill an additional 5 minutes. Yield: 4 servings.

**Note:** Chops may be baked on a lightly greased rack in a broiler pan at 350° for 30 minutes, turning once. Brush with apricot mixture, and bake 5 minutes. Turn chops, brush with apricot mixture, and bake an additional 5 minutes.

*Michele Baker*
*Montezuma, Georgia*

# Great Layered Salads

It's supper club this weekend, and you've signed up to bring a salad. In place of the usual greens and tomatoes, try these spectacular versions, which are layered with cheese, meat, fresh greens, and vegetables or fruit or both. They can be made a day in advance and are easy to transport.

Use a clear bowl for our layered salads to show off the colorful rows of ingredients. Straight-sided ones—like trifle bowls—work best.

Once layered, cover the salad tightly, and chill to allow flavors to blend. Simply toss the salad before serving, or let each guest delve into the layers himself or herself.

## LAYERED TURKEY SALAD

4 cups torn iceburg lettuce
½ pound smoked turkey, cut into thin strips
1 large sweet red pepper, chopped
1 cup sliced celery (about 3 stalks)
2 cups (8 ounces) shredded Jarlsberg or baby Swiss cheese
2 cups seedless red grapes (about ¾ pound)
½ cup mayonnaise
½ cup sour cream
⅛ teaspoon ground white pepper

Layer first 6 ingredients in a 2½-quart bowl; set aside.

Combine mayonnaise, sour cream, and white pepper; spread over salad, sealing to edge of bowl. Cover and chill 8 hours. Toss gently before serving, if desired. Yield: 6 servings.

## LAYERED ANTIPASTO SALAD

2 (6½-ounce) jars marinated artichoke hearts, undrained
3 tablespoons olive oil
2 tablespoons white wine vinegar
1 clove garlic, minced
6 cups torn romaine lettuce
4 medium tomatoes, cut into wedges
1 (3½-ounce) package sliced pepperoni
8 ounces mozzarella cheese, cut into thin strips
1 small purple onion, sliced and separated into rings
½ cup whole pitted ripe olives
8 pickled banana peppers, sliced
4 slices bacon, cooked and crumbled
Garnish: whole pickled banana pepper

Drain artichokes, reserving marinade; set aside artichokes. Combine marinade, olive oil, vinegar, and garlic in a jar; cover tightly, and shake vigorously. Set aside.

Layer one-third of lettuce and half of tomato wedges in a 4-quart bowl; top with artichoke hearts and pepperoni. Layer with one-third of lettuce, cheese, onion, and olives; drizzle with half of dressing. Top with remaining lettuce, remaining tomato, and banana pepper slices. Drizzle with remaining dressing, and sprinkle with bacon. Cover and chill at least 3 hours. Toss gently before serving, if desired. Garnish, if desired. Yield: 8 servings.

*Margie Owen*
*Sheffield, Alabama*

## CITRUS-BLUE CHEESE SALAD

2 pink grapefruit
1 (0.7-ounce) envelope Italian salad dressing mix
½ cup vegetable oil
2 tablespoons water
10 cups mixed salad greens
2 oranges, peeled, seeded, and sectioned
1 (4-ounce) package crumbled blue cheese

Peel and section grapefruit over a small bowl, reserving ¼ cup juice; set grapefruit sections aside. Combine juice, salad dressing mix, oil, and water in a jar; cover tightly, and shake vigorously. Chill at least 3 hours.

Layer half each of salad greens, grapefruit sections, and orange sections in a 4-quart bowl. Repeat procedure, and sprinkle with blue cheese. Cover and chill at least 3 hours. Just before serving, pour dressing over salad, and toss mixture gently. Yield: 6 servings.

**Note:** Leaf, romaine, and Bibb lettuces and spinach all work well in this citrus-cheese salad.

## EASY CONFETTI-PASTA SALAD

1 (8-ounce) package shell macaroni, uncooked
3 cups fresh broccoli flowerets
1 (6-ounce drained weight) can small pitted ripe olives, drained
1 sweet red pepper, cut into thin strips
1 cup small cherry tomatoes
2 small yellow squash, sliced
2 carrots, scraped and sliced
¼ cup thinly sliced green onions
¼ cup grated Parmesan cheese
1 (8-ounce) bottle Caesar salad dressing

Cook macaroni according to package directions; drain. Rinse with cold water, and drain.

Layer half each of pasta and next 8 ingredients in a 2½-quart bowl; drizzle with half of salad dressing. Repeat procedure. Cover and chill at least 8 hours. Toss gently before serving, if desired. Yield: 10 to 12 servings.

**Tip:** *Keep in mind that you cook pasta only until it's tender and slightly firm to the bite; overcooking makes it soft and mushy.*

*Creamy Pumpkin-Pear Soup and Butternut Spice Loaf pay tribute to the season's fresh fruits and vegetables (Recipes begin on page 234.)*

*Lowcountry cooking starts with fresh produce and seafood. (Above) Red Rice and (above top) Frogmore Stew are regional specialties. (Recipes begin on page 235.)*

*Commercial piecrust makes Pineapple-Coconut Chess Pie (page 214) simple to prepare.*

# ON THE LIGHT SIDE

## Reap The Benefits Of Autumn Apples

Apples have much to boast nutritionally. For only 81 calories per medium apple, you get a generous 21 grams of carbohydrate, a good shot of vitamin C and potassium, and only a trace of fat. Also, Mother Nature's addition of pectin makes the apple a rich source of soluble fiber, a known cholesterol-reducer.

Using applesauce to lower the fat content of cakes and quick breads is a growing trend. Simply replace some or all of the oil, butter, or shortening with an equal amount of applesauce.

Check for fruit that has good color and smooth skin without bruises. The variety of apple you choose depends on how you plan to use it. Any type is fine for eating out of hand, but for cooking or baking, be sure to try one of the following: Golden Delicious, McIntosh, Rome Beauty, York Imperial, Granny Smith, Stayman, or Winesap.

### APPLE SPICE CAKE

Vegetable cooking spray
1¾ cups sugar
¼ cup vegetable oil
½ cup egg substitute
3 cups all-purpose flour
1 teaspoon baking soda
¾ teaspoon baking powder
1 teaspoon ground allspice
1 teaspoon ground cinnamon
½ cup plain nonfat yogurt
¾ cup unsweetened applesauce
3 cups unpeeled, cored, finely
    chopped Granny Smith apple
1 cup chopped walnuts
1 teaspoon vanilla extract
½ teaspoon rum flavoring
½ teaspoon black walnut flavoring
½ teaspoon butter flavoring

Coat a 10-inch Bundt pan with cooking spray; dust with flour, and set aside.

Beat sugar and oil at medium speed with an electric mixer 1 minute. Add egg substitute, ¼ cup at a time, beating after each addition.

Combine flour and next 4 ingredients; add to sugar mixture alternately with yogurt and applesauce, beginning and ending with flour mixture. Mix after each addition. Stir in apple and remaining ingredients. Pour batter into prepared pan. Bake at 350° for 55 to 60 minutes or until a wooden pick inserted in center of cake comes out clean. Cool in pan on a wire rack 10 minutes; remove from pan, and cool on a wire rack. Yield: 24 servings (174 calories [26% from fat] per serving).

□ *2.9g protein, 5.1g fat (0.7g saturated, 1.3g monounsaturated, 2.8g polyunsaturated), 29.9g carbohydrate, 0mg cholesterol, 56mg sodium, and 33mg calcium.*          *Suzi Rife*
*Germanton, North Carolina*

### APPLE-CHEESE BAKE

Vegetable cooking spray
⅓ cup honey
1½ tablespoons reduced-calorie
    margarine, melted
¼ teaspoon ground cinnamon
¼ teaspoon ground nutmeg
¼ teaspoon ground coriander
6 (8-ounce) cooking apples,
    unpeeled, cored, and cut into 8
    wedges
½ cup granola cereal
¼ cup firmly packed brown
    sugar
¼ cup all-purpose flour
3 tablespoons reduced-calorie
    margarine, softened
½ cup (2 ounces) shredded,
    40%-less-fat Cheddar cheese

Coat a 15- x 10- x 1-inch jellyroll pan with cooking spray.

Combine honey and next 4 ingredients in a large bowl. Add apple wedges; stir gently to coat. Drain and arrange in jellyroll pan.

Combine cereal and next 3 ingredients, stirring with a fork until crumbly; sprinkle evenly over apples. Bake at 350° for 30 minutes or until apples are tender. Sprinkle evenly with cheese; bake 5 minutes or until cheese melts. Yield: 12 servings (149 calories [26% from fat] per 4 wedges).

□ *2.3g protein, 4.3g fat (0.6g saturated, 0.1g monounsaturated, 0.2g polyunsaturated), 27.6g carbohydrate, 3.6g fiber, 3mg cholesterol, 74mg sodium, and 51mg calcium.*

**Tip:** *To prevent fruit or nuts from sinking to the bottom of bread or cake batter, shake them in a bag with a small amount of flour to dust lightly before adding to batter.*

## TART APPLE CRISP

6½ cups unpeeled, sliced Granny
  Smith apple (2 pounds)
¼ cup honey
2 tablespoons lemon juice
½ teaspoon ground cinnamon
⅛ teaspoon ground cloves
Vegetable cooking spray
¾ cup whole wheat flour
⅓ cup firmly packed brown sugar
¼ cup wheat germ
3 tablespoons reduced-calorie
  margarine
1 tablespoon vegetable oil
¼ cup chopped pecans

Combine first 5 ingredients, tossing to coat apples. Place in a 2-quart baking dish coated with cooking spray; set aside. Combine whole wheat flour, brown sugar, and wheat germ; cut in margarine with a pastry blender until mixture is crumbly. Stir in oil and pecans, and sprinkle over apples. Bake at 350° for 45 minutes. Serve warm. Yield: 8 servings (233 calories [28% from fat] per ¾-cup serving).

☐ *2.7g protein, 7.9g fat (0.7g saturated, 2.2g monounsaturated, 1.8g polyunsaturated), 41.9g carbohydrate, 4.9g fiber, 0mg cholesterol, 46mg sodium, and 23mg calcium.*

*Sandra Russell*
*Gainesville, Florida*

## APPLE-SESAME-CHICKEN
## STIR-FRY

1 tablespoon reduced-calorie
  margarine
2 (4-ounce) skinned, boned chicken
  breast halves, cut into thin strips
3 cups fresh broccoli flowerets
1 cup unpeeled, cubed cooking
  apple
¾ cup sliced fresh mushrooms
¼ cup thinly sliced celery
1 tablespoon water
¼ teaspoon salt
¼ teaspoon curry powder
½ teaspoon sesame seeds, toasted

Melt margarine in a large nonstick skillet; add chicken, and stir-fry about

3 minutes. Add broccoli and next 6 ingredients; cover and simmer 5 minutes or until crisp-tender. Sprinkle with sesame seeds. Yield: 2 servings (229 calories [27% from fat] per 1¾-cup serving).

☐ *23.4g protein, 7.4g fat (0.9g saturated, 1g monounsaturated, 1.1g polyunsaturated), 22.6g carbohydrate, 9g fiber, 42mg cholesterol, 462mg sodium, and 166mg calcium.*

*Angie Kinney*
*Dallas, Texas*

## DRIED APPLE SIDE DISH

1 (8-ounce) package sliced dried
  apples
2½ cups water
¾ cup raisins
½ cup firmly packed brown sugar
1 tablespoon reduced-calorie
  margarine
¼ teaspoon butter flavoring

Combine apples and water in a medium saucepan; bring to a boil. Reduce heat and simmer, uncovered, 25 minutes. Add raisins and remaining ingredients; simmer 5 minutes. Yield: 8 servings (112 calories [5% from fat] per ⅔-cup serving).

☐ *0.5g protein, 0.7g fat (0g saturated, 0g monounsaturated, 0g polyunsaturated), 28.5g carbohydrate, 1g fiber, 0mg cholesterol, 29mg sodium, and 15mg calcium.*

*Ramona Johnson*
*Statesville, North Carolina*

**Tip:** *When food boils over in the oven, sprinkle the burned surface with a little salt. This will stop smoke and odor from forming and make the spot easier to clean. Also, rubbing damp salt on dishes in which food has been baked will help remove brown spots.*

## LIGHT FAVORITE

# Old-Fashioned Cinnamon Rolls

We took a classic and shaped it up to meet today's healthy standards. But these cinnamon rolls are so moist that you'll be too busy swooning to notice that half the fat and all the cholesterol are gone.

## OLD-FASHIONED
## CINNAMON ROLLS
*(pictured on page 257)*

⅓ cup skim milk
⅓ cup reduced-calorie margarine
¼ cup firmly packed brown sugar
1 teaspoon salt
1 package dry yeast
½ cup warm water (105° to 115°)
½ cup egg substitute
3½ cups bread flour, divided
¾ cup quick-cooking oats,
  uncooked
Vegetable cooking spray
¼ cup reduced-calorie margarine,
  softened and divided
¾ cup firmly packed brown sugar
¼ cup raisins
2 teaspoons ground cinnamon
1 cup sifted powdered sugar
2 tablespoons water

Combine skim milk and next 3 ingredients in a saucepan; heat until margarine melts, stirring occasionally. Cool mixture to 105° to 115°.

Combine yeast and warm water in a 1-cup liquid measuring cup; let stand 5 minutes. Combine yeast mixture, milk mixture, egg substitute, 1 cup flour, and oats in a large mixing bowl, mixing well. Gradually stir in enough remaining flour to make a soft dough.

Turn dough out onto a lightly floured surface; knead until smooth and elastic (about 8 minutes). Place dough in a large bowl coated with cooking spray, turning to grease top. Cover and let rise in a warm place

(85°), free from drafts, 1 hour or until doubled in bulk.

Punch dough down; cover and let rest 10 minutes. Divide dough in half, and roll each into a 12-inch square. Spread each square of dough with 2 tablespoons margarine. Combine ¾ cup brown sugar, raisins, and cinnamon; sprinkle mixture over each square. Roll up jellyroll fashion; pinch seam to seal (do not seal ends). Cut each roll into 1-inch slices, and place in two 8-inch square pans coated with cooking spray.

Cover and let rise in a warm place, free from drafts, about 30 minutes or until almost doubled in bulk. Bake at 375° for 15 to 20 minutes or until golden brown. Combine powdered sugar and 2 tablespoons water; drizzle over warm rolls. Yield: 2 dozen (157 calories [19% from fat] per roll).

□ *3.2g protein, 3.4g fat (0.1g saturated, 0.1g monounsaturated, 0.2g polyunsaturated), 29.4g carbohydrate, 0.5g fiber, 0mg cholesterol, 153mg sodium, and 21mg calcium.*

| COMPARE THE NUTRIENTS | | |
|---|---|---|
| (per serving) | | |
| | Traditional | Light |
| Calories | 226 | 157 |
| Fat | 7.7g | 3.4g |
| Cholesterol | 18mg | 0mg |

# LIGHT MENU

# Guiltless Goulash

For a hurry-up meal when you're hungry for a healthy supper, make a batch of Hungarian Goulash. Lean, boneless top round steak reduces fat and calories in this colorful main dish.

The entire meal can be put together in less than an hour. While the goulash is simmering, prepare Light Glazed Carrots and brown rice. Slice the carrots diagonally for a more finished appearance. We suggest using an instant brown rice that requires only 10 minutes to cook. The rice will also add color and fiber to the meal.

Next, cut and toss an assortment of mixed greens; then top with a commercial fat-free salad dressing of your choice. Fruited Cheese Pie can be made a day in advance and refrigerated until dessert time.

## EASY FALL MENU

**Hungarian Goulash
With brown rice
Light Glazed Carrots
Tossed green salad with
Commercial fat-free dressing
Fruited Cheese Pie**

## HUNGARIAN GOULASH

1 pound lean, boneless top round
  steak
2 teaspoons vegetable oil
1¼ cups coarsely chopped onion
1 cup green pepper strips
2½ cups chopped fresh tomatoes
1¼ to 1½ cups water
1 tablespoon paprika
½ teaspoon salt
¼ teaspoon pepper
2 cups hot cooked brown rice
  (cooked without salt or fat)

Trim all visible fat from steak; cut steak into bite-size pieces. Cook in hot oil in a large skillet over medium heat until browned, stirring often. Add onion and green pepper; cook 5 minutes, stirring often. Stir in tomatoes and next 4 ingredients. Bring to a boil; cover, reduce heat, and cook 45 minutes or until tender, adding additional water, if necessary. Serve over rice. Yield: 4 servings (341 calories [22% from fat] per ¾ cup meat mixture and ½ cup rice).

□ *31g protein, 8.5g fat (2.4g saturated, 3g monounsaturated, 2g polyunsaturated), 35.6g carbohydrate, 5g fiber, 65mg cholesterol, 370mg sodium, and 37mg calcium.* Betsy Heatwole
Harrisonburg, Virginia

## LIGHT GLAZED CARROTS

4½ cups sliced carrots (about 2
  pounds)
1 tablespoon reduced-calorie
  margarine
1½ tablespoons honey
1 tablespoon lemon juice

Arrange carrots in a vegetable steamer over boiling water. Cover and steam 4 to 8 minutes or until desired degree of doneness. Remove from steamer, and keep warm.

Melt margarine in a large skillet over medium heat; add honey and lemon juice, stirring until smooth. Add carrots, tossing gently. Yield: 4 servings (113 calories [5% from fat] per 1-cup serving).

□ *1.7g protein, 2.1g fat (0.3g saturated, 0.5g monounsaturated, 0.8g polyunsaturated), 24.1g carbohydrate, 5.4g fiber, 0mg cholesterol, 87mg sodium, and 47mg calcium.*

Elizabeth M. Haney
Dublin, Virginia

## FRUITED CHEESE PIE

1 cup graham cracker crumbs
3 tablespoons reduced-calorie
  margarine, melted
2 tablespoons sugar
Butter-flavored cooking spray
1 envelope unflavored gelatin
¼ cup cold water
1 cup nonfat cottage cheese
½ cup plain nonfat yogurt
¼ cup sugar
½ cup unsweetened pineapple juice
1 teaspoon lemon juice
⅛ teaspoon ground cinnamon
1 (11-ounce) can mandarin orange
  sections, drained
2 tablespoons low-sugar orange
  marmalade, melted

Combine first 3 ingredients in a small mixing bowl; firmly press crumb mixture over bottom and up sides of a 9-inch pieplate. Coat crust with cooking spray; bake at 350° for 7 to 9 minutes. Cool on a wire rack.

Sprinkle gelatin over water in a small saucepan; let stand 1 minute. Cook over low heat, stirring until gelatin dissolves (about 2 minutes).

Combine cottage cheese and next 5 ingredients in container of an electric blender; process until smooth, stopping once to scrape down sides. With blender on high, gradually add gelatin. Pour into prepared crust; chill until firm. Arrange oranges on top; drizzle with orange marmalade. Yield: 10 servings (144 calories [25% from fat] per serving).

□ *4.7g protein, 2.7g fat (0g saturated, 0.6g monounsaturated, 0.7g polyunsaturated), 25.2g carbohydrate, 0g fiber, 1mg cholesterol, 202mg sodium, and 46mg calcium.* Dorothy Martin
Woodburn, Kentucky

# QUICK!

## Easy Stuffed Potatoes

Need some fresh ideas for a speedy meal? Try a stuffed potato that's micro-baked. Baking potatoes in the microwave dramatically reduces overall preparation and cooking time.

To eliminate the guesswork, our Test Kitchens staff has developed a reference chart (on facing page). Identify the size and number you are preparing; the recommended baking time is listed to the right. Times may vary slightly depending on the number, size, and shape. All potatoes should be micro-baked on HIGH.

### BLUE CHEESE STUFFED POTATOES

4 slices bacon
4 medium baking potatoes (about
  1½ pounds)
½ cup sour cream
¼ cup (1 ounce) crumbled blue
  cheese
¼ cup milk
¼ cup butter or margarine, melted
¼ teaspoon salt
⅛ teaspoon pepper

Place bacon slices on a rack in an 11- x 7- x 1½-inch baking dish; cover with paper towels. Microwave at HIGH 3½ to 4½ minutes or until crisp. Drain and crumble; set aside.

Scrub potatoes; prick several times with a fork. Place potatoes 1 inch apart on a microwave-safe rack or paper towels. Microwave at HIGH 10 to 13 minutes, turning and rearranging once; let stand 2 minutes. Cut a 1-inch lengthwise strip from the top of each potato. Carefully scoop out potato pulp, leaving a ¼-inch shell intact; mash pulp. Combine potato pulp, sour cream, and next 5 ingredients. Spoon potato mixture into shells. Place on a microwave-safe plate. Microwave at HIGH 2 minutes or until thoroughly heated. Sprinkle with crumbled bacon. Yield: 4 servings. Lucia Crull
Charleston, South Carolina

### BROCCOLI-SHRIMP STUFFED POTATOES

2 large baking potatoes (about 1¼
  pounds)
⅓ cup loaf process cheese spread
2 tablespoons milk
1 cup fresh broccoli flowerets
1 (6-ounce) can shrimp, drained *
1 green onion, chopped

Scrub potatoes; prick several times with a fork. Place potatoes 1 inch apart on a microwave-safe rack or paper towels. Microwave at HIGH 10 to 13 minutes, turning and rearranging once; let stand 2 minutes. Cut an X to within ½ inch of bottom of each potato. Squeeze potatoes from opposite sides, and opposite ends to open; fluff with a fork.

Combine cheese spread and milk in a heavy saucepan; cook over low heat until cheese melts, stirring often. Remove from heat, and set aside.

Place broccoli in a 9-inch pieplate; cover and microwave at HIGH 2 to 3 minutes or until tender. Arrange broccoli and shrimp in potatoes. Spoon cheese sauce over potatoes, and sprinkle with green onions. Yield: 2 servings.

\* One-third cup fresh or frozen cooked shrimp may be substituted for canned shrimp, if desired. *Terri Fort Goodview, Virginia*

---

### POTATO MICRO-BAKING GUIDE
**(Based on size and number)**

| Number/Size | Micro-baking Time at HIGH (700 watts) |
|---|---|
| **5 ounces or less:** | |
| 1 small | 3 minutes |
| 2 small | 5 minutes |
| 3 small | 6 minutes |
| 4 small | 8 minutes |
| **6 to 8 ounces:** | |
| 1 medium | 5 minutes |
| 2 medium | 8 minutes |
| 3 medium | 10 minutes |
| 4 medium | 11 minutes |
| **9 ounces or more:** | |
| 1 large | 6 minutes |
| 2 large | 10 minutes |
| 3 large | 12 minutes |
| 4 large | 14 minutes |

---

# Teenage Cook Loves The Kitchen

Leanne Baker of Johnson City, Tennessee, enjoys cooking for friends her own age. Here's a simple dinner menu of Leanne's that most 17-year-olds could prepare, although the White Chocolate Roulage, she confesses, "is a little more complicated." It beat 64 other entries and won a first-prize ribbon at the Appalachian District Fair.

### EASY MEAT LOAF DINNER

**Fresh fruit tray**
**Tossed green salad**
**Choice of commercial dressing**
**Individual Meat Loaves**
**Cheesy Potato Casserole**
**Honey-Glazed Carrots**
**Buttered green peas**
**Commercial dinner rolls**
**White Chocolate Roulage**

### INDIVIDUAL MEAT LOAVES

1½ pounds lean ground beef
½ pound hot ground pork sausage
1 small onion, finely chopped
1 teaspoon salt
¼ teaspoon pepper
½ teaspoon poultry seasoning
2 tablespoons Worcestershire sauce
5 slices white bread
2 large eggs
½ cup milk
1½ cups soft breadcrumbs
1½ cups chili sauce
½ cup boiling water
Garnish: fresh parsley sprigs

Combine first 7 ingredients; set aside. Remove crust from bread; cut bread into cubes. Combine bread cubes, eggs, and milk in a large mixing bowl; beat at medium speed with an electric mixer until smooth. Stir in meat mixture, and shape into 6 individual loaves; roll each loaf in breadcrumbs.

Place in a lightly greased 13- x 9- x 2-inch pan. Spread chili sauce over loaves. Pour boiling water into dish. Bake, uncovered, at 350° for 1 hour. Transfer loaves to a serving platter; garnish, if desired. Yield: 6 servings.

### CHEESY POTATO CASSEROLE

7 medium potatoes (about 2 pounds)
¼ cup butter or margarine, melted
1 small onion, chopped
1 teaspoon salt
¼ teaspoon pepper
1 (8-ounce) carton sour cream
1 (10¾-ounce) can cream of chicken soup, undiluted
2 cups (8 ounces) shredded Cheddar cheese
3 tablespoons butter or margarine, melted
1½ cups herb-seasoned stuffing mix

Cook potatoes in boiling water to cover 30 minutes or until tender. Drain; let cool to touch. Peel and cut into ¼-inch strips; set aside.

Combine ¼ cup butter and next 5 ingredients in a large bowl; gently stir in potatoes and cheese. Spoon into a lightly greased 13- x 9- x 2-inch baking dish. Combine 3 tablespoons butter and stuffing mix; sprinkle over potato mixture. Bake, uncovered, at 350° for 25 minutes or until thoroughly heated. Yield: 8 servings.

### HONEY-GLAZED CARROTS

2 pounds carrots, scraped and thinly sliced
½ cup water
3 tablespoons honey
3 tablespoons brown sugar
2 tablespoons butter or margarine

Combine carrots and water in a medium saucepan. Bring to a boil; cover, reduce heat, and simmer 8 minutes or until crisp-tender. Drain and return to pan. Add honey and remaining ingredients; cook over low heat, stirring gently, until butter and sugar melt. Yield: 6 to 8 servings.

## WHITE CHOCOLATE ROULAGE

4 large eggs, separated
¾ cup sugar, divided
1 tablespoon vegetable oil
1 teaspoon vanilla extract
⅔ cup sifted cake flour
1 teaspoon baking powder
¼ teaspoon salt
1 to 2 tablespoons powdered sugar
White Chocolate Cream Filling
Buttercream Frosting
Garnish: white chocolate curls

Lightly oil bottom and sides of a 15- x 10- x 1-inch jellyroll pan with vegetable oil; line with wax paper, and lightly oil and flour wax paper. Set prepared pan aside.

Beat egg yolks at high speed with an electric mixer until foamy. Gradually add ¼ cup sugar; beat until mixture is thick and pale (about 5 minutes). Stir in vegetable oil and vanilla; set aside.

Beat egg whites at high speed with an electric mixer until foamy. Gradually add remaining ½ cup sugar, 1 tablespoon at a time, beating until stiff peaks form and sugar dissolves; fold into yolk mixture. Combine flour, baking powder, and salt; gradually fold into egg mixture. Spread batter evenly into pan. Bake at 350° for 8 to 10 minutes.

Sift powdered sugar in 15- x 10-inch rectangle on a cloth towel. When cake is done, immediately loosen from sides of pan, and turn out onto towel. Carefully peel off wax paper. Starting at narrow end, roll up cake and towel together; cool completely on a wire rack, seam side down.

Unroll cake; spread with White Chocolate Cream Filling, and carefully reroll. Place cake on platter, seam side down. Spread Buttercream Frosting on all sides. Garnish, if desired. Yield: 10 to 12 servings.

### White Chocolate Cream Filling

¾ teaspoon unflavored gelatin
1½ tablespoons cold water
3 ounces white chocolate-flavored baking bar, grated
⅔ cup whipping cream
½ teaspoon vanilla extract

Sprinkle gelatin over water in a small saucepan; let stand 1 minute. Cook over low heat, stirring until gelatin dissolves. Add white chocolate, stirring constantly, until chocolate melts; cool 5 minutes.

Combine whipping cream and gelatin mixture in a small mixing bowl; beat at medium speed with an electric mixer until thickened (do not overbeat). Stir in vanilla, and chill mixture. Yield: 1½ cups.

### Buttercream Frosting

½ cup butter or margarine, softened
2 cups sifted powdered sugar
1 to 3 teaspoons milk
½ teaspoon vanilla extract

Beat butter at medium speed with an electric mixer; gradually add sugar, beating until light and fluffy. Add 1 teaspoon milk; beat until spreading consistency. Add additional milk, if needed. Stir in vanilla. Yield: 1½ cups.

**Note:** To make white chocolate curls, melt 3 ounces white chocolate-flavored baking bar; pour onto wax paper in a 3-inch-wide strip. Let cool until chocolate feels slightly tacky but is not firm. Pull a vegetable peeler or cheese plane across chocolate until curl forms.

# Sweets Of The Southwest

Contrary to popular belief, Southwestern cuisine isn't limited to spicy dishes; it's also known for many desserts. The list is as colorful as a Texas sunset: biscochitos, capirotada, flan, buñuelos, and empanadas.

Egg custards and puddings are the most common because their light textures and flavors complement a fiery Southwestern meal. But other desserts abound as well. Some are traditionally associated with holidays, such as biscochitos (anise-flavored cookies) and empanadas (turnovers) at Christmas, and capirotada (bread pudding) at Lent.

## BISCOCHITOS

2 cups shortening
1 cup sugar
2 large eggs
1 teaspoon anise seeds, crushed
5½ cups all-purpose flour
1 tablespoon baking powder
1 teaspoon salt
¼ cup white wine or dry sherry
½ cup sugar
1 teaspoon ground cinnamon

Beat shortening at medium speed with an electric mixer until fluffy. Gradually add 1 cup sugar; beat well. Add eggs and anise seeds; mix well.

Combine flour, baking powder, and salt, and add to shortening mixture alternately with wine, beginning and ending with flour mixture. Mix after each addition.

Shape dough into a ball; roll to ¼-inch thickness on a floured surface. Cut with 3-inch cookie cutters, and place on lightly greased cookie sheets. Combine ½ cup sugar and cinnamon; sprinkle over cookies. Bake at 350° for 8 to 10 minutes or until lightly browned. Transfer to wire racks to cool. Yield: about 6 dozen.

*Toni Pemberton*
*Roswell, New Mexico*

## JALAPEÑO JELLY

1 pound green peppers
¼ pound jalapeño peppers
5½ cups sugar
1¼ cups white vinegar (5% acidity)
⅓ cup fresh lemon juice
2 (3-ounce) packages liquid fruit pectin

Wash peppers; pat dry. Trim, seed, and remove veins in peppers; cut into quarters, and set aside.

Position steel blade in food processor bowl. Add peppers; process about 1½ minutes or until smooth (pulp will be visible). Combine peppers, sugar, and vinegar in a Dutch oven; bring to a boil. Boil 5 minutes, stirring constantly. Stir in lemon juice, and return to a boil. Add fruit pectin; return to a boil, and boil 1 minute, stirring constantly. Remove from heat, and skim off foam with a metal spoon.

Quickly pour jelly into hot sterilized jars, filling to ¼-inch from top; wipe jar rims. Cover at once with metal lids, and screw on bands. Process in boiling-water bath 5 minutes, or let cool 12 hours and store in refrigerator. Serve over cream cheese with fresh fruit and Biscochitos. Yield: 8 half pints.

**Note:** When working with hot peppers, such as jalapeños, always wear rubber gloves.         *Kay Cruse*
*Christoval, Texas*

## BAKED FLAN WITH CARAMEL

1 cup sugar
¼ cup water
¼ teaspoon cream of tartar
3 large eggs
1 egg yolk
½ cup sugar
1 teaspoon vanilla extract
1 cup whipping cream
1 cup milk

Combine first 3 ingredients in a heavy saucepan; bring to a boil. Reduce heat and simmer, stirring frequently, until mixture turns a light golden brown (about 15 minutes). Pour syrup into four 10-ounce custard cups; let cool.

Combine eggs, egg yolk, and ½ cup sugar with a wire whisk; stir in vanilla.

Combine whipping cream and milk in a saucepan; heat until bubbles form around edge of pan. Gradually stir about one-fourth of hot milk mixture into egg mixture; add to remaining hot milk mixture, stirring constantly. Pour evenly into custard cups. Place custard cups in a 13- x 9- x 2-inch pan; add hot water to pan to depth of 1 inch. Cover with aluminum foil.

Bake at 325° for 45 minutes or until a knife inserted in center of each cup comes out clean. Remove cups from water; let custard cool. Cover and chill at least 8 hours.

To serve, loosen edges of custard with a spatula; invert onto individual plates, letting caramelized sugar mixture drizzle over top. Yield: 4 servings.         *Priscilla Sims*
*Lubbock, Texas*

# Colorful Grilled Vegetables

Next time you cook out, don't forget the vegetables. There are two ways of cooking them on the grill: bare or wrapped in aluminum foil. Foil wrapping opens the way to cooking almost any vegetables or combination of them.

## VEGETABLE MARINADE

¼ cup olive or vegetable oil
½ cup apple cider
2 teaspoons fines herbes
½ teaspoon freshly ground pepper

Combine all ingredients in a jar. Cover tightly; shake vigorously. Brush vegetables with marinade before and during grilling. Yield: ¾ cup.

## GRILLED VEGETABLES

**Bell pepper (red, yellow, or green):** Place whole peppers on grill rack, and grill, uncovered, over medium coals (300° to 350°) 8 to 10 minutes or until done, turning frequently. Omit basting.
**Cabbage:** Core cabbage, and cut into 8 wedges; brush with marinade. Place on grill rack, and grill, uncovered, over medium coals (300° to 350°) 8 to 10 minutes, turning once and basting occasionally.
**Carrots:** Scrub (do not scrape) and trim ends from one bunch of carrots. Arrange on lightly oiled heavy-duty aluminum foil; brush with marinade or add 2 tablespoons water, and seal. Place on grill rack, and grill, uncovered, over medium coals (300° to 350°) 30 minutes, turning once.
**Corn:** Turn back husks, and remove corn silks. Lay husks back in position, and soak corn in cold water 20 minutes. Place on grill rack, and grill, uncovered, over medium coals (300° to 350°) 45 minutes, turning frequently. Omit basting.
**Mushrooms:** Trim off stem ends. Grill large mushrooms whole; thread small ones on metal skewers. Place on grill rack, and grill, uncovered, over medium coals (300° to 350°) 9 minutes or until done, turning frequently and basting occasionally.
**Onions:** Remove outside leaves of medium to large onions; brush with marinade. Wrap individually in heavy-duty aluminum foil. Place on grill rack, and grill, uncovered, over medium coals (300° to 350°) 45 minutes or until tender when squeezed with an oven mitt; turn frequently. Or cut onion into 1-inch-thick slices; brush with marinade. Grill 15 to 20 minutes.
**Potatoes:** Scrub and dry thoroughly. Wrap individually in heavy-duty aluminum foil. Grill over medium coals (300° to 350°) 50 minutes or until tender when squeezed with an oven mitt; turn after 30 minutes. Omit basting.
**Summer Squash:** Trim off stem ends of medium zucchini or yellow squash. Cut in half lengthwise. Place in a shallow dish; pour marinade over squash, and refrigerate 30 minutes, turning once. Remove from marinade; place on grill rack. Grill, uncovered, over medium-hot coals (350° to 400°) 10 to 15 minutes, turning frequently and basting occasionally.
**Tomatoes:** Cut firm, ripe tomatoes in half, and brush with marinade. Wrap loosely in heavy-duty aluminum foil; place tomato halves on grill rack. Grill over medium-hot coals (350° to 400°) 8 to 12 minutes.

# A Cut Above The Rest

All you need is a sharp knife and a little imagination to cure the same old side-dish blues. These quick tricks make even the simplest recipes more tempting.

When considering cooking times for vegetables, 8 to 10 minutes is a good rule of thumb for steaming, microwaving, or grilling. But remember, the maturity and variety of the vegetables will make a little difference in the cooking time you need to allow. For example, if you have a mature pole bean, it will take longer to cook than a young, tender snap bean.

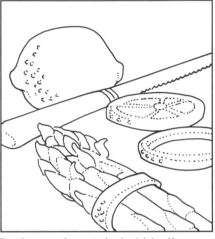

*Make vegetable fans by cutting ¼-inch slices to, but not through, the top of the vegetable; brush with commercial Italian salad dressing, place in a grilling basket, and grill.*

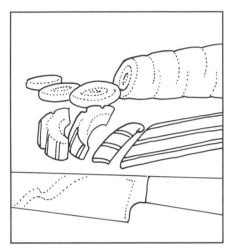

*Slice carrots, celery, or other long, skinny vegetables diagonally for an appealing shape. Steam 8 minutes or until tender; season with butter, lemon juice, and herbs.*

*Cut lemons into ½-inch-thick slices. Remove pulp, reserving round rings. Squeeze pulp into melted butter. Place fresh, cooked asparagus in rings, drizzle with lemon butter, and serve.*

*Peel midsection of new potatoes, and cook. Steam broccoli flowerets, and arrange around potatoes; drizzle with olive oil, and sprinkle with freshly ground pepper.*

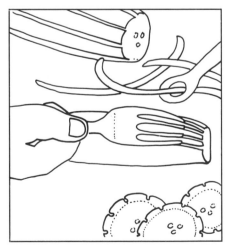

*Score zucchini or cucumber by pulling the tines of a fork down the length of the vegetable; repeat on all sides. Or remove lengthwise strips with a zester. Slice; use in salads or with a dip.*

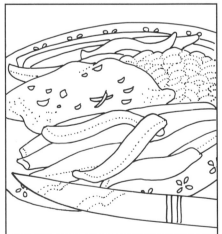

*Slice red peppers into thin strips. Cook the pepper strips and green beans in a small amount of oil over medium-high heat, stirring constantly, until crisp-tender.*

# OCTOBER

*Salute the 500th anniversary of Christopher Columbus's*

*legacy by exploring the world of lighter fare, and discover*

*sausage in a new light. For another taste discovery, sample*

*the versatile tomatillo. And just in time for Halloween are*

*those special treats—cookies. Invite the children to take part*

*in a hands-on cookie-decorating session. And speaking of*

*sweets, don't miss the selections in 30-Minute Desserts. We've*

*cut preparation time to mere minutes without sacrificing*

*a rich flavor.*

# Welcome The Flavors Of Fall

At roadside stands, portly pumpkins and squash signal fall's arrival. In the kitchen, spices replace herbs, and the red-checked tablecloths of summer are put aside.

It is the season for soup—fragrant with pear, wine, and pumpkin. It is a time for baking. Fresh from the oven come pies ripe with the smell of apples or toasty with the scent of pecans. A sense of pleasant urgency fills the kitchen as the freshest fall vegetables and fruits demand immediate attention. The chill in the air hints that winter is just around the corner, but for now, all is golden.

## SWEET POTATO-BEEF TZIMMES

1 (3-pound) beef brisket
2 tablespoons vegetable oil
4 cups boiling water
1½ teaspoons salt
¼ teaspoon pepper
¼ teaspoon ground nutmeg
1 pound carrots, scraped and sliced
4 sweet potatoes, peeled and cut into quarters
⅓ cup firmly packed brown sugar
½ cup golden raisins

Brown brisket in oil in an ovenproof Dutch oven; add water and next 3 ingredients. Bring to a boil; cover, reduce heat, and simmer 1½ hours. Add carrots and remaining ingredients; cover and bake at 350° for 1½ hours.

To serve, slice brisket, and arrange on serving platter with carrots and sweet potatoes. Yield: 8 servings.

*Jenny Heinzmann*
*Lothian, Maryland*

## PUMPKIN-PEAR SOUP
*(pictured on page 221)*

3 ripe pears, peeled and thinly sliced
¼ cup chopped onion
2 tablespoons butter, melted
2 cups canned or cooked, mashed pumpkin
2 (14½-ounce) cans ready-to-serve chicken broth
½ cup water
¼ cup Chablis or other dry white wine
¼ teaspoon salt
1 (3-inch) stick cinnamon
⅓ cup half-and-half
Garnishes: sour cream, green onion strips

Cook pears and onion in butter in a large skillet over medium-high heat, stirring constantly, until tender. Position knife blade in food processor bowl; add pear mixture and pumpkin. Process until smooth. Transfer to a large saucepan; add chicken broth and next 4 ingredients. Bring to a boil. Reduce heat and simmer, uncovered, 20 minutes; remove cinnamon stick. Stir in half-and-half, and heat thoroughly (do not boil). Garnish, if desired. Yield: 6 cups.

*Nick Cairns*
*Alabaster, Alabama*

## APPLE PARTY SANDWICHES

1 (8-ounce) package cream cheese, softened
½ cup firmly packed brown sugar
1 teaspoon vanilla extract
1 (16-ounce) loaf cinnamon-raisin bread
2 Red or Golden Delicious apples, unpeeled
1 to 2 tablespoons orange juice
¼ to ⅓ cup chopped salted peanuts

Combine cream cheese, brown sugar, and vanilla; beat at medium speed with an electric mixer 1 minute or until smooth. Set aside.

Cut each bread slice into a 3-inch round. Core apples; cut each apple horizontally into 7 slices, and brush with orange juice. Spread 1 tablespoon cheese mixture onto each bread round; top with an apple slice. Sprinkle peanuts in center. Yield: 14 sandwiches.

*Ginger Gentry*
*Sutherlin, Virginia*

## PECAN PIE

1½ cups light corn syrup
1 (3-ounce) package vanilla instant pudding mix
4 large eggs
¼ cup butter or margarine, melted
2 cups pecan halves
1 unbaked 9-inch pastry shell

Combine first 4 ingredients; stir in pecans. Pour into pastry shell. Bake at 350° for 50 to 55 minutes. Yield: one 9-inch pie.

*Nanette Wesley*
*Jackson, Georgia*

## APPLE-CHEESE CRISP

6 cups peeled, sliced cooking apples
1 tablespoon water
½ teaspoon lemon juice
1 cup (4 ounces) shredded Cheddar
  cheese
1 cup all-purpose flour
½ cup firmly packed brown sugar
2 tablespoons sugar
¼ teaspoon ground cinnamon
¼ teaspoon ground nutmeg
½ cup butter or margarine
Vanilla ice cream
Toasted sliced almonds (optional)

Arrange apples in a lightly greased 8-inch square baking dish. Combine water and lemon juice; sprinkle over apples. Top with cheese.

Combine flour and next 4 ingredients; cut in butter with a fork or pastry blender until mixture is crumbly. Sprinkle over cheese. Bake at 350° for 40 minutes or until tender. Serve warm topped with ice cream; sprinkle with almonds, if desired. Yield: 6 to 8 servings.

*Valerie Stutsman*
*Norfolk, Virginia*

## PUMPKIN POUND CAKE

1 cup butter or margarine, softened
3 cups sugar
5 large eggs
3 cups all-purpose flour
2 teaspoons baking powder
½ teaspoon baking soda
½ teaspoon salt
2 teaspoons ground cinnamon
¼ teaspoon ground cloves
⅛ teaspoon apple pie spice
2 cups canned or cooked, mashed
  pumpkin
⅓ cup rum

Beat butter at medium speed with an electric mixer about 2 minutes or until soft and creamy. Gradually add sugar, beating at medium speed 5 to 7 minutes. Add eggs, one at a time, beating just until yellow disappears.

Combine flour and next 6 ingredients. Combine pumpkin and rum. Add flour mixture to creamed mixture alternately with pumpkin mixture, beginning and ending with flour mixture. Mix at lowest speed just until blended after each addition.

Pour batter into a greased and floured 10-inch tube pan. Bake at 325° for 1 hour and 25 to 30 minutes or until a wooden pick inserted in center comes out clean. Cool in pan on a wire rack 10 minutes; remove from pan, and let cool completely on wire rack. Yield: one 10-inch cake. *Helen Phifer*
*New Bern, North Carolina*

## BUTTERNUT SPICE LOAF
*(pictured on page 221)*

1 (2-pound) butternut squash
½ cup butter or margarine,
  softened
1½ cups sugar
2 large eggs
2 cups self-rising flour
1 teaspoon ground cinnamon
½ teaspoon ground nutmeg
½ teaspoon ground allspice
¼ teaspoon ground ginger
½ cup chopped pecans

Cut squash in half lengthwise; remove seeds. Place cut side down in a shallow pan; add water to depth of ½ inch. Cover with foil, and bake at 400° for 1 hour or until tender; drain. Scoop out pulp; mash. Discard shell. Measure 1¾ cups pulp; reserve any remaining pulp for other uses.

Beat butter at medium speed with an electric mixer until creamy; gradually add sugar, beating mixture well. Add eggs, one at a time, beating after each addition.

Combine flour and spices; add to butter mixture alternately with squash, beginning and ending with flour mixture. Stir in pecans. Spoon batter into a greased and floured 9- x 5- x 3-inch loafpan; bake at 350° for 1 hour to 1 hour and 10 minutes or until a wooden pick inserted in center comes out clean. Cool in pan on a wire rack 10 minutes. Remove from pan, and let cool completely on wire rack. Yield: 1 loaf. *Loretta Wuest*
*Cantonment, Florida*

# What's Cooking In The Lowcountry

Here, in the Lowcountry, body and soul are nourished by the land. Locals of the Lowcountry, which encompasses the coastline and estuaries from Myrtle Beach, South Carolina, south to Savannah, Georgia, serve shrimp and grits for breakfast, and fresh seafood fills every dinner table.

Only in the Lowcountry can you sample a ragoût of grits and wild mushrooms, and then go to the restaurant next door for a pone of cornbread sweetened with a tablespoon of sugar. These regional recipes confirm that the food is worthy of its special reputation.

■ This traditional Lowcountry recipe of rice cooked in tomato sauce is similar to the African-American dish of Jollof Rice—rice cooked in a rich broth, soup, or stew to which meat is added. This recipe comes from *Sea Island Seasons,* a cookbook published by the Beaufort County Open Land Trust, Inc.

## RED RICE
*(pictured on page 223)*

5 slices bacon
1 medium onion, chopped
2 cups chopped, peeled tomato
1 cup long-grain rice, uncooked
1 cup finely chopped cooked ham
½ teaspoon salt
¼ teaspoon pepper
⅛ teaspoon hot sauce

Cook bacon in a large skillet until crisp; remove bacon, reserving 2 tablespoons drippings in skillet. Crumble bacon, and set aside. Cook onion in drippings over medium-high heat, stirring constantly, until tender. Add crumbled bacon, tomato, and remaining ingredients to skillet; cover and cook over low heat 10 minutes. Spoon mixture into a lightly greased 1-quart baking dish. Cover and bake at 350° for 1 hour, stirring every 15 minutes. Yield: 6 to 8 servings.

■ Opinions vary on the best recipe for Frogmore Stew, also known as Low-country Boil, Down Ya Stew, and Beaufort Stew.

## FROGMORE STEW
*(pictured on page 223)*

¼ cup Old Bay seasoning
4 pounds small red potatoes
2 pounds kielbasa or hot, smoked link sausage, cut into 1½-inch slices
6 ears fresh corn, halved
4 pounds unpeeled, large fresh shrimp
Additional Old Bay seasoning
Commercial cocktail sauce

Fill large container of a propane cooker halfway with water; add ¼ cup Old Bay seasoning. Bring to a boil, following manufacturer's instructions. Add potatoes, return to a boil, and cook 10 minutes. Add sausage and corn; return to a boil, and cook 10 minutes or until potatoes are tender. Add shrimp; cook 3 to 5 minutes or until shrimp turn pink. Remove with a slotted spoon onto a serving platter or newspaper-lined table. Serve with additional Old Bay seasoning and cocktail sauce. Yield: 12 servings.

**Note:** Frogmore Stew may be cooked indoors in a large Dutch oven on a cook top surface, over high heat, if desired.

■ Shrimp and grits are familiar fare to Lowcountry natives. Some people even enjoy a hearty casserole like this one for breakfast. Here's the dinner version.

## MISS HANNAH'S CASSEROLE

5 cups water
1½ pounds unpeeled, medium-size fresh shrimp
3¼ cups water
½ teaspoon salt
1 cup regular grits, uncooked
2 large eggs, lightly beaten
¼ cup milk
2 cloves garlic, minced
1½ cups (6 ounces) shredded Cheddar cheese, divided
Garnish: chopped fresh parsley

Bring 5 cups water to a boil; add shrimp, and cook 3 to 5 minutes or until shrimp turn pink. Drain well; rinse with cold water. Peel and devein shrimp; set aside.

Bring 3¼ cups water and salt to a boil in a medium saucepan; stir in grits. Cover, reduce heat, and simmer 10 minutes. Remove from heat.

Combine eggs and milk; gradually stir into grits. Stir in shrimp, garlic, and 1 cup cheese. Spoon into a lightly greased 11- x 7- x 1½-inch baking dish. Sprinkle with remaining ½ cup cheese. Bake at 350° for 30 minutes. Let stand 5 minutes. Garnish, if desired. Yield: 6 servings.
*The Gullah House Restaurant*
*St. Helena Island, South Carolina*

■ Magnolias Uptown/Down South Restaurant on East Bay Street in Charleston, South Carolina, serves food true to its name. Chef Donald Barickman uses some Southern ingredients, such as grits, in mouthwatering combinations.

## SPICY SHRIMP AND SAUSAGE OVER CREAMY GRITS WITH TASSO GRAVY

1½ pounds Italian sausage
1½ pounds unpeeled, medium-size fresh shrimp
2 tablespoons unsalted butter
Tasso Gravy
¼ cup whipping cream
Creamy Grits
¼ cup chopped fresh parsley

Prick sausage several times with a fork; place on rack in broiler pan. Bake at 350° for 20 minutes, turning after 10 minutes; set aside.

Peel and devein shrimp; cook in butter in a large skillet 3 to 5 minutes or until shrimp turn pink. Add sausage and 2½ cups Tasso Gravy; cook over medium heat 1 to 2 minutes. Stir in whipping cream; cook until thoroughly heated. If mixture is too thick, thin with water or chicken broth.

Spoon about 1 cup Creamy Grits into each shallow bowl; spoon shrimp-sausage mixture over grits. Sprinkle with parsley; serve with remaining Tasso Gravy. Yield: 8 to 10 servings.

### Tasso Gravy

¼ cup butter
½ cup all-purpose flour
3 (10¾-ounce) cans condensed chicken broth, undiluted
3 ounces tasso, chopped (about ¾ cup) *

Melt butter in a heavy saucepan over low heat; add flour, stirring until smooth. Cook over low heat, stirring constantly, 3 to 5 minutes or until lightly browned. Gradually add broth to mixture; cook over medium heat, stirring constantly with a whisk, until mixture is thickened. Bring to a boil; reduce heat, and simmer 10 to 15

---

## What is Frogmore Stew?

Frogmore Stew is a mixture of sausage, potatoes, corn, and shrimp, seasoned with a prepared spice mix such as Old Bay seasoning, and boiled until everything is tender and the shrimp have turned pink.

The name Frogmore is the namesake of an old fishing community on St. Helena Island, South Carolina. According to legend, a fisherman developed the recipe when he couldn't find fish for stew. He scavenged for leftovers, added what shrimp and crab he did catch, and the delicious result has become a hallmark recipe of the Lowcountry.

minutes, stirring occasionally. Stir in chopped tasso. Yield: 3¾ cups.

\* Tasso is cured pork or beef that has been richly seasoned with Cajun spices and smoked. Three ounces smoked, boneless pork loin, cubed, and ½ teaspoon hot sauce may be substituted for tasso.

### Creamy Grits

6 (10¾-ounce) cans condensed chicken broth, undiluted
2½ cups coarsely ground regular white grits, uncooked
1 cup whipping cream
½ teaspoon ground white pepper

Bring chicken broth to a boil in a large, heavy Dutch oven; stir in grits. Bring mixture to a boil. Cover, reduce heat, and simmer 25 minutes or until broth is absorbed and grits are soft, stirring frequently. Stir in whipping cream and pepper; cook 20 minutes over low heat, stirring frequently. Yield: about 10 cups.
*Donald Barickman*
*Magnolias*
*Uptown/Down South Restaurant*
*Charleston, South Carolina*

■ Traditionally, she-crab soup is made with crabmeat and crab roe (the eggs of the crab), and it's seasoned with sherry and Worcestershire sauce. Today, roe is no longer used, so here's an easy, updated version.

### PLANTATION CRAB SOUP

1 quart whipping cream
⅛ teaspoon salt
⅛ teaspoon pepper
¼ cup unsalted butter
⅓ cup all-purpose flour
2 cups Homemade Fish Stock or bottled clam juice
2 tablespoons lemon juice
1 teaspoon ground nutmeg
½ pound fresh lump crabmeat, drained
Garnish: chopped parsley
Sherry

Combine first 3 ingredients in a heavy saucepan; bring to a boil over medium heat. Reduce heat, and simmer, uncovered, 1 hour. Set aside.
Melt butter in a large, heavy saucepan over low heat; add flour, stirring until smooth. Cook 1 minute, stirring constantly. Gradually add Homemade Fish Stock; cook over medium heat until thickened. Stir in cream mixture, and cook until thoroughly heated. Add lemon juice, nutmeg, and crabmeat. Garnish, if desired. Spoon sherry over soup. Yield: 5½ cups.

### Homemade Fish Stock

1 pound mild fish bones
1 quart water
1 bunch fresh parsley stems
1 medium onion, thinly sliced

Combine all ingredients in a large saucepan. Bring to a boil; cover, reduce heat, and simmer 2 hours. Pour mixture through a wire-mesh strainer, discarding bones, parsley, and onion. Yield: 2½ cups.
*Jeff Tuttle*
*Pawleys Plantation*
*Golf and Country Club*
*Pawleys Island, South Carolina*

### Some Lowcountry Pronunciations

■ If you're looking for luck in this region, find a benne seed. Benne (pronounced BEHN-ee) seeds are actually sesame seeds. They were brought to America by slaves. Look for Benne Wafers from the Byrd Cookie Company, the oldest producer of the cookies in the area.
■ The first syllable of Beaufort, South Carolina, rhymes with the word "new" as opposed to the pronunciation of the first syllable of Beaufort, North Carolina, which rhymes with "row."

■ This gumbo is different from those traditionally made on the Gulf Coast. It's thickened with okra rather than a roux and boasts a rich tomato color.

### THE GULLAH HOUSE GUMBO

1 (3- to 3½-pound) broiler-fryer
1 onion, quartered
Celery leaves
1 teaspoon salt
6 slices bacon, finely chopped
1 pound smoked sausage, cut into ¼-inch slices
2 large onions, chopped
2 green peppers, chopped
2 stalks celery, chopped
3 cloves garlic, minced
3 tomatoes, peeled and chopped
1 (16-ounce) can tomato puree
1 cup fresh corn, cut from cob, or 1 (10-ounce) package frozen whole kernel corn, thawed
1 cup fresh okra, sliced, or 1 (10-ounce) package frozen sliced okra, thawed
1 tablespoon chopped fresh thyme or 1 teaspoon dried thyme

Combine first 4 ingredients in a Dutch oven; add water to cover. Bring to a boil; cover, reduce heat, and simmer 40 minutes or until chicken is tender. Remove chicken, reserving broth and discarding onion and celery leaves. Skin, bone, and cut chicken into bite-size pieces. Set aside.
Cook bacon and sausage in a large Dutch oven over medium heat until bacon is crisp. Remove bacon and sausage, reserving 1 tablespoon drippings in Dutch oven. Crumble bacon; set bacon and sausage aside. Add 2 onions, pepper, celery, and garlic to Dutch oven; cook over medium heat, stirring constantly, until vegetables are tender. Add chicken, bacon, sausage, reserved broth, tomatoes, and remaining ingredients. Bring to a boil; reduce heat, and simmer, uncovered, 1½ hours. Yield: 11 cups.
*The Gullah House Restaurant*
*St. Helena Island, South Carolina*

■ Seasonings make this crab soup a tasty departure from the more traditional ones.

## BEAUFORT CRAB SOUP

3 stalks celery, cut into 1-inch pieces
1 medium onion, quartered
1 medium leek (white portion only), quartered
1 carrot, cut into 1-inch pieces
1 shallot, halved
3 tablespoons butter, divided
1 clove garlic, minced
¼ cup all-purpose flour
2 cups chicken broth
2 cups milk
2 bay leaves
1 tablespoon Old Bay seasoning
Pinch of powdered saffron
1 teaspoon Worcestershire sauce
½ teaspoon salt
¼ teaspoon ground mace
¼ teaspoon ground red pepper
1 pound lump crabmeat, drained
¼ cup brandy
1 cup half-and-half
1½ teaspoons fresh chopped parsley

Position knife blade in food processor bowl; add first 5 ingredients, and process until finely chopped. Melt 2 tablespoons butter in a Dutch oven over medium heat. Add finely chopped vegetables and garlic; cover and cook 8 minutes, lifting lid to stir occasionally. Uncover and stir in flour; cook 1 minute, stirring constantly. Gradually stir in broth and milk. Bring to a simmer; add next 7 ingredients, and cook 10 minutes, stirring occasionally.

Melt remaining 1 tablespoon butter in a small skillet; add crabmeat. Toss gently, and cook over medium heat until thoroughly heated; add brandy. Stir crabmeat mixture and next 2 ingredients into soup; discard bay leaves. Yield: about 2 quarts.
*Kevin Adams*
*Dataw Island, South Carolina*

■ Wild mushrooms—including varieties such as enoki, shiitake, oyster, and chanterelle—are available at large supermarkets. Regular mushrooms may be substituted, but avoid mushrooms gathered from the wild.

## RAGOÛT OF WILD MUSHROOMS WITH CREAMY GRITS

2 cups fresh wild mushrooms, sliced
¼ cup olive oil
¼ cup finely chopped shallots
3 cups chicken broth
2 tablespoons chopped fresh parsley
2 tablespoons chopped fresh chervil or 2 teaspoons dried chervil
3 tablespoons unsalted butter, softened
¼ teaspoon salt
¼ teaspoon pepper
Creamy Grits
Thin sheets of fresh Parmesan cheese

Cook mushrooms in olive oil in a large skillet over medium heat, stirring constantly, 2 minutes. Add shallots; cook 1 minute. Gradually add broth; increase heat to high, and cook 25 minutes (broth will be reduced and slightly thickened). Stir in parsley and next 4 ingredients. Serve over Creamy Grits, and top with Parmesan cheese. Yield: 4 main-dish servings or 6 appetizer servings.

### Creamy Grits

4 cups milk
1 teaspoon salt
¼ teaspoon pepper
1 cup regular white grits, uncooked
1 cup whipping cream
3 tablespoons unsalted butter

Combine first 3 ingredients in a large saucepan; bring to a boil over medium heat. Stir in grits; cook 10 minutes or until soft. Add whipping cream and butter, stirring mixture until smooth. Grits may be thinned with a few drops of water if they are too thick. Yield: 4 cups.
*Louis Osteen*
*Louis's Charleston Grill*
*Charleston, South Carolina*

■ Kendall Levin based this recipe on one of her favorites from *Sea Island Seasons*. This cookbook, published by the Beaufort County Open Land Trust, Inc., raises money to preserve Beaufort County's scenic vistas of marshes, creeks, rivers, and islands.

## ISLAND TRIFLE

6 large eggs, beaten
¾ cup sugar
6 cups half-and-half
1½ teaspoons vanilla extract
1 (16-ounce) frozen pound cake, thawed and cut into ½-inch cubes
3 to 4 tablespoons bourbon, divided
2 Red Delicious apples, unpeeled, cored, and chopped
2 cups seedless green grapes, halved

Combine eggs and sugar in a heavy saucepan; gradually stir in half-and-half. Cook over medium heat, stirring constantly with a wire whisk, until mixture thickens and coats a spoon (about 30 minutes). Stir in vanilla.

Place half of cake in bottom of a 16-cup trifle bowl; sprinkle with 1½ tablespoons bourbon. Pour half of custard over cake. Repeat procedure with remaining cake, bourbon, and custard. Cover and chill 3 to 4 hours.

Combine chopped apple and grapes; serve with trifle. Yield: 12 to 15 servings.
*Kendall Levin*
*Beaufort, South Carolina*

# A Hands-On Halloween

Susan Logan plans an annual cookie-decorating session as the prelude to the Altadena Woods Halloween parade. Colorfully costumed children in the Birmingham, Alabama, suburb are dressed for a Sunday afternoon march around the neighborhood. The parade is complete with a firetruck, sirens, and a table of goodies at the end of the route. Everyone enjoys the decorated cookies as a finale.

Before the parade, she bakes cookies and the children decorate them.

## No Trick to These Treats

Keep things simple so that the children have a good time and don't have to worry about perfection. Here are some ideas:

**Ghoulish Sugar Cookies:** Use refrigerated sliceable sugar cookie dough, and cut into ¼-inch slices; shape into pumpkins, cats, witches's hats, and ghosts.

Decorate with Vanilla Buttercream Frosting or commercial ready-to-spread frosting; add desired amounts of paste food coloring to frosting. Place red cinnamon candies, candy corn, chocolate morsels, and raisins in foil cupcake pans or custard cups for easy access when decorating. Cookies can be stored in an airtight container for a few days.

**Halloween Pretzels:** Dip pretzels into melted vanilla-flavored candy coating. (This is often called almond bark although it contains no almonds.) Place pretzels on a baking sheet or wax paper to dry. When pretzels are dry, drizzle with orange and brown edible writing gel (available at supermarkets or variety stores). Let dry. Store pretzels in an airtight container for one day.

**Pumpkin Faces:** Melt vanilla-flavored candy coating. Stir in desired amount of orange paste food coloring. Dip cream-filled chocolate sandwich cookies into coating, and place on cookie sheets or wax paper to dry. Drizzle remaining candy coating over any spots not covered. Use brown edible writing gel to decorate pumpkin faces as desired. Store in an airtight container for a few days.

**Note:** For Halloween Pretzels and Pumpkin Faces, melt candy coating in a heavy saucepan, following package directions, or melt in a microwave-safe container. If the mixture gets too hot, the coating becomes gloppy.

## VANILLA BUTTERCREAM FROSTING

1½ cups butter or margarine, softened
4 cups sifted powdered sugar
2 tablespoons milk
Paste food coloring (optional)
1 teaspoon vanilla or almond extract

Beat butter at medium speed with an electric mixer until soft and creamy; gradually add sifted powdered sugar, beating until light and fluffy. Add 2 tablespoons milk and, if desired, food coloring; beat until frosting reaches spreading consistency. Stir in vanilla or almond extract. Yield: 3 cups.

# QUICK!
## 30-Minute Desserts

For a sweet ending to a busy day or a welcoming treat for unexpected company, try one of these time-saving desserts. By keeping the ingredients on hand, you can prepare these delicious treats in less than a half hour.

## EASY INDIVIDUAL TRIFLES

1 (3-ounce) package ladyfingers
¼ cup seedless raspberry jam
2 tablespoons dry sherry
2 tablespoons orange juice
2 cups milk
1 (3.4-ounce) package vanilla instant pudding mix
1 (8.5-ounce) can refrigerated instant whipped cream
2 tablespoons slivered almonds, toasted

Split ladyfingers in half lengthwise. Spread 1 teaspoon raspberry jam on bottom half of each ladyfinger; cover each with top, and cut in half crosswise. Arrange 4 filled halves in each individual serving dish; drizzle each with 1 teaspoon sherry and 1 teaspoon orange juice.

Combine milk and pudding mix in a 1-quart container; cover tightly, and shake 45 seconds. Pour over ladyfingers. Chill, if desired. Just before serving, top with whipped cream and almonds. Yield: 6 servings.

## HOT APPLE SPICE SUNDAE

2 tablespoons butter or margarine
2 tablespoons brown sugar
½ teaspoon ground cinnamon
1 (21-ounce) can apple pie filling
¼ cup chopped walnuts
1 quart vanilla ice cream

Melt butter in a saucepan; stir in brown sugar, cinnamon, and pie filling. Bring to a boil; remove from heat, and stir in walnuts. Serve warm over ice cream. Yield: 6 to 8 servings.

*Margaret L. Hunter*
*Princeton, Kentucky*

## PRALINE GRAHAMS

1 package graham crackers (⅓ of a 16-ounce box)
¾ cup butter or margarine
½ cup sugar
1 cup chopped pecans

Separate each graham cracker into four sections. Arrange in a jellyroll pan with edges touching. Melt butter in a saucepan; stir in sugar and pecans. Bring to a boil; cook 3 minutes, stirring frequently. Spread mixture evenly over graham crackers. Bake at 300° for 12 minutes. Remove from pan, and let cool on wax paper. Yield: 3½ dozen.
*Mrs. Dale Blackston*
*Ducktown, Tennessee*

## CREAMY PEANUT BUTTER FUDGE

3 cups sugar
¾ cup butter or margarine
⅔ cup evaporated milk
1 (10-ounce) package peanut butter-flavored morsels
1 (7-ounce) jar marshmallow creme
1 teaspoon vanilla extract

Combine first 3 ingredients in a large, heavy saucepan. Bring to a boil over medium-high heat, stirring constantly. Cover and cook 3 minutes without stirring; uncover and boil 5 minutes. (Do not stir.) Remove from heat; add morsels, stirring until morsels melt. Stir in marshmallow creme and vanilla. Pour into a buttered 13- x 9- x 2-inch pan. Place in freezer for 10 minutes, or let cool at room temperature. Yield: 3 pounds.          *Jan Spivey*
*Birmingham, Alabama*

## CHOCOLATE CREAM CHEESE PIE

1 (8-ounce) package cream cheese, softened
¾ cup sifted powdered sugar
¼ cup cocoa
1 (8-ounce) container frozen whipped topping, thawed
1 (6-ounce) chocolate-flavored crumb crust
½ cup coarsely chopped pecans

Combine first 3 ingredients in a mixing bowl; beat at medium speed with an electric mixer until soft and creamy. Add whipped topping, folding until smooth. Spread over crumb crust, and sprinkle with pecans. Serve immediately, or store in refrigerator. Yield: one 9-inch pie.

*Gleneerah Nesbit*
*Alexandria, Virginia*

# Go Nuts For Peanut Brittle

The closest most people come to making peanut brittle is watching professionals make it in candy store windows. However, it's easier than you think. The key is to bring the sugar, corn syrup, water, and peanuts to a temperature of 300°. Once it has reached the correct temperature, stir in butter and baking soda, and pour into a buttered pan.

Ruth Clegg, from Fort Worth, Texas, sent her recipe, which called for raw peanuts, but they can be difficult to find. So try our substitutions.

## PEANUT BRITTLE

2 cups sugar
½ cup light corn syrup
¼ cup boiling water
2 cups dry-roasted peanuts *
1 tablespoon butter or margarine
1 teaspoon baking soda

Combine first 3 ingredients in a large, heavy saucepan; cook over low heat, stirring constantly, until sugar dissolves. Cover and cook over medium heat 2 to 3 minutes to melt sugar crystals on sides of pan. Uncover, add peanuts, and cook, stirring occasionally, to hard crack stage (300°). Stir in butter and soda. Pour into a buttered 15- x 10- x 1-inch jellyroll pan, spreading thinly. Let brittle cool, and break into pieces. Yield: 1½ pounds.

* 1 cup pecan pieces and 1 cup dry-roasted peanuts may be substituted for 2 cups dry-roasted peanuts.

---

### No Candy Thermometer?

If you don't have a candy thermometer, test for doneness by dropping a small amount of syrup into a cup of very cold water. When the correct temperature is reached, the syrup will separate into threads that are hard and brittle. If the threads are still pliable or hard but not brittle, continue cooking the mixture.

---

# Seeds Of Change

Everyone knows that Christopher Columbus's journey was one of courageous adventure aboard tiny ships, with the exciting discovery of unexpected lands and cultures. So where do mundane-by-comparison corn, potatoes, and sugar fit in? Corn, potatoes, and sugar were "seeds" or elements of change found long ago by Columbus that set the New World in motion.

## RED ROCK CANDY

2 cups sugar
1 cup light corn syrup
½ cup water
½ cup red cinnamon candies
1 teaspoon butter or margarine

Combine first 3 ingredients in a heavy 3-quart saucepan; cook over low heat, stirring constantly, until sugar dissolves. Cook over medium heat, stirring often, about 10 minutes or until mixture reaches soft ball stage or a candy thermometer reaches 234°.

Add cinnamon candies; cook, stirring constantly, to hard crack stage or a candy thermometer reaches 300°. Remove from heat; stir in butter. Quickly pour into a buttered 13- x 9- x 2-inch pan; cool. To serve, break into small pieces. Yield: 1½ pounds.

*Betty Lamb*
*Dothan, Alabama*

## CREAMY POTATO SALAD

7 cups peeled, cubed red potatoes
    (about 2 pounds)
4 slices bacon, cooked and
    crumbled
3 hard-cooked eggs, peeled and
    chopped
1 (2-ounce) jar diced pimiento,
    drained
½ cup sliced green onions
½ cup chopped green pepper
½ cup chopped celery
3 tablespoons chopped fresh parsley
    or cilantro
Creamy Dressing

Cook potatoes in salted boiling water
to cover 10 minutes or until tender;
drain. Combine potatoes and remaining ingredients in a large bowl. Toss
potato mixture gently; cover and chill.
Yield: 8 servings.

### Creamy Dressing

¾ cup mayonnaise or salad
    dressing
½ cup plain yogurt
1 tablespoon sugar
1 tablespoon Dijon mustard
1 tablespoon cider vinegar
1½ teaspoons salt
½ teaspoon dry mustard
¼ teaspoon celery seeds
¼ teaspoon paprika
⅛ teaspoon garlic powder

Combine all ingredients; mixing well
Yield: 1¼ cups.     *Cynda A. Spoon*
            *Broken Arrow, Oklahoma*

### CORN RELISH

¼ cup sugar
1 tablespoon cornstarch
1 teaspoon ground turmeric
½ teaspoon celery seeds
¼ cup white vinegar
¼ cup water
1 tablespoon chopped onion
1 (10-ounce) package frozen whole
    kernel corn, thawed
2 tablespoons chopped green pepper
1 tablespoon diced pimiento

Combine first 4 ingredients in a saucepan; add vinegar and water, stirring
until smooth. Add onion. Cook over
medium heat, stirring constantly, until
mixture boils; boil 1 minute. Remove
from heat; stir in corn and remaining
ingredients. Cover and chill. Serve
with meats. Yield: 1⅔ cups.
            *Dorothy L. Driggers*
            *Claxton, Georgia*

---

# ON THE LIGHT SIDE

# Sausage Sees
# The Light

Move over, impostors; make room for
these positively lean and sassy sausages. Because commercial "light"
sausages often boast low fat percent-
ages that conceal their high-fat content, we felt challenged to develop a
genuinely lean (less than 30% total fat
and less than 10% saturated fat) product that beats the competition.

We developed a basic meat mixture
of ground white turkey meat and
ground pork loin. Each spice blend
was added to 1 pound of this base to
yield Kielbasa (Polish), Country, Italian, Chorizo (Mexican), and Andouille
(Cajun) sausages. We used a food
processor with metal blade to grind
the meat.

Low-fat ground beef product is
added to give flavor to the basic meat
base in Kielbasa (traditionally a pork-
based sausage).

We used a sausage funnel with a
¾-inch tip (¾-cup capacity) to stuff
the sausage casings. (Purchase sausage casings from a local butcher.)
Simply fit one open end of the casing
over the tip of the funnel. While holding the casing firmly in place with one
hand, use a wooden spoon to push the
meat mixture through. Use kitchen
shears to snip off the ends of the casings, leaving about 1½ inches at each
end for twisting or tying off.

## BASIC MEAT MIXTURE

4 pounds boneless, skinless turkey
    breast
2 pounds boneless pork loin
2 tablespoons browning-and-
    seasoning sauce
1 teaspoon salt

Position knife blade in food processor
bowl; add half of turkey, pork, and
seasonings. Process until smooth. Repeat procedure with remaining ingredients. Yield: 6 pounds (585 calories
[24.6% from fat] per pound).

## CHORIZO

1 pound Basic Meat Mixture
¼ cup white vinegar
1 tablespoon dry sherry
2 teaspoons paprika
2 teaspoons chili powder
½ teaspoon dried oregano
½ teaspoon ground cumin
¼ teaspoon pepper
⅛ teaspoon ground cinnamon
⅛ teaspoon ground cloves
Pinch of ground coriander
Pinch of ground ginger
½ teaspoon browning-and-
    seasoning sauce
2 cloves garlic, crushed
1 yard sausage casing
½ cup water

Combine first 14 ingredients; divide
into four (4-ounce) portions. Cut casing into four (8-inch) pieces; slip one
end of each casing over sausage funnel
tip. Force each portion through funnel
into each casing; twist ends.

Bring water to a boil in a nonstick
skillet; add sausage. Cover, reduce
heat, and simmer 10 minutes. Uncover and cook over medium heat 5
minutes or until browned, turning occasionally. Yield: 4 servings (190 calories [23% from fat] per sausage).

□ *30.8g protein, 4.9g fat (1.4g saturated), 3.7g carbohydrate, 0.8g fiber,
88mg cholesterol, 174mg sodium, and
28mg calcium.*

## COUNTRY SAUSAGE

1 pound Basic Meat Mixture
1 teaspoon rubbed sage
½ teaspoon black pepper
¼ teaspoon dried crushed red
   pepper
Vegetable cooking spray

Combine first 4 ingredients; shape into eight (2-ounce) patties. Coat a nonstick skillet with cooking spray; place over medium heat until hot. Cook sausage patties 3 minutes on each side or until browned. Yield: 4 servings (172 calories [23% from fat] per patty).

□ 30.3g protein, 4.5g fat (1.4g saturated), 0.3g carbohydrate, 0.1g fiber, 88mg cholesterol, 158mg sodium, and 16mg calcium.

## KIELBASA

Hickory chips
1 pound Basic Meat Mixture
4 ounces low-fat ground beef
1 clove garlic, crushed
½ teaspoon finely chopped onion
1½ teaspoons ground coriander
½ teaspoon ground mace
½ teaspoon sugar
1⅛ yards sausage casing

Soak chips in water 1 hour; drain. Wrap chips in aluminum foil, and make several holes on top and sides of foil. Light gas grill on one side; place foil-wrapped chips directly on hot coals. Place grill rack over chips, and place a pan of water on rack. Let burn 10 to 15 minutes.
   Position knife blade in food processor bowl; add Basic Meat Mixture and next 6 ingredients. Process until smooth, stopping once to scrape down sides. Divide into five (4-ounce) portions. Cut casing into five (8-inch) pieces; slip one end of each casing over sausage funnel tip. Using the handle of a wooden spoon, force each portion of meat mixture through funnel into each casing; twist ends.

Arrange sausage on prepared grill rack opposite water; cook, covered, 45 minutes or until internal meat thermometer registers 170°, turning occasionally. Yield: 5 servings (170 calories [27% from fat] per sausage).

□ 28.6g protein, 5.1g fat (1.6g saturated), 1.4g carbohydrate, 0.1g fiber, 85mg cholesterol, 174mg sodium, and 15mg calcium.

## ITALIAN SAUSAGE

1 pound Basic Meat Mixture
1 teaspoon fennel seeds, crushed
¾ teaspoon coriander seeds,
   crushed
¾ teaspoon dried parsley flakes
½ teaspoon pepper
¼ teaspoon salt
⅛ teaspoon garlic powder
1 yard sausage casing
Vegetable cooking spray

Combine first 7 ingredients; divide into four (4-ounce) portions. Cut casing into four (8-inch) pieces; slip one end of each casing over sausage funnel tip. Force each portion of meat mixture through funnel into each casing; twist ends. Coat a large nonstick skillet with cooking spray. Place over medium heat until hot. Cook sausage until browned, turning occasionally. Yield: 4 servings (174 calories [23% from fat] per link or 2 patties).

□ 31.3g protein, 4.6g fat (1.3g saturated), 2.1g carbohydrate, 0.9g fiber, 88mg cholesterol, 304mg sodium, and 23mg calcium.

**Note:** To make eight (2-ounce) patties, cook meat in a nonstick skillet coated with cooking spray over medium heat 3 minutes on each side.

## ANDOUILLE

1 pound Basic Meat Mixture
¼ teaspoon pepper
¼ teaspoon rubbed sage
¼ teaspoon ground marjoram
¼ teaspoon dried thyme
Dash of ground bay leaves
⅛ teaspoon minced garlic
1 tablespoon dry white wine
1 yard sausage casing
½ cup water

Combine first 8 ingredients; divide into four (4-ounce) portions. Cut casing into four (8-inch) pieces; slip one end of each casing over sausage funnel tip. Force each portion of meat mixture through funnel into each casing; twist ends.
   Bring water to a boil in a nonstick skillet; add sausage. Cover, reduce heat, and simmer 10 minutes. Uncover and cook 5 minutes or until browned, turning occasionally. Yield: 4 servings (174 calories [22% from fat] per link or 2 patties).

□ 30.3g protein, 4.4g fat (1.4g saturated), 1.3g carbohydrate, 0.1g fiber, 88mg cholesterol, 162mg sodium, and 17mg calcium.

**Note:** To make eight (2-ounce) patties, cook meat in a nonstick skillet coated with cooking spray over medium heat 3 minutes on each side or until browned.

## LIGHT MENU

# Serve An Indian Summer Supper

When Mother Nature grants you a spell of unseasonably warm weather this fall, enjoy an afternoon outdoors followed by a simple supper to re-energize. Bean-and-Cornbread Casserole, along with a healthy side dish of

Apple-Carrot Slaw, is a satisfying way to replenish your body.

This easy menu packs plenty of vital complex carbohydrates and 9.8 grams of fiber for under 630 calories and 30% fat. Complete the meal with commercial chocolate nonfat frozen yogurt and Mocha Sauce for a refreshing way to really cool down.

## SIMPLE SUPPER FOR EIGHT

**Apple-Carrot Slaw
Bean-and-Cornbread Casserole
Mocha Sauce With
Chocolate Yogurt**

## APPLE-CARROT SLAW

4   cups shredded cabbage
2   cups shredded carrots
1¾  cups unpeeled, chopped Red
    Delicious apple
⅔   cup fat-free mayonnaise
2   tablespoons sugar
⅓   cup white vinegar
1   teaspoon celery seeds
8   cabbage leaves (optional)

Combine first 3 ingredients in a large bowl. Combine mayonnaise and next 3 ingredients; pour over cabbage mixture, tossing gently to coat. Cover and chill. Serve on cabbage leaves, if desired. Yield: 8 servings (72 calories [3.7% from fat] per 1-cup serving).

□ *1.1g protein, 0.3g fat (0g saturated), 17.6g carbohydrate, 3.2g fiber, 0mg cholesterol, 275mg sodium, and 44mg calcium.*

## BEAN-AND-CORNBREAD CASSEROLE

Vegetable cooking spray
1 cup chopped onion
½ cup chopped green pepper
2 cloves garlic, minced
1 (16-ounce) can kidney beans, drained
1 (16-ounce) can pinto beans, drained
1 (16-ounce) can no-salt-added tomatoes, undrained and chopped
1 (8-ounce) can no-salt-added tomato sauce
1 teaspoon chili powder
½ teaspoon pepper
½ teaspoon prepared mustard
⅛ teaspoon hot sauce
1 cup yellow cornmeal
1 cup all-purpose flour
2½ teaspoons baking powder
½ teaspoon salt
1 tablespoon sugar
1¼ cups skim milk
½ cup egg substitute
3 tablespoons vegetable oil
1 (8½-ounce) can no-salt-added, cream-style corn
Garnish: green pepper strips

Coat a large, nonstick skillet with cooking spray; place over medium-high heat until hot. Add onion, green pepper, and garlic; cook, stirring constantly, until tender. Stir in kidney beans and next 7 ingredients. Cover and cook 5 minutes; pour into a 13- x 9- x 2-inch baking dish coated with cooking spray. Set aside.

Combine cornmeal and next 4 ingredients in a medium bowl. Combine milk and next 3 ingredients; add to dry mixture, stirring until dry ingredients are moistened. Spoon evenly over bean mixture to within 1 inch of edges of dish. Bake at 375° for 30 to 35 minutes or until cornbread is done. Cut into 8 squares. Garnish with green pepper strips, if desired. Yield: 8 servings (397 calories [14.7% from fat] per serving).

□ *17.1g protein, 6.5g fat (1.2g saturated), 69.2g carbohydrate, 6.6g fiber, 1mg cholesterol, 564mg sodium, and 181mg calcium.*

## MOCHA SAUCE
## WITH CHOCOLATE YOGURT

½ cup sugar
⅓ cup unsweetened cocoa
⅓ cup light corn syrup
⅓ cup water
2½ tablespoons semisweet chocolate morsels
1 teaspoon instant coffee granules
½ teaspoon vanilla extract
½ gallon chocolate nonfat frozen yogurt

Combine first 4 ingredients in a saucepan. Bring to a boil over medium heat, stirring frequently. Add chocolate morsels and coffee granules, stirring just until morsels melt. Remove from heat and cool. Stir in vanilla. Spoon over nonfat frozen yogurt. Yield: 16 servings (153 calories [5% from fat] per 1 tablespoon sauce with ½ cup chocolate nonfat frozen yogurt).

□ *4.4g protein, 0.9g fat (0.5g saturated), 33.3g carbohydrate, 0g fiber, 0mg cholesterol, 76mg sodium, and 147mg calcium.*

## Good Old Greens Go Lean

There's hardly a food as naturally nutritious as greens. But unfortunately, fat overwhelms the healthy greens in many traditional Southern recipes.

Here, we feature a reduced-fat, cholesterol-free recipe for greens—not collard or turnip greens, but kale. Kale rates higher in vitamin A (in the form of beta carotene) than the other two greens. To clean kale, rinse thoroughly, but do not soak, to preserve its rich supply of water-soluble B-complex and C vitamins. Our recipe calls for gentle steaming to enhance flavor and retain nutrients, color, and texture.

### KALE WITH TOMATO AND ONION

1½ pounds fresh kale
2 teaspoons vegetable oil
1 cup chopped tomato
¾ cup chopped onion
2 teaspoons lemon juice
1 clove garlic, minced
½ to ¾ teaspoon pepper

Remove stems from kale. Wash leaves thoroughly (do not dry); tear into small pieces. Place wet kale into a large Dutch oven (do not add water). Cook, uncovered, 20 to 30 minutes or until tender.

Heat oil in a large skillet over low heat. Add tomato and onion; cook over medium-high heat, stirring constantly, until tender. Add cooked greens and remaining ingredients; cook, stirring constantly, 4 to 5 minutes. Yield: 7 servings (86 calories [26% from fat] per 1-cup serving).

□ 4.3g protein, 2.5g fat (0.4g saturated), 15.2g carbohydrate, 2.6g fiber, 0mg cholesterol, 52mg sodium, and 161mg calcium.

| COMPARE THE NUTRIENTS | | |
|---|---|---|
| (per serving) | | |
| | Traditional | Light |
| Calories | 162 | 86 |
| Fat | 11.7g | 2.5g |
| Cholesterol | 13mg | 0mg |

## There's Plenty Of Spaghetti

Whether you're serving spaghetti to family, friends, or a crowd, try Easy Spaghetti Meat Sauce. Flo Burtnett of Gage, Oklahoma, shared this recipe for 4; with some adjustments, it can also serve 25. When serving numbers in between, double or triple the recipe for 4. When doubling the recipe, don't automatically double the water. Larger batches of sauce need less water proportionately than smaller ones.

This recipe for 25 fills an 8-quart Dutch oven almost to the top. So if you're serving more than 25 people and don't have institutional cooking equipment, make several batches.

### EASY SPAGHETTI MEAT SAUCE FOR 4

1 pound ground beef
1 (8-ounce) can tomato sauce
1 cup water
2 tablespoons dried onion flakes
2 teaspoons Worcestershire sauce
½ teaspoon garlic powder
¼ teaspoon pepper
1 (14-ounce) jar spaghetti sauce (1⅔ cups)
8 ounces spaghetti, uncooked
Grated Parmesan cheese

Brown ground beef in a small Dutch oven, stirring until it crumbles; drain well. Stir in tomato sauce, water, dried onion flakes, Worcestershire sauce, garlic powder, and pepper. Bring to a boil over medium heat. Cover, reduce heat, and simmer 20 minutes, stirring occasionally. Add spaghetti sauce, and simmer, uncovered, 20 minutes, stirring occasionally. Cook spaghetti according to package directions, and drain. Spoon meat sauce over cooked spaghetti, and sprinkle with Parmesan cheese. Yield: 4 servings.

**Note:** Sauce can be frozen in an airtight container up to 3 months.

## EASY SPAGHETTI MEAT SAUCE FOR 25

6 pounds ground beef
3 (15-ounce) cans tomato sauce
4 cups water
¾ cup dried onion flakes
¼ cup Worcestershire sauce
1 tablespoon garlic powder
1½ teaspoons pepper
3 (28-ounce) jars spaghetti sauce
3 (16-ounce) packages spaghetti, uncooked
Grated Parmesan cheese

Brown ground beef in an 8-quart Dutch oven, stirring until it crumbles. Drain well. Stir in tomato sauce and next 5 ingredients. Bring to a boil over medium heat. Cover, reduce heat, and simmer 20 minutes, stirring occasionally. Add spaghetti sauce, and simmer, uncovered, 20 minutes, stirring occasionally. Cook spaghetti according to package directions; drain. Spoon meat sauce over cooked spaghetti, and sprinkle with Parmesan cheese. Yield: 25 servings.

**Note:** Sauce can be frozen in an airtight container up to 3 months.

### Complete the Menu

■ Allow 1 cup tossed salad (about ¾ cup salad greens and ¼ cup other salad ingredients) per person. When serving a crowd, it's best to buy salad greens by weight. A pound of greens yields about 5 cups of torn leaves (enough for 6 servings).
■ Plan on 16 to 32 servings from a 16-ounce bottle of salad dressing because most people like 1 to 2 tablespoons on a salad.
■ Allow two slices of French bread per person. A 16-ounce loaf of French bread yields about 16 (1-inch) slices.
■ Count on 1½ gallons of tea to serve 25. Fill 20-ounce glasses with ice, and add 1 cup of tea to each glass.

# The Versatile Tomatillo

The Southwestern food boom has withstood the test of time. No longer a trend, this food phenomenon shows no signs of waning. Interest in things Southwestern has also introduced a newcomer to Southern produce sections in supermarkets—tomatillos (tohm-ah-TEE-ohs).

Available year-round, the best are firm and dry with parchment-like husks that show no signs of deterioration. Tomatillos vary from the size of a cherry tomato to the size of a peach; so when purchasing them for recipes, buy by the pound. Remove the husk, and wash away the sticky residue to uncover what appears to be a simple green tomato.

Tomatillos have a sharply acidic flavor when served raw. Use them in salads or on sandwiches, and try Open-Faced Tomatillo Sandwiches for an easy lunch recipe.

Cook tomatillos to soften their pulp and bring out their lemon-herb flavor. Tomatillo Salsa makes the perfect accompaniment to grilled or pan-seared fish, as well as tortillas, tacos, and tostadas.

### TOMATILLO SALSA

¾ pound fresh tomatillos
½ cup finely chopped onion
½ cup finely chopped celery
¼ cup finely chopped green pepper
2 cloves garlic, minced
2 tablespoons olive oil
1 (4-ounce) can chopped green chiles, undrained
½ cup clam juice
2 tablespoons lime juice
1 teaspoon ground cumin
1 teaspoon chopped fresh cilantro or parsley
½ teaspoon dried oregano
¼ teaspoon salt
¼ teaspoon ground white pepper
¼ teaspoon ground red pepper

Remove husks, rinse, and finely chop tomatillos. Cook tomatillos and next 4 ingredients in olive oil in a large skillet over medium heat, stirring frequently, 5 minutes. Add green chiles and remaining ingredients; simmer, uncovered, 15 minutes, stirring often. Remove from heat; cool. Serve with fish, chicken, or chips. Yield: 2 cups.

*Ginny Munsterman*
*Garland, Texas*

### TOMATILLO SOUP WITH CRUNCHY JICAMA

½ pound fresh tomatillos
¼ cup chopped onion
2 tablespoons seeded, chopped poblano peppers
1 tablespoon chopped fresh cilantro or parsley
1 tablespoon lime juice
½ teaspoon salt
½ teaspoon ground cumin
¼ teaspoon sugar
1 clove garlic, minced
1 cup half-and-half
1 cup peeled, finely chopped jicama
Garnishes: tomatillo slices, fresh cilantro sprigs

Remove husks, and rinse tomatillos. Place in a saucepan; add water to cover. Bring to a boil; reduce heat, and simmer 6 minutes or until tender. Drain and cool.

Combine tomatillos, onion, and next 7 ingredients in container of an electric blender; process until smooth, stopping once to scrape down sides. Transfer mixture to a large bowl; stir in half-and-half and jicama. Cover and chill. Serve in individual bowls; garnish, if desired. Yield: 3 cups.

## OPEN-FACED TOMATILLO SANDWICHES

2 small fresh tomatillos
1 (6-ounce) package sliced mozzarella cheese
4 (¾-inch-thick) slices Italian bread, toasted
1½ tablespoons commercial pesto
1 small tomato, thinly sliced
Cracked black pepper

Remove husks, rinse, and thinly slice tomatillos; set aside. Arrange cheese evenly on bread slices; broil 5 inches from heat (with electric oven door partially opened) 2 minutes or until cheese melts. Gently spread pesto evenly over melted cheese. Top with tomatillos and tomato; sprinkle with pepper. Serve immediately. Yield: 4 servings.

# The Fruits Of His Labor

If Robert Barnum invites you over for dinner, you should go. But expect a refreshingly different menu and an evening that's, well, a little exotic. He owns Possum Trot Nursery, a tropical fruit farm near Homestead, Florida.

"I cook by art—not science," he explains. Today, he handily stuffs chayotes, mixes Florida Fruit Punch, and checks on the chicken grilling just outside the door. His artist's palette of flavors includes ingredients from many cuisines. For his barbecue sauce, he mixes Asian teriyaki flavors with Florida limes and carambola for a sweet-sour chicken. His Avocado Salad is a surprising blend of capers, lime juice, herbs, and Italy's Gorgonzola cheese.

"The secret to a good recipe is flavor and texture. Every part of the tongue should be touched by what you cook," he says. "You've got four basic things to consider: acid, salt, sugar, and the body of the food. You have to

hit the front, middle, sides, back, and top of the palate. You must create intricate flavors and learn how to balance all that. *That's* cooking in a nutshell."

Tired of having a "bored palate," he threw himself into cooking years ago and even worked at a restaurant in Grenada before coming back to his family's nursery. Passion fruit, avocado, guava, carambola, and other delicacies from the nursery provide inspiration for his cooking. Here, he shares some of his recipes.

For more information on exotic fruits, see "From Our Kitchen To Yours" on page 248.

## A MENU FROM SOUTH FLORIDA FOR EIGHT

Avocado Salad
Carambola-Glazed Barbecued Chicken
Stuffed Chayote
Boniato Chips
Tropical Trilogy Parfait
Guava Puffs
Florida Fruit Punch

■ Robert Barnum says October is a prime month to get good avocados from Florida.

### AVOCADO SALAD

1 ripe avocado, cubed
2 tomatoes, cubed
1 small onion, sliced
3 to 4 ounces Gorgonzola cheese, crumbled
3 tablespoons fresh lime juice
1 tablespoon olive oil
1 tablespoon balsamic or red wine vinegar
2 teaspoons capers
½ teaspoon seasoned salt
½ teaspoon pepper
½ teaspoon garlic powder
½ teaspoon dried marjoram
½ teaspoon dried thyme
8 cups mixed salad greens
Garnish: carambola slices

Combine first 13 ingredients in a medium bowl. Arrange salad greens on individual plates, and top with avocado mixture. Garnish, if desired. Yield: 8 servings.

■ Carambola, also called "star fruit," is good eaten out of hand or used as a garnish. Here, Robert Barnum blends it with juice and other seasonings to make a basting sauce.

### CARAMBOLA-GLAZED BARBECUED CHICKEN

2 (3- to 3½-pound) broiler-fryers, quartered
1 cup corn oil
1 cup white wine vinegar
½ cup dry sherry or white wine
1 teaspoon garlic powder
1 teaspoon seasoned salt
1 teaspoon pepper
½ teaspoon poultry seasoning
2 carambolas, sliced
¼ cup lime juice
¼ cup honey
2 tablespoons white wine vinegar
1 tablespoon soy sauce
1 clove garlic
½ teaspoon seasoned salt
½ teaspoon pepper
Dash of hot sauce

Place chicken quarters in a shallow dish. Combine corn oil and next 6 ingredients. Reserve 1 cup of marinade, and set aside. Pour remaining marinade over chicken. Cover and refrigerate 3 to 4 hours. Remove chicken from marinade; reserve marinade. Grill chicken, uncovered, over medium coals (300° to 350°) for 1 hour, turning occasionally and basting with marinade after each turn.

Place carambolas in container of an electric blender; add lime juice and remaining ingredients. Process until smooth, stopping to scrape down sides. Gradually add 1 cup reserved marinade; blend until smooth. Brush glaze over chicken; grill 20 additional minutes or until chicken is done, turning occasionally and basting with any additional glaze after each turn. Yield: 8 servings.

■ In Louisiana, chayotes are called "mirlitons." Shaped like a pear, chayote may be cooked like squash.

## STUFFED CHAYOTE

4 chayotes, cut in half
3 slices bacon, chopped
1 small onion, chopped
1 clove garlic, minced
½ teaspoon salt
¼ teaspoon pepper
¼ teaspoon dried thyme
¼ teaspoon dried marjoram
¼ cup (1 ounce) shredded Cheddar cheese
2 tablespoons soft breadcrumbs
2 tablespoons chopped fresh parsley
2 teaspoons grated Parmesan cheese

Cook chayotes in boiling water to cover 10 minutes; drain. Let cool to touch. Using a melon baller or spoon, carefully scoop out pulp, leaving shells intact; set pulp and shells aside.

Cook bacon and next 6 ingredients in a large skillet over medium-high heat until bacon is crisp; drain. Combine bacon mixture, chayote pulp, Cheddar cheese, breadcrumbs, and parsley; spoon into shells, and sprinkle with Parmesan cheese. Bake at 350° for 45 minutes or until tender. Yield: 8 servings.

■ Boniato chips are similar to potato chips, but they have more flavor. The boniato is not quite as easy to peel as a potato.

## BONIATO CHIPS

2 boniatos, peeled (about 1½ pounds)
Vegetable or peanut oil

Using a very sharp knife, slice boniatos crosswise into ⅛-inch slices; place in cool water to prevent discoloring. Pour oil to depth of 2 inches into a Dutch oven; heat to 375°. Drain boniato slices on paper towels, and fry 2 to 3 minutes or until golden brown. Drain slices on paper towels. Yield: 6 to 8 servings.

■ This parfait combines three fruits—banana, pineapple, and mango. Robert Barnum often uses other combinations, such as apple, peach, and pear.

## TROPICAL TRILOGY PARFAIT

1 (14-ounce) can sweetened condensed milk
¼ cup lime juice
¼ cup passion fruit juice
1 cup whipping cream
⅓ cup sifted powdered sugar
½ teaspoon cream of tartar
2 bananas, sliced
2 cups fresh pineapple cubes
1 mango, peeled and finely chopped
Garnishes: carambola slices, maraschino cherries

Combine sweetened condensed milk, lime juice, and passion fruit juice in a large mixing bowl; beat at low speed with an electric mixer until thickened.

Beat whipping cream, powdered sugar, and cream of tartar at medium speed with an electric mixer until stiff peaks form. Fold into condensed milk mixture. Carefully fold in fruits; spoon into parfait glasses, and garnish, if desired. Serve with cookies or Guava Puffs. Yield: 8 servings.

■ Goya is the company most likely to market guava paste in the South. Ask your grocer if he stocks the paste or can order it for you.

## GUAVA PUFFS

1 (17¼-ounce) package commercial frozen puff pastry, thawed *
1 (14-ounce) can guava paste

Roll each sheet of pastry dough to a 12-inch square; cut into 16 (3-inch) squares. Place 1 teaspoon paste in center of each pastry square. Brush edges with water; fold edges to form a triangle, pressing to seal. Crimp edges with fork; place on ungreased baking sheets. Bake at 350° for 20 to 22 minutes. Yield: 32 pastries.

* 2 (8-ounce) cans refrigerated crescent dinner rolls may be substituted for frozen puff pastry. Roll each can of rolls into a 12-inch square, and cut into 16 (3-inch) squares. Fill with paste and bake at 350° for 10 to 12 minutes.

**Note:** Puffs may be brushed with egg whites before baking.

■ Passion fruit can be expensive, so don't be afraid to try this beverage without it or substitute other juices.

## FLORIDA FRUIT PUNCH

2 quarts fresh orange juice
1 quart fresh grapefruit juice
1⅓ cups sugar
1 cup fresh lime juice
1 cup passion fruit juice
⅓ cup grenadine
10 cups water
2 cups rum (optional)
Garnishes: orange and carambola slices, maraschino cherries

Combine first 7 ingredients, stirring until sugar dissolves; chill. Add rum, if desired. Serve over ice. Skewer orange and carambola slices and maraschino cherries onto wooden picks for garnish, if desired. Yield: 6½ quarts.

# From Our Kitchen To Yours

Passion fruit, mango, chayote, and boniato might be unfamiliar to you now, but they won't be strangers for long. These newcomers to the produce section of many supermarkets are waiting to be discovered.

Before testing recipes using this exotic produce (beginning on page 246), the Test Kitchens staff had many questions about taste, selection, storage, and preparation. We found the taste sensations refreshing and the preparation simple. It's just as easy to cook a boniato as it is a sweet potato, and chayote can be prepared like summer squash. Here is a guide from our tropical food adventure.

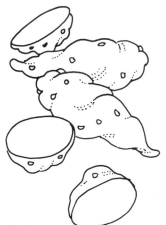

## Boniato

Boniato (bow-knee-AHH-toe) or Cuban sweet potato, is an irregularly shaped, starchy tuber resembling a cross between a Louisiana yam and an Idaho russet. When cooked, the white flesh has a creamy texture with a nutty, mildly sweet flavor.

**Selection and storage:** Choose rock-hard vegetables without shrinkage or decay. Try to buy small ones; they're more tender. The skin may have tones of pink, purple, cream, or red. Keep at room temperature in a well-ventilated area no more than a few days.

**Preparation:** To prevent discoloration, peel under running water; then immediately drop peeled portions into cold water. To boil, cover with water. Do not overwhelm the subtle flavor with heavy seasoning. Cook as you would a sweet potato—bake, boil, fry, mash, or combine in custards, puddings, pies, and muffins.

**Serving suggestions:** Season mashed or cubed boniato with garlic butter and cilantro; or bake at 400° for 1 hour (skin will be crunchy and hard). Enrich the pulp with cream, honey, and allspice.

**Substitution:** Sweet potato.

**Nutrition:** Good source of vitamin C.

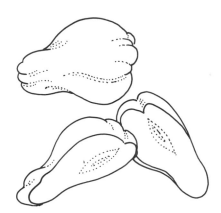

## Chayote

Chayote (chy-OH-tay), also known as mirliton, is a firm-textured, gourdlike fruit that resembles a pale-green gnarled pear with uneven furrows running its length. The skin may be fairly smooth, or have a hairbrush-like covering of prickles. Beneath the pale-green skin is a white, bland-tasting flesh, which surrounds a soft seed. Its taste and texture are between a cucumber and a zucchini.

**Selection and storage:** Choose firm, unblemished ones; smaller chayotes are slightly more tender. Refrigerate vegetables in a plastic bag up to two weeks.

**Preparation:** Prepare as you would summer squash, but allow longer cooking time (20 to 25 minutes) due to the firmer texture. Peel chayotes either before or after cooking. Use a vegetable peeler on uncooked ones. A slippery substance may ooze out as you peel raw chayote; it's neater to work under running water. The fruit can be boiled, steamed, pureed for soups, or stuffed. Before stuffing, partially cook fruit in boiling water 10 minutes.

**Serving suggestions:** Slice peeled fruit, and use instead of water chestnuts in stir-frys; peel, shred, and combine with shredded carrots, and cook quickly in herb butter; or grate peeled fruit, soak in cold water 10 minutes, squeeze out water, and use raw in slaw. The flavor blends well with seafood or ham.

**Substitution:** Summer squash.

**Nutrition:** A good source of vitamin C and potassium.

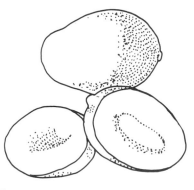

## Mango

Mango (MANG-go), called the "apple" of the tropics, can be oval, round, or kidney-shaped. As the fruit ripens, the thin, tough, green skin turns yellow with a red blush. Yellow or golden-orange flesh, which tastes like a blend of peach, apricot, and pineapple, clings to a large flat seed. Unripe fruit is bitter.

**Selection and storage:** Look for full, firm, partially ripe fruit showing some yellow or red, although color is not a reliable sign of ripeness. Aroma determines ripeness. Sniff the stem end; a pleasant scent hints of rich flavor. Keep at room temperature until tender and aromatic; refrigerate ripened fruit in a plastic bag up to a few days. For longer storage, cube peeled flesh, process in a food processor or electric blender until smooth, pour through a wire-mesh strainer, pressing with back of a spoon, and freeze in small airtight containers.

**Preparation:** To peel, score skin in quarters from the top to stem end; peel like a banana. Cut flesh into small cubes by crisscrossing it with a knife; then cut cubes away from the seed.

For slicing, score peeled flesh in quarters, remove from the seed, and slice. Processed pulp has a smoothness similar to a sweetened, cooked, and thickened sauce, but it is lighter. If desired, add lime juice and sugar to processed pulp, and freeze as a base for making ices, ice creams, sorbets, and parfaits.

**Serving suggestions:** Cube and add to chicken, fruit, and vegetable salads; dice and use as a filling for crêpes, or add to seafood, meat, or poultry stir-frys; add fruit liqueur or lime juice to pureed fruit, and serve over fresh fruit, ice cream, or pound cake; drizzle fruit slices with orange liqueur for serving with yogurt or cake. For a refreshing shake, combine sliced fruit in an electric blender with milk, a splash of fresh lime juice, sugar or honey, and ice.

**Substitution:** Peaches may be used in most recipes.

**Nutrition:** Excellent source of vitamin A and vitamin C; good source of potassium.

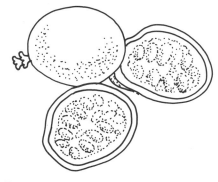

## Passion Fruit

Passion fruit looks like a small, round, dimpled pink, purple, or yellow ball. Its sweet/tart flavor is often preferred sweetened with a little sugar. The thin, hard shell of the fruit encloses a small quantity of juice, as well as a translucent pulp of teardrop-shaped golden capsules containing tiny edible dark seeds.

**Selection and storage:** Choose large, heavy, firm fruit. Don't be misled by a wrinkled or dimpled shell and a sloshy sound that actually ensure a delicious interior. To ripen fruit, let stand at room temperature until wrinkled. Store ripened fruit in the refrigerator up to five days; for longer storage, place whole fruit in plastic bags, and freeze.

**Preparation:** Many recipes call for strained pulp with seeds removed. Holding fruit over a bowl, slice and remove the shell tip, scoop out all the pulp, and stir in a little sugar to help break up the pulp. Pour pulp through a wire-mesh strainer (be sure that you don't use an aluminum one), pressing with back of a spoon to squeeze out juice; discard seeds.

**Serving suggestions:** Cut in half crosswise and carefully open; add whipping cream, and eat with a spoon. Flavor prepared punches, sauces, sorbets, ice creams, and fruit and gelatin salads with pulp. Combine juice and powdered sugar; toss with fresh fruit. Lightly sweeten pulp with sugar or a sweet liqueur, and pour over fresh fruit or yogurt; for a richer topping, blend pulp with sugar, and fold in whipped cream. Combine vanilla yogurt with juice for a fruit dip. Use juice as a flavoring as you would an extract.

**Substitutions:** Canned passion fruit juice is available in many supermarkets, or orange juice may be used in some recipes.

**Nutrition:** Excellent source of vitamin C; good source of vitamin A.

## Carambola

Carambola (kair-ahm-BOH-lah or kah-rahm-BO-la), or star fruit, is easily recognizable with its golden yellow, glossy skin. The matching translucent flesh, dotted occasionally with a dark seed, is very juicy. Its five wings or ribs create a star shape when sliced crosswise. When sweet, the flavor suggests a blend of plums, apples, and grapes with a citrus edge. When sour, it is sharp as a lemon, but less harsh and more fruity.

**Selection and storage:** Choose full, firm yellow fruit. Sweet varieties often have thicker, wider ribs, while tart varieties have very narrow ribs. Store green or green-tinged fruit at room temperature; when golden, refrigerate in plastic bags up to one week. For longer storage, freeze whole fruit in plastic bags.

**Preparation:** This easy-to-prepare fruit requires no peeling or seeding. Scrape off the tiny brown stripe running down the ribs with a vegetable peeler or knife, if desired.

**Serving suggestions:** Garnish entrées and desserts; float slices in beverages; make a daiquiri; add to green, fruit, or poultry salads; puree for ices or sherbets; slice and arrange on cheesecake with fresh mint; dip into melted chocolate. Stir-fry slices with strips of green pepper and onion; add chicken and shrimp for an entrée. Quickly cook in a skillet with a touch of sugar to glaze, and serve as an accompaniment to fish or poultry; combine with other fruit for a strudel filling.

**Substitution:** There is no good substitute for carambolas.

**Nutrition:** Good source of vitamin A and vitamin C.

## Avocado

Avocado (a-voh-CAH-doh) varieties differ in shape and size, ranging from round to pear-shaped with thick to thin, green to purplish black, smooth to corrugated skin. The pale yellow-green flesh surrounds a seed and has a buttery consistency with a rich, nutty flavor.

**Selection and storage:** Firm, unripe ones are usually found in the market. Never use hard fruit—it has little flavor and is difficult to peel. Ripe avocados yield to gentle palm pressure. To speed the ripening process, enclose in a paper bag at room temperature two to four days. Refrigerate ripe avocados, but for longer storage, mash with a little lemon or lime juice, and freeze. (Whole or sliced fruit does not freeze well.)

**Preparation:** Cut lengthwise around the seed; then turn halves in opposite directions to separate. Lift seed out with fingers or a spoon. Using a knife or your fingers, gently peel off skin; cut as desired. To prevent discoloration of cut surfaces, sprinkle with lemon or lime juice. Very soft flesh is best for mashing; slightly firmer flesh should be used for slicing and cutting into chunks. Add cubes or slices to a recipe at the last moment, and include lemon or lime juice in dishes calling for mashed avocado. Add to hot foods at the last minute; prolonged heat causes a bitter flavor.

**Serving suggestions:** Add to seafood, pasta, fruit, and green salads; mash and spread in pita pockets, and fill with fresh vegetables; toss with hot pasta and seafood; use as a pizza topping; float thin slices on soups as a garnish; fill halves with chilled salads; combine with artichoke hearts and a vinaigrette.

**Substitution:** There is no good substitute for avocados.

**Nutrition:** Excellent source of vitamin A; good source of vitamin E and potassium.

# Celebrating Jewish Heritage

When most of us think of Jewish observances, Hanukkah and Passover quickly come to mind. You may be surprised to know that the community observes three holidays each fall—Rosh Hashanah, Yom Kippur, and Sukkot—all within a month. Each is a special occasion with its own symbolism and its own place in our Jewish readers' hearts and homes. Enjoy both the recipes and heritage they have shared with us.

## Rosh Hashanah

While most associate the New Year with January, Jewish families begin their calendar in autumn with Rosh Hashanah. Families celebrate different holiday traditions, depending on whether they practice Orthodox, Conservative, or Reform Judaism.

But like Southerners of different backgrounds who serve black-eyed peas for luck on New Year's Day, many Jewish families enjoy sugary foods for Rosh Hashanah to bring a "sweet" future in the coming year.

### HONEY CAKE

1 cup honey
1 cup vegetable oil
1 cup sugar
4 large eggs
2½ cups all-purpose flour
1½ teaspoons baking powder
½ teaspoon baking soda
½ teaspoon ground allspice
½ teaspoon instant coffee granules
½ cup hot water
1 teaspoon vanilla extract
½ teaspoon lemon extract
½ teaspoon almond extract
¼ cup sugar
¼ cup chopped pecans
½ teaspoon ground cinnamon

Beat first 4 ingredients at medium speed with an electric mixer. Combine flour and next 3 ingredients; gradually add to honey mixture, mixing well. Dissolve coffee granules in hot water and add to mixture, beating well. Stir in flavorings. Pour into two greased and floured 9- x 5- x 3-inch loafpans. Combine ¼ cup sugar, pecans, and cinnamon; sprinkle over loaves. Bake at 325° for 1 hour to 1 hour and 15 minutes or until a wooden pick inserted in center comes out clean. Cool loaves in pans 10 minutes; remove from pans, and let cool on a wire rack. Yield: 2 loaves. *Terri Cohen*
*North Potomac, Maryland*

## Pan Tips

■ When a recipe calls for a "greased pan," be sure to grease the pan with solid shortening or an oil unless specified.

■ Use shiny cookie sheets and cakepans for baking. Dark cookie sheets and pans absorb more heat and cause baked products to overbrown.

## Yom Kippur

Also called the Day of Atonement, this observance always comes eight days after Rosh Hashanah. The mood turns from festive to somber as a day of fasting from both food and drink begins in recognition of the past year's sins. After fasting, many gather with family and friends at sunset to "break the fast." Light dairy or breakfast foods are common.

### CHEESE BLINTZ CASSEROLE

2 (8-ounce) packages cream cheese, softened
2 (8-ounce) packages farmer cheese
2 large eggs
¼ cup sugar
2½ teaspoons lemon juice
½ cup butter or margarine, softened
¼ cup sugar
2 large eggs
¾ cup milk
1¼ cups all-purpose flour
1 teaspoon baking powder

Beat first 5 ingredients at low speed with an electric mixer; set cheese mixture aside.

Beat butter and ¼ cup sugar at medium speed until fluffy. Add 2 eggs and milk, mixing well. Combine flour and baking powder; stir into butter mixture. Pour half of butter mixture into a greased 11- x 7- x 1½-inch baking dish. Spoon cheese mixture on top, and pour remaining butter mixture over cheese mixture. Bake at 350° for 45 minutes. Yield: 8 to 10 servings.

**Note:** You may freeze baked casserole. To serve, thaw in refrigerator, and bake at 350° for 20 minutes or until thoroughly heated.

*Rosalyn Bloomston*
*Birmingham, Alabama*

### APRICOT NOODLE KUGEL

3 (16-ounce) cans apricot halves, undrained and divided
16 ounces wide egg noodles, uncooked
1 (8-ounce) package cream cheese, softened
6 large eggs
1 cup sugar
1 (16-ounce) carton sour cream
½ cup butter or margarine, melted
½ cup graham cracker crumbs
1 teaspoon sugar
1 teaspoon ground cinnamon

Drain 2 cans of apricot halves; chop and set aside.

Cook noodles according to package directions; drain and set aside.

Beat cream cheese and next 4 ingredients at medium speed with an electric mixer until blended. Stir in chopped apricots and cooked noodles. Spoon apricot-noodle mixture into a lightly greased 13- x 9- x 2-inch baking dish.

Drain remaining can of apricot halves and place on noodle mixture. Combine graham cracker crumbs, 1 teaspoon sugar, and cinnamon; sprinkle mixture evenly over apricots. Bake casserole at 350° for 1 hour. Yield: 15 servings.

*Rosalyn Bloomston*
*Birmingham, Alabama*

## Sukkot

Sukkot celebrates the bountiful fall harvest and the beginning of autumn. In addition to feasting on fruits, vegetables, and occasionally cookies and punch, some observers build the traditional "sukka," a temporary outdoor shelter or booth reminiscent of the desert dwelling places used when the Israelites were delivered from Egypt. Today, these shelters are festively decorated with fresh produce and used for eating or sleeping during this holiday, which is also known as the Feast of Booths.

### STUFFED CABBAGE ROLLS

2 medium cabbages (about 5 pounds)
3 onions, chopped
¼ cup vegetable oil
1 cup brown rice, uncooked
2 pounds ground beef
1 teaspoon salt
½ teaspoon pepper
1 (16-ounce) can sauerkraut, drained and divided
¾ cup firmly packed brown sugar, divided
1 (46-ounce) can tomato juice

Freeze cabbages 8 hours; thaw. Separate leaves, and set aside.

Cook onion in oil in a large skillet over medium-high heat, stirring constantly, until crisp-tender. Add rice, and cook 3 to 5 minutes over medium heat, stirring constantly. Cool rice mixture slightly.

Combine rice mixture, ground beef, salt, and pepper. Reserving smaller cabbage leaves, spoon about ¼ cup beef mixture in center of each large cabbage leaf. Fold left and right sides of leaf over, and roll up, beginning at bottom. Repeat procedure with remaining large cabbage leaves. Chill rolls overnight, if desired, or proceed immediately.

Arrange reserved small cabbage leaves in bottom of a large Dutch oven or stockpot. Spoon half of sauerkraut and half of brown sugar over small cabbage leaves. Top with half of cabbage rolls, seam side down. Repeat layers with remaining sauerkraut, brown sugar, and cabbage rolls. Pour tomato juice over assembled layers; bring to a boil, and simmer, covered, 2 hours or until rice is done. Serve immediately. Yield: about 2½ dozen cabbage rolls.

**Note:** Instead of freezing cabbages, you may cover them with boiling water in a large stockpot and let stand 10 minutes.
*Holly Berkowitz Clegg*
*Baton Rouge, Louisiana*

## SPAGHETTI SQUASH WITH SESAME EGGPLANT

1 (3-pound) spaghetti squash
1 large eggplant
Salt
3 tablespoons olive oil
1 (2⅛-ounce) jar sesame seeds,
  toasted
1 cup grated Parmesan cheese,
  divided
2 tablespoons butter or margarine
2 or 3 cloves garlic, minced
¼ teaspoon salt
¼ teaspoon pepper

Cut spaghetti squash in half lengthwise, and remove seeds. Place halves, cut side down, in a 13- x 9- x 2-inch pan; add water to a depth of 1½ inches. Bake at 350° for 45 minutes or until tender; drain. Cool slightly. Using a fork, scrape squash into spaghetti-like strands; set aside, discarding shells.

Trim ends from eggplant (do not peel); cut lengthwise into 8 slices. Sprinkle slices with salt, and place in a large bowl; let stand about 20 minutes. Rinse slices with water; pat dry. Brush both sides of each slice with olive oil; place in a single layer on a lightly greased baking sheet. Bake at 450° for 15 to 20 minutes or until slices begin to soften. Remove from oven, and sprinkle one side of each slice with sesame seeds. Turn slices over, and sprinkle 1 tablespoon Parmesan cheese on each; set remaining ½ cup Parmesan cheese aside. Roll slices up, starting at end, and secure with wooden picks. Set aside, and keep warm.

Melt butter in a large skillet over low heat; add garlic, and cook 2 minutes, stirring constantly. Add squash, remaining ½ cup Parmesan cheese, salt, and pepper; cook until thoroughly heated, tossing gently. Arrange on a serving plate; place eggplant rolls over squash. Remove wooden picks. Yield: 6 servings.

**Note:** To cook squash in microwave oven, cut squash in half lengthwise, and remove seeds. Place halves, cut side down, in a large baking dish; add ¼ cup water. Cover tightly with heavy-duty plastic wrap; fold back a small edge of wrap to allow steam to escape. Microwave at HIGH 8 to 10 minutes or until tender; drain.

*Carole Sheldon*
*Houston, Texas*

## RUGELACH

1 cup butter or margarine, softened
1 (8-ounce) package cream cheese,
  softened
2 cups all-purpose flour
½ cup sugar
1 teaspoon ground cinnamon
1 cup chopped pecans
½ cup raisins

Beat butter and cream cheese at medium speed with an electric mixer until smooth and creamy. Gradually add flour, beating until smooth. Cover and chill 1 hour.

Combine sugar and remaining ingredients; set aside.

Divide dough in half; roll each portion into a 14-inch circle on a lightly floured surface. Sprinkle each circle with sugar mixture, and cut each circle into 12 wedges. Roll up each wedge, beginning at wide end; place on ungreased baking sheets, point side down. Bake at 350° for 15 to 18 minutes or until golden brown. Yield: 2 dozen.

**Note:** For strawberry filling, omit sugar, cinnamon, and raisins, and reduce pecans to ½ cup. Spread ¼ cup strawberry jam on each circle, and sprinkle each with ¼ cup chopped pecans. Cut, roll, and bake as directed.

*Terri Cohen*
*North Potomac, Maryland*

# Bake A Batch Of Savory Muffins

Check out these four muffin recipes to determine which ones fit into your next meal. All of them feature major ingredients that aren't sweet but are very versatile. Match them with a soup, salad, or main dish, or warm them up to solo as a snack or as a quick breakfast.

## HAM-AND-CHEESE MUFFINS

1¾ cups all-purpose flour
⅓ cup rye flour
2 teaspoons baking powder
¼ teaspoon salt
1 tablespoon light brown sugar
⅓ cup finely chopped cooked ham
½ cup (2 ounces) shredded Swiss
  cheese
1 large egg, lightly beaten
1 cup milk
¼ cup vegetable oil
¾ teaspoon spicy brown mustard
½ teaspoon Worcestershire sauce
3 drops of hot sauce

Combine first 5 ingredients in a large bowl; stir in ham and cheese. Make a well in center of mixture. Combine egg and next 5 ingredients; add to dry ingredients, stirring just until moistened. Spoon into greased muffin pans, filling two-thirds full. Bake at 400° for 22 to 25 minutes. Remove from pans immediately. Yield: 1 dozen.

## CHEESY SAUSAGE MUFFINS

¼ pound ground pork sausage,
  cooked and drained
1 (3-ounce) package cream cheese,
  cut into small cubes
½ cup (2 ounces) shredded
  Cheddar cheese
¼ cup chopped green onions
1 cup biscuit mix
2 large eggs, lightly beaten
⅔ cup milk

Combine first 5 ingredients in a large bowl; make a well in center of mixture. Combine eggs and milk; add to sausage mixture, stirring just until moistened. Spoon into greased miniature muffin pans, filling three-fourths full. Bake at 350° for 35 to 40 minutes. Remove from pans immediately. Yield: 2 dozen.

*Ginny Whitt*
*Mount Washington, Kentucky*

## TEX-MEX CORN MUFFINS

1½ cups yellow cornmeal
½ teaspoon baking soda
½ teaspoon salt
1 (2-ounce) jar diced pimiento, drained
1 cup (4 ounces) shredded Cheddar cheese
½ cup finely chopped onion
¼ cup chopped green chiles
1 clove garlic, minced
2 large eggs, lightly beaten
1 cup milk
1 (8¾-ounce) can yellow cream-style corn

Heat ungreased muffin pans in a 400° oven 10 minutes or until hot.

Combine cornmeal, soda, and salt in a large bowl; stir in pimiento and next 4 ingredients. Make a well in center of mixture. Combine eggs, milk, and corn; add to dry ingredients, stirring just until moistened. Spoon into prepared muffin pans, filling three-fourths full. Bake at 400° for 30 minutes or until golden. Remove from pans immediately. Yield: 1½ dozen.

*Joy Allard*
*San Antonio, Texas*

## ONION-DILL MUFFINS

1½ cups wheat bran cereal
1¼ cups milk
2 large eggs, lightly beaten
3 tablespoons vegetable oil
1 cup all-purpose flour
¾ cup whole wheat flour
1 tablespoon baking powder
½ teaspoon salt
2 tablespoons sugar
½ teaspoon dried dillweed
½ teaspoon dry mustard
½ cup finely chopped onion

Combine cereal and milk in a bowl; let stand 2 minutes or until cereal is softened. Stir in eggs and oil.

Combine flours and next 5 ingredients in a large bowl; stir in onion. Make a well in center of mixture; add cereal mixture, stirring just until moistened. Spoon into greased muffin pans, filling three-fourths full. Bake at 400° for 18 minutes or until golden brown. Remove from pan immediately. Yield: 1 dozen.

# Here's To The Weekend Cook

For easy weekend entertaining, invite a few friends over for an enticing meal starring crowd-pleasing Oriental Beef Pot Pie. The casserole of sirloin tip and vegetables in a puff pastry can be complemented with a salad and bread for a complete meal.

## ORIENTAL BEEF POT PIE

2 pounds sirloin tip roast
1 clove garlic, minced
2 tablespoons vegetable oil
½ cup all-purpose flour
1 (10¾-ounce) can condensed beef broth, undiluted
1⅓ cups water
¾ teaspoon ground ginger
½ teaspoon pepper
2 teaspoons soy sauce
1 (16-ounce) package frozen broccoli, green beans, pearl onions, and red peppers, thawed
1 (8-ounce) can sliced water chestnuts, drained
1 (4-ounce) can sliced mushrooms, drained
½ (17¼-ounce) package commercial frozen puff pastry, thawed

Trim excess fat from roast; cut meat into bite-size pieces. Sauté meat and garlic in hot oil in a large skillet. Remove meat from skillet, and set aside.

Add flour to pan drippings; stir until smooth. Cook 1 minute, stirring constantly. Gradually add broth and water. Cook over medium heat, stirring constantly, until thickened. Stir in ginger, pepper, and soy sauce. Combine broth mixture, meat, mixed vegetables, water chestnuts, and mushrooms. Spoon into a lightly greased 13- x 9- x 2-inch baking dish.

Roll pastry on a lightly floured surface; cut into ½-inch strips, and arrange diagonally over casserole. Bake at 350° for 30 minutes or until golden brown. Yield: 8 servings.

# It's A Good Year For Oysters

Oyster lovers, rejoice—you can still enjoy cooked oysters without fear. According to the food safety experts, oysters are safe to eat when properly handled and cooked.

"Cooking an oyster might be compared to cooking pork or chicken. The cooking process destroys bacteria, resulting in a safe product," explains Dr. Louise McFarland of the Louisiana Office of Public Health.

So, oyster lovers, start cooking. Roland Ormrod of Towson, Maryland, shares his recipe for Oysters Chesapeake, baked oysters on the half shell adorned with country ham and Swiss cheese. Or try Crusty Oyster Loaf as a casual supper.

## CRUSTY OYSTER LOAF

1 (16-ounce) loaf unsliced French
  bread
⅓ cup butter or margarine, melted
2 large eggs
1 tablespoon milk
1½ cups Italian-seasoned
  breadcrumbs
1 cup all-purpose flour
1 teaspoon salt
¾ teaspoon paprika
3 (12-ounce) containers fresh Select
  oysters, drained
Vegetable oil
Coastal Cocktail Sauce

Trim a 1-inch slice off top of loaf, and set aside. Scoop out inside of loaf, leaving a 1-inch-thick shell; reserve inside of loaf for other uses. Brush melted butter over inside and outside of loaf. Place on a baking sheet, and bake at 400° for 8 minutes. Cool.

Combine eggs and milk. Combine breadcrumbs and next 3 ingredients.

Dip oysters in egg mixture, and dredge in breadcrumb mixture.

Pour oil to depth of 1 inch into a large, heavy skillet. Fry oysters in hot oil (375°) over medium-high heat about 3 minutes, turning once. Drain well on paper towels. Arrange oysters in bread loaf, and cover with 1-inch slice from top of loaf. Slice, and serve immediately with Coastal Cocktail Sauce. Yield: 3 to 4 servings.

### Coastal Cocktail Sauce

1 cup catsup
2 tablespoons lemon juice
1 tablespoon prepared
  horseradish
1 tablespoon Worcestershire
  sauce
1 teaspoon hot sauce
¼ teaspoon garlic salt
¼ teaspoon onion powder

Combine all ingredients; cover and refrigerate. Yield: about 1¼ cups.

## OYSTERS CHESAPEAKE

Rock salt
5 cloves garlic, minced
¼ cup butter or margarine,
  melted
2 medium onions, finely chopped
2½ cups finely chopped cooked
  country ham
½ cup dry white wine
2½ dozen fresh oysters on the half
  shell
4 (¾-ounce) slices Swiss cheese,
  cut into 30 strips

Sprinkle a thin layer of rock salt in two 15- x 10- x 1-inch jellyroll pans; set pans aside.

Cook garlic in butter in a large skillet over medium heat, stirring constantly, until slightly brown. Add chopped onion and cook, stirring constantly, until tender. Stir in ham, and cook until moisture evaporates (about 5 minutes). Add wine, and simmer 5 minutes.

Arrange oysters (in shells) over rock salt. Spoon 1 heaping tablespoon ham mixture on each oyster; top with cheese. Bake at 400° for 10 minutes or until cheese melts. Serve immediately. Yield: 2½ dozen.

## CREAMED OYSTERS

½ cup green onions, chopped
2 tablespoons chopped fresh parsley
¼ cup butter or margarine, melted
2 (10-ounce) containers fresh
  oysters, drained and chopped
1 (10¾-ounce) can cream of
  mushroom soup, undiluted
1 (4.5-ounce) jar sliced mushrooms,
  drained and chopped
2 (9½-ounce) packages commercial
  frozen mini puff pastry shells,
  baked

Cook green onions and parsley in butter in a large skillet over medium heat, stirring constantly, until tender. Add oysters, and cook until edges curl (about 5 minutes); drain and return to skillet. Stir in mushroom soup and mushrooms, and cook 5 minutes, stirring frequently. Serve in pastry shells. Yield: 48 appetizer servings.

*Margaret Chilquelin*
*Baton Rouge, Louisiana*

# Barbecue On A Salad

Residents of Memphis, Tennessee, have long enjoyed barbecue salads. But John Wills of John Wills Bar-B-Que Bar and Grill wasn't satisfied serving his "Pig in the Garden" Salad with the usual salad dressings. He added various items to his barbecue sauce and developed Cheesy-Barbecue Salad Dressing.

## "PIG IN THE GARDEN" SALAD

9 cups mixed salad greens
¾ cup sliced celery
¾ cup chopped green pepper
1 cup (4 ounces) shredded Monterey Jack cheese
1 cup (4 ounces) shredded Cheddar cheese
3 cups warm shredded or chopped, grilled or smoked pork
6 small tomatoes, cut into wedges
Cheesy-Barbecue Salad Dressing

Combine first 3 ingredients; toss and arrange on plates. Combine cheeses; sprinkle over greens. Top with pork; arrange tomatoes on plates. Serve with Cheesy-Barbecue Salad Dressing. Yield: 6 servings.

### Cheesy-Barbecue Salad Dressing

1 cup John Wills's Barbecue Sauce
1 (9-ounce) can Cheddar cheese dip
⅓ cup sour cream
½ cup buttermilk
½ cup mayonnaise or salad dressing
1 tablespoon sugar

Combine all ingredients using a wire whisk; chill. Yield: 3 cups.

### John Wills's Barbecue Sauce

1 (8-ounce) can tomato sauce
½ cup spicy honey mustard
1 cup catsup
1 cup red wine vinegar
½ cup Worcestershire sauce
¼ cup butter or margarine
2 tablespoons hot sauce
1 tablespoon lemon juice
2 tablespoons brown sugar
1 tablespoon paprika
1 tablespoon seasoned salt
1½ teaspoons garlic powder
⅛ teaspoon chili powder
⅛ teaspoon ground red pepper
⅛ teaspoon black pepper

Combine all ingredients in a Dutch oven. Bring to a boil; reduce heat, and simmer 30 minutes, stirring occasionally. Yield: 1 quart.

# Vegetables In A Flash

One little, two little, three little . . . ingredients. The song applies well to these vegetable recipes, but you'll have to stop singing at six instead of ten—the recipes are that simple. And the best part about them is you probably have all the ingredients on hand.

Most of these dishes don't take very long to cook, either. Glazed Baby Carrots (on page 256) will be on the table in less than 10 minutes if you buy them scraped in 1-pound packages, as you can in many markets.

## ZUCCHINI TOSS

1 pound fresh zucchini, cut into ¼-inch slices
1 tablespoon olive oil
1 tablespoon freshly grated Parmesan cheese
⅛ to ¼ teaspoon grated lemon rind
¼ teaspoon salt
¼ teaspoon pepper

Sauté zucchini in hot oil 5 minutes or until crisp-tender. Remove from heat; cover and let stand 5 minutes. Spoon into serving dish.

Combine cheese and remaining ingredients. Sprinkle over squash; toss gently. Serve immediately. Yield: 3 servings.

*Shirley McGehee*
*Spring Branch, Texas*

## MUSHROOM-BACON GREEN BEANS

4 slices bacon
½ pound fresh mushrooms, sliced
1 medium onion, chopped
2 (16-ounce) cans green beans, drained
⅛ teaspoon pepper

Cook bacon in a large skillet until crisp; remove bacon, reserving 2 tablespoons drippings in skillet. Crumble bacon, and set aside.

Add mushrooms and onion to drippings in skillet; sauté until onions are tender. Add beans and pepper; cook until thoroughly heated. Spoon into serving dish; sprinkle with bacon. Yield: 6 servings.

*Karen Wood*
*Crescent, Oklahoma*

## GLAZED BABY CARROTS

1 (16-ounce) package baby carrots,
   scraped
2 tablespoons butter or margarine
3 tablespoons brown sugar
2 to 3 tablespoons pineapple juice
½ teaspoon ground ginger
Garnish: chopped parsley

Cook carrots in a small amount of boiling water 5 minutes or until crisp-tender; drain.

Melt butter in a small saucepan; add brown sugar, pineapple juice, and ginger. Pour mixture over carrots, and toss gently; garnish, if desired. Yield: 4 servings.
*Linda Wright*
*Tulsa, Oklahoma*


## BROCCOLI
## WITH LEMON SAUCE

1½ pounds fresh broccoli
½ clove garlic, minced
2 tablespoons olive oil
2 tablespoons lemon juice

Remove large leaves from broccoli, and cut off tough ends of lower stalks; discard. Wash broccoli thoroughly, and cut into spears. Cook in a small amount of boiling water 6 to 8 minutes or just until tender; drain.

Sauté garlic in hot olive oil until tender. Add lemon juice; pour over broccoli, tossing gently. Yield: 6 servings.
*Caroline W. Kennedy*
*Newborn, Georgia*


## APPLESAUCE
## SWEET POTATOES

4 medium-size sweet potatoes
   (about 2 pounds)
1 cup unsweetened applesauce
⅔ cup firmly packed brown sugar
2½ tablespoons butter or
   margarine, melted
¼ teaspoon salt

Cook sweet potatoes in boiling water to cover 30 minutes or until they are tender. Let cool to touch; peel potatoes, and slice ½ inch thick. Arrange slices in a lightly greased, 1½-quart baking dish.

Combine applesauce and remaining ingredients; pour over potatoes. Bake, uncovered, at 350° for 20 minutes or until thoroughly heated. Yield: 6 to 8 servings.

**Microwave Directions:** Peel sweet potatoes, and slice ½ inch thick. Arrange in a shallow 2-quart baking dish; add ¼ cup water. Cover tightly with heavy-duty plastic wrap; fold back a small corner of wrap to allow steam to escape. Microwave at HIGH 15 minutes, stirring after 10 minutes. Drain. Arrange slices in a lightly greased 1½-quart baking dish.

Combine applesauce and remaining ingredients; pour mixture over potatoes. Microwave, uncovered, at HIGH 4 minutes.
*Mrs. Marvin Jackson*
*Silas, Alabama*


## Get the Most Out of Vegetables

■ Remember that overcooking vegetables destroys their nutrients. Warm leftovers carefully in a double boiler or a microwave. Even better, just mix them cold in a salad.

■ Store onions in a cool, dark place with air circulation to prevent sprouting.

■ Always wash or chop vegetables, and open cans before you begin preparing any recipe. It is also a good idea to have most ingredients measured before beginning to cook.

■ Winter squash is mature when it doesn't yield to pressure when you give it a slight squeeze. If the squash has a soft skin, it means the squash is old and past its peak.

■ Wipe fresh mushrooms clean or quickly rinse them in a colander immediately before using; never immerse fresh mushrooms in water.

■ Marinate leftover vegetables (beets, carrots, beans, broccoli, cauliflower, corn, and brussels sprouts) in pourable salad dressing for relishes and salads.

■ When selecting fresh cabbage, choose heads that are solid and heavy in relation to their size. The cabbage leaves should be fresh, crisp, and free from bruises.

■ Fold leftover vegetables into a cream sauce to serve over a plain omelet; add to fritter batter or marinate vegetables in French dressing for a delicious salad.

*These classic Old-Fashioned Cinnamon Rolls (page 226) have new-fashioned appeal to meet today's healthy standards.*

Above: *Celebrate holidays and other special occasions with Creamy Ham-and-Chicken Medley (page 272).*

Left: *Add Cranberry Gelatin Mold (page 271) to your Thanksgiving or Christmas menu.*

Far Left: *On Christmas Eve, a family needs a simple, relaxing meal, such as delicious Chicken-Vegetable Spaghetti and Spinach Salad. (Recipes, page 281.)*

*For a night of dining and fun, set out tortilla-lined bowls, White Lightning Texas Chili, and Mexican Salad With Avocado Dressing buffet-style so that friends and family can help themselves. (Recipes begin on page 321.)*

# NOVEMBER

*Ring in the holidays with festive menus from our special section, "Holiday Dinners." In this chapter, you'll find traditional recipes for Thanksgiving, plus a few surprises for Christmas and New Year's Eve with the accent on contemporary. As the holiday excitement builds, entertain the little ones with a tea party that features a Teddy Bear Cake for show and eating, too. And just in the nick of time are different kinds of cookies to bake as sweet endings to your holiday meals or to leave for Santa.*

# Quick & Easy!

If you think your life is hectic, just try to keep up with these people. Between family, friends, work, school, community projects, and hobbies, they have little time to spare. Their days revolve around a different mix of activities, but all have at least one thing in common—they're busy people who love to cook.

We asked each person to share a favorite quick recipe and a little about himself or herself.

■ Michelle Vachris of Arlington, Virginia, remembers what it was like to hold down a full-time job and go to school at the same time.

Evening meals had to be quick, but they were often the only time she and her husband, Scott, had together, so Michelle wanted the food to be special. She learned to add her own touch to recipes by experimenting with seasonings.

## CREOLE CHICKEN AND RICE

¾ cup water
¼ teaspoon salt
¾ cup instant rice, uncooked
Vegetable cooking spray
2 skinned and boned chicken breast
　halves
1 (8-ounce) can tomato sauce
¼ cup water
¼ cup chopped onion
2 tablespoons chopped green pepper
1 clove garlic, minced
½ teaspoon dried basil
⅛ teaspoon pepper
Garnish: fresh basil leaves

Combine ¾ cup water and salt in a small saucepan; bring to a boil. Remove from heat; stir in rice, cover, and let stand 5 minutes, or until all liquid is absorbed. Keep warm.

Coat a large, nonstick skillet with cooking spray; place over medium-high heat until hot. Add chicken; cook until lightly browned, turning once. Add tomato sauce and next 6 ingredients; bring to a boil. Cover, reduce heat, and simmer 6 minutes, stirring occasionally. Serve with rice. Garnish, if desired. Yield: 2 servings.

■ As an airline flight attendant, Jane Micol Schatzman of Winston-Salem, North Carolina, is out of town 12 to 15 days each month. When she's not flying, she loves to cook, calling it her "substitute for golf, tennis, and bridge."

## FILET MIGNON
## WITH HORSERADISH GRAVY

1 (¾-ounce) package brown gravy
　mix
1 to 2 tablespoons prepared
　horseradish
1 (4-ounce) can sliced mushrooms,
　drained
4 (5-ounce) beef tenderloin steaks
¼ teaspoon salt
¼ teaspoon pepper
Garnishes: tomato wedges, fresh
　parsley sprigs

Prepare gravy according to package directions; stir in horseradish and mushrooms. Set aside.

Heat a heavy, nonstick skillet over medium-high heat until hot. Add steaks, and cook 1 minute on each side. Steaks will be rare. Place in a lightly greased 1-quart baking dish; sprinkle with salt and pepper. Pour gravy over steaks; bake at 350°, uncovered, for 15 minutes or until desired degree of doneness. Garnish, if desired. Yield: 4 servings.

■ When it snows in Springfield, Virginia, Tom Hayes has two jobs. In addition to working four 10-hour days managing the video teleconferencing network for the Army Materiel Command Headquarters, he runs a snowplow business.

## EASY CHILI WITH BEANS

1 pound lean ground beef
1 medium onion, chopped
1 clove garlic, minced
1 tablespoon olive oil
3 (8-ounce) cans tomato sauce
1 tablespoon chili powder
1 milk chocolate kiss
1 (15-ounce) can kidney beans,
　undrained
Garnish: shredded Cheddar cheese

Cook first 3 ingredients in olive oil in a Dutch oven over medium-high heat, stirring until ground beef crumbles; drain. Return mixture to Dutch oven; stir in tomato sauce, chili powder, and chocolate kiss. Cook over low heat 15 minutes, stirring occasionally. Add kidney beans, and cook until thoroughly heated. Garnish, if desired. Yield: 5½ cups.

■ Sandra B. Connell of Stockton, Georgia, plans menus and mentally makes a shopping list during her 30-minute commute to Valdosta High School where she works as a media specialist.

To make time for all her activities, Sandra cooks more than she needs so she has leftovers in the refrigerator or freezer for other meals. She also uses a microwave oven to thaw and reheat foods quickly.

## FIESTA DIP

1 (8-ounce) package cream cheese, softened
1 (8-ounce) jar mild picante sauce
Garnish: sliced green onions

Combine cream cheese and picante sauce; beat mixture at low speed with an electric mixer until smooth. Garnish, if desired. Serve with corn chips. Yield: 2 cups.

■ Susan Lee of Conway, Arkansas, gets up at 4:45 a.m. to drive 45 minutes to her job as a licensed practical nurse (LPN) at North Little Rock's Baptist Memorial Medical Center. When she gets home at 4 p.m., she quickly prepares the evening meal for her family.

## FESTIVE CORN SALAD

1 (11-ounce) can white whole kernel corn, drained and rinsed
1 medium-size green pepper, chopped
1 medium tomato, chopped
1 medium-size purple onion, chopped
¼ teaspoon pepper
½ cup commercial Italian salad dressing *
Lettuce leaves

Combine first 6 ingredients. Spoon into a bowl lined with lettuce leaves. Serve with a slotted spoon. Yield: 4 to 6 servings.

* Mayonnaise or salad dressing may be substituted for Italian salad dressing in the salad.

■ Marine Biologist Byron White of Charleston, South Carolina, has spent the past seven years on and off the sea. Currently, he's working with the South Carolina Wildlife and Marine Resources Department.

## POTATO SOUP

1 cup peeled, cubed potatoes
½ cup chopped onion
1 (14½-ounce) can ready-to-serve chicken broth
1 cup milk
⅛ to ¼ teaspoon salt
¼ teaspoon dried thyme
¼ teaspoon pepper
1 teaspoon butter or margarine
3 to 4 tablespoons instant mashed potato flakes
Garnish: fresh thyme sprigs

Combine first 3 ingredients in a large saucepan. Bring to a boil; cover, reduce heat, and simmer 15 minutes or until potatoes are tender. Add milk and next 4 ingredients. Gradually add potato flakes; cook over medium heat, stirring constantly, until thoroughly heated. Garnish with thyme sprigs, if desired, and serve immediately. Yield: 3⅓ cups.

■ Mary Jackson of Maryville, Missouri, calls herself a "lazy" cook. She says if any recipes in her cookbooks have yeast in them, she turns the page.

She keeps her favorite kitchen convenience, the freezer, full most of the time. She likes to have something ready for guests so she can be with them instead of in the kitchen.

## CINNAMON TEA ROLLS

1 (8-ounce) can refrigerated crescent dinner rolls
2 tablespoons butter or margarine, melted
⅓ cup sugar
¼ teaspoon ground cinnamon
Orange Glaze

Unroll dough onto lightly floured wax paper; press perforations to seal.

brush with melted butter. Combine sugar and cinnamon; sprinkle over dough. Roll up jellyroll fashion, starting at long side; cut into 1-inch slices. Place in a lightly greased miniature muffin pan. Bake at 375° for 8 to 10 minutes or until golden brown. Remove from pan, and drizzle with Orange Glaze. Yield: 9 rolls.

### Orange Glaze

⅓ cup sifted powdered sugar
1 tablespoon frozen orange juice concentrate, thawed and undiluted
1 teaspoon water

Combine all ingredients, stirring until smooth. Yield: 2½ tablespoons.

# Coffee With A Kick

Many hosts and hostesses enjoy serving coffee with a splash of a favorite liqueur. But try adding extra flavor with chocolate, cinnamon, ice cream, whipped cream, or eggnog.

## AMARETTO ESPRESSO

¼ cup semisweet chocolate morsels
1½ tablespoons sugar
1 tablespoon water
2 cups hot brewed espresso
¼ cup amaretto
Whipped cream
⅓ cup crushed amaretti cookies

Combine first 3 ingredients in a small saucepan; cook over low heat, stirring constantly, until smooth. Stir in espresso. Remove from heat; stir in amaretto. Pour into espresso or coffee cups; top with whipped cream, and sprinkle with cookies. Yield: 2½ cups.

## GERMAN CHOCOLATE CAFÉ AU LAIT

3½ tablespoons ground Dutch
    Almond coffee *
1 cup water
½ cup hot milk
2 tablespoons CocoRibe or other
    coconut-flavored liqueur
2 tablespoons Frangelico or other
    hazelnut liqueur
¼ cup whipped cream
2 teaspoons grated sweet baking
    chocolate

Prepare coffee according to manufacturer's directions using 3½ tablespoons ground coffee and 1 cup water. Stir in milk and liqueurs. Pour into mugs; top with whipped cream and grated chocolate. Yield: 1¾ cups.

* 3 tablespoons instant Swiss Mocha coffee powder may be substituted for ground coffee. Dissolve coffee in 1 cup boiling water and proceed as directed above.

## COFFEE EGGNOG PUNCH

1 tablespoon instant coffee granules
½ cup milk
3 cups commercial eggnog
⅓ cup bourbon
⅓ cup Kahlúa or other
    coffee-flavored liqueur
1 cup whipping cream, whipped
Garnishes: ground cinnamon,
    ground nutmeg

Combine coffee granules and milk in a small saucepan; cook over medium heat until granules dissolve, stirring often. Let cool.

Combine milk mixture, eggnog, bourbon, and Kahlúa; chill. Fold in whipped cream. Garnish, if desired. Yield: 6 cups.

**Tip:** *For best results, use freshly brewed coffee. If coffee must be held before serving, keep it no longer than one hour in an automatic pot or reheat over low heat; do not allow it to boil.*

## CAPPUCCINO COFFEE DESSERT

2 teaspoons instant coffee granules
1 cup boiling water
2 tablespoons Frangelico or other
    hazelnut liqueur
½ teaspoon vanilla extract
1 scoop vanilla ice cream

Combine coffee granules and water in a coffee mug. Stir in liqueur and vanilla; top with ice cream. Yield: 1 cup.
*Zita Pavey*
*Miami Shores, Florida*

# Add Chocolate To The Cheese

Melanie Smith of Monroe, North Carolina, loves chocolate. Her family and friends were never surprised when she whipped up wonderful desserts made with this rich confection—until the day she laced a cheese spread with chocolate nuggets.

It sounds unusual, but the combination really works. She stirs cinnamon and powdered sugar into the mixture of cream cheese and chocolate morsels, and serves the clever concoction with gingersnaps she bakes from scratch.

## CHOCOLATE CHIP CHEESE LOAVES

3 (8-ounce) packages cream cheese,
    softened
1½ cups semisweet chocolate mini-
    morsels
1 cup sifted powdered sugar
1 tablespoon ground cinnamon
1 (7-ounce) milk chocolate candy
    bar
1¼ cups chopped pecans
Gingersnaps

Combine first 4 ingredients, stirring until blended; divide mixture in half, and spoon each half into a plastic wrap-lined 7½- x 3- x 2-inch loafpan. Cover and chill 5 hours or until ready to serve.

Pull a vegetable peeler down long edge of candy bar, letting chocolate curl up on vegetable peeler.

To serve, invert each cheese loaf onto a serving plate; remove plastic wrap. Press pecans around sides of loaves. Sprinkle chocolate curls on top. Serve with Gingersnaps. Yield: 2 (2-cup) cheese loaves.

### Gingersnaps

¾ cup shortening
1 cup sugar
1 large egg
¼ cup molasses
2 cups all-purpose flour
2 teaspoons baking soda
¼ teaspoon salt
1 tablespoon ground ginger
1 teaspoon ground cinnamon
Sugar

Beat shortening in a large bowl at medium speed with an electric mixer; gradually add 1 cup sugar, beating well. Add egg and molasses, mixing thoroughly.

Combine flour and next 4 ingredients; add flour mixture one-fourth at a time to creamed mixture, mixing after each addition.

Shape dough into ¾-inch balls, and roll in sugar. Place on ungreased cookie sheets, and bake at 350° for 8 minutes. (Tops will crack.) Remove to wire racks to cool. Yield: 8 dozen.

**Note:** To make larger gingersnaps, shape cookie dough into 1-inch balls, and bake 10 minutes; the yield will be 4 dozen.

# Over The River . . .

And through the woods—Thanksgiving day is here. Pull up a chair and tuck in that napkin. This family celebration features golden brown turkey, crunchy apple salad, and moist cornbread dressing.

This is a meal like grandma used to make—but updated for today's busy cooks. There's a choice of entrées: turkey or an easy Cornish hen casserole. Both have five or fewer ingredients. (The casserole includes rice, so you won't need to make dressing.)

Two desserts are also offered. Pumpkin Pie With Meringue is for traditionalists. Raspberry Ice is for those who prefer a lighter ending to a day of feasting, and it can be made ahead.

All the recipes that go into the oven are adjusted to bake together at 350° except Pumpkin Pie With Meringue; it's intended to go in at 400° early that morning, before all the "serious" cooking starts.

Here's to a bountiful season. Celebrate with family and friends.

## A FAMILY THANKSGIVING
## MENU FOR EIGHT OR TWELVE

**Cranberry Spritzer**
**Broccoli-Cheese Appetizer**
**Stuffed Apple Salad**
**Herbed Turkey Breast with Cornbread Dressing**
**or**
*****Cornish Hens-and-Rice Casserole**
**Buttered green beans   Boiled new potatoes**
**Commercial rolls**
**Pumpkin Pie With Meringue**
**or**
*****Raspberry Ice**
*****(Serves eight)**

■ Aromatic bitters, a blend of herbs, spices, and alcohol, spike this recipe with a little extra flavor. If you're serving the drink to both adults and children, mix just the fruit juices for the children, then shake bitters into drinks for adults.

### CRANBERRY SPRITZER
*(pictured on page 293)*

1 (48-ounce) bottle cranberry juice cocktail
2 cups pineapple juice
¼ cup Angostura bitters (optional)

Combine all ingredients in a large pitcher, stirring well. Serve beverage chilled or poured over ice. Yield: 2 quarts.

■ Skip the traditional broccoli-cheese casserole in favor of this appetizer, hot and savory with Parmesan cheese and even a bit of chili powder.

### BROCCOLI-CHEESE APPETIZER
*(pictured on page 293)*

1 (10-ounce) package frozen chopped broccoli, thawed and drained
1 cup mayonnaise or salad dressing
⅔ cup grated Parmesan cheese
½ cup chopped fresh chives
½ cup chopped fresh parsley
1 tablespoon dried basil
1 tablespoon lemon juice
½ teaspoon chili powder

Combine all ingredients in a lightly greased 1-quart baking dish. Bake, uncovered, at 350° for 20 minutes or until thoroughly heated. Serve with crackers and turnip or other vegetable sticks. Yield: 2½ cups.

**Note:** For extra color when serving, place turnip or other vegetable sticks into a halved, seeded, sweet red pepper.
*Grace Bravos*
*Timonium, Maryland*

## A Picture-Perfect Platter

Cooks often agonize over how to garnish their turkeys. Sometimes, the best garnish is more food—such as buttered green beans and boiled new potatoes served in mouth-watering mounds alongside the turkey breast.

**How to do it:** Cook vegetables the way you deem easiest—steamed, microwaved, or boiled. When we tried it, we cooked 2 (9-ounce) packages of frozen French-style green beans according to package directions, and then tossed them with melted butter or margarine, salt, and pepper. We boiled the new potatoes for 15 minutes, drained

them, drizzled them with olive oil, and then sprinkled them with freshly ground pepper. (One pound of new potatoes will serve 3 to 4. Cook 3 pounds of new potatoes to serve 12.)

When you transfer the turkey from a baking dish to a platter, simply arrange the cooked vegetables around it for an attractive presentation.

■ Red cinnamon candies—the kind you ate at Halloween as a child—give this apple salad its appealing color and unique flavor. The stuffing tastes like Waldorf salad.

### STUFFED APPLE SALAD
*(pictured on pages 294 and 295)*

6 large cooking apples, peeled
2 cups water
1 cup red cinnamon candies
1 cup raisins or currants
½ cup chopped celery
⅓ cup chopped, toasted pecans
⅓ cup mayonnaise or
  salad dressing
Lettuce leaves

Cut apples in half crosswise; core each with a sharp knife or melon baller, leaving a 1-inch hole in center. Set aside.

Combine water and candies in a Dutch oven; bring to a boil, stirring constantly. Add half of apple halves; cover and simmer 3 to 4 minutes or until tender. Remove cooked apples with a slotted spoon, and set aside. Add remaining apple halves to Dutch oven, and repeat procedure. Cool.

Combine raisins and next 3 ingredients; spoon into center of apple halves. Cover and chill at least 2 hours; serve on a bed of lettuce on a platter or salad plates. Yield: 12 servings.
*Jeanne Dobson*
*New Orleans, Louisiana*

■ Serving a turkey breast versus a whole turkey eliminates waste and is especially helpful if your family prefers white meat. Use the leftover bone to flavor soup or make broth.

### HERBED TURKEY BREAST
*(pictured on page 294)*

¼ cup olive oil
3 cloves garlic, minced
1 teaspoon dried rosemary
1 (5- to 5½-pound) bone-in turkey
  breast

Combine first 3 ingredients. Loosen skin from turkey breast without totally

## Little Details Count

You might think that writing out the menu for each guest is silly until you ask your teenager (who recently learned calligraphy) to do it. Chances are, the project will turn out letter-perfect. If you prefer a little less formality, ask the younger children who just can't wait for the turkey to get done to write out menus. (This project should keep them occupied for at least 30 minutes!)

If you're the creative one in the family, consider writing each menu on stiff paper, or have copies made at a nearby copy center. Your creative doodlings just might find their way into someone's family scrapbook as a treasured memento of Thanksgiving.

detaching skin; brush about one-third of olive oil mixture under skin. Replace skin. Place breast in a lightly greased 11- x 7- x 1½-inch baking dish. Cover with aluminum foil; bake at 325° for 1 hour. Uncover and bake 1 hour or until a meat thermometer reaches 170°, basting with remaining olive oil mixture every 15 minutes. Yield: 10 to 12 servings.

**Note:** For an even, golden brown turkey, add a few drops of a browning-and-seasoning sauce, such as Kitchen Bouquet, to the olive oil mixture.

■ Ann Sturdivant bakes her cornbread in an 8-inch iron skillet; she says 1½ rounds or batches make 8 cups of crumbs. She saves the remaining cornbread for dinner that night. If you're short on time, bake a commercial mix and use it in the dressing.

### CORNBREAD DRESSING
*(pictured on page 294)*

1 bunch celery, chopped
2 large green peppers, chopped
2 medium-size yellow onions, chopped
1 bunch green onions, chopped
¼ cup vegetable oil
8 cups cornbread crumbs
1 (14½-ounce) can ready-to-serve chicken broth
2 (10½-ounce) cans cream of chicken soup, undiluted
3 large eggs, beaten
1 teaspoon garlic powder
1 teaspoon rubbed sage
¼ teaspoon pepper
Garnish: sweet red and green pepper strips

Cook first 4 ingredients in oil in a large skillet over medium-high heat, stirring constantly, until tender (about 5 minutes). Combine cooked vegetables, cornbread crumbs, and next 6 ingredients in a large bowl; spoon into a lightly greased 13- x 9- x 2-inch baking dish. Bake at 325° for 1 hour and 10 minutes or until a knife inserted in center comes out clean. Garnish, if desired. Yield: 12 servings.

*Ann Sturdivant*
*McComb, Mississippi*

■ To feed eight guests, you'll need to bake this recipe in two 11- x 7- x 1½-inch baking dishes. This recipe can also be made ahead of time, refrigerated, and reheated (covered with foil).

### CORNISH HENS-AND-RICE CASSEROLE

2 cups long grain rice, uncooked
1 (0.6 ounce) envelope Italian salad dressing mix
4 cups boiling water
2 (10½-ounce) cans condensed cream of chicken soup, undiluted
4 (1¼-pound) Cornish hens, split

Spread rice into two lightly greased 11- x 7- x 1½-inch baking dishes; bake at 350°, stirring occasionally, for 15 to 20 minutes, or until golden brown.

Combine salad dressing mix, water, and soup in a large saucepan; stir in rice. Divide in half, and return to baking dishes; place hens, cut side down, on rice mixture.

Bake, uncovered, at 350° for 1 hour. (Cover with foil if Cornish hens begin getting too brown.) Yield: 8 servings.

**Note:** The casserole may also be baked in one 13- x 9- x 2-inch baking dish and one 11- x 7- x 1½-inch baking dish according to the directions above.

*Irene Graham*
*Union, South Carolina*

### A Head Start

**Up to three months ahead:**
■ Assemble Cornbread Dressing, and freeze, thaw in the refrigerator the day before serving, and bake at 325° for 1 hour and 15 minutes.
■ Make and freeze Raspberry Ice. Remove from freezer 10 minutes before serving, and let stand.

**The day before:**
■ Mix juices for Cranberry Spritzer, and chill.
■ Combine ingredients for Broccoli-Cheese Appetizer, and chill; cut up vegetables, and chill.
■ Refrigerate stuffing and cooked apples for Stuffed Apple Salad separately.
■ Mix filling for Pumpkin Pie With Meringue, and chill; the morning of the meal, make the meringue, and bake pie.

**About two to three hours before the meal:**
■ Bake Broccoli-Cheese Appetizer; serve with Cranberry Spritzer as an appetizer in the kitchen while you cook.
■ Bake Herbed Turkey Breast or Cornish Hens-and-Rice Casserole.
■ Stuff filling into apples for Stuffed Apple Salad; place salads on beds of lettuce. Chill serving platter or salad plates in refrigerator if you have room for them.

**A half hour before serving:**
■ Cook green beans and new potatoes; assemble on platter with turkey. (See "A Picture-Perfect Platter" on facing page for tips.)
■ Heat commercial rolls in oven (about 10 minutes) or microwave (about 2 minutes).

# Holiday Dinners

■ To shield a pie or piecrust means to cover the edges of the crust with strips of aluminum foil so the crust doesn't get too brown.

### PUMPKIN PIE WITH MERINGUE
*(pictured on page 295)*

1 (9-inch) refrigerated piecrust
1 (16-ounce) can mashed, cooked pumpkin
3 large eggs, separated
1 (14-ounce) can sweetened condensed milk
½ cup flaked coconut
¼ cup water
1 teaspoon ground cinnamon
½ teaspoon ground ginger
½ teaspoon ground nutmeg
Dash of salt
¼ teaspoon cream of tartar
½ cup sugar

Place piecrust in a 9-inch pieplate; trim off excess pastry along edges. Fold edges under and crimp. Prick bottom and sides of piecrust with a fork. Bake at 425° for 5 minutes on lowest oven rack.

Combine pumpkin, egg yolks, sweetened condensed milk, and next 6 ingredients; pour into piecrust. Shield crust with aluminum foil, and bake at 400° for 30 minutes in center of oven.

Beat egg whites and cream of tartar at high speed with an electric mixer until foamy. Gradually add sugar, 1 tablespoon at a time, beating until stiff peaks form and sugar dissolves (2 to 4 minutes). Spread over hot filling, sealing to edge of pastry. Shield crust, and bake at 325° for 25 to 28 minutes or until golden brown; cool on a wire rack. Yield: one 9-inch pie.

*Sandra Russell*
*Gainesville, Florida*

■ This dessert can be made several days ahead of time. Your favorite sugar cookies can also be made in advance, if desired. Or serve Raspberry Ice with specialty cookies from the bakery instead.

### RASPBERRY ICE

3 (10-ounce) packages frozen raspberries, thawed
¼ cup Grand Marnier or other orange-flavored liqueur
3 tablespoons sugar
1 tablespoon lemon juice
Garnish: orange rind strips

Position knife blade in food processor bowl; add first 4 ingredients. Process 30 seconds, scraping the sides of bowl once. Pour mixture through a wire-mesh strainer, pressing the back of a spoon against the sides of strainer to squeeze out juice. (Discard pulp and seeds remaining in strainer.) Pour juice mixture into an 8-inch square pan; freeze until almost firm.

Spoon mixture into a mixing bowl; beat at medium speed with an electric mixer until color turns lighter. Return mixture to pan, and freeze until firm. To serve, let mixture stand at room temperature 10 minutes. Garnish, if desired, and serve with sugar cookies. Yield: 4 cups. *Dorothy Eggert*
*Greensboro, North Carolina*

# Passing Along Family Recipes

If you want to know something about a family's history, you might first reach for a treasured, yellowed photo album. But you'd be surprised how much you can learn by thumbing through favorite dog-eared recipes scrawled on scraps of paper from generations past.

Our readers recognize the importance of this preservation and have shared family recipes with our magazine for more than 25 years. This holiday season, why not give a gift from both the heart and the home, sharing some of your own recipes with loved ones on your Christmas list? They'll appreciate your one-of-a-kind gift for years to come.

■ Our mailboxes bulge with recipes sent by readers each month, and we treasure those contributions. Lemon Tea Bread is a favorite one sent by a reader years ago.

### LEMON TEA BREAD

½ cup shortening
1 cup sugar
2 large eggs
1½ cups all-purpose flour
1½ teaspoons baking powder
¼ teaspoon salt
½ cup milk
Grated rind of 1 lemon
½ cup chopped pecans (optional)
Lemon Glaze

Beat shortening at medium speed with an electric mixer until fluffy; gradually add sugar, beating mixture well. Add eggs, one at a time, beating after each addition.

Combine flour, baking powder, and salt; add to creamed mixture alternately with milk, beginning and ending with flour mixture. Stir in lemon rind and, if desired, pecans.

Pour batter into a greased and floured 9- x 5- x 3-inch loafpan. Bake at 350° for 50 to 55 minutes or until a wooden pick inserted in center comes out clean. Cool in pan on a wire rack

10 to 15 minutes; remove from pan, and let cool completely on a wire rack. Pour Lemon Glaze over bread. Yield: 1 loaf.

### Lemon Glaze

1 cup sifted powdered sugar
2 tablespoons lemon juice

Combine ingredients, stirring until smooth. Yield: about ⅓ cup.

■ In the line of duty, one of our former Foods editors met Willard Scott of NBC's "Today Show" and learned of his love for biscuits. We sent our favorite biscuit recipe to him, and two of our Test Kitchens home economists created a clever gift basket to go with it.

Along with *The Southern Living Cookbook* containing our favorite version, Quick Buttermilk Biscuits, we packaged a rolling pin, flour, biscuit cutters, oven mitt, wooden spoons, and a pastry blender. As Willard attested, he tried the recipe and highly approved.

## QUICK BUTTERMILK BISCUITS

½ cup butter or margarine
2 cups self-rising flour
¾ cup buttermilk
Butter or margarine, melted

Cut ½ cup butter into flour with a pastry blender until mixture is crumbly. Add buttermilk, stirring until dry ingredients are moistened. Turn dough out onto a lightly floured surface, and knead lightly 3 or 4 times.

Roll dough to ¾-inch thickness. Cut with a 2-inch biscuit cutter, and place on a lightly greased baking sheet. Bake at 425° for 13 to 15 minutes. Brush biscuits with melted butter. Yield: 1 dozen.

■ Diane Brown of Earleville, Maryland, compiled a small recipe book for her family. She typed it herself and had it printed and bound professionally. Cranberry Sauce and Apple Strudel give you a taste of her work.

## CRANBERRY SAUCE

½ cup sugar
1 cup water
2 cups fresh cranberries
1 (3-ounce) package raspberry-flavored gelatin
1 (20-ounce) can pineapple tidbits, undrained

Combine sugar and water in a saucepan; bring to a boil over medium heat, stirring until sugar dissolves. Add cranberries, and bring to a boil. Boil 5 to 10 minutes or until cranberry skins pop. Remove from heat; add gelatin, stirring 2 minutes or until gelatin dissolves. Stir in pineapple; cover and chill 8 hours. Yield: 4 cups.

## APPLE STRUDEL

1 (17¼-ounce) package commercial frozen puff pastry sheets, thawed
2 tablespoons butter or margarine, melted and divided
¼ cup firmly packed brown sugar
1 teaspoon grated lemon rind
½ cup chopped pecans, divided
½ cup raisins, divided
1 (21-ounce) can apple pie filling, chopped

Roll each sheet of pastry into a 12- x 9-inch rectangle. Brush one rectangle with 1 tablespoon melted butter. Combine brown sugar and lemon rind; sprinkle half of brown sugar mixture on buttered pastry. Sprinkle half of pecans and raisins over brown sugar mixture. Brush remaining 1 tablespoon melted butter over second sheet of pastry, and place on top of

first sheet. Sprinkle with remaining brown sugar mixture, chopped pecans, and raisins.

Spoon pie filling down one 12-inch edge of pastry; starting with long side, roll up jellyroll fashion. Place strudel, seam side down, on a lightly greased baking sheet. With a knife, make diagonal 2-inch slits in top of pastry every 1 to 2 inches. Bake at 400° for 40 minutes or until golden. Yield: one 12-inch strudel.

■ One of our own travel writers, Carolanne Griffith-Roberts, once had a cookbook like Diane Brown's until her mother took it even a step further. Now when Carolanne needs a family favorite, she pops a floppy diskette into her home computer, thanks to mom. She calls up the needed recipe on her computer, complete with anecdotes of family history.

## PINK PEPPERMINT BIRTHDAY CAKE FROSTING

1½ cups sugar
½ cup water
2 egg whites
1 tablespoon light corn syrup
⅛ teaspoon salt
¼ teaspoon peppermint extract
2 to 3 drops red food coloring (optional)

Combine first 5 ingredients in top of a large double boiler. Before placing top of double boiler over boiling water, beat mixture at low speed with a handheld electric mixer 1 minute or just until blended.

Place over boiling water; beat at high speed 7 minutes or until stiff peaks form. Remove from heat. Add peppermint extract and, if desired, food coloring. Beat at high speed 2 minutes or until thick enough to spread. Yield: 7 cups. *Ann Griffith
Charleston, West Virginia*

# Meet The Pros

Some people wonder if we really try all the recipes we print in the magazine. You bet we do, and some of the recipes are tried time and time again. In the *Southern Living* kitchens, any day you'll find six talented Test Kitchens home economists busily preparing and perfecting some of the thousands of recipes our readers send us each month.

With over 60 years combined experience, this is an accomplished team of food experts, and we want you to meet them. Each month you see what they've been preparing in the Test Kitchens, but many ask what they cook at home. Find out as each one shares a favorite holiday recipe she traditionally serves to her own family and friends.

■ Every Christmas, Test Kitchens Director and Recipe Editor **Kaye Mabry Adams** serves hot Cinnamon Rolls. Kaye started the tradition of serving brunch right after opening presents. She makes the rolls ahead and freezes them. On Christmas, she serves the rolls, ham-and-egg casserole, and fresh fruit.

## CINNAMON ROLLS

½ cup water
½ cup milk
⅓ cup butter or margarine
4 to 4½ cups all-purpose flour,
    divided
1 teaspoon salt
¼ cup firmly packed brown sugar
1 package rapid-rise yeast
2 large eggs
1 cup firmly packed brown sugar
⅓ cup butter or margarine,
    softened
2 teaspoons ground cinnamon
2 cups sifted powdered sugar
3 to 4 tablespoons milk
¼ teaspoon vanilla extract

Combine water, ½ cup milk, and ⅓ cup butter in a saucepan over medium heat; cook until butter melts, stirring occasionally. Let mixture cool to 125° to 130°.

Combine 3 cups flour and next 3 ingredients in a large mixing bowl. Gradually add milk mixture to flour mixture, beating at low speed with an electric mixer. Add eggs, and beat 2 minutes at medium speed.

Gradually add 1 additional cup flour, beating 2 minutes. Gradually stir in enough remaining flour to make a soft dough.

Turn dough out onto a well-floured surface, and knead 5 minutes or until smooth, elastic, and no longer sticky. Cover and let rest 10 minutes. Divide dough in half, and roll each half into a 12-inch square. Combine 1 cup brown sugar, ⅓ cup butter, and cinnamon; spread evenly over both squares of dough. Roll dough, jellyroll fashion; pinch seams to seal. Cut each roll into 1-inch slices. Place rolls, cut side down, in two lightly greased 8-inch square pans.

Cover and let rise in a warm place (85°), free from drafts, 45 minutes or until doubled in bulk. Bake at 375° for 15 to 20 minutes or until golden brown. Combine powdered sugar, milk, and vanilla; drizzle over warm rolls. Yield: 2 dozen.

**Note:** Baked Cinnamon Rolls may be frozen without glaze. Cover with aluminum foil; freeze up to three months. Thaw in refrigerator overnight, and bake in foil at 375° for 10 to 15 minutes or until thoroughly heated. Drizzle with glaze.

■ If you think there's no room for other cooks in these professionals' home kitchens, visit **Diane Hogan** and her husband, Jim, on Christmas Eve morning. They prepare breakfast for 15 to 20 family members and friends. They set up a buffet of eggs, cheese grits, sweet rolls, juice, hot tea, coffee, and their favorite— Biscuits and Sausage Gravy.

## BISCUITS AND SAUSAGE GRAVY

3 cups self-rising soft wheat flour
¼ teaspoon baking soda
1 teaspoon sugar
½ cup butter-flavored shortening
1¼ cups buttermilk
Butter or margarine, melted
Sausage Gravy

Combine first 3 ingredients in a large bowl; cut in shortening with a pastry blender until mixture is crumbly. Add buttermilk, stirring just until dry ingredients are moistened. Turn dough out onto a lightly floured surface, and knead lightly 4 or 5 times.

Roll dough to ¾-inch thickness; cut with a 2½-inch biscuit cutter. Place on a lightly greased baking sheet. Bake at 425° for 12 minutes or until golden. Brush tops with butter. Split biscuits open; serve with Sausage Gravy. Yield: 12 to 14 servings.

### Sausage Gravy

½ pound ground pork sausage
¼ cup butter or margarine
⅓ cup all-purpose flour
3¼ cups 1% low-fat or whole milk
½ teaspoon salt
½ teaspoon pepper
⅛ teaspoon Italian seasoning

Brown sausage in a skillet, stirring until it crumbles. Drain, reserving 1 tablespoon drippings in skillet. Set sausage aside.

Add butter to drippings; heat over low heat until butter melts. Add flour, stirring until smooth. Cook 1 minute, stirring constantly. Gradually add milk; cook over medium heat, stirring constantly, until thickened and bubbly. Stir in seasonings and sausage. Cook until thoroughly heated, stirring constantly. Yield: 3¾ cups.

■ For **Judy Feagin,** the more the merrier. She enjoys mixing china and flatware patterns to accommodate her lengthy guest lists. Friends and family always enjoy her lively parties, but each Thanksgiving, they eagerly anticipate an old favorite, Cranberry Gelatin Mold.

### CRANBERRY GELATIN MOLD
*(pictured on page 259)*

1 large orange, seeded and
  quartered
4 cups fresh cranberries
2 cups sugar
1 envelope unflavored gelatin
¼ cup cold water
2 (3-ounce) packages
  lemon-flavored gelatin
3 cups boiling water
Lettuce leaves
Garnishes: orange slices, fresh
  cranberries, lettuce leaves

Position knife blade in food processor bowl; add orange. Process 30 seconds or until chopped. Add cranberries, and process 1 minute. Combine cranberry mixture and sugar in a bowl; let stand 15 minutes or until sugar dissolves.

Sprinkle unflavored gelatin over cold water in a bowl; stir and let stand 1 minute. Add lemon-flavored gelatin and boiling water; stir 2 minutes or until gelatin dissolves. Chill until the consistency of unbeaten egg white.

Stir cranberry mixture into gelatin mixture. Pour into a lightly oiled 12-cup Bundt pan or mold. Cover and chill until firm. Unmold onto a lettuce-lined plate, and garnish, if desired. Yield: 20 servings.

■ Marketing Manager **Peggy Smith** keeps six *Southern Living* pantries stocked. With 20 years of professional shopping behind her, she remembers when frozen foods first became popular. She tried serving her family a frozen pot pie, but they insisted on her Old-Fashioned Chicken Pot Pie.

### OLD-FASHIONED
### CHICKEN POT PIE

1 (3½-pound) broiler-fryer
2 quarts water
1 teaspoon salt
½ teaspoon pepper
1 stalk celery, cut into 2-inch
  pieces
1 medium onion, quartered
1 bay leaf
1 (16-ounce) package frozen mixed
  vegetables
2 large potatoes, peeled and cubed
½ cup butter or margarine
½ cup all-purpose flour
1 cup milk
1½ teaspoons salt
1¼ teaspoons pepper
¼ teaspoon dried thyme
2 hard-cooked eggs, sliced
1 (9-inch) refrigerated piecrust

Combine first 7 ingredients in a large Dutch oven; bring to a boil. Cover, reduce heat, and simmer 1 hour or until chicken is tender. Remove chicken, reserving broth in Dutch oven; discard vegetables and bay leaf. Let chicken cool; skin, bone, and cut into bite-size pieces.

With a large spoon, skim fat (oily liquid) from surface of broth reserved in Dutch oven; bring broth to a boil. Add frozen vegetables and potatoes; return to a boil. Reduce heat, cover, and simmer 8 minutes or until tender. Remove vegetables from broth, and set aside. Measure 3 cups broth; set aside. Reserve remaining broth for other uses.

Melt butter in Dutch oven over low heat; add flour, stirring until smooth. Cook 1 minute, stirring constantly. Gradually add 3 cups broth and milk; cook over medium heat, stirring constantly, until mixture is thickened and bubbly. Stir in 1½ teaspoons salt, 1¼ teaspoons pepper, and thyme. Add vegetables, chicken, and hard-cooked eggs; stir gently. Spoon into a lightly greased 13- x 9- x 2-inch baking dish; set aside.

Roll out piecrust on a lightly floured surface into a 15- x 11-inch rectangle (piecrust will be very thin). Place over chicken mixture; crimp edges, pressing against sides of baking dish. Cut slits in top for steam to escape; bake at 400° for 20 minutes or until golden brown. Yield: 6 to 8 servings.

**Tip:** *Fresh meat, poultry, and fish should be loosely wrapped and refrigerated; use in a few days. Loosely wrap fresh ground meat, liver, and kidneys; use in one or two days. Frankfurters, bacon, and sliced sandwich meats can be stored in original wrappings in the refrigerator. Store all meat in the coldest part of the refrigerator.*

■ Where there's a reason to celebrate, there's **Jane Cairns** ready to whip up just the right dish for the special occasion.

Her Creamy Ham-and-Chicken Medley has become a staff favorite. And you can enjoy this dish served over pasta with breadsticks and green salad or with fresh fruit and sweet rolls. It's perfect for a wedding brunch or farewell party. Perhaps you'll find just the occasion to try Jane's recipe.

### CREAMY HAM-AND-CHICKEN MEDLEY
*(pictured on page 259)*

1 tablespoon butter or margarine
½ cup sliced fresh mushrooms
⅓ cup butter or margarine
⅓ cup all-purpose flour
2½ to 3 cups milk, divided
1 cup whipping cream
1 cup freshly grated Parmesan cheese
½ teaspoon salt
¼ teaspoon freshly ground black pepper
¼ teaspoon ground nutmeg
Dash of ground red pepper
2 cups chopped cooked chicken
2 cups chopped cooked ham
2 (10-ounce) packages commercial frozen puff pastry shells, baked
Paprika

Melt 1 tablespoon butter in a large saucepan over medium heat; add mushrooms, and cook until tender, stirring constantly. Remove from saucepan; set aside.

Melt ⅓ cup butter in saucepan over low heat; add flour, stirring until smooth. Cook 1 minute, stirring constantly. Gradually add 2½ cups milk; cook over medium heat, stirring constantly, until thickened and bubbly. Stir in whipping cream and next 5 ingredients. Cook, stirring constantly, until cheese melts and mixture is smooth; stir in chicken and ham. Add enough of remaining ½ cup milk for a thinner consistency, if desired. To serve, spoon into shells, and sprinkle with paprika. Yield: 12 servings.

**Note:** Creamy Ham-and-Chicken Medley may be served over hot, cooked angel hair pasta instead of pastry. Sprinkle with freshly grated Parmesan cheese, if desired.

■ You might think our home economists would tire of cooking by the end of a day, but come the holidays there's no stopping Assistant Test Kitchens Director **Patty Vann**. This Christmas season, Patty's kitchen will once again become a cookie and candy factory while she cranks out 150 dozen, yes, dozen goodies as gifts.

### FROSTED PEANUT BUTTER BROWNIES

1 cup butter or margarine
⅓ cup cocoa
2 cups sugar
1½ cups all-purpose flour
½ teaspoon salt
4 large eggs
1 teaspoon vanilla extract
1 (12-ounce) jar chunky peanut butter
½ cup butter or margarine
¼ cup cocoa
⅓ cup milk
10 large marshmallows
1 (16-ounce) package powdered sugar, sifted

Combine 1 cup butter and ⅓ cup cocoa in a saucepan over low heat; cook, stirring frequently, until butter melts. Remove from heat, and cool slightly.

Combine sugar, flour, and salt in a large mixing bowl. Add chocolate mixture, and beat at medium speed with an electric mixer until blended. Add eggs and vanilla, mixing well. Spread into a well-greased 13- x 9- x 2-inch pan. Bake at 350° for 20 to 25 minutes or until a wooden pick inserted in center comes out clean.

Remove lid from peanut butter jar; microwave at MEDIUM (50% power) 2 to 3 minutes or until peanut butter melts, stirring at 1-minute intervals. Spread over warm brownies. Chill about 30 minutes or until set.

Combine ½ cup butter and next 3 ingredients in a saucepan over medium heat; cook, stirring frequently, until marshmallows melt. Remove from heat, and add powdered sugar, stirring until smooth. Spread over peanut butter, and chill until set. Store in refrigerator. Yield: 4 dozen.

**Note:** Freeze brownies in airtight containers up to three months.

# I'll Swap You A Baker's Dozen

Instead of turning your kitchen into a bakery for several days, pick just one afternoon and one cookie recipe. Here's the key: With our 13 recipes (that's a "baker's dozen"—12, plus 1 for good measure), you can invite 12 friends to do the same and pool your efforts in a "cookie swap." And you'll end up with yummy cookies to enjoy or give as gifts.

### EASY PEANUT BUTTER COOKIES

1 large egg, lightly beaten
1 cup crunchy peanut butter
1 cup sugar
36 milk chocolate kisses, unwrapped

Combine first 3 ingredients; shape into ¾-inch balls. Place on ungreased cookie sheets; bake at 350° for 10 minutes. Immediately press a chocolate kiss in center of each cookie; remove to wire racks to cool. Yield: about 3 dozen.    *Sandra Pichon*
*Slidell, Louisiana*

## TOASTED OATMEAL COOKIES

1½ cups butter, divided
3 cups regular or quick-cooking
   oats, uncooked
1 cup chopped pecans
¾ cup firmly packed brown sugar
½ cup sugar
1 large egg
1 teaspoon vanilla extract
1½ cups all-purpose flour
1 teaspoon baking soda
½ teaspoon salt
1 teaspoon ground cinnamon
1 cup raisins

Melt ½ cup butter in a 15- x 10- x 1-inch jellyroll pan at 425°. Remove from oven; add oats and pecans, stirring to coat. Bake at 425° for 15 to 18 minutes, stirring occasionally, until lightly browned; set aside to cool.

Beat remaining 1 cup butter at medium speed with an electric mixer until soft and creamy. Gradually add sugars, beating well. Add egg and vanilla, mixing well. Combine flour and next 3 ingredients; add to butter mixture, mixing well. Stir in oat mixture and raisins.

Drop by rounded tablespoonfuls onto lightly greased cookie sheets; bake at 375° for 10 to 12 minutes or until lightly browned. Cool 1 minute on cookie sheets; remove cookies to wire racks to cool completely. Yield: 5 dozen.    *Delana Smith*
*Birmingham, Alabama*

## ALMOND SNAPS

½ cup shortening
½ cup almond paste
½ cup sugar
½ cup firmly packed brown sugar
1 large egg
2 tablespoons milk
1 teaspoon vanilla extract
1¾ cups all-purpose flour
1 teaspoon baking soda
½ teaspoon salt
¼ cup sugar

Beat shortening and almond paste at medium speed with an electric mixer. Add ½ cup sugar and next 4 ingredients, beating well. Combine flour, soda, and salt; gradually add to shortening mixture, mixing well.

Roll into 1-inch balls; roll in ¼ cup sugar, and place 2 inches apart on lightly greased cookie sheets. Bake at 375° for 12 to 14 minutes or until lightly browned; cool about 2 minutes on cookie sheets. Remove to wire racks to cool. Yield: 4½ dozen.
*Elaine M. Dubrosky*
*Waynesville, Missouri*

## OLD-FASHIONED CUTOUT COOKIES

1 cup butter, softened
1 cup sifted powdered sugar
2¼ cups all-purpose flour
1 teaspoon vanilla extract
½ cup flaked coconut

Beat butter at medium speed with an electric mixer until soft and creamy; gradually add sugar, beating well. Add flour and vanilla, mixing well. Roll to ⅛-inch thickness on a lightly floured surface. Cut with a 3-inch lamb-shaped or other shaped cookie cutter; place on ungreased cookie sheets. Sprinkle with flaked coconut. Bake at 375° for 7 to 9 minutes or until edges begin to brown. Yield: 2 dozen.

## Cookie Tips

■ For consistent results, form drop cookies using either a teaspoon or a tablespoon.
■ When making bar cookies, use the size of pan called for in the recipe. Altering the pan size will affect the consistency of the cookies.
■ If the dough for rolled cookies is sticky and hard to work with, chill it for a few minutes in the freezer before continuing.
■ Grease cookie sheet only if specified in the recipe.
■ For chewy cookies, choose the low range of a recipe's baking time. For crisp cookies, bake for the longer time.
■ To prevent overbaking, let cookies cool on cookie sheets 1 minute; then remove to wire racks to cool completely (unless recipe specifies differently).
■ Cool bar cookies completely before cutting.
■ To soften cookies that have become hard, place an apple wedge in an airtight container with them. Remove apple the next day.

## A Head Start

■ Most cookie doughs can be tightly wrapped and stored in the refrigerator up to one week or in freezer up to six months before baking.
■ You can bake and freeze these cookies up to eight months in advance. (Snow Flurries should be frozen unassembled.) Package the cookies in airtight containers to keep them as fresh as possible. (Frozen cookies usually thaw in 10 to 15 minutes at room temperature.)

## SUGAR-COATED CHOCOLATE COOKIES

½ cup butter or margarine
3 (1-ounce) squares unsweetened
  chocolate
2 cups sugar
2 cups all-purpose flour
2 teaspoons baking powder
3 large eggs, lightly beaten
2 teaspoons vanilla extract
¾ cup sifted powdered
  sugar

Melt butter and chocolate in a heavy saucepan over low heat. Combine sugar, flour, and baking powder in a large bowl. Add chocolate mixture, eggs, and vanilla, mixing until smooth (mixture will be very thin). Cover and chill at least two hours.

Roll dough into 1-inch balls, and roll balls in powdered sugar. Place 2 inches apart on lightly greased cookie sheets; bake at 375° for 10 to 12 minutes. Remove to wire racks to cool. Yield: 8 dozen. *Darlene Reynolds*
*Nashville, Tennessee*

## Cookie Tips

■ To shape cookies without rolling and cutting, roll dough into 1-inch balls and place on cookie sheet 2 inches apart; flatten each ball with bottom of glass dipped in sugar.

■ Let cookies cool completely before storing. To keep cookies fresh, store soft and chewy ones in an airtight container and crisp cookies in a jar with a loose-fitting lid.

## EGGNOG LOGS

1 cup butter or margarine, softened
¾ cup sugar
1 large egg
2 teaspoons vanilla extract
1 teaspoon rum flavoring
3 cups all-purpose flour
1 teaspoon ground nutmeg
Vanilla Frosting
¾ cup chopped pecans, toasted

Beat butter at medium speed with an electric mixer until soft and creamy; gradually add sugar, beating well. Add egg and flavorings, mixing well. Combine flour and nutmeg; gradually add to butter mixture, mixing well.

Divide dough into 10 portions. Roll each portion into a 15-inch-long rope, and cut each rope into 5 (3-inch) logs. Place 2 inches apart on ungreased cookie sheets; bake at 350° for 10 to 12 minutes. Cool on wire racks.

Dip log ends into Vanilla Frosting; roll in pecans. Yield: 50 cookies.

### Vanilla Frosting

¼ cup butter or margarine,
  softened
2 cups sifted powdered sugar
2 tablespoons milk
1 teaspoon vanilla extract

Beat butter at medium speed with an electric mixer until soft and creamy. Add sugar and milk alternately, beating mixture after each addition. Add vanilla; beat until smooth and mixture reaches spreading consistency. Yield: about 1 cup.

## MACADAMIA-OAT SNOWBALLS

1 cup butter or margarine, softened
½ cup sifted powdered sugar
1 teaspoon vanilla extract
2 cups all-purpose flour
¾ cup quick-cooking oats, uncooked
1 (3½-ounce) jar macadamia nuts,
  chopped
Powdered sugar

Beat butter at medium speed with an electric mixer until soft and creamy; gradually add ½ cup powdered sugar, beating well. Add vanilla and flour, mixing well. Stir in oats and nuts. Shape into 1-inch balls; place on ungreased cookie sheets. Bake at 375° for 12 minutes. Remove from pan; roll in powdered sugar, and cool on wire racks. Yield: 4 dozen.

*Evelyn Weisman*
*Corpus Christi, Texas*

## RASPBERRY BROWNIES

½ cup butter or margarine,
  softened
1 cup sugar
2 large eggs
2 (1-ounce) squares unsweetened
  chocolate, melted
¾ cup all-purpose flour
1 cup chopped walnuts
⅓ cup raspberry jam

Beat butter at medium speed with an electric mixer until soft and creamy; gradually add sugar, beating well. Add eggs and chocolate, mixing well. Add flour to butter mixture, mixing well; stir in walnuts.

Spoon half of batter into a greased and floured 9-inch square pan. Spread raspberry jam over batter; top with remaining batter. Bake mixture at 350° for about 28 to 30 minutes. Yield: 3 dozen brownies.

*Mrs. Harland J. Stone*
*Ocala, Florida*

## CHERRY CROWNS

1 cup butter or margarine, softened
1 (3-ounce) package cream cheese, softened
1 cup sugar
1 large egg, separated
1 teaspoon almond extract
2½ cups all-purpose flour
1 cup finely ground blanched almonds
30 red candied cherries, halved

Beat butter and cream cheese at medium speed with an electric mixer until soft and creamy; gradually add sugar, beating well. Add egg yolk and almond extract, mixing well; gradually stir in flour. Cover and chill 1 hour.

Shape dough into 1-inch balls; dip tops of balls in lightly beaten egg white, then almonds. Place 2 inches apart on lightly greased cookie sheets. Press a candied cherry half in center of each ball. Bake at 350° for 15 minutes. Remove to wire racks to cool. Yield: 5 dozen.          *Jean Voan*
*Shepherd, Texas*

## SNOW FLURRIES

½ cup butter or margarine, softened
½ cup shortening
1 cup sugar
2 large eggs
1 tablespoon grated lemon rind
1 teaspoon vanilla extract
½ teaspoon almond extract
3½ cups all-purpose flour
½ teaspoon baking powder
½ teaspoon salt
⅓ cup raspberry jam
1 cup sifted powdered sugar

Beat butter and shortening at medium speed with an electric mixer until soft and creamy; gradually add 1 cup sugar, beating well. Add eggs, lemon rind, and flavorings, mixing well.

Combine flour, baking powder, and salt; gradually add to butter mixture, mixing well. Cover; chill 1 hour.

Divide dough in half; store one portion in refrigerator. Roll remaining portion to ⅛-inch thickness on a lightly floured surface. Cut with a 2½-inch star-shaped cookie cutter, and place on ungreased cookie sheets. Bake at 375° for 7 to 8 minutes or until lightly browned; cool 2 minutes on cookie sheets. Remove to wire racks to cool. Repeat with remaining dough.

Just before serving, spread center of half of cookies with about ¼ teaspoon raspberry jam. Place a second cookie on top, alternating points of stars of top and bottom cookies. Sprinkle generously with powdered sugar. Yield: 5 dozen.   *Edith Askins*
*Greenville, Texas*

## FRUITCAKE DROP COOKIES

2 cups chopped red candied cherries
1 cup chopped green candied pineapple
1 cup chopped pecans
1 cup chopped almonds
1 cup chopped dates
1 cup golden raisins
1 cup butter or margarine, softened
2 cups firmly packed brown sugar
3 large eggs, lightly beaten
¼ cup honey
1 teaspoon lemon juice
1 teaspoon vanilla extract
3½ cups all-purpose flour
1 teaspoon baking powder
1 teaspoon baking soda
1 teaspoon ground cinnamon
½ teaspoon ground cloves
½ teaspoon ground nutmeg

Combine first 6 ingredients; set fruit mixture aside.

Beat butter at medium speed with an electric mixer until soft and creamy; gradually add brown sugar, beating well. Add eggs and next 3 ingredients, beating well. Combine flour and next 5 ingredients; gradually add to butter mixture, beating well. Stir in fruit mixture. Drop by rounded teaspoonfuls onto lightly greased cookie sheets; bake at 350° for 15 minutes. Cool on wire racks. Yield: 12½ dozen.
*Aleisha Dawn Humphrey*
*Stanardsville, Virginia*

### How to Plan A Cookie Swap

■ Have each person bake a dozen or half-dozen cookies for each person attending the party. (Keep the guest list manageable. The more people you invite, the more each person will have to bake, but each guest will take home a greater variety, too.)
■ Ask participants to bring extra cookies for sampling during the party. So, the only refreshment you have to prepare, besides your cookies, is a beverage.
■ Tell everyone how to bring their cookies for trading. They can package them for each guest by the dozen or half-dozen, or the participants can bring the whole batch in one container plus an empty container for collecting their share of cookies from the other bakers.
■ Because someone's sure to ask, have guests bring copies of their cookie recipes.

## BRAIDED CANDY CANES AND WREATHS

¾ cup butter or margarine, softened
1 cup sugar
3 large eggs
1 tablespoon vanilla extract
4 cups all-purpose flour
1 tablespoon baking powder
½ teaspoon baking soda
1 egg white
Red decorator sugar crystals or sesame seeds

Beat butter at medium speed with an electric mixer until soft and creamy; gradually add sugar, beating well. Add eggs and vanilla, mixing well. Combine flour, baking powder, and soda; gradually add flour mixture to butter mixture, mixing at low speed just until blended.

Divide dough into fourths. Divide each fourth of dough into 14 portions, and roll each portion into an 8-inch rope. Fold each rope in half and twist. Shape twists into candy canes or wreaths; brush with lightly beaten egg white, and sprinkle with sugar crystals or sesame seeds.

Place cookies 2 inches apart on lightly greased cookie sheets; bake at 350° for 15 to 18 minutes or until the edges begin to brown. Remove to wire racks to cool. Yield: 4½ dozen.

*Kelly Barbee*
*Savannah, Georgia*

## Packaging Ideas

■ Check stores for holiday tins, serving containers, bags, baskets, and gift boxes. Line with paper or cloth napkins, colored plastic wrap, or colored tissue paper.
■ Create your own gift bags from white, colored, or small brown paper food-grade bags. Decorate with holiday stencils or rubber stamps and ink. Use pinking shears or cut scallops on the top edge of the bags. Fold down the top, and seal with holiday stickers, or weave ribbon through holes punched in the bag to close.
■ Ask local Chinese restaurants if you can buy traditional cardboard carryout containers with wire handles. Also check gift shops, candy stores, or import retailers. Use rubber stamps and ink to decorate the outside, and seal with holiday stickers or ribbon.
■ To protect fragile cookies, place each cookie in its own foil or paper baking cup.

## MOLASSES CRINKLES

¾ cup shortening
1 cup firmly packed brown sugar
1 large egg
¼ cup molasses
2¼ cups all-purpose flour
2 teaspoons baking soda
½ teaspoon salt
1 teaspoon ground cinnamon
1 teaspoon ground ginger
½ teaspoon ground cloves
½ cup sugar

Beat shortening at medium speed with an electric mixer until soft and creamy; gradually add brown sugar, beating well. Add egg and molasses, mixing well. Combine flour and next 5 ingredients; add flour mixture to shortening mixture, mixing well. Cover; chill 2 hours.

Shape dough into 1-inch balls, and roll balls in sugar. Place 2 inches apart on lightly greased cookie sheets; bake at 350° for 12 to 15 minutes. Remove crinkles to wire racks to cool. Yield: 4½ dozen.

*Alice Rhodes*
*Harrisonburg, Virginia*

# Teddy Bear Tea Party

"Bring your special teddy bear. Come play dress up with me, and stay for tea," read the invitations to this Teddy Bear Tea. Favorite playmates, furry friends, vintage clothes, and dainty foods guarantee a fun-filled afternoon.

Drape a cloth over a small table or desk, fill a teapot with roses, and let the young hostess set her tea table. If you haven't saved favorite old garments, browse through secondhand stores or scout grandmother's attic. The menu is simple; you can choose either made-from-scratch or quick-and-easy recipes.

## TEDDY BEAR TEA FOR EIGHT

**Cheese Tea Sandwiches**
or
**Peppermint Sandwich Cookies**
**Simple Petit Fours**
or
**Red-Bellied Bears**
**Chocolate-Peanut Butter Tarts**
**Snowflake Cookies**
**Teddy Bear Cakes**
**Fresh strawberries**
**Fruit punch**

## CHEESE TEA SANDWICHES
*(pictured on page 334)*

½ cup whipped cream cheese
½ cup (2 ounces) shredded Cheddar cheese
½ teaspoon prepared mustard
¼ teaspoon Worcestershire sauce
⅛ teaspoon ground red pepper (optional)
16 unpeeled cucumber slices (optional)
16 slices white sandwich bread

Combine first 4 ingredients; add red pepper, if desired, and set aside. With a 1¾-inch cookie cutter, cut two rounds out of each bread slice. Spread half of bread rounds with cheese filling; top with cucumber slices, if desired, and remaining bread rounds. Place in a shallow container, and cover with plastic wrap; top with a dampened dish towel, and refrigerate 8 hours. Yield: 16 sandwiches.

**Note:** Sandwiches may be frozen, omitting cucumber; thaw in refrigerator, and add cucumber before serving, if desired. Flavored cream cheese may be substituted for the cheese filling.

### PEPPERMINT SANDWICH COOKIES
*(pictured on page 334)*

⅔ cup ready-to-spread vanilla frosting
3 tablespoons crushed hard peppermint candy
¼ teaspoon peppermint extract
20 chocolate wafers

Combine first 3 ingredients; spread on half of chocolate wafers. Top with remaining chocolate wafers. Yield: 10 sandwich cookies.

**Note:** Cookies may be assembled in advance and refrigerated up to eight hours. (They will soften slightly.)

### SIMPLE PETIT FOURS
*(pictured on page 334)*

1 (18.5-ounce) package white cake mix with pudding
1 (16-ounce) container ready-to-spread vanilla frosting
Teddy bear-shaped chocolate graham cracker cookies
1 (4.25-ounce) tube red decorating frosting (optional)

Prepare cake mix according to package directions; spread batter in a greased and floured 15- x 10- x 1-inch jellyroll pan. Bake at 350° for 20 minutes. Let cake cool in pan on a wire rack. Spread vanilla frosting on top; cover and chill 8 hours.

Decorate cookies with red frosting, if desired; set aside.

Cut cake into 1½-inch squares; place each square in miniature paper baking cups, and top with graham cracker cookies. Yield: 5 dozen.

### RED-BELLIED BEARS
*(pictured on page 334)*

½ cup butter or margarine, softened
¾ cup sugar
1 large egg
¼ cup molasses
1½ tablespoons orange juice
3½ to 4 cups all-purpose flour
1 teaspoon baking soda
½ teaspoon salt
2 to 3 teaspoons ground ginger
1 teaspoon ground cinnamon
Red decorator sugar crystals
Red cinnamon candies

Beat butter at medium speed with an electric mixer until soft and creamy; gradually add sugar, beating well. Add egg, molasses, and orange juice, beating well. Combine flour and next 4 ingredients; gradually add to butter mixture, beating until blended.

Divide dough into thirds; roll each portion to ¼-inch thickness on lightly greased cookie sheets. Cut cookies close together with a 3½-inch, bear-shaped cookie cutter. Remove excess dough from cookie sheets. Decorate with sugar crystals and candies. Bake at 350° for 10 minutes; remove to wire racks to cool. Yield: 3 dozen.

**Note:** Freeze in airtight containers up to six months. *Rosey Sommerville Chapel Hill, North Carolina*

### CHOCOLATE-PEANUT BUTTER TARTS
*(pictured on page 334)*

½ (20-ounce) package refrigerated sliceable peanut butter cookie dough
2 (4-ounce) containers refrigerated chocolate pudding
Frozen whipped topping, thawed

Cut cookie dough into ¾-inch slices; cut each slice into quarters, and roll dough into balls. Place balls into ungreased miniature (1¾-inch) muffin pans. Bake at 350° for 10 minutes. Remove cookies from oven, and immediately press the center of each cookie down with a tart tamper or the end of a wooden spoon handle, forming a tart shell. Return cookies to oven; bake at 350° for an additional 10 minutes.

Carefully loosen outer edges of tart shells with a small knife; let cool. Remove shells from pans, and store in an airtight container up to three days. (Or freeze shells in airtight containers up to six months.) Just before serving, fill shells with pudding, and top each with a dollop of whipped topping. Yield: 20 tarts.

## SNOWFLAKE COOKIES
*(pictured on page 334)*

1 cup butter or margarine, softened
½ cup sugar
2 tablespoons milk
1 tablespoon lemon rind
½ teaspoon vanilla extract
¼ teaspoon lemon extract
2½ cups all-purpose flour
Sifted powdered sugar

Beat butter at medium speed with an electric mixer until creamy; gradually add sugar, beating well. Stir in milk, lemon rind, and flavorings. Gradually add flour, mixing after each addition.

Roll dough to ⅛-inch thickness on an ungreased cookie sheet; cut close together with a 2-inch round cookie cutter. Carefully remove excess dough from cookie sheet. Using a drinking straw, randomly cut holes in dough, removing dough by slightly twisting straw. Bake at 375° for 6 to 7 minutes. (Cookies will not brown.) Remove cookies to wire racks to cool. Sprinkle with powdered sugar. Yield: 6 dozen.

**Note:** Freeze cookies in airtight containers up to six months.

---

### A Head Start

■ Gather vintage clothes, cuddly teddy bears, and a tea set **up to a month ahead.**
■ Assemble and freeze Cheese Tea Sandwiches without cucumbers **up to a month ahead,** or make and chill **the day before.**
■ Bake and freeze unfilled shells for Chocolate-Peanut Butter Tarts **up to a month ahead,** or bake and store in an airtight container **up to three days before.** Fill just before serving.
■ Bake and freeze Snowflake Cookies and Red-Bellied Bears **up to a month ahead,** or bake and store in an airtight container **one or two days before.**
■ Make and chill Simple Petit Fours **the day before.** Decorate with cookies before serving.
■ Make Teddy Bear Cakes **the day before.** Decorate up to two hours before serving.
■ Assemble Peppermint Sandwich Cookies **the morning of the party,** if desired, but they will be fresher if made just before the event.

---

### TEDDY BEAR CAKES

2 (16-ounce) packages pound cake mix
1 (16-ounce) container ready-to-spread vanilla frosting
Flaked coconut
Round peppermint candies
Semisweet chocolate morsels
Red cinnamon candies

Prepare cake mix according to package directions; spread batter in a greased and floured 15- x 10- x 1-inch jellyroll pan. Bake at 350° for 30 to 35 minutes or until a wooden pick inserted in center comes out clean. Let cool in pan on a wire rack 10 minutes; remove from pan, and let cool completely on wire rack.

With cookie cutters, cut 8 (3½-inch) circles and 8 (1¾-inch) circles. Cut small circles in half. Position large circle on plate; spread frosting on sides and top of cake. Arrange half-circles for ears, and spread with frosting. Pat coconut around sides, and decorate as desired. (Add peppermint last as it will bleed onto frosting after 2 hours.) Yield: 8 cakes.

---

# In The Nick Of Time!

Just before Santa makes his Christmas Eve delivery, let the children have a party of their own with old Saint Nick as the guest of honor. Watch their faces light up as he arrives to hear their Christmas wish lists. And since this party is *for* children, let them help with everything, from making invitations to assembling the food.

### SAINT NICK PARTY FOR EIGHT

**Easy Cheesy Bobolis or
Christmas Tree Sandwiches
Santa's Hat
Christmas Confetti Dip
Reindeer Nibbles
Frosted Pretzels**

■ Bobolis are cellophane-wrapped, baked pizza crusts available in the deli section of many grocery stores. Set out the ingredients before guests begin to arrive, and let them assemble their own.

### EASY CHEESY BOBOLIS

8 (6-inch) Bobolis *
1 (14-ounce) jar pizza sauce
1 (3½-ounce) package pepperoni slices
1 (8-ounce) package shredded mozzarella cheese

Spread each Boboli with ¼ to ⅓ cup pizza sauce. Top each with 6 to 8 pepperoni slices and ¼ cup cheese. Bake at 350° for 15 minutes or until cheese melts. Yield: 8 servings.

\* 8 (6-inch) pita bread rounds may be substituted for Bobolis.

■ Mix the sandwich filling the day before, and let children use cookie cutters to cut the bread slices into tree shapes. Help them spread the filling and cut "ornaments" from chewy fruit rolls to decorate the sandwiches.

### CHRISTMAS TREE SANDWICHES

1 (3-ounce) package cream cheese, softened
¼ cup finely chopped pecans
¼ cup chopped dates
¼ cup crushed pineapple, well drained
16 slices wheat or white sandwich bread
Cherry-flavored chewy fruit rolls (optional)

Combine first 4 ingredients; set mixture aside.

With a 3½-inch tree-shaped cookie cutter, cut 32 Christmas trees from bread slices. Spread about 1½ teaspoons filling on half of trees; top with remaining trees. Unroll fruit rolls; cut into small circles and triangles. Place on tree sandwiches as ornaments, if desired. Yield: 16 sandwiches.
*DeLea Lonadier*
*Montgomery, Louisiana*

■ The children can spoon ice cream into glasses or mugs and pour a little ginger ale over it. Then comes the best part—squirting canned instant whipped cream to make the "hat."

### SANTA'S HAT

½ gallon cherry-vanilla ice cream
1 (33.8-ounce) bottle ginger ale
1 (8.75-ounce) can refrigerated instant whipped cream
Red decorator sugar crystals
8 long-stemmed maraschino cherries

Spoon 1 cup ice cream into each of 8 glasses or mugs; pour ½ cup ginger ale over each. Top each with whipped cream, sugar crystals, and a cherry. Yield: 8 servings.

■ The day before, let the children help measure and stir the dip and wash the vegetables, but leave the slicing and chopping to adults.

### CHRISTMAS CONFETTI DIP

⅔ cup sour cream
⅓ cup mayonnaise or salad dressing
1 (2-ounce) jar diced pimiento, drained
2 tablespoons finely chopped chives
1 tablespoon finely chopped onion
¼ teaspoon garlic powder

Combine all ingredients. Cover and chill up to 2 days, or serve immediately with assorted fresh vegetables. Yield: about 1¼ cups. *Carrie Treichel*
*Johnson City, Tennessee*

## A Head Start

■ Due to the hectic holiday season, mail or hand-deliver party invitations a bit earlier than usual. Your guests will need enough time to get the party date on their parents' calendars.
■ Enlist a "Santa," and fill him in on all the details. Suggest ahead of time that he tell a story or two about his favorite Christmas adventures after he has chatted with each child.
■ Ask older children or parents to help you and Santa at this party. Youngsters will need guidance as they assemble Easy Cheesy Bobolis, Christmas Tree Sandwiches, and Santa's Hat.

■ For an easy holiday centerpiece, make a Reindeer Tree. Bake Reindeer Nibbles **a day or two ahead,** and let the children wrap them in cellophane holiday bags. Hang the bags on a miniature Christmas tree. For a finishing touch, drape popcorn or cranberry strings around the tree.

## Irresistible Invitations

Attention-grabbing invitations don't have to break the budget. The ones for this party look great yet are reasonably priced and easy enough for the children to make. Start with Saint Nick stationery and envelopes. Using a versatile and reusable "It's a Party" rubber stamp and an ink pad, the children can print their own invitations.

After first practicing on scratch paper, let older children stamp the stationery and fill in the party details with markers. Younger ones can slip the invitations into envelopes and seal them with fun Christmas stickers.

■ This is a granola Rudolph, Donner, and even Blitzen would love. But these nibbles are for children only.

### REINDEER NIBBLES

⅔ cup creamy peanut butter
⅔ cup honey
½ teaspoon ground cinnamon
1 teaspoon vanilla extract
4 cups regular oats, uncooked
1 cup unsalted peanuts
1½ cups raisins

Combine first 3 ingredients in a small saucepan. Cook over medium heat, stirring constantly, until thoroughly heated (do not boil). Stir in vanilla.

Spread oats in a lightly greased 15- x 10- x 1-inch jellyroll pan. Pour peanut butter mixture over oats; stir to coat evenly. Bake at 300° for 35 minutes, stirring occasionally. Stir in peanuts. Turn oven off, and cool in oven 1½ hours with door closed, stirring occasionally. Remove from oven; stir in raisins. Yield: 8 cups.

*Velma P. Kestner*
*Berwind, West Virginia*

# 'Twas The Night Before...

Christmas and all through the house, not a creature was stirring . . . except the cook, of course. After stirring and stirring in preparation for tomorrow's feast, the wearer of the apron needs a break. The packages are wrapped, the cards are in the mail, and the stockings are hung by a carefully trimmed tree. It's time for your family to enjoy the approach of the big day quietly by sharing a simple Christmas Eve meal.

Because the cook is likely up to her elbows in turkey and cornbread dressing, this Christmas Eve menu is easy enough for the rest of the family. Festive, yet casual, these recipes ensure a relaxed evening.

### CHRISTMAS EVE DINNER FOR FOUR

**Easy Brunswick Stew**
**Overnight Slaw**
**Santa Claus Milk**
**Sugar Plums**
or
**Chicken-Vegetable Spaghetti**
**Spinach Salad**
**Praline Sauce over sliced bananas**
or
**Frozen yogurt**

■ The morning of the party, melt the frosting in a microwave; then let the children dip the pretzels. Dry pretzels on wax paper for a couple of hours.

### FROSTED PRETZELS

1 cup ready-to-spread vanilla
   frosting
1 (10-ounce) bag large pretzel
   twists

Place frosting in a 2-cup glass measure; microwave at HIGH 30 to 45 seconds or until frosting melts, stirring once. Dip half of each pretzel into frosting, allowing excess to drip. Place on wax paper; let dry 2 hours or until no longer sticky. Serve same day. Yield: 2 dozen. *Chris Bryant*
*Johnson City, Tennessee*

■ What could be easier than opening cans and heating the contents at the last minute? You'll be surprised at how good something so simple can be.

### EASY BRUNSWICK STEW

1 (20-ounce) can Brunswick stew
1 (10-ounce) can pork with
   barbecue sauce
1 (10-ounce) can barbecue beef
1 (17-ounce) can lima beans, rinsed
   and drained
1 (11-ounce) can whole kernel corn,
   undrained
¼ cup commercial barbecue sauce
1 teaspoon lemon juice

Combine all ingredients in a 5-quart Dutch oven; cook, covered, over medium heat 20 minutes, lifting lid and stirring occasionally. Yield: 7 cups.

■ Let an adult or older child shred the cabbage in a food processor or chop it by hand; then a younger child can toss the slaw with the dressing.

### OVERNIGHT SLAW

4 cups shredded cabbage
¼ cup chopped purple onion
¾ cup sugar
¾ cup white vinegar
¾ cup water
2 teaspoons salt

Combine cabbage and purple onion in a large bowl. Combine sugar and remaining ingredients, stirring until sugar dissolves. Pour over cabbage mixture; toss gently. Cover and chill 8 hours. Serve with a slotted spoon. Yield: 4 servings. *Linda Turney*
*Jonesboro, Arkansas*

■ Ruth Fulton Tiedemann tells us her recipe dates back to colonial times when families gathered around the hearth for Christmas songs and stories and warmed their spirits with this comforting drink. Prepare Santa Clause Milk just before bedtime, and serve warm with Sugar Plums.

## SANTA CLAUS MILK

4 cups milk
1 (2-inch) stick cinnamon
3 to 4 whole cloves
¼ cup sugar
1 tablespoon cornstarch
2 tablespoons cold milk
Ground nutmeg

Combine first 3 ingredients in a saucepan; cook over medium heat 15 minutes, stirring occasionally. (Heat thoroughly, but do not boil.) Remove and discard cinnamon and cloves.

Combine sugar and cornstarch; add 2 tablespoons cold milk, stirring mixture until smooth. Add cold milk mixture to hot milk mixture, stirring constantly; cook 2 minutes, stirring constantly. Ladle into mugs, and sprinkle with nutmeg. Yield: 4 cups.
*Ruth Fulton Tiedemann*
*Bartlesville, Oklahoma*

■ After an adult or teenager chops the mixture in a food processor, youngsters will be eager to get their hands "dirty" rolling the balls.

## SUGAR PLUMS

1 (12-ounce) package pitted prunes
1 (8-ounce) package chopped dates
1 (6-ounce) package dried apricots
½ cup ground pecans
¼ cup graham cracker crumbs
1 teaspoon grated orange rind
½ teaspoon grated lemon rind
⅔ cup sugar

Position knife blade in food processor bowl; add first 3 ingredients. Process 1 minute or until finely chopped, stopping to scrape down sides as needed. Transfer to a large bowl; add pecans, graham cracker crumbs, and rinds, mixing well. Cover and chill 2 hours. Shape into ¾-inch balls, and roll in sugar. Cover and chill 1 hour. Yield: 5½ dozen.

■ This recipe is simple enough for a teenager to prepare alone. Younger children can shred the cheese and stir ingredients.

## CHICKEN-VEGETABLE SPAGHETTI
*(pictured on page 258)*

2 tablespoons olive oil
4 skinned and boned chicken breast halves, cut into 2-inch strips
3 medium zucchini, cut in half lengthwise and sliced (about 1 pound)
1 large green pepper, coarsely chopped
½ pound fresh mushrooms, sliced
¼ cup chopped onion
1 clove garlic, minced
1 (30-ounce) jar spaghetti sauce
2 cups (8 ounces) shredded mozzarella cheese, divided
8 to 12 ounces spaghetti, uncooked
2 tablespoons chopped fresh parsley

Heat oil in a large skillet. Add chicken; cook, stirring constantly, until no longer pink. Drain chicken, and set aside, reserving 1 tablespoon drippings in skillet.

Add zucchini, chopped green pepper, mushroom slices, chopped onion, and garlic to skillet; cook over medium heat, stirring constantly, until crisp-tender. Stir in chicken and spaghetti sauce; cook until thoroughly heated, stirring occasionally. Stir in 1 cup

mozzerella cheese; cook until cheese melts, stirring often.

Cook spaghetti according to package directions; drain. Arrange noodles on a large platter; top with sauce mixture, and sprinkle with remaining 1 cup cheese and parsley. Yield: 4 to 6 servings.
*Yvonne M. Greer*
*Mauldin, South Carolina*

■ A child can stem and wash spinach and would *love* to mix and shake the dressing in a jar.

## SPINACH SALAD
*(pictured on page 258)*

1 pound fresh spinach
1 apple, unpeeled, cored, and cut into thin wedges
2 tablespoons lemon juice
3 green onions, sliced
1 (2-ounce) package sliced almonds, toasted
2 slices bacon, cooked and crumbled (optional)
⅓ cup vegetable oil
⅓ cup red wine vinegar
2 to 3 teaspoons sugar
¾ teaspoon dry mustard
¼ teaspoon salt
¼ teaspoon pepper

Remove stems from spinach; wash leaves thoroughly, and pat dry. Tear into bite-size pieces. Toss apple wedges in lemon juice; drain. Combine spinach, apple wedges, green onions, and almonds; toss with bacon, if desired.

Combine oil and remaining ingredients in a jar. Cover tightly, and shake vigorously. Before serving, pour dressing over spinach mixture; toss. Yield: 6 servings. *Eleanor K. Brandt*
*Arlington, Texas*

■ Just a few ingredients and a few minutes and you can prepare this quick dessert sauce. If you're serving it with bananas, slice them just before spooning the sauce over them to prevent them from turning brown.

### PRALINE SAUCE

⅓ cup water
⅓ cup firmly packed dark brown
   sugar
1 cup light corn syrup
1 cup chopped pecans

Bring water to a boil in a small saucepan; stir in brown sugar and corn syrup. Bring mixture to a boil, stirring constantly; remove from heat, and add pecans. Cover and chill. Serve over sliced bananas or frozen yogurt. Yield: 2 cups.          *Bobbie Derbes*
                       *Metairie, Louisiana*

---

## A Head Start

■ Make Praline Sauce up to **five days ahead,** and store in the refrigerator.
■ Prepare Overnight Slaw or dressing for Spinach Salad **the day before.**
■ Make Sugar Plums **a day ahead,** and chill.
■ Stem and wash spinach, cook bacon, and toast almonds for Spinach Salad **a few hours before** dinner.

---

# A White, Quiet Christmas

Depending on where you live in the South, you may not have experienced a "White Christmas" Bing Crosby-style. But who needs snow when you can snuggle up with your honey and celebrate a quiet holiday?

This menu for two, which gives a choice of beef entrées, will make Christmas memories, no matter what the weather.

### A MENU FOR TWO

**Teriyaki London Broil
or
Beef With Tomatoes and
Artichokes
Mock Caesar Salad
Creamy Fettuccine
Commercial rolls
Brandy Alexander**

### TERIYAKI LONDON BROIL

1 (1- to 1½-pound) flank steak
½ cup vegetable oil
½ cup red wine vinegar
¼ cup teriyaki sauce
2 tablespoons Worcestershire sauce
1 clove garlic, minced
2 teaspoons dry mustard
½ teaspoon freshly ground black
   pepper
Dash of ground red pepper
Dash of hot sauce

Trim excess fat from steak; score on both sides in 1½-inch squares. Place in a large shallow dish or heavy-duty, zip-top plastic bag.

Combine oil and remaining ingredients; reserve ¼ cup mixture. Pour remaining mixture over steak. Cover or seal; marinate in refrigerator 8 hours or overnight, turning occasionally.

Drain steak, discarding marinade. Grill, covered, over medium coals (300° to 350°) 6 to 8 minutes on each side or to desired degree of doneness, basting twice with ¼ cup reserved mixture. To serve, slice steak across the grain into thin slices. Yield: 4 to 6 servings.          *Stanlay Webber,*
          *Winston-Salem, North Carolina*

### BEEF WITH TOMATOES AND ARTICHOKES
*(pictured on page 298)*

2 (1¼-inch-thick) beef tenderloin
   steaks (filet mignon)
Marinade
½ cup commercial oil-packed dried
   tomatoes
1½ tablespoons green onions,
   finely chopped
1 clove garlic, finely chopped
1 (14-ounce) can artichoke hearts,
   drained and quartered
¼ teaspoon dried basil

Place steaks in an 8-inch square dish; pour Marinade over steaks; cover and chill 8 hours, turning steaks several times. Drain, discarding Marinade. Grill uncovered, over medium-hot coals (350° to 400°) 4 to 5 minutes on each side or until desired degree of doneness. Keep warm.

Drain tomatoes, reserving 1 tablespoon of oil from tomatoes in a large skillet. Chop tomatoes; set aside. Cook green onions and garlic in reserved oil in skillet over medium-high heat, stirring constantly, 2 minutes. Add tomatoes, artichoke hearts, and basil; cook 5 minutes, stirring often. Thinly slice steaks, and serve with tomato mixture. Yield: 2 servings.

### Marinade

1 tablespoon olive oil
2 teaspoons red wine vinegar
1 tablespoon finely chopped onion
1 clove garlic, minced
½ teaspoon mustard
¼ teaspoon dried basil
¼ teaspoon dried rosemary
⅛ teaspoon salt
⅛ teaspoon pepper

Combine all ingredients in a container. Yield: 3 tablespoons.

### MOCK CAESAR SALAD
*(pictured on page 298)*

1 clove garlic
¼ cup water
⅛ teaspoon salt
1 tablespoon white wine vinegar
½ teaspoon Dijon mustard
¼ cup olive oil
2 cups firmly packed torn romaine lettuce
2 tablespoons freshly grated Parmesan cheese
2 tablespoons pine nuts, toasted
⅛ teaspoon freshly ground pepper

Combine garlic and water in a small saucepan; bring to a boil. Cover, reduce heat, and simmer 10 minutes or until soft; drain. Place garlic in a salad bowl; add salt. Mash into a paste, using the back of a spoon. Stir in vinegar and mustard with a wire whisk. Add olive oil in a slow, steady stream, beating with a whisk until blended. Add lettuce, and gently toss. Sprinkle with cheese, pine nuts, and pepper. Yield: 2 servings. *Nicka Thornton Greensboro, North Carolina*

### CREAMY FETTUCCINE
*(pictured on page 298)*

6 ounces fettuccine, uncooked
¼ cup butter or margarine
2 tablespoons all-purpose flour
½ cup half-and-half
½ cup water
½ cup freshly grated Parmesan cheese
2 teaspoons dried parsley flakes
½ teaspoon coarsely ground pepper
½ teaspoon garlic powder
½ teaspoon poppy seeds
¼ teaspoon salt

Cook fettuccine according to package directions, omitting salt; drain. Melt butter in a heavy saucepan over low heat; add flour, stirring until smooth. Cook 1 minute, stirring constantly. Gradually add half-and-half and water; cook over medium heat, stirring constantly, until mixture is thickened and bubbly. Stir in Parmesan cheese and remaining ingredients. Toss with fettuccine. Serve immediately. Yield: 2 servings. *Lynne Teal Weeks Columbus, Georgia*

### BRANDY ALEXANDER
*(pictured on page 299)*

2 cups vanilla ice cream
3 to 4 tablespoons brandy
3 to 4 tablespoons white crème de cacao
Garnish: white chocolate shavings

Combine first 3 ingredients in container of an electric blender; process until smooth. Spoon into glasses. Garnish, if desired. Serve immediately. Yield: 2 servings.
*Rebecca Salisbury Rice Murfreesboro, Tennessee*

## ON THE LIGHT SIDE

# Have Yourself
# A Merry "Little" Christmas

If the threat of unwanted pounds brings holiday worries, lighten up! Combat seasonal weight gain *before* excessive fat and calories stack up. For starters, try our healthy holiday party, complete with a delicious menu under 550 calories.

These guilt-free goodies command accolades from guests. Featuring sweet and savory finger foods and beverages, the menu offers several options for versatility. No matter which combination you choose, you won't break your calorie budget.

### LIGHT APPETIZER BUFFET FOR TWENTY

**Chicken Wontons**
**Tortellini With Rosemary-Parmesan Sauce**
**Festive Crab Dip with vegetables**
or
**Lentil Pâté with crackers**
**Apricot-Orange Bread**
**Chocolate-Kahlúa Truffles**
or
**Cran-Raspberry Meringue Tarts**
**Holiday Hot Fruit Punch**
or
**Bourbon Blizzard**

### CHICKEN WONTONS
*(pictured on pages 296 and 297)*

2 (4-ounce) boned and skinned chicken breast halves, cut into ¼-inch strips
1 clove garlic, minced
½ cup shredded carrot
¼ cup finely chopped celery
1 tablespoon low-sodium soy sauce
1 tablespoon dry sherry
1 tablespoon fresh lime juice
1 teaspoon ground ginger
2 teaspoons cornstarch
½ (16-ounce) package wonton wrappers (32 wrappers)
Butter-flavored cooking spray

Position knife blade in food processor bowl; add chicken. Process 1 minute or until ground. Cook chicken with garlic in a nonstick skillet over medium heat, stirring constantly, until chicken is no longer pink; drain. Combine chicken, shredded carrot, and next 6 ingredients.

Spoon 1 rounded teaspoon into center of each wonton wrapper; moisten edges with water. Carefully bring 2 opposite points of wrapper to center over filling; pinch points together. Bring two remaining opposite points to center, and pinch together.

Place filled wontons on a baking sheet coated with cooking spray.

Lightly coat each wonton with cooking spray. Bake at 375° for 8 to 10 minutes or until lightly browned. Yield: 2½ dozen (20 calories [27% from fat] per wonton).

□ *1.9g protein, 0.6g fat (0.1g saturated), 1.4g carbohydrate, 0.1g fiber, 10mg cholesterol, 30mg sodium, and 3mg calcium.*

### TORTELLINI WITH ROSEMARY-PARMESAN SAUCE
*(pictured on pages 296 and 297)*

2½ tablespoons nonfat dry milk
⅔ cup skim milk
1⅔ cups nonfat cottage cheese
¼ cup grated Parmesan cheese
¼ cup chopped fresh chives
1¾ teaspoons chopped fresh rosemary
1 tablespoon lemon juice
¼ teaspoon pepper
¼ teaspoon salt
1 (9-ounce) package refrigerated cheese-filled tortellini, cooked without salt or fat
1 (9-ounce) package refrigerated cheese-filled spinach tortellini, cooked without salt or fat
Garnish: fresh chives

Position knife blade in food processor bowl; add dry milk and skim milk. Process 10 seconds or until blended. Add cottage cheese and next 6 ingredients; process 1 minute, stopping to scrape down sides of bowl.

Cover and chill thoroughly. Serve sauce with tortellini and garnish, if desired. Yield: 20 servings (101 calories [19% from fat] per 2 tablespoons sauce and 8 tortellini).

□ *6.8g protein, 2.1g fat (0.7g saturated), 13.2g carbohydrate, 0g fiber, 14mg cholesterol, 203mg sodium, and 45mg calcium.*

## FESTIVE CRAB DIP
*(pictured on pages 296 and 297)*

1 (6-ounce) can lump crabmeat, drained
1 cup fat-free mayonnaise
¼ cup plain nonfat yogurt
¼ cup nonfat sour cream alternative
1 tablespoon chopped fresh parsley
1 tablespoon diced pimiento, drained
1 tablespoon dry sherry
1 teaspoon lemon juice
¼ teaspoon celery seeds
⅛ teaspoon pepper

Combine all ingredients; cover and chill. Serve with assorted fresh vegetables. Yield: 2 cups (35 calories [10% from fat] per 1 tablespoon dip and ½ cup vegetables).

☐ *2.1g protein, 0.4g fat (0.1g saturated), 6g carbohydrate, 1.2g fiber, 5mg cholesterol, 119mg sodium, and 13mg calcium.* JoAnn Conway
Guyton, Georgia

## LENTIL PÂTÉ

¾ cup dried lentils
3 cups water
2 hard-cooked eggs
1½ cups coarsely chopped onion
1 tablespoon vegetable oil
2 cloves garlic, minced
½ teaspoon salt
¼ teaspoon pepper
⅛ teaspoon ground nutmeg
¼ teaspoon hot sauce
⅛ teaspoon liquid smoke

Combine lentils and water in a small saucepan; bring to a boil. Cover, reduce heat, and simmer 30 to 35 minutes; drain. Set aside.
Peel eggs, and discard shells and yolks; set whites aside.

Cook onion in oil in a medium skillet over medium heat, stirring constantly, until tender.
Position knife blade in food processor bowl. Add lentils, egg whites, onion, garlic, and remaining ingredients; process 2 minutes or until smooth, stopping to scrape down sides. Cover and chill. Serve with water crackers. Yield: 2 cups (71 calories [27% from fat] per 1 tablespoon pâté and ½ ounce [approximately 4] crackers).

☐ *2.2g protein, 2.1g fat (0.2g saturated), 11.3g carbohydrate, 0.7g fiber, 0mg cholesterol, 123mg sodium, and 5mg calcium.*

## APRICOT-ORANGE BREAD
*(pictured on pages 296 and 297)*

1 (6-ounce) package dried apricots, diced
¾ cup firmly packed brown sugar
1 cup nonfat buttermilk
½ cup egg substitute
3 tablespoons vegetable oil
1 tablespoon grated orange rind
1¼ teaspoons vanilla extract
¼ teaspoon almond extract
1½ cups all-purpose flour
¾ cup whole wheat flour
1½ teaspoons baking powder
1 teaspoon baking soda
½ teaspoon salt
Vegetable cooking spray
Garnishes: dried apricots, orange rind strips, cinnamon sticks, grape leaves

Combine first 8 ingredients; let stand 5 minutes. Combine all-purpose flour and next 4 ingredients in a large bowl; make a well in center of mixture. Add apricot mixture to dry ingredients, stirring just until moistened. Coat either a 6-cup Bundt pan or 9- x 5- x 3-inch loafpan with cooking spray. Spoon batter into pan. Bake at 350°

for 35 minutes or until a wooden pick inserted in center comes out clean. Cool in pan on a wire rack 10 minutes; remove from pan, and cool on a wire rack. Garnish, if desired. Yield: 21 servings (119 calories [17% from fat] per slice).

☐ *2.7g protein, 2.3g fat (0.4g saturated), 22.6g carbohydrate, 1g fiber, 0mg cholesterol, 146mg sodium, and 52mg calcium.* Edna Mae Sharp
Sun City Center, Florida

## CHOCOLATE-KAHLÚA TRUFFLES
*(pictured on page 296)*

1 (10-ounce) package teddy bear-shaped chocolate graham cracker cookies
6 tablespoons skim milk
¼ cup nonfat dry milk
1 tablespoon Kahlúa or other coffee-flavored liqueur
⅔ cup finely chopped pitted whole dates
⅓ cup finely chopped pecans

Place knife blade in food processor bowl; add cookies, and process until cookies turn to crumbs. Combine skim milk, dry milk, and Kahlúa in a large bowl; stir in crumbs. Add dates, stirring until mixture forms a soft dough; shape into ¾-inch balls. Roll in chopped pecans; cover and chill. Serve in miniature paper baking cups. Yield: 4½ dozen (74 calories [30% from fat] per 2 truffles).

☐ *1.4g protein, 2.4g fat (0g saturated), 11.8g carbohydrate, 0.8g fiber, 0.2mg cholesterol, 54mg sodium, and 20mg calcium.*

## CRAN-RASPBERRY MERINGUE TARTS
*(pictured on page 296)*

3 egg whites
¼ teaspoon cream of tartar
1 cup sugar
1 teaspoon vanilla extract
½ cup no-sugar-added raspberry-
  cranberry fruit spread

Beat egg whites and cream of tartar at high speed with an electric mixer 1 minute. Gradually add sugar, 1 tablespoon at a time, beating until stiff peaks form and sugar dissolves (about 2 to 4 minutes). Stir in vanilla.

Drop heaping teaspoonfuls onto cookie sheets lined with unglazed brown paper. (Do not use recycled paper.) Using the back of a teaspoon, make a small indention in center of each meringue. Bake at 250° for 45 minutes; turn off heat and leave meringues in oven, with door closed, at least 2 hours.

Carefully peel meringues from brown paper. Just before serving, fill each with ½ teaspoon fruit spread. Yield: 50 tarts (36 calories [0% from fat] per 2 tarts).

□ *0.4g protein, 0g fat (0g saturated), 9g carbohydrate, 0g fiber, 0mg cholesterol, 8mg sodium, and 0mg calcium.*

## HOLIDAY HOT FRUIT PUNCH
*(pictured on page 296)*

1 (48-ounce) can unsweetened
  apple juice
1 teaspoon ground nutmeg
1 (3-inch) stick cinnamon
1 (46-ounce) can unsweetened
  pineapple juice
1 (46-ounce) can unsweetened
  orange juice
¼ cup sugar
2 medium oranges
2 teaspoons whole cloves

Combine first 3 ingredients in a Dutch oven; cook, covered, over low heat 20 minutes. Add remaining juices and sugar. Stud oranges with cloves, and add to liquid. Cook 5 minutes (do not boil). Serve immediately. Yield: about 4½ quarts (87 calories [0% from fat] per 6-ounce serving).

□ *0.6g protein, 0.2g fat (0g saturated), 21.4g carbohydrate, 0.3g fiber, 0mg cholesterol, 3mg sodium, and 20mg calcium.*
*Betty Haygood*
*Liberty, Mississippi*

### A Head Start

■ Bake Apricot-Orange Bread up to **two days before the party.** Store in an airtight container.
■ Prepare and chill Festive Crab Dip or Lentil Pâté, Rosemary-Parmesan Sauce for tortellini, filling for Chicken Wontons, and Chocolate-Kahlúa Truffles **the day before the party.**
■ Bake shells for Cran-Raspberry Meringue Tarts, and cut vegetables for Festive Crab Dip **the morning of the party.**
■ **One hour before the party,** fill meringue shells or place truffles in miniature paper baking cups, make beverage, and arrange crackers for pâté.
■ Fill and bake wontons **30 minutes before,** and garnish dishes to be served.

### Serving from a Samovar

Enjoy a warming beverage fit for a czar by serving Holiday Hot Fruit Punch in a samovar (SAM-uh-var). Originating in Russia in the early 1800s, the urn was used for heating water to make tea. The Russian word "samo" means self, and "var" means to cook or boil.

The most elegant samovars—usually found in silver and antiques shops—are sterling silver or silver plate. Reproductions, in copper and other metals, are less expensive and are becoming popular. Try local flea markets and estate sales for unique samovars with charm and history.

Some of the newer urns have a place for an electric plug in the back. True antiques are heated by first pouring boiling water into the urn, letting it sit for a minute, then pouring the water out. Immediately add the hot beverage to the warm samovar.

Surround the samovar with a collection of demitasse cups and saucers for entertaining or for display. Keep your samovar shiny with copper, brass, or silver polish. Clean the inside between uses, being careful not to submerge the samovar in water if it has an electrical plug.

This elegant piece is a wonderful alternative to the standard coffee urn or teapot. If you happen to run across a samovar that has seen better days, don't pass it up. They make wonderful lamp bases, too.

## BOURBON BLIZZARD

½ gallon vanilla ice milk, divided
½ gallon 1% low-fat milk, divided
¾ cup bourbon
¼ cup vanilla extract
1 tablespoon ground nutmeg
Additional ground nutmeg

Combine 2 cups ice milk, 2 cups milk, bourbon, vanilla, and nutmeg in container of an electric blender; process until smooth. Pour into a large bowl. Add one-third each of remaining ice milk and milk to blender; process until smooth, and add to bowl. Repeat procedure twice with remaining ice milk and milk. Stir with a wire whisk to blend. Cover and chill. To serve, pour into punch cups, and sprinkle with additional nutmeg. Yield: 13 cups (145 calories [21% from fat] per 5-ounce serving).

□ *5.3g protein, 3.4g fat (2.1g saturated), 17.3g carbohydrate, 11mg cholesterol, 91mg sodium, and 191mg calcium.*

# Sweet Memories Of 1992

Believe it or not, another year has flown by, and we must bid it farewell. That inevitable tug of dietary guilt is just around the corner, but there's time for one last fling. So bring on the sweets for a New Year's Eve dessert buffet.

Because most of the recipes are make-ahead, there's no last-minute rush, so you can relax and enjoy the party just as much as your guests. (If you have fewer guests, just pick three or four of the recipes to serve a smaller group.)

At the stroke of midnight, raise a glass and toast the good times, good friends, and sweet memories of the past year. And worry about those resolutions tomorrow.

### NEW YEAR'S EVE DESSERT BUFFET FOR TWENTY

**Irish Cream-and-Coffee Pound Cake**
**White Chocolate Fondue**
**Tiny Chocolate Cheesecakes with fresh strawberries**
**Orange-Walnut Fudge**
**Peanut Clusters**
or
**Creamy Pralines**
**Pecan Pie Cookies**
**Kahlúa-Pecan Brie**
or
**Peachy Cream Cheese**
**Citrus Party Punch**
or
**Champagne**

### IRISH CREAM-AND-COFFEE POUND CAKE

1½ cups butter or margarine, softened
3 cups sugar
6 large eggs
1½ tablespoons instant coffee granules
¼ cup boiling water
½ cup Irish cream liqueur
4 cups all-purpose flour
1 teaspoon vanilla extract
1 teaspoon almond extract
Irish Cream Glaze
2 to 3 tablespoons sliced almonds, toasted

Beat butter at medium speed with an electric mixer about 2 minutes or until soft and creamy. Gradually add sugar, beating at medium speed 5 to 7 minutes. Add eggs, one at time, beating just until yellow disappears.

Dissolve coffee granules in boiling water; stir in liqueur. Add flour to butter mixture alternately with coffee mixture, beginning and ending with flour mixture. Mix at low speed just until blended after each addition. Stir in flavorings.

Pour batter into a greased and floured 13-cup Bundt pan. Bake at 300° for 1 hour and 40 minutes or until a wooden pick inserted in center of cake comes out clean. Cool in pan on a wire rack 10 to 15 minutes; remove from pan, and let cool 30 minutes on wire rack. Brush with Irish Cream Glaze, and sprinkle with toasted almonds. Let cool completely. Yield: one 10-inch cake.

### Irish Cream Glaze

1 teaspoon instant coffee granules
2 tablespoons boiling water
1½ tablespoons Irish cream liqueur
⅔ cup sifted powdered sugar

Dissolve coffee granules in water; add liqueur and powdered sugar, stirring until blended. Yield: about ½ cup.

**Note:** Glazed cake may be frozen up to one month. *H. W. Asbell*
*Tallahassee, Florida*

### WHITE CHOCOLATE FONDUE

1 pound vanilla-flavored candy coating
½ cup half-and-half
2 tablespoons brandy

Melt candy coating in a heavy saucepan over low heat, stirring constantly. Gradually add half-and-half, stirring constantly until blended. Stir in brandy. Serve at room temperature with strawberries or assorted fruits. Yield: 2 cups. *Ann Ruff*
*Bellaire, Texas*

## A Head Start

■ Bake, glaze, and freeze Irish Cream-and-Coffee Pound Cake **up to a month ahead,** or bake and glaze **a day ahead** and store in an airtight container.
■ Bake and freeze Pecan Pie Cookies **up to a month ahead,** or bake **a day ahead** and store in an airtight container.
■ Assemble and freeze Tiny Chocolate Cheesecakes **up to a month ahead** without whipped cream and morsels, or chill **up to two days ahead**. Garnish before serving.
■ Make Citrus Party Punch and minted ice cubes **up to three days before the party**.
■ Make Orange-Walnut Fudge and Creamy Pralines or Peanut Clusters **a day ahead,** and store in an airtight container. (Fudge and pralines will be a better texture made the day of the party.)
■ Assemble and refrigerate Peachy Cream Cheese or Kahlúa-Pecan Brie **up to four hours before the party**.
■ Make White Chocolate Fondue **an hour before the party**, and serve at room temperature.

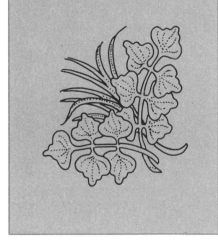

## TINY CHOCOLATE CHEESECAKES

¼ cup butter or margarine, softened
¾ cup chocolate wafer crumbs
2 (8-ounce) packages cream cheese, softened
½ cup sugar
2 large eggs
1 cup semisweet chocolate mini-morsels, melted
Garnishes: whipped cream, semisweet chocolate mini-morsels

Grease miniature (1¾-inch) muffin pans with butter. Sprinkle each muffin cup (5 dozen) with 1 teaspoon chocolate crumbs; turn pans upside down to discard excess crumbs.

Beat cream cheese at high speed with an electric mixer until light and fluffy; gradually add sugar, beating well. Add eggs, one at a time, beating well after each addition; stir in melted chocolate. Spoon about 1 tablespoon into each prepared muffin cup. Bake at 350° for 20 minutes. Cool in pans on wire racks about 5 minutes. Carefully remove to wire racks to cool completely. Chill up to two days or freeze up to one month. Garnish, if desired. Yield: 5 dozen.

**Note:** To make 3-inch cheesecakes, substitute 24 cream-filled chocolate sandwich cookies for chocolate wafer crumbs. Place cookies in greased muffin pans. Spoon chocolate mixture evenly over cookies. Bake at 350° for 25 minutes. Cool in pans on wire racks about 5 minutes. Carefully remove to wire racks to cool completely. Chill up to two days or freeze up to one month. Yield: 2 dozen
*Peggy C. Brown*
*Winston-Salem, North Carolina*

## ORANGE-WALNUT FUDGE

3 cups sugar
½ cup orange juice
½ cup water
1 (12-ounce) package semisweet chocolate morsels
1 tablespoon grated orange rind
4 cups coarsely chopped walnuts

Combine first 3 ingredients in a large saucepan. Cook over medium heat, stirring constantly, until sugar dissolves and mixture boils. Cook, stirring occasionally, until mixture reaches softball stage or candy thermometer reads 234°. Remove from heat. Add chocolate morsels and orange rind; stir until chocolate melts. Stir in walnuts. Pour into a buttered 13- x 9- x 2-inch pan; cool. Cut into 1-inch squares, and store in an airtight container at room temperature. Yield: 9 dozen.
*Sandra Russell*
*Gainesville, Florida*

## PEANUT CLUSTERS

2 cups peanut butter morsels or butterscotch morsels
1 (6-ounce) package semisweet chocolate morsels
1 (12-ounce) can salted peanuts

Combine peanut butter morsels and chocolate morsels in a heavy saucepan; cook over low heat, stirring frequently, until morsels melt.

Remove melted morsels from heat; add peanuts, stirring to coat. Drop by rounded teaspoonfuls onto wax paper. Cool completely, and store covered at room temperature. Yield: about 4 dozen.
*Judy Hughes*
*Indian Harbour Beach, Florida*

## CREAMY PRALINES

Butter or margarine
1 cup sugar
1 cup firmly packed light brown
 sugar
1 (14-ounce) can sweetened
 condensed milk
¾ cup butter or margarine, cut into
 ½-inch pieces
½ cup light corn syrup
⅛ teaspoon salt
3 cups pecan pieces
1 teaspoon vanilla extract
½ to 1 teaspoon almond extract

Grease wax paper sheet with butter, and set aside.

Combine sugar and next 5 ingredients in a large heavy saucepan. Cook over low heat, stirring gently, until butter melts. Cook over medium heat, stirring constantly, until mixture reaches soft ball stage or candy thermometer reads 238° (about 15 minutes). Remove from heat; stir in pecans and flavorings. Beat with a wooden spoon just until mixture begins to thicken. Working rapidly, drop by rounded tablespoonfuls onto prepared wax paper; let stand until firm. Yield: 4 dozen.       *Mrs. Elton Krause*
*Spicewood, Texas*

## PECAN PIE COOKIES

1 cup butter or margarine, softened
½ cup sugar
½ cup dark corn syrup
2 large eggs, separated
2½ cups all-purpose flour
½ cup sifted powdered sugar
¼ cup butter or margarine
3 tablespoons dark corn syrup
½ cup chopped pecans

Beat 1 cup butter and sugar at medium speed with an electric mixer until light and fluffy. Add ½ cup corn syrup

and egg yolks; beat well. Stir in flour; cover and chill 2 hours.

Combine powdered sugar, ¼ cup butter, and 3 tablespoons corn syrup in a heavy saucepan. Cook over medium heat, stirring constantly, until mixture boils. Stir in pecans; chill 30 minutes. Shape mixture by ½ teaspoonfuls into ¼-inch balls; set aside.

Shape cookie dough into ¾-inch balls; place 2 inches apart on ungreased cookie sheets. Beat egg whites until foamy; brush on dough balls. Bake at 350° for 6 minutes; remove from oven. Place pecan ball in center of each cookie. Return to oven, and bake 5 minutes or until lightly browned. Cool 2 minutes on cookie sheets; remove to wire racks to cool completely. Store in an airtight container. Yield: 6 dozen.

**Note:** Cookies may be frozen up to one month.       *Margie G. McGee*
*Richmond, Virginia*

## KAHLÚA-PECAN BRIE

1 (15-ounce) mini-Brie
½ cup finely chopped pecans,
 toasted
2 tablespoons Kahlúa or other
 coffee-flavored liqueur
1½ tablespoons brown sugar

Remove rind from top of cheese, cutting to within ½ inch of outside edges. Place on an oven-safe dish.

Combine pecans, Kahlúa, and brown sugar; spread over top of cheese. Bake at 350° for 3 to 5 minutes or just until soft. Serve immediately with apple slices or gingersnaps. Yield: 12 to 15 servings.

**Note:** To make ahead, assemble and chill up to 4 hours; let stand at room temperature 10 to 15 minutes before baking. You may also slice apples

ahead and chill in a zip-top plastic bag with orange or pineapple juice to cover to prevent browning.
*Janis Bevers*
*Tulsa, Oklahoma*

## PEACHY CREAM CHEESE

1 (8-ounce) package cream cheese,
 softened
½ cup peach preserves
½ teaspoon ground ginger

Shape cream cheese into a 4½-inch circle on a serving dish; chill. Just before serving, combine preserves and ginger; spread over cheese. Serve with date bread or gingersnaps. Yield: 8 to 10 servings.       *Evelyn Foster*
*Salisbury, North Carolina*

## CITRUS PARTY PUNCH

2½ dozen small fresh mint leaves
2 cups sugar
1 gallon water
1½ cups lemon juice
1 (12-ounce) can frozen orange
 juice concentrate, thawed and
 undiluted
1 (46-ounce) can unsweetened
 pineapple juice
1 tablespoon vanilla extract
1½ teaspoons almond extract

Place 1 mint leaf in each compartment of 2 ice cube trays. Fill trays with water, making sure mint leaves do not float; freeze.

Combine sugar and water in a large punch bowl, stirring until sugar dissolves. Stir in lemon juice and remaining ingredients. To serve, add minted ice cubes. Yield: 1½ gallons.
*Elizabeth M. Haney*
*Dublin, Virginia*

# Tools Of The Trade

Any cook who's faced the rigors of holiday dinner parties and festive family meals—in addition to the usual daily dose of cooking—can be downright weary and grumpy about now.

That's why we're offering an early present—a list of can't-miss gadgets that will make this holiday season a breeze. Many of them can be found in supermarkets, cookware specialty shops, or mail-order catalogs.

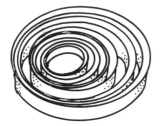

A set of **nested round cutters** has every size for making Snowflake Cookies, Cheese Tea Sandwiches, and Teddy Bear Cakes (see page 278). Thirteen rounds (ranging from 7/8 inch to 4½ inches) with sharp cutting edges nestle in a tin box. Graduated cutters are also available in heart, daisy, and star shapes.

Use **miniature paper baking cups** for no-bake Chocolate-Kahlúa Truffles (see page 285).

Use a **stainless steel wire whisk** or **whip** to make Sour Cream Gravy, a smooth sauce for Roasted Pork Loin With Mushrooms and Garlic (see page 301). The looped wires also prevent lumping when dry ingredients are added to liquids in the Irish Cream Glaze brushed on Irish Cream-and-Coffee Pound Cake (see page 287) and quickly combine dressing ingredients for Mock Caesar Salad (see page 283). Use a large whisk to incorporate air into egg whites or whipping cream for Frozen Yogurt Salad (see page 303), and you won't need an electric mixer. A slimmer whisk with fewer wires mixes cream sauces for Creamy Fettuccine (see page 283) and Creamy Ham-and-Chicken Medley (see page 272), and smooths cornstarch with orange juice for Gingered Carrots (see page 302).

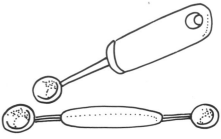

With a quick twist of the wrist, a **melon baller** cuts the flesh of cantaloupe, honeydew melon, and watermelon into balls. You can also use this bowl-shaped tool to quickly scoop out the centers of cucumbers, cherry tomatoes, and zucchini for stuffing, and then use it to add a filling. Try this tool to core the apples for Stuffed Apple Salad (see page 266). Several varieties of ballers are available; choose one scoop with a cushioned handle or two scoops connected by a single wooden handle.

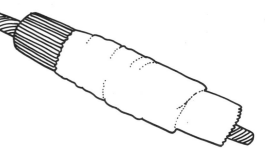

Slide a **rolling pin cover** over the rolling pin before rolling out cookies, pastry, biscuits, and bread dough. The 100% cotton knit cover doesn't slip, stretch, or stick to dough and is machine washable, so cleanup is quick and easy.

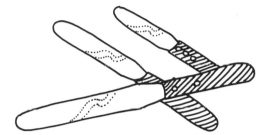

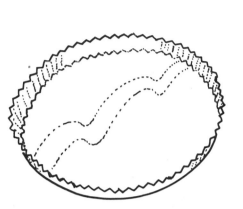

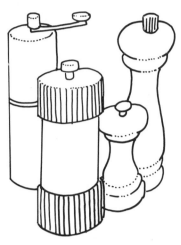

Finding ways to use **spatulas** is easy. The flexible, straight metal blade smoothly spreads frosting or fillings on flat surfaces. Use an 11- or 12-inch spatula for spreading peanut butter and chocolate frosting on Frosted Peanut Butter Brownies (see page 272), and try a shorter 4-inch blade for finer work—such as shaping cream cheese for Peachy Cream Cheese (see page 289) and frosting Teddy Bear Cakes (see page 278).

Crush dry peppercorns with a hand-held **pepper mill.** The internal grinding mechanism is generally stainless steel and adjusts to produce fine or coarse grinds. You'll be pleased with the sharp, zesty flavor of freshly ground pepper.

With scalloped sides and a removable bottom, a **tart pan** is designed to bake desserts with shallow sides like Black Bottom Mocha-Cream Tart (see page 304). To serve, simply remove the rim and slip the tart and bottom of the tart pan onto a serving plate. Be careful not to burn your arm when removing the rim from a hot tart pan. Because there is no rim to obstruct a knife when serving, slices cut neatly, and the scalloped edge makes a holiday dessert pretty.

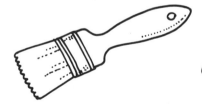

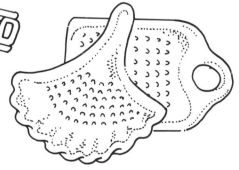

Use an all-purpose **pastry brush** to apply egg white on Pecan Pie Cookies (see page 289), butter puff pastry sheets for Apple Strudel (see page 269), moisten wonton wrappers for Chicken Wontons (see page 284), and grease cakepans, loafpans, and muffin pans. Keep one brush on hand to dust excess flour from biscuit or cookie dough, and another for basting meats. Choose a brush 1 to 1½ inches wide with natural—not nylon—bristles; they are softer, hold more liquid, and don't melt, shred, or leave any marks.

The best way to measure the temperature while making Creamy Pralines (see page 289) and other candies is with a **candy-deep fry thermometer.** Use it to read the temperature of sugar syrup for Orange-Walnut Fudge (see page 288) and warm water when adding yeast to Cinnamon Rolls (see page 270). Choose a thermometer that registers from 100° to 400°, is easy to read, and has an adjustable clip on the back to attach to the side of the saucepan.

Ceramic "teeth" of a **ginger grater** remove spicy pulp from peeled fresh gingerroot. You can also use this handy tool for grating small amounts of lemon rind and hard cheeses, or as a spoon rest or soap dish.

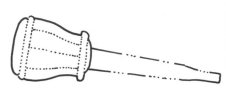

Try a **bulb baster** to moisten Herbed Turkey Breast with an olive oil mixture (see page 266). This tool works like a syringe; squeeze the bulb first to extract liquid from the baking pan, then again to squirt the pan juices back over the meats. It's quicker and neater than using a spoon to baste and prevents burns since you don't have to handle the hot pan as much. Also use a bulb baster to skim fat from liquids, such as chicken broth for Old-Fashioned Chicken Pot Pie (see page 271).

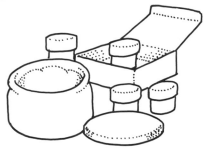

We receive many questions about **paste food coloring** and **meringue powder.** Concentrated paste food coloring has a rich creamy base which doesn't change frosting's consistency. For true holiday colors, try Red-Red, Tulip Red, or Christmas Red and Leaf or Forest Green. Meringue powder beaten with water according to package directions replaces beaten raw egg whites in royal icing. The powder and coloring are both available at cake decorating supply stores.

To sprinkle Snowflake Cookies (see page 278), place powdered sugar in a small **wire-mesh strainer,** and lightly tap with finger. This gadget also gives cakes a light dusting with powdered sugar or cocoa and sifts out lumps in small amounts of flour and sugar. It can also be used to strain juices.

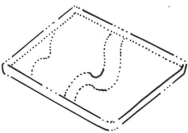

Traditionally, a heavy aluminum **jellyroll pan** with a polished surface bakes thin sheet and sponge cakes that are filled and rolled into jellyrolls. This 15- x 10- x 1-inch pan is used for Simple Petit Fours (page 277) and Teddy Bear Cakes (page 278). Don't confuse it with a flat baking sheet; if a jellyroll pan is used to bake cookies, the steam trapped by the sides of the pan could make them soggy.

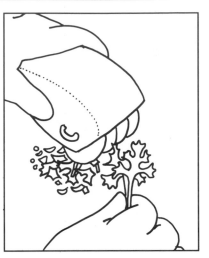

Speedily mince or finely chop using a **rolling mincer.** Five sharp stainless steel blades covered with a comfortable plastic handgrip easily roll over leafy herbs, garlic, and green onions.

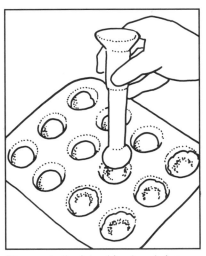

Place a ball of cookie dough into each cup of a **miniature muffin pan,** and press down with a **tart tamper** to form a shell for Chocolate-Peanut Butter Tarts (see page 277). The pan also shapes bite-size Tiny Chocolate Cheesecakes (see page 288).

*For starters at your holiday gatherings, you and your guests can munch on Broccoli-Cheese Appetizer (page 265) and sip Cranberry Spritzer (page 265) in the kitchen.*

*Herbed Turkey Breast, Cornbread Dressing, Stuffed Apple Salad, green beans, and new potatoes welcome the family home for Thanksgiving. (Recipes begin on page 266.)*

*Red cinnamon candies color the apples for Stuffed Apple Salad (page 266).*

*In Pumpkin Pie With Meringue (page 268), meringue adds new flavor and texture to traditional pumpkin pie.*

Above: *Throughout the evening, keep Holiday Hot Fruit Punch warm in a samovar (urn). For dessert, serve Cran-Raspberry Meringue Tarts or Chocolate-Kahlúa Truffles. (Recipes, pages 285 and 286.)*

Right: *Present your friends with a pretty palette of light holiday appetizers: (clockwise from top) Festive Crab Dip with vegetables, Chicken Wontons, Apricot-Orange Bread, and Tortellini With Rosemary-Parmesan Sauce. (Appetizer recipes begin on page 284.)*

*Settle in by a glowing fire and enjoy a romantic dinner for two, serving (left) Beef With Tomatoes and Artichokes, Creamy Fettuccine, and Mock Caesar Salad. For dessert, (above) sip Brandy Alexander, a creamy blend of vanilla ice cream, brandy, and crème de cacao. (Recipes begin on page 282.)*

Roasted Pork Loin With Mushrooms
and Garlic, Gingered Carrots,
Mandarin Orange Tossed Salad,
Broccoli With Bacon, and Holiday
Potato Casserole fill the buffet table.
(Recipes begin on page 301.)

# I'll Be Home For Christmas...

Most of us yearn to be home for Christmas. It's a family time when you visit with neighbors and old friends.

If you're the cook who keeps the home fires burning, you'll want the meal to be as perfect as the occasion. But you don't want to spend this special holiday in the kitchen. Our menu offers several simple recipes with make-ahead tips, and you can choose your own menu combination from several options.

To make Christmas dinner enjoyable for all, do as much advance preparation as possible. Then let everyone share in the remaining tasks.

solidified fat. Reserve 2 tablespoons pan drippings for Sour Cream Gravy. Serve roast with gravy. Garnish, if desired. Yield: 8 to 10 servings.

### Sour Cream Gravy

- 1 teaspoon cornstarch
- 1 tablespoon water
- 2 tablespoons reserved pan drippings from roast
- 1 (8-ounce) carton sour cream
- ⅛ teaspoon freshly ground pepper

Combine cornstarch and water in a saucepan; stir until cornstarch dissolves; gradually stir in reserved pan drippings, sour cream, and pepper. Cook sour cream mixture over low heat; stir constantly just until gravy is thickened and heated. Do not boil. Yield: 1 cup. *Mrs. Thad Sharp, Jr. Sims, North Carolina*

## CHRISTMAS DINNER FOR EIGHT

Roasted Pork Loin
With Mushrooms and Garlic
or
Pork Tenderloin With Mustard Sauce
Holiday Potato Casserole
Gingered Carrots   Broccoli With Bacon
Mandarin Orange Tossed Salad
or
Frozen Yogurt Salad
Velvet Cream Biscuits
Black Bottom Mocha-Cream Tart
or
Cran-Apple Pie

### A Head Start

- Bake and freeze Velvet Cream Biscuits **up to three months ahead.** Make Frozen Yogurt Salad **up to one month ahead.**
- Prepare Vinaigrette Dressing and Caramelized Almonds for Mandarin Orange Tossed Salad **up to three days ahead,** and chill.
- Prepare Holiday Potato Casserole and Mustard Sauce for the pork **up to two days ahead.** Store both in the refrigerator.
- Prepare Black Bottom Mocha-Cream Tart or Cran-Apple Pie **the day before Christmas.**
- Prepare ingredients for Mandarin Orange Tossed Salad **up to three hours ahead.**

### ROASTED PORK LOIN WITH MUSHROOMS AND GARLIC
*(pictured on page 300)*

- 1 (3- to 4-pound) boneless pork loin roast
- 2 tablespoons lemon juice
- 1½ teaspoons salt, divided
- ½ teaspoon freshly ground pepper
- 4 to 5 cloves garlic
- 1 cup fresh mushrooms
- Sour Cream Gravy
- Garnishes: fresh mushroom slices, fresh rosemary sprigs

Place roast, fat side up, on a rack in a shallow roasting pan. Cut ½-inch slits at 1-inch intervals in diagonal rows on top of roast. Brush with lemon juice, and sprinkle with 1¼ teaspoons salt and ½ teaspoon pepper. Insert meat thermometer in thickest portion of roast, making sure it does not touch fat; set aside.

Cut garlic into ⅛-inch slices and slice mushrooms into ¼-inch strips; sprinkle with remaining ¼ teaspoon salt. Insert a garlic slice and a strip of mushroom into each ½-inch slit. Bake, uncovered, at 325° for 1 hour and 10 minutes or until meat thermometer registers 160°. Let stand 10 to 15 minutes before slicing. Quickly chill pan drippings in freezer; discard

## PORK TENDERLOIN WITH MUSTARD SAUCE

¼ cup soy sauce
¼ cup bourbon
2 tablespoons brown sugar
2 (1- to 1½-pound) packages pork
  tenderloins
Mustard Sauce

Combine first 3 ingredients in an 11- x 7- x 1½-inch baking dish; add tenderloins. Cover and refrigerate at least 2 hours, turning occasionally. Remove from marinade, discarding marinade; place on a rack in a shallow roasting pan. Bake at 325° for 45 minutes or until a meat thermometer inserted into thickest portion registers 160°. Serve with Mustard Sauce. Yield: 8 servings.

### Mustard Sauce

⅔ cup sour cream
⅔ cup mayonnaise
2 tablespoons dry mustard
3 to 4 green onions, finely chopped

Combine all ingredients; cover and chill. Yield: 1⅓ cups.

## HOLIDAY POTATO CASSEROLE
*(pictured on page 300)*

3 pounds potatoes, peeled and
  quartered
½ cup butter or margarine
2 (3-ounce) packages cream cheese,
  softened
1 cup (4 ounces) shredded Cheddar
  cheese, divided
1 (2-ounce) jar diced pimiento,
  drained
1 small green pepper, finely
  chopped
1 bunch green onions, finely chopped
½ cup grated Parmesan cheese
¼ cup milk
1 teaspoon salt

Cook potatoes in boiling water to cover 15 minutes or until tender; drain and mash. Add butter and cream cheese; beat at medium speed with an electric mixer until smooth. Stir in ½ cup Cheddar cheese and next 6 ingredients; spoon into a lightly greased 11- x 7- x 1½-inch baking dish. Cover and chill, if desired.

Remove casserole from refrigerator, and let stand at room temperature 30 minutes. Bake at 350° for 40 minutes or until thoroughly heated. Sprinkle with remaining ½ cup Cheddar cheese; bake 5 minutes or until cheese melts. Yield: 8 servings.

**Note:** You can bake casserole immediately instead of chilling. (Baking time may be less than 40 minutes.)
*Clairiece Gilbert Humphrey*
*Charlottesville, Virginia*

## GINGERED CARROTS
*(pictured on page 300)*

2 pounds carrots, scraped
2 tablespoons sugar
2 teaspoons cornstarch
½ teaspoon salt
½ teaspoon ground ginger
½ cup orange juice
2 tablespoons butter or margarine
Garnish: chopped fresh parsley

Cut carrots diagonally into ¼-inch slices. Cook carrots in boiling water to cover 7 minutes or until tender; drain. Keep warm in a serving dish.

Combine next 4 ingredients in saucepan; gradually add orange juice, stirring well. Bring to a boil over medium heat, stirring constantly. Boil 1 minute, stirring constantly; stir in butter. Pour over carrots; toss well. Garnish, if desired. Yield: 8 servings.
*Romanza O. Johnson*
*Bowling Green, Kentucky*

## BROCCOLI WITH BACON
*(pictured on page 300)*

2 pounds fresh broccoli
6 slices bacon
¾ cup coarsely chopped walnuts
  (optional)
½ cup chopped green onions

Remove broccoli leaves, and cut off tough ends of stalks; discard. Wash broccoli, and cut into spears. Cook in a small amount of boiling water 6 to 8 minutes or just until tender; drain. Place in a serving dish; keep warm.

### Deck the Halls

Southern magnolia leaves can add special touches to your holiday table. Here are the "how-to's."

**Centerpiece:** Place a fresh ivy topiary tree in a basket, and attach a large bow with streamers to the top. Arrange swirls of raffia (strawlike ribbon) around the basket. "Gild" fruit, such as pears, apples, lemons, oranges, and grapes, by placing fruit on newspaper outdoors and lightly spraying fruit with gold metallic floral spray paint. Let dry 30 minutes. Angle fruit on the table around the basket, adding grapes last—they are the most fragile and will drape over larger fruits to fill in gaps.

**Place cards:** Lightly paint pears (choose those with nice stems and flat bases) as directed above. Write guests' names on large magnolia leaves with a metallic gold paint pen. After setting the table, place pears upright next to each plate; then spear stems of painted leaves into pears.

Cook bacon in a skillet until crisp, reserving 2 tablespoons drippings in skillet. Crumble bacon, and set aside. Cook walnuts, if desired, in bacon drippings over medium-high heat, stirring constantly, 3 minutes. Add green onions, and cook, stirring constantly, 2 minutes. Spoon over broccoli; sprinkle with bacon. Yield: 8 servings.

*Sue-Sue Hartstern*
*Louisville, Kentucky*

### MANDARIN ORANGE TOSSED SALAD
*(pictured on page 300)*

1  head leaf lettuce, torn
3  stalks celery, thinly sliced
4  green onions, sliced
1  (11-ounce) can mandarin orange
    sections, drained
Vinaigrette Dressing
Caramelized Almonds

Combine first 4 ingredients in a salad bowl; cover and chill up to 3 hours, if desired. Just before serving, toss with Vinaigrette Dressing, and sprinkle with Caramelized Almonds. Yield: 6 to 8 servings.

#### Vinaigrette Dressing

¼  cup vegetable oil
2  tablespoons sugar
1  tablespoon white vinegar
½  teaspoon salt
¼  teaspoon pepper
5  drops hot sauce

Combine all ingredients, and chill. Stir well before serving. Yield: ⅓ cup.

#### Caramelized Almonds

¼  cup slivered almonds
2  tablespoons sugar

Combine ingredients in a heavy saucepan; cook over medium heat, stirring

constantly, until golden. Pour onto wax paper, and cool. Break into pieces, and store in an airtight container. Yield: ¼ cup.

*Margy Shedd*
*Athens, Georgia*

### FROZEN YOGURT SALAD

1  cup whipping cream
2  tablespoons honey
1  (8-ounce) carton strawberry
    yogurt
1  (15¼-ounce) can pineapple
    tidbits, drained
1  cup sliced fresh strawberries
Lettuce leaves

Beat whipping cream at medium speed with a mixer until soft peaks form; gradually add honey, beating until stiff peaks form. Fold in yogurt and fruit; spoon into 10 lightly oiled ½-cup molds; cover and freeze at least 8 hours. To serve, let stand 10 to 15 minutes at room temperature. Run a knife blade around edges to release from molds, and serve on lettuce-lined plates. Yield: 10 servings.

**Note:** You may also freeze mixture in an 8-inch square dish. To serve, let stand at room temperature 10 to 15 minutes; cut into squares. Either version may be frozen up to 1 month.

*Jeni Meredith*
*Franklin, North Carolina*

### VELVET CREAM BISCUITS

4  cups all-purpose flour
2  tablespoons baking powder
1  teaspoon salt
2  tablespoons sugar
2½  cups whipping cream
¼  cup butter or margarine, melted

Combine first 4 ingredients; add whipping cream, stirring until dry ingredients are moistened. Turn dough out onto a well-floured surface, and knead 10 to 12 times.

Roll dough to ½-inch thickness; cut with a 2-inch biscuit cutter. Place on lightly greased baking sheets; brush with melted butter. Bake at 425° for 12 to 14 minutes. Yield: 2½ dozen.

**Note:** To make ahead, bake biscuits only 7 to 8 minutes. Cool on wire racks; freeze. To serve, thaw at room temperature, and bake at 425° for 5 to 6 minutes.

*LaJuan Coward*
*Jasper, Texas*

## Simple Holiday Chargers

Do you like the look of chargers or service plates but don't want to spend the money on brass or silver ones for a Christmas dinner crowd? Then make your own spectacular but affordable magnolia-leaf chargers for the occasion. You'll need fresh **magnolia leaves, cardboard cake circles** from a cake decorating supply or crafts store, a **hot-glue gun,** and **clear polyurethane floral spray** from the florist.

Simply use a hot glue gun to glue leaves (overlapping them) onto circles with tips pointing outward. Press leaves onto cardboard circles with a cloth to avoid burning your fingers. Then spray clear floral spray on the leaves for a shiny, protective finish. (You can vary the look with silver or gold metallic floral spray paint.) The leaves will last about a week, so you can make your chargers before the holiday rush.

## BLACK BOTTOM MOCHA-CREAM TART

1½ cups all-purpose flour
½ cup butter or margarine
2½ tablespoons orange juice
½ cup finely chopped pecans
1 (6-ounce) package semisweet
  chocolate morsels
1 (5-ounce) can evaporated milk
2 tablespoons brown sugar
1 tablespoon butter or margarine
½ teaspoon vanilla extract
1 envelope unflavored gelatin
1¼ cups milk, divided
⅓ cup sugar
2 to 3 teaspoons instant coffee
  granules
2 egg yolks, beaten
¼ teaspoon almond extract
2 cups frozen whipped topping,
  thawed
Garnishes: whipped topping,
  chocolate shavings

Position knife blade in food processor bowl. Add flour, and cover with lid. With processor running, drop ½ cup butter, one tablespoon at a time, through food chute. Process until mixture is crumbly. Add orange juice and pecans through food chute; process until mixture forms a ball.

Place dough on lightly floured wax paper, and roll to a 13-inch circle. Place dough in an 11-inch round tart pan with removable bottom; trim off excess pastry around edges. Prick bottom and sides with a fork; bake at 350° for 20 to 25 minutes.

Combine chocolate morsels and next 3 ingredients in a small saucepan. Cook over low heat, stirring frequently, until chocolate melts. Stir in vanilla; spoon into pastry. Set aside.

Sprinkle gelatin over ½ cup milk in a small saucepan; let stand 1 minute. Add remaining ¾ cup milk, ⅓ cup sugar, and coffee granules. Cook over low heat, stirring until gelatin and coffee granules dissolve (about 2 minutes). Gradually stir about one-fourth of hot mixture into egg yolks, stirring constantly; add to remaining hot mixture. Cook about 1 minute or until mixture reaches 160° (do not boil). Remove from heat; stir in almond extract. Chill until consistency of unbeaten egg white.

Fold whipped topping into gelatin mixture; spoon into pastry over chocolate layer. Cover and refrigerate until firm. To serve, remove sides of pan, and garnish, if desired. Yield: one 11-inch tart.
*Wanda Edwards*
*Fayetteville, North Carolina*

## CRAN-APPLE PIE

2 cups peeled, sliced cooking apples
⅔ cup sugar
⅓ cup firmly packed light brown
  sugar
3 tablespoons cornstarch
1 tablespoon apple jelly
½ teaspoon ground cinnamon
3 tablespoons butter or margarine
2 cups fresh cranberries
1 unbaked 9-inch pastry shell
⅓ cup chopped pecans

Combine first 7 ingredients in a heavy saucepan; bring to a boil over medium heat, stirring constantly. Cook 1 minute, stirring constantly; stir in cranberries. Pour into pastry shell; sprinkle with pecans. Bake at 400° for 35 to 40 minutes or until set, covering edges with aluminum foil after 20 minutes. Cool on a wire rack. Yield: one 9-inch pie.
*Cathy Darling*

## Pastry Tips

■ Pans used for pastry never need greasing. The pastry shell or crumb crust will not stick to the sides of the pan.

■ Roll pie pastry on a lightly floured surface, but remember that too much flour toughens the crust. A stockinette rolling pin cover minimizes the amount of flour needed during rolling.

■ Make a quick job of rolling pastry. Roll lightly; keep in mind that too much handling will result in a tough crust.

■ To prevent a soggy crust in custard pies or quiche, brush slightly beaten egg white on the uncooked pastry shell; bake at 425° for 5 to 10 minutes. Add filling, and bake according to the recipe directions.

■ Slip a cookie sheet or a sheet of foil under a cobbler or fruit pie when baking in the oven in order to catch any run over.

■ Add a finishing touch to pies: Garnish with an ingredient used in the pie, such as lemon slices on a lemon pie or peanuts on a peanut butter pie.

■ To give the top crust of a pie a golden brown color and increase the flakiness, brush pastry lightly with milk before baking pie.

# A Real Fish Story

At the Sembler Marina in Sebastian, Florida, the sky is clear and bright. Eighty-degree days mark the arrival of the holiday season, yet Christmas seems months away. Schools of mullet shimmer like silver in the Indian River, and occasionally, you notice a needlefish brooding near the boat dock. Frank Lawlor approaches the marina, breaking the tranquil mood and setting the stage for a fish smoke with his buddies.

## Smoking Fish at Home

Frank Lawlor, the "smoke master," says you can use either a gas grill or a traditional smoker if you don't have a smokehouse handy. After testing these methods, our Foods staff found the fish to be tender and well seasoned no matter which way it was smoked. We worked with 5 pounds of fish, but you can smoke larger portions, based on the size of your smoker and your dedication to the task at hand.

Frank also let us borrow a few of the smoked fish recipes that he's tried over the years. Be sure to try all of his suggestions.

You might also be tempted to toss the fish in pasta or try it in a sandwich. For a simple yet enticing appetizer, serve smoked fish with crackers. Whether served alone or in recipes, it's sure to be delicious.

Combine all ingredients; mix well. Yield: about ⅓ cup.

**Note:** To use gas grill for smoking, soak hickory chips in water 30 minutes; drain. Wrap chips in aluminum foil, and make several holes in foil. Light gas grill on one side; place foil-wrapped chips directly on hot coals. Coat grill rack with cooking spray. Place rack over chips; let burn 10 to 15 minutes. Arrange fish on grill rack; cover and cook 1 hour or until fish flakes easily when tested with a fork.

## SMOKED FISH SPREAD

½ cup mayonnaise
1 tablespoon finely chopped sweet pickles
1 tablespoon chopped fresh parsley
1 clove garlic, minced
1 teaspoon finely chopped celery
1 teaspoon finely chopped onion
Dash of Worcestershire sauce
1¾ cups flaked, smoked fish (about ½ pound)

Combine all ingredients; cover and refrigerate. Serve with assorted crackers. Yield: 1¾ cups.

## SMOKED FISH

¾ cup kosher salt (not iodized or ice-cream salt)
1 quart water
2½ tablespoons sugar
2 tablespoons lemon juice
1½ teaspoons onion powder
1 teaspoon garlic powder
½ teaspoon seafood seasoning
5 pounds fillets of amberjack, bluefish, or mullet
Hickory chips
Vegetable cooking spray
GOPPS Seasoning Mix

Dissolve salt in water; stir in sugar and next 4 ingredients. Cut fish into serving-size pieces, if desired. Submerge fish in salt solution; cover and refrigerate overnight.

Soak hickory chips in water 30 minutes. Prepare charcoal fire in smoker; let burn 15 to 20 minutes. Place hickory chips on hot coals. Place water pan in smoker, but do not fill with water. Coat food rack with cooking spray, and place in smoker.

Remove fish from brine; pat dry. Sprinkle with GOPPS Seasoning Mix. Place fish on food rack. Cover with smoker lid; cook 2 hours or until fish flakes easily when tested with a fork. Yield: about 5 pounds smoked fish.

### GOPPS Seasoning Mix

1 tablespoon garlic powder
1 tablespoon onion powder
1 tablespoon paprika
1 tablespoon pepper
1 tablespoon brown sugar

## When You Try It . . .

- Debone fish when you clean them. Skin may be left on one side of the fish to hold it together (this is optional). Frank recommends using 1-inch-thick fillets. If the fish are smaller, they will cook more quickly and may also taste salty.
- Soak fish in brine at least four hours, but overnight is best. The salt in the brine serves two purposes: food safety and flavor.
- Bear in mind that we didn't make a mistake in omitting water from the water pan of the smoker. Dry heat works best when smoking the fish.

## SMOKED FISH HASH

4 cups peeled, finely chopped potato
2½ cups flaked, smoked fish (about ¾ pound)
6 slices bacon, cooked and crumbled
2 tablespoons chopped onion
2 tablespoons chopped fresh parsley
⅛ teaspoon pepper
⅓ cup vegetable oil
½ cup water
Paprika

Combine first 6 ingredients; set aside. Heat oil in a heavy nonstick skillet; stir in potato mixture. Add water; cover, reduce heat, and simmer 7 minutes. Uncover and cook 8 to 10 minutes, stirring occasionally, or until browned. Spoon into a serving dish; sprinkle with paprika. Serve immediately. Yield: 6 servings.

## FISH-STUFFED POTATOES

6 medium baking potatoes
½ cup butter or margarine, melted
1 (5-ounce) can evaporated milk
2 teaspoons salt
½ teaspoon black pepper
¼ teaspoon ground red pepper
2 cups flaked, smoked fish (about ½ pound)
1 cup (4 ounces) grated Cheddar cheese
3 tablespoons finely chopped greens onions or chives
Paprika

Scrub potatoes. Wrap each potato in foil; bake at 400° for 1 hour or until done. Cut potatoes in half lengthwise; carefully scoop out pulp, leaving shells approximately ¼ inch thick.
Combine potato pulp, butter, and next 4 ingredients. Stir in flaked fish, cheese, and green onions. Stuff shells with mixture; sprinkle with paprika. Bake at 350° for 10 minutes or until thoroughly heated. Yield: 6 servings.

## ON THE LIGHT SIDE

# Fine Food For Good Friends

A crisp autumn night that hints of winter makes the perfect backdrop for a candlelit dinner with close friends. Faces will beam with pleasure when elegant Steak Diane is served. Worcestershire sauce and lemon highlight the exquisite flavor of this tender cut of beef.
While the bold color of Sweet Potato Puree attracts the eye, it's the cinnamon in the dish that excites the palate. And for a sophisticated and healthful dessert, sprinkling pecans on Poached Pears With Honey-Yogurt Sauce completes the menu.

### ELEGANT DINNER FOR SIX

**Steak Diane**
**Sweet Potato Puree**
**Steamed broccoli**
**Commercial French bread**
**Poached Pears With**
**Honey-Yogurt Sauce**
**Wine**

### STEAK DIANE

6 (4-ounce) beef tenderloin steaks (1 inch thick)
1½ teaspoons salt-free lemon-pepper seasoning
Butter-flavored cooking spray
1 teaspoon margarine
2 tablespoons lemon juice
2 teaspoons Worcestershire sauce
1 teaspoon Dijon mustard
Garnish: lemon twists

Sprinkle steaks with lemon-pepper seasoning. Coat a large, nonstick skillet with cooking spray; add margarine. Place over medium-high heat until margarine melts. Add steaks, and cook 5 minutes on each side or until

desired degree of doneness. Transfer to a platter; keep warm.
Add lemon juice, Worcestershire sauce, and mustard to skillet; bring to a boil, stirring constantly. Pour over steaks. Garnish, if desired, and serve immediately. Yield: 6 servings (179 calories [41% from fat] per 1 steak and 1½ teaspoons sauce).

☐ *23.7g protein, 8.2g fat (3.1g saturated), 1.1g carbohydrate, 0.1g fiber, 70mg cholesterol, 110mg sodium, and 11mg calcium.*

### SWEET POTATO PUREE

3 cups thinly sliced carrot
1 (16-ounce) can cut sweet potatoes in light syrup, drained
¼ cup firmly packed brown sugar
2 tablespoons unsweetened orange juice
½ teaspoon ground cinnamon
⅛ teaspoon salt
¼ teaspoon vanilla extract

Cook carrots in boiling water to cover 15 minutes or until very tender; drain.
Position knife blade in food processor bowl; add carrots and remaining ingredients. Process until smooth, stopping to scrape down sides. Yield: 6 servings (112 calories [2% from fat] per ½-cup serving).

☐ *1.2g protein, 0.3g fat (0.1g saturated), 27.2g carbohydrate, 2.7g fiber, 0mg cholesterol, 88mg sodium, and 34mg calcium.*

### POACHED PEARS
### WITH HONEY-YOGURT SAUCE
*(pictured on back cover)*

1 cup water
1 tablespoon lemon juice
6 medium ripe pears (3 pounds)
6 cups unsweetened apple juice
Honey-Yogurt Sauce
3 tablespoons chopped pecans, toasted

Combine water and lemon juice in a medium bowl; set aside. Peel pears, and remove core from bottom end, leaving stems intact. Dip in lemon juice mixture; set aside.

Place apple juice in a Dutch oven; bring to a boil, and cook over high heat until reduced to 1½ cups (about 12 minutes). Place pears, stem end up, in pan; cover, reduce heat, and simmer 12 minutes or until tender. Remove with a slotted spoon, and cool slightly. Discard remaining apple juice. Cut pears lengthwise into 4 or 5 slices, leaving stem end intact.

To serve, spoon 2 tablespoons Honey-Yogurt Sauce onto each plate, and arrange pears on sauce. Sprinkle each with 1½ teaspoons pecans. Yield: 6 servings (186 calories [16% from fat] per pear and 2 tablespoons Honey-Yogurt Sauce).

□ *2g protein, 3.4g fat (0.4g saturated), 40.7g carbohydrate, 4.5g fiber, 1mg cholesterol, 16mg sodium, and 59mg calcium.*

### Honey-Yogurt Sauce

½ cup plus 1 tablespoon vanilla
   low-fat yogurt
3 tablespoons honey

Combine yogurt and honey, stirring until blended. Yield: ¾ cup (25 calories [4% from fat] per 1 tablespoon).

□ *0.5g protein, 0.1g fat (0.1g saturated), 5.8g carbohydrate, 0g fiber, 1mg cholesterol, 7mg sodium, and 18mg calcium.*

**Tip:** *Fruited and flavored yogurts add a rich texture to desserts, shakes, and snacks with less fat and cholesterol. Use lemon or vanilla yogurt in fruit dishes, sauces, and some salad dressings or as toppings for desserts.*

---

## MORE LIGHT RECIPES

# Discover Rice— The Amazing Grain

Rice has been cultivated for centuries, and today it is the dietary staple for almost half the world's population. The vast array of rices available offers a marvelous palette of textures, aromas, and appearances. And the quick-cooking varieties make preparing rice faster than ever.

### SHRIMP-AND-RICE SALAD
*(pictured on page 4)*

3 cups water
1 pound unpeeled, medium-size
   fresh shrimp
2 cups cooked white rice (cooked
   without salt or fat)
½ cup chopped celery
½ cup chopped green pepper
¼ cup sliced pimiento-stuffed olives
¼ cup chopped onion
2 tablespoons diced pimiento
3 tablespoons commercial oil-free
   Italian dressing
2 tablespoons reduced-calorie
   mayonnaise
2 tablespoons prepared mustard
1 tablespoon lemon juice
1 teaspoon salt-free lemon-pepper
   seasoning
⅛ teaspoon pepper
Lettuce leaves
Garnishes: fresh parsley sprig,
   cooked shrimp, and
   pimiento-stuffed olive

Bring water to a boil; add shrimp, and cook 3 to 5 minutes or until shrimp turn pink. Drain well; rinse with cold water. Chill. Peel and devein shrimp.

Combine shrimp and next 6 ingredients in a medium bowl. Combine Italian dressing and next 5 ingredients, stirring until well blended. Pour over shrimp mixture, and toss gently to coat. Cover and chill 3 to 4 hours. Line a serving plate with lettuce leaves. Spoon salad onto plate, and garnish, if desired. Yield: 5 servings (185 calories [15% from fat] per 1-cup serving).

□ *13.4g protein, 3.1g fat (0.3g saturated), 25.3g carbohydrate, 1.5g fiber, 101mg cholesterol, 408mg sodium, and 55mg calcium.*          Betty J. Casey
                              Montgomery, Alabama

### CHICKEN BREASTS WITH FRUITED RICE PILAF

½ cup unsweetened apple juice
½ cup no-salt-added chicken broth
1 cup chopped dried apricots
¼ cup raisins
Butter-flavored cooking spray
1 cup chopped onion
½ cup chopped celery
½ cup chopped fresh parsley
2 cups cooked brown rice (cooked
   without salt or fat)
½ teaspoon salt
½ teaspoon pepper
½ teaspoon rubbed sage
¼ teaspoon poultry seasoning
4 (6-ounce) skinned chicken breast
   halves
¼ teaspoon pepper

Combine juice and broth in a saucepan; bring to a boil. Stir in apricots and raisins; remove from heat. Cover and let stand 1 hour. (Do not drain.)

Coat a nonstick skillet with cooking spray; place over medium-high heat until hot. Add onion, celery, and parsley; cook, stirring constantly, until tender. Remove mixture from heat; stir in apricot mixture, rice, and next 4 ingredients.

Place chicken in an 11- x 7- x 1½-inch baking dish coated with cooking spray; sprinkle with ¼ teaspoon pepper. Spoon rice around chicken. Cover and bake at 350° for 35 minutes; uncover and bake 10 minutes or until chicken is done. Yield: 4 servings (413 calories [7% from fat] per 1 breast half and 1 cup rice pilaf).

□ *31.6g protein, 3.1g fat (0.6g saturated), 66.9g carbohydrate, 7.2g fiber, 66mg cholesterol, 396mg sodium, and 79mg calcium.*

## EASY BLACK BEANS AND YELLOW RICE

Vegetable cooking spray
½ cup chopped onion
¼ cup chopped celery
¼ cup chopped green pepper
1 (15-ounce) can black beans, drained
1 (14½-ounce) can no-salt-added whole tomatoes, undrained and chopped
1 teaspoon sugar
¾ teaspoon dried Italian seasoning
¼ teaspoon garlic powder
¼ teaspoon pepper
⅛ teaspoon salt
⅛ teaspoon hot sauce
¾ cup water
⅓ cup long-grain white rice, uncooked
¼ teaspoon ground turmeric

Coat a medium saucepan with cooking spray, and place over medium-high heat until hot. Add onion, celery, and green pepper; cook, stirring constantly, until tender. Stir in drained beans and next 7 ingredients; bring to a boil. Reduce heat, and simmer, uncovered, 15 minutes or until thickened, stirring frequently; set aside.

Combine water, rice, and turmeric in a saucepan; bring to a boil. Cover, reduce heat, and simmer 20 minutes. Remove rice from heat; let stand 5 minutes or until liquid is absorbed. Serve black bean mixture over rice. Yield: 2 servings (370 calories [4% from fat] per 1¼ cups bean mixture and ½ cup rice).

□ *17g protein, 1.8g fat (0.3g saturated), 74.8g carbohydrate, 8.6g fiber, 0mg cholesterol, 562mg sodium, and 150mg calcium.*

## BAKED RICE CUSTARD

⅔ cup sugar
2 teaspoons cornstarch
¼ teaspoon salt
2¾ cups 2% low-fat milk
2 large eggs
1 egg white
1 cup cooked white rice (cooked without salt or fat)
¼ cup raisins
½ teaspoon vanilla extract
Vegetable cooking spray
⅛ teaspoon ground nutmeg

Combine first 3 ingredients; set aside. Place milk in a heavy saucepan; cook over medium heat, stirring constantly, until almost boiling. Remove from heat, and gradually stir in sugar mixture. Beat eggs and egg white until frothy. Gradually stir one-fourth of hot mixture into eggs; add to remaining hot mixture, stirring constantly. Stir in rice, raisins, and vanilla. Pour into a 1½-quart baking dish coated with cooking spray.

Place baking dish in a 13- x 9- x 2-inch baking dish. Add water to pan to depth of 1 inch. Bake at 325° for 30 minutes. Stir custard gently, and bake 10 minutes. Stir custard, and sprinkle with nutmeg; bake 10 to 15 minutes or until a knife inserted halfway between center and edge of dish comes out clean. Remove baking dish from water; cool. Cover and chill 3 to 4 hours. Yield: 9 servings (153 calories [16% from fat] per ½-cup serving).

□ *4.8g protein, 2.7g fat (1.3g saturated), 27.8g carbohydrate, 0.3g fiber, 53mg cholesterol, 123mg sodium, and 101mg calcium.*

## Discover Types of Rice

Regular-milled white rice, sometimes called polished rice, is the most common variety in this country and cooks in about 15 minutes. Because the milling process strips away the nutrient-rich bran on the outside of the grain, white rice is almost always enriched with vitamins and minerals. Parboiled or "converted" white rice, which takes about 25 minutes to cook, has undergone a steam-pressure process to make the cooked grains extra fluffy.

The tan color of brown rice comes from the bran left on the grains. The bran adds fiber and increases the cooking time to about 45 minutes. Cooked brown rice has a nutty flavor and slightly chewy texture.

Precooked rice has been completely cooked and dehydrated and is often sold in boil-in-bag packages. It takes only 5 minutes to prepare; precooked brown rice takes 10 to 15 minutes.

White and brown rices are divided into classes according to the length of their grains—short, medium, or long. Long grains of rice remain separate and fluffy when cooked; medium and short grains, which are more moist and tender, tend to stick together.

Arborio and basmati rice are becoming more widely available. Arborio rice, used in risotto, is a short-grain variety from northern Italy that cooks up firm but creamy. (Any medium-grain rice can be substituted.) Basmati rice, grown in the foothills of the Himalayas, has slender, long grains with a nutty aroma and flavor. Texmati rice, a basmati-type rice grown in this country, has similar characteristics.

## Crispy Cheesy Catfish

Nothing gets taste buds tingling like the sound of catfish frying in a skillet. But fish doesn't have to sizzle in oil to taste good. Catfish is terrific (and much more healthful) when it's dredged in a spicy Parmesan cheese mixture, then popped under the broiler for a few minutes.

### PARMESAN CATFISH

½ cup grated Parmesan cheese
2 tablespoons yellow cornmeal
1 teaspoon paprika
⅛ teaspoon ground red pepper
8 (4-ounce) farm-raised catfish
 fillets
Vegetable cooking spray

Combine first 4 ingredients in a large, zip-top plastic bag. Add fillets; seal bag, and shake to coat fillets with cheese mixture. Place on broiler pan coated with cooking spray; discard remaining cheese mixture. Broil 3 inches from heat (with electric oven door partially opened) 10 minutes or until fish flakes easily when tested with a fork. Yield: 8 servings (148 calories [35% from fat] per serving).

□ *21.8g protein, 5.7g fat (1.6g saturated), 1g carbohydrate, 0.1g fiber, 68mg cholesterol, 118mg sodium, and 80mg calcium.*

| COMPARE THE NUTRIENTS | | |
|---|---|---|
| (per serving) | | |
| | Traditional | Light |
| Calories | 272 | 148 |
| Fat | 14.9g | 5.7g |
| Cholesterol | 68mg | 68mg |

## Leftover Turkey Makes The Salad

Do you have trouble deciding what size turkey to buy for Thanksgiving? The rule of thumb is 1 pound per person (1¼ pounds if it's prestuffed), but most buy extra, not realizing that this figure already allows for leftovers.

### HONEY-MUSTARD TURKEY SALAD

2 cups chopped cooked turkey
6 slices bacon, cooked and
 crumbled
1 (4.5-ounce) jar whole mushrooms,
 drained
¼ cup thin sweet red pepper strips
¼ cup sliced green onions
½ cup mayonnaise or salad
 dressing
2 tablespoons honey
1½ tablespoons Dijon mustard
¾ teaspoon soy sauce
¾ teaspoon lemon juice
1 (2-ounce) package roasted
 cashews
Lettuce leaves
Sweet red pepper rings
Chow mein noodles

Combine first 5 ingredients; set aside. Combine mayonnaise and next 4 ingredients; fold into turkey mixture. Cover and refrigerate. Just before serving, stir in cashews. Serve on lettuce leaves and pepper rings; sprinkle with chow mein noodles. Yield: 4 to 6 servings.

*Laurie McIntyre*
*Houston, Texas*

## Relishes, Chutneys, And Sauces

For a different taste treat, consider crowning a beef or pork roast, ham, or turkey with one of these sauces. Any of these combinations—whether sweet and tart or hot and spicy—will add a spark to your holiday meal.

### APPLE CHUTNEY

½ cup raisins
½ cup dry white wine
6 medium-size Red Delicious
 apples, peeled, cored, and
 chopped
½ cup sugar
½ cup butter or margarine
1 tablespoon lemon juice
1 teaspoon ground cinnamon

Combine raisins and wine; let stand 2 hours. Drain and set aside.

Combine apples, sugar, butter, lemon juice, and ground cinnamon in a 3-quart saucepan; bring to a boil, stirring constantly. Reduce heat and simmer, uncovered, 30 to 35 minutes or until thickened, stirring occasionally.

Stir in raisins, and cook 1 minute or until hot, stirring constantly. Serve with ham or pork. Yield: 3½ cups.

*Debbie Wall*
*Richmond, Texas*

### CUMBERLAND SAUCE

1⅓ cups red currant jelly
⅓ cup port
1½ tablespoons white vinegar
2 tablespoons water
2 teaspoons dry mustard

Combine all ingredients in a saucepan; cook over medium heat 10 minutes, stirring occasionally. Serve warm with pork or ham. Yield: 1⅓ cups.

*Sharon McClatchey*
*Muskogee, Oklahoma*

## JALAPEÑO-CRANBERRY SAUCE

1 (16-ounce) can whole-berry
  cranberry sauce
½ cup hot jalapeño pepper jelly

Combine ingredients in a small sauce-pan; cook over medium heat, stirring frequently, until jelly melts. Serve warm with lamb, pork, or poultry. Yield: 2 cups.


## TIPSY CRANBERRY RELISH

4 cups fresh or frozen cranberries,
  thawed
1½ cups sugar
⅓ to ½ cup brandy
½ cup chopped walnuts

Combine cranberries and sugar in a microwave-safe 1½-quart casserole; microwave at MEDIUM (50% power) 12 to 13 minutes, stirring once. Stir in brandy and walnuts; cool. Cover and refrigerate 2 to 3 hours. Serve with poultry or pork. Yield: 2½ cups.

*Elsie R. Fraga*
*New Bedford, Massachusetts*


## RAISIN RELISH

1 cup raisins
1 cup golden raisins
½ cup white vinegar
4 cloves garlic, crushed
1½ tablespoons sugar
2 teaspoons peeled, minced
  gingerroot or ½ teaspoon
  ground ginger
¼ teaspoon salt
½ teaspoon mustard seeds
½ teaspoon ground red pepper

Combine all ingredients; cover and re-frigerate at least 8 hours. Serve with ham. Yield: 2 cups.      *Gwen Louer*
*Roswell, Georgia*


# Some Like It Jalapeño Hot

Jalapeños are the hands-down winner of the pepper popularity contest. Largely due to their exposure as the finishing touch to nachos, these hot and flavorful peppers have quickly worked their way into most supermar-kets as a common item.

Fresh jalapeños, available in the produce section, should be smooth, dark green, and about 2 inches long.


## EASY CHICKEN JALAPEÑO

4 skinned and boned chicken breast
  halves
2 tablespoons butter or margarine,
  melted
½ cup jalapeño jelly

Place chicken breasts between two sheets of heavy-duty plastic wrap, and flatten to ¼-inch thickness, using a meat mallet or rolling pin.

Cook chicken in butter in a large skillet over medium-high heat 5 min-utes on each side. Remove to a serv-ing platter, and keep warm. Add jelly to pan drippings; bring to a boil, stir-ring until smooth. Spoon over chicken. Yield: 4 servings.

*Juanita Alexander*
*Bradenton, Florida*


### Too Hot to Handle

When peeling and chopping fresh jalapeño peppers, always wear rubber gloves, and keep your hands away from your face and eyes. After all, the compound that causes the peppers' hot fla-vor—capsaicin—is a potent skin irritant.

## HOT PEPPER RICE

3 cups cooked long-grain rice
1 (8-ounce) carton sour cream
1 (4-ounce) can chopped green
  chiles, drained
1 medium fresh jalapeño pepper,
  seeded and diced
1 (8-ounce) package Monterey
  Jack cheese, thinly sliced
  and divided
½ cup (2 ounces) shredded Cheddar
  cheese

Combine first 4 ingredients. Layer half of rice mixture in a lightly greased 10- x 6- x 2-inch baking dish; top with half of Monterey Jack cheese. Repeat pro-cedure; sprinkle with Cheddar cheese. Bake at 350° for 15 minutes. Yield: 6 to 8 servings.      *Patricia Pashby*
*Memphis, Tennessee*


## SPINACH-BACON SPREAD

8 slices bacon, cooked and
  crumbled
2 (10-ounce) packages frozen
  chopped spinach, thawed and well
  drained
4 (8-ounce) packages Monterey Jack
  cheese with jalapeño peppers,
  shredded
1 (11-ounce) can Cheddar cheese
  soup, undiluted
1 (8-ounce) package cream cheese,
  softened
1 teaspoon Greek seasoning
½ teaspoon onion powder
1 teaspoon hot sauce
1 (2-ounce) jar diced pimiento,
  drained
Paprika (optional)

Combine first 8 ingredients in a lightly greased 11- x 7- x 1½-inch baking dish; microwave at HIGH 3 minutes. Reduce heat to MEDIUM (50% power), and microwave 7 to 9 min-utes, stirring at 1½ minute intervals.

Sprinkle mixture with pimiento and paprika, if desired. Serve spread with crackers or bagel chips. Yield: about 1½ quarts.      *Barbara Morawietz*
*Seguin, Texas*

## FIERY SWEET MELON BALLS

2 cups honeydew melon balls
2 cups cantaloupe balls
2 tablespoons white wine
 vinegar
2 tablespoons vegetable oil
1 tablespoon water
1 tablespoon seeded and minced
 fresh jalapeño pepper
2 teaspoons sugar
½ teaspoon paprika
⅛ teaspoon pepper

Place melon balls in a shallow dish. Combine vinegar and remaining ingredients in a small bowl; pour mixture over melon balls. Cover fruit and chill. Yield: 6 to 8 servings.

# An Apple For The Teacher

Why not add a bit of diversity to an age-old custom this season? Take the traditional presentation of an apple to the teacher and revise it. The result is a great package for anyone—including a favorite teacher.

Apple-Filled Cookies offers an oatmeal exterior with a hidden apple filling. If you have several people to remember, try Apple Butter, which combines tangy apples with subtle spices for a delicious spread.

## APPLE BUTTER

5 pounds Granny Smith apples,
 peeled, cored, and sliced
3 cups water
3 cups sugar
3 cups firmly packed brown sugar
1 (1¾-ounce) box powdered pectin
1 tablespoon ground cinnamon
1 teaspoon ground allspice
¼ teaspoon ground cloves
¼ teaspoon ground nutmeg

Combine apples and water in a large Dutch oven; bring to a boil. Reduce heat, and cook 20 to 25 minutes or until tender. Mash. Stir in sugars and remaining ingredients. Bring to a boil; cook 2 minutes, stirring constantly. Quickly pour mixture into hot sterilized jars, filling to ¼ inch from top; wipe jar rims. Cover jars at once with metal lids, and screw on bands. Process in boiling-water bath 5 minutes. Yield: 6 pints.

**Note:** Unprocessed Apple Butter may be refrigerated in a covered container up to one month. *Mary Lynn Butler Decaturville, Tennessee*

## APPLE SQUARES

4 cups all-purpose flour
1 teaspoon salt
2 cups shortening
1 (8-ounce) carton sour cream
6 large cooking apples, peeled,
 cored, and sliced
1 cup sugar
½ cup firmly packed brown sugar
1½ tablespoons lemon juice
¼ cup graham cracker crumbs
¼ cup fine, dry breadcrumbs

Combine flour and salt; cut in shortening with pastry blender until mixture is crumbly. Add sour cream; stir with a fork until flour mixture is moistened. Cover and chill.

Combine apples and next 3 ingredients; set aside.

Divide flour mixture in half; roll one portion into a 15- x 10-inch rectangle on wax paper. Place in a 15- x 10- x 1-inch jellyroll pan. Sprinkle with graham cracker crumbs and breadcrumbs. Arrange apple mixture over crumbs. Roll remaining pastry into a 16- x 12-inch rectangle; place over apple mixture. Fold edges under, and crimp. Bake at 375° for 1 hour. Let cool on a wire rack. Cut into 2-inch squares. Yield: about 3 dozen.

**Note:** Baked Apple Squares may be frozen in airtight containers up to eight months. *Mary Prischak Ladson, South Carolina*

## APPLE-FILLED COOKIES

1 cup peeled, chopped cooking
 apple
¼ cup raisins
¼ cup chopped walnuts
½ cup sugar
2 tablespoons water
1 cup butter or margarine,
 softened
½ cup sugar
1 cup firmly packed brown sugar
1 large egg
1 teaspoon vanilla extract
1½ cups all-purpose flour
½ teaspoon baking soda
½ teaspoon salt
3 cups regular oats, uncooked
1 cup flaked coconut

Combine chopped apple, raisins, chopped walnuts, ½ cup sugar, and water in a small saucepan. Cook over low heat, stirring frequently, 15 minutes or until thickened; cool.

Beat butter at medium speed with an electric mixer until soft and creamy; gradually add sugars, beating well. Add egg and vanilla, mixing well. Combine flour, soda, and salt; add to butter mixture, mixing well. Stir in oats and coconut.

Reserve ¼ of dough. Shape remaining dough into 1-inch balls; place about 2 inches apart on ungreased cookie sheets. Press thumb in center of each ball to make an indentation. Spoon ¼ teaspoon apple mixture into each indentation. Pinch off small portion of reserved dough; flatten, place over filling, and seal edges. Bake at 375° for 10 minutes. Yield: 3 dozen.
*Mary Alice Carmichael Birmingham, Alabama*

# Tasty Teaching Methods

Louise Smith has a reputation among her friends in Columbus, Georgia, as a gourmet cook, but her 4-year-old students at Brookstone School know her best as the "Gingerbread Lady." She opens her class each fall with a lively segment based on the gingerbread man, and the students don't stop cooking—or eating—all year.

Trained as a home economics teacher, she's been teaching the young set for the last 17 years, and they have reaped the benefits of her training and her love of food.

## YEAST GINGERBREAD MEN

1 package dry yeast
¼ cup warm water (105° to 115°)
¾ cup milk
½ cup sugar
⅓ cup butter or margarine
1 teaspoon salt
1 large egg
3 cups all-purpose flour, divided
1 cup graham cracker crumbs
½ teaspoon ground cinnamon
½ teaspoon ground cloves
½ teaspoon ground ginger
¼ cup currants or raisins
1 large egg, beaten

Combine yeast and warm water in a 1-cup liquid measuring cup; let stand 5 minutes.

Combine milk and next 3 ingredients in a saucepan; heat until butter melts, stirring occasionally. Cool to 105° to 115°. Combine milk mixture, yeast mixture, 1 egg, 1 cup flour, and next 4 ingredients in a mixing bowl; beat at medium speed with an electric mixer until smooth. Gradually stir in remaining 2 cups flour. Cover and let rise in a warm place (85°), free from drafts, 1 hour or until doubled in bulk.

Punch dough down, and divide into six equal portions; set five portions aside. Form three-fourths of one portion of dough into an oblong shape about 5 inches long; place on a lightly greased baking sheet. Cut a lengthwise slit halfway through bottom to form legs. Divide remaining one-fourth of that portion into three equal parts. Shape one part into a head and remaining two parts into arms; gently press each to attach to body. Gently push currants into dough for eyes and buttons. Repeat procedure with remaining five portions of dough.

Cover and let rise in a warm place (85°), free from drafts, 40 minutes. Gently brush each with beaten egg. Bake at 350° for 15 minutes or until golden. Cool on wire racks. Yield: 6 gingerbread men.

## GINGERBREAD MIX

4 cups all-purpose flour
2 tablespoons baking powder
1 teaspoon salt
½ teaspoon baking soda
1 cup firmly packed dark brown sugar
1 to 2 teaspoons ground ginger
1 teaspoon ground cinnamon
1 cup butter-flavored shortening

Position knife blade in food processor bowl; add all ingredients. Pulse 5 or 6 times or until mixture is crumbly. Store in an airtight container in a cool place up to 6 weeks. Yield: 6½ cups.

## GINGERBREAD PEOPLE

3 cups Gingerbread Mix (recipe above)
¼ cup all-purpose flour
⅓ cup molasses
1 large egg
Frosting

Combine first 4 ingredients; beat at medium speed with an electric mixer until dry ingredients are moistened. Shape into a ball; cover and chill at least 1 hour. Roll to ¼-inch thickness on a lightly floured surface. Cut with 5-inch gingerbread cutters, and place on lightly greased cookie sheets. Bake at 350° for 10 to 12 minutes. Cool 2 minutes on cookie sheets; transfer to wire racks to cool completely. Pipe Frosting as desired. Yield: 1 dozen.

### Frosting

2 cups sifted powdered sugar
3 tablespoons butter or margarine, melted
1 teaspoon vanilla extract
2 to 3 teaspoons milk
Paste food coloring

Combine first 4 ingredients; beat at medium speed with an electric mixer 1 minute or until piping consistency. Stir in food coloring as desired. Yield: about 1 cup.

## NO-MOLASSES GINGERBREAD

1 teaspoon baking soda
½ cup cane syrup
½ cup butter or margarine, softened
½ cup sugar
2 large eggs, lightly beaten
1½ cups all-purpose flour
1 teaspoon ground cinnamon
½ teaspoon ground ginger
¼ teaspoon ground cloves
¼ teaspoon salt
½ cup water

Combine soda and syrup; set aside. Beat butter at medium speed with an electric mixer until soft and creamy. Gradually add sugar, beating well. Add eggs, one at a time, beating after each addition. Stir in syrup mixture.

Combine flour and next 4 ingredients; add to butter mixture alternately with water, beginning and ending with flour mixture. Mix after each addition.

Pour batter into a greased and floured 9-inch square pan. Bake at 350° for 30 minutes or until a wooden pick inserted in center comes out clean. Cool at least 10 minutes before serving. Yield: 9 to 12 servings.

# Not Just Plain Pralines

Let's get this straight: Is that "pray-leen" or "praw-leen"? Just utter "pray-leen" to many a New Orleanian and their cringe will quickly let you know you've goofed. Cooking instructor and humorist Joe Cahn of New Orleans knows a good praline when he makes one and advises students, "If it's smooth and creamy, it's a 'praw-leen'; if it's coarse and gritty, then it's a 'pray-leen'."

Although candymaking can be a science, Joe takes the fear out of (and puts the fun into) stirring up a batch of perfect pralines. "If you screw up, don't tell everyone it's a failure. Just change the name of the recipe!" he jokes. (See Joe's "Quick Fixes for Praline Problems" on this page.)

At the New Orleans School of Cooking and Louisiana General Store in Jax Brewery, Joe's employees are always cranking out his basic praline recipe while passersby watch, sample, and praise. But one version isn't enough for Joe's creativity. Here, he shares 10 variations of the pecan candy with us, each calling for just one or two extra ingredients tossed into the pot for a new twist.

Where does Joe get his inspiration? Anywhere—you name it. Stirring in a few "bed mints" (as he calls them) from the pillows of hotel rooms, he jests, "You travel, steal those little bitty things, throw them in the pot, and you've got Chocolate-Mint Pralines." It's as simple as that.

## BASIC PRALINES

Vegetable cooking spray
1½ cups sugar
¾ cup firmly packed brown sugar
¼ cup plus 2 tablespoons butter
½ cup milk
1½ cups chopped pecans

Lightly coat wax paper with vegetable cooking spray; set aside. Combine sugar and remaining ingredients in a heavy 3-quart saucepan. Bring to a boil over medium heat, stirring constantly. Boil, uncovered, stirring constantly, 1 to 2 minutes or until a candy thermometer reaches 220°. (You may need to lower the heat with a thinner saucepan, and rely on the candy thermometer instead of the timer.)

Remove from heat, and beat with a wooden spoon 4 to 6 minutes or just until mixture begins to thicken. Working rapidly, drop by tablespoonfuls onto prepared wax paper; let stand until firm. Yield: 2½ dozen.

**Orange Pralines:** Add 3 tablespoons Cointreau or other orange-flavored liqueur before cooking.

**Café au Lait Pralines:** Add 1½ tablespoons instant coffee granules before cooking.

**Mocha Pralines:** Add 1½ to 2 tablespoons instant coffee granules and ½ cup semisweet chocolate morsels before cooking.

**Chocolate-Peanut Butter Pralines:** Add ½ cup semisweet chocolate morsels and ¼ cup creamy peanut butter before cooking.

**Peanut Butter Pralines:** Add 2 tablespoons creamy peanut butter before cooking and 1 teaspoon vanilla extract to cooked mixture before beating.

**Chocolate-Mint Pralines:** Add 5 (½-ounce) chocolate-covered peppermint patties before cooking.

**Hot Spicy Pralines:** Add ½ teaspoon ground red pepper to mixture before cooking.

**Bourbon Pralines:** Add 3 tablespoons bourbon before cooking.

**Chocolate Pralines:** Add 2 (1-ounce) squares unsweetened chocolate before cooking.

**Vanilla Pralines:** Stir 1 teaspoon vanilla extract into cooked mixture before beating.

---

## Quick Fixes For Praline Problems

■ If your pralines don't harden as they should, fold them into softened vanilla ice cream for **Praline Ice Cream**. Or you can scrape the soft mixture up, chill, and roll it into 1-inch balls. Dip pralines into melted chocolate to make **Praline-Chocolate Truffles**.

■ If the candy mixture hardens in the pot, break it into pieces and fold it into softened vanilla ice cream, and you have **Praline Crunch Ice Cream**, or sprinkle the crumbled mixture over a commercial cheesecake and serve **Praline Cheesecake**.

# From Our Kitchen To Yours

Mastering the art of cooking requires practice and experience. Here are some tips that our readers and the Test Kitchens staff have learned over the years.

When Reba Stephens of Wilmington, North Carolina, works with dough, she dampens the work surface before covering it with wax paper. "The dampness holds the wax paper in place and keeps it from slipping when using the rolling pin. Also, when the work is finished, I roll up the wax paper and discard it—there's no more cleaning up to do."

Marie Schulmeister of Crescent City, Florida, tells us the quickest and easiest way to grease pans is to slip your hand into a sandwich bag and then into the shortening can. "Smear away and come out with a clean hand. When finished, turn the bag inside out, and discard." When baking a chocolate cake, she suggests using cocoa to flour the greased pan.

"My mother taught me how to bake pies without the crust getting soggy," writes Mildred Johnson of Pfafftown, North Carolina. "For custard pies, such as pumpkin, sprinkle a tablespoon each of flour and sugar on the crust, and rub gently with fingertips before adding the filling."

## Test Kitchens Tips

■ Prevent piecrust edges from overbrowning by folding a 12-inch square of aluminum foil into quarters. Cut out the center, leaving an 8-inch hole. Unfold and place foil over the partially baked piecrust to shield the edges.
■ Lightly flour the knife blade before chopping nuts in a food processor.
■ Dip a sharp knife in warm water or coat it with vegetable cooking spray before slicing a cheesecake.
■ Squeeze a small piece of onion through a garlic press to grate a small amount of onion. Quickly chop onion without using a food processor by rolling a pizza cutter over onion slices.
■ Check doneness of yeast breads by inserting an instant-read thermometer into the center of bread; thermometer should register 190°.
■ Spray a grater with vegetable cooking spray before grating cheese or citrus fruit for easy cleanup.
■ Store leftover fresh gingerroot up to three months wrapped in a white paper towel in the refrigerator's vegetable drawer. For longer storage, slice gingerroot and place in pale dry sherry up to one year; use gingerroot slices when stir-frying and ginger-flavored sherry in other recipes.
■ Freeze leftover almond paste up to three months.
■ Store leftover fresh mushrooms in a paper bag to prevent dampness, which causes them to turn brown.
■ Buy cranberries when they're in season and freeze them in the 12-ounce plastic bag they come in up to one year.
■ Purchase candied fruit on sale after the holiday season, and store in the refrigerator for next year's baking.
■ Freeze leftover buttermilk up to three months and leftover eggnog up to six months. To reuse, thaw overnight in the refrigerator, and stir vigorously before using.

## Just Ask Us

*Why does a jellyroll cake sometimes crack when rolling?* To prevent a jellyroll cake from cracking, roll the cake immediately after it's removed from the oven, while it's still warm and flexible. Carefully loosen cake from the sides of the jellyroll pan with a knife. Invert it onto a towel dusted with powdered sugar, and lift off pan. Quickly roll the cake up with the towel; let cool on a wire rack 10 to 15 minutes. Unroll the cake and spread with filling.

*My favorite desserts contain sweetened, beaten, raw egg whites; what can be substituted?* Meringue powder (found in specialty shops) replaces raw egg whites in many recipes. Follow the package directions for making Cold Meringue; the recipe yields 3½ cups, which is equivalent to 4 egg whites beaten with ½ cup sugar.

*How can I make a clearer raspberry sauce?* Place raspberries in a large, wire-mesh strainer, and let juice drain into a bowl; do not stir or mash.

*How are perfect cake layers made?* Use pan size specified in recipe; incorrect pan size can cause the cake to be flat and shrunken or to rise to a peak and fall. Stagger the pans on the center rack so they do not touch each other or the sides of the oven during baking. If all pans will not fit on one rack, bake a layer by itself; do not place one pan underneath another.

*What causes chocolate to harden or seize when melting?* High heat and drops of water cause chocolate to harden. To return it to its melted consistency, stir in 1 teaspoon shortening or vegetable oil (not butter) for every 2 ounces of chocolate.

*What are substitutes for alcohol in recipes?* The following substitutes are similiar in flavor and work in most dishes. Substitute unsweetened fruit juice with half the specified amount of brandy, rum, or bourbon. For a sweet recipe, use an equal amount of unsweetened grape juice to replace red wine and unsweetened apple juice to replace white wine. Beef or chicken broth replaces either red or white wine in savory dishes.

## Unmold with Ease

Removing a congealed salad from the mold need not be tricky. Before filling the mold, coat it with vegetable cooking spray. To remove, carefully ease the set gelatin away from the edge of the mold with a knife to let in air and break the suction. Invert mold onto a lettuce-lined platter, and shake gently up and down until the salad drops out. If nothing happens, leave mold inverted and cover with a warm, damp towel for several seconds. Remove towel, and shake gently.

# DECEMBER

*Capture the spirit of the holiday season with a*

*tree-trimming party, and serve White Lightning Texas*

*Chili cooled by Mexican Salad With Avocado Dressing. For a*

*change of pace on Christmas morning, try an eye-opening*

*breakfast featuring trout cakes, country ham, sweet potato*

*hash, and steaming buttermilk raisin biscuits. And before you*

*resolve to shape up and trim down next year, feast on Spirited*

*Mince Pie, an updated version of mincemeat pie, or*

*Cranberry-Pecan Pie, robust with those*

*scarlet berries now in peak season.*

# Desserts As Easy As Pie

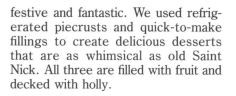

*Deck the halls with boughs of holly. Fa-la-la-la-la, la-la-la-la.* And while you're at it, why not deck the pies with boughs of holly, too.

Using our easy directions, you can serve a pie this holiday season that is festive and fantastic. We used refrigerated piecrusts and quick-to-make fillings to create delicious desserts that are as whimsical as old Saint Nick. All three are filled with fruit and decked with holly.

Combine raisins and brandy in a large bowl; let stand 2 hours.

Unfold 1 piecrust, and press out fold lines; sprinkle with flour, spreading over surface. Place, floured side down, in a 9-inch pieplate; fold edges under, and flute. Set aside.

Combine raisin mixture, mincemeat, and remaining ingredients; spoon into pastry shell. Roll remaining piecrust on a lightly floured surface to press out fold lines; cut with a 3¼-inch leaf-shaped cutter, and mark veins using a pastry wheel or knife. Roll pastry scraps into balls. Arrange on top of filling as desired. Bake at 375° for 10 minutes; shield edges with aluminum foil, and bake an additional 25 minutes. Cool on a wire rack. Yield: one 9-inch pie.

* Orange juice may be substituted for brandy.               *Robert W. Nolen*
*Falls Church, Virginia*

### CHERRY-BERRY PIE
*(pictured on cover)*

1 (10-ounce) package frozen red raspberries, thawed
1 (16-ounce) can pitted red cherries, undrained
1 cup sugar
¼ cup cornstarch
¼ cup butter or margarine
¼ teaspoon almond extract
¼ teaspoon red liquid food coloring
1 (15-ounce) package refrigerated piecrusts
1 teaspoon all-purpose flour
Garnishes: fresh raspberries, powdered sugar

Drain raspberries and cherries, reserving 1 cup combined juices; set fruit aside. Combine sugar and cornstarch in a medium saucepan; gradually stir in juices. Cook over medium heat, stirring constantly, until mixture begins to boil. Cook 1 minute, stirring constantly. Remove from heat; stir in butter, almond extract, and food coloring. Gently fold in reserved fruit; cool slightly.

Unfold 1 piecrust, and press out fold lines; sprinkle with flour, spreading over surface. Place, floured side down, in a 9-inch pieplate; fold edges under, and flute. Spoon in filling. Roll remaining piecrust to press out fold lines. Cut 5 leaves with a 3¼-inch leaf-shaped cutter, and mark veins using a pastry wheel or knife; set aside. Cut remaining pastry into ½-inch strips, and arrange in a lattice design over filling. Top with pastry leaves. Bake at 375° for 45 minutes. Cool on a wire rack. Garnish, if desired. Yield: one 9-inch pie.               *Mary Ealey*
*Smithfield, Virginia*

### SPIRITED MINCE PIE
*(pictured on page 336)*

¾ cup raisins
3 tablespoons brandy *
1 (15-ounce) package refrigerated piecrusts
1 teaspoon all-purpose flour
1 (27-ounce) jar mincemeat
1 large cooking apple, cored and finely chopped
1 cup chopped walnuts
¼ cup firmly packed brown sugar
1 teaspoon grated lemon or orange rind
1 tablespoon lemon juice

### CRANBERRY-PECAN PIE
*(pictured on page 336)*

1 (15-ounce) package refrigerated piecrusts
1 teaspoon all-purpose flour
3½ cups fresh or frozen cranberries, divided
½ cup raisins, divided
¾ cup chopped pecans
1½ cups sugar
3 tablespoons all-purpose flour
¼ cup light corn syrup
1 teaspoon grated orange rind
Garnish: fresh or frozen cranberries

Unfold 1 piecrust, and press out fold lines; sprinkle with 1 teaspoon flour, spreading over surface. Place crust, floured side down, in a 9-inch pieplate; fold edges under, and flute. Set aside.

Roll remaining piecrust to press out fold lines; cut with a 3¾-inch leaf-shaped cutter, and mark veins using a pastry wheel or knife. Drape leaves over small balls of aluminum foil on a baking sheet. Bake at 350° for 7 minutes; remove foil balls, and bake 3 additional minutes. Let cool.

Position knife blade in food processor bowl; add 1¾ cups cranberries and ¼ cup raisins. Pulse 5 or 6 times or until coarsely chopped, stopping once to scrape down sides. Transfer to a large bowl. Repeat procedure with remaining fruit. Combine cranberry mixture, pecans, and next 4 ingredients; spoon into pastry shell. Bake at 350° for 20 minutes; shield edges with foil, and bake an additional 20 minutes. Let cool on a wire rack. Arrange pastry leaves around edges, and garnish, if desired. Yield: one 9-inch pie.

# It's Time For Treats

Has the whirlwind of seasonal activities kept you a little too busy to bake a batch of cookies? If the answer is yes, don't panic. There's still time left for cookie baking, candy making, and treat taking. We're here to help get you going. Our holiday recipes will join the "must-have" list for your family.

## WHITE CHOCOLATE FUDGE

1 (8-ounce) package cream cheese, softened
4 cups sifted powdered sugar
1½ teaspoons vanilla extract
12 ounces vanilla-flavored candy coating, melted
¾ cup chopped pecans

Beat cream cheese at medium speed with an electric mixer until smooth; gradually add sugar and vanilla, beating well. Stir in candy coating and pecans. Spread into a buttered 8-inch square pan; refrigerate until firm. Cut into small squares. Yield: 2 pounds.
*Elizabeth Thompson*
*Connelly Springs, North Carolina*

## CHOCOLATE-PEANUT BUTTER BITES

1 cup sugar
1 cup light corn syrup
1½ cups creamy peanut butter
5 cups high-protein rice-and-wheat cereal
¾ cup semisweet chocolate morsels
¾ cup peanut butter or butterscotch morsels

Combine sugar and corn syrup in a large microwave-safe bowl; microwave at HIGH 3½ minutes. Stir and microwave 1 minute; stir in peanut butter and cereal. Press into a lightly greased 15- x 10- x 1-inch jellyroll pan; set aside.
Combine chocolate morsels and peanut butter morsels in a small glass bowl; microwave at MEDIUM HIGH (70% power) 1 to 2 minutes or until morsels melt, stirring once. Spread over cereal mixture; let cool. Cut into squares. Yield: about 3 pounds.
*Nancy Pope*
*Auburndale, Florida*

## MICROWAVE TOFFEE

½ cup finely chopped pecans
½ cup butter or margarine
1 cup sugar
1 teaspoon salt
¼ cup water
¾ cup semisweet chocolate morsels
¼ cup finely chopped pecans

Sprinkle ½ cup pecans in a 9-inch circle on a greased cookie sheet; set aside. Coat the top 2 inches of a 2½-quart glass bowl with butter; place remaining butter in bowl. Add sugar, salt, and water; do not stir. Microwave at HIGH 11 minutes or until mixture just begins to turn light brown; pour over pecans. Sprinkle with morsels; let stand 1 minute. Spread morsels over sugar mixture, and sprinkle with ¼ cup chopped pecans. Chill until firm. Break into bite-size pieces. Yield: 1 pound.
*Jan Ramsey*
*Quitaque, Texas*

## NUTTY CARAMEL CORN

6 quarts freshly popped corn (about 1 cup unpopped corn)
1 cup pecan halves
1 cup cashews
1 cup butter or margarine
2 cups firmly packed brown sugar
½ cup light corn syrup
1 teaspoon salt
½ teaspoon baking soda
1 teaspoon vanilla extract

Combine first 3 ingredients in a large roasting pan; set aside.
Melt butter in a large saucepan; stir in brown sugar, corn syrup, and salt. Bring to a boil over medium heat, stirring constantly. Boil 5 minutes, without stirring (temperature will register about 250°). Remove from heat; stir in soda and vanilla. Pour over popped corn and nuts; stir well. Bake at 225° for 1 hour, stirring every 15 minutes. Cool and break into pieces, if desired. Store in an airtight container. Yield: 5 quarts.
*Marion Hall*
*Knoxville, Tennessee*

## HOLIDAY BUTTER COOKIES

1½ cups butter, softened
¾ cup sugar
1 large egg
3 cups all-purpose flour
¼ cup orange juice
1 (4¼-ounce) tube green decorator frosting
Red cinnamon candies

Beat butter at medium speed with an electric mixer until soft and creamy; gradually add sugar, beating well. Add egg, mixing well. Add flour to creamed mixture, alternately with juice, beginning and ending with flour.
Use a cookie gun fitted with a star-shaped disk to shape wreaths; follow manufacturer's directions. Place on ungreased cookie sheets. Bake at 375° for 8 minutes or until edges begin to brown. Remove to wire racks to cool completely. Decorate cookies with frosting and candies as desired. Yield: 6 dozen.
*Emily Tempel*
*Higginville, Missouri*

## CHOCO-PEANUT CHIP COOKIES

1 cup butter or margarine, softened
½ cup sugar
½ cup firmly packed brown sugar
2 large eggs
1 teaspoon vanilla extract
2½ cups all-purpose flour
1 teaspoon baking soda
½ teaspoon salt
1 cup semisweet chocolate morsels
1 cup peanut butter morsels
1 cup chopped unsalted peanuts

Beat butter at medium speed with an electric mixer until soft and creamy; gradually add sugars, beating well. Add eggs and vanilla, mixing well. Combine flour, soda, and salt; add to creamed mixture, mixing well. Stir in morsels and peanuts.

Drop dough by tablespoonfuls onto ungreased cookie sheets. Bake at 350° for 10 to 12 minutes. Remove to wire racks to cool completely. Yield: 5 dozen.

*Polly A. Hughes*
*Hickory, North Carolina*

# Give A Gift Of Chocolate

If chocolate fanciers appear on your holiday gift list, we think you'll find the ultimate confection to capture their hearts in this selection of chocolate recipes.

Gather accessories for packaging these treats. Pretty baskets, platters, trays, tins, and boxes transport these treasures while doubling as part of the gift. Line containers with colorful cloth napkins to cushion and protect baked goods. For an added surprise, tuck smaller, inedible gifts, such as holiday candles and cookie cutters, among the goodies.

To keep baked gifts fresh, wrap containers with plastic wrap, gather at the top, and secure with a bow. Or wrap each food separately. Plastic food bags and boxes with holiday motifs make functional yet fun presentations for your gifts.

## MOCHA VELVET TORTE

1 tablespoon instant coffee granules
1 cup boiling water
1½ cups sugar
2½ cups semisweet chocolate morsels
1½ cups butter, melted
6 large eggs
1 teaspoon vanilla extract
Ganache Cream
Garnishes: chocolate leaves, chocolate-covered coffee beans

Grease bottom of a 9-inch springform pan; line with wax paper. Grease wax paper, and set aside.

Dissolve coffee granules in boiling water. Add sugar, stirring until sugar dissolves; set coffee mixture aside. Position knife blade in food processor bowl; add chocolate morsels. Process 1½ minutes or until finely chopped, stopping once to scrape down sides. Pour coffee mixture through food chute with processor running, stopping once to scrape down sides. Pour melted butter through food chute with processor running. Add eggs, one at a time, through food chute, pulsing after each addition. Add vanilla, and pulse once.

Pour into prepared pan; bake at 225° for 2½ hours or until slightly firm to touch. Cool completely on a wire rack. Run a knife around edge; release sides of springform pan. Invert torte onto an 8-inch cardboard round, and place on a rack over a shallow pan. Pour Ganache Cream over top and sides, covering completely. Chill 8 hours; garnish, if desired. Yield: one 9-inch torte.

### Ganache Cream

1 cup whipping cream
2 (4-ounce) packages bittersweet chocolate, chopped and divided
1½ tablespoons butter, divided

Combine whipping cream and two-thirds of chocolate in top of a double boiler; bring water to a boil. Reduce heat to low; cook until chocolate melts, stirring often. Remove from heat. Add remaining chocolate, stirring until chocolate melts and mixture is smooth. Add one-third of butter, beating until butter melts and mixture is smooth. Repeat procedure with remaining butter. Let cool until mixture is slightly thickened and pouring consistency. Yield: 1¼ cups.

**Note:** If room is cool, ganache may become too thick to pour. Mixture may be reheated in a double boiler over simmering water until the proper consistency is reached.

*Sherry Johnson*
*Asheboro, North Carolina*

## FOUR CHIPS FUDGE

¾ cup butter or margarine
1 (14-ounce) can sweetened condensed milk
3 tablespoons milk
1 (12-ounce) package semisweet chocolate morsels
1 (11½-ounce) package milk chocolate morsels
1 (10-ounce) package peanut butter-flavored morsels
1 cup butterscotch-flavored morsels
1 (7-ounce) jar marshmallow cream
1½ teaspoons vanilla extract
½ to 1 teaspoon almond extract
1 pound walnuts, coarsely chopped

Melt butter in a heavy Dutch oven over low heat; stir in condensed milk and milk. Add all morsels, stirring constantly, until mixture is smooth. Remove from heat; stir in marshmallow cream and flavorings. Stir in walnuts. Spoon into a buttered 15- x 10- x 1-inch jellyroll pan; spread evenly. Chill and cut into squares. Store in the refrigerator. Yield: 5 pounds.

*Annie Grace*
*Walkertown, North Carolina*

## BITTERSWEET CHOCOLATE SAUCE

8 (1-ounce) squares unsweetened
  chocolate
2 cups sugar
1 (12-ounce) can evaporated milk
½ teaspoon instant coffee granules
2 tablespoons boiling water
1 teaspoon vanilla extract
¼ cup butter or margarine

Melt chocolate in a heavy saucepan over low heat; stir in sugar. Gradually add evaporated milk, and cook over medium heat, stirring constantly, 10 minutes or until thickened.

Dissolve coffee granules in boiling water; add coffee mixture, vanilla, and butter to chocolate mixture, stirring until butter melts. Yield: 3⅓ cups.

*Sandi Pichon*
*Slidell, Louisiana*

## TRIPLE DECKER BROWNIES

1½ cups quick-cooking oats,
  toasted
1 cup all-purpose flour
1 cup firmly packed brown sugar
½ teaspoon baking soda
¼ teaspoon salt
¾ cup butter or margarine, melted
2 (1-ounce) squares unsweetened
  chocolate
½ cup butter or margarine
1½ cups sugar
2 large eggs
1⅓ cups all-purpose flour
½ teaspoon baking powder
¼ teaspoon salt
½ cup milk
1 teaspoon vanilla extract
1 cup chopped pecans
Chocolate Frosting

Combine oats, flour, brown sugar, soda, and salt in a large bowl; add ¾ cup melted butter, stirring well. Press mixture into bottom of two greased 8-inch square pans. Bake at 350° for 10 minutes.

Melt chocolate and ½ cup butter in a large, heavy saucepan over low heat; remove from heat. Add sugar and eggs, mixing well. Combine 1⅓

cups flour, baking powder, and ¼ teaspoon salt; add to chocolate mixture alternately with milk. Stir in vanilla and pecans. Spread over crust, and bake at 350° for 20 to 25 minutes. Cool on wire racks. Spread with Chocolate Frosting. Cut into 2-inch squares. Yield: 32 brownies.

### Chocolate Frosting

2 (1-ounce) squares unsweetened
  chocolate
¼ cup butter or margarine
3 cups sifted powdered sugar
2 teaspoons vanilla extract
3 to 4 tablespoons hot water

Melt chocolate and butter in a heavy saucepan over low heat; remove from heat. Stir in powdered sugar, vanilla, and 1 tablespoon water. Stir in additional water until desired spreading consistency. Yield: 1½ cups.

## CARAMEL-FILLED CHOCOLATE COOKIES

1 cup butter or margarine, softened
1 cup sugar
1 cup firmly packed brown sugar
2 large eggs
2¼ cups all-purpose flour
¾ cup cocoa
1 teaspoon baking soda
2 teaspoons vanilla extract
1 cup chopped pecans, divided
1 tablespoon sugar
1 (9-ounce) package chewy
  caramels in milk chocolate

Beat butter at medium speed with an electric mixer until creamy. Gradually add sugars, beating well. Add eggs, beating well.

Combine flour, cocoa, and soda; add to butter mixture, mixing well. Stir in vanilla and ½ cup chopped pecans. Cover cookie dough and refrigerate 1 hour.

Combine remaining ½ cup pecans and 1 tablespoon sugar; set aside. Gently press 1 tablespoon cookie dough around each candy, forming a ball. Dip one side of cookie in pecan

mixture. Place, pecan side up, 2 inches apart on ungreased cookie sheets. Bake at 375° for 8 minutes. (Cookies will look soft.) Let cool 1 minute on cookie sheets. Remove to wire racks to cool. Yield: 4 dozen.

*Krista Kiger*
*Winston-Salem, North Carolina*

# QUICK!

## Spreadable Edibles

Spread the word: Butter just got better, and mayonnaise marvelous. Stirring in just a couple of ingredients can do wonders. Add a little garlic powder and dillweed to mayonnaise before making that ordinary sandwich, or blend orange marmalade into butter for your breakfast toast. Try some of these spreads on meats and vegetable dishes, too.

### ORANGE BUTTER

1 cup butter or margarine, softened
1 (10-ounce) jar orange marmalade

Combine both ingredients; beat at medium speed with an electric mixer until creamy. Cover and refrigerate. Yield: 2 cups.

*Debie Hayse*
*Lexington, Kentucky*

### CINNAMON BUTTER

½ cup butter or margarine,
  softened
1½ tablespoons maple syrup
½ teaspoon ground cinnamon
⅛ teaspoon ground nutmeg

Combine all ingredients; beat at medium speed with an electric mixer until creamy. Cover and refrigerate. Yield: ½ cup.

## Spread the Idea

Now you've made the spread recipe, and you're wondering how to serve it. Each makes at least a ½ cup of spread (more than you can—or should—eat in one sitting), so you can keep it on hand for multiple uses. Here are some quick ideas for delicious ways to enjoy these recipes.

**Sweet Butters:**
- Slather it on warm pancakes and waffles. Serve them with or without syrup.
- Put a pat on hot breakfast muffins, biscuits, and other quick breads.
- Spread on bread slices, and quickly broil in the oven for toast.
- Slather on warm flour tortillas, roll up, and enjoy for breakfast or dessert.

**Savory Butters:**
- Dollop on hot baked potatoes.
- Put a pat on hot-off-the-grill fish, steak, or chicken.
- Spread on corn muffins or cornbread, rolls, biscuits, or French bread.
- Use on corn on the cob.

**Mayonnaises:**
- Substitute flavored versions for regular mayonnaise on both hot and cold sandwiches.
- Toss with cooked, cubed potatoes for quick potato salad.
- Stir into shredded cabbage for easy coleslaw.
- Substitute for tartar sauce with fried fish.

## SOUTHWESTERN BUTTER

½ cup butter or margarine, softened
2 teaspoons grated lime rind
¼ teaspoon chili powder
⅛ teaspoon ground cumin

Combine all ingredients; beat at medium speed with an electric mixer until creamy. Cover and refrigerate. Yield: ½ cup.

## ITALIAN HERBED MAYONNAISE

½ cup mayonnaise or salad dressing
1 teaspoon dried basil or 1 tablespoon chopped fresh basil
½ teaspoon dried oregano or 1½ teaspoons chopped fresh oregano

Combine all ingredients; cover and chill at least 2 hours. Yield: ½ cup.

## DILL-GARLIC MAYONNAISE

½ cup mayonnaise or salad dressing
½ teaspoon dried dillweed or 1½ teaspoons chopped fresh dillweed
¼ teaspoon garlic powder
Garnish: fresh dillweed

Combine first 3 ingredients; cover and refrigerate. Garnish, if desired. Yield: ½ cup.

# A Night Of Dining And Decorating

The tree is steady and straight, and the twinkling lights are finally just right. Out comes the old cardboard box, jingling and rattling with both regal and ragged Christmas treasures.

A similar scene probably plays in your own living room year after year and you wouldn't have it any other way. This time, invite a few friends or in-town relatives to share your memories and a meal.

## TREE-TRIMMING SUPPER FOR EIGHT

Spiced White Grape Juice
Bite-Size Cheese Balls
Sweet-And-Spicy Pecans
White Lightning Texas Chili
Mexican Salad With Avocado Dressing
Cranberry-Peach Cobbler
or
Chocolate-Peanut Butter Drops

- This beverage will warm you up, while spreading the sweet aroma of Christmas all through the house.

### SPICED WHITE GRAPE JUICE

4 (2-inch) sticks cinnamon
2 whole nutmegs
32 whole cloves
2 (24-ounce) bottles white grape juice
6 cups water
⅓ cup lemon juice
¼ cup sugar

Cut a 6-inch square of cheesecloth, and place first 3 ingredients in center; tie with string. Combine white grape juice and water in a Dutch oven. Add spice bag, and bring to a boil. Reduce heat, and simmer 20 minutes. Remove and discard spice bag, and stir in lemon juice and sugar. Serve hot. Yield: 3 quarts.      *Marcia Jeffries*
*Oklahoma City, Oklahoma*

■ Here's a job for your youngsters. You just combine the ingredients and chill; then let the children roll the mixture into balls and—the best part—insert a pretzel stick into each one for easy pickup.

## BITE-SIZE CHEESE BALLS

1 (3-ounce) package cream cheese, softened
1 cup (4 ounces) finely shredded Cheddar cheese
¾ cup finely shredded carrot
1 teaspoon honey
½ cup finely chopped pecans
24 pretzel sticks

Combine first 4 ingredients; cover and chill 1 hour. Shape into 1-inch balls, and roll in pecans; cover and chill. To serve, place a pretzel into each. Yield: 2 dozen.
*Edith Askins*
*Greenville, Texas*

■ You can make this easy appetizer the day before and store it at room temperature in an airtight container.

## SWEET-AND-SPICY PECANS

2 cups pecan halves
2 tablespoons butter, melted
1 tablespoon sugar
½ teaspoon ground cumin
½ teaspoon chili powder
¼ teaspoon dried crushed red pepper
⅛ teaspoon salt

Toss pecans in butter. Combine sugar and remaining ingredients; sprinkle over pecans, tossing to coat. Spread on a baking sheet; bake at 325° for 15 minutes, stirring occasionally. Cool. Yield: 2 cups.

■ Start soaking the beans that morning and they'll be ready to go into the chili by afternoon. This rib-sticker simmers for 3 hours—about the time it takes to put up the tree, string the lights, and bring out the decorations. (Or you can make the chili the day before, refrigerate, and then reheat to serve.)

## WHITE LIGHTNING TEXAS CHILI
### (pictured on page 260)

1 pound dried navy beans
4 (14½-ounce) cans ready-to-serve chicken broth, divided
1 large onion, chopped
2 cloves garlic, minced
1 tablespoon ground white pepper
1 tablespoon dried oregano
1 tablespoon ground cumin
1 teaspoon salt
½ teaspoon ground cloves
5 cups chopped cooked chicken
2 (4-ounce) cans chopped green chiles
1 cup water
1 jalapeño pepper, seeded and chopped
8 (8-inch) flour tortillas
Shredded Monterey Jack cheese
Commercial salsa
Sour cream

Sort and wash beans; place in a large Dutch oven. Cover with water 2 inches above beans. Soak 8 hours; drain beans, and return to Dutch oven. Discard liquid. Add 3 cans chicken broth and next 7 ingredients; bring mixture to a boil. Reduce heat and simmer, covered, 2 hours or until beans are tender, stirring occasionally. Add remaining can of chicken broth, chicken, and next 3 ingredients. Cover and simmer 1 hour, stirring occasionally.

With kitchen shears, make 4 cuts in each tortilla toward, but not through, center. Line serving bowls with tortillas, overlapping cut edges of tortillas. Spoon in chili, and top with cheese, salsa, and sour cream. Serve immediately. Yield: 12 cups.
*Beverly Germany*
*Fort Worth, Texas*

■ You can assemble the salad and make the dressing in the afternoon. Just refrigerate; then arrange on the buffet table come chowtime.

## MEXICAN SALAD WITH AVOCADO DRESSING
### (pictured on page 260)

3 tomatoes, cut into wedges
¾ cup sliced ripe olives
1 small purple onion, sliced and separated into rings
6 cups shredded iceberg lettuce
3 tablespoons chopped fresh cilantro or parsley
Avocado Dressing

Arrange first 3 ingredients on shredded lettuce; sprinkle with cilantro. Serve with Avocado Dressing. Yield: 8 to 10 servings.

### Avocado Dressing

1 ripe avocado, peeled and mashed
¾ cup sour cream
1½ tablespoons lime juice
2 cloves garlic, crushed
½ teaspoon ground cumin
¼ teaspoon salt
¼ teaspoon ground red pepper
2 tablespoons vegetable oil

Combine first 7 ingredients in a mixing bowl; beat at medium speed with an electric mixer until smooth. Add oil, 1 tablespoon at a time, beating until blended. Cover and chill at least 3 hours. Yield: 1½ cups.

## Vitamin-rich Foods

■ Deep green, yellow, and orange fruit and vegetables are good sources of vitamin A.
■ Citrus fruit, deep green vegetables, and potatoes are rich in vitamin C.
■ Buy fresh citrus fruits with smooth, blemish-free skins. Indications of high juice content are that fruits feel firm and are heavy for their size.

■ A version of what some call "dump" cake, this recipe calls for little more than opening packages and "dumping" them into a baking dish. It's easy enough for older children to make by themselves. Ask them to assemble and bake the cobbler while you're serving dinner. By the time the family is finished eating, the dessert will be ready. Serve it warm, topped with ice cream.

## CRANBERRY-PEACH COBBLER

1 (21-ounce) can peach pie filling
1 (16-ounce) can whole-berry cranberry sauce
1 (18.25-ounce) package yellow cake mix without pudding
½ teaspoon ground cinnamon
¼ teaspoon ground nutmeg
½ cup butter or margarine
½ cup chopped pecans

Combine pie filling and cranberry sauce in a lightly greased 13- x 9- x 2-inch baking dish; set aside.
Combine cake mix and spices. Cut in butter with a pastry blender until mixture is crumbly; stir in pecans. Sprinkle over fruit mixture; bake at 350° for 45 minutes. Serve warm with ice cream. Yield: 12 servings.

*LaJuan Coward*
*Jasper, Texas*

■ While you're stringing the lights on the tree, let excited children stir these ingredients together and spoon them onto wax paper. (You can take a quick break from decorating to do the cooking portion of the recipe if your children are too young.)

## CHOCOLATE-PEANUT BUTTER DROPS

1 cup sugar
½ cup light corn syrup
¼ cup honey
1 (12-ounce) jar chunky peanut butter
4 cups chocolate-flavored frosted corn puff cereal

Combine first 3 ingredients in a Dutch oven; bring to a boil, stirring constantly. Remove from heat; add peanut butter, stirring until blended. Stir in cereal; drop by tablespoonfuls onto wax paper. Let cool. Yield: 4 dozen.

*Hattie McNeely*
*Archer City, Texas*

---

## ON THE LIGHT SIDE

# Say Cheers With Mocktails

Fun and good friends are essential ingredients for great celebrations. This year, add one more: mocktails—mixed drinks minus the calories and side effects of alcohol. The only thing intoxicating is the flavor.

For your next holiday party, dust off the blender and stock the bar with ingredients to concoct these beverages. Then, proudly treat your guests to our assortment—including everything from spunky Spiced Pineapple Sparkle to dreamy Mock Black Russian. All are under 165 calories, and many have less than half the fat of their traditional counterparts.

## SPICED PINEAPPLE SPARKLE

1½ cups water
6 (3-inch) sticks cinnamon
12 whole cloves
½ cup sugar
1 (46-ounce) can unsweetened pineapple juice, chilled
1½ cups unsweetened orange juice, chilled
½ cup lemon juice, chilled
3 (12-ounce) bottles lemon-lime carbonated beverage, chilled
Garnishes: orange slices, maraschino cherries

Combine first 3 ingredients in a saucepan; bring to a boil. Reduce heat, cover, and simmer 15 minutes. Remove from heat, and stir in sugar; let cool. Pour mixture through a large, wire-mesh strainer into a punch bowl, discarding spices; stir in juices and lemon-lime beverage. Garnish, if desired. Yield: 12 cups (149 calories [0% from fat] per 8-ounce serving).

□ 0.6g protein, 0.2g fat (0g saturated), 37.7g carbohydrate, 0.4g fiber, 0mg cholesterol, 12mg sodium, and 39mg calcium.
*Barbara Davis*
*Atlanta, Georgia*

## MOCK PIÑA COLADA

1 (8-ounce) can crushed pineapple
2½ cups vanilla ice milk
1 teaspoon rum extract
1 teaspoon coconut extract
1 tablespoon powdered sugar

Combine first 5 ingredients in container of an electric blender. Add enough ice cubes to measure 4 cups; blend until smooth. Serve immediately. Yield: 4 cups (162 calories [20% from fat] per 8-ounce serving).

□ 3.5g protein, 3.6g fat (2.2g saturated), 28.9g carbohydrate, 0.4g fiber, 11mg cholesterol, 66mg sodium, and 118mg calcium.

## MOCK BLACK RUSSIAN

1½ tablespoons instant coffee granules
1 cup boiling water
1 quart vanilla ice milk, divided
½ cup chocolate syrup, divided
2 teaspoons vanilla extract
2 teaspoons semisweet chocolate shavings

Dissolve coffee granules in boiling water; let cool. Place half of ice milk and half of chocolate syrup in container of an electric blender; process until smooth, stopping to scrape down sides. Repeat with remaining ice milk and syrup. Add coffee and vanilla; process until smooth. Pour into glasses; sprinkle each with ¼ teaspoon chocolate shavings. Serve immediately. Yield: 5 cups (150 calories [20% from fat] per 5-ounce serving).

□ *3.3g protein, 3.4g fat (1.8g saturated), 26.4g carbohydrate, 0g fiber, 9mg cholesterol, 65mg sodium, and 92mg calcium.*

## MOCK EGGNOG WITH ORANGE AND NUTMEG

2 tablespoons sugar
2 tablespoons cornstarch
1 quart skim milk
1 teaspoon vanilla extract
½ teaspoon rum extract
½ teaspoon grated orange rind
⅛ teaspoon salt
⅓ cup sugar, divided
1 tablespoon meringue powder
½ cup cold water
Ground nutmeg (optional)

Combine first 2 ingredients in a medium saucepan; stir in milk. Bring to a boil over medium heat, stirring constantly. Boil mixture 1 minute, stirring constantly. Remove from heat; stir in vanilla and next 3 ingredients; cover and chill.

Just before serving, combine 3 tablespoons sugar, meringue powder, and water in a large mixing bowl. Beat at high speed with an electric mixer 5 minutes; gradually add remaining 2⅓ tablespoons sugar, beating until soft peaks form. Fold into milk mixture. Sprinkle with nutmeg, if desired. Yield: 5¼ cups (115 calories [0% from fat] per 6-ounce serving).

□ *5g protein, 0.2g fat (0.1g saturated), 22.7g carbohydrate, 0g fiber, 3mg cholesterol, 117mg sodium, and 173mg calcium.*

## SPICY VIRGIN MARY

1 (48-ounce) can low-sodium tomato juice
1 (13¾-ounce) can ready-to-serve, no-salt-added beef broth
¼ cup low-sodium Worcestershire sauce
3 tablespoons lime juice
1½ teaspoons seasoned salt
1 teaspoon celery seeds
½ teaspoon onion powder
½ teaspoon freshly ground pepper
⅛ teaspoon garlic powder
¼ teaspoon hot sauce
Ice cubes
Garnish: celery stalks

Combine first 10 ingredients; chill. Serve over ice and garnish, if desired. Yield: 8 cups (49 calories [1% from fat] per 8-ounce serving without ice).

□ *1.9g protein, 0.1g fat (0g saturated), 11.4g carbohydrate, 0.1g fiber, 0mg cholesterol, 432mg sodium, and 6mg calcium.*

---

## LIGHT MENU

# Healthy Lunch For Hungry Shoppers

You've made your list and checked it twice, and it no longer matters if anyone's been naughty or nice—you're headed for a Christmas shopping expedition. Armed with walking shoes and joined by a squadron of seasoned shopper friends, you are confident that many great deals lie ahead.

And your day's strategic plan provides a made-ahead lunch for your returning troop. The menu includes soup, salad, rolls, and a delectable dessert satisfying enough to curb the appetites of bargain-hungry pals. But with only 540 calories, it's conservative enough not to threaten cautious calorie counters.

## POST-SHOPPING LUNCH FOR SIX

**Gazpacho Molded Salad
Chicken, Artichoke, And Mushroom Soup
Commercial multigrain hard rolls
Warm Chocolate Pudding Cake**

## GAZPACHO MOLDED SALAD

2 envelopes unflavored gelatin
¼ cup cold water
1½ cups no-salt-added cocktail vegetable juice
¼ cup red wine vinegar
¼ teaspoon hot sauce
1 clove garlic, minced
¼ cup fat-free mayonnaise
1 cup finely chopped cucumber
½ cup finely chopped green pepper
½ cup finely chopped onion
Vegetable cooking spray
6 lettuce leaves
Garnish: cucumber slices

Sprinkle gelatin over cold water in a medium saucepan; let stand 1 minute. Add vegetable juice and next 3 ingredients. Cook over medium heat, stirring until gelatin dissolves (about 2 minutes). Add mayonnaise; whisk until blended. Chill until the consistency of unbeaten egg white. Fold in cucumber, green pepper, and onion; spoon into six ½-cup molds lightly coated with cooking spray. Cover and chill at least 8 hours. Unmold onto lettuce leaves, and garnish, if desired. Yield: 6 servings (60 calories [1% from fat] per serving).

□ *4g protein, 0.5g fat (0g saturated), 11g carbohydrate, 0.9g fiber, 0mg cholesterol, 157mg sodium, and 39mg calcium.*
Nancy Collins
Charlotte, North Carolina

## CHICKEN, ARTICHOKE, AND MUSHROOM SOUP

3 (4-ounce) skinned, boned chicken breast halves
2½ cups water
Vegetable cooking spray
¾ cup chopped onion
½ cup chopped celery
3 (10½-ounce) cans ready-to-serve, no-salt-added chicken broth
1 bay leaf
½ teaspoon salt
½ teaspoon pepper
Dash of ground nutmeg
¾ cup thinly sliced fresh mushrooms
1 (14-ounce) can artichoke hearts, drained and chopped
¼ cup grated Parmesan cheese

Combine chicken and water in a large Dutch oven; bring to a boil. Reduce heat, cover and simmer 20 minutes or until tender. Remove chicken from broth; cool slightly and shred. Reserve broth.

Coat Dutch oven with cooking spray; place over medium-high heat until hot. Add onion and celery; cook, stirring constantly, until crisp-tender. Add reserved chicken broth, canned chicken broth, and next 4 ingredients. Bring to a boil; reduce heat, cover and simmer 15 minutes. Add mushrooms, and cook 10 minutes. Add shredded chicken and artichoke hearts, and cook until thoroughly heated. Top each serving equally with Parmesan cheese. Yield: 6 cups (137 calories [19% from fat] per 1-cup serving).

□ *16.4g protein, 2.9g fat (1.1g saturated), 8.7g carbohydrate, 1.1g fiber, 39mg cholesterol, 328mg sodium, and 81mg calcium.* Georgie O'Neill
Welaka, Florida

## WARM CHOCOLATE PUDDING CAKE

1 cup all-purpose flour
2 teaspoons baking powder
⅛ teaspoon salt
½ cup sugar
2 tablespoons unsweetened cocoa
Vegetable cooking spray
½ cup skim milk
3 tablespoons reduced-calorie margarine, melted
1 teaspoon vanilla extract
¼ cup sugar
¼ cup firmly packed brown sugar
¼ cup unsweetened cocoa
1½ cups warm water
2 cups vanilla ice milk

Combine first 5 ingredients in a 9-inch square pan coated with cooking spray; stir in milk, reduced-calorie margarine, and vanilla. Spread evenly in pan.

Combine ¼ cup sugar and next 2 ingredients; sprinkle evenly over batter. Pour warm water over top. Bake at 350° for 30 minutes. Top each serving with ¼-cup ice milk. Yield: 8 servings (233 calories [17% from fat] per serving).

□ *4.5g protein, 4.3g fat (1.6g saturated), 44.4g carbohydrate, 0.4g fiber, 5mg cholesterol, 200mg sodium, and 124mg calcium.*

## LIGHT FAVORITE

# Cornbread Dressing

If cornbread dressing accompanies your traditional Christmas meal, try a healthful modification. Spices and vegetables lighten this version by boosting flavor without significantly adding sodium, fat, or cholesterol. Save time during the holidays by preparing and freezing Light Cornbread Dressing up to three months in advance.

## LIGHT CORNBREAD DRESSING

Vegetable cooking spray
1 cup chopped celery
½ cup chopped onion
Cornbread
2 (16-ounce) cans low-sodium, fat-free, ready-to-serve chicken broth
½ cup egg substitute
2 teaspoons rubbed sage
½ teaspoon salt
⅛ teaspoon pepper

Coat a large nonstick skillet with cooking spray; place over medium-high heat. Cook celery and onion, stirring constantly, until vegetables are tender. Transfer to a large mixing bowl; add 8 cups crumbled cornbread. Stir in chicken broth, egg substitute, rubbed sage, salt, and pepper. (Dressing mixture will be wet.) Spoon dressing into a 13- x 9- x 2-inch baking dish; cover and chill 8 hours. Remove dressing from refrigerator, and let stand at room temperature 30 minutes. Bake at 400° for 40 minutes or until edges are lightly browned. Yield: 8 servings (277 calories [27% from fat] per 1-cup serving).

### Cornbread

2 cups white cornmeal
¾ cup all-purpose flour
2½ teaspoons baking powder
¾ teaspoon baking soda
2 teaspoons sugar
2¼ cups nonfat buttermilk
¾ cup egg substitute
¼ cup vegetable oil
Vegetable cooking spray

Heat a 10-inch cast-iron skillet in a 425° oven 5 minutes. Combine white cornmeal, flour, baking powder, soda, and sugar in a large bowl; make a well in center of mixture. Combine buttermilk, egg substitute, and oil; add to dry ingredients, stirring just until moistened.

Remove skillet from oven, and coat with cooking spray; pour batter into skillet. Bake at 450° for 25 to 30 minutes or until golden brown. Let cool. Yield: 8 cups crumbled cornbread or 8 servings (252 calories [30% from fat] per serving).

☐ *10.3g protein, 8.4g fat (1.6g saturated), 39.5g carbohydrate, 4.2g fiber, 2.2mg cholesterol, 472mg sodium, and 19.1mg calcium.*

**Note:** To freeze dressing, line baking dish with aluminum foil, leaving at least a 1½-inch foil collar; fill with dressing. Cover with a sheet of foil, folding edges together; freeze. When dressing is frozen solid, lift the foil package from dish, and return to freezer. Dressing may be frozen up to three months. To serve, remove foil, and return to same baking dish; thaw in refrigerator 24 hours; remove from refrigerator, and let stand at room temperature 30 minutes. Bake at 400° for 45 minutes.

| COMPARE THE NUTRIENTS (per serving) | | |
|---|---|---|
| | Traditional | Light |
| Calories | 327 | 277 |
| Fat | 11.5g | 8.4g |
| Cholesterol | 145mg | 2.2mg |

# A Cook With An Eye On Africa

Merriam McLendon may have grown up in Birmingham, Alabama, but her palate yearns for the flavors of West Africa—fiery, spicy foods that tingle the lips and warm the soul—foods such as Jollof Rice Dinner.

"It plays tricks with your taste buds," says Merriam's sister, Kausandra Jones. She describes Jollof Rice Dinner as a meal-in-one recipe.

Merriam first learned about the foods of Africa while living in Chicago.

"One of my favorite dishes was jollof rice. I wanted to learn to cook it, so I begged—you know, people are kind of close with their recipes—but this guy from Gambia gave me the recipe."

When Merriam serves Jollof Rice Dinner at her dinner parties, guests immediately acknowledge the hot, pungent flavor of the dish. Although Merriam admits to going easy on the red pepper when people are unaccustomed to it, she adds a hot pepper on the side for those from the region who like it *really* hot. Although yams would be used in Africa, Merriam substitutes sweet potatoes.

## JOLLOF RICE DINNER

3   medium sweet potatoes (1¼ pounds), peeled and cut into large cubes
1   (1¾-pound) cabbage, cut into 8 wedges
2   pounds frozen whiting fish fillets, thawed and cut into pieces
½   cup vegetable oil
1   pound medium-size fresh shrimp, peeled and deveined
2   tablespoons vegetable oil
1   large onion, coarsely chopped
1   medium-size green pepper, coarsely chopped
4   large carrots, scraped and cut into pieces
7   cloves garlic, chopped
1   (6-ounce) can tomato paste
6½  cups hot water, divided
2   teaspoons salt
1   to 2 tablespoons ground red pepper
1   tablespoon dried oregano
2   cups long-grain rice, uncooked

Cook sweet potatoes in boiling water 6 minutes or until tender; drain and set aside. Cook cabbage in boiling water 8 minutes or until crisp-tender; drain and set aside.

Cook one-third of fish fillets in ½ cup oil in skillet until lightly browned, turning once. Remove from skillet, reserving drippings in skillet. Repeat procedure twice with remaining fish. Add shrimp to skillet; cook over medium heat, stirring constantly 3 minutes or until shrimp turn pink. Remove shrimp from skillet, and set aside.

Transfer oil from skillet to Dutch oven; add 2 tablespoons oil to Dutch oven. Add onion and next 3 ingredients; cook over medium heat, stirring constantly, until crisp-tender. Stir in tomato paste, and cook 5 to 7 minutes, stirring often. Add 5 cups water and next 3 ingredients. Simmer 30 minutes over low heat, stirring occasionally. Remove vegetables using a slotted spoon; set vegetables aside.

Add sweet potatoes to sauce mixture, and heat thoroughly. Remove to serving platter, and keep warm. Repeat procedure with cabbage, fish, and shrimp.

Add remaining 1½ cups water to sauce mixture; bring to a boil. Add rice, and cook 20 minutes or until rice is tender, stirring often. Add additional water, if necessary. Spoon into serving bowl. Serve sweet potatoes, cabbage, fish, and shrimp over rice. Yield: 8 servings.

## You Say Sweet Potato, I Say Yam

What's in a name? More than you might guess when it comes to yams and sweet potatoes. Most Southern cooks substitute yams for sweet potatoes with no hesitation—that's because they're often the same product. If you venture outside the United States, however, you'll find some clear distinctions.

Real yams (known as Dioscorea bulbifera) are rarely grown in the United States; the tuber of this tropical vine may grow up to seven feet long. It's sweeter than the sweet potato and is used in Latin-American and African cooking.

# Appetizing Appetizers

Appetizers are the forgotten food of casual dining. Few of us serve a starter before the main meal, unless it's a special occasion. So why not make a meal out of these neglected appetizers?

Who can resist Spinach-Mushroom Cheesecake? It's smooth and creamy and flavored with mushrooms, garlic, spinach, and feta cheese. You can make it two days in advance and refrigerate. On the day of the party, bring it to room temperature and serve with crackers. Crisp German Meatballs offers a fun twist, incorporating sauerkraut with sausage meatballs. These and other recipes provide a bountiful buffet.

## SPINACH-MUSHROOM CHEESECAKE

Butter or margarine
¾ cup Italian-seasoned breadcrumbs, divided
¼ cup butter or margarine, melted and divided
1 (10-ounce) package chopped frozen spinach, thawed
1 cup chopped fresh mushrooms
¼ cup finely chopped onion
2 cloves garlic, minced
1 (2-ounce) jar diced pimiento, drained
3 (8-ounce) packages cream cheese, softened
1 (7-ounce) package feta cheese, drained
⅓ cup milk
4 large eggs
¾ teaspoon salt
¼ teaspoon ground red pepper
¼ teaspoon black pepper
⅛ teaspoon ground nutmeg

Grease bottom and sides of a 9-inch springform pan with butter. Dust sides of pan with 1 tablespoon breadcrumbs. Combine remaining breadcrumbs and 2 tablespoons melted butter; firmly press into bottom of pan. Set aside.

Drain spinach on paper towels; set aside. Cook chopped mushrooms, chopped onion, and minced garlic in remaining 2 tablespoons melted butter in a large skillet over medium-high heat, stirring constantly, 3 minutes or until crisp-tender. Stir in spinach and pimiento. Set aside.

Beat cream cheese at medium speed with an electric mixer until creamy. Add feta cheese, beating until blended. Gradually add milk, beating at low speed until blended. Add eggs, one at a time, beating after each addition. Stir in spinach mixture, salt, and remaining ingredients. Pour into prepared pan.

Bake at 300° for 1 hour or until almost set. Turn oven off, and partially open oven door; leave cheesecake in oven 1 hour. Remove cheesecake from oven, and let cool completely on a wire rack. Cover and chill until serving time. Serve cheesecake with crackers. Yield: 25 appetizer servings.
*Rachel Jennings*
*Sparta, Tennessee*

## DATE-NUT BALL

1 (8-ounce) package cream cheese, softened
1 (8-ounce) package chopped dates
1 cup chopped pecans, toasted and divided

Combine cream cheese, dates, and ½ cup pecans; cover and chill 30 minutes. Shape into a ball, and roll in remaining ½ cup pecans. Serve ball with apple wedges or gingersnaps. Yield: 2 cups.
*Delma Ford Marshall*
*De Ridder, Louisiana*

## CRISP GERMAN MEATBALLS

½ pound ground pork sausage
¼ cup chopped onion
1 (16-ounce) can chopped sauerkraut, drained
2 tablespoons fine, dry breadcrumbs
1 (3-ounce) package cream cheese, softened
2 tablespoons chopped fresh parsley
1 teaspoon prepared mustard
¼ teaspoon garlic salt
⅛ teaspoon pepper
1 cup mayonnaise or salad dressing
¼ cup prepared mustard
2 large eggs
¼ cup milk
½ cup all-purpose flour
1 cup fine, dry breadcrumbs
Vegetable oil

Combine sausage and onion in a large skillet; cook until sausage is browned, stirring until it crumbles. Drain well. Stir in sauerkraut and 2 tablespoons breadcrumbs.

Combine cream cheese and next 4 ingredients in a large bowl; add sausage mixture, stirring well. Cover and chill 2 hours.

Combine mayonnaise and ¼ cup mustard; set aside.

Combine eggs and milk in a small bowl; set aside. Shape sausage mixture into ¾-inch balls; roll in flour. Dip each ball in reserved egg mixture; roll balls in 1 cup breadcrumbs. Pour oil to a depth of 2 inches into a Dutch oven; heat to 375°. Fry, a few at a time, 2 minutes or until golden brown. Drain on paper towels. Serve with mayonnaise mixture. Yield: 5 dozen.

Note: Crisp German Meatballs may be cooked and frozen. To reheat, place frozen meatballs in a single layer in a 15- x 10- x 1-inch jellyroll pan. Bake at 375° for 10 minutes or until meatballs are thoroughly heated.

*Elise Walker*
*Greenbrier, Tennessee*

### CATFISH MOUSSE

2½ pounds farm-raised catfish
   fillets
2 envelopes unflavored gelatin
¼ cup cold water
1 (8-ounce) package cream cheese,
   softened
1 cup sour cream
½ cup mayonnaise or salad
   dressing
1 (2-ounce) jar diced pimento,
   drained
½ cup chopped celery
½ cup chopped green onions
¼ cup chopped fresh parsley
¼ cup lemon juice
1 teaspoon dried dillweed
1 teaspoon Creole seasoning
½ teaspoon salt
½ teaspoon liquid smoke
¼ teaspoon ground red pepper
Vegetable cooking spray
Lettuce leaves

Arrange catfish on a 15- x 10- x 1-inch jellyroll pan; bake at 350° for 15 minutes or until fish flakes easily when tested with a fork. Drain and flake.

Sprinkle gelatin over cold water in a small saucepan; let stand 1 minute. Cook over low heat, stirring constantly, until gelatin dissolves (about 2 minutes); set aside. Beat cream cheese at medium speed with an electric mixer until creamy; stir in gelatin mixture. Add sour cream and next 11 ingredients, stirring until blended. Fold in fish. Spoon into an 8-cup mold coated with cooking spray. Cover, and chill 8 hours. Unmold onto lettuce leaves. Serve with crackers. Yield: 25 appetizer servings.

*Betsy Neill*
*Leland, Mississippi*

### TURKEY-MUSHROOM PÂTÉ IN PASTRY

1 cup chopped fresh mushrooms
1 tablespoon butter or margarine,
   melted
2 cloves garlic
12 ounces smoked turkey, cut into
   1-inch pieces
1½ cups pecans, chopped and
   toasted
¾ cup mayonnaise or salad
   dressing
½ teaspoon salt
¼ teaspoon ground red pepper
½ cup finely chopped green onions
2 tablespoons soy sauce
1 (17¼-ounce) package frozen puff
   pastry sheets, thawed

Cook mushrooms in butter in a large skillet over medium heat, stirring constantly, until tender and liquid evaporates; set aside.

Position knife blade in food processor bowl; drop garlic through food chute with processor running, and process 10 seconds or until garlic is minced. Gradually add turkey and pecans; process 20 seconds after each addition or until finely ground. Transfer mixture to a large bowl; stir in mushroom mixture, mayonnaise, and next 4 ingredients. Spoon into a plastic wrap-lined 8½- x 4½- x 3-inch loafpan. Cover and chill 8 hours.

Unfold one pastry sheet, and roll on a lightly floured surface into a 14- x 12-inch rectangle. Unmold turkey mixture, and place in center of pastry. Lightly moisten pastry edges with water. Fold ends and sides over mixture, pressing to seal. Place wrapped loaf, seam side down, on a lightly greased baking sheet.

Cut decorative shapes from remaining pastry sheet. Brush back of cutouts with water, and arrange cutouts on wrapped loaf. Bake loaf at 400° for 20 minutes or until pastry is golden. Serve loaf with crackers. Yield: one 8-inch loaf.

---

## How to Stock the Bar

### Wines

White wines are the most popular for cocktail parties. They should be on the dry (not sweet) side, or they can be slightly sweet. (Avoid very sweet wines.) Sauvignon Blanc, Reisling, Chablis, and Chenin Blanc are good possibilities. To help in planning, you can estimate that there are four (6-ounce) servings in each 750-milliliter bottle of wine.

### Cocktails

A well-stocked bar is usually composed of the following: vodka, scotch, rum, gin, and bourbon, plus mixers including sparkling water, club soda, tonic water, ginger ale, soft drinks, orange juice, and tomato juice. Each 750-milliliter bottle of liquor is equivalent to 17 drinks when 1½ ounces are used per drink. One 10-ounce bottle of mixer per person is usually sufficient. You may decide to offer one special cocktail during the evening. Prepare those that can be made up in quantity and served from pitchers. Some may prefer a refreshing beverage without the liquor. See "Say Cheers With Mocktails" (beginning on page 322) for suggestions.

### Beer

Many people prefer beer over wine or liquor. Offer a variety including light beer, imported beer, and dark beer. Frosted mugs are an added touch.

## MARINATED MUSHROOMS

1 pound small fresh mushrooms
1 (8-ounce) bottle red wine vinaigrette dressing
1 small onion, thinly sliced
1 tablespoon brown sugar
2 teaspoons dried parsley flakes
1 teaspoon dry mustard
¼ teaspoon salt

Clean mushrooms with damp paper towels; trim ends from stems. Set mushrooms aside.

Combine red wine vinaigrette and next 5 ingredients in a saucepan; bring to a boil. Stir in mushrooms; reduce heat, and simmer 5 minutes. Remove from heat; cool. Cover and chill at least 8 hours, stirring occasionally. Drain before serving. Yield: 12 to 15 appetizer servings.

*Peggy Fowler Revels*
*Woodruff, South Carolina*

## COCONUT-CRANBERRY CHEESE SPREAD

1 (8-ounce) package cream cheese, softened
¼ cup whole-berry cranberry sauce
1 teaspoon grated orange rind
⅛ teaspoon salt
2 tablespoons flaked coconut

Combine first 4 ingredients, stirring until well blended. Spoon into a serving dish, and sprinkle with coconut. Serve spread with gingersnaps. Yield: 1¼ cups.

*Kathy Reeves-Miller*
*Sparta, North Carolina*

# Elegant Entrées, Etc.

Having a special dinner? Relax. Try one of these incredibly wonderful (but not incredibly difficult) main dishes; then take our suggestions for easy side dishes you can prepare *without* recipes. Simple steamed vegetables and deli and bakery items complement the entrée, making a full meal without complicating the cooking.

**Greek Chicken Phyllo Pie**
**Piped mashed sweet potatoes**
**Steamed asparagus in**
**sweet red pepper rings**
**Coffee**
**Assorted bakery cookies**

## GREEK CHICKEN PHYLLO PIE

1 (3- to 3½-pound) broiler-fryer, cut up
5 cups water
1 onion, chopped
1 stalk celery, cut into 1-inch pieces
1 bay leaf
1 teaspoon salt
¼ cup butter or margarine
⅓ cup all-purpose flour
3 large eggs, lightly beaten
¼ cup grated Romano or Parmesan cheese
½ teaspoon salt
¼ teaspoon ground white pepper
¼ teaspoon black pepper
⅛ teaspoon ground nutmeg (optional)
1 (17-ounce) package commercial frozen phyllo pastry, thawed
Butter-flavored cooking spray *
Garnish: celery leaves

Combine first 6 ingredients in a Dutch oven. Bring to a boil; cover, reduce heat, and simmer 40 minutes or until tender. Remove chicken, and cool slightly. Bone chicken, cutting meat into bite-size pieces; set aside. Remove and discard celery and bay leaf, reserving 3 cups broth and onion mixture; set aside.

Melt butter in a Dutch oven over low heat; add flour, stirring until smooth. Cook 1 minute, stirring constantly. Gradually add reserved broth mixture; cook over medium heat, stirring constantly, until thickened. Gradually stir about one-fourth of hot mixture into eggs; add to remaining hot mixture, stirring constantly. Add cheese and next 4 ingredients. Cook over low heat, stirring constantly, about 3 minutes or until thickened. Add chicken, and set aside.

Unfold phyllo, and cut the stack of sheets in half crosswise. Trim each half to a 13- x 9-inch rectangle. Cover with a slightly damp towel to prevent pastry from drying out.

Coat bottom and sides of a 13- x 9- x 2-inch pan with cooking spray. Layer 15 trimmed phyllo sheets in pan, spraying each with cooking spray. Spread half of chicken mixture evenly over phyllo. Top with 12 additional trimmed phyllo sheets, spraying each with cooking spray. Spread remaining chicken mixture over phyllo; top mixture with remaining trimmed phyllo sheets, spraying each sheet with cooking spray.

With a sharp knife, cut through only the top layer of phyllo to make 12 servings. Bake, uncovered, on lowest rack in oven at 375° for 1 hour. Let stand 10 minutes. Garnish, if desired. Yield: 12 servings.

* 1 cup melted butter or margarine may be substituted for cooking spray. Brush on each phyllo sheet.

*Ouida Hamilton*
*Birmingham, Alabama*

**Tuna Steaks**
**With Tarragon Butter**
**Steamed or sautéed carrots,**
**yellow squash, and zucchini**
**Buttered orzo and parsley**
**Raspberry or lemon sherbet**

## TUNA STEAKS WITH TARRAGON BUTTER

2 tablespoons butter or margarine, softened
¼ teaspoon lemon juice
½ teaspoon minced fresh tarragon or ¼ teaspoon dried tarragon
2 (½-pound) tuna steaks (about ¾ inch thick)
¼ teaspoon salt
¼ teaspoon freshly ground pepper
1 tablespoon olive oil

Combine first 3 ingredients; shape into a 1-inch-thick log; cover and chill until firm.

Sprinkle tuna with salt and pepper on all sides. Heat olive oil in a nonstick skillet over medium heat; cook tuna 5 minutes on each side or until desired degree of doneness. Slice tarragon butter, and serve with tuna. Yield: 2 servings.

Wine or sparkling water
Fruit, cheese, and crackers
Herbed Shrimp And Pasta
Red, green, and yellow
pepper strips
Commercial rolls

### HERBED SHRIMP AND PASTA

1 pound unpeeled, medium-size
fresh shrimp
4 ounces angel hair pasta,
uncooked
½ cup butter
2 cloves garlic, minced
1 cup half-and-half
¼ cup chopped fresh parsley
1 teaspoon chopped fresh dillweed
or ½ teaspoon dried dillweed
¼ teaspoon salt
⅛ teaspoon pepper

Peel and devein shrimp; set aside. Cook pasta according to package directions. Drain and set aside; keep warm. Melt butter in a heavy skillet over medium-high heat; add shrimp and garlic. Cook 3 to 5 minutes, stirring constantly; remove shrimp, and set aside, reserving garlic and butter in skillet.

Add half-and-half to skillet; bring to a boil, stirring constantly. Reduce heat to low, and simmer about 15 minutes or until thickened, stirring occasionally. Add shrimp, parsley, and seasonings; stir until blended. Serve over angel hair pasta with steamed or sautéed red, green, and yellow pepper strips. Yield: 2 or 3 servings.
*Martha S. Richardson*
*Deer Park, Texas*

Crabmeat Ravigote
Steamed whole green beans
Carrots tossed in
lemon juice and butter
Winter fruit salad or compote

### CRABMEAT RAVIGOTE

½ cup finely chopped green
pepper
⅓ cup sliced green onions
1 (4-ounce) can stems and pieces
mushrooms, drained
⅓ cup butter or margarine,
melted
1 (2-ounce) jar diced pimiento,
drained
⅓ cup dry sherry
1 tablespoon chopped fresh parsley
½ teaspoon garlic salt
½ teaspoon ground white pepper
½ teaspoon celery seeds
1 pound lump crabmeat
½ cup soft breadcrumbs, divided

Cook first 3 ingredients in butter in a large skillet over medium-high heat, stirring constantly, until vegetables are tender. Stir in pimiento and next 5 ingredients. Fold in crabmeat and half of breadcrumbs. Spoon into 6 lightly greased (6-ounce) individual ramekins; sprinkle with remaining breadcrumbs. Broil 6 inches from heat (with electric oven door partially opened) 1 to 2 minutes or until lightly browned. Yield: 6 servings.
*Beverly Lafaye Clark*
*New Orleans, Louisiana*

Stuffed Veal Cutlets
Spinach-orange salad
French bread
Sparkling wine or champagne
Assorted chocolates

### STUFFED VEAL CUTLETS

6 (4-ounce) veal cutlets
6 slices prosciutto (about 5 ounces)
4 ounces fontina cheese, cut into 5
strips
¼ teaspoon salt
¼ teaspoon pepper
½ cup all-purpose flour
1 tablespoon butter or margarine,
melted
1 tablespoon vegetable oil
1 cup dry white wine
Hot cooked spaghetti

Place cutlets between sheets of heavy-duty plastic wrap; flatten to ⅛-inch thickness using a pounder or rolling pin. Wrap a prosciutto slice around each cheese strip, and place in center of each cutlet. Fold ends of veal cutlets over prosciutto and cheese; fold sides over, and secure with a wooden pick.

Sprinkle with salt and pepper; dredge in flour. Brown on all sides in butter and oil in a heavy skillet. Remove and keep warm. Add wine to skillet; boil until wine is reduced by half. Add veal; cover and simmer 5 minutes. Serve on a bed of spaghetti. Yield: 6 servings.
*Sue-Sue Hartstern*
*Louisville, Kentucky*

## Pointers on Pasta

■ Allow 2 ounces of uncooked pasta and 1 to 1½ cups cooked pasta per person.

■ Cooking times vary with pasta's size, shape, and moisture content. Fresh pasta cooks in 1 to 3 minutes, while dried pasta requires 4 to 15 minutes.

■ When cooked *al dente*, pasta can be reheated. To do this, drop cooked pasta in boiling water that has been removed from heat 1 to 2 minutes.

■ Adding 1 or 2 tablespoons of vegetable oil to the cooking water keeps pasta separated.

# One Potato, Two Potato, Three Potato, Four...

... five potato, six potato, seven potato, more. Welcome this children's rhyme to your table with a foolproof, basic recipe for mashed potatoes *plus* seven unexpected variations. Blue cheese in mashed potatoes? You bet! Try feta cheese, garlic, or pesto for more delightful surprises. We don't mean you should abandon your favorite just-the-way-mama-makes-'em mashed potatoes, but when you're in the mood for a little adventure, try one of these new renditions.

## To Mash or to Whip?

Who would have thought the simple pleasure of mashed potatoes could get so complicated? While testing these recipes, forks were drawn in the debate over whether to mash potatoes by hand or whip with an electric mixer. Not able to settle the issue ourselves, we called on a few Southern food authorities for answers.

■ **Nathalie Dupree,** Atlanta food columnist, author, cooking instructor, and public television series host, safely rides the fence on the issue. "It's a matter of personal preference," she rationalizes. "If your mother made lumpy mashed potatoes, there's nothing you can do about it, and that's what you're going to want. If she whipped them, then that's the way you like them."

When pushed a little farther, she finally admits to using a mixer. "It's what I'm used to," she explains. Nathalie insists on adding *hot* cream instead of cold to the potatoes and beating with a portable mixer over heat for the best texture.

■ Mississippi-born **Craig Claiborne,** *New York Times* columnist and cookbook author, chooses neither option. Instead, he first puts his cooked potatoes through a ricer (a tool that looks like a large garlic press); then he beats them with a wooden spoon. He always uses a hot bowl (heated by rinsing in hot water) and never uses cream, only milk.

Remembering his days in the Delta, he comments, "Oh, we always had mashed potatoes. We had them with every other supper." Craig learned to make this favorite side dish from the cooks in his mother's boardinghouse. Today mashed potatoes are right at home in his New York City kitchen where he still enjoys them often. "I love them!" he says.

■ Author and designer **Lee Bailey,** another Southern transplant in New York City, also treasures his culinary roots. He reacts to the matter of mashed potatoes seriously. "You shouldn't ever really beat them. They should always be mashed," he advises. "Beating releases too much gluten, and that's what makes them sticky."

Surprisingly, instead of boiling, he bakes potatoes before mashing them. He says it makes them drier and more flavorful since the flavor isn't poured out with the water.

■ **John Egerton** of Nashville, Tennessee, is known by others as a food historian and author, but calls himself an "eater." His expertise in that arena came in handy for his book, *Southern Food.* Authenticity figures into his decision on mashed potatoes. "The masher certainly preceded the mixer since stainless steel preceded electricity," he explains. "I tend to be a purist about that sort of thing."

But the tool isn't the key for Egerton. He is more concerned about ingredients; in fact, he rues the day instant potato flakes were invented. "I keep my eye on whether the potatoes are real or not and have all that good stuff in them—butter, milk, salt, and pepper. But I'm not going to pass them up, no matter what."

## BASIC MASHED POTATOES

4  medium baking potatoes, peeled and cut into eighths (about 1½ pounds)
⅓ to ½ cup milk
3  tablespoons butter or margarine
¾  teaspoon salt
¼  teaspoon pepper

Cook potatoes in boiling water to cover, 15 minutes or until tender; drain and mash. Stir in milk and remaining ingredients. Serve immediately. Yield: 4 servings.

**Mexican Mashed Potatoes:** Prepare Basic Mashed Potatoes, except reduce salt to ½ teaspoon and add 2 to 3 tablespoons canned chopped green chiles and 1 cup (4 ounces) shredded Monterey Jack cheese.

**Garlic Mashed Potatoes:** Melt 3 tablespoons butter in a small skillet. Add 4 to 6 cloves garlic, crushed, and cook over medium heat, stirring constantly, 1 minute or until lightly browned. Prepare Basic Mashed Potatoes, replacing butter with garlic mixture.

**Feta Mashed Potatoes:** Boil, drain, and mash potatoes as directed. Combine ¾ cup crumbled feta cheese with the milk and pepper (no salt) in container of electric blender; process until smooth. Stir butter and feta cheese mixture into mashed potatoes.

**Blue Cheese Mashed Potatoes**: Boil, drain, and mash potatoes as directed. Combine ½ cup crumbled blue cheese, milk, ¼ teaspoon salt, and pepper in container of an electric blender; process until smooth. Stir butter and blue cheese mixture into mashed potatoes.

**Pesto Mashed Potatoes:** Prepare Basic Mashed Potatoes, except delete butter, decrease salt to ¼ teaspoon, and add ⅓ cup commercial pesto.

**Dill-Sour Cream Mashed Potatoes:** Prepare Basic Mashed Potatoes, except decrease milk to 3 tablespoons, and add ⅓ cup sour cream and ½ teaspoon dried dillweed.

**Chive-Cream Cheese Mashed Potatoes:** Prepare Basic Mashed Potatoes; delete butter, and add ½ cup chive-flavored cream cheese.

# Heartwarming Soups

Some people follow rules for eating soup, such as placing the bowl-shaped spoon in the proper place and meticulously filling the spoon from the front of the bowl to the back. Relax and throw out that regimen. These soups are for savoring without a lot of fuss.

Center a casual wintertime dinner around Italian Spinach Soup With Meatballs or a savory chowder.

## ITALIAN SPINACH SOUP WITH MEATBALLS

3 quarts chicken broth
2 stalks celery, cut into chunks
2 carrots, scraped and cut into chunks
1 large onion, quartered
½ teaspoon salt
1 pound lean ground beef
1½ slices bread, crumbled
1 large egg, lightly beaten
2 tablespoons grated Parmesan cheese
1½ tablespoons chopped fresh parsley
½ teaspoon salt
¼ teaspoon ground white pepper
1 (16-ounce) can crushed Italian-style tomatoes, undrained
1 (10-ounce) package frozen chopped spinach, thawed and drained
2 tablespoons grated Parmesan cheese
3 tablespoons olive oil
2 tablespoons lemon juice
2 teaspoons dried basil
4 cloves garlic, crushed

Combine first 5 ingredients in a large Dutch oven. Bring to a boil; reduce heat, and simmer, uncovered, 30 minutes. Remove vegetables, and discard. Set broth aside.

Combine ground beef and next 6 ingredients; shape into 1-inch meatballs, and cook in a large nonstick skillet over medium heat until browned. Drain on paper towels.

Bring broth to a boil; add meatballs. Reduce heat, and simmer 10 minutes. Stir in tomatoes and remaining ingredients, and simmer 10 to 15 minutes. Yield: 3 quarts.          *Barbara Carson*
*Tifton, Georgia*

## CHUNKY FISH CHOWDER

2 tablespoons butter or margarine
½ cup chopped onion
1 clove garlic, minced
2 cups water
2 medium potatoes, peeled and diced
1 (10-ounce) package frozen baby lima beans, unthawed
⅓ cup dry white wine
1 pound cod fillets, cut into 1-inch pieces
1 (16-ounce) can whole tomatoes, drained and chopped
1 (10¾-ounce) can cream of mushroom soup, undiluted
1 (10-ounce) package frozen whole kernel corn, unthawed
1 teaspoon lemon-pepper seasoning
1 teaspoon Worcestershire sauce
4 drops hot sauce
1 cup evaporated skimmed milk

Melt butter in a Dutch oven; add onion and garlic. Cook, stirring constantly, until tender. Add water, diced potato, lima beans, and wine. Bring to a boil; cover, reduce heat, and simmer 15 minutes, stirring occasionally. Add fish and next 6 ingredients; cover and simmer 15 minutes, stirring occasionally. Stir in milk; cook 2 minutes or until thoroughly heated. Yield: 2 quarts.          *Vivian Levine*
*Oak Ridge, Tennessee*

## MUSHROOM-POTATO CHOWDER

2 tablespoons butter or margarine
1 small onion, chopped
1 stalk celery, chopped
½ small green pepper, chopped
1 (8-ounce) package sliced fresh mushrooms
2 cups peeled and diced red potato
2 cups chicken broth
½ teaspoon dried thyme
2 cups milk, divided
½ teaspoon salt
½ teaspoon pepper
3 tablespoons all-purpose flour

Melt butter in a large Dutch oven; add onion, celery, green pepper, and mushrooms. Cook, stirring frequently, until tender. Stir in potato, chicken broth, and thyme. Bring to a boil; reduce heat, and simmer, uncovered, 30 minutes or until potatoes are tender.

Stir in 1½ cups milk, salt, and pepper. Combine remaining ½ cup milk and flour, stirring until smooth. Stir into chowder and simmer, uncovered, stirring frequently, until slightly thickened. Yield: 1½ quarts.

# Begin The Weekend With Homemade Breakfast

December weekends filled with holiday shopping and decorating deserve more than cold cereal and frozen waffles for breakfast. These recipes leave you with plenty of time and energy to face the new day, and may just start another tradition at your house.

## HAM-AND-CHEESE TART

1 (9-inch) refrigerated piecrust
8 (1-ounce) slices process American cheese, divided
2 cups finely chopped, cooked ham
2 cups chopped onion
2 tablespoons butter or margarine, melted
2 large eggs, lightly beaten
½ cup milk
3 tablespoons grated Parmesan cheese
Dash of pepper

Roll piecrust into a 13-inch circle; place onto a 12-inch pizza pan. Fold edges under, and crimp; prick with a fork. Bake at 425° for 10 minutes; cool. Arrange 6 cheese slices, overlapping, on baked crust; sprinkle with cooked ham.

Cook onion in butter in a large skillet over medium-high heat, stirring constantly, until tender. Remove from heat; stir in eggs and next 3 ingredients. Spoon over ham. Cut each of the remaining 2 cheese slices into 9 squares; arrange on top. Bake at 425° on lower rack of oven 15 minutes or until set. Let stand 10 minutes before serving. Yield: one 12-inch tart.

*Ana Desmarás*
*Fort Benning, Georgia*

## EGG PILLOWS

3 tablespoons butter or margarine, divided
5 fresh mushrooms, sliced
1 tablespoon dry white wine
4 large eggs, lightly beaten
¼ teaspoon salt
¼ teaspoon pepper
½ cup (2 ounces) shredded Swiss cheese
2 (6-inch) pita bread rounds, cut in half and toasted

Melt 1 tablespoon butter in an 8-inch skillet over medium heat; add mushrooms, and cook 1 minute, stirring constantly. Add wine, and cook until most of the liquid evaporates. Remove from skillet, and set aside.

Combine eggs, salt, and pepper. Melt remaining 2 tablespoons butter in skillet over medium heat, tilting to coat bottom; pour in egg mixture. Cook without stirring until mixture begins to set on bottom. Sprinkle cheese and mushroom mixture over eggs. Draw a spatula across bottom of pan to form large curds. Continue to cook until eggs are thickened, but moist. Spoon into pita halves. Yield: 4 servings.

*Deborah A. Varnadore*
*Jacksonville, Florida*

## CURRANT SCONES

1 cup all-purpose flour
1 teaspoon baking powder
⅛ teaspoon baking soda
1½ tablespoons sugar
¼ teaspoon grated orange rind
¼ cup butter or margarine
¼ cup currants
¼ cup buttermilk
½ teaspoon sugar
⅛ teaspoon ground cinnamon

Combine first 5 ingredients; cut in butter with a pastry blender until mixture is crumbly. Add currants, tossing lightly. Add buttermilk, stirring until dry ingredients are moistened. Turn dough out onto a lightly floured surface, and knead 6 times; shape into a ball. Place in a greased 8-inch round cakepan, and flatten to a 7-inch circle. Combine ½ teaspoon sugar and cinnamon; sprinkle over top. Bake at 375° for 10 minutes. Remove from oven; make an X about ½ inch deep across top. Bake an additional 20 minutes or until golden brown. Serve warm. Yield: 4 to 6 servings.

*Kathleen Stone*
*Houston, Texas*

## APPLE BREAKFAST SANDWICHES

⅓ cup firmly packed brown sugar
2 tablespoons all-purpose flour
½ teaspoon ground cinnamon
1 (10-ounce) can refrigerated buttermilk biscuits
1 cup (4 ounces) shredded sharp Cheddar cheese
2 large apples, peeled, cored, and cut into rings
1 tablespoon butter or margarine, melted

Combine first 3 ingredients in a small bowl; set aside.

Separate biscuits, and press each into a 3-inch circle. Place on lightly greased baking sheets; sprinkle with cheese, and top each with an apple ring. Sprinkle with reserved sugar mixture, and drizzle with melted butter. Bake at 350° for 15 minutes or until crust is golden. Serve immediately. Yield: 10 servings.

*Cathy Darling*
*Grafton, West Virginia*

---

Right: *A Christmas-morning brunch, Tennessee-style, features Mountain Trout Cakes With Lemon-Butter Sauce, Sweet Potato Hash, Sautéed Roma Tomatoes, Country Ham Chips, and Buttermilk-Raisin Biscuits. (Recipes begin on page 337.)*

*Half the fun of going to a tea party is playing dress up. Seated left to right are Laura Byers, Holly Bradford, and Sarah Byers. Their tea table, on facing page, features a beverage and (clockwise in foreground) Red-Bellied Bears, Snowflake Cookies, Chocolate-Peanut Butter Tarts, and Cheese Tea Sandwiches. Additional recipes in background include Peppermint Sandwich Cookies and Simple Petits Fours. (Recipes begin on page 276.)*

*These may look hard, but here's the secret—piecrusts from the grocer's refrigerator and easy fillings. You don't make the pastry—just the magic for (left) Spirited Mince Pie and Cranberry-Pecan Pie. (Recipes begin on page 316.)*

# Holiday Recipes With Tennessee Style

Christmas is coming to The Inn at Blackberry Farm, the country house hotel Kreis and Sandy Beall of Mobile, Alabama, own. There, in the Great Smoky Mountains, Kreis's recipe for a joyful holiday includes creative decorating of the inn and their farmhouse (see box on page 338).

The Bealls and their sons, Sam and David, especially look forward to Christmas in the mountains and their farmhouse, an often-visited retreat near the inn.

Christmas brunch at the farmhouse is inspired by the previous afternoon's fishing trip to Hesse Creek. For example, she transforms the day's catch of rainbow trout into tender, flaky trout cakes served with a classic French lemon-butter sauce. And what Southerner wouldn't warm to her Country Ham Chips, slivers of country ham deep-fried until crisp. Her Sweet Potato Hash is a fresh, seasonal alternative to hashbrowns. Kreis also puts her signature on Sautéed Roma Tomatoes. Even her biscuits, Buttermilk-Raisin Biscuits, boast a surprise—raisins soaked in applejack. Try her special Christmas brunch menu or create your own holiday supper from some of her favorite seasonal recipes that reflect her Tennessee heritage.

## CHRISTMAS BRUNCH AT THE FARMHOUSE

**Mountain Trout Cakes With Lemon-Butter Sauce**
**Sweet Potato Hash     Sautéed Roma Tomatoes**
**Country Ham Chips**
**Buttermilk-Raisin Biscuits**

## MOUNTAIN TROUT CAKES WITH LEMON-BUTTER SAUCE
*(pictured on page 333)*

2 pounds trout fillets
3 large eggs, lightly beaten
3 tablespoons whipping cream
1 tablespoon Dijon mustard
2 teaspoons Old Bay seasoning
1 teaspoon Worcestershire sauce
⅛ teaspoon ground red pepper
¼ teaspoon freshly ground black pepper
½ cup mayonnaise
3 tablespoons finely chopped scallions
2 tablespoons finely chopped fresh parsley
1 cup saltine cracker crumbs
1 cup fine, dry breadcrumbs
¼ cup butter, divided
¼ cup vegetable oil, divided
Lemon-Butter Sauce
Garnish: fresh thyme springs, lemon slices

Place trout fillets in a lightly greased 13- x 9- x 2-inch pan; bake at 350° for 20 to 25 minutes or until fish flakes easily with a fork. Let fillets cool; flake fish, carefully removing any bones. Set aside.

Combine eggs trout, whipping cream, mustard, Old Bay seasoning, Worcestershire sauce, red pepper, and pepper in a large bowl; beat with a fork until blended. Combine mayonnaise scallions, and parsley; fold into egg mixture. Stir in fish and cracker crumbs. Cover and chill 1 hour; shape mixture into 8 large or 16 small patties (mixture will be somewhat sticky). Coat patties with breadcrumbs.

Heat 2 tablespoons butter and 2 tablespoons oil in a large skillet; cook half the patties 3 to 4 minutes on each side or until golden. Drain on paper towels; keep warm. Repeat procedure. Serve with Lemon-Butter Sauce. Garnish, if desired. Yield: 8 servings.

### Lemon-Butter Sauce

1 cup dry, white wine
2½ tablespoons grated lemon rind
½ cup fresh lemon juice
2 bay leaves
1 teaspoon black peppercorns
1 teaspoon white peppercorns
¼ cup whipping cream
1 pound unsalted butter, cubed

Combine first 6 ingredients in a small saucepan; bring to a boil, and cook, uncovered, 10 to 12 minutes or until liquid is reduced to 1 tablespoon. Stir in whipping cream. Transfer mixture to top of a double boiler; place over hot, not boiling water, and add butter cubes, one at a time, beating with a wire whisk until blended. Pour mixture through a wire-mesh strainer. Yield: 2 cups.

**Note:** To keep sauce warm for up to one hour, let stand over hot water and whisk occasionally.

## SWEET POTATO HASH
*(pictured on page 333)*

3¼ pounds sweet potatoes, peeled and cut into 1-inch cubes
3 quarts water
1 teaspoon salt
2 tablespoons butter or margarine
2 tablespoons vegetable oil
3 cups chopped onions
½ teaspoon ground white pepper

Combine first 3 ingredients in a Dutch oven; bring to a boil. Cover and cook 3 minutes. Drain immediately, and cover with cold water; drain. Pat dry or let stand 15 minutes.

Heat butter and oil in Dutch oven over medium heat. Add onion, and cook, stirring constantly, until tender. Add potatoes and pepper; cook about 5 to 8 minutes or until thoroughly heated, stirring often. Yield: 8 to 10 servings.

## SAUTÉED ROMA TOMATOES
*(pictured on page 333)*

3 tablespoons butter or margarine
1 pint Roma or cherry tomatoes
Chopped fresh parsley

Heat butter in a large skillet over medium heat. Add tomatoes; cook 2 to 3 minutes or until thoroughly heated, stirring often. (Be careful that skins do not burst.) Sprinkle with parsley. Use as a garnish or a complement to other side dishes. Yield: about 2 cups.

## COUNTRY HAM CHIPS
*(pictured on page 333)*

16 pieces thinly sliced country ham
    or prosciutto (1 to 1½ pounds)
Vegetable oil

Remove any fat from ham and cut into 1½-inch strips. Pour oil to depth of 3 inches into a Dutch oven; heat to 375°. Fry ham strips until crisp. Drain on paper towels, and serve immediately. Yield: 8 side-dish servings.

## BUTTERMILK-RAISIN BISCUITS
*(pictured on page 333)*

½ cup raisins
¾ cup applejack
4 cups self-rising soft wheat flour
1 teaspoon sugar
⅔ cup shortening
1¾ cups milk
¼ cup unsalted butter, melted

Soak raisins in applejack 4 to 8 hours; drain, discarding applejack, and set raisins aside.

Combine flour and sugar in a large bowl; cut in shortening with a fork or pastry blender until shortening is the size of peas. Add milk, stirring with a fork until dry ingredients are moistened. (Dough will resemble cottage cheese and be sticky.) Turn dough out onto a heavily floured surface; add raisins. Knead lightly 10 to 12 times. Roll dough to ½-inch thickness; cut with a 2½-inch round cutter. Bake at 475° for 12 to 15 minutes on an ungreased baking sheet. Brush with unsalted butter. Yield: 2 dozen.

**Note:** Soft wheat flour is made from wheat grown and milled in regions that produce soft wheat. You'll find it under labels such as White Lily, Martha White, and other regional brands. Applejack is a potent brandy made from apple cider. Purchase it where liqueurs or other alcoholic beverages are sold.

## A Knack for Hospitality

At The Inn at Blackberry Farm, you immediately sense Kreis's attention to detail. Gold ribbons, softened by hundreds of dried roses, establish a warm and welcoming tone at the inn.

"I just like to *do* things," Kreis says as she strides through the generous rooms of the inn. Included in that "doing" is creating settings for marvelous meals and special moments.

Kreis is just as adamant about food as she is about decorating. She prefers a crusty cobbler or a homey upside-down cake, and she holds the inn and its team of chefs to her high standards.

## Decorating with Abundance and Simplicity

Kreis Beall often combines luxurious elements with ordinary items to achieve excellent results. Here are her tips:

■ Boxed gifts are wrapped in brown kraft paper and highlighted with the gold metallic ribbon that is used for decorations at the inn. The white liner of the ribbon is also put to use in wrapping any packages.
■ Purchasing one type of ribbon by the roll rather than several different types of ribbon by the yard will save money.
■ Gift bottles of flavored oils and vinegars, jellies and preserves boast a plump raffia bow rather than an expensive wrap. When she needs a container, Kreis pulls from the stash of cheese and fruit cases she has saved throughout the year.
■ A blue-and-white color scheme used throughout the farmhouse unifies and simplifies interior decorating. Kreis lets the style of the farmhouse suggest appropriate decorations, rather than impose a formal or red-and-green holiday theme.
■ The most common of materials—fresh fruit, traditional spices, and narcissus bulbs—are bought in bulk at considerable savings and used generously in decorating the farmhouse.
■ Crates of small Lady apples, oranges, tangerines, kumquats, lemons, and limes are ordered from a wholesale grocer. All arrive seven to ten days before Christmas. Kreis mounds the fruit in bowls and sets them around the farmhouse.
■ An occasional small bowl of spices—cloves or precious star of anise—are slipped among the bowls of fruit to enhance both the fragrance and visual appeal of the display.
■ Spices ordered in bulk usually come in 5-pound bags. Kreis uses them in her cooking throughout the coming year.

## Enjoy a Country Christmas Supper

When Kreis begins to think about which recipes she might make for a holiday supper, several favorites come to mind. The Crispy Cornbread recipe comes from Kreis's mom. Instead of spooning the batter into pans or molds, pour the batter onto two large jellyroll pans. Then, spread the batter thinly and bake into crispy sheets of cornbread. The secret is heating the pans before adding the batter.

If you make Kreis's Deep-Fried Turkey, you might ask someone to assist you. This recipe should be prepared outdoors with a propane cooker. Vegetable or peanut oils are the best to use. Also, be cautious when heating the oil, and make sure someone watches it at all times. When filled with hot oil, the pot for the propane cooker is heavy; it may take more than one person to empty the pot safely.

A small 8- to 10-pound turkey will heat to the correct temperature, making it safe to eat. If you want to cook a larger turkey, roast the turkey in the oven.

Mix and match Kreis's recipes for a Christmas meal—Tennessee style. Or try them with some of your family's favorites this holiday season.

Bring 6 cups chicken broth to a boil in a large saucepan. Add rice; cover tightly, and simmer 50 to 60 minutes. (Drain rice after cooking if all chicken broth is not absorbed; discard broth.) Toss rice with 2 tablespoons melted butter.

Cook oysters, mushrooms, celery, and onion in 2 tablespoons butter in a large skillet over medium heat, stirring occasionally, until edges of oysters begin to curl. Drain well, and set aside.

Pour remaining 4 tablespoons butter into a large, heavy saucepan or Dutch oven; add flour, stirring until smooth. Cook over low heat 1 minute, stirring constantly. Gradually add 1 cup chicken broth and whipping cream; cook over medium heat, stirring constantly, until mixture is thickened and bubbly. Stir in curry powder and next 5 ingredients. Add wild rice and oyster mixture, stirring well; spoon into a lightly greased 3½-quart casserole. Bake at 350° for 30 minutes or until bubbly. Sprinkle with parsley. Yield: 10 to 12 servings.

**Note:** To garnish, butter the rim of a casserole dish, and sprinkle it with parsley.

---

### DEEP-FRIED TURKEY

1 (8-ounce) bottle Caesar salad
   dressing
1 (8- to 10-pound) turkey
1 to 2 gallons vegetable or peanut
   oil

Fill the injector needle of a bulb baster with salad dressing, and squirt under skin. Tie legs together with one end of a 30-inch string. Pour oil to depth of 5 to 6 inches into a deep pot of a propane cooker; heat to 325°. Carefully lower turkey into hot oil, using string; fry 30 minutes or until meat thermometer inserted in turkey registers 185°. (Temperature of oil drops immediately after turkey is placed in it; oil may not reach 325° again.) Remove turkey from oil, and cool slightly before slicing. Yield: 12 to 14 servings.

### WILD RICE AND OYSTERS

6 cups chicken broth
2 (6-ounce) packages wild rice
½ cup butter or margarine,
   melted and divided
2 quarts oysters, drained
1 pound fresh mushrooms,
   sliced
½ cup chopped celery
½ cup chopped onion
½ cup all-purpose flour
1 cup chicken broth
1 cup whipping cream
1 to 1½ tablespoons curry
   powder
1 teaspoon onion powder
1 teaspoon dried thyme
½ teaspoon salt
¼ teaspoon pepper
¼ teaspoon hot sauce
½ cup chopped fresh parsley

### FRESH TURNIP GREENS

8 pounds fresh turnip or collard
   greens
¾ cup olive oil
⅓ cup butter or margarine
¼ cup minced fresh garlic
1 teaspoon salt
½ teaspoon pepper

Remove and discard stems and any discolored spots from greens. Wash thoroughly and drain; tear into bite-size pieces. Set aside.

Combine olive oil and butter in a large stock pot; add garlic, and cook over medium heat, stirring constantly, until tender. Add greens; cover and bring to a boil. Reduce heat, and simmer, covered, 35 to 45 minutes or until tender, stirring occasionally. Stir in salt and pepper. Yield: 12 servings.

## SPAGHETTI SQUASH

1 large spaghetti squash
2 tablespoons butter or margarine,
  melted
½ teaspoon salt
¼ teaspoon pepper
Garnish: 2 tablespoons chopped
  fresh chives

Cut squash in half lengthwise, and re-move seeds. Place squash halves, cut side down, in a 13- x 9- x 2-inch pan, and add boiling water to pan to a depth of 1½ inches. Bake at 350° for 50 min-utes or until tender. Remove from oven; let cool slightly. Using a fork, remove spaghetti-like strands of squash. Combine squash, butter, salt, and pepper in a bowl; toss until coated. Transfer to a serving platter, and garnish, if desired. Serve immedi-ately. Yield: 8 to 10 servings.

## ROASTED VIDALIA ONIONS WITH PECANS AND ROASTED CARROTS

6 large Vidalia or sweet onions
½ cup unsalted butter or
  margarine, melted and divided
¼ teaspoon salt (optional)
¼ teaspoon pepper (optional)
¼ cup chopped pecans, toasted
Roasted Carrots

Wash and peel onions; set on root ends on a cutting board. Cut vertical slices into onions at ¼-inch intervals, cutting to within ½ inch of root end. Turn onion and cut in same manner, making a crisscross pattern. The on-ions will look like flower blossoms. Ar-range in a 13- x 9- x 2-inch baking dish, leaving enough room between each to allow onions to open up. Driz-zle with half of butter, and sprinkle with salt and pepper, if desired. Bake at 350° for 30 minutes, basting occa-sionally with butter. Sprinkle with pe-cans, and bake an additional 15 to 20 minutes or until onion tops are deep golden brown. Serve with Roasted Carrots. Yield: 12 servings.

### Roasted Carrots

36 carrots (about 3 pounds)
2 tablespoons butter or margarine,
  melted
2 tablespoons vegetable oil
¼ teaspoon salt
¼ teaspoon pepper

Scrape carrots; cut large carrots into lengthwise slices. Place in a 13- x 9- x 2-inch baking dish. Combine butter and oil; drizzle over carrots. Sprinkle with salt and pepper. Bake at 350° for 30 minutes; turn carrots, and bake an additional 30 minutes or until tender. Yield: 12 servings.

## A Rose Is a Rose Is . . .

When Kreis Beall talks about her Mobile, Alabama, flower garden, conversation waxes, well, down-right poetic.

"My earliest memories are of roses," she says. "My mother said whatever I did, I always came out smelling like a rose. They are the most pleasurable flower. That once-a-year bloom is the most cherished, wonderful thing." So cherished, in fact, that she cut over 275 roses from her garden last Thanksgiving alone. From Kreis's experience of using roses in decorating at Blackberry Farm, come these tips.

■ Miniature spray roses are the best to order in winter.

■ Wear heavy gloves to protect skin from thorns.
■ Drying roses in silica gel yields the best color. The gel is avail-able at floral shops or gardening or crafts centers. Simply follow the directions on the package for best results.
■ Don't be afraid to mix colors.
■ Revive roses that have not been placed in arrangements by placing them in a large sink or bucket filled with cool water.
■ Grouping roses in assorted silver vases can make a stunning arrangement. Be sure to vary heights and shapes of the vases as well as the size and color of the roses.

## CRISPY CORNBREAD

2 cups white cornmeal
½ teaspoon salt
½ teaspoon baking soda
½ cup shortening
2 cups buttermilk
Cornmeal

Grease two 15- x 10- x 1-inch jellyroll pans, and place in a 425° oven for 5 minutes. Combine first 3 ingredients; cut in shortening with a fork or pastry blender until mixture is crumbly. Add buttermilk, stirring until dry ingredi-ents are moistened. Remove jellyroll pans from oven, and sprinkle with cornmeal. Divide batter between two pans, spreading evenly (do not spread batter to edge of pan). Bake at 425° for 20 minutes or until light golden brown and edges are crisp. Yield: 10 to 12 servings.

**Note:** Mix cornbread while pans heat.

## CRANBERRY RELISH

2 (12-ounce) packages fresh
   cranberries
2 cups sugar
2 cups water

Combine all ingredients in a saucepan; bring to a boil. Reduce heat to medium-high, and cook 5 minutes or until cranberry skins pop; cool. Serve with meats. Yield: 5½ cups.

# Weeknight Family Fare

Are you on the lookout for a streamlined menu for your famished family? Your search may end here. Follow our game plan to have supper on the table in about an hour.

The recipe for All-American Meat Loaf makes two loaves. Simply freeze the additional loaf for another meal. Recruit younger family members to perform easy jobs such as making the salad and setting the table. With everybody helping, dinner will be ready before you know it.

## ALL-AMERICAN MEAT LOAF

2 pounds ground chuck
¾ cup quick-cooking oats,
   uncooked
1 medium onion, chopped
½ cup catsup
¼ cup milk
2 large eggs, lightly beaten
1 tablespoon prepared horseradish
1 teaspoon salt
¼ teaspoon pepper
½ cup catsup
1 tablespoon prepared horseradish
3 tablespoons brown sugar
2 teaspoons prepared mustard

Combine first 9 ingredients; shape into two 7½- x 4-inch loaves. Place on a lightly greased rack of a broiler pan; bake at 350° for 40 minutes.

Combine ½ cup catsup, 1 tablespoon horseradish, and remaining ingredients; spoon over meat loaf, and bake an additional 5 minutes. Yield: 2 loaves or 8 servings.

**Note:** Freeze one meat loaf after cooking. Cool and wrap in heavy-duty aluminum foil. Seal, label, and freeze up to three months. To reheat, thaw in refrigerator eight hours. Bake, in foil, at 350° for 45 minutes or until thoroughly heated. *Sabrina McFarling*
*Hawesville, Kentucky*

## SPINACH SALAD

1 pound fresh spinach
1 (11-ounce) can mandarin oranges,
   drained
1 medium-size purple onion, thinly
   sliced and separated into rings
Tangy Orange Vinaigrette Dressing

Remove stems from spinach; wash leaves thoroughly, and pat dry. Tear leaves into bite-size pieces. Combine spinach, oranges, and onion rings; toss with Tangy Orange Vinaigrette Dressing. Serve immediately. Yield: 4 to 6 servings.

### Tangy Orange Vinaigrette Dressing

1½ teaspoons grated orange rind
1½ teaspoons Dijon mustard
½ teaspoon minced garlic
¼ teaspoon hot sauce
¼ cup cider vinegar
½ cup vegetable oil

Position knife blade in food processor bowl. Add first 5 ingredients, and pulse 2 or 3 times or until blended. With processor running, pour oil through food chute in a slow, steady stream; process until blended. Yield: ¾ cup. *Trudy Dunn*
*Dallas, Texas*

## PARMESAN POTATOES

2 tablespoons butter or margarine
½ cup chopped green pepper
⅓ cup chopped onion
¼ cup grated Parmesan cheese
½ teaspoon seasoned salt
½ teaspoon seasoned pepper
¼ teaspoon garlic powder
2 pounds potatoes, peeled and cut
   into ¼-inch slices
Paprika

Place butter in a 2-quart baking dish; microwave at HIGH 30 seconds or until butter melts. Add green pepper and next 5 ingredients, stirring well. Stir in potatoes. Cover tightly with heavy-duty plastic wrap; fold back a small corner of wrap to allow steam to escape. Microwave at HIGH 12 to 14 minutes or until tender, uncovering and stirring every 5 minutes. Sprinkle with paprika. Yield: 4 servings.
*Mrs. Charles DeHaven*
*Owensboro, Kentucky*

### Game Plan For a Timely Meal

■ Dissolve flavored gelatin for pie, and place in refrigerator to chill.
■ Prepare meat loaf, and place in oven to bake.
■ Assemble pie, and place in refrigerator to set.
■ Prepare Parmesan Potatoes; put in the microwave to cook.
■ Combine spinach and fruit for salad; make dressing.

## LEMON FLUFF PIE

1 (3-ounce) package lemon-flavored gelatin
1 cup boiling water
½ cup cold water
1 (8-ounce) carton lemon yogurt
1 (8-ounce) container frozen whipped topping, thawed
1 (9-ounce) graham cracker crust

Combine lemon-flavored gelatin and 1 cup boiling water in a small bowl, stirring mixture 2 minutes or until gelatin dissolves. Add ½ cup cold water to gelatin. Chill gelatin until the consistency of unbeaten egg white. Fold yogurt and whipped topping into gelatin; pour gelatin mixture into graham cracker crust. Refrigerate until firm. Yield: one 9-inch pie.

# Side Dishes That Please

Once you choose a main dish, the next question is what to serve with it. During the holidays, it's nice to have something other than plain vegetables. Whether you're serving a family meal or entertaining friends, there's a dish here for you.

# Give Napkins a Ring

The dining experience has come a long way since the Middle Ages. Back then there were no permanent dining tables or individual chairs, and, instead of plates, diners were handed thick, square slices of old bread. No forks, no spoons—just dig in with your fingers.

But by the 19th century, things were downright elegant. So much so that, in 1869, a patent for napkin rings was granted. The ring's main use was to mark each person's napkin because it was difficult to wash linens daily.

With today's strong emphasis on recycling, many people are coming back to cloth napkins, and along with them come some unique napkin rings.

## Facts That Ring True

■ In rural areas, bamboo was cut into pieces to be used as napkin rings in the early 1900s.

■ If you are a guest at someone's home, it is not proper to put your napkin back into the ring after the meal is over; napkins are returned to the ring only if you are a frequent visitor to that table.

## Napkin Rings You Can Make

■ A 15-inch piece of fresh ivy can be woven into a 3-inch ring for any occasion.
■ White cotton rope, available at most hardware stores, knotted at each end and then tied into a square knot, makes a simple napkin ring for casual events. For additional color, use multicolored rappelling rope from an outdoor equipment store. Allow ½ to ⅔ yard of rappelling rope to make each napkin ring.
■ Plastic toy watches found in variety stores are not only fun for children as party favors, but they can serve as napkin rings, too.

## CHEESY BROCCOLI CASSEROLE

2 (10-ounce) packages frozen chopped broccoli, thawed and drained
2 large eggs, lightly beaten
1 (10¾-ounce) can cream of mushroom soup, undiluted
1 cup (4 ounces) shredded mozzarella cheese
1 cup mayonnaise or salad dressing
½ cup herb-seasoned stuffing mix

Combine broccoli and next 4 ingredients. Spoon into a lightly greased 2-quart shallow casserole; sprinkle with stuffing mix. Bake at 350° for 30 minutes. Yield: 6 to 8 servings.

*Ruth D. Whitehead*
*West Columbia, South Carolina*

## SQUASH CASSEROLE

2 (16-ounce) packages frozen sliced yellow squash
1 cup chopped onion
1 cup mayonnaise or salad dressing
3 large eggs, lightly beaten
½ cup crushed unsalted saltine crackers
1 (0.4-ounce) envelope buttermilk Ranch-style salad dressing mix
1 cup (4 ounces) shredded sharp Cheddar cheese
1 cup soft breadcrumbs
1 tablespoon butter or margarine, melted

Cook squash with onion according to directions on squash package, omitting salt; drain well, pressing between paper towels. Combine squash mixture, mayonnaise, and next 4 ingredients in a lightly greased 2-quart shallow casserole. Combine breadcrumbs and butter; sprinkle over top. Bake at 350° for 20 to 25 minutes. Yield: 8 servings. *Chloe S. Pearch*
*Isola, Mississippi*

### CASHEW PEA PODS

Vegetable cooking spray
2 cups sliced fresh mushrooms
⅓ cup sliced green onions
1 (6-ounce) package frozen snow pea pods, thawed and drained
1 (8-ounce) can sliced water chestnuts, drained
1½ teaspoons cornstarch
1 teaspoon sugar
⅛ teaspoon garlic powder
¼ cup ready-to-serve, no-salt-added chicken broth
2 tablespoons reduced-sodium soy sauce
3 tablespoons unsalted cashews, toasted

Coat a large nonstick skillet with cooking spray; place over medium heat until hot. Add mushrooms and green onions; cook, stirring constantly, 3 minutes. Stir in snow peas and water chestnuts.

Combine cornstarch and next 4 ingredients; add to vegetables. Bring to a boil, stirring constantly. Cook 1 minute, stirring constantly. Remove from heat; sprinkle with cashews. Yield: 4 servings. *Kathy Nelson*
*El Paso, Texas*

**Tip:** *After purchasing fresh mushrooms, refrigerate immediately in their original container. If mushrooms are in a plastic bag, make a few holes in the bag for ventilation. Always store mushrooms with cool air circulating around them.*

# All In The Gingerbread Family

Like sweet memories of sugarplums from a childhood fairy tale, our gingerbread family will dance its way into your thoughts this month. Using a basic gingerbread cookie recipe, plus lots of imagination, you and your family can form whimsical creations that are as much at home on your fireplace mantel as they are in the kitchen.

You can decorate these cookies any way you like. Use cinnamon candies for red-hot lips, commercial candies for buttons and bows, and decorator sprinkles to dazzle. And don't forget a plump white beard for old Saint Nick. Use decorator frosting to make hair and clothes and to hold the candies in place.

For even more fun, bake the cookies ahead, and invite neighborhood children in for a party. You'll find that they will love piling on the goodies and creating their own fantasy figures.

Once the figures dry, add candy canes to the back; then prop the gingerbread family on the mantel. You're sure to have sweet dreams.

### GINGERBREAD COOKIES

1¾ cups sugar
¾ cup honey
¼ cup butter or margarine
1 tablespoon grated lemon rind
⅓ cup lemon juice
6 cups all-purpose flour
¼ cup baking powder
⅛ teaspoon salt
1½ teaspoons ground ginger
1 teaspoon ground cinnamon
¼ teaspoon ground nutmeg
¼ teaspoon ground cloves
1 large egg, lightly beaten
1 egg yolk, lightly beaten
Assorted colors of decorator frosting in tubes
Assorted candies
Ready-to-spread vanilla frosting
40 to 50 (3½-inch) candy canes

Combine first 3 ingredients in a 4-quart Dutch oven; bring to a boil, stirring constantly, until sugar dissolves. Remove from heat; stir in lemon rind and lemon juice. Let cool to room temperature.

Combine flour and next 6 ingredients; add 2 cups flour mixture, egg, and egg yolk to sugar mixture, stirring well. Gradually add remaining flour mixture, mixing well. Shape dough into a ball; knead on a floured surface until smooth. (Dough will appear dry before kneading.)

Divide dough in half; roll to about ¼-inch thickness on a floured surface. Cut out with a 4- or 6-inch gingerbread cutter; place on lightly greased cookie sheets. Bake at 325° for 15 to 18 minutes or until golden brown and firm. Loosen cookies with a spatula, and let cool 1 minute on cookie sheet. Transfer to wire racks to cool. Repeat procedure.

Decorate cookies with decorator frosting and assorted candies as desired; let dry. Turn cookies over; carefully attach two candy canes to back of each cookie with commercial frosting, and let dry before standing. Yield: 20 to 25 (4- or 6-inch) cookies.

**Note:** Store gingerbread in a cardboard box at room temperature or freeze in airtight containers. Avoid making cookies during humid weather because they may pick up moisture and soften. Even though these cookies are edible, they are very hard and are best used for decorative purposes. To keep the little ones from eating their creations, supply milk and other cookies for snacking.

# From Our Kitchen To Yours

When you're in the middle of preparing a recipe and discover an ingredient is missing, there isn't always time for a trip to the supermarket. Keep this emergency substitution chart nearby—the solution could be on your pantry shelf. For easy access, post the chart in a handy area of your kitchen.

*Needed Ingredient*

*Substitute*

**Baking products:**

1 cup powdered sugar — 1 cup sugar plus 1 tablespoon cornstarch (processed in food processor)
1¼ cups sugar plus ¼ cup water
1 cup honey — 1 cup regular oats, toasted (in baked products)
1 cup chopped pecans — 1 cup sugar plus ¼ cup water
1 cup light corn syrup — 1 (16-ounce) package marshmallows, melted, plus 3½ tablespoons light corn syrup
1 (7-ounce) jar marshmallow cream
1 teaspoon baking powder — ⅓ teaspoon baking soda plus ½ teaspoon cream of tartar

**Dairy Products:**

1 cup milk — ½ cup evaporated milk plus ½ cup water
1 cup whipping cream — ¾ cup milk plus ⅓ cup melted butter (for baking only; will not whip)
1 cup plain yogurt — 1 cup buttermilk
1 cup sour cream — 1 cup yogurt plus 3 tablespoons melted butter or 1 cup yogurt plus 1 tablespoon cornstarch

**Vegetable Products:**

1 pound fresh mushrooms, sliced — 1 (8-ounce) can sliced mushrooms, drained, or 3 ounces dried mushrooms
1 small onion, chopped — 1 tablespoon instant minced onion or 1 teaspoon onion powder
3 tablespoons chopped sweet red or green pepper — 1 tablespoon dried red or green pepper flakes
3 tablespoons chopped sweet red pepper — 2 tablespoons chopped pimiento
3 tablespoons chopped shallots — 2 tablespoons chopped onion plus 1 tablespoon chopped garlic

**Seasoning Products:**

1 clove garlic — ⅛ teaspoon garlic powder or minced dried garlic
1 tablespoon chopped chives — 1 tablespoon chopped green onions tops
1 tablespoon grated fresh gingerroot — ⅛ teaspoon ground ginger
1 tablespoon grated fresh horseradish — 2 tablespoons prepared horseradish
1 tablespoon dried orange peel — 1½ teaspoons orange extract or 1 tablespoon grated orange rind
1 tablespoon candied ginger — ⅛ teaspoon ground ginger
1 (1-inch) vanilla bean — 1 teaspoon vanilla extract
1 teaspoon garlic salt — ⅛ teaspoon garlic powder plus ⅞ teaspoon salt
1 teaspoon ground allspice — ½ teaspoon ground cinnamon plus ½ teaspoon ground cloves
1 teaspoon apple pie spice — ½ teaspoon ground cinnamon, ¼ teaspoon ground nutmeg, plus ⅛ teaspoon ground cardamom
1 teaspoon pumpkin pie spice — ½ teaspoon ground cinnamon, ¼ teaspoon ground ginger, ⅛ teaspoon ground allspice, plus ⅛ teaspoon ground nutmeg
1 teaspoon dry mustard — 1 tablespoon prepared mustard

**Miscellaneous Products:**

¼ cup Marsala — ¼ cup dry white wine plus 1 teaspoon brandy
1 tablespoon brandy — ¼ teaspoon brandy extract plus 1 tablespoon water
½ cup balsamic vinegar — ½ cup red wine vinegar (slight flavor difference)
1 cup tomato juice — ½ cup tomato sauce plus ½ cup water
2 cups tomato sauce — ¾ cup tomato paste plus 1 cup water

# Recipe Title Index

*An alphabetical listing of every recipe by exact title*
*All microwave recipe page numbers are preceded by an "M."*

# Month-by-Month Index

*An alphabetical listing within the month of every food article and accompanying recipes*
*All microwave recipe page numbers are preceded by an "M."*

# General Recipe Index

*A listing of every recipe by food category and/or major ingredient*
*All microwave recipe page numbers are preceded by an "M."*

# Favorite Recipes

*Record your favorite recipes below for quick and handy reference.*

| Recipe | Source/Page | Remarks |
| --- | --- | --- |
| | | |